MAYFLOWER FAMILIES
Through
Five Generations

DESCENDANTS OF THE PILGRIMS
WHO LANDED AT
PLYMOUTH, MASS. DECEMBER 1620

VOLUME TWO

edited by

Robert M. Sherman, F.A.S.G.

FAMILIES
JAMES CHILTON — *Robert M. Sherman & Verle D. Vincent*
RICHARD MORE — *Robert S. Wakefield & Lydia R. D. Finlay*
THOMAS ROGERS — *Alice W. A. Westgate*

Published by
General Society of Mayflower Descendants
1978

First printing, November 1978

Signatures on endpapers were reproduced from the
following sources:

> *Mary Chilton:* MD 1:65
> *Richard More:* MD 21:97
> *John[3] Rogers:* MD 20:opposite page 1

Library of Congress Cataloging in Publication Data   (Revised)
Main entry under title:

Mayflower families through five generations.

   Vol. 1 edited by L. M. Kellogg; v. 2: R. M. Sherman.
   Includes bibliographical references and indexes.
   CONTENTS: v. 1. Families: Francis Eaton, Samuel
Fuller, William White.--v. 2. Families: James Chilton,
Richard More, Thomas Rogers.
   1. Massachusetts--Genealogy. I. Kellogg, Lucy
Mary. II. Sherman, Robert M. III. Society of May-
flower Descendants.
F63.M39   929'.2'0973   75-30145
ISBN 0-930270-01-0 (v. 2)

IN MEMORY OF

L U C Y   M A R Y   K E L L O G G

1892-1973

FIRST EDITOR

FIVE GENERATIONS PROJECT

1970-1973

She devoted her expertise and
the boundless energy of her last three years
to editing the
Five Generations Project

HISTORY OF THE PROJECT

The idea of tracing both male and female descendants
of the Pilgrims down to Revolutionary times was announced
in 1899 by George E. Bowman, founder of the Massachusetts
Mayflower Society, first Secretary General and fifth Historian General. As editor of the *Mayflower Descendant*
(1899-1937) and of *Pilgrim Notes and Queries*, he devoted
many years to seeking out and publishing authentic data on
the Pilgrims and their descendants. The Bowman manuscripts
fill several file cabinets at the office of the Massachusetts Society. In 1956 the first three generations of his
findings were published by the Massachusetts Society as
Families of the Pilgrims.

Meanwhile Herbert Folger, first historian of the California Society, prepared a pamphlet listing the names of
men who married daughters, granddaughters and great-granddaughters of Mayflower passengers. Mr. Folger's research
fills 82 ledgers at the California Mayflower Society office. During the twenties and thirties Dr. Frank T. Calef
of the Rhode Island Mayflower Society compiled from printed sources five or more generations from the Mayflower
passengers. His 41 manuscript volumes are to be found at
the Rhode Island Historical Society.

As proven lineages accumulated at the office of the
General Society, it was recognized that a printed compilation of all accepted descendants would help those seeking
Pilgrim ancestry. William A. McAuslan of the Rhode Island
Society, while Historian General, compiled the *Mayflower
Index*, using an adaptation of Mr. Folger's numbering system. This Index included all names appearing in lineage
papers accepted to 1932, with a numbering system to trace
parentage, generation by generation, back to the Mayflower
ancestor. In 1959 Lewis E. Neff of the Oklahoma Society,
Historian General and later Governor General, corrected,
revised and expanded the *Mayflower Index* to include lineages of all members through 1959.

In 1959 Mr. Neff presented to the General Board of the
Mayflower Society, with the support of Carroll Alton Means
of the Connecticut Society, a resolution to endorse "publication of the tracing out of five generations of all the
descendants of all Mayflower passengers from whom descent
can be proved." All possible lines both male and female
were to be followed, down to around Revolutionary times.
To Lewis E. Neff belongs credit for the idea of recruiting
separate volunteer genealogists to work on each Pilgrim

family. Besides recruiting several family workers, he also
solicited funds for research and publication. Thus was
born the Five Generations Project.

Mr. Neff remained in charge of the Project until his
death in 1966. His successor, Mr. Means, expanded the
Committee, added family workers, and arranged a meeting of
the workers. In 1967 Dr. Lee D. van Antwerp, Surgeon General and later Governor General, became Chairman; under his
leadership volunteer workers were found for the remaining
families, contributions sought, Committee meetings sched-
uled regularly, and an editor found.

Miss Lucy Mary Kellogg, Historian of the Michigan Mayflower Society, was recruited in 1970 to be the Project's
first Editor. The following year she was elected a Fellow
of the American Society of Genealogists [FASG]. She stan-
dardized the format of the Families in a modified Register
style, included names of the sixth generation, and assis-
ted, encouraged and, in many instances, visited the workers. She insisted that each family compilation should be
"authentic, explicit, easy to use," and as complete as possible.

Upon her death in 1973 five Families had been subjec-
ted to Miss Kellogg's preliminary editing. The three
closest to completion--Eaton, Samuel Fuller and White--
were published sacrificing strict adherence to format in
favor of prompt publication.

In 1975 Robert M. Sherman of the Rhode Island Society,
co-worker with Mrs. Sherman on the Samson and White families, was appointed Chairman to succeed Dr. van Antwerp.
Three months later both Mr. and Mrs. Sherman were elected
Fellows of the American Society of Genealogists. With the
assistance of Prof. Claude W. Barlow, F.A.S.G., worker on
the Billington and Warren families, of Mrs. Sherman, and of
Dr. van Antwerp. Mr. Sherman supervised final preparation
of the first volume of *Mayflower Families*.

Early in 1976 the Project lost its most experienced
worker--Professor Barlow. To him more than to any one
other person belongs credit for the appearance in 1975 of
volume one. Nearly 3000 copies were sold during the first
twelve months; a second printing of 2000 copies, incorpo-
rating minor corrections, was sold out during 1978.

Additional research into primary sources was conducted
on the three families in this volume during 1977 and 1978
by Mr. and Mrs. Sherman, and by Robert S. Wakefield, the
Brown family worker. Evaluation of the manuscript was un-
dertaken by these three together with Robert C. Anderson.

Three significant changes should make this volume easier to follow: separation of generation four from generations five and six, use of closer spacing of the smaller type, and use of roman rather than italic type in the index.

Each worker donated the time spent on researching and writing his family; the Chairman, who also served as Editor, the three primary source researchers, the four evaluators, the typist and the indexer also donated their time and expertise. The Project continues a labor of love!

Robert M. Sherman

OFFICERS OF THE GENERAL SOCIETY

1975-1978

GOVERNOR GENERAL   Dr. Robert L. Thomas
ASSISTANT GOVERNOR GENERAL   E. Roy Chesney
SECRETARY GENERAL   Mrs. Robert M. Sherman
TREASURER GENERAL   E. Frederick Low
HISTORIAN GENERAL   Mrs. Lester A. Hall
ELDER GENERAL   Dr. E. Bradford Davis
CAPTAIN GENERAL   Evan M. Day
SURGEON GENERAL   Dr. Herbert M. Giffin
COUNSELLOR GENERAL   Hewitt A. Conway

MEMBERS AT LARGE, EXECUTIVE COMMITTEE

Hershel W. Anderson, Lynmar Brock, Jr.,
Mrs. John R. Orndorff

FIVE GENERATIONS PROJECT COMMITTEE

1978

John D. Austin, Jr., F.A.S.G.
Mrs. W. Carroll Barnes
Mrs. Lester A. Hall
Mrs. Robert M. Sherman, F.A.S.G.
Col. John Soule
Dr. Lee D. van Antwerp, C.G.
Robert S. Wakefield, F.A.S.G.
Robert M. Sherman, F.A.S.G.,
    chairman and editor

Information about the editor, Robert M. Sherman,
appears on page 2.

THE SOCIETY EXPRESSES THANKS

To everyone involved in preparing this book. Some names have unfortunately escaped the record, but the contribution of each is appreciated and herewith acknowledged.

RESEARCH ASSISTANCE: Substantial work in primary sources for the Rogers family, Ruth W. Sherman, F.A.S.G. (RI Soc.). Help in one or more families by Robert C. Anderson, F.A.S.G. (of MA), John D. Austin, F.A.S.G. (OK Soc.), the late Claude W. Barlow, F.A.S.G. (MA Soc.), Frederick R. Boyle, G.R.S. (of MA), Nettie Bradford (UT Soc.), Roberta G. Bratti (of MA), Natalie S. Butler (ME Soc.), Sandra N. Calverley (RI Soc.), Charles W. Farnham, F.A.S.G. (of RI), Ernest A. Harris (NH Soc.), the late Lucy Mary Kellogg, F.A.S.G. (MI Soc.), Marjorie Lewis (of Barbados), Stuart P. Lloyd (NJ Soc.), William G. Murphy (of Nova Scotia), Marjorie P. Nutt (CT Soc.), Claire A. Richardson (MD Soc.), Robert M. Sherman, F.A.S.G. (RI Soc.), Arthur W. Soper (NC Soc.), Dorothy T. Stillwell (VT Soc.), Kenn Stryker-Rodda, F.A.S.G. (of NJ), Caroline W. Thompson (MA Soc.), Arthur H. & Dorothy F. Vollertsen (VA Soc.), Robert S. Wakefield, F.A.S.G. (CA Soc.), Elizabeth C. White (NY Soc.) and Ralph V. Wood, Jr. (MA Soc.).

RESEARCH FINANCING: State Societies and Colonies, individual members and non-members, whose contributions made this work possible.

LIBRARIES: Berkshire Athenaeum; CA Genealogical Society; CA Mayflower Society; CT State Library; Essex Institute (Salem); Knight Memorial Library (Providence RI); LDS Genealogical Society (Salt Lake City and Oakland CA); Los Angeles Public Library; MA Mayflower Society's Bowman files, courtesy Adele W. Allen; Middleboro Public Library; New Bedford Public Library; New England Historic Genealogical Society; Old Colony Historical Society (Taunton); RI Historical Society; Sandwich Public Library; Sturgis Library (Barnstable); Sutro Library (San Francisco CA); Taunton Public Library; and General Society Library and lineage papers (Plymouth), courtesy Corinne D. Hall (MA Soc.) and Florence F. deVries (IL Soc.).

EDITING and PROOFREADING: Robert C. Anderson and Robert M. Sherman. Charles W. Farnham, Committee consultant.

KEY TO ABBREVIATED TITLES: Ruth W. Sherman and Milton E. Terry. (NJ Soc.).

INDEXES: Milton E. Terry.

ART WORK: Charles F. Mathewson (of Leyden Press, Plymouth).

TYPING: Lee D. van Antwerp, C.G. (IL Soc.), preliminary typing; Cathryn P. Lanham (MI Soc.), final copy.

TABLE OF CONTENTS

xi

ERRATA AND ADDENDA

December 1978

Page 201, footnote line 5: *For* Gidoen *read* Gideon

Page 261, line 24: *For* (BRADORD) *read* (BRADFORD)

Page 285, 4th line up: *For* Crance *read* Crane

Page 294, at bottom of page: *Add:*

Mary[5] Richmond m. (2) Taunton 6 Nov. 1738
STEPHEN ANDREWS, b. bef. 1679; d. Taunton 4
March 1770. He m. (1) Bethia ----- by whom he
had seven children b. Rochester 1699-1713. He
had no children by Mary.

The will of Stephen Andrews of Taunton
husbandman, made 20 Oct. 1762, witnesses deposed 30 April 1770, names wife Mary to have
moveables she had before her marriage; grandsons Stephen and Thomas Andrews; his daughters
Mary Doty wife of Edward, Hannah Coombs wife of
Ashemar, Deborah Mitchell, and Bethia Winslow.

Page 296, 4th line up: *For* (Richard) *read* (Rickard)

Page 303, lines 31 and 33: *For* Eliakim *read* Elnathan

TO THE READER

Among the immigrants to Massachusetts between 1620 and 1650 were at least twenty-four named More or Moore, and fifteen named Rogers (MA PIONEERS). At least two immigrants to Virginia in the same period were named Chilton (CAVALIERS & PIONEERS). These figures permit the reader to estimate the chance that his early Massachusetts More, Rogers or Chilton ancestor is a member of one of the families in this book.

The authors have assembled families as correctly and as completely as circumstances permitted. Their work is based largely on carefully researched articles in genealogical journals and family histories, together with probate and land records, and town and church vital statistics. Family tradition, in the absence of confirmatory evidence, has not been accepted as proof of a line. This has, regretfully, resulted in the rejection of a few lines which the Society accepted in its early years, but based on insufficient or erroneous evidence. On the other hand, many new potential lines have been uncovered.

Paucity of records sometimes renders it virtually impossible to follow a family or individual to another town: An entire family disappears, or one or more children are labelled "n.f.r." (no further record found). The authors often offer tentative identifications using the word probably, when evidence is nearly conclusive, and possibly, when evidence is merely suggestive. This is done in the hope that a reader, tracing back his ancestry through such clues, may come upon real proof and so establish the new line.

Spelling was far from consistent even after the Revolution. To a great extent names in this book have been spelled as found in each record. This often provides different spellings of an individual's name at his birth, upon marriage, and in a deed or will. For example, Hayward is found as Heywood and even Howard for the same person; Marcy and Mercy are many times interchangeable. With variant spellings so commonplace, use of "(*sic*)" is restricted to exceptional examples. To assist the reader, most variant spellings of a name are clumped together in the Index, rather than separately alphabetized.

A reader who finds either an error or additional information regarding any family or individual in this volume down to *the birth of sixth generation children*, but not beyond, is urgently requested to send such material to: FIVE GENERATIONS PROJECT, P.O. BOX 297, PLYMOUTH MA 02360.

J A M E S   C H I L T O N

of the

M A Y F L O W E R

Compiled by

Robert Moody Sherman, C.G., F.A.S.G.

and

Verle Delano Vincent

Robert Moody Sherman is a descendant of
Pilgrims John Alden, William Brewster and
Richard Warren. He has served as Governor of
the Rhode Island Mayflower Society, and is
presently Deputy Governor General from Rhode
Island, and Chairman of the Five Generations
Project and Project Editor. He holds an S.B.
in chemistry from M.I.T., and is currently
Chairman of the Division of Mathematics and
Science at Bristol Community College in Fall
River. A Certified Genealogist and a Fellow
of the American Society of Genealogists, he is
known for articles on Pilgrim families and for
his transcriptions of the Marshfield and Yarmouth MA vital records. Co-author of the William White family in volume one of *Mayflower
Families*, he has done much research on anoth-
er--the Henry Samson family. He is responsible for research into primary sources for the
Chilton family.

Verle Delano Vincent is a descendant of
Pilgrims William Brewster, James Chilton,
Francis Cooke, Edward Doty and Richard Warren.
He has served as Chaplain and Governor of the
California Society's Alameda Colony, and as
Treasurer and Governor of the California Mayflower Society. He is retired as Assistant
Treasurer of the Pacific Gas and Electric Company at San Francisco. Mr. Vincent has conducted extensive research into the Cape Cod
Vincent families, as well as into the descendants of immigrant Richard Lowden (manuscript
at the New England Historic Genealogical Society); he has articles published on the Randall
and Stites families (New York Genealogical and
Biographical Record). He is responsible for
research into published sources for the Chilton family.

JAMES CHILTON

James Chilton was the oldest passenger on the *Mayflower*, with the possible exception of Elder William Brewster. James was born before 1563 in Canterbury, Kent County, England, where the surname appears in the annals as far back as 1339 when Robert Chilton was a representative to Parliament from Canterbury. James' grandfather Richard Chilton of St. Paul's Parish, Canterbury, in a will dated and proved in 1549, mentioned his deceased wife Isabell, and bequeathed the bulk of his estate to his son Lyonell.

The will of Lyonell "Chylton," a yeoman of considerable property residing in St. Paul's Parish, dated 7 Sept. 1582 and proved 13 Feb. 1582/3, named sons John and James Chilton; daughters Alice, Anne and Margaret; wife Isabell and her children--Thomas Furner and Susanna Furner. To son James he left two tenements in Canterbury. Isabell was evidently a recent second wife of Lyonell, and not James' mother (whose name is unknown).

James Chilton, tailor, was listed as a freeman of Canterbury in 1583. He married before 1587 just possibly Susanna Furner, daughter of his step-mother and her first husband Francis Furner. Seven children were baptized in Canterbury to James, then about 1600 the family moved to neighboring Sandwich where three more children were baptized, including youngest daughter Mary, who was baptized at St. Peter's in 1607. Here he undoubtedly met Moses Fletcher, who was destined to be a fellow *Mayflower* passenger, as well as other Pilgrims who later went to Holland, and so was drawn into the Pilgrim movement.

From 1607 to 1620 we lose sight of James, but since his daughter "Ysabel Tgiltron spinster from Canterbury" was married in Leyden, Holland in 1615, and probably a second daughter Ingle, listed as "Engeltgen Gilten," was married there in 1622, it is likely that James took his family to Holland, where Leyden betrothal records include several Pilgrims from Sandwich and Canterbury. On the other hand, James Chilton's name has not been found in Leyden as owner of property, as a citizen, as friend of a betrothed couple, or even as witness at the betrothal of his own daughter. Possibly this apparent lack of record might be ascribed to the difficulty the Dutch had with writing the name Chilton.

Descent from James Chilton has been proved through only his eldest daughter Isabella and his youngest daughter Mary. "Engeltgen Gilten" mentioned above, who married

Robert Nelson, could not be followed further. None of the other children appears to have lived to maturity.

Governor Bradford wrote that among those on the *May-flower* were James Chilton and his wife, and Mary their daughter; they had another daughter that was married, came afterward. In 1650 he wrote "James Chilton and his wife also died in the first infection, but their daughter Mary is still living and hath nine children; and one daughter is married and hath a child. So their increase is ten." James died on 18 December 1620, scarcely a month after signing the Mayflower Compact--the only signer who died at Cape Cod. His wife shortly followed him, dying during the First Sickness at Plymouth sometime after 21 January 1620/1.

At thirteen Mary Chilton was thus left an orphan at Plymouth. No record reveals with whom she spent the next few years, but perhaps for at least a part of the time she was a member of either the Alden or the Standish household; in the 1623 land division "Marie" Chilton received her share (undoubtedly three acres--one for herself and one for each parent) between the shares of John Alden and Myles Standish. By the time of the cattle division of May 1627, Mary had married John Winslow, and the couple were included with John Shaw's group.

References: NEHGR 63:201. TAG 38:244-5. STODDARD pp. 100, 120, 124. FAM OF PILGRIMS pp. 60-1. BANKS ENGLISH ANCESTRY p. 45. BRADFORD'S HIST (1952) pp. 442, 446. MQ 26(4):2; 27(1):5-6; 33:43-5; 38:101-3; 40:8-13; 43:56. SAVAGE 1:379. LEYDEN DOCUMENTS pp. 21, 48. PLYMOUTH COLONY RECS 1:9; 12:4, 11.

FIRST GENERATION

1 JAMES[1] CHILTON b. prob. Canterbury, Kent Co., England
bef. 1563; d. Cape Cod Harbor (now Provincetown) aboard the
Mayflower 18 Dec. 1620; son of Lyonell Chylton. [Lyonell's
second wife, the widow Isabell Furner, was not the mother
of his children.]
    He m. England bef. 1587 pos. SUSANNA FURNER, dau. of
his step-mother; his wife d. Plymouth shortly after 11 Jan.
1620/1.

    Children (CHILTON) b. Kent Co., England:

2   i ISABELLA[2] bp. St. Paul's Parish, Canterbury, 15 Jan. 1586/7.
    ii JANE bp. St. Paul's Parish, Canterbury, 8 June 1589; n.f.r.
   iii MARY b. Canterbury; bur. St. Martin's Parish 23 Nov. 1593.
    iv JOEL b. Canterbury; bur. St. Martin's Parish 2 Nov. 1593.
     v ELIZABETH bp. St. Martin's Parish, Canterbury, 14 July
          1594; n.f.r.
    vi JAMES bp. St. Martin's Parish, Canterbury, 22 Aug. 1596;
          d.y.
   vii INGLE bp. St. Paul's Parish, Canterbury, 29 April 1599;
          prob. the "Engeltgen Gilten" who m. Leyden, Holland, 27
          Aug. 1622 ROBERT NELSON; n.f.r.
  viii CHRISTIAN (dau.) bp. St. Peter's Parish, Sandwich, 26 July
          1601; n.f.r.
    ix JAMES bp. St. Peter's Parish, Sandwich, 11 Sept. 1603; n.f.r.
3   x MARY bp. St. Peter's Parish, Sandwich, 30 May 1607.

References: MD 1:87; 6:244. MQ 26(4):2; 27(1):5-6; 38:101[some dates
          in error]; 43:56. SAVAGE 1:379. TAG 38:244-5. NEHGR
63-201. BANKS ENGLISH ANCESTRY p. 45. FAM OF PILGRIMS pp. 60-1.
LEYDEN DOCUMENTS p. 48. BRADFORD'S HIST (1952) pp. 442, 446. Register, St. Peter's Christenings, Sandwich (now at Canterbury Cathedral).

SECOND GENERATION

2 ISABELLA[2] CHILTON (James[1]) bp. St. Paul's Parish,
Canterbury, Kent Co., England, 15 Jan. 1586/7; no death re-
cord found. In fact, Bradford's statement that James Chil-
ton "had an other doughter, that was married, came after-
ward," provides the only evidence that Isabella came to
Plymouth.
    She m. Leyden, Holland, 21 July 1615 ROGER CHANDLER
(Rogier Kandelaer batchelor from Colchester, England); d.
bet. 1658 and 3 Oct. 1665 prob. Duxbury.
    The Leyden poll tax of 15 Oct. 1622 includes "Rogier
Chandelaer, Isabel Chandelaer" his wife, and children
Samuel and Sara. Roger and his family probably came to
Plymouth in 1629 or 1630, when according to Bradford the

Leyden contingent arrived. He was taxed in Plymouth 25
March 1633, and listed as a freeman the same year--the
earliest record of him in this country. He was enumerated
among those able to bear arms in Duxbury in 1643, and sold
land there in 1644; he was listed among freemen of Duxbury
in a tally presumed taken in 1658.

In October 1665 the Plymouth Court granted 150 acres
of land to the three (unnamed) daughters of Roger Chandler
deceased. Articles in TAG indicate their names and husbands.

        Children (CHANDLER):

        i   SAMUEL[3] b. Leyden, Holland, bef. 15 Oct. 1622; prob. d.y.*
   4   ii   SARAH b. Leyden bef. 15 Oct. 1622
   5 iii   MARY b. after 1622 prob. Leyden
   6   iv   MARTHA b. after 1622 prob. Leyden

References: MD 6:244; 11:129; 14:69. LEYDEN DOCUMENTS p. 21. FAM OF
            PILGRIMS pp. 61-2. TAG 27:1-6; 37:212-7. SMALL DESC
2:855-70. SAVAGE 1:358. NEHGR 63:201. BRADFORD'S HIST (1952) p. 442;
also (1912) 2:400. DUXBURY RECS p. 19. PLYMOUTH COLONY RECS 1:4, 10,
11, 27, 165; 2:98; 4:110; 8:174, 198; 12:109. ARBER p. 273. Leyden
Poll Tax. MA PIONEERS p. 93.

    3 MARY[2] CHILTON (James[1]) bp. St. Peter's Parish, Sand-
wich, Kent Co., England, 31 May 1607; d. Boston MA bef. 1
May 1679.
    She m. Plymouth bet. July 1623 and 22 May 1627 JOHN
WINSLOW, b. Droitwich, Worcestershire, England, 16 April
1597; d. Boston bef. 21 May 1674; son of Edward and Magda-
len (Ollyver) Winslow, and brother of Pilgrim Edward Winslow. Both John and Mary are buried in King's Chapel Burying Ground, Boston.
    John Winslow arrived at Plymouth in 1621 on the *For-
tune*. He was listed a freeman in 1633, and became active
in the government of the colony, setting off and appraising
land and serving on jury; in 1653 he became a member of "a
counsell of warr." With wife Mary he moved to Boston in
1657. His will, attested 21 May 1674, preserved in Boston,
reads:

    "In the name of God Amen the twelveth day of March in the yeare
of our Lord according to the Computacon of the Church of England one
thousand six hundred seaventy and three Annoq Regni Regis Car: Secundi
Anglia &c xxvj, I John Winslow Sen[r] of Boston in the Countie of Suf-
folke in New England Merchant ...

---

*Neither Samuel Chandler of Duxbury nor the one of Dorchester seems to
be a son of Roger. Samuel of Duxbury was the son of Edmund Chandler,
and Samuel of Dorchester was taxed in Plymouth in 1633, so appears to
be too old to be Roger's son. Further, in the 1665 grant to Roger's
three daughters, no mention was made of a son.

"Item I give and bequeath unto my Deare and well beloved wife
Mary Winslow the use of my now dwelling house with the gardens and
yards thereunto belonging for and during the tearme of her naturall
life. Item I give and bequeath unto my said wife the use of all my
househould goods for her to dispose of as she shall thinke meet. Item
I give unto my said wife the sume of Foure hundred pounds in lawfull
mony of New England...

"Item after the death of my said wife I give and bequeath my said
dwelling house with all the Land belonging to the same unto my sone
John Winslow and to his heires for ever, he or they paying when they
come to possesse & enjoy the same the sume of Fifty pounds of Lawfull
mony of New England unto William Payne the sone of my Daughter Sarah
Meddlecott, and also to Parnell Winslow Daughter to my Son Isaack
Winslow the full sume of Fifty pounds of like Lawfull mony. And my
Will is that both the said sums be paid into the hands of my overseers
to be improved for them untill they come to age or the day of Marriage... But in case both of them should dye before they come to age:
My Will is that then the said sums shall be Equally divided amongst
the Daughters of my Daughter Latham to be paid unto them as they come
to age or marriage...

"Item my Will is that my Katch Speedwell (whereof I am the sole
owner) and the produce of the Cargo that I sent out in her be (at her
returne to Boston) disposed of by my Overseers hereafter named, and
the neate produce thereof be Equally divided amongst my Children my
sone John Winslow onely Excepted and to have no part thereof. Item I
give and bequeath unto my sone Benjamin the full sume of one hundred
pounds to be paid him by my Executo^r or overseers hereafter named when
he shall attaine the Age of twenty one yeares. Item my Will is that
if my sone Edward Winslow shall see cause to relinquish his s^d part
and intrest in the s^d Katch Speedwell and her proceeds, then my Will
is that he shall have one quarter part of my Katch John's Adventure
unto his owne proper use. And then the said Katch and Cargo to be
Equally divided among my other Children, my son John Excepted as
afforesaid togather with my sone Edward from haveing any part in the
afforesaid Katch or Cargo.

"Item I give and bequeath unto my grandchild Susanna Latham the
sume of thirty pounds in mony to be paid her at the day of her marriage. And to the rest of my Daughter Latham's Children I give and
bequeath unto Each of them five pounds pr peece to be paid unto them
as they shall come to age or the day of marriage. Item I give and
bequeath unto my sone Edward Winslows Children the sume of five
pounds pr peece to be paid unto them as they shall come to age or the
day of Marriage. Item I give and bequeath unto my sone Edward Grey
his children that he had by my Daughter Mary Grey the sume of twenty
pounds pr peece to be paid unto them when they come to age or the day
of their respective marriages. Item I give unto my sone Joseph Winslow's two Children five pounds pr peece to be paid unto them as
afforesaid. Item I give unto my Grandchild Mercy Harris her two
Children five pounds apeece to be paid unto them as afforesaid.

"Item I give and bequeath unto my Kinsman Josiah Winslow now
Governo^r of New Plimoth the sume of twenty pounds to be paid unto him
by my overseers in Goods. Item I give unto my Brother Josiah Winslow

the sume of twenty pounds to be paid unto him by my overseers in Goods
...   Item I give unto my kinswoman Eleano[r] Baker the Daughter of
my Brother Kenelem Winslow five pounds...

"Item my will is that what my Estate shall amount unto more then
will pay funerall Charges My Debts and Legacyes in this my will given
and bequeathed it shall be divided (after the Decease of my said wife)
among my seaven Children in Equall proportions Except any one of my
said Children shall have any Extraordinary providence befall them by
way of any Eminent Losse, then that part of my Estate that shall re-
maine as afforesaid shall be divided & distributed according to the
prudence and discression of my overseers hereafter named or any two of
them.   Item my will is that in case any of my now children shall dye
before my said wife, that then his or their proportion of the said re-
maineing Estate shall be disposed of to his or their Children if they
have any; if not, then that part or parts shall be equally divided
amongst the survivors of my said Children.

"Item I give to M[r] Paddyes Widow five pounds as a token of my
love.   Item my will is that my Negro Girle Jane (after she hath served
twenty yeares from the date hereof) shall be free, and that she shall
serve my wife during her live and after my wifes decease she shall be
disposed of according to the discression of my overseers...

"Item I doe nominate and appoint my sone John Winslow the sole
Executo[r] of this my last Will and testament.   Item I doe hereby nominate & appoint my love[torn] Friends M[r] Thomas Brattle, M[r] William
Tailer and M[r] John Winsley my Overseers...In witnesse whereof I the
said John Winslow Sen[r] have hereunto set my hand & seale the day and
yeare first above written.

                                        John Winslow (seal)"

        A tradition, apparently true, persists that Mary Chil-
ton was the first female to reach shore from the *Mayflower;*
less certain is whether this was accomplished at Cape Cod
or at Plymouth.   However it is certain that she left the
only will of a female passenger, a paper today preserved
at the Suffolk County Registry of Probate in Boston.   (In
fact only two other written wills of *Mayflower* passengers
are known to exist, those of Edward Winslow, with other
probate records in London, and Peregrine White at Pilgrim
Hall in Plymouth MA.   William Mullins left a nuncupative
will.)   Mary (Chilton) Winslow's will reads as follows:

"In the name of God Amen the thirty first day of July in the
yeare of our Lord one thousand Six hundred seventy and Six I Mary
Winslow of Boston in New England Widdow being weake of Body but of
Sound and perfect memory praysed be almighty God for the same, Knowing the uncertainety of this present life and being desirous to settle
the outward Estate the Lord hath Lent me.   I doe make this my last
Will and Testam[t] in manner and forme following (that is to say) First
and principally I comend my Soule into the hands of Almighty God my
Creato[r] hopeing to receive full pardon and remission of all my sins;
and Salvation through the alone merrits of Jesus Christ my redeemer:
And my body to the Earth to be buried in Such Decent manner as to my

Executo[r] hereafter named shall be thought meet and convenient and as
touching such worldly Estate as the Lord hath Lent me my Will and
meaneing is the same shall be imployed and bestowed as hereafter in
and by this my Will is Exprest.

"Imp[s] I doe hereby revoake renounce and make voide all Wills by
me formerly made and declaire and apoint this my Last Will and Testam[t].
Item I will that all the Debts that I Justly owe to any manner of person or persons whatsoever shall be well and truely paid or ordained to
be paid in convenient time after my decease by my Executo[r] hereafter
named. Item I give and bequeath into my Sone John Winslow my great
Square table. Item I give and bequeath unto my Daughter Sarah Middlecott my Best gowne and Pettecoat and my Silver beare bowle and to each
of her children a Silver Cup with an handle: Also I give unto my
grandchild William Paine my Great silver tankard: Item I give unto my
Daughter Susanna Latham my long Table: Six Joyned Stooles and my
great Cupboard: a bedstead Bedd and furniture there unto belonging
that is in the Chamber over the roome where I now Lye; my small silver
Tankard: Six Silver Spoones, a case of Bottles with all my wearing
apparell: (except onely what I have hereby bequeathed unto my Daughter
Meddlecott & my Grandchild Susanna Latham:)

"Item I give and bequeath unto my Grandchild Ann Gray that trunke
of Linning that I have alreddy delivered to her and is in her possession and also one Bedstead, Bedd Boulster and Pillows that are in the
Chamber over the Hall: Also the sume of ten pounds in mony to be paid
unto her within Six months next after my decease: Also my will is that
my Executo[r] shall pay foure pounds in mony pr ann for three yeares
unto M[rs] Tappin out of the Intrest of my mony now in Goodman Cleares
hands for and towards the maintenance of the said Ann Gray according
to my agreem[t] with M[rs] Tappin: Item I give and bequeath unto Mary
Winslow Daughter of my sone Edward Winslow my largest Silver Cupp with
two handles: and unto Sarah Daughter of the said Edward my lesser Silver cupp with two handles: Also I give unto my Said Sone Edwards
children Six Silver Spoones to be divided between them:

"Item I give and bequeath unto my grandchild Parnell Winslow the
Sume of five pounds in mony to be improved by my Executo[r] untill he
(sic) come of age: and then paid unto him (sic) with the improvem[t].
Item I give & bequeath unto My grandchild Chilton Latham the sum of
five pounds in mony to be improved for him untill he come of Age and
then paid to him with the improvem[t]. Item my will is that the rest of
my spoones be divided among my grandchildren according to the discression of My Daughter Middlecott: Item I give unto my Grandchild Mercy
Harris my White Rugg: Item I give unto my Grandchild Mary Pollard
forty shillings in mony. Item I give unto my grandchild Susanna
Latham my Petty Coate with the silke Lace: Item I give unto Mary
Winslow Daughter of my Sone Joseph Winslow the Sume of twenty pounds
in mony to be paid out of the sume my said Sone Joseph now owes to be
improved by my Executo[r] for the said Mary and paid unto her when She
Shall attaine the Age of eighteene yeares or day of Marriage which of
them shall first happen.

"Item I give and bequeath the full remainder of my Estate whatsoever it is or wheresoever it may be found unto my children Namely
John Winslow Edward Winslow Joseph Winslow Samuell Winslow:

Susanna Latham and Sarah Middlecott to be equally divided betweene them. Item I doe hereby nominate constitute authorize and appoint my trusty friend M[r] William Tailer of Boston afores[d] merchant the Sole Executo[r] of this my last Will and testam[t]: In Witness whereof I the said Mary Winslow have hereunto set my hand and Seale the daye and yeare first above written.

    "Memorandum I doe hereby also Give and bequeath unto M[r] Thomas Thacher paster of the third Church in Boston the Sume of five pounds in mony to be pd convenient time after my decease by my Execut[r].

                               Mary   Winslow
                                her   marke"

    Mary's will was proved 11 July 1679. It would appear that she died before 1 May 1679, however, upon which date Mr. William Tailer renounced the executorship of her estate. Administration of her estate was granted 24 July 1679 to her son John Winslow and son-in-law Richard Middlecott.

       Children (WINSLOW) b. Plymouth after 22 May 1627:

7	i	JOHN[3]	b. prob. bef. 1630
8	ii	SUSANNA	b. prob. bef. 1630
9	iii	MARY	b. about 1631
10	iv	EDWARD	b. ca. 1635
11	v	SARAH	b. ca. 1638
12	vi	SAMUEL	b. ca. 1641
13	vii	JOSEPH	
14	viii	ISAAC	b. 1644
	ix	a child	b. bef. 1650; prob. d.y., certainly d. bef. 12 March 1673 (date father's will)
	x	BENJAMIN	b. 12 Aug. 1653; d. between 12 March 1673/4 and 31 July 1676; unm.

References: MD 1:65-71, 151; 2:116; 3:129-33; 17:70. MQ 33:43-5; 38:101-3. FAM OF PILGRIMS pp. 62-3[no primary source found for mar. date 10 Oct. 1624]. STODDARD pp. 100, 125. BANKS ENGLISH ANCESTRY pp. 45, 130. BRADFORD'S HIST (1952) pp. 442, 446. NEHGR 17:159-60. PLYMOUTH COLONY RECS 1:3, 9; 8:17; 12:11(John & Mary Winslow in a division). PLYMOUTH BY THACHER p. 95. MARY CHILTON. SAVAGE 1:379; 4:601.

THIRD GENERATION

    4   SARAH CHANDLER[3] (Isabella[2] Chilton, James[1]) b. Leyden, Holland, bef. 15 Oct. 1622; d. Bridgewater bef. 27 Oct. 1675.

    She m. Duxbury ca. 1640 SOLOMON LEONARD (or Lenner or Leonardson), b. prob. Monmouthshire, England, ca. 1610; d. Bridgewater bef. 1 May 1671.

Solomon Leonard was first recorded in Duxbury 1637, and in May 1638 was "promised lands on Duxburrow side, (in part of those due to him for his service)." This was probably the usual recompense to a servant; since normal service was seven years, we surmise that Solomon prob. arrived in Plymouth ca. 1631. In Feb. 1638/9 he received a grant of 25 acres. In 1645 he received a share of land in what later became Bridgewater, to which he removed soon after 1649. He was living there in 1658/9.

On 1 May 1671 Samuel Leonard of Bridgewater confirmed that his deceased father, Solomon Leonard, had given land to "my brother John Leonard." Strangely, Samuel did not post bond as administrator of his father, Solomon deceased, until 27 Oct. 1675, at which time the failure to mention the widow of Solomon implies that Sarah had already died. In the disposition of this estate, "Samuel Leanardson" is called eldest son, John second son, with equal division among the "rest of the children." In a deed 10 May 1677 to his brother "Isack Leonardson," Samuel Leonardson mentions brothers John, Jacob and Solomon.

Children (LEONARD) all b. Duxbury, last two prob. in that part later called Bridgewater:

15	i	SAMUEL[4]	b. ca. 1643
16	ii	JOHN	b. ca. 1645
17	iii	JACOB	b. ca. 1647
18	iv	ISAAC	b. ca. 1650
19	v	SOLOMON	b. after 1650
20	vi	MARY	b. ca. 1650

References: TAG 27:1-6; 37:213. SAVAGE 3:80[incorrect wife and death]. BRIDGEWATER BY MITCHELL p. 244[confounds Solomon with son Solomon]. (PLYMOUTH) ANC LANDMARKS p. 172. FAM OF PILGRIMS p. 62. Plymouth Col. LR 3:199; 4:217-8(Samuel Leonard). Plymouth Co. PR #12697(Solomon Leonardson). LEONARD FAM pp. 13-33. PLYMOUTH COLONY RECS 1:83, 112; 3:159-60; 5:179-80; 8:189; 12:113. MA HIST COLL(Second Series) 7:138.

5   MARY CHANDLER[3] (Isabella[2] Chilton, James[1]) b. prob. Leyden, Holland, after 1622; with virtual certainty the "Mary wife of Edmund Burfe" who d. Boston 15 Aug. 1658.

She m. EDMUND BRUFF (or Braugh, Brough, Burfe, or Burph), who prob. d. soon after his wife.

Edmund Brough was first recorded in a Plymouth arbitration in Nov. 1640; he was in Marshfield in 1643, and moved to Boston about 1654. Nothing further was found in Suffolk County probate or land records.

Child (BRUFF) b. pos. Marshfield:

21   i STEPHEN b. bef. 1653

References: TAG 37:212-7. SAVAGE 1:263, 302. BOSTON VR 9:67. MA
            PIONEERS p. 71. PLYMOUTH COLONY RECS 1:164; 2:58; 8:196.

6   MARTHA CHANDLER[3] (Isabella[2] Chilton, James[1]) b. prob.
Leyden, Holland, after 1622; d. Taunton 1 May 1674.
      She m. bef. 1649 JOHN BUNDY, b. England ca. 1617; d.
Taunton after April but bef. 29 Oct. 1681 ae 64. His
mother was sister to Susanna, wife of Phillip Alley of
Boston. He m. (2) Taunton 1676 Ruth (Ratchell?) Gurney of
Mendon; they had sons John, Joseph and Edward. His widow
Ruth m. Guido Bailey of Bridgewater.
      John Bundy was in Boston in 1635; in Plymouth by 1636,
indentured to William Brewster, where he was listed as able
to bear arms in 1643; and served in the Narragansett expedition of 1645. He returned to Boston by 1649, and by
1662 was in Taunton.
      The will of John Bundy "aged 64 or therabout of Tan-
ton", dated April 1681 and proved 29 Oct. 1681, mentions
his wife (unnamed), "the children", son "Jeames Bundy",
"my sons", and "the sons by this wife".

      Children (BUNDY) born to John and Martha, first two born in Bos-
      ton, last three in Taunton:

         i   MARTHA[4] b. 2 Nov. 1649; n.f.r.
   22   ii   MARY b. 5 Oct. 1653
        iii PATIENCE b. ?; d. Taunton 27 March 1665.
   23   iv   JAMES b. 29 Sept. (or Dec.) 1664
         v   SARAH b. 4 March 1668; n.f.r.
  pos. vi   SAMUEL b. 4 Oct. 1670 ["son of Samuel"--an apparent
             error?]; n.f.r.

References: TAG 27:1-6; 33:138, 141; 37:212. SAVAGE 1:298. VR TAUN-
            TON. BOSTON VR 9:29, 41. NEHGR 116:18-9. SEATTLE BUL
5(6):333-5; 6(8):451-3(Bundy). Plymouth Co. PR #3310(John Bundy).
PLYMOUTH COLONY RECS 1:51, 107; 2:90; 4:20; 8:35, 36, 39, 55, 65, 70,
82, 85. SUFFOLK COUNTY CT pp. 210-1(John Bundy, plaintiff). MA
PIONEERS pp. 72a, 79. KING PHILIP's WAR p. 458.

7   JOHN WINSLOW[3] (Mary[2] Chilton, James[1]) b. Plymouth
prob. bef. 1630; d. Boston bet. 3 and 12 Oct. 1683.
      He m.(1) bef. 1664 ELIZABETH -----, living Boston 7
Aug. 1670.
      He m.(2) JUDITH -----, b. ca. 1625(?); bur. Boston 18
Dec. 1714 ae near 90.

The record-book copy of the will of John Winslow merchant of Boston, dated 3 Oct. proved 12 Oct. 1683, remem-
bered each son "of my three brothers: Edward Winslow,
Joseph Winslow and Samuel Winslow"; "the two sons of my
sister Susanna Latham decd (*sic*)"; "my only son John Winslow" under 21 years; wife Judith. His dwelling and land
were to go to son John when he became 21; if John died
while a minor, then to the sons of "my three brothers."
Wife Judith was to receive one-third, and son John two-
thirds, of the rest of all his real and personal estate.
No probate or land records were located for Judith in
Bristol, Plymouth or Suffolk Counties.

Children (WINSLOW) b. Boston to John and Elizabeth:*

   i   RICHARD[4] b. 18 April 1664; d.y.
   ii ELIZABETH b. 14 March 1665; n.f.r. She is not the Eliza-
         beth Winslow, according to Wyman, who m. Charlestown 1689
         Edward Thomas, and d. Boston 1699 ae 33 "wife of Edward
         Thomas." In fact Edward Thomas actually married an Eliza-
         beth Winsley, as can be shown through Suffolk County deeds.
24 iii JOHN b. 22 May 1669
   iv ANN b. 7 Aug. 1670; prob. d.y.

References: MD 10:54-5. FAM OF PILGRIMS p. 62. SAVAGE 4:601[omits
          some children]. BOSTON VR 9:94, 98, 112, 116; 28:16;
30:291. WINSLOW MEM 2:Appendix p. 16. MA HIST COLL (fifth series)
7:30(Sewall Diary). (BOSTON) GRANARY BUR GD p. 227. BOSTON REC COM
7:219. NEHGR 29:71. CHARLESTOWN BY WYMAN 2:939. SUFFOLK CO. LR 22:247.

  8 SUSANNA WINSLOW[3] (Mary[2] Chilton, James[1]) b. Plymouth
prob. bef. 1630; d. E. Bridgewater after 14 Nov. 1685.
    She m. prob. at Plymouth ca. 1649 ROBERT LATHAM, b.
prob. England ca. 1623; d. E. Bridgewater bef. 28 Feb.
1688/9 ae 76.
    He lived with the Rev. Thomas Shepard in Cambridge
for two years, prior to 12 Nov. 1646, then moved to Plymouth, later to Marshfield by 1650 where he was constable
in 1653. Although all his property was confiscated by the
court in 1655, he was accepted as a freeman two years
later; and after he and Susanna removed to E. Bridgewater

---

*The Mayflower Society has accepted lineages through a purported
daughter Judith. No evidence has been found to substantiate this
claim of a daughter Judith born to John and Judith Winslow, as reported in FAMS OF PILGRIMS and in COL. FAMS OF AMERICA 1:56; nor has
the Judith Winslow who married Taunton 1688 John Packer been identified.

about 1660 they evidently moved up the economic ladder,
for after his death his children sold land originally belonging to him.

Although the record-book copy of the will of John
Winslow (#7) dated October 1683 mentions "the two sons of
my sister Susanna Latham decd", three sons were then alive,
and Susanna would acknowledge a deed in Nov. 1685.   The
disappearance of the original will is a matter of regret!

No probate records exist for either Robert or Susanna
Latham.   But on 28 Feb. 1688/9 Joseph Latham of Bridge-
water sold land bought by "my father Robert Latham late of
Bridgewater decd."; on 13 Aug. 1714 Joseph Washborn Sr., of
Bridgewater [husband of Hannah Latham] surrendered rights
to land "of my father-in-law Robert Latham decd."; and on
18 April 1715 James Latham of Bridgewater quitclaimed to
his brother Chilton Latham rights to land "of our father
Robert Latham."   In addition the will of Mary (Chilton)
Winslow (#3) names three grandchildren in the order Mercy
Harris, Mary Pollard and Susanna Latham--the only record
of Mary, and aside from a mention in John Winslow's will,
the only record of Susanna.   Since Mary Pollard's name
occurs between those of Mercy Harris and Susanna Latham,
both daughters of Robert and Susanna, it is possible, although far from certain, that Mary was also theirs.

Although no birth, probate or land record substanti-
ates a daughter Elizabeth, Mr. Bowman's acceptance of her,
a marriage record of an otherwise unplaced Elizabeth
Latham, and the names Robert and Susanna given to her
firstborn children--all warrant her inclusion in this
family.   On the other hand, no proof was found to substantiate the claim by Mitchell and by Savage for a daughter
Sarah Latham.   The daughter Sarah is here replaced by Susanna, based on Williams Latham's suggestion in "Bridgewater Corrections" and reasoning offered in *Mary Chilton's
Title to Celebrity.*

      Children (LATHAM) last four prob. b. Bridgewater:

25   i   MERCY[4] b. Plymouth 2 June 1650
prob. ii MARY b. ca. 1653; m. ----- POLLARD, pos. Samuel Pollard, b.
            Boston 24th 11mo 1645; d. there 29 May 1678; son of
            William and Anne (-----) Pollard.   However, the situation
            is complicated by two stubborn records: Buried in the
            Granary Burial Ground is "Mary Pollard late wife to Samuel
            Pollard died 30 Sept. 1706 ae 56y 6m" [an age which fails
            to jibe]; and the will of Joseph Taynter of Watertown
            dated 18 Feb. 1689/90 names a daughter Mary Pollard not
            otherwise placed and of unrecorded birth.
26   iii SUSANNA b. ca. 1656
27   iv JAMES b. ca. 1659
28   v HANNAH

29 vi   JOSEPH b. ca. 1663
30 vii   ELIZABETH b. ca. 1665
31 viii   CHILTON b. ca. 1672

References: PN&Q 1:10-11; 4:91-5. FAM OF PILGRIMS p. 62. BRIDGE-
WATER BY MITCHELL pp. 230-1, 409. BRIDGEWATER EPITAPHS
p. 209. VR E. BRIDGEWATER. SAVAGE 3:58, 449; 4:601. MA PIONEERS p.
279. MD 1:65-7; 3:129-34; 10:54; 16:235; 18:147; 23:76. WINSLOW MEM
2:Appendix p. 17. CAMBRIDGE HIST p. 598. PEIRCE'S LISTS p. 44. MARY
CHILTON pp. 18-23. PLYMOUTH COLONY RECS 3:71-3, 82; 8:178. Plymouth
Col. LR 3:7(Robert Latham); 3:37(Edward Gray). Plymouth Co. LR 2:26
(Jos. Latham); 5:28(Robt. Latham); 11:40(Jos. Washburn); 12:52(James
Latham). Bridgewater Corrections p. 14. BOSTON VR 9:20. WATERTOWN
BY BOND pp. 596-7. (BOSTON) GRANARY BUR GD p. 190. POLLARD FAM
1:47, 60-1, 65. Suffolk Co. PR 12:29, 361; 1:137[ns](Samuel Pollard).

9 MARY WINSLOW[3] (Mary[2] Chilton, James[1]) b. Plymouth ca.
1631; d. there after 28 Oct. 1663 and bef. Nov. 1665.
    She m. Plymouth 16 Jan. 1650/1 EDWARD GRAY, b. ca.
1629; d. Plymouth "ye last of June" 1681 aged ca. 52. He
m.(2) Plymouth 1665 Dorothy Lettice, by whom he had Edward,
Thomas, Samuel, Susanna, Rebecca and Lydia.
    Edward arrived in Plymouth about 1643, took the free-
man's oath in 1657, and was constable in 1666. A merchant,
he amassed an estate inventoried at £2751, largest at the
time in Plymouth Colony.
    In 1664 John Winslow of Boston gave land to his two
granddaughters Sarah and Anna Gray, naming their father
Edward Gray. On 2 Nov. 1665 Edward Gray "being about to
marry a second wife" made provision for his *five* daughters
by his first wife.
    The inventory of Edward Gray's estate was taken in
July 1681. In a financial settlement 24 Aug. 1681 are mentioned three sons and three daughters of the widow; double
portion to John Gray; and single portions to Nathaniel and
Desire Southworth, Seth and Elizabeth Arnold, Sarah Gray
and Anna Gray. Land of Edward Gray was divided 30 Oct.
1684 among Nathaniel Thomas and Dorothy Gray, as guardians
of Edward, Thomas, Samuel, Susanna, Rebecca and Lydia
(children of Mr. Edward Gray late of Plymouth deceased);
Nathaniel Southworth and wife Desire; Seth Arnold and wife
Elizabeth; Samuel Little and wife Sarah; Capt. John
Whalley, as guardian of Anna Gray; and eldest son John
Gray.

    Children (GRAY) b. Plymouth to Edward and Mary:

32   i   DESIRE[4] b. 6 Nov. 1651
    ii   MARY b. 18 Sept. 1653; living Nov. 1665, but d. bef. 24
         Aug. 1681 leaving no issue (not mentioned in settlement of
         the estate of her father Edward Gray).

33	iii	ELIZABETH b. "11 Feb. 165x" [prob. 1655, 1656 or 1657]
34	iv	SARAH b. 12 Aug. 1659
35	v	JOHN b. 1 Oct. 1661
36	vi	ANNA b. ca. 1664

References: PN&Q 4:91-5. MA PIONEERS p. 197. PLYMOUTH COLONY RECS
     4:123; 5:223-9; 8:11, 12, 15, 22, 31, 181. MD 1:66;
3:129-33; 14:64; 16:235, 237; 17:70, 183; 18:56; 21:62; 34:84. (PLYM-
OUTH) BURIAL HILL p. 3. SAVAGE 2:298; 4:601. FAM OF PILGRIMS p. 62.
PLYMOUTH BY THACHER p. 325. LITTLE COMPTON FAMS p. 292 [assigns wrong
mother to dau. Anna, incorrect husband to dau. Sarah]. SOUTHWORTH GEN
p. 85. Plymouth Col. LR 3:24(John Winslow); 3:45; 5:223, 229-30(Edward Gray).

   10 EDWARD WINSLOW[3] (Mary[2] Chilton, James[1]) b. Plymouth
ca. 1635; d. Boston 19 Nov. 1682 in 48th yr.
     He m. (1) bef. 1661 SARAH HILTON, b. Newbury in June
1641; d. Boston 4 April 1667 ae 26; dau. of William and
Sarah (Greenleaf) Hilton.
     He m. (2) Boston 8 Feb. 1668 ELIZABETH HUTCHINSON, b.
Boston 4 Nov. 1639 (bp. "10 day 9 mo."); d. there 16 Sept.
1728 in 89 yr; dau. of Edward and Catherine (Hanly) Hutchinson. The will of Edward Hutchinson Sr. of Boston,
proved 1675, mentions daughter Elizabeth Winslow.
     The will of Edward Winslow mariner of Boston, dated
8 Nov. 1680 and proved 1 Feb. 1682, names wife Elizabeth;
sons John and Edward, each to receive a double portion; his
children to receive their portions when they become of age
or marry; widow Elizabeth to be executrix. A list of inhabitants of Boston in 1695 includes John Winslow and
mother; these would appear to be son John[4] and his step-
mother, Elizabeth.

     Children (WINSLOW) b. Boston to Edward and Sarah:

     i JOHN[4] b. 18 June 1661; living Boston in 1695; d. there 22
          April 1699.
     ii SARAH b. 10 April 1663; living 31 July 1676 (will of Mary
          (Chilton) Winslow); n.f.r.
  37 iii MARY b. 30 April 1665

     Children (WINSLOW) b. Boston to Edward and Elizabeth:

  38 iv EDWARD b. 1 Nov. 1669
  39 v KATHERINE b. 2 June 1672
  40 vi ELIZABETH b. 22 March 1673/4
     vii SUSANNA b. 31 July 1675; d. after 17 Sept. 1734 (executrix'
          account); m. Boston 22 Nov. 1722 JOHN[3] ALDEN, b. Boston 12
          March 1663; d. there 1 Feb. 1729/30 in 67 yr; son of John[2]
          and Elizabeth (Phillips) Alden, grandson of Pilgrim John

Alden, and widower of Elizabeth Phelps, by whom he had 12
children. John and Susanna had no children.

41 viii   ANNA   b. 7 Aug. 1678

References: MD 1:65-71, 90; 10:53-4, 80; 12:129.   SAVAGE 2:423; 4:600.
NEHGR 1:300; 17:159-60; 19:15; 124:88, 104-6.   VR NEWBURY.
BOSTON VR 9:8, 80, 87, 89, 98, 112, 125, 130, 147, 252; 28:104.   BOS-
TON REC COM (REVISED) 1:170.   ME-NH GEN DICT p. 335.   CHARLESTOWN BY
WYMAN p. 504.   (PLYMOUTH) ANC LANDMARKS p. 289.   CABOT GEN pp. 219,
361.   FAMS OF PILGRIMS p. 62.   (BOSTON) KINGS CHAPEL p. 158.   BOSTON
MEM HIST 2:551.   Suffolk Co. PR 6(1):159(Edw. Hutchinson).   BOSTON
NEWS OBITS 1:4(John Alden).   DOWSE FAM p. 122.   (BOSTON) COPPS HILL
p. 44.

11   SARAH WINSLOW[3] (Mary[2] Chilton, James[1])   b. Plymouth
ca. 1638; d. Boston 9 April 1726 ae 88.
     She m.(1) Boston 19 July 1660 MYLES STANDISH Jr., b.
Plymouth after 22 May 1627; disappeared at sea ca. 1660;
son of Pilgrim Myles and Barbara (-----) Standish.   They
had no children.
     She m.(2) Boston in Nov. 1666 or 1667 TOBIAS PAYNE of
Fownhope, Hereford, England; d. Boston 12 Sept. 1669.   He
came to Boston in 1666 from the West Indies.   The nuncupative will of Tobias Payne, dated 11 Sept. 1669, mentions
"our little sonn"; administration granted his relict Sarah
Payne on behalf of herself and of son William 21 Sept.
1669.
     She m.(3) 1672 RICHARD MIDDLECOTT, b. Wiltshire
County, England, ca. 1640; d. Boston 13 June 1704; son of
Edward and Mary (-----) Middlecott.
     The will of Richard Middlecot merchant of Boston,
dated 22 June 1700 proved 20 June 1704, mentions son Edward
Middlecot "besides Such Estate in Lands which I have formerly Settled upon him in Old England", dau. Mary Gibbs and
son-in-law Henry Gibbs, daus. Sarah Middlecot and Jane Middlecot, son-in-law William Payne, and wife Sara Middlecot.
     A petition received by the General Court sought divi-
sion of land in Boston among Edward Middlecot of Worminster
in Great Britain, Sarah Boucher, Elisha Cook and wife Jane
(Edward, Sarah and Jane being three children of Richard
Middlecot late of Boston decd.) and also the children of
Mrs. Mary Haggat deceased, another daughter.   The division
was ordered 2 Jan. 1727.
     Administration was granted 12 May 1726 on the estate
of Sarah Middlecott late of Boston widow deceased, their
mother, to widow Sarah Boucher and to Elisha Cooke and wife
Jane of Boston.   In a settlement 26 May 1729 one share was
awarded to Mrs. Sarah Boucher, one share to Elisha Cooke
and wife Jane, a double share to William Payne, one share
to the heirs of Mary Hagget deceased, and one share to the
heirs of Edward Middlecott deceased.

Child (PAYNE) b. Boston to Tobias and Sarah:

42   i WILLIAM[4] b. 21 or 22 Jan. 1668/9

Children (MIDDLECOTT) b. to Richard and Sarah:

43   ii   MARY b. Boston 1 July 1674
44   iii EDWARD b. ca. 1676 (?)
45   iv   SARAH b. Boston 20 May 1678
46   v   JANE b. 16 Sept. 1682

References: MD 1:65-71; 3:129-33; 21:1-10. SAVAGE 3:205, 337; 4:162,
         601. FAM OF PILGRIMS p. 62, 147. BOSTON MEM HIST 1:581-
2; 2:549. BOSTON VR 9:76, 108, 133, 146. BRIDGEWATER BY MITCHELL p.
323. MA HIST PROC 13:405(Payne & Gore Fams.). NEHGR 15:308; 124:88.
MA BAY ACTS & RESOLVES 11:120, 207.

12 SAMUEL WINSLOW[3] (Mary[2] Chilton, James[1]) b. Plymouth
ca. 1641; d. Boston 14 Oct. 1680 ae 39.
      He m. bef. 22 June 1675 HANNAH BRIGGS, b. Scituate
ca. 1650; living Boston 4 Nov. 1714 (deed); dau. of Walter
and Mary (-----) Briggs. She m. (2) Capt. Thomas Jolls.
The will of Walter Briggs of Scituate, dated 16 Jan. 1676
probated 1684, names dau. Hannah Winslow.
      Samuel Winslow apparently moved to Maryland, where in
1664 two plots of land called "Intention" and "Cabbin Neck"
were laid out to him. During 1665 he was granted 1100
acres in Talbot County, including "Intention" and "Cabbin
Neck"; and he was foreman of a jury there in 1666. On 10
Oct. 1668 "Joseph Winsloe of Kequetan in Elizabeth Citty
County in Virginia mariner" sold "Boston Clift" and "Plain
Dealing" to "Samuel Winsloe of Talbott in the province of
Maryland, mariner." But little more than a month later, 17
Nov. 1668, "Samuel Winsloe" was styled "merchant of the
City of Boston in New England, formerly of the province of
Maryland and the County of Talbot" when he sold "Plain
Dealing" and "Cabbin Neck".
      Samuel Winslow of Boston, merchant, on 23 Aug. 1669
hired the ketch *Adventure*; and on 4 Sept. 1669 gave power
of attorney to Phillip LeConsteur. Pursuant to an agreement with Walter Briggs of Scituate, Samuel Winslow of
Boston merchant made over to his wife Hannah 22 June 1675
his dwelling in Boston, to the use of whichever of them
lived longer, then to go to their children. (This was undoubtedly the house Samuel purchased from John and Elizabeth Winsley 14 Feb. 1673.)
      The will of Samuel Winslow, mariner of Boston, dated
7 Oct. 1680 proved 26 Jan. 1680/1, names wife Hannah, son
Richard (under 21), daughter Mary Winslow (under 18), and
brothers-in-law Richard Middlecott of Boston and John
Briggs of Scituate. The will of Richard Winslow, merchant
of Boston, dated 31 March 1697 proved 26 Feb. 1707, names

mother Hannah Jolls, widow of Boston, as executor to receive his whole estate; brother John Jolls; uncles John
Briggs deceased, James Briggs, and Cornelius Briggs
deceased, all of Cohasset.

On 4 Nov. 1714 Hannah Jolls of Boston sold land in
Boston which her former husband, Samuel Winslow, had
bought of John Winsley and his wife Elizabeth on 14 Feb.
1673.

Children (WINSLOW) bp. Scituate:

   i RICHARD[4] b. bef. 10 July 1678; bp. 30 March 1679; d. Bos-
      ton bef. 26 Feb. 1707 unm.
  ii MARY b. 8 June 1678; bp. 30 March 1679; d. Boston 2 June
      1681 ae 3 yrs.

References: MD 10:52-3, 55-6. BOSTON VR 9:147. VR SCITUATE. FAM OF
          PILGRIMS p. 63. NEHGR 57:182; 124:88. SAVAGE 1:252;
4:603. (BOSTON) COPP'S HILL pp. 4, 50. BRIGGS FAM 1:69-71, 183-6.
Plymouth Col. LR 4:192(Walter Briggs to Richard Winslow). Suffolk Co.
PR 6:347(Samuel Winslow); 16:413(Richard Winslow). Suffolk Co. LR
28:180(Hannah Jolles). SUFFOLK DEEDS 6:134; 8:407-9; 9:212(Samuel
Winslow). MD EARLY SETTLERS p. 514. MD Archives EE #6 pp. 113-4;
Talbot Co. MD LR A#1:53-4, 66. Calvert Papers, Quit rents, Talbot Co.
1707, reel 1355 p. 21 (MD Hist. Soc., Baltimore). MD ARCHIVES 54:401,
404; 57:396.

13 JOSEPH WINSLOW[3] (Mary[2] Chilton, James[1]) b. Plymouth;
d. Long Island NY bef. 7 Aug. 1679.

He pos. m. (1) ----- ----- (in a deed Sarah called
"his now wife").

He m. (2) by 1668 SARAH LAWRENCE, prob. d. bef. 1693;
dau. of Capt. Thomas Lawrence of Newtown, Long Island, NY.
She m. (2) Charles LeBros. She is not mentioned in her
father's will dated 1693.

An Admiralty Court held at St. John, Maryland, 8 May
1663 confiscated the *Content* of Boston in New England,
Joseph Winslow master. Apparently Joseph remained in Maryland, for in 1663 a 680 acre tract in Talbot County was
laid out to "Joseph Winslow of this province Marriner,"
which he named "Boston Cliff," patented to him in 1665;
also laid out to him and patented was "Plaine Dealing" in
1664. On 10 Oct. 1668 "Joseph Winsloe of Kequetan [now
Hampton] in Elizabeth Citty County in Virginia, Mariner"
sold "Boston Clift" and "Plaine Dealing"; "the said Joseph
Winsloe and Sarah his now wife" guaranteed the title. In
Nov. 1668 in sale of this land by Samuel, Joseph is called
"Marinor of Boston." [No Virginia records to indicate
Joseph resided in that state were found in searches at
Hampton Court House, Marinare's Museum in Newport News, VA
State Library, VA State Hist. Soc., Swem Library College of
William and Mary, the Research Dept. Colonial Williamsburg,
or the State Library and Archives at Raleigh.]

No proof was found that Joseph was the father of Timothy Winslow, of age in Perquimans County NC in 1702, and founder there of a family. Although Joseph Winslow was asked to serve as foreman of a jury 1677-78 in Perquimans County NC, he is called "another New England traider" in the NC COL REC, which thus does not prove he owned land or resided there.

Meantime, Joseph Winslow of Boston, mariner, bought a house of John Drury in Boston 29 Aug. 1674, and adjoining land 15 Sept. 1675. The Suffolk County Court ordered 7 Aug. 1679 the remainder of Mary Winslow's (#3) estate to be distributed, including the children of her deceased son Joseph. Administration on Joseph Winslow, mariner of Boston, was granted 3 Oct. 1679 to brother John Winslow and to Capt. Elisha Hutchinson "in the right of the widow and children." Administration was also granted in New York 26 Jan. 1679/80 to Capt. Thomas Lawrence, Sarah's father.

Children (WINSLOW) last two b. Boston:

	i	child[4] living March 1673/4 ⎫
	ii	child living March 1673/4 ⎬ in grandfather's will; n.f.r.
47	iii	MARY b. 25 Sept. 1674
48	iv	JOSEPH b. 16 June 1677

References: TAG 17:74-6. FAM OF PILGRIMS p. 62. SAVAGE 4:602. MD 1:65-71; 3:129-33; 10:52. BOSTON VR 9:134, 143. NEWTON LI ANNALS p. 284. NEWTON LI MINUTES p. 132. NY HIST COLL (1892) vol. 1 (1665-1707 Abstracts of Wills) p. 64; also Corrections p. 8. NY Surrogate Court Wills 1/2:260. NY HIST COLL: NY Tax List: East Ward vol. 2. NEHGR 124:88. PERQUIMANS CO. (VA) HIST pp. 438-9. SUFFOLK CO. DEEDS 9:16, 246. Col. Rec. NC(old series) 1:274. Talbot Co. MD LR A#1:53-4, 66. Comm. Land Office, Annapolis MD, Rec. of Provincial Court BB:23-4. MS. prepared 20 May 1969 by Mrs. A. Waldo Jones of Vinings GA. MD ARCHIVES 49:23, 49. Calvert Papers, Quit rents, Talbot Co. 1707, reel 1355 pp. 16, 21, 108(MD Hist. Soc., Baltimore). NC COL RECS 1:274.

14 ISAAC WINSLOW[3] (Mary[2] Chilton, James[1]) b. Plymouth 1644; d. Port Royal, Jamaica, bet. 26 and 29 Aug. 1670.

He m. Charlestown 14 Aug. 1666 MARY NOWELL, b. there 26 (3) 1643; d. Charlestown bef. 23 Jan. 1729; dau. of Increase and Parnell (Gray) Nowell. She m. (2) Charlestown, John Long (also his second m.), by whom she had four children.

The will of Isaac Winslow of Middlesex County in New England, dated 26 Aug. 1670 in Port Royal, Jamaica, and probated 29 Aug. 1670, mentions wife Mary, dau. "Parnill" Winslow, and child unborn when he left on 12 July. The will of Mary Long, dated 14 April 1720 and probated 23 Jan. 1729, mentions grandchildren Foster.

Children (WINSLOW) b. Charlestown to Isaac and Mary:

49   i   PARNELL[4] b. 14 Nov. 1667
     ii   ISAAC b. 22 July 1670; d. Charlestown 24 Aug. 1670.

References: MD 3:130. SAVAGE 3:107-8; 4:600. FAM OF PILGRIMS p. 62.
         CHARLESTOWN BY WYMAN pp. 626, 711, 1042. WINSLOW MEM
2:Appendix p. 16. Middlesex Co. PR #25344(Isaac Winslow). NEHGR
124:88.

FOURTH GENERATION

    15 SAMUEL LEONARD[4] (or Leonardson) (Sarah Chandler[3],
Isabella[2] Chilton, James[1]) b. Duxbury ca. 1643; d. Preston
CT after 30 Nov. 1720.
         He m. (1) bef. 7 March 1675/6 ABIGAIL WOOD, b. Plym-
outh ca. 1645; d. prob. Worcester; dau. of John and Sarah
(Masterson) Wood (or Attwood). A division of the estate of
John Wood "formerly of Plymouth" 7 March 1675/6 includes
his child Abigail Leonard.
         He m. (2) DEBORAH -----, prob. d. Preston between 21
March 1718/9 and 30 Nov. 1720.
         He lived in Bridgewater from before 1683 until after
10 Jan. 1687/8 when he and wife Abigail sold lands in
Bridgewater in a deed acknowledged at Boston 31 Jan. 1687/8.
He went to Worcester where he was living in 1692. Driven
out by Indians in 1697, he moved with his family to Preston
CT, where in Nov. 1698 he was among the twelve founders of
the First Church.
         Samuel Leonard of Preston sold 140 acres of land in
Worcester 21 March 1718/9, his wife Deborah releasing her
dower right. Also in 1718 Samuel "Lenard" of Preston sold
to Thomas Clark of Norwich [husband of his daughter Eliza-
beth] his rights to "all ye commons and unlaid out lands in
Preston." Together with his daughter Mercy and her husband,
and Lydia, widow of his son Samuel, he was among founders
of the Second Church in Preston 30 Nov. 1720.

    Children (LEONARD or LEONARDSON) b. Bridgewater to Samuel and
       Abigail:*

50   i   MERCY[5]
51   ii   ELIZABETH
52 iii   SAMUEL b. ca. 1683

---

*No confirmation was found for daughters Mary and Abigail suggested in
LEONARD FAM. The Mayflower Society has accepted lineages based on a
daughter Mary, for whom no substantiating proof was found.

Child (LEONARD or LEONARDSON) b. to Samuel and Deborah:

53   iv   PHEBE   bp. Preston CT 7 or 17 Oct. 1703

References: LEONARD FAM pp. 35-6. PLYMOUTH COLONY RECS 5:188; 6:161-3
             (John Wood). TAG 27:1-6. Plymouth Col. LR 3:199; 4:5
(Samuel Leonard). CSL Barbour Index:Preston. Plymouth Co. PR 1:338-9
(John Wood). PRESTON CH pp. 129, 138. Middlesex Co. LR 20:233(Samuel
Leonard). Preston CT LR 3:159(Samuel Lenard). WORCESTER BY NUTT p.
168.

16   JOHN LEONARD[4] (Sarah Chandler[3], Isabella[2] Chilton,
James[1]) b. Duxbury ca. 1645; d. Bridgewater bef. 21 Nov.
1699 (inventory).
        He m. ca. 1670 SARAH -----, living 30 Aug. 1701.*
     Widow Sarah Leonard and son Joseph Leonard were ap-
pointed administrators 23 Jan. 1699/1700 on the estate of
John Leonard late of Bridgewater deceased. In a division
of this estate the widow was to receive her thirds; John
Leonard the eldest son's share; other shares to sons
Enoch, Moses, Josiah and Joseph, and to daughter Sarah
Leonard when she was 18. On 30 Aug. 1701 signing receipts
were: widow Leonard, John Leonard, Joseph Leonard and
Josiah Leonard. No Plymouth County probate or land records were found to reveal anything further regarding
either the mother or the daughter Sarah.

     Children (LEONARD) all prob. b. Bridgewater:

        i   JOHN[5] living Bridgewater 1710(deed); prob. living with
             brother Moses in Worcester 25 Feb. 1726; prob. d. unm.**
54   ii   ENOCH
55   iii   MOSES   b. ca. 1677
56   iv   JOSIAH
        v   JOSEPH b. bef. 1681(signed receipt 1701); living Bridge-
             water 1725(deed, see #54); n.f.r.
       vi   SARAH   b. after 1683; pos. the Sarah who m. Bridgewater 28
             July 1708 THOMAS WASHBURN; no known issue.

References: TAG 27:1-6[no daughter Martha found]. SAVAGE 3:79. VR
             BRIDGEWATER. LEONARD FAM pp. 37-8. BRIDGEWATER BY
MITCHELL pp. 245, 341[no evidence found that the above Joseph was the
one who married Hannah and moved to Pomfret CT--see #65]. Plymouth
Co. PR 1:321, 360(John Leonard). Plymouth Co. LR 31:204(Enoch Leonard & Joseph Leonard).

---

*Not a daughter of Roger Chandler as claimed in LEONARD FAM.

**Mitchell attributes children born in the 1730's to this John; they
are more likely of a younger John.

17   JACOB LEONARD[4] (or Lenerson)   (Sarah Chandler[3], Isabella[2] Chilton, James[1]) b. Duxbury ca. 1647; d. Bridgewater bet. 9 May and 19 Dec. 1717.

He m.(1) ----- -----, d. bef. 1680.

He m.(2) ca. 1680 SUSANNA KING, b. Weymouth 6 May 1659; living Bridgewater 14 Dec. 1716; dau. of Samuel and Experience (Phillips) King.

Jacob served in King Philip's War 1676; he was in Weymouth by 1679, apparently in Worcester by 1684, but returned to Bridgewater from which he was warned in 1693. Evidently he spent most of his later life in Bridgewater, although he was in Taunton when he purchased a Bridgewater house in 1697, and in Hingham in Dec. 1713. Jacob "Lennard" of Bridgewater sold to Moses "Lennard" (#55) of Marlboro a purchase right in "Woster" (Worcester) 9 May 1717.

The will of Jacob Leonard of Bridgewater husbandman, dated 14 Dec. 1716 presented 19 Dec. 1717 left land in "Woster" to two eldest daughters, Abigail "Washbourne" and Susanna Hill; names three younger daughters, Experience Leonard, Mary Leonard and Sarah Leonard; two sons Solomon and Jacob Leonard; "my present wife Susanna Leonard their mother."

A son Joseph by an earlier wife is indicated in LEONARD FAM and BRIDGEWATER BY MITCHELL, as well as in "Bridgewater Corrections." VR BRIDGEWATER cites gravestones and a "framed record in the possession of the New England Historic Genealogical Society" indicating a son Joseph. It is curious that although the phrase "my present wife" in his will suggests an earlier wife, Jacob did not mention a son Joseph, or Joseph's heirs, either in his will or in any deeds.

Child (LEONARD) b. to Jacob and first wife, prob. Duxbury:

57   i   JOSEPH[5] b. ca. 1672*

Children (LEONARD) b. to Jacob and Susanna:

58   ii   ABIGAIL   b. Weymouth 11 Nov. 1680
59   iii   SUSANNA   b. Weymouth 27 Dec. 1683
      iv   EXPERIENCE   living 14 Dec. 1716; n.f.r.
60   v   MARY
61   vi   SOLOMON   b. ca. 1693
62   vii   SARAH   b. Bridgewater 11 June 1699
  viii   JACOB   b. Bridgewater 13 June 1702; d. there 6 Dec. 1722;
           Solomon granted administration of his brother Jacob, 21
           Dec. 1728 (_sic_); no other probate papers.

---

*The Mayflower Society accepts descent through this Joseph although the evidence is skimpy. No evidence was located to indicate the name of Jacob's purported first wife.

References: SAVAGE 3:79. VR BRIDGEWATER, WEYMOUTH. LEONARD FAM pp.
38-43. WEYMOUTH BY CHAMBERLAIN 3:351, 367. BRIDGEWATER
BY MITCHELL pp. 245, 423. EASTON HIST p. 43. NEHGR 33:246. Bridgewater Corrections p. 17. TAG 27:4. Plymouth Co. PR 4:31; #12617 and
5:408(Jacob Leonard). Plymouth Co. LR 6:82(Harris to Leonard); 10:337
(Allen to Leonard). Middlesex Co. LR 21:295(Jacob Lennard). VR
BRIDGEWATER 1:14 "P.R. 107." KING PHILIP'S WAR p. 221.

18 ISAAC LEONARD[4] (Sarah Chandler[3], Isabella[2] Chilton,
James[1]) b. Duxbury ca. 1650; d. Bridgewater after 10 Dec.
1717 and before 9 March 1719/20 (deed).
He m. ca. 1675 DELIVERANCE -----, living Bridgewater
in March 1719/20 (pos. dau. of William and Hannah (-----)
Ames b. Braintree 12 mo. 6th 1653).
Isaac took part in the Narragansett Expedition in
1675, for which son Isaac Leonard of Bridgewater claimed a
grant in 1733. He was a weaver. Isaac of Bridgewater and
wife Deliverance sold land with dwelling and barn in Bridgewater 29 Feb. 1705/6. He owned land in Mendon and Worcester. He was of Bridgewater 27 March 1717 when he transferred Worcester land, wife Deliverance consenting 7 March
1719/20; son Benjamin on 9 March 1719/20 attested he saw
Isaac sign. On 5 April 1717, acknowledged 10 Dec. 1717,
Isaac Leonard of Bridgewater gave to son Joseph Leonard his
homestead in Bridgewater, on condition Isaac have lifetime
use. No Plymouth County probate or land records were found
to connect probable child Deliverance.

    Children (LEONARD) presumably b. Bridgewater:

63   i ISAAC[5]
64   ii HANNAH b. 15 March 1679/80
prob.iii DELIVERANCE m. Bridgewater 9 Jan. 1701 SAMUEL WASHBURN JR.,
            b. Bridgewater 6 April 1678; d. 1752; son of Samuel and
            Deborah (Packard) Washburn. He m.(2) 1703 Abigail Leonard
            (#58). Samuel and Deliverance had no issue.
65   iv JOSEPH
66   v BENJAMIN b. ca. 1686-90

References: VR BRIDGEWATER. BRAINTREE VR p. 633. TAG 46:121.
BRIDGEWATER BY MITCHELL pp. 245, 341. NEHGR 16:145.
LEONARD FAM pp. 44-5. KING PHILIP'S WAR p. 428. BOSTON TRANSCRIPT 19
Feb. 1917 #6058-10. Plymouth Co. LR 8:65; 14:94(Isaac Leonard); 38:201
(Benjamin Leonard). Middlesex Co. LR 21:70(Isaac Leonard).

19 SOLOMON LEONARD (or Lenerson)[4] (Sarah Chandler[3],
Isabella Chilton[2], James[1]) b. Duxbury or Bridgewater after
1650; d. Bridgewater 14 May 1686 (inventory).
He m. MARY -----, d. after 15 June 1686. The inventory of the estate of Solomon Lenerson of Bridgewater was

taken 21 May 1686, and sworn to be true by Mary Lenerson 15 June 1686.

Isaac Hayward and his wife Martha in 1739 transferred all rights to lands of "our father Solomon Leonard" late of Bridgewater deceased.

Children (LEONARD) prob. b. Bridgewater:*

67   i   MARTHA[5] b. ca. 1685

References: BRIDGEWATER BY MITCHELL pp. 244-5, 277, 288[confounds two Solomons, father and son]. LEONARD FAM pp. 46-8. Plymouth Co. PR 1:1(Solomon Leonard). Plymouth Co. LR 33:46(Isaac Hayward).

20 MARY LEONARD[4] (Sarah Leonard[3], Isabella[2] Chilton, James[1]) b. Duxbury or Bridgewater after 1650; living Taunton 3 March 1724/5.

She m. Taunton 24 Dec. 1673 JOHN POLLARD, b. Boston 4th day 4th month 1644; living Taunton 7 May 1722; son of William and Anne (-----) Pollard. He m.(1) Deliverance Willis, by whom he had Deliverance, Hannah and William.

John was head of a family in Taunton in 1675, then moved to Boston; he returned to Taunton before Feb. 1692/3 when he bought land of Nicholas Stoughton. John Pollard Sr. was a press master for troops in July 1695; John Pollard Jr. was impressed for service in May 1697. On 7 May 1722 John Pollard of Taunton, cooper, released rights to one-eighth of a house called the "Horse Show" [Horse Shoe] in Boston to Jonathan Pollard of Boston, innholder; wife Mary signed the deed. Mary Pollard of Taunton testified 3 March 1724/5 aged about 75 years.

Children (POLLARD) b. to John and Mary:

     i   JOHN[5] b. Taunton 20 March 1675; disappears after 1710, unless he is the John Polden of Plymouth.
    ii   MARY b. Boston 8 March 1677; n.f.r.**
68 iii   SAMUEL b. Boston 16 Jan. 1679
pos. iv JOSEPH bp. Boston 1685/6; n.f.r.

References: SAVAGE 3:80, 449. VR TAUNTON. BOSTON VR 9:18, 101, 108, 115, 142, 149. MD 21:57. LEONARD FAM p. 48. POLLARD FAM 1:47, 50-3[erroneously indicates John Pollard m. Mary dau. of Solomon

---

*No evidence was found to support the claim in LEONARD FAM for two other "supposed" daughters, Sarah and Lydia. The Sarah Leonard who m. 1710 Samuel Perry of "Sandwitch," and Lydia Leonard who m. 1712 Joseph Pratt Jr. have not been placed.

**This Mary was not the wife of Solomon Kneeland, since one of the sons of Solomon and Mary Kneeland had Samuel Pollard for a grandfather.

and Mary Leonard; proposes the family lived in Essex County and had additional children]. PLYMOUTH COLONY RECS 8:55, 66. Suffolk Co. LR 33:261(John Pollard). Bristol Co. LR 4:68(Stoughton to Pollard); 14:208(John Pollard); 16:93(Mary Pollard). TAUNTON HIST pp. 93, 399, 400. [John Pollard and wife Deborah Campbell of Norton 1724 (see Bristol Co. LR 18:225) have not been placed.]

21 STEPHEN BRUFF[4] (or Broof, Brosse, Brust, Burfe, Burph) (Mary Chandler[3], Isabella[2] Chilton, James[1]) b. pos. Marshfield bef. 1653; d. bef. 21 Jan. 1719.
    He m.(1) Rehoboth 29 May 1674 ELIZABETH PERRY, b. there 25 Oct. 1650; dau. of Anthony and Elizabeth (-----) Perry. The will of Anthony Perry, dated Rehoboth 20 Feb., proved 15 March 1682, mentions wife Elizabeth, eldest daughter Elizabeth Bruff, and three grandchildren [but none of them named Bruff].
    He m.(2) Boston ca. 1697 DAMARIS THREENEEDLES, b. Boston 26 Oct. 1670; d. bef. 21 Jan. 1719; dau. of Bartholomew and Damaris (Hawkins) Threeneedles.
    The will of Bartholomew Threeneedles of Boston, dated 2 April 1700 probated 7 Oct. 1702, names wife Damaris, daughter Damaris Broffe, and granddaughter Elizabeth Broffe. An agreement dated 18 Jan. 1719 between Damaris Threeneedles of Boston, widow of the late Bartholomew deceased, and children of Bartholomew, includes "David Gibbins" of Boston mariner and wife Elizabeth, both for themselves and for Damaris Bruff, a minor, Elizabeth and Damaris being the only two children of Damaris Bruff, deceased, daughter of Bartholomew.

    Child (BRUFF) prob. b. to Stephen and Elizabeth:

    i JOHN[5] b. after 1681; m. Boston 5 Nov. 1706 MARY BRICKNEL, b. Boston 15 Sept. 1689; dau. of Edward and Mary (Kemble) Bricknel. No children found. Did she m.(2) Boston 1708 John Pumery, and d. bef. Dec. 1711, when he remarried?

    Children (BRUFF) b. to Stephen and Damaris:

69   ii   ELIZABETH b. ca. 1699
70   iii DAMARIS b. Boston 27 Oct. 1701

References: MD 19:70. TAG 37:212-7. SAVAGE 1:305. BOSTON REC COM 1:152. REHOBOTH VR pp. 74, 715. Plymouth Col. PR 4:2:29 (Anthony Perry). PLYMOUTH COLONY RECS 8:53. BOSTON VR 9:116, 183; 24:5; 28:8, 20. Suffolk Co. PR 9:363; 14:8, 13, 62(Edw. Bricknell); 15:77(Bartholomew Threeneedles). Suffolk Co. LR 34:145(Damaris Threeneedles et al.).

22 MARY BUNDY[4] (Martha Chandler[3], Isabella[2] Chilton, James[1]) b. Boston 5 Oct. 1653; living Taunton in Feb. 1694 (deed).

      She m. Taunton 5 Jan. 1673 ANDREW SMITH, b. Taunton 10 April 1648; living 4 Feb. 1722/3 (deed). Andrew Smith of Taunton and wife Mary sold land in Taunton 15 Feb. 1694.

      Andrew Smith of Taunton gave land to son Samuel Smith of Taunton 6 May 1706, and acknowledged the deed 4 Feb. 1722/3. He gave land to son John Smith of Taunton 4 Sept. 1710. On 10 Dec. 1714 Giles Gilbert, Andrew Smith and John Briggs of Taunton sold land in Taunton and Norton to Samuel and John Smith of Taunton, sons of Andrew. On 10 Dec. 1716 Andrew Smith Sr. of Taunton gave land in Norton to son Andrew Smith Jr. of Taunton. No probate records were found in Bristol County for Andrew or Mary Smith. Smith deeds were searched in Bristol County; few clearly applied to this family, and insufficient identification makes following the children difficult. An in-depth study of Taunton court records might be fruitful.

     Children (SMITH) b. Taunton:

    i   MARY[5] b. 30 March (or 3 Oct.) 1675; n.f.r.
   ii   SAMUEL b. 15 May 1678; was he the Samuel who d. Taunton
          "old, April soposed 1765"? On 11 May 1756 a Samuel Smith
          aged about 78 pointed out a bound in Taunton.
  iii SUSANNA b. 2 Nov. 1680; n.f.r.
   iv ANDREW b. 2 April 1683; d. Taunton bef. 18 Aug. 1724. He
          pos. m.(1) int. Norton 15 Dec. 1722 MARY VERY; m.(2) SARAH
          -----; living 13 Sept. 1742. She m.(2) ----- Morris after
          18 April 1727. Andrew Smith Jr. of Taunton sold a swamp
          in Norton 26 June 1719, acknowledged in 1722. Sarah Smith
          widow of Andrew Smith of Taunton deceased was appointed
          administratrix of her husband's estate 18 Aug. 1724. In
          her account 4 Sept. 1725 she included "provision spent in
          ye family," which implies there were children. On 18
          April 1727 Sarah Smith widow of Andrew late of Taunton
          sold land, formerly Andrew's homestead, acknowledged 13
          Sept. 1742 by Sarah Morris formerly Smith.
    v   JOHN b. 23 Aug. 1685; d. 6 Sept. 1685
71   vi MARTHA b. 20 Oct. 1686
  vii JOHN b. 3 June 1689; living Taunton 9 Oct. 1736 when Benja-
          min Smith of Stoughton sold to "John Smith of Taunton, son
          of Andrew Smith late of Taunton deceased," land in Taun-
          ton, part granted in 1702 to Giles Gilbert, the rest to
          the right of James Phillips in 1721 for Andrew Smith. On
          11 May 1756 a John Smith aged about 68 pointed out a
          bound in Taunton.

      viii JOSEPH b. 18 Jan. 1691; n.f.r.*
       ix BENJAMIN b. 4 Feb. 1695; was he the Benjamin of Stoughton
            who sold land to John above? n.f.r.

References: VR TAUNTON. PLYMOUTH COLONY RECS 8:58, 66, 69, 82, 86.
         SEATTLE BUL 6(8):454. Bristol Co. LR 5:303; 9:608;
10:701; 15:72, 81; 16:72, 261; 50:518(Andrew Smith); 42:23(Saml. &
John Smith); 26:101(Benjamin Smith); 31:86(Sarah Smith). Bristol Co.
PR 4:339; 5:66, 158(Andrew Smith).

    23 JAMES BUNDY[4] (Martha Chandler[3], Isabella[2] Chilton,
James[1]) b. Taunton 29 Sept. or Dec. 1664; d. East Greenwich RI 25 Sept. 1721 (inventory).
      He m. MARY -----, d. South Kingstown RI bef. 6 Feb.
1736/7 (inventory presented).
      On 6 Jan. 1690 James Bundy of Braintree sold land in
Taunton. On 31 May 1703 James Bundy of "Narrigansett country near Point Judah," eldest surviving son of John Bundy
formerly of Taunton, transferred land in Taunton. James
Bundy of "Kings Town" cooper sold all rights to house and
land which had been his for 16 years, near Point Judith RI
in 1719/20. In 1720 James of Kingstown gave to his son
Samuel Bundy of Kingstown, laborer, part of his East Greenwich farm. On 15 Sept. 1721 James of East Greenwich sold
to Samuel Bundy of East Greenwich, cooper, and Ebenezer
Bundy of Preston CT, yeoman, all his land, houses, etc. in
East Greenwich; Ebenezer Bundy transferred his share to his
"brother Samuel" on 20 Nov. 1721.
      On 25 Nov. 1721 Mary Bundy, widow of James Bundy of
East Greenwich deceased, and three sons of James--James,
Samuel and Ebenezer--appeared regarding an administrator.
On 10 March 1721/2 Samuel Bundy "son of deceased" was appointed administrator of the estate of James Bundy of East
Greenwich, cooper; the inventory was dated 8 Nov. 1721.
      In depositions on 30 Jan. 1730/1 Samuel Bundy aged 37
of East Greenwich and Joseph Bundy aged 30 of North Kingstown mentioned their father James Bundy. Ebenezer Bundy
deposed 31 March 1719 aged "19 years and upward" mentioning
his father James Bundy. No evidence was found to prove
that the following were also children of James as has been
claimed: John, who married Norwich CT Lydia Smallbent;
Lydia; Benjamin, of Voluntown and possibly later of Stratford CT; and Nathaniel, who married Mary Palmister in
Westerly RI.

---

*Although the SEATTLE BUL claims Joseph Smith was of Canterbury CT,
this is incorrect. The Joseph of Canterbury was originally from Newton MA [VR NEWTON, CAMBRIDGE. Canterbury CT LR 1:143(Frost & Woodward
to Joseph Smith)].

Children (BUNDY):

72 i   JAMES[5] b. ca. 1690
73 ii   SAMUEL b. ca. 1694
74 iii EBENEZER b. ca. 1699
75 iv   JOSEPH b. ca. 1701

References: E. Greenwich RI PR 1:21(James Bundy). E. Greenwich LR
3A:74(James Reinolds); 3A:185, 256, 257(James Bundy). E.
Greenwich Council Rec.1715-1729:20(Mary Bundy). Bristol Co. MA LR
4:147; 7:554(James Bundy). RI Rec Ctr(deposition Ebenezer Bundy). No.
Kingstown RI LR 4:192(James Bundy). So. Kingstown RI LR 1:127(James
Bundy); 3:355(deposition Samuel Bundy). So. Kingstown RI Council &
Probate Rec 3:46(Mary Bundy). SEATTLE BUL 6(8):454-5, 469(Bundy).

24 JOHN WINSLOW[4] (John[3], Mary[2] Chilton, James[1]) b.
Boston 22 May 1669; d. there 1 Jan. 1694/5.
   He m. Boston 18 June 1689 ABIGAIL ATKINSON, b. Boston
13 Dec. 1672; d. bef. 31 Dec. 1739; dau. of Theodore and
Elizabeth (Mitchelson) Atkinson Jr. She m.(2) Boston 1702
James Oborn, by whom she had Abigail and James; she m.(3)
Boston 1714 Samuel Penhallow of Portsmouth NH.
   The will of John Winslow merchant of Boston, dated 21
April 1690 proved 4 Nov. 1695, "being now goeing abroad in
their Ma[ties] Service to war against the comon Enemy" names
his mother Mrs. Judith Winslow and wife Abigail, mentioning
her heirs and assignes.
   Sarah Winslow (widow of John[5]) 31 Dec. 1739 renounced
administration of the estate of her "mother" Penhallow. On
30 April 1740 administration of the estate of Abigail Penhallow was granted to her son-in-law William King of Portsmouth.
   John Winslow of Boston mariner, Alexander Todd of Boston mariner and wife Elizabeth (Elizabeth and John being
the only children and heirs of John Winslow late of Boston
mariner deceased) conveyed 12 Oct. 1719 all rights in the
estate of their father in a deed acknowledged by all three
19 Sept. 1720.

   Children (WINSLOW) b. Boston:

76 i   ELIZABETH[5] b. 2 April 1693 (_sic_) [was 1692 intended?]
77 ii   JOHN b. 31 Dec. 1693 (_sic_)

References: BOSTON VR 9:122, 208, 209; 24:16, 50; 28:5, 54. BOSTON
NEWS OBITS 3:226. MD 10:55. ME-NH GEN DICT p. 765.
NEHGR 24:15-6; 29:110; 32:31. Suffolk Co. PR(new series) 6:487(James
Oborne). Suffolk Co. LR 34:268(John Winslow et al.). NH STATE PAPERS
32:283-7(Samuel Penhallow); 32:773(Abigail Penhallow).

25 MERCY LATHAM[4] (Susanna Winslow[3], Mary[2] Chilton,
James[1]) b. Plymouth 2 June 1650; d. Bridgewater after 2
Feb. 1684 (deed) and bef. June 1698.
    She m. bef. 29 Oct. 1668 ISAAC HARRIS, b. Duxbury ca.
1644; d. Bridgewater 22 Jan. 1706/7; son of Arthur and Martha (-----) Harris. He m.(2) Hingham 1698 Mary Dunbar, by
whom he had children Benjamin and Martha.
    Robert Latham and his daughter Mercy, wife of "Isaack
Harris," complained to the General Court at Plymouth that
Harris "departed the government" leaving her with her
child; the court took action 5 July 1669. In July 1679
Martha Harris, widow of Arthur late of Boston deceased,
deeded land to her son Isaac Harris of Bridgewater. Isaac
was living in Bridgewater in 1684 and in 1706 (deeds).
    Sons-in-law Peletiah Smith and John Kingman were ap-
pointed administrators of the estate of Isaac Harris late
of Bridgewater on 7 March 1706/7. On the same day Peletiah
was appointed guardian to Isaac's daughter Mercy "Harrice"
aged over 14; and Peter Dunbar was appointed guardian to
Isaac's two children by his wife Mary, Peter's sister. A
19 June 1708 account and division of Isaac's estate names
Isaac Harris as eldest living son, other sons Samuel and
Benjamin, daughters Desire wife of John Kingman, Jane wife
of Peletiah Smith, Susanna "Nuland," Mary, Mercy and
Martha.

        Children (HARRIS) b. to Isaac and Mercy:

78   i   DESIRE[5] b. prob. Bridgewater bef. 5 July 1669
79 ii   JANE b. Bridgewater 19 July 1671
80 iii   SUSANNA b. bef. 1680
    iv   ARTHUR prob. d. at sea ca. 1703
81   v   ISAAC
82 vi   SAMUEL b. prob. bef. 1685
83 vii   MARY b. Bridgewater bef. 1690
84 viii MERCY b. Bridgewater bet. 1688 and 1693

References: VR BRIDGEWATER. MD 1:67; 3:129-31. SAVAGE 2:361.
        BRIDGEWATER BY MITCHELL pp. 176, 231 [Arthur's wife was
not Martha Lake; both this and Savage err in assigning dau. Mercy too
early a birth and the wrong husband]. HINGHAM HIST pp. 195-6, 298.
ANNAPOLIS CO NS HIST p. 523. Plymouth Co. PR 2:85-6, 91; 3:12-3(Isaac
Harris). Plymouth Co. LR 7:17; 18:39(Isaac Harris); 14:174(Martha
Harris). PLYMOUTH COLONY RECS 5:10, 23.

26 SUSANNA LATHAM[4] (Susanna Winslow[3], Mary[2] Chilton,
James[1]) b. prob. Bridgewater ca. 1656; d. bef. June 1703.
    She prob. m. ca. 1680 Ensign John Haward (or Howard)
Jr., b. ca. 1653; d. Bridgewater bet. July 1725 and 3 Oct.
1726; son of Lt. John and Martha (Hayward) Haward. He m.
(2) bef. 28 June 1703 Sarah -----. Both John Haward and
his father were innholders in Bridgewater.

A study of Plymouth County deeds provides strong cir-
cumstantial evidence that John Haward married a daughter of
Robert Latham. In addition, two of John's children were
named Robert and Susanna--names rare in the Haward family.
Mary Chilton's Title to Celebrity urges accepting the
known daughter Susanna Latham, rather than an otherwise unknown daughter Sarah Latham, as John's Latham wife. Because
on 28 June 1703 a wife Sarah signed a deed with John Haward,
Mitchell, perhaps aware of the Latham-Haward connection,
evidently assumed that Sarah was a Latham. We prefer the
assumption that John had a second wife, Sarah -----.
     Absence of appropriate vital, land or probate records
linking Susanna Latham to John Haward makes it impossible
to prove their marriage. We do not even know when Susanna
died. Not all of John's children need be Susanna's; but if
Robert was named for his Latham grandfather, then at least
the first five bore Latham blood.
     Edward Howard of Bridgewater on 3 Oct. 1726 was appoin-
ted administrator of his father John Haward (or Howard) late
of Bridgewater deceased. A division was made 12 May 1729
among eldest son Edward, son Robert, daughter Martha wife of
David Perkins of Bridgewater, daughter Sarah wife of David
Turner of Rehoboth, daughter Susanna wife of Nathaniel Eames
of Bridgewater, and daughter Bethiah wife of John Hays of
Providence RI. In a 13 Feb. 1732 settlement, five children
were living, and mention is made of "the children of Susanna
Eames deceased."

        Children (HAWARD or HOWARD) b. to John in Bridgewater, probably
by Susanna:*

    84A   i   MARTHA[5] b. ca. 1681
    84B   ii   SUSANNA b. ca. 1683
    84C   iii EDWARD b. 7 Feb. 1686/7
    84D   iv   BETHIA b. ca. 1691
    84E   v   ROBERT b. ca. 1699
    84F   vi   SARAH b. ca. 1701

        for 84A-F refer to pages 317-320

References: MARY CHILTON pp. 18-27. VR BRIDGEWATER. BRIDGEWATER BY
          MITCHELL pp. 197-8, 231[indicates a Sarah Latham]. SAVAGE
2:472[indicates a Samuel instead of Susanna]. HOWARD GEN pp. 1-6[in-
dicates a Sarah Latham]. Bridgewater Corrections p. 14. Plymouth Co.
PR 5:139, 720-7; 6:357, 363(John Howard). Plymouth Co. LR 5:159(John
Haward & wife Sarah); 22:123, 131; 23:134(John Haward).

---

*The Mayflower Society has accepted lineages through all six of these
as children of Sarah Latham, purported daughter of Robert. No evidence
was found for this daughter Sarah; but the children are probably grandchildren of Robert Latham.

27 JAMES LATHAM[4] (Susanna Winslow[3], Mary[2] Chilton,
James[1]) b. ca. 1659; d. Bridgewater bef. 6 Feb. 1738/9 ae
ca. 80.

He m. E. Bridgewater bef. 9 April 1690 (deed) DELIVER-
ANCE ALGER, b. W. Bridgewater; d. E. Bridgewater bef. 1
Jan. 1749; dau. of Thomas and Elizabeth (Packard) Alger.

On 6 Feb. 1738 administration was granted to Joseph
Latham of Bridgewater on the estate of his deceased father
James Latham. The inventory includes real estate already
settled by deeds of gift to son Joseph, to Nathaniel Har-
den, to Nicholas Wade, to son Thomas Latham, and to Daniel
Johnson's wife. Necessaries were set off to the widow
Deliverance Latham 2 April 1739. On 3 Sept. 1750 the
estate was settled naming sons Thomas and Joseph Latham,
dividing residue among Ann Wade, Susanna Harden and Betty
John (*sic*).

On 1 Jan. 1749 Joseph Latham was appointed administrator on the estate of "your mother Deliverance Latham,
widow, late of Bridgewater." Her estate was settled 7 Oct.
1751 with payments to Nicholas Wade and Nathaniel Harden.

Children (LATHAM) prob. all b. Bridgewater:

85   i   THOMAS[5] b. bef. 1693
86   ii   ANNE b. ca. 1693
87   iii SUSANNA b. bef. 1697
88   iv   JOSEPH b. bef. 1697
89   v   BETTY b. ca. 1701; bp. E. Bridgewater 6 June 1725

References: Plymouth Co. PR 8:4; 10:355; 11:414(James Latham); 11:310;
        12:392(Deliverance Latham). Plymouth Co. LR 6:103(James
Latham and wife). MD 16:256; 22:118-21. VR BRIDGEWATER, E. BRIDGE-
WATER. BRIDGEWATER BY MITCHELL p. 231. BRIDGEWATER EPITAPHS p. 210.
SAVAGE 1:28.

28 HANNAH LATHAM[4] (Susanna Winslow[3], Mary[2] Chilton,
James[1]) b. prob. Bridgewater; d. after 1 July 1725.

She m. Marshfield ca. 1680 JOSEPH WASHBURN, b. Bridge-
water 7 July 1653; d. there 20 April 1733 ae ca. 80; son of
John and Elizabeth (Mitchell) Washburn, and a descendant of
Pilgrim Francis Cooke. Joseph was a blacksmith.

Joseph Washburn of Bridgewater in 1714 transferred land
to son Joseph Washburn, naming father-in-law Robert Latham.
In 1718 Joseph of Plympton, blacksmith, transferred Bridgewater land to son Jonathan. Still of Plympton he transferred land in 1720 to son Ebenezer Washburn of Bridgewater,
and in 1723 to son Miles Washburn of Plympton. On 1 July
1725 Joseph Washburn and wife Hannah acknowledged a deed
of their homestead in Bridgewater. In 1738 Miles and Edward Washburn of Plympton sold a meadow bought by their father Joseph Washburn. The sons Ephraim and Benjamin are
named as uncles by Seth Washburn (MD 2:67). No probate,
land or vital records were found to confirm proposed daugh-

ters Hepzibah and Hannah. However, a process of elimination indicates Joseph to be the likely parent of Hepzibah who married Benjamin Leach; Benjamin and Hepzibah named their first son Joseph (for her father?); and Benjamin witnessed a deed of Joseph Washburn.

Children (WASHBURN) prob. b. Bridgewater:

```
90     i   JONATHAN⁵
91    ii   JOSEPH
92   iii   MILES
93    iv   EBENEZER
94     v   EPHRAIM
95    vi   EDWARD
96   vii   BENJAMIN
96A viii   prob. HEPZIBAH* (see page 320).
```

References: MD 2:66-70; 15:247; 21:40-2. VR BRIDGEWATER. SAVAGE 4:430. BRIDGEWATER BY MITCHELL pp. 231, 339. WASHBURN DESC pp. 53, 54, 56b-57[not all are accepted]. Plymouth Co. LR 10:528; 11:40; 14:195, 256; 15:41, 204; 12:153; 18:109; 19:98(Jos. Washburn); 36:189(Miles & Edward Washburn).

29 JOSEPH LATHAM⁴ (Susanna Winslow³, Mary² Chilton, James¹) prob. b. Bridgewater ca. 1663; living 20 May 1706, prob. d. before 9 July 1723.
      He m. ca. 1688 PHEBE FENNER, b. Providence RI ca. 1665; living there April 1710, and prob. living 30 June 1716; dau. of Arthur and Mehitable (Waterman) Fenner. In 1702 Arthur Fenner of Providence made over to his son-in-law Joseph Latham of Providence a legacy for daughter Phebe Fenner, now wife of Joseph.
      Joseph Latham of Bridgewater sold land 28 Feb. 1688/9, which "my father Robert Latham bought," in a deed acknowledged by Joseph and wife Phebe. But Joseph was an "inhabitant of Providence" when he sold other Bridgewater land 12 April 1690. Living in Providence he bought and sold several tracts, the last was the sale on 24 May 1705 of "a mantion hous" and all his lands in Providence. Joseph left his family, and in Oct. 1705 was in Saybrook CT when he granted his wife Phebe power of attorney. He appeared at Bristol RI in May 1706. On 12 July 1706 Phebe, wife of Joseph Latham, relinquished her dower rights in land "formerly belonging to Joseph Latham formerly of Providence."

---

*The Mayflower Society has accepted lineages through this daughter Hepzibah, as claimed in the LEACH FAM. No confirming evidence was found in probate, land or vital records, other than her marriage record.

Joseph was last reported seen in Tappan NY in 1707, by a
visitor to Providence.
    Account books of Thomas Fenner mention his sister
Phebe Latham, her husband Joseph, and their son Robert; the
latest reference to Phebe was a promise to pay her dated 30
June 1716. Josiah Westcot had promised to pay Phebe Latham
"of Providence" 24 April 1710. On 9 July 1723 Phebe Latham
of Providence, daughter of Joseph Latham deceased, made a
deposition "being of lawful age." (No evidence of either a
probate record or a death was found for Joseph).

        Children (LATHAM) b. prob. Providence RI:

    97   i   ROBERT[5]
    98   ii PHEBE

References: WATERMAN GEN 3:7. TAG 15:83. RI GEN DICT pp. 74, 315[no
        evidence found for dau. Sarah]. RI HIST MAG 7:1:19-37.
BRIDGEWATER BY MITCHELL p. 231. Plymouth Co. LR 2:26; 10:147, 148
(Joseph Latham). Providence RI LR 2:42(Brown to Latham); 2:43(Arthur
Fenner); 2:163(Westcot to pay Phebe Latham). RI Land Rec (Archives,
Statehouse) 2:264-5(354-5)(Joseph Latham & Phebe Latham). Providence
RI Town Papers (originals, RI Hist. Soc.) #0723, #16823, #16875,
#16981(Phebe Latham); #0930, #16713, #16725, #16805(Joseph Latham).
PROVIDENCE TOWN PAPERS 4:61, 131; 5:37, 136; 11:55, 86(Joseph Latham);
6:228-30(Arthur Fenner's will).

    30 ELIZABETH LATHAM[4] (Susanna Winslow[3], Mary[2] Chilton,
James[1]) b. prob. Bridgewater ca. 1665; d. Kingston 16 Nov.
1730 in 66 yr.
    She m. Plymouth 2 Aug. 1687 FRANCIS COOKE, b. Plymouth
5 Jan. 1662/3; d. Kingston bef. 18 Sept. 1746; son of Jacob
and Damaris (Hopkins) Cooke, and a grandson of Pilgrims
Francis Cooke and Stephen Hopkins.
    The will of Francis Cooke of Kingston, dated 28 Oct.
1732 probated 18 Sept. 1746, refers to son Caleb Cook;
children of son Robert Cook deceased; children of son Francis Cook deceased; three daus. (or their representatives):
Susanna Stertevant, children of dau. Sarah Cole, dau.
Elizabeth Cook; son Caleb was to be executor.

        Children (COOKE):

    99   i   SUSANNA[5] b. ca. 1689, bp. Plymouth 1693
   100   ii   ROBERT b. ca. 1691, bp. Plymouth 1693
   101   iii CALEB b. ca. 1694
   102   iv   FRANCIS b. ca. 1696
   103   v   SARAH b. ca. 1698
   104   vi   ELIZABETH b. ca. 1707

References: VR KINGSTON. MD 7:26; 13:204; 17:183; 18:147; 29:87.
        PN&Q 4:39. BRIDGEWATER BY MITCHELL p. 231. PLYMOUTH

CH RECS 1:280.

31 CHILTON LATHAM[4] (Susanna Winslow[3], Mary[2] Chilton,
James[1]) b. Bridgewater ca. 1672; d. there 6 Aug. 1751 in
80 yr.
He m. Bridgewater 6 Dec. 1699 SUSANNA KINGMAN, b. Weymouth 12 April 1679; d. E. Bridgewater 23 June 1776 ae 97y
2m; dau. of John and Elizabeth (Edson) Kingman. Chilton
Latham and wife Susanna both of Bridgewater in 1724 surrendered rights to the estate of "our father John Kingman deceased."
     Chilton Latham of Bridgewater gave land where his
house stands to son Arthur Latham of Bridgewater 7 Nov.
1734. On 7 Oct. 1751 Susanna Latham widow of Bridgewater
was appointed administratrix of the estate of Chilton
Latham late of Bridgewater deceased <u>intestate</u>. The <u>will</u> of
Chilton Latham gentleman of Bridgewater, dated 13 June 1748
sworn 2 March 1752, names wife Susanna; sons Charles, James,
Robert and Joseph; two grandchildren Nehemiah and Jean
Latham "besides what I have given their father Arthur deceased"; daughters Susanna "Wate" wife of Thomas "Waid" Jr.
of Bridgewater, and Mary wife of Jonathan Allen of Bridgewater; son Robert to be executor.

          Children (LATHAM) b. Bridgewater:

105   i   CHARLES[5] b. 18 March 1701
      ii   JANE b. 13 June 1703; d. bef. 13 June 1748, prob. d.y.
106 iii   ARTHUR b. 16 Sept. 1705
107   iv   JAMES b. 16 Aug. 1708
108   v   ROBERT b. 16 Aug. 1711
      vi   JOSEPH b. 24 July 1714; d. E. Bridgewater 7 Feb. 1777 ae 62
             unm.
109 vii   SUSANNA b. 20 May 1717
110 viii   MARY b. 6 July 1720

References: SAVAGE 3:27. WEYMOUTH BY CHAMBERLAIN 3:356. MD 14:46.
          BRIDGEWATER BY MITCHELL pp. 183, 195, 225, 231-2, 256.
NEHGR 59:107. VR BRIDGEWATER, E. BRIDGEWATER, WEYMOUTH. BOSTON NEWS
OBITS 3:42. KINGMAN DESC pp. 22, 30-1. BRIDGEWATER EPITAPHS pp. 195,
209. Plymouth Co. PR 12:382, 444(Chilton Latham). Plymouth Co. LR
27:125; 29:217(Chilton Latham).

32 DESIRE GRAY[4] (Mary Winslow[3], Mary[2] Chilton, James[1])
b. Plymouth 6 Nov. 1651; d. there 4 Dec. 1690 ae 39.
     She m. Plymouth 10 Jan. 1671/2 NATHANIEL SOUTHWORTH,
b. Plymouth May 1648; d. Middleboro 14 Jan. 1710/11 in 62
yr; son of Constant and Elizabeth (Collier) Southworth.
     They lived in Plymouth, then moved to Middleboro by
1708. The will of Nathanel Southworth Sr. of Middleboro,
dated 18 Sept. 1708 probated 8 March 1710/1, names sons
Ichabod, Nathanel and Edward Southworth; daus. Elizabeth

Southworth and Mary Rider; sons Ichabod and Nathanel, executors.

        Children (SOUTHWORTH) b. or bp. Plymouth:

        i   CONSTANT[5] b. 12 Aug. 1674; d. Tiverton RI between 14 Jan.
            1702 and 5 Feb. 1705 unm. The will of Constant Southworth
            of Tiverton "being bound on a Voyage to Sea" names brothers
            Nathaniel and Edward Southworth; cousin Edward Grey Jr., of
            Tiverton, son of "my Unkle Edward Grey of said Town";
            brother Ichabod Southworth "of Plimouth."
111   ii   MARY b. 3 April 1676
112   iii   ICHABOD b. ca. middle of March 1678/9
113   iv   NATHANIEL b. 18 May 1684, bp. 1685
114   v   ELIZABETH bp. 1687
115   vi   EDWARD b. 1688 or 1689, bp. 1690

References: MD 1:142; 16:62, 237; 18:68; 21:24-8. SAVAGE 4:153.
        MIDDLEBORO DEATHS pp. 171-2. BRIDGEWATER BY MITCHELL pp.
319-20, 385-6. PLYMOUTH COLONY RECS 8:33. SOUTHWORTH GEN pp. 85-6.
PLYMOUTH CH RECS pp. 257, 260, 268.

        33 ELIZABETH GRAY[4] (Mary Winslow[3], Mary[2] Chilton,
James[1]) b. Plymouth "11 Feb. 165x" [prob. 1655, 6, or 7];
d. after 22 Dec. 1721.
        She m. bef. 1680 Capt. SETH ARNOLD, d. Duxbury bet. 15
May 1719 and 31 Oct 1721; son of the Rev. Samuel and Elizabeth (-----) Arnold.
        Seth Arnold and wife Elizabeth of "Duxborough" on 27
Sept. 1689 sold their share of land which fell to Elizabeth
in the division of her father Edward Gray's estate.
        The will of Seth Arnold of Duxborough, dated 11 Dec.
1715 sworn 31 Oct. 1721, names sons Edward, James and Benjamin Arnold; dau. Elizabeth Waterman; Sarah Bartlet and
Seth Bartlet, the two children of deceased dau. Desire;
wife Elizabeth to be executrix.

        Children (ARNOLD):

116   i   EDWARD[5] b. Marshfield 20 March 1679/80
      ii   PENELOPE b. Marshfield 21 April 1682; d. bef. 11 Dec. 1715
            (not mentioned in father's will).
117   iii   DESIRE
118   iv   BENJAMIN
119   v   ELIZABETH
120   vi   JAMES bp. Marshfield 20 Oct. 1700

References: MARSHFIELD VR pp. 11, 13. MD 11:122; 25:35-7; 33:18.
        SAVAGE 1:66. TAG 37:143-4.

34   SARAH GRAY[4] (Mary Winslow[3], Mary[2] Chilton, James[1])
b. Plymouth 12 Aug. 1659; d. Bristol RI 14 Feb. 1736/7.
She m. Marshfield 18 May 1682 SAMUEL LITTLE, b. Marsh-
field ca. 1656; d. Bristol 16 Jan. 1707; son of Thomas and
Anna (Warren) Little, and a grandson of Pilgrim Richard
Warren. He moved to Bristol (now RI) soon after 1691.
   The will of Samuel Little of Bristol, joyner, dated 13
Jan. 1707 probated 3 March 1707/8, mentions wife Sarah,
eldest son Samuel Little, youngest son Edward Little, dau.
Sarah wife of Mr. Richard Billings of Little Compton,
granddau. Sarah Billings Jr., and grandson Richard Billings
Jr.; wife Sarah, executrix.
   Samuel Little of Bristol, gentleman, was appointed 19
April 1737 administrator of the estate of his mother Sarah
Little, widow, late of Bristol, who died intestate.

   Children (LITTLE) first b. Duxbury, others Marshfield:

      i   THOMAS[5] b. 28 June 1683, bp. Marshfield 2 April 1699; d.
         bef. 1707
121 ii SARAH b. 23 July 1685
122 iii SAMUEL b. 7 Nov. 1691
123 iv EDWARD bp. Marshfield 17 July 1698

References: VR DUXBURY. MARSHFIELD VR pp. 19, 20. RI VR:Bristol p.
        145. NGSQ 60:83. PN&Q 4:91. MD 2:248; 11:38, 39;
17:82-7. Bristol Co. PR 2:196(Samuel Little); 8:463, 505(Sarah
Little). LITTLE COMPTON FAMS p. 399.

   35   JOHN GRAY[4] (Mary Winslow[3], Mary[2] Chilton, James[1])
b. Plymouth 1 Oct. 1661; d. Kingston 29 May 1732 in 71 yr.
   He m. Plymouth 9 Dec. 1686 JOANNA MORTON, living 23
Aug. 1738; dau. of Ephraim and Ann (Cooper) Morton.*
   The will of Ephraim Morton Sr. of Plymouth, dated 27
Sept. proved 2 Nov. 1693, names wife Mary, son Nathaniel,
dau. Patience wife of John Nelson, dau. Mercy Norton, sons
George, Josiah, Thomas and Eliezer Morton. Although this
will omits mention of son Ephraim and daus. Joanna and
Rebecca, the will of his son Nathaniel Morton of Plymouth,
dated 23 June and proved 1 Oct. 1709, names brother Josiah
deceased; brothers George, Ephraim, Thomas and Eliezer;
sisters Rebecker Wood, Patience Nelson; and Anna Gray
daughter of his sister Joanna Gray.
   The will of John Gray of Kingston, dated 23 Sept. 1728
probated 21 July 1732, names wife Johannah Gray, son Samuel,
son-in-law John Tincom, daus. Marcy Gray, Anne Tincom and
Johannah Fuller. Receipts were signed 23 Aug. 1738 by Joanna Gray, widow of John; Ebenezer and wife Joanna Fuller;

---

*Not the dau. of George and Joanna (Kempton) Morton, who was b. 1673!

Jabez and wife Mercy Fuller, acquitting Samuel Gray only
son and executor. [Ann and her husband both died in 1730.]

       Children (GRAY) b. Plymouth:

       i   EDWARD[5] b. 21 Sept. 1687; d. 20 Feb. 1687/8
       ii MARY b. 7 Dec. 1688; d. 17 March 1703 [1703/4] in 16 yr.
  124 iii ANN b. 5 Aug. 1691
       iv DESIRE b. 1 Dec. 169[3]; d. 6 Dec. 1695
  125   v JOANNA(H) b. 29 Jan. 1695/6
  126 vi SAMUEL b."23 Dec. 1701/2"
  127 vii MARCY (or Mercy) b. 4 Feb. 1703/4

References: MD 1:145; 7:88; 13:86, 204, 205; 17:46; 21:62-4. VR KING-
           STON. PLYMOUTH BY THACHER p. 325. (PLYMOUTH) BURIAL HILL
p. 8. PLYMOUTH COLONY RECS 8:22. (PLYMOUTH) ANCIENT LANDMARKS p. 188.
Plymouth Co. PR 1:179 & #14264(Ephraim Morton); 2:156(Nath'l. Morton).

       36 ANN (or Anna) GRAY[4] (Mary Winslow[3], Mary[2] Chilton,
James[1]) b. ca. 1664; d. Boston 28 July 1728 (deed).
       She m. bef. 1690 JAMES LEBLOND(E), d. Boston bef. 10
Nov. 1713. Was he the James Leblond who made deposition on
the island of Nevis 13 June 1682?
       James Leblond merchant of Boston and wife Anna on 29
Jan. 1691 sold land in Little Compton which was set off to
Anna from the estate of her father Edward Gray late of
Plymouth deceased. The will of James Leblond of Boston,
merchant, dated 17 Oct. 1700 probated 10 Nov. 1713, names
wife Anna Leblond, and mentions "all my children." In two
accounts Mrs. Ann Leblond, executrix of her husband James
late of Boston merchant deceased, mentions sons James,
Gabriel, daus. Ph)lleppa, Mary, and son Alexander. [It is
not clear why, although the will was probated 10 Nov. *1713*,
the inventory is dated 11 June *1719* and sworn to by Ann 17
Sept. *1719*.]
       Mrs. Ann Leblond was an innholder in Boston in July
1714, and in June 1720. On 30 Nov. 1730 James Leblond of
Boston merchant was appointed administrator of his mother
Ann Leblond widow deceased.
       On 19 June 1718 Peter Leblond of Boston merchant sold
to his brother James Leblond all his rights in the estate
of his father James Leblond deceased. On 20 Sept. 1721
Gabriel Leblond merchant of Boston, child and legatee of
James Leblond late of Boston deceased, sold to his brother
James Leblond of Boston his rights in the estate of his
late father, acknowledged 18 July 1722. On 30 Nov. 1734
Alexander Leblond merchant of Boston sold 1/6 part of a
messuage wherein James Leblond dwells. A narrative deed of
12 Feb. 1735 recapitulates: James Leblond left property to
his children equally; his wife Ann held it until her death
28 July 1728, when the surviving children were James,

Gabriel and Alexander, merchants, and Phillipa Leblond and
Mary Leblond, spinsters, all of Boston; Gabriel sold his
share in 1721; James sold part of his in 1732; Alexander
sold and mortgaged his in 1734; James, Alexander, Phillipa
and Mary Ann now sell all holdings in their father's estate, and all four acknowledged the deed 12 April 1736. No
evidence was found for a marriage or children of any of the
following.
    On 20 Dec. 1786 Edward Payne Esq. by right of inheri-
tance sought possession of a tomb in the "Common Burying
Place" that formerly belonged to the family of Leblonds.

    Children (LEBLOND) b. Boston:

    i   JAMES[5] b. 17 April 1690; d.y.
    ii   JAMES b. in June 1691; living 12 April 1736, merchant.
    iii ANN b. 8 April 1693; d.y.
    iv   PETER b. 1 Jan. 1694/5; living 19 June 1718, merchant; d.
         bef. 28 July 1728.
    v   GABRIEL b. 5 March 1697/8; living 28 July 1728, merchant.
    vi   ANN b. 12 Dec. 1700; prob. d.y.
    vii ALEXANDER b. 31 March 1703; d.y.
    viii PHILLIPPA b. 19 April 1704; living unm. 19 April 1769; prob.
         alive Boston 6 Jan. 1773.
    ix   MARIAN (or Mary Ann) b. 4 March 1705; living unm. 13 Feb.
         1771; prob. alive Boston 6 Jan. 1773. Either Phillippa or
         Mary Ann may have been the Mrs. Leblond alive Boston 3
         Feb. 1775.
    x   ALEXANDER b. 1 Sept. 1709; d. Boston 20 Jan. 1770 "French-
         man." He was a merchant and was chosen constable in Bos-
         ton in 1753 and 1754.

References: MD 3:131; 13:64; 34:84. SAVAGE 3:71. BOSTON VR 9:190,
            196, 207, 215, 233, 241; 24:3, 22, 29, 39, 65. BOSTON REC
COM 1:165; 11:212; 13:70; 14:233, 245; 23:14, 76, 159, 244; 25:335.
BOSTON NEWS OBITS 3:51. NEHGR 84:262. Bristol Co. LR 6:259(James
Leblond). Suffolk Co. PR 18:185; 21:474; 22:63, 220(James Leblond);
28:245(Ann Leblond). Suffolk Co. LR 36:79(Gabriel Leblond); 33:19-20
(Peter Leblond); 47:59-60(James Leblond); 47:162(Wm. Cooper to Le-
blond); 47:278-9; 49:147-8(Alexander Leblond); 52:128(four Leblonds).
CALENDAR OF STATE PAPERS, COLONIAL SERIES, AMERICA AND WEST INDIES
1681-1685, Hon. J. W. Fortescue, editor, (London 1898) 6:263(item 602
xviii).

    37 MARY WINSLOW[4] (Edward[3], Mary[2] Chilton, James[1]) b.
Boston 30 April 1665; d. there 17 July 1733.
    She m. Boston 26 Dec. 1693 JONATHAN POLLARD, b. Boston
12 April 1666; d. there 31 July 1725 in 60th yr. "Capt.";
son of William and Ann (-----) Pollard. He was proprietor
of the Horseshoe Tavern, and a tailor. Mary's cousin, Mary
Leonard, m. Jonathan's brother John Pollard (see p. 25).

The will of Jonathan Pollard, gentleman, of Boston,
dated 3 June 1725 probated 9 Aug. 1725, names wife Mary
Pollard, son Benjamin Pollard, dau. Anne wife of William
Robie mariner of Boston; wife and both children to be executors. On 4 April 1726 Mary Pollard and Benjamin Pollard,
surviving executors, swore to inventory.

Children (POLLARD) b. Boston:

128   i BENJAMIN⁵ b. 6 June 1696
       ii ANN b. 22 Jan. 1697; buried Boston 22 Dec. 1725; m. Boston
          6 Dec. 1722 WILLIAM ROBIE, bp. 1 Nov. 1690; son of William
          and Elizabeth (Greenough) Robie. He m.(1) 1719 Lois(e)
          Burrell, and had son William by her, of whom he was made
          guardian in 1732. The only child of William and Ann Robie
          was buried 8 Dec. 1725 in the arms of her great grand-
          mother, Ann Pollard.

References: BOSTON VR 9:101, 210, 228, 234; 28:84, 109. BOSTON NEWS
             OBITS 1:241. POLLARD FAM 1:48, 68-70; 2:124. (BOSTON)
OLD SOU CH p. 230. SAVAGE 3:449, 549. Suffolk Co. PR 24:163, 438,
440(Jonathan Pollard); 31:142(William Roby gdn.). NEHGR 30:441. MA
HIST COLL (5th Series) 7:363, 368.

38 EDWARD WINSLOW⁴ (Edward³, Mary² Chilton, James¹) b.
Boston 1 Nov. 1669; d. there 30 Nov. or 1 Dec. 1753 in 85th
yr.
     He m.(1) 30 June 1692 HANNAH MOODY, b. Boston 17 Sept.
1672; d. there 25 April 1711; dau. of the Rev. Joshua and
Martha (Collins) Moody of Portsmouth NH.
     He. m.(2) Boston 22 May 1712 ELIZABETH (DIXEY) PEMBER-
TON, b. 3 Oct. 1669; d. 18 Sept. 1740; dau. of John and
Elizabeth (Allen) Dixey of Swansea, and widow of Benjamin
Pemberton.
     He m.(3) Boston 27 March 1744 SUSANNA (FARNUM) LYMAN,
b. 1687 or 88; widow of Caleb Lyman.
     Edward was a goldsmith, a sheriff of Suffolk County,
justice of the Court of Common Pleas and a colonel in the
Boston Regiment. His will, dated Boston 3 Aug. 1748 proved
14 Dec. 1753, names wife Susanna, who was to care for his
grandchild Rebecca Winslow; daus. Davis and Clarke; son
Joshua, and "my granddau. Hanna Winslow"; son Samuel's estate and his children: Sarah, Edward, Joshua and Rebecca;
three widowed daus-in-law: Hanna widow of son Edward,
Rebecca widow of son Samuel, Elizabeth widow of son William; son Joshua and his heirs; sons John and Isaac; Dixe
Goffe, grandson to "my late wife"; son Joshua to be executor. A codicil dated 1748 includes "my mother Farnum."
     On 2 Oct. acknowledged by all 5 Oct. 1758, Joshua
Winslow Esq., John Winslow merchant, Hannah Davis widow,

Richard Clark Esq. and wife Elizabeth, all of Boston,
and Isaac Winslow of Roxbury Esq. sold a dwelling and
land in Boston.

Children (WINSLOW) b. Boston to Edward and Hannah:

	i	EDWARD[5] b. 15 April 1693; d. Oct. 1702
129	ii	JOSHUA b. 12 Feb. 1694 [1694/5]
130	iii	HANNAH b. 8 March 1697
	iv	JOHN b. 24 Dec. 1698; d. 22 April 1699
	v	JOHN b. 14 April 1700; d. Dunstable 3 Nov. 1788 ae 88. He

m. Chelmsford 4 Sept. 1760 SARAH TYNG ("he of Boston, she
of Dunstable"), b. Dunstable 22 April 1720; d. Tyngsboro 29
Oct. 1791 ae 72; dau. of Col. Eleazer and Sarah (Alford)
Tyng. He was a merchant of Boston in a deed of date 1758.
They had no surviving children. John's will dated Dun-
stable 17 Oct. 1788 names wife Sarah; niece Elizabeth
Minot; kinsman Mr. Samuel Hinckes; children of late brother
Isaac Winslow; niece Sarah Winslow dau. of late brother
Samuel; nephew Isaac Winslow; nieces Margaret Pollard,
Katherine Malbone and Martha Winslow children of late bro-
ther Joshua; children of Rev. Edward Winslow formerly of
Braintree; children of late nephews Joshua and Edward Wins-
low, sons of brother Samuel.

	vi	WILLIAM b. 24 March 1701; d. 23 March 1702
131	vii	EDWARD b. 8 Feb. 1702/3
132	viii	SAMUEL b. 29 May 1705
	ix	WILLIAM b. 13 Feb. 1707; d. Louisburg, N.S., 14 Sept. 1746;

m. Boston 11 Dec. 1735 ELIZABETH CLARKE. No children
found. On 27 Oct. 1746 Isaac Winslow of Boston was appointed administrator of "Your Brother William Winslow late
of Boston...last Resident in Louisburg on ye Island of Cape
Breton Merchant." A 1759 account indicates the estate to
be insolvent, and includes "necessary implements of Household allowed ye widow."

133	x	ISAAC b. 2 May 1709

Child (WINSLOW) b. Boston to Edward and Elizabeth:

134	xi	ELIZABETH b. 16 Feb. 1712/3

References: BOSTON VR 9:208, 216, 234, 242, 252; 24:4, 12, 24, 38, 52,
64, 87; 28:43, 194, 267; 30:291. NEHGR 13:248; 17:160;
67:211. VR CHELMSFORD, DUNSTABLE, TYNGSBORO. ME-NH GEN DICT p. 487.
MD 10:106-11; 24:165. BOSTON NEWS OBITS 1:332; 3:580, 581. MA OBITS
1784-1840 5:5004. BOSTON MEM HIST 2:551. PLYMOUTH BY THACHER pp. 96-
7. CABOT GEN pp. 214, 219. POLLARD FAM 2:125[differs on some birth
dates]. Swansea VR p. 5 in rec. book births; mar. John Dixse and
Elizabeth Allen(no page). Suffolk Co. LR 92:70(Joshua Winslow et al.).
Middlesex Co. PR #25345(John Winslow).

39 KATHERINE WINSLOW[4] (Edward[3], Mary[2] Chilton, James[1])
b. Boston 2 June 1672; d. 1742 prob. Charlestown.
      She m.(1) int. Boston 16 July 1695 JAQUES HERBERT, d.
bef. July 1701; n.f.r.
      She m.(2) Boston 3 July 1701 JONATHAN DOWSE, b. ca.
1661; d. Charlestown 28 Jan. 1744/5; son of Lawrence and
Margery (Rand) Dowse. He m.(1) 1694 Elizabeth (Ballard or
Ballatt) Gilbert, by whom he had Jonathan, Elizabeth d.y.,
Samuel d.y., and Samuel. He was a shipwright and justice
of the Court of Common Pleas.
      The will of Jonathan Dowse of Charlestown, dated 2
Oct. 1744 presented 6 Feb. 1744/5, mentions dau. Katherine,
grandson Jonathan Dowse, sons Nathaniel, Joseph and Samuel
Dowse, dau. Elizabeth and her present husband and children.

      Children (DOWSE) b. Charlestown to Jonathan and Katherine:

      i   EDWARD[5] b. 6 Aug. 1703; d. 19 Aug. 1704
      ii   EDWARD b. 1 March 1705; graduated Harvard College 1725; d.
             bet. 1730 and 1733.
135   iii KATHERINE b. 17 May 1706
136   iv   JOSEPH b. 14 Jan. 1708/9
137   v   ELIZABETH b. 13.Nov. 1710
      vi   LAWRENCE b. 5 Aug. 1712; living 1733-4; d. bef. 2 Oct. 1744
138   vii NATHANIEL bp. 6 Feb. 1714/5

References: CHARLESTOWN BY WYMAN 1:305-6. BOSTON VR 28:3, 348. HAR-
          VARD GRADS 7:510. DOWSE DESC pp. 122-6[corrects second
wife of Jonathan, in error in DOWSE FAM]. DOWSE FAM pp. 5, 8-18.
Middlesex Co. PR #6394(Jonathan Dowse).

40 ELIZABETH WINSLOW[4] (Edward[3], Mary[2] Chilton, James[1])
b. Boston 22 March 1673/4; living 1725.
      She m.(1) Boston 18 Jan. 1693/4 JOSEPH SCOTT, d. Bos-
ton bef. 1712.
      She m.(2) Greenland NH 29 March 1712 SAMUEL HINCK(E)S,
b. Portsmouth NH ca. 1680; d. prob. Portsmouth bet. 1758
and 1761; son of John and Elizabeth (Fryer) Hincks.
      Samuel graduated from Harvard in 1701. He was a mer-
chant of Portsmouth in 1719, and a proprietor of Barrington
NH in 1722. He commanded Fort Mary at Winter Harbor (near
Saco, now Biddeford, ME) from 1722 to 1727. During the de-
predations of the Indians in 1725, he sent his family to
Boston, where he later joined them. He is said to have
been still living there in 1753. No appropriate probate
records were found in either Suffolk County or in the published NH records.

      Child (SCOTT) b. Boston to Joseph and Elizabeth:

139   i   JOSEPH[5] b. 23 Nov. 1694

Children (HINCKS) bp. Portsmouth, last two to Samuel and Eliza:

pos. ii ELIZABETH bp. 26 July 1713 [no parents named]
     iii KATHARINE ANN bp. 2 Jan. 1714/5; m. Boston 25 Aug. 1736
          FRANCIS SKINNER, living 14 Feb. 1769. No children found.
          Was he the Francis Skinner b. Boston 14 Feb. 1708 to Wil-
          liam and Deborah Skinner? A Francis Skinner, scrivener of
          Boston, took a mortgage on land in Walpole in 1771; he sold
          the mortgage, acknowledged by him 2 June 1774. Francis
          Skinner and William Sherburn, scriveners of Boston, bought
          land and dwelling in Boston from Isaac McDaniel of Boston
          mariner, in 1773. Was he clerk of Council of Mass. who
          was at Halifax NS in July 1776? Or was he late of Boston
          deceased intestate in 1786, gentleman?
140   iv SAMUEL bp. 19 April 1717

References: SAVAGE 2:426. NEHGR 29:315; 81:426; 84:257, 379. HARVARD
             GRADS 5:69-73. BOSTON VR 9:210, 216; 24:59; 28:198. RI
GEN DICT pp. 338, 614. BARRINGTON NH HIST p. 22. MA BAY ACTS & RE-
SOLVES 10:245; 11:265(Capt. Samuel Hincks). ME-NH GEN DICT p. 338. NH
GEN REC 4:97. Suffolk Co. LR 119:151(Levi Lindley to Francis Skinner);
124:17(Isaac McDaniel); 126:23(Francis Skinner). Suffolk Co. PR
85:485(Francis Skinner estate, Henry Skinner admr. 26 July 1786).
LOYALISTS BY SABINE 2:577.

   41 ANN WINSLOW[4] (Edward[3], Mary[2] Chilton, James[1]) b.
Boston 7 Aug. 1678; d. Milton 24 May 1773 ae 95 "widow of
Kenelm Winslow of Marshfield."
     She m.(1) Boston 1 or 5 Nov. 1702 JOHN TAYLOR, b. Bos-
ton 21 or 22 Nov. 1674; d. Jamaica, West Indies, bef. 29
Jan. 1719/20; son of John and Rebecca (Tainter) Taylor.
John Taylor, cooper, of Boston wrote his will 9 April 1703
leaving everything to wife Ann, and after her decease to
her heirs "by me lawfully begotten." He then moved with
his family to Jamaica about 1705. As the result of a letter from Ann Taylor, executrix of the will, sent from
Jamaica 29 Jan. 1719/20, the will was presented by Edward
Winslow Esq. and probated in Boston 4 April 1720.
     She m.(2) Boston 14 April or 7 Sept. 1730 [Boston and
Marshfield records differ] KENELM WINSLOW "of Marshfield,"
b. Marshfield 22 Sept. 1675; d. there 10 June 1757 ae 82;
son of Nathaniel and Faith (Miller) Winslow. He m.(1) ca.
1703 Abigail Waterman, by whom he had three sons and three
daughters. No children were born to Kenelm and Ann.
     The will of Kenelm Winslow of Marshfield, dated 5 Jan.
1749 presented 19 July 1757, names wife Ann and his three
sons and three daughters.

Children (TAYLOR) b. to John and Ann, first b. Boston, rest b. "Jemico"[Jamaica]:

141   i   JOHN[5] b. 30 Aug. 1704
142   ii   ELIZABETH b. 8 Nov. 1712
143 iii   WILLIAM b. 18 May 1714
144   iv   REBECCA b. 25 Feb. 1715
       v   ANN (or Nancy) b. 14 May 1718; n.f.r.

References: MD 1:89-90; 21:121; 24:145; 32:145-7. MARSHFIELD VR pp. 8, 33, 34, 352, 390. BOSTON VR 9:134; 24:31; 28:6, 157. HARVARD GRADS 6:569. VR MILTON. MILTON HIST p. 255. WATERMAN GEN 1:61. Suffolk Co. PR 21:687(John Taylor). Plymouth Co. PR 14:293 (Kenelm Winslow).

42 WILLIAM PAYNE[4] (Sarah Winslow[3], Mary[2] Chilton, James[1]) b. Boston 21 or 22 Jan. 1668/9; d. 10 June 1735 in 66 yr.

He m.(1) Boston 11 Oct. 1694 MARY TAYLOR, b. 25 Jan. 1675; d. Boston 6 Jan. 1700/1; dau. of James and Elizabeth (-----) Taylor.

He m.(2) 12 May 1703 MARGARET STEWART, b. Limerick, Ireland,in May 1683; d. Boston bet. 3 July and 28 Nov. 1760; dau. of William and Ann (-----) Stewart.

William graduated from Harvard College in 1689, then continued for his master's degree. He was Collector of Excise 1699-70 and in 1716, and was a sheriff of Suffolk County 1714-15. The will of William Payne gentleman of Boston,dated 25 Jan. 1733 presented 1 July 1735, names son Tobias Payne and daughter Mary Sewall, children of his late wife Mary who was daughter of James Taylor Esq., deceased; his other children by wife Margaret: Sarah, Anne, John, Margaret, Richard, Edward and Jane Payne (several under age); his father Tobias Payne deceased; his wife Margaret, executrix.

On 23 Sept. 1747 an agreement was signed between John Payne gentleman, Mary Sewall widow, John Coleman Jr. distiller and wife Sarah, Ann Payne singlewoman, Margaret Phillips widow, Richard Payne brazier, Edward Payne merchant, Jane Payne singlewoman, and Kenelm Winslow Jr. brazier as guardian of Mary Payne, infant and only child of Tobias Payne late of Boston deceased, all of Boston, being the children and heirs of William Payne esquire late of Boston deceased, to convey a lot in Boston including buildings and dwelling where William died.

The will of Margaret Payne of Boston widow, dated 3 July presented 28 Nov. 1760, names son Edward, grandsons John and Benjamin Colman, three daughters: Ann Payne, Margaret Phillips and Jane Payne.

Children (PAYNE) b. Boston to William and Mary:

       i   WILLIAM[5] b. 23 or 25 Nov. 1695; d. Feb. 1705
145   ii TOBIAS b. 25 June 1697
     iii SARAH b. 16 Jan. or July 1699; d.y.
146   iv MARY b. 6 Jan. 1700/1

Children (PAYNE) b. Boston to William and Margaret:

147   v SARAH b. 15 June 1704
      vi WILLIAM b. 19 Sept. 1706; d.y.
     vii WILLIAM b. 26 Jan 1707/8; d.y.
   viii EDWARD b. 17 March 1708/9; d.y.
     ix ANN b. 8 June 1711; living unm. 4 June 1771
      x JOHN b. 9 Feb. 1712/3; d. 17 Nov. 1759 unm. His will left
            everything to his mother.
     xi EDWARD b. 1 or 7 Oct. 1714; d.y.
    xii MARGARET b. 22 May 1716; d. Boston bet. 4 June 1771 and 31
            March 1775. She m. Boston 17 Oct. 1741 JOHN PHILLIPS, d.
            Boston bef. 12 June 1747. They had no children. He m.(1)
            Boston 1732 Sarah Cooke (see #156) by whom he had five
            children. The will of Margaret Phillips of Boston widow,
            dated 4 June 1771 presented 31 March 1775, names sister
            Jane Payne, Mary Phillips wife of William the son of my
            late husband John Phillips deceased, brother Thomas
            Phillips, sister Anne Payne.
   xiii RICHARD b. 4 April 1718
   xiv THOMAS b. 23 April 1720; d.y.
148   xv EDWARD b. 4 Feb. 1721/2
   xvi JANE b. 17 Feb. 1723; living unm. 15 Feb. 1787.

References: PAYNE & GORE FAM pp. 10-1, 15-9. BOSTON VR 9:218, 223, 248; 24:3, 30, 43, 50, 63, 80, 85, 119, 134, 148, 152, 162; 28:179, 257. SAVAGE 3:338. BOSTON MEM HIST 1:581; 2:549[claim of twins unsubstantiated]. BOSTON NEWS OBITS 3:217. HARVARD GRADS 3:409-12. Suffolk Co. PR 32:176; 40:272(William Payne); 57:370(Margaret Payne); 74:381(Margaret Phillips). MA HIST COLL 7(fifth series):95. Suffolk Co. LR 74:221(John Payne et al.).

43 MARY MIDDLECOTT[4] (Sarah Winslow[3], Mary[2] Chilton, James[1]) b. Boston 1 July 1674; d. at sea coming from Barbados to Boston, June 1718 in her 45th year. She resided in Barbados from 1701 to 1718.
     She m.(1) ca. 1696 HENRY GIBBS, b. Boston 8 Oct. 1668; d. Boston bef. 24 Oct. 1705; son of Robert and Elizabeth (-----) Gibbs of Barbados. The will of Henry Gibbes of Boston merchant, dated 2 Dec. 1698 probated 24 Oct. 1705, mentions wife Mary, son John, daughter Sarah (both under 21), and the child "my wife is now carrying"; executors to be wife Mary, William Payne, Edward Lyde, and "my father" Richard Middlecott of Boston. (Administrators were

appointed because Edward Lyde refused to serve, and Richard
Middlecott was deceased.) Will was also recorded in Barbados.

   She m.(2) Barbados? [no record found] ca. 1705
OTHANIEL (or Othniel) HAGGET, d. Barbados bef. 18 Nov.
1729; son of Othaniel Hagget. Othaniel travelled to Boston
in 1718 with the three youngest children, returning to Bar-
bados the following year with Sarah Gibbs, John Gibbs and
Mary Hagget. Othaniel m.(2) Barbados after 1718 Susanna
(-----) Lambert, widow of Simon Lambert of Barbados and
Bristol, England, who had daughters Ruth and Jane.

   The will of Othaniel Haggatt (*sic*), probated 18 Nov.
1729 in Barbados, names wife Susanna, sons Othaniel,
Nathaniel and William, and daughter Mary; refers to
Othaniel Haggatt the elder of Bristol as making deeds with
testator, Othaniel the younger.

   Children (GIBBS) b. Boston to Henry and Mary:

149   i   SARAH^5 b. 13 Sept. 1696
     ii   JOHN b. 14 Dec. 1697; went to Barbados in 1719 where he died
          unmar.
    iii   HENRY b. ca. 1699; went with mother to Barbados ca. 1701;
          later returned to Boston, and lived with William Payne "to
          be educated." Supposedly he later returned to Barbados,
          where he married and had children (not found). Is he pos-
          sibly the Henry Gibbs, late of Barbados, who was of Charles
          Town SC in his appointment as attorney in March 1726? The
          town house in Boston of Mr. Henry Gibbs is mentioned 29
          Nov. 1736. [The will of Henry Gibbs of Barbados dated 25
          Dec. 1731 entered 6 Jan. 1732 names a granddau. and so
          cannot belong to this Henry; similarly the burial of Henry
          31 Dec. 1731 in St. Michael's Parish, Barbados, must belong
          to the Henry of the will.]

   Children (HAGGET) b. Barbados to Othaniel and Mary:

150   iv OTHANIEL
151   v NATHANIEL
      vi MARY went to Boston 1718, returned to Barbados 1719; did she
          subsequently remove to Bristol, England?
152 vii WILLIAM
    viii SARAH prob. d. bef. Nov. 1729

References: PAYNE & GORE FAM pp. 12-14. CARIBBEANA pp. 166-71. BOS-
           TON VR 9:107, 203, 227, 232. BOSTON MEM HIST 1:582;
2:549. Suffolk Co. PR 16:63(Henry Gibbs). BOSTON REC COM 15:12(house
Henry Gibbs). Barbados Archives RB6 vol. 6 p. 59(Henry Gibbs "late of
Boston deceased"); RB6 vol. 16 p. 520(Othaniel Haggatt); RB6 vol. 37
p. 163(Henry Gibbs--1732); RL1 vol. 2 p. 365(bur. Henry Gibbs); RB7
vol. 32 p. 211(Henry Gibbs of Charles Town).

44 EDWARD MIDDLECOTT[4] (Sarah Winslow[3], Mary[2] Chilton, James[1]) b. prob. Boston ca. 1676 [Savage appears in error when he says he came with father from England]; d. Warminster, Wilts., England, bur. 15 Nov. 1727.

He m. in England, MARY -----. She m.(2) ----- Oliver.

Edward returned to England after learning the merchant's trade, and "purchased his Father's Life in an estate at Worminster of £300 per annum, which was entailed to him by his Uncle."

Mary Middlecott of Warminster, widow of Edward Middlecott 1618-1660 of Warminster, in a will, dated 26 April 1700 proved 20 May 1701, bequeathed "unto the servants that are now in service with my grandson Edward Middlecott of Warminster" who is "son of Richard Middlecott," and appointed this same Edward to be her executor.

Edward Middlecott of Warminster [brother of Richard[3] and so uncle of Edward[4]] in a will, dated 2 Nov. 1686 admin. 1 Feb. 1704, left "all remaining property at Warminster... on trust: for use of my brother Richard Middlecott for life, and after his decease to his eldest son and his heirs ..." In a revision of the will "Whereas I purchased property of the Manor of Furnax Grove for the heirs of John Middlecott & William Middlecott, after the death, surrender or forfeiture of Mary Middlecott, my mother, and of me, the said Edward Middlecott, my will is that my brother Richard Middlecott shall have the sole advantage of the said copyhold estate...and the said Richard Middlecott shall come and reside at the Mansion House wherein I do now dwell. No action to be taken regarding surrender of copyhold without the consent of said Richard Middlecott."

Administration of the estate of Edward Middlecott of Warminster deceased was granted 17 March 1728 to Edward Middlecott his son, "Maria Olliver" widow and relict having renounced the administration.

Child (MIDDLECOTT) b. Warminster, England:

153   i EDWARD[5] b. bef. 1708

References: PAYNE & GORE FAM p. 13. BOSTON MEM HIST 1:582. MA BAY ACTS & RESOLVES 11:120, 207. SAVAGE 3:205. Warminster, Wilts., England Parish Registers: Burials 1727/29. P.C.C. Wills and Admin. 1650/1730: 1705 Edward Middlecott and Revision; 1728 Edward Middlecott. Archdeaconry & Consistory Courts of Sarum, Wilts., Eng: 1701 Mary Middlecott.

45 SARAH MIDDLECOTT[4] (Sarah Winslow[3], Mary[2] Chilton, James[1]) b. Boston 2 June 1678; d. Cambridge 27 Dec. 1764 ae 87 "widow of Lewis Boucher."

She m. Boston 26 March 1702 LOUIS BOUCHER from
Rochelle, France; d. at sea on way to England 1715. He
was a merchant.
     The will of Sarah Boucher of Cambridge widow, dated
27 Sept. 1759, left five shillings to dau. Sarah Foye,
wife of John Foye; the rest of her property to dau. Jane
Boucher and her heirs; dau. Jane executor.

     Children (BOUCHER) b. Boston:

154   i   ANNE[5] b. 7 April 1703
155   ii SARAH b. 6 Oct. 1706
       iii MARY b. 1708; d.y.
       iv MARY b. 1710; d.y.
       v   LEWIS b. 1713; d.y.
       vi JANE b. 6 June 1716; living unm. 27 Sept. 1759; d. Cam-
              bridge 11 or 13 March 1800 ae 78 or 88(?).

References: VR CAMBRIDGE. BOSTON VR 28:3; 24:19, 119, 356. BOSTON
             MEM HIST 1:582; 2:549. PAYNE & GORE FAM pp. 13-5. MD
21:1-10. BOSTON NEWS OBITS 2:109. CHARLESTOWN BY WYMAN 1:100. CAM-
BRIDGE FIRST CH pp. 150, 506. Middlesex Co. PR #2240(Sarah Boucher).

     46 JANE MIDDLECOTT[4] (Sarah Winslow[3], Mary[2] Chilton,
James[1]) b. Boston 16 Sept. 1682; d. Sept. 1743 ae 61.
     She m. Boston 7 Jan. 1702 ELISHA COOKE Jr., b. Boston
20 Dec. 1678; d. there 24 Aug. 1737 in 59th yr; son of Dr.
Elisha and Elizabeth (Leverett) Cooke. This is not a Mayflower Cooke line. Elisha was a physician, graduated from
Harvard College in 1697 and received an MA in 1700; he was
also active in politics.
     The will of Elisha Cooke of Boston, dated 19 Aug. pro-
bated 6 Sept. 1737, names son Middlecott; son-in-law John
Phillips and dau. Sarah; dau. Mary; wife Jane and son
Middlecott executors. An account of Middlecott Cooke executor dated Sept. 1743 includes "sundries at my mother's
funeral." A division of the estate of Elisha Cooke deceased was made 23 April 1747 between Mary Saltonstall
wife of Richard; Elisha Cooke Phillips, John Phillips Jr.,
and William Phillips, children of Sarah Phillips deceased;
and only son Middlecott Cooke.

     Children (COOKE) b. Boston:

     i   ELISHA[5] b. 3 Nov. 1703; d.y.
     ii MIDDLECOTT b. 13 Aug. 1705; d. there 1 May 1771 ae 67 yrs.
            He never married. Middlecott was a selectman and clerk of
            the Court of Common Pleas. He graduated from Harvard 1723.
            The will of Middlecott Cooke of Boston, gentleman, dated
            24 April 1771 probated 7 May 1771, left to nephew Nathaniel
            Saltonstall; sister Harrod; Mrs. Sarah Green and Mrs. Sarah

Morby widow; niece Mary Saltonstall; nephew Leveret Saltonstall under 21; nephew William Phillips.
- iii ELIZABETH b. Feb. 1708; bur. Boston 26 June 1725 ae ca. 17.
- 156 iv SARAH b. April 1711
- v ELISHA d.y.
- vi ELISHA d.y.
- vii JANE d.y.
- viii JANE d.y.
- ix JANE d.y.
- 157 x MARY b. ca. 1723

References: PAYNE & GORE FAM pp. 13-4. BOSTON MEM HIST 1:579, 582;
2:549. SAVAGE 1:445. BOSTON VR 9:145; 24:20, 33; 28:3.
HARVARD GRADS 4:349-56(Elisha Cooke); 7:160-3(Middlecott Cooke). Suffolk Co. PR 33:274; 62:513, 520(Elisha Cooke); 70:277; 71:105(Middlecott Cooke). BOSTON NEWS OBITS 1:71; 2:243. MA HIST COLL (series 5)
7:361.

47 MARY WINSLOW[4] (Joseph[3], Mary[2] Chilton, James[1]) b.
Boston 25 Sept. 1674.
    She m. New York NY ca. 1695 ROBERT CRANNELL (or Crenil
or Craunil), b. Devonshire, England, ca. 1670; d. New York
NY 18 Jan. 1734[1734/5]; son of William Crannell. Robert
came to New York, and at the time of his death was overseer of the watch of New York City.
    In a 1703 census, Robert Crannell was in the West Ward
of New York City with one female, two male children, and
two female children. In 1717 William, son of Robert, was
apprenticed for seven years. Robert Crannell Jr. was
ordered to assist taking stock of the powder house in 1734/
5 upon his father's death. No estate of Robert or Mary has
been found.

        Children (CRANNELL) prob. b. New York City:

- 158 i ROBERT[5] b. ca. 1696
- ii MARY b. ca. 1698; m. (Jamaica NY) licensed at Hell Gate 23
  Nov. 1716 SOLOMON RIDLEY; n.f.r.
- 159 iii WILLIAM b. ca. 1703 (based on apprenticeship date)
- iv daughter

References: NY BY VALENTINE p. 348. HUDSON-MOHAWK GEN 4:1412[errone-
ously shows Mary dau. of *Gov*. Winslow]. AM ANC p. 19.
MIN COUNCIL NY 4:203-4. 1703 CENSUS NEW YORK. NEW YORK WEEKLY JOUR-
NAL, 21 Jan. 1734. NYGBR 19:55(Parish Reg., Jamaica NY).

48 JOSEPH WINSLOW[4] (Joseph[3], Mary[2] Chilton, James[1]) b.
Boston 16 June 1677; d. Dutchess Co. NY bet. 6 April 1760
and 18 April 1761.

He m.(1) New York City 24 Nov. 1721 ABIGAIL SNETHEN.
[Although he was 44 at the time, no evidence was found for
an earlier marriage--other Winslows married comparatively
late in life.]
    He m.(2) Fishkill, Dutchess Co., NY 28 June 1742 the
widow MARRIGRIET (-----) HEYSER, d. bef. 6 April 1760.
    Joseph was taxed at either Fishkill or Rumbout in
1735/6, 1739/40, 1741/2, and as late as June 1757. The
will of Joseph Winslow "Seanor" of the Fishkills, Dutchess
County, yeoman, dated 6 April 1760 attested 18 April 1761,
mentions his children (unnamed), his grandchildren (unnamed) by his daughter Sarah, sons Samuel and Joseph Winslow to be executors. Son Joseph was sworn in as executor
28 April 1761 in New York City. It is possible there were
other children, such as the John Winslow who witnessed a
will in Beakmans Precinct in 1751, and Hannah Winslow whose
marriage in 1757 is recorded in the Rumbout Presbyterian
Church; however, no evidence was found connecting them to
Joseph.

    Children (WINSLOW) b. to Joseph and Abigail:

160   i SAMUEL[5] b. ca. 1725
      ii JOSEPH b. ca. 1725-30; living Dutchess Co. NY 26 May 1769.
          He m. Rumbout, Dutchess Co., NY 21 Aug. 1753 MARGARET STORM,
          pos. b. Fishkill 1735; dau. of Johannes and Martha (-----)
          Storm. Joseph was in Rumbout when sued in Oct. 1765. He
          witnessed a will, farmer, 26 May 1769. No children found.
161   iii SARAH b. ca. 1725-30

References: NYGBR 69:285; 83:95. NY WILLS pp. 106, 462, 485. Tax
             Records, Dutchess Co. (Letter from Mrs. Wm. R. White).
REFORMED DUTCH CHURCH OF NYC REC p. 136(Marriages). Hist. Doc. Coll.,
Queen's College of NY, #AW34(will Jos. Winslow Sr.).

    49 PARNELL WINSLOW[4] (Isaac[3], Mary[2] Chilton, James[1]) b.
Charlestown 14 Nov. 1667; d. 15 April 1751.
    She m. Charlestown 4 May 1686 Capt. RICHARD FOSTER, b.
Charlestown 10 Aug. 1666; d. bef. 14 Jan. 1745; son of
Capt. William and Anne (Brackenbury) Foster.
    The will of Richard Foster of Charlestown Esq., dated
22 Jan. 1735/6 probated 14 Jan. 1745, left his entire estate to wife Parnel; names sons Richard and Isaac; daughters Parnel Codman, Ann Perkins, Sarah Calef and Elizabeth
McDaniel; grandsons Samuel and Richard Cary; executors wife
and sons Richard and Isaac. The inventory of 24 April 1751
states wife Parnel is deceased. An account of Richard Foster, executor, dated May 1751 includes "provisions for
Parnel to 15 April 1751."

Children (FOSTER) b. Charlestown:

	i	PARNELL[5] b. 23 Feb. 1686/7; d. 14 Nov. 1687
	ii	RICHARD b. 28 Nov. 1689; d. 11 Feb. 1693/4
162	iii	MARY b. 16 Feb. 1691/2
163	iv	RICHARD b. 23 March 1693/4
164	v	PARNELL b. 25 Aug. 1696
165	vi	ANNE b. 8 Nov. 1699
166	vii	SARAH b. 16 Nov. 1701
167	viii	ISAAC b. 3 Jan. 1703/4
168	ix	ELIZABETH b. 21 Aug. 1706
	x	KATHARINE b. 6 April 1713; d. 11 Feb. 1715/6

References: CHARLESTOWN BY WYMAN 1:362; 2:1042. NEHGR 25:69. FOSTER GEN 2:502-4. SAVAGE 2:190. Middlesex Co. PR #8250 (Richard Foster).

FIFTH GENERATION

50 MERCY LEONARD[5] (Samuel[4], Sarah Chandler[3], Isabella[2] Chilton, James[1]) b. Bridgewater; d. Preston CT 24 Dec. 1749 "Marcy wife of Richard Adams."
    She m. RICHARD ADAMS of Preston, perhaps son of William Adams, b. 22 Oct. 1678; d. Preston 12 April 1749.
    Richard Adams and wife Mercy renewed the covenant at the First Congregational Church of Preston in Jan. 1709, where their three children were baptized. The will of Richard Adams of Preston, dated 19 Jan. 1748/9 and probated 4 May 1749, names wife Mercy, daughters Elizabeth and Abigail, and son Richard; son Richard and his wife Susanna were named as executors.

Children (ADAMS) first b. Canterbury CT, others b. Preston: ELIZABETH[6] b. 1705; RICHARD b. 1708; and ABIGAIL b. 1717/8.

References: PRESTON CH pp. 135, 139, 143. LEONARD FAM p. 50. CSL Barbour Index: Canterbury, Preston. CT PR Norwich Dist #103(Richard Adams).

51 ELIZABETH LEONARD[5] (Samuel[4], Sarah Chandler[3], Isabella[2] Chilton, James[1]) b. Bridgewater; living Norwich CT 25 Sept. 1746.
    She m. Norwich CT 10 July 1703 THOMAS CLARK of Norwich, b. Ipswich MA 15 Jan. 1674; d. Norwich CT bef. 12 Oct. 1752; son of John and Mary (Burnam) Clark.
    The will of Thomas Clark of Norwich, dated 25 Sept. 1746 and sworn 12 Oct. 1752, names wife Elizabeth; sons

Thomas and Joseph; grandson Simeon son of Robert Gates of
Preston; dau. Ruth; dau. Mary's children; son Thomas, executor.

Children (CLARK) b. Norwich CT (all bp. at PRESTON CH except
Ruth): MARY[6] b. 1705; THOMAS b. 1709, bp. 1708(*sic*); ELIZABETH b.
1711; JOSEPH b. 1713/4; and RUTH b. 1722.

References: PRESTON CH pp. 138, 139, 140, 141. NORWICH CT VR 1:96.
            VR IPSWICH. LEONARD FAM pp. 50-1. Clarke Fams of CT, MS.
(CT State Library). CT PR Norwich Dist #2515(Thomas Clark).

   52 SAMUEL LEONARD[5] (or Lenerson or Leonardson)
(Samuel[4], Sarah Chandler[3], Isabella[2] Chilton, James[1]) b.
Bridgewater ca. 1683; d. Preston CT 11 May 1718.
     He m. ca. 1706 LYDIA COOKE, bp. Stonington CT 27 April
1679; dau. of Richard Cooke of Norwich CT. This is not a
Mayflower Cooke line. Samuel Leonard and wife Lydia in 1716
acknowledged receipt of her share of the estate of her
father Richard Cooke of Norwich. She m.(2) Preston (now
Griswold) CT 1720 Nicholas Williams, pos. he d. Sprague-
Hanover Church rec. Nov. 1776 ae 97.
     Living with his family in Worcester MA, Samuel aged 12
was kidnapped by Indians in the fall of 1695. He was still
with the Indians when in 1697 they captured Hannah Dustin
of Haverhill. He subsequently escaped with her to Haverhill, then rejoined his family in Connecticut. Samuel
Lenerson Jr. traded land over the years 1705 to 1718 while
living in Preston. Four of his children (except Jane) were
baptized there, after his wife Lydia renewed the covenant.
     Samuel Leonard of Preston, a son of Samuel Leonard de-
ceased, chose his father-in-law [step-father] Nicholas Williams as guardian 30 Aug. 1729. [No guardianships were
found for the other children.] A division of lands was
made 7 Jan. 1741/2 "Whereas our Honrd father Mr. Samuel
Lennard late of Preston died and left an estate in lands to
several of us miners, and there being three of us survive-
ing...Ebenezer Lennard and Samuell Lennard...to our loveing
brother Nathan Lennard of sd Preston." This was acknowledged by Ebenezer and Samuel at Norwich 18 May 1756.

Children (LEONARD or LEONARDSON) b. Preston: LYDIA[6] b. 170-, bp.
1708; EBENEZER b. 1709/10; SAMUEL b. 1712; JANE b. 1714; and NATHAN b.
1717.

References: CSL Barbour Index: Preston. CSL Ch Rec: Sprague-Hanover.
            PRESTON CH pp. 131, 135, 139, 140, 141, 143. STONINGTON
CH p. 195. GRISWOLD CH 1:251. NEHGR 52:271. LEONARD FAM pp. 51-7.
WORCESTER BY NUTT p. 168. Norwich CT LR 3A:411(Saml. Leonard). CT PR
New London Dist #3171(Samuel Leonard gdn.). Preston CT LR 2:17, 431;
3:68, 116(Samuel Leonard); 7:69(Ebenezer and Saml. Lennard). WORCESTER

SUNDAY TELEGRAM, Bill Moile's Column, 30 Nov. 1975 and 4 Jan. 1976(Memorial to Samuel Leonard's capture).

53 PHEBE LEONARD[5] (Samuel[4], Sarah Chandler[3], Isabella[2] Chilton, James[1]) bp. Preston CT 7 or 17 Oct. 1703.
     She m. Windham CT 21 Jan. 1729/30 ISAAC CANADA (or Canaday or Kennedy), b. bef. 1697; d. Windham bef. 5 July 1754; son of Daniel and Hannah (Cooke) Canaday.
     Isaac Canada of Windham bought land 18 Dec. 1717 in Windham. He owned the covenant there about 1723-4. He was living in Windham during several land transactions; a final sale was acknowledged 23 March 1737/8. James Flint of Windham posted bond 5 July 1754 as administrator of the estate of Isaac Canaday late of Windham deceased; the inventory, including no land, was exhibited 2 Sept. 1754.
     An Isaac Kennedy was living in Windham in 1790 with one male over 16, two under 16, and four females.

     Children (CANADA or KENNEDY) b. Windham CT: ISAAC[6] b. 1732; and SAMUEL b. 1739.

References: CSL Barbour Index: Windham. PRESTON CH p. 138. WINDHAM CO CT BY LARNED 1:100, 566. CT PR Windham Dist #2253; also Windham Dist PR(special) 2:455(Isaac Canady). 1790 CT CENSUS p. 152. Windham CT LR E:234(Ichabod Allen); E:295, 306; F:281, 306; G:490, 491(Isaac Canada); F:60, 305(John Fitch); G:487(John Ayres).

54 ENOCH LEONARD[5] (John[4], Sarah Chandler[3], Isabella[2] Chilton, James[1]) b. prob. Bridgewater; prob. d. Mendum, Morris Co., NJ bet. 16 Sept. and 19 Oct. 1757.
     He m. Bridgewater 12 Feb. 1706 ELIZABETH HOOPER (or Hupper), b. Reading 8 July 1689; prob. living Mendum 16 Sept. 1757; dau. of William and Susanna (-----) Hooper.
     On 30 Jan. 1724/5 Joseph, Josiah and Enoch Leonard all of Bridgewater sold their rights to a cedar swamp. In 1737/8 Enoch Leonard of Bridgewater sold "my farm or homestead on which I now live" together with all rights to lands in Bridgewater.
     On 17 April 1744 Enoch Leonard cordwainer [is this Enoch[6]?] and wife Abigail of Bridgewater sold 20 acres of "our homestead," acknowledged the same day. No further records of Enoch or his family were found in Plymouth County.
     There is a will of Enoch Leonard of Mendum, Morris Co., NJ, signed 16 Sept. probated 19 Oct. 1757, leaving to wife Elizabeth "all my estate in New England"; naming grandson John Arnold (not of age); appointing Robert Arnold to be executor. Although this is probably the will of Enoch[5], it is not proved to be so.

Children (LEONARD) b. Bridgewater: ENOCH[6] b. 1707; and ELIZABETH
b. 1719.

References: BRIDGEWATER BY MITCHELL p. 245. VR BRIDGEWATER. LEONARD
            FAM pp. 37-8. MD 14:204. CORY ANCY 2:(1):88. Plymouth
Co. LR 27:189; 31:204; 36:191; 42:164(Enoch Leonard). NJ ARCH, first
series, 32:195(Enoch Leonard); 37:17(Wills 8, est. Robt. Arnold).

    55 MOSES LEONARD[5] (or Lennardson) (John[4], Sarah Chand-
ler[3], Isabella[2] Chilton, James[1]) b. prob. Bridgewater ca.
1677; d. Barre 10 Dec. 1775 ae ca. 98 "Lt."
    He m.(1) Marlboro 15 May 1705 MERCY NEWTON, b. Marl-
boro 16 Feb. 1685; d. there 1 Dec. 1714; dau. of Moses and
Johannah (Larkin) Newton. The will of Moses Newton of
Marlborough, dated 3 April 1724, mentions granddaughter
Mercy Leonard, committed to his care when his daughter
Mercy Leonard died, also the "children of daughter Mercy
deceased."
    He m.(2) Marlboro 8 Aug. 1716 HANNAH (WOODS) WITHERBY,
b. Marlboro 4 Aug. 1677; prob. d. 7 Sept. 1751; dau. of
John and Lydia (-----) Woods, and widow of Thomas Witherby.
Moses and Hannah Leonard of Marlboro are mentioned among
the children of Deacon John Woods late of Marlboro, in a
division of his estate.
    He very probably m.(3) int. Dudley 12 Nov. 1757 SARAH
(-----) HALL, widow of Thomas Hall; living in 1770.
    Moses Leonard of Marlboro bought land there in 1708,
and in 1709 sold to Joseph Leonard land in Bridgewater
called Eagles Nest. He received grants of land in Worcester in 1714 and 1715, and bought additional land there in
1717 from his uncle Jacob Leonard (#17) of Bridgewater.
He was in Worcester from 1717 until at least 1729, when he
sold his homestead and moved first to Brookfield, then to
Hardwick, and about 1735 to Leicester. By 1757 he was in
Rutland, at the time of his third marriage. Here he spent
the remainder of his life, living first in that part which
became Oakham, and later in the part which became Barre.
Moses Leonard[6] transferred land in Rutland District [now
Barre] 27 April 1759 to "my father Moses Leonard late of
Rutland Westwing Precinct" [now Oakham] "now living in
said District Gentleman"; Moses and wife Beulah acknowl-
edged their signatures 10 Sept. 1760.

    Children (LEONARD) b. Marlboro to Moses and Mercy: MOSES[6] b.
1706; EZRA b. 1711; and MERCY b. 1714.
    Children (LEONARD) b. to Moses and Hannah, first b. Marlboro,
second Worcester: JONAS b. 1717; and ANDREW b. 1719.

References: VR BARRE, MARLBORO, DUDLEY, WORCESTER(Collec. Worcester
            Soc. Antiq. XII). WORCESTER BY NUTT pp. 168-9. MARLBORO
HIST pp. 421, 473. BRIDGEWATER BY MITCHELL p. 245. NEWTON GEN pp.

31-41. LEONARD FAM pp. 57-60. Plymouth Co. LR 11:56(Moses Leonard).
Middlesex Co. PR #25457(John Woods). Middlesex Co. LR 21:294(Jonathan
Rugg); 21:295(Jacob Leonard); 24:233(Woods); 24:593; 30:372(Moses
Leonard). Worcester Co. PR (old series) #43331(Moses Newton). Wor-
cester Co. LR 44:17(Moses Leonard).

56   JOSIAH LEONARD[5]   (John[4], Sarah Chandler[3], Isabella[2]
Chilton, James[1])   prob. b. Bridgewater; d. there bef. 21
May 1745.
       He m.(1) Bridgewater 2 Nov. 1699 MARJORAM WASHBURN,
dau. of Phillip and Elizabeth (Irish) Washburn.
       He m.(2) Bridgewater 21 Nov. 1717 ABIGAIL WASHBURN, b.
Bridgewater 2 June 1688; dau. of John and Rebecca (Lapham)
Washburn; d. bef. 6 Feb. 1743. On 11 April 1724, acknowl-
edged in June 1731 by all three, Josiah and William Wash-
burn and Abigail Leonard, all of Bridgewater, quitclaimed to
brother John Washburn.
       The will of Josiah Leonard of Bridgewater, dated 6
Feb. 1743 and presented 21 May 1745, names eldest son John,
other sons Josiah, Ezekiel, Samuel and Nathan; daughters
Elizabeth Washburne, Mary Herrington and Margene Pratt; son
Josiah was named executor. It has not been possible to de-
termine which wife was the mother of his last six children.

       Children (LEONARD) b. Bridgewater, at least the first two by wife
Marjoram: JOHN[6]; JOSIAH b. ca. 1710; EZEKIEL; SAMUEL; NATHAN; ELIZA-
BETH; MARY; and MARGENE.

References: VR BRIDGEWATER. BRIDGEWATER BY MITCHELL pp. 245, 339.
            MD 15:247. Plymouth Co. PR 9:458-63(Josiah Leonard).
Plymouth Co. LR 27:38(Josiah Washburn). LEONARD FAM pp. 60-1. BRIDGE-
WATER EPITAPHS p. 94.

57   JOSEPH LEONARD[5]   (Jacob[4], Sarah Chandler[3], Isabella[2]
Chilton, James[1])   b. prob. Duxbury ca. 1672; d. Bridgewater
29 Jan. 1749. No primary evidence was located to connect
Joseph with his purported father Jacob.
       He m. 1695 MARTHA ORCUTT, b. Scituate 1671, bp. there
23 April 1671; pos. the unnamed "widow Lenard" who d.
Bridgewater 30 Sept. 1752; dau. of William and Martha
(-----) Orcutt. An agreement dated 5 Dec. 1694 between
Martha Orcutt of Bridgewater, widow of William Orcutt who
died in 1693, and her children, includes daughter Martha
Orcutt.
       No will for Joseph, nor deeds from him to his children
were found. LEONARD FAM, BRIDGEWATER BY MITCHELL, "Bridgewater Corrections" and VR BRIDGEWATER concur in the following children, for whom other evidence is lacking.

Probable children (LEONARD) b. Bridgewater:* JOSEPH[6] b. ca. 1696 (calculated from his d.); EPHRAIM; MARTHA; and prob. others.

References: VR BRIDGEWATER, SCITUATE. LEONARD FAM pp. 40-43, 62-3.
          EDDY GEN p. 890. BRIDGEWATER BY MITCHELL pp. 260, 423.
NEHGR 33:246. Bridgewater Corrections p. 17. Plymouth Co. PR 1:215
(widow Martha Orcutt).

58 ABIGAIL LEONARD[5] (Jacob[4], Sarah Chandler[3], Isabella[2] Chilton, James[1]) b. Weymouth 11 Nov. 1680; alive 8 April 1735 (deed).
     She m. 1703 SAMUEL WASHBURN Jr., b. Bridgewater 6 April 1678; living 8 April 1735; son of Samuel and Deborah (Packard) Washburn, and a descendant of Pilgrim Francis Cooke. He m.(1) Bridgewater 1701 Deliverance Leonard (#18 iii). They had no issue.
     Samuel Washburn and wife Abigail of Bridgewater on 8 Dec. 1734 sold their homestead "where we now dwell" in Bridgewater, and a cedar swamp "which my father Samuel Washburn died seized of," together with all rights yet to come in the will of his father. It was acknowledged by both 8 April 1735. It sounds as though they planned either on leaving town, or moving in with a child.

     Children (WASHBURN) b. Bridgewater: DAVID[6] b. 1704; DELIVERANCE b. 1706; SOLOMON b. 1708; SAMUEL b. 1710; ABIGAIL b. 1712; SUSANNA b. 1714; and TABITHA b. 1716.

References: BRIDGEWATER BY MITCHELL p. 341. LEONARD FAM p. 43[incor-
          rectly names Abigail's husband as Thomas Washburn]. MD
16:47. VR BRIDGEWATER, WEYMOUTH.

59 SUSANNA LEONARD[5] (Jacob[4], Sarah Chandler[3], Isabella[2] Chilton, James[1]) b. Weymouth 27 Dec. 1683; d. Bridgewater 19 Nov. 1764.
     She m. Bridgewater 22 March 1714 EBENEZER HILL, b. Bridgewater 9 Nov. 1686; d. there 6 July 1760; son of Ebenezer and Ruth (-----) Hill. Ebenezer was a blacksmith.
     In a division 6 April 1761 of the estate of Ebenezer Hill, son Eleazer of Bridgewater was to pay his brothers Ebenezer, Jacob and Israel.

     Children (HILL) b. Bridgewater: EBENEZER[6] b. 1715; JACOB b. 1717; ISRAEL b. 1719; MOSES b. 1722, d. 1737; HEZEKIAH b. 1727, d. 1745; and ELIEZER b. 1730.

References: VR BRIDGEWATER. BRIDGEWATER BY MITCHELL p. 192[attrib-
          utes Ebenezer to wrong parents]. LEONARD FAM pp. 43, 63.
Plymouth Co. PR 15:551; 16:59(Ebenezer Hill). OLD TIMES p. 346.

---

*The Mayflower Society accepts lines through Joseph[6] despite the lack of primary evidence.

60 MARY LEONARD[5] (Jacob[4], Sarah Chandler[3], Isabella[2]
Chilton, James[1]) d. Bridgewater 20 April 1733.
    She m. Bridgewater 27 Nov. 1719 BENJAMIN WILLIS Jr.,
b. 1696; d. Bridgewater 13 Feb. 1779; son of Benjamin and
Susanna (Whitman) Willis. Benjamin Willis Esq. of Bridge-
water was appointed administrator of the estate of Benjamin
Willis, late of Bridgewater deceased, 1 March 1779.

    Children (WILLIS) b. Bridgewater: BENJAMIN[6] b. 1720; child d.
1731; and another child d. 1733.

References: HARVARD GRADS 10:540[erroneously gives Benjamin Willis[6]
            as grandson of Samuel Willis]. VR BRIDGEWATER. Plymouth
Co. PR 27:12(Benj. Willis). BRIDGEWATER BY MITCHELL pp. 365-366.
LEONARD FAM p. 43.

61 SOLOMON LEONARD[5] (Jacob[4], Sarah Chandler[3], Isabella[2]
Chilton, James[1]) b. Bridgewater ca. 1693; d. Bridgewater
29 May 1761 in 69 yr., "Capt.".
    He m. 1730 ELIZABETH PERKINS (pos. his(2) wife), b.
Bridgewater 29 March 1707; d. there 19 April 1781 "widow of
Capt. Solomon," unnamed; dau. of David and Martha (Howard)
Perkins. In a settlement of the estate of David Perkins,
the widow's thirds were set off to Mrs. Martha Perkins, and
one-tenth of the remainder went to daughter Elizabeth Lenard wife of Solomon Lenard of Bridgewater 11 Oct. 1738.
    Solomon Leonard of Bridgewater was appointed adminis-
trator of Solomon Leonard late of Bridgewater 3 Aug. 1761;
the inventory, taken by Benjamin Willis Jr., John Washburn
and Jonathan Cary, included household goods received by
Elizabeth Hooper.
    Hezekiah Hooper of Bridgewater blacksmith and wife
Elizabeth, and Samuel Whitman of Bridgewater and wife Susanna, heirs of Solomon Leonard of Bridgewater gentleman deceased, sold to Solomon Leonard of Bridgewater all rights
to homestead which Solomon died seized of, reserving to the
widow her dower; Elizabeth Leonard widow, in exchange for
dower set off to her, yielded any rights to the remainder
11 Dec. 1761. Also Experience Leonard of Bridgewater spinster sold to Solomon Leonard of Bridgewater all rights to
her deceased father's land, except widow's thirds, 9 May
acknowledged 30 Oct. 1765.

    Children (LEONARD) b. Bridgewater: EXPERIENCE[6] b. 1732, d.y.;
SOLOMON b. 1733; ELIZABETH b. 1737; SUSANNA b. 1740; EXPERIENCE b.
1743.

References: BRIDGEWATER BY MITCHELL pp. 245, 277. VR BRIDGEWATER.
            LEONARD FAM p. 43, 63-6. Plymouth Co. PR 16:238; 17:49
(Solomon Leonard); 7:327, 336, 451(David Perkins). BRIDGEWATER

EPITAPHS p. 92(Solomon Leonard). Plymouth Co. LR 67:161(Experience Leonard); 47:117(Hezekiah Hooper et al.). NEHGR 50:36.

62   SARAH LEONARD[5] (Jacob[4], Sarah Chandler[3], Isabella[2] Chilton, James[1]) b. Bridgewater 11 June 1699; living Stafford CT 1743.
        She m. Bridgewater 27 Feb. 1720/1 WILLIAM ORCUTT Jr., pos. b. Weymouth 13 Aug. 1695; living Stafford in 1743; pos. son of Andrew and Frances (Ward) Orcutt.
        William Orcutt Jr. "of Bridwatter" MA bought land in Stafford CT 13 March 1728 of Joseph Orcutt. A William Orcutt of Stafford posted bond as administrator of the estate of William Orcutt of Willington CT, with Josiah Converse as security, 25 Feb. 1776; the William of Willington was said to have married ----- Converse.

        Children (ORCUTT) b. to William and Sarah, the first at Bridgewater, others recorded at Stafford CT: JACOB[6] b. 1723, d. Stafford 1745; WILLIAM b. 1725; SUSANNA b. 1727, d. Stafford 1744; SOLOMON b. 1730; SIMEON b. 1732; LEMUEL b. 1735; MOSES b. 1737; SARAH b. 1740; and JANE b. 1743.

References: VR BRIDGEWATER, WEYMOUTH. CSL Barbour Index: Stafford.
            BRIDGEWATER BY MITCHELL pp. 245, 260. LEONARD FAM p. 43. WEYMOUTH BY CHAMBERLAIN 4:447. Stafford CT LR 1:292(Jos. to Wm. Orcutt). CT PR Stafford Dist #1592(Wm. Orcutt).

63   ISAAC LEONARD[5] (Isaac[4], Sarah Chandler[3], Isabella[2] Chilton, James[1]) living 2 March 1736/7 "in York government."
        He m. Bridgewater 16 April 1701 MARY (GURNEY?) RANDALL of "North Purchase," widow of Samuel Randall.
        Isaac Leonard Jr. of Bridgewater bought land in Taunton "North Purchase" in 1702. When he moved there is uncertain, but he was living in North Purchase in 1713 and in 1720 when he bought land there. He was of Norton "east precinct" in 1722/3 when he purchased land in Easton. Isaac Leonard of Easton and wife Mary sold their home lot with dwelling in Easton March 1725/6.
        Isaac Leonard of "Pomphret" CT sold two tracts in Easton 9 Sept. 1727, and Isaac "late of Easton now of Pomfret CT" sold his share in an iron mine in Easton 4 Jan. 1729, in a deed acknowledged 19 March 1730/1. Listed as inhabitants of Pomfret in 1731 were: Isaac Leonard Sr. and Jr., David Leonard and Thomas Leonard. Isaac was in Pomfret in 1732/3 when he traded land with a Joseph Leonard. (In one instance the land, sold by Joseph to Isaac[6], was bounded by land of Joseph's brother Isaac[5].) After 1734 Joseph Leonard and wife, and Isaac Leonard, were admitted to the Second Church in Pomfret. In a deed signed 2 Feb. 1736/7

Isaac Leonard "late of Pomfret" was "now resident in Worcester shire in York government"* when he sold his holdings in Pomfret. No further records were found in CT for
Isaac or sons David and Thomas.

   Probable children (LEONARD): ISAAC[6], DAVID, and THOMAS.

References: VR BRIDGEWATER. BRIDGEWATER BY MITCHELL pp. 106, 245.
         LEONARD FAM pp. 66-7. TAG 33:137-41. NEHGR 116:18-9.
EATON HIST p. 48. WINDHAM CO CT BY LARNED 1:343, 349. Pomfret CT LR
2:156, 160; 3:38(Isaac Leonard). Bristol Co. LR 7:454(Benjamin Snow);
13:119(Thos. Randall Jr.); 13:121(Jeremiah Willis & Samuel Smith); 18:
145(Wm. Hayward); 18:510; 19:487; 20:50(Isaac Leonard).

   64 HANNAH LEONARD[5] (Isaac[4], Sarah Chandler[3], Isabella[2]
Chilton, James[1]) b. Bridgewater 15 March 1679/80; d. Eas-
ton 22 April 1753.
   She m. (1) Marlboro 11 March 1697 DAVID NEWTON, b.
Marlboro 12 March 1671/2; d. there 4 April 1702; son of
Moses and Joanna (Larkin) Newton. David Newton's will,
dated Marlboro 3 April 1702 sworn 26 May 1702, names wife
Hannah, three "small daughters" Hannah, Lydia and Thank-
full, and father Moses Newton Sr. as overseer. The will of
Moses Newton of Marlborough, dated 3 April 1724, mentions
"children of my sons David and Edward Newton deceased."
   She m. (2) bet. 1702 and 1708 NATHANIEL MANLEY, b.
Weymouth 27 May 1684; d. Easton 21 April 1753; son of Wil-
liam and Rebecca (-----) Manley of Easton.
   In 1716 Nathaniel Manley living in the easterly end of
Taunton North Purchase gave rights in iron ore to his
brother-in-law Isaac Leonard of Taunton. The same year he
sold land and dwelling, his share from his father William
Manley and his brothers Thomas and William Manley.
Nathaniel was of Easton when he next sold land in 1726, and
in 1727/8, which he and wife Hannah both acknowledged 5 May
1738. On 20 April 1753 Nathaniel Manley of Easton sold to
Ichabod Manley of Easton several lots in Easton; on the
second Tuesday of June 1754 one of the witnesses attested
that Nathaniel Manley, since deceased, signed the deed.

   Children (NEWTON) b. Marlboro to David and Hannah: HANNAH[6] b.
1697; LIDIAH b. 1699; and THANKFULL b. 1701.

   Children (MANLEY) b. Easton to Nathaniel and Hannah: ICHABOD b.
1709; HANNAH b. 1711; REBECCA b. 1714; ELIZABETH b. 1716; and MARY b.
1720, d. 1739.

References: VR BRIDGEWATER, HARDWICK(b. Ichabod), MARLBORO, WEYMOUTH.
         LEONARD FAM pp. 44-5. NEHGR 16:145. NEWTON GEN pp. 166-9.

_____
*"Worcester shire in York government" has not been surely located,
though Westchester NY has been suggested.

WEYMOUTH BY CHAMBERLAIN 3:414. EASTON HIST pp. 47-8. Easton VR(copy
of original record book at town hall). Middlesex Co. PR #15885 and
10:459(David Newton). Bristol Co. LR 13:117; 20:214; 27:406; 36:292;
40:402(Nathaniel Manley). Worcester Co. PR, old series, #43331 (Moses
Newton).

65 JOSEPH LEONARD[5] (Isaac[4], Sarah Chandler[3], Isabella[2]
Chilton, James[1]) b. prob. Bridgewater; living Pomfret CT
6 April 1736.
        He m. Bridgewater 19 Nov. 1712 HANNAH JENNINGS, dau.
of Richard Jennings. Richard's will, signed in Bridgewater
27 April 1739 proved 1751, names daughter Hannah wife of
Joseph Leonard.
        In 1725 Mary Bailey sold rights to Joseph Leonard of
Bridgewater "son of Isaac Leonard decd." Joseph Leonard
Jr. of Bridgewater sold 20 March 1728 "my homestead where I
dwell" in Bridgewater, and wife Hannah released right of
dower. On 8 April 1728 Joseph Leonard of Bridgewater,
cooper, bought land in Pomfret, bounded on the south by
land of Isaac Leonard. Joseph Leonard of Pomfret husbandman on 9 Jan. 1732/3 sold to Isaac Leonard of Pomfret "the
farm whereon I now live" bounded by land of "my brother
Isaac Leonard," witnessed by an Isaac Leonard. On 5 April
1736 Joseph Leonard of Pomfret sold land in Pomfret, acknowledged the next day; he and his family then disappear
from the records of Connecticut.

        Children (LEONARD) all except last b. Bridgewater: twins HANNAH[6]
and JOSEPH b. 1713; MOSES b. 1714; SETH b. 1715; TIMOTHY b. 1718;
REBECCA b. 1721; MEHETABEL b. 1724; THANKFUL b. 1726; EBENEZER b. 1728;
and BETTE b. Pomfret CT 1730.

References: CSL Barbour Index:Pomfret. VR BRIDGEWATER. BRIDGEWATER
            BY MITCHELL pp. 210, 245. LEONARD FAM p. 61[clearly has
the incorrect Joseph going to Pomfret]. Plymouth Co. PR 12:385(Richard
Jennings). Plymouth Co. LR 19:168(Mary Bailey); 23:151(Joseph Leonard). WINDHAM CO. CT BY LARNED 1:349. Pomfret CT LR 2:59(John Adams);
2:155, 156, 157, 160, 161, 162(Joseph Leonard & Isaac Leonard).

66 BENJAMIN LEONARD[5] (Isaac[4], Sarah Chandler[3], Isa-
bella[2] Chilton, James[1]) b. prob. Bridgewater ca. 1686 to
1690; d. Mendham NJ by July 1749.
        He m. (1) Bridgewater 15 Aug. 1715 or 1716 HANNAH
PHILLIPS, d. ca. 1730; dau. of William and Hannah (Gilbert)
Phillips of Taunton. On 15 Nov. 1717 Benjamin and Hannah
Leonard of Bridgewater received of "our grandfather Thomas
Gilbert of Taunton, administrator of the estate of William
Phillips late of Taunton deceased, our father," their share
of his estate.

He m. (2) Freetown 13 June 1734 MARY CUDWORTH, b.
Freetown 14 Nov. 1702; very prob. d. Morristown NJ 5 Nov.
1778 ae 75; dau. of James and Betsey (Hatch) Cudworth.

Benjamin Leonard, cooper, of Bridgewater sold his
homestead in Bridgewater in 1720, and the same year he and
wife Hannah sold land in Dighton, set off to her from her
father's estate. In 1722 Benjamin bought land in Dighton,
and was living in the part which later became Berkley in
July 1723 with wife Hannah. Benjamin was of Berkley when
he sold land in 1735, and also when he sold his homestead
in 1737, wife Mary relinquishing dower. Both he and Mary
still of Berkley acknowledged a sale 7 Dec. 1738. His last
sale was acknowledged in Berkley 3 Sept. 1739.

About 1740 Benjamin and family moved to Mendham,
Morris Co., NJ. No probate or land records have been located for either Benjamin or Mary in NJ.

Children (LEONARD) b. to Benjamin and Hannah, first two b. Bridgewater, all recorded Dighton: JEMIMA[6] b. 1717; LYDIA b. 1718; HANNAH b.
1720; BENJAMIN b. 1722; WILLIAM b. 1724; and CALEB b. 1726.

Children (LEONARD) b. to Benjamin and Mary, only Henry certain,
others probable (marriages for Ephraim, Sarah, Dorothea and Hannah
found at Morristown NJ 1753-61): EPHRAIM; HENRY bp. Berkley 1738;
SARAH; DOROTHEA; HANNAH; and possibly SUSANNA.

References: VR BRIDGEWATER. Dighton VR 1:42, 91. Freetown VR, type-
                script, pp. 17, 79; and marriages p. 40. TAG 46:121.
BRIDGEWATER BY MITCHELL p. 247. LEONARD FAM pp. 67-8. CORY ANCY 2:
1:87-90. Plymouth Co. LR 38:201(Benj. Leonard). BERKLEY HIST p. 6.
Berkley Baptisms by Rev. Samuel Tobey, typescript at Old Colony Hist.
Soc., Taunton. Bristol Co. LR 13:139, 565; 15:16, 255; 35:355;
40:276; 57:199(Benj. Leonard); 15:5(James Leonard Jr.). NJ ARCHIVES,
WILLS 2:478(Jos. Thompson will mentions Benj. Leonard deceased).

67 MARTHA LEONARD[5] (Solomon[4], Sarah Chandler[3], Isabella[2] Chilton, James[1]) b. prob. Bridgewater ca. 1685; d.
1761.

She m. (1) Bridgewater 9 Nov. 1709 NATHAN PERKINS, bp.
Beverly 13 Sept. 1685; d. Bridgewater bef. 4 June 1723 (inventory); son of David and Elizabeth (Brown) Perkins. A
division of the estate of Nathan Perkins of Bridgewater
deceased was made 12 June 1730 among Martha Hayward wife of
Isaac, formerly widow of Nathan Perkins; his sons Nathan,
Solomon, Timothy and James; and his daus. Martha and
Silence. Also the will of David Perkins dated 21 Jan.
1735/6 proved 5 Oct. 1736, names grandsons Nathan, James,
Timothy and Solomon "my son Nathan's children"; and their
sisters Martha and Silence.

She m. (2) Bridgewater 15 May 1728 ISAAC HAYWARD, b.
Bridgewater 16 Oct. 1691; living there 4 Feb. 1741/2; son

of Nathaniel and Elizabeth (-----) Hayward. They had no
children. Isaac Hayward of Bridgewater and wife Martha
transferred to Solomon Perkins of Bridgewater, joiner, 24
Aug. 1739, upon his bond to support and care for Martha,
all rights to lands "our father Solomon Leonard" late of
Bridgewater died siezed of. Isaac of Bridgewater sold a
meadow in Bridgewater, acknowledged 4 Feb. 1741/2.

    Children (PERKINS) b. Bridgewater to Nathan and Martha: NATHAN[6]
b. 1710; SOLOMON b. 1712; TIMOTHY b. 1714/5; MARTHA b. 1717; JAMES b.
1720/1; and SILENCE b. 1723.

References: VR BEVERLY, BRIDGEWATER. BRIDGEWATER BY MITCHELL pp. 182,
             184, 277. LEONARD FAM pp. 47, 63. NEHGR 50:37. Plym-
outh Co. PR 4:383, 455; 5:717-20(Nathan Perkins); 7:246(David Perkins).
Plymouth Co. LR 33:46; 34:160; 39:255(Isaac Hayward).

    68 SAMUEL POLLARD[5] (Mary Leonard[4], Sarah Chandler[3],
Isabella[2] Chilton, James[1]) b. Boston 16 Jan. 1679; pos. d.
Taunton 24 April 1768 (or was this his son?)
    He m. ----- -----, pos. the "Old Mrs. Pollard" who d.
Taunton 31 Aug. 1771 (though this may be the widow of his
son Samuel).
    In 1713 Samuel commenced an involvement in land trans-
actions, in which he was of Taunton, often called cooper.
He had a son Samuel[6], and distinguishing between the two is
difficult. Samuel Pollard Jr. mar. in Easton 13 Nov. 1740
Abigail Smith dau. of Joseph Smith. This Samuel, also of
Taunton, often sold land, and wife Abigail also signed. On
8 Nov. 1748 Samuel Pollard second of Taunton, cooper, and
wife Abigail sold 1/6 part of land of "our father Joseph
Smith late of Easton deceased." On 19 April 1757 Samuel
Pollard transferred land and "my dwelling" to son Samuel,
together with his carpenter and cooper tools, under the
condition that Samuel support and care for him and his
"present wife" Abigail. Abigail's latest acknowledgment of
a deed was dated 11 May 1757; Samuel's 31 May 1760. [In
little of the above is it clear with just which Samuel we
are dealing.]

    Children (POLLARD) b. Taunton: SAMUEL[6] b. ca. 1700; and prob.
others.

References: VR TAUNTON. POLLARD FAM 1:57. Bristol Co. LR 8:91
             (Stoughton to Pollard); 9:594; 18:385; 35:260, 261, 634;
37:457; 42:265, 313, 419; 44:261(Samuel Pollard); 46:428(Dean to
Samuel Pollard et al.).

69 ELIZABETH BRUFF[5] (Stephen[4], Mary Chandler[3], Isabella[2] Chilton, James[1]) b. ca. 1699; living 1725.
      She m. (1) Boston 22 May 1716 DAVID GIBSON (or Gib-
bons), b. Boston 20 Nov. 1691; living Boston 18 Jan. 1719;
son of William and Hannah (Phippen) Gibson. He was a mariner. "David Gibbins" and wife Elizabeth were included in
an agreement dated 18 Jan. 1719 (see #21). No children.
      She m. (2) Boston 11 Oct. 1722 JOHN GALPIN(E), living
1724. On 30 Oct. 1723 Thomas Millins and wife Mary, Thomas Weymouth and wife Susannah, two daughters of Bartholomew Threeneedles; John Galpin, tinplate worker, and wife
Elizabeth, and William Dorrington, cordwainer, and wife
Damaris, two daughters of Bartholomew's daughter Damaris
deceased, all of Boston, sold "our dwelling" in Boston. No
other deeds or probate found in Suffolk Co.

      Children (GALPINE) b. Boston to John and Elizabeth: JOHN[6] b.
1723; and ELIZABETH b. 1725.

References: BOSTON VR 9:196; 24:160, 171; 28:63, 106. TAG 37:217.
            GALPIN FAM p. 239. Suffolk Co. LR 34:145(Damaris Three-
needles et al); 37:140(Thos. Millins et al.).

70 DAMARIS BRUFF[5] (Stephen[4], Mary Chandler[3], Isabella[2]
Chilton, James[1]) b. Boston 27 Oct. 1701; prob. the "Mrs.
Dorrington" who d. Boston in Sept. 1775.
      She m. Boston 26 March 1723 WILLIAM DORRINGTON, d.
Boston bef. 28 Feb. 1778.
      See deed of 1723 under family #69. A petition for ad-
ministration of William's estate is dated 28 Feb. 1778.
The inventory of the estate of William Dorrington cordwainer deceased late of Boston was presented 19 Feb. 1779
by John Merritt, administrator. Their children are found
in TAG.

      Children (DORRINGTON) first four b. Boston: WILLIAM[6] b. 1724;
MARY b. 1725; STEPHEN b. 1728; ELIZABETH b. 1731; JOHN; and pos. SARAH.

References: TAG 37:217. BOSTON VR 24:5, 164, 170, 186, 202; 28:112.
            NEHGR 85:120. Suffolk Co. PR 77:305; 78:148(Wm. Dorring-
ton).

71 MARTHA SMITH[5] (Mary Bundy[4], Martha Chandler[3], Isabella[2] Chilton, James[1]) b. Taunton 20 Oct. 1686; prob. the
"Mrs. Prisbery, old" d. Taunton 1 Jan. 1778.
      She prob. m. Norton 9 Dec. 1714 JOSEPH PRISBERY (or
Presbry), d. Taunton 22 March 1771 ae 84.
      On 7 Feb. 1765 Joseph Presbrey of Taunton transferred
to his sons Joseph Presbrey Jr. and William Presbrey, both
of Taunton, his homestead farm with buildings in Taunton,

reserving same to his use during his lifetime. Upon petition, William Presbery of Taunton was appointed guardian of
Martha Presbery of Taunton, widow, 27 April 1772. As a result of a petition by Martha 29 June 1772, Joseph Presbry
of Taunton was appointed guardian 8 July 1772 in place of
William. In Martha's petition, both William and Joseph are
called her sons.

Children (PRISBERY or PRISBERRY) b. Taunton to Joseph: HANNAH[6] b.
1715; JOSEPH; and WILLIAM.

References: VR NORTON, TAUNTON. Bristol Co. PR 22:236, 490, and orig.
papers(Martha Presbery); 22:515(Wm. Presbry). Bristol Co.
LR 47:366(Jos. Presbrey).

72 JAMES BUNDY[5] (James[4], Martha Chandler[3], Isabella[2]
Chilton, James[1]) b. ca. 1690; d. prob. Preston CT bet.
1752 and 1762.
He m. ca. 1710 MARY [JOHNSON?], d. Preston 4 May 1766.
James Bundy of Preston 5 Sept. 1748 gave land in Pres-
ton to his son James Bundy Jr. On 13 Jan. 1748/9 James of
Preston gave land in Preston to his son Peter Bundy.

Children (BUNDY) b. Preston CT to James and Mary, and all except
first Isaac were baptized at Griswold First Congregational Church 25
July 1728: HANNAH[6] b. 1711 or 1712; DEBORAH b. 1713/4; JAMES b. 1715;
MARY b. 1717; EUNICE b. 1719; PETER b. 1720/1; ISAAC b. 1722, d. 1725;
JOHN b. 1724; and ISAAC b. 1726.

References: WALPOLE NH HIST 2:41. CSL Barbour Index: Preston.
SEATTLE BUL 6(8):455(Bundy). Preston CT LR 6:142, 144
(James Bundy).

73 SAMUEL BUNDY[5] (James[4], Martha Chandler[3], Isabella[2]
Chilton, James[1]) b. ca. 1694; living West Greenwich RI 3
Sept. 1747.
He m. ABIGAIL -----, living 14 Aug. 1725 (deed).
Samuel Bundy, cooper, of E. Greenwich RI sold land in
E. Greenwich in 1722, and again 14 Aug. 1725 with consent
of wife Abigail. In a deposition Jan. 1730/1 in E. Greenwich he stated he was aged 37. His last sale as resident
of E. Greenwich, cooper, was made 16 Feb. 1738. In 1743,
resident in W. Greenwich, he purchased land there, which he
sold back to the original owner 3 Sept. 1747 in his latest
sale of record, still called cooper.
Of his children, only Lydia is identified as his
daughter (in her marriage record). The following may be
his children as indicated in SEATTLE BUL, but no proof of
such connection has been found: Sarah m. E. Greenwich

1735; Rebecca m. E. Greenwich 1739; Samuel m. W. Greenwich 1741; Martha m. W. Greenwich 1752; and Thier and Jonathan.

Child (BUNDY) b. to Samuel: LYDIA[6] b. ca. 1723; and pos. others.

References: S. Kingston LR 1:272; 3:355(Samuel Bundy). E. Greenwich LR 3A:260; 4:245; 5:453(Samuel Bundy); 5:235(Thos. Rathbone). W. Greenwich LR 1-2:349(Samuel Bundy); 1-2:162(Saml. Reynolds). RI VR: E. Greenwich pp. 5, 15; W. Greenwich p. 9. SEATTLE BUL 6(8):456.

   74 EBENEZER BUNDY[5] (James[4], Martha Chandler[3], Isabella[2] Chilton, James[1]) b. ca. 1699; d. bef. 1743.
   He m. Preston CT 11 June 1724 ("both of Plainfield") MARTHA CLARK, b. Plainfield CT ca. 1700; dau. of Benjamin and Mary (-----) Clark. She m. (2) bef. 1743 ----- Aldredge. The will of Benjamin Clark of Plainfield, dated 1743/4 probated 1750, names dau. Martha Aldridg (*sic*).
   Ebenezer deposed ae 19 and upward at Kingstown RI 31 March 1719. He was living in Preston CT in 1721, but was living in Plainfield when he married, and apparently for some time thereafter. No evidence was found for the two sons, Silas b. ca. 1726, and Ebenezer b. 1729/30, claimed in SEATTLE BUL; no probate records at either Plainfield or Windham districts.

References: SEATTLE BUL 6(8):458. CT MARR 4:32. E. Greenwich RI LR 3A:256(James and Ebenezer Bundy). RI Rec Ctr(depos. Ebenezer Bundy). Plainfield CT Dist PR 2:111(Benjamin Clark).

   75 JOSEPH BUNDY[5] (James[4], Martha Chandler[3], Isabella[2] Chilton, James[1]) b. ca. 1701; d. Hopkinton RI bef. 8 April 1771.
   He m. (1) ABIGAIL JOHNSON, d. bef. Oct. 1758.
   He m. (2) Westerly RI 30 Oct. 1758 MARY (REYNOLDS) TEFFT, living 4 Sept. 1773; widow of John Tefft.
   Joseph was living in N. Kingstown RI in 1731, but by 1736 was in Preston CT; he returned to N. Kingstown by 1741, but was in Charlestown RI in 1747, and in Hopkinton RI by 1760. He was a cordwainer.
   The will of Joseph Bundy of Hopkinton, dated 1 Dec. 1770 approved 1 July 1771, names wife Mary, son Ezekiel of Preston, dau. Elizabeth Teft, dau. Dorcas Harrick, wife's dau. Mary Burdick; friend Thomas West, executor. Widow Mary was appointed administrator in place of Thomas West 8 April 1771. On Sept. 1773 Elijah Burdick posted bond to care for widow Mary Bunday. No proof was found for sons Caleb and George claimed in SEATTLE BUL.

Children (BUNDY) b. to Joseph and Abigail: ELIZABETH[6] b. ca. 1730; EZEKIEL b. Preston 1736; and DORCAS.

References: S. Kingstown RI LR 3:355(Samuel & Joseph Bundy); 3:379 (Jos. Bundy). RI VR: Westerly p. 15. CSL Barbour Index: Preston. SEATTLE BUL 6(8):457-8. Hopkinton RI PR 2:11-12, 18(Jos. Bundy). Hopkinton RI LR 1:301(Button to Bundy); 2:412(Elijah Burdick).

76 ELIZABETH WINSLOW[5] (John[4-3], Mary[2] Chilton, James[1]) b. Boston 2 April 1693; living Boston 1723.
     She m. Portsmouth NH July 1715 ALEXANDER TODD, b. Northern Ireland; son of James and Rachel (Nelson) Todd. Alexander was a graduate of the University of Edinburgh, Scotland, and a mariner of Boston from 1719 to at least 1723. See the deed abstracted under family #24.

Children (TODD) b. Boston: ABIGAIL[6] b. 1721; ELIZABETH b. 1723; and prob. another dau.

References: BOSTON VR 24:153, 162. ME-NH GEN DICT p. 765. Suffolk Co. LR 34:268(John Winslow, Alexander Todd). LONDONDERRY HIST p. 301.

77 JOHN WINSLOW[5] (John[4-3], Mary[2] Chilton, James[1]) b. Boston 31 Dec. 1693; d. at sea 13 Oct. 1731 ae 38.
     He m. Portsmouth NH 21 Sept. 1721 SARAH PIERCE (or Peirce), b. Portsmouth 30 April 1697; d. there 21 Aug. 1771; dau. of Joshua and Elizabeth (Hall) Pierce. She m. (2) 1749 Nathaniel Sargent, physician of Hampton NH. The will of Joshua Peirce of Portsmouth NH dated 13 Nov. 1742 (inventory March 1742/3) names wife Elizabeth, and children including Joshua Peirce and Sarah Winslow.
     The will of Joshua Peirce of Portsmouth, dated 18 July 1754 proved 28 Aug. 1754, left to "my sister Sargent" and to her sons John Winslow and Joshua Winslow. The will of Nathaniel Sargent of Portsmouth physician, dated 24 Oct. 1760 proved 18 May 1762, mentions contract before marriage with Sarah Winslow, now his wife.
     John Winslow[5] went to Portsmouth NH with his mother after her marriage to Samuel Penhallow. John was a mariner of Boston in 1719.

Children (WINSLOW) b. to John and Sarah: SARAH[6] b. 1722 (prob. the Sarah Jr. received into full communion 1741 at South Church of Portsmouth); JOHN b. Boston 1724, d.y.; JOHN b. Portsmouth 1725/6; and JOSHUA b. Portsmouth 1726/7.

References: BOSTON VR 24:168. NEHGR 23:269; 24:14-5; 29:110; 81:452. HAMPTON NH BY DOW p. 962. NH STATE PAPERS 33:131;

35:133(Joshua Peirce); 37:31(Nathaniel Sargent). ME-NH GEN DICT pp. 553, 608, 765.

78 DESIRE HARRIS[5] (Mercy Latham[4], Susanna Winslow[3], Mary[2] Chilton, James[1]) b. prob. Bridgewater bef. 5 July 1669; d. Bridgewater early in 1698.
    She m. by 1690 JOHN KINGMAN JR., b. Weymouth 20 April 1664; d. Bridgewater 8 Jan. 1755 in 95 yr; son of John and Elizabeth (Edson) Kingman. He m. (2) Bridgewater 1698 the widow Bethiah (-----) Newcomb, and had by her Abigail, Bethia, David, Ebenezer, Isaac, John, Joseph and Josiah.
    The will of John Kingman of Bridgewater, dated 21 Jan. 1744/5 proved 3 Feb. 1755, names wife Bethiah; sons Isaac, John, Josiah, David and Ebenezer; daughters Mary Copeland, Deliverance Orcutt, Abigail Allen; grandson John Orcutt and granddaughter Susanna Orcutt, children of deceased daughter Desire Orcutt; son-in-law John Orcutt; grandson Ebenezer Allen and granddaughter Bethiah Allen, children of deceased daughter Bethiah Allen; son-in-law James Allen.

    Children (KINGMAN) b. Bridgewater to John and Desire: DESIRE[6] b. 1690; MARY b. 1692; JOHN b. 1694, d.y.; SETH b. 1696; and DELIVERANCE b. 1698.

References: VR BRIDGEWATER. BRIDGEWATER BY MITCHELL p. 225. Plym-
              outh Co. PR 13:389(John Kingman). WEYMOUTH BY CHAMBER-
LAIN 3:356.

79 JANE HARRIS[5] (Mercy Latham[4], Susanna Winslow[3], Mary[2] Chilton, James[1]) b. Bridgewater 19 July 1671; d. Bellingham 8 Nov. 1746 in 77 yr. "wife of Zurial Hall, formerly widow of Pelatiah Smith."
    She m. (1) ca. 1689 JAMES DUNBAR, b. Hingham 5 June 1644; d. Bridgewater 12 Dec. 1690; son of Robert and Rose (-----) Dunbar. Jane, relict widow of James, was appoint-
ed administratrix of the estate of James Dunbar of Bridge-
water deceased 17 March 1690/1. A settlement dated the same day names Jane relict and son Robert, under 21.
    She m. (2) Bridgewater ca. 1691 PELATIAH SMITH, b. Malden(?); d. Bellingham 10 or 18 Sept. 1727; son of Michael and Joan (-----) Smith. He m. (1) Sarah -----, by whom he had Eleanor, Ruhamah and Sarah.
    Peletiah Smith of Bridgewater bought in 1713 a house between Mansfield and Mendon. He was of Bellingham, black-
smith, when in 1722 he gave part of his homestead to son Samuel Smith. The will of Peletiah Smith of Bellingham, blacksmith, dated 28 April sworn 1 Nov. 1727, left all real estate to wife Jane; she and son James to be executors. A declaration 12 Feb. 1730 claims that whereas Peletiah Smith died seized of a messuage and leaving nine children and the daughter of one other who predeceased him, and failed to

mention any of his children or grandchild in his will, so the children and grandchild were entitled to all his real estate. One of the daughters, Jane Smith of Bellingham "simster", released her rights to her brother James Smith of Bellingham. Benjamin Smith of Bellingham 16 March 1737 sold to his brothers James and Robert Smith of Bellingham all rights to the estate of his father Peletiah Smith deceased.

Jane m. (3) int. Bellingham 14 Dec. 1742 ZURIAL HALL, b. ca. 1678; d. Bellingham 3 April 1765 in 88 yr; son of Zurial and Elizabeth (Tripp) Hall. He m. (1) Susanna -----, by whom he had eight children: Elizabeth, Mary, Susanna, Patience, Seth, Urania, Abigail and Ruth. Zurial and Jane had no children.

Child (DUNBAR) b. Bridgewater to James and Jane: ROBERT[6] b. 1689.

Children (SMITH) b. Bridgewater to Peletiah and Jane: JANE b. 1692; PELETIAH b. 1695; JAMES b. 1696/7; SAMUEL b. 1699; DESIRE b. 1701; JOANNA b. 1703; RUHAMAH b. 1705; ROBERT b. 1708; and JOSEPH b. 1710.

References: VR BELLINGHAM, BRIDGEWATER, MALDEN (pp. 79, 181-2).
        BRIDGEWATER BY MITCHELL pp. 149, 308. BELLINGHAM HIST pp. 68-9. CHARLESTOWN BY WYMAN 2:873. MD 2:243; 14:181-2; 31:15-6. HINGHAM HIST 2:195-6 [erroneously assigns sons Elisha, James and Samuel to James and Jane]. Plymouth Co. PR 1:97-8 (James Dunbar). Suffolk Co. PR 25:540; 27:151; (new series) 15:248 (Peletiah Smith). Suffolk Co. LR 29:247 (Sandford to Smith); 70:51 ("whereas Peletiah Smith..."); 70:52 (Benjamin Smith).

80   SUSANNA HARRIS[5]   (Mercy Latham[4], Susanna Winslow[3], Mary[2] Chilton, James[1]) b. bef. 1680; living 24 Aug. 1730.
She m. (1) Bridgewater 7 April 1696 JEREMIAH NEWLAND, b. Taunton 8 Feb. 1667; d. Bridgewater bef. 1711; son of Jeremiah Newland.
Their children are revealed in the following deed abstracts. (1) Jeremiah[6] Newland of "Plimton" and [his sister] Keturah Newland of Pembroke sold to Samuel Harris 13 July 1722 3/7 part of house and land of their father Jeremiah Newland late of Bridgewater deceased; the deed was acknowledged by Keturah 9 March 1723, and on that same day witnesses Mercy Harris, now Mulford, and Joshua Pearce testified they saw Jeremiah sign. (2) John Newland of Bridgewater on 7 Jan. 1725/6 sold his part of land "from my father Jeremiah Newland" late of Bridgewater deceased, and also rights to the estate of his brother Jeremiah Newland late of Pembroke deceased. (3) Seth Cushman and wife Susanna of Taunton on 10 March 1725/6 sold their rights to land of Jeremiah Newland of Bridgewater deceased "who was

father of Susanna." (4) Jabez Newland of "Plimton" sold
his 1/7 part of real estate of his father Jeremiah Newland
formerly of Bridgewater deceased in a deed acknowledged 16
May 1727. (5) Priscilla Newland of Plymouth spinstress on
17 May 1727 sold her 1/7 part of real estate that her
father Jeremiah Newland formerly of Bridgewater died seized
of, and also her rights in the estate of her brother Jeremiah Newland late of Pembroke deceased. All sales, except
Jeremiah and Keturah's, were made to Isaac Harris of
Bridgewater, innholder.

Susanna m. (2) Bridgewater 26 Jan. 1710/11 JOHN PEARCE
(or Pierce or Peirce) "of Pembroke"; d. Bridgewater bef. 1
Feb. 1726/7. By a first wife, John had several children
including Caleb, Nehemiah, Elinor, Abraham and prob. Mary,
Priscilla, Thankful and Joshua. Nehemiah of Pembroke 24
Aug. 1730 sold to Joshua Pearce 1/10 of the last habita-
tion of John Pearse, reserving dower of the widow Susanna
Pearce (Caleb, Elinor and Abraham executed similar trans-
fers).

On 7 Oct. 1723 John Peirce of Pembroke was granted administration on the estate of his son-in-law [step-son]
Jeremiah Newland[6] late of Pembroke deceased. On 12 Oct.
1725 Caleb Peirce of Yarmouth was appointed administrator
on the estate of his father John Peirce late of Pembroke
deceased. No other children are mentioned in the estate
records. Four children were baptized to John Pearse in
Pembroke in 1712; it therefore seems likely that dau.
Mercy baptized in 1714 was born to wife Susanna.

Children (NEWLAND) b. to Jeremiah and Susanna: JEREMIAH[6] b. ca.
1698; SUSANNA; KETURAH b. bef. 1704; JOHN; PRISCILLA; and JABEZ b. ca.
1707.

Child (PEARCE) baptized to John at Pembroke, prob. dau. of Susanna: MERCY bp. 1714.

References: VR BRIDGEWATER, PEMBROKE, PLYMPTON, TAUNTON. TAG 40:196-
8; 52:181. Plymouth Co. PR #14614 and 4:375, 401-2(Jeremiah Newland); 5:90(John Peirce); 5:165(gdn. of Nehemiah Peirce); 30:
141-2(Jabez Newland); 33:161-2(Sarah Newland). Plymouth Co. LR 20:28
(John Newland); 20:85(Seth Cushman); 22:65(Jabez Newland, Priscilla
Newland); 23:185(Caleb Pearce); 23:186(Elija Bisbee & wife Eleanor);
23:187(Abraham Pearce Jr.); 24:219-20(Jeremiah Newland); 26:41
(Nehemiah Pearce).

81 ISAAC HARRIS[5] (Mercy Latham[4], Susanna Winslow[3],
Mary[2] Chilton, James[1]) d. Bridgewater bef. 30 Oct. 1738.
He m. (1) Scituate 27 March 1707 JANE COOKE, b. Plym-
outh 16 March 1688/9; d. Bridgewater 8 Feb. 1716/7; dau.
of Caleb and Jane (-----) Cooke and great granddaughter of
Pilgrim Francis Cooke. The will of Caleb Cooke of

Plymouth, dated 10 Feb. 1721, mentions wife Jean and his grandchildren, children of daughter Jean Harris.

He m. (2) Bridgewater 22 July 1717 ELIZABETH (SHAW) WASHBURN, living 20 May 1740; dau. of Joseph and Judith (Whitmarsh) Shaw, and widow of Noah Washburn.

On 9 April 1722 Isaac Harris of Bridgewater was appointed guardian to his sons and daughters, all under 14, namely: Elizabeth, Arthur, Jane, Anne and Abner Harris. Arthur Harris was appointed administrator 30 Oct. 1738 of the estate of Isaac Harris deceased. An agreement 20 May 1740 after the widow's thirds were set aside mentions the children of Isaac: Arthur, Abner, John Holman Jr., and wife Ann, all of Bridgewater, and Jane Johnson of Middletown CT.

Children (HARRIS) b. Bridgewater to Isaac and Jane:* ARTHUR[6] b. 1708; ABNER b. 1710; ANNE b. 1712; ELIZABETH b. 1714; and JANE b. 1716/7.

Child (HARRIS) b. Bridgewater to Isaac and Elizabeth: ISAAC b. 1720.

References: VR BRIDGEWATER, SCITUATE. MD 4:111; 15:136-9; 24:44.
BRIDGEWATER BY MITCHELL pp. 176, 304. Plymouth Co. PR #9321(Isaac Harris gdn.); 7:434; 8:193-5(Isaac Harris Jr.).

82 SAMUEL HARRIS[5] (Mercy Latham[4], Susanna Winslow[3], Mary[2] Chilton, James[1]) b. bef. 1685; d. after 20 Sept. 1729 and bef. 27 June 1731.

He m. Bridgewater 10 Jan. 1709/10 ABIGAIL HARDEN (or Harding), pos. dau. of John and Hannah (-----) Harden, b. Braintree 20 May 1689; living 5 March 1729/30.

On 20 Sept. 1729 Samuel Harris of Bridgewater sold to Isaac Harris of Bridgewater all rights to land in Plymouth County derived from the purchase rights of his father Isaac Harris deceased, together with rights on account of Isaac's eldest son Arthur deceased. On 13 Sept. 1729 Samuel Harris of Bridgewater with the consent of his wife Abigail sold 3/7 part of land with dwelling and orchard near the dwelling formerly of Isaac Harris deceased; he acknowledged the deed 16 Sept. 1729, wife Abigail acknowledged 5 March 1729/ 30. No Plymouth probate or land records connect children.

Children (HARRIS) first six bp. E. Bridgewater to Samuel: ABIGAIL[6] bp. 1725; MARY bp. 1725; SUSANNA bp. 1725; SETH bp. 1726; SAMUEL bp. 1727/8; ISAAC bp. 27 June 1731 "son of Samuel deceased"; and pos. JOSEPH** b. ca. 1712.

---

*More detail and a further generation will be found in the *Francis Cooke Family*.

**The Mayflower Society has accepted membership through Joseph. No proof was found that Joseph was Samuel's son.

References: VR BRIDGEWATER, E. BRIDGEWATER. BRAINTREE VR p. 666.
        BRIDGEWATER BY MITCHELL pp. 174, 176. MIDDLEBORO DEATHS
p. 82. Plymouth Co. LR 24:220; 25:77(Samuel Harris). ANNAPOLIS CO NS
HIST p. 523. ANNAPOLIS CO SUP p. 75.

83 MARY HARRIS[5] (Mercy Latham[4], Susanna Winslow[3], Mary[2]
Chilton, James[1]) b. Bridgewater before 1690 (no guardian
1707); d. there 22 April 1727.
        She m. Bridgewater 2 Dec. 1713 DANIEL PACKARD, d. 21
March 1731/2 (inventory); son of Samuel and Elizabeth
(Lothrop) Packard.
        The will of Daniel Packard of Bridgewater, dated 16
March 1731/2 proved 20 April 1732, names sons Isaac Packard and Daniel Packard; daus. Sarah Packard, Mary Packard
and Susanna Packard; son Nehemiah Packard; dau. Martha;
his brother Samuel Packard, executor. In Dec. 1732 guardians were appointed for all children except Mary (presumed
dead). In an account of the estate by Samuel Packard 7
Oct. 1745, son Isaac was called deceased.

        Children (PACKARD) b. Bridgewater: SARAH[6] b. 1714; MARY b. 1716;
SUSANNA b. 1718; MARTHA b. 1720; DANIEL b. 1722; ISAAC b. 1724; and
NEHEMIAH b. 1727.

References: Plymouth Co. PR 6:172-3, 182; 10:35(Daniel Packard); 6:
        259, 265-6; 9:242; 10:248(guardians of children). VR
BRIDGEWATER. BRIDGEWATER BY MITCHELL p. 264. SAVAGE 3:327.

84 MERCY HARRIS[5] (Mercy Latham[4], Susanna Winslow[3],
Mary[2] Chilton, James[1]) b. Bridgewater bet. 1688 and 1693
[not 1680 as Mitchell claims]; living Eastham 15 Aug. 1739
(birth of child).
        She m. (1) Eastham 25 Dec. 1723 JOHN MULFORD, b. East-
ham in July 1670; d. there 20 April 1730 in 59 yr; son of
Thomas and Elizabeth (Barnes) Mulford. He m. (1) Eastham
1699 Jemima Higgins, but they had no issue.
        She m. (2) Eastham 14 Oct. 1731 JOHN BEE of Harwich,
living 1738. He m. (1) 1728/9 Martha "Nickason."
        Mercy Mulford of Eastham was appointed administratrix
of the estate of her late husband, John Mulford of Eastham
deceased, 17 March 1730/1; on 22 April 1731 she was made
guardian of three minor children of John Mulford: Mercy,
John and Jemima Mulford. On 4 Aug. 1736 "Mercy Bee once
Mulford" rendered an acount of all three. On 8 June 1743
Thomas Mulford Jr. was appointed guardian of three minor
children of John Mulford late of Eastham deceased: John,
Jemima and Mercy. At this time Ralph Smith, who had been
their guardian for about seven years, was released from
same, and transferred his accounts to Thomas Mulford Jr.
in August 1743.

Children (MULFORD) b. Eastham to John and Mercy: JEMIMA[6] b. 1724; MERCY b. 1725/6; and JOHN b. 1728.

Children (BEE) b. Eastham to John and Mercy: REBECCA b. 1732; MARCY b. 1733; and MARTHA b. 1739.

References: TAG 40:196-8. BRIDGEWATER BY MITCHELL pp. 176, 303[errors in Mercy's birth and husband]. MD 3:229; 4:210; 8:4, 245; 13:59; 16:34; 17:29, 79; 28:113[Mercy misnamed Martha Harris], 174. Plymouth Co. LR 24:219-20(Jeremiah Newland). Barnstable Co. PR 4:592(John Mulford); 5:41, 45-6(Mercy Mulford gdn.); 5:79-80(John Mulford); 5:273(Mercy Bee acct.); 6:313-5(Thos. Mulford and Ralph Smith gdns.).

85 THOMAS LATHAM[5] (James[4], Susanna Winslow[3], Mary[2] Chilton, James[1]) b. prob. Bridgewater bef. 1693; d. E. Bridgewater 1769.
     He m. Bridgewater 19 March 1711/12 DEBORAH HARDIN, prob. dau. of John and Anna (-----) Hardin, b. Braintree 29 July 1694; living 5 Sept. 1732.
     In deeds from his father, Thomas was living in Bridgewater in 1721, 1724 and 1726, although he is called "late of Bridgewater, now of Middleboro" in one dated 24 June 1724. On 11 April 1728 Thomas Latham of Bridgewater sold his homestead "where I now dwell," bounded by his father James' homestead; wife Deborah released dower. Sometime before June 1731 Thomas appears to have moved to N. Yarmouth ME, when his house is mentioned in a deed. He bought and sold land there in 1732, the latest sale being dated 22 Aug. 1732, signed also by Deborah, and acknowledged by both Thomas and Deborah in Boston 5 Sept. 1732.
     Of the children indicated by Mitchell, no confirming evidence was located for Joseph or Deliverance. For four there are baptismal records; for Anne, the fact that she named a son Rotheus (presumably for her brother); for Jennet (or Jane,) her marriage in 1732 in N. Yarmouth at just the time her parents were living there; and for Rhoda, the gift of Thomas Latham to dau. Rhoda Conant and her husband David of land on the Kennebec River in 1753.
     Thomas of Bridgewater sold land in Bridgewater 2 Jan. 1759, acknowledged 21 May 1759. No probate records were found for either Thomas or Deborah Latham.

     Children (LATHAM) all prob. b. Bridgewater except Micajah. JENNET[6] (or Jane) b. ca. 1714; ANNE b. ca. 1718; RHODA b. ca. 1723; ROTHEUS bp. E. Bridgewater 1726; BERIAH bp. E. Bridgewater 1727/8; JOHN bp. E. Bridgewater 1730; and MICAJAH bp. N. Yarmouth ME 1732.

References: VR BRIDGEWATER, E. BRIDGEWATER. BRAINTREE VR p. 671. MD 22:118. BRIDGEWATER BY MITCHELL pp. 174, 231. BRIDGEWATER EPITAPHS p. 210. OLD TIMES pp. 491, 658, 684-5, 742, 1143.

York Co. ME LR 15:310-12(Thos. Latham). Plymouth Co. LR 15:153;
18:63(two deeds); 20:210(James Latham); 17:167; 20:189; 22:228;
42:183; 45:186(Thos. Latham).

86   ANNE LATHAM[5] (James[4], Susanna Winslow[3], Mary[2] Chilton, James[1]) b. prob. Bridgewater ca. 1693; d. E. Bridgewater 15 May 1770 ae 77.
     She m. Bridgewater 17 Feb. 1714/5 NICHOLAS WADE, b. ca. 1693; d. bet. 20 Jan. and 22 May 1767; prob. son of Nicholas Wade Jr. of Scituate.
     The will of Nicholas Wade of Bridgewater, dated 20 Jan. proved 22 May 1767, names sons Samuel, Thomas, John, James, Nicholas and Amasa; dau. Mary Mitchel; wife Ann; son Thomas Wade, executor. Payments were made to the widow and to Mary Mitchel, daughter, 20 Oct. 1767. No evidence was found to confirm a dau. Elizabeth mentioned in Mitchell.

     Children (WADE) prob. b. E. Bridgewater: SAMUEL[6]; THOMAS b. ca. 1721; JOHN; MARY b. ca. 1726; JAMES b. ca. 1728; NICHOLAS b. ca. 1731; and AMASA.

References: VR BRIDGEWATER, E. BRIDGEWATER. BRIDGEWATER BY MITCHELL
              p. 336. Plymouth Co. PR 19:476, 493, 553(Nicholas Wade).

87   SUSANNA LATHAM[5] (James[4], Susanna Winslow[3], Mary[2] Chilton, James[1]) b. prob. Bridgewater bef. 1697; living Pembroke 15 Oct. 1772.
     She m. Bridgewater 17 Feb. 1714/5 NATHANIEL HARDEN, b Braintree 7 Jan. 1691/2; d. Pembroke bet. 23 Feb. 1769 and 15 April 1771; son of John and Hannah (-----) Harden. The will of John Harden of Bridgewater, dated 1718, names wife Hannah and son Nathaniel.
     On 31 Oct. 1765 Nathaniel Harden of Pembroke, yeoman, sold land to grandsons Samuel and Reuben Harden. [A Samuel was born 1744 to Abraham Harden, and a Reuben 1755 to Seth Harden, both in Pembroke; this would indicate that Nathaniel had sons named Abraham and Seth.] On 11 Aug. 1766 Nathaniel Harden gave to grandson Jephthah Dawes of Halifax land next to land of "my son Nathaniel Harden." [A Mary Harden had a son baptized in E. Bridgewater 1741 named Jephthae Harden, who married in Halifax 1757 as "Jeptha Harden allias Jeptha Dorz"; this would indicate that Nathaniel had a daughter Mary.] Nathaniel's last recorded act was his acknowledgement of a deed 23 Feb. 1769. John Turner of Pembroke was made administrator 15 April 1771 of the estate of Nathaniel Harden late of Pembroke deceased. On 15 Oct. 1772 Susanna Harden, widow of Pembroke, quitclaimed land in Halifax given to her and her late deceased husband, Nathaniel Harden, by her father James Latham, late of Bridgewater deceased.

Children (HARDEN) prob. b. Bridgewater: ABRAHAM[6]; NATHANIEL b.
E. Bridgewater 1726/7; SETH bp. E. Bridgewater 1731; and MARY.

References: VR BRIDGEWATER, E. BRIDGEWATER, PEMBROKE. HALIFAX VR pp.
         36, 59. BRAINTREE VR p. 666. BRIDGEWATER BY MITCHELL p.
174. Plymouth Co. PR 4:191-2(John Harden); 20:512-3; 21:169(Nathaniel
Harden). Plymouth Co. LR 46:113, 130; 52:174; 53:266; 54:231
(Nathaniel Harden); 57:18(Susanna Harden).

    88 JOSEPH LATHAM[5] (James[4], Susanna Winslow[3], Mary[2]
Chilton, James[1]) b. prob. Bridgewater bef. 1697; d. E.
Bridgewater between 2 June and 9 Oct. 1758.
    He m. Bridgewater 27 Nov. 1717 SARAH HAYWARD, b.
Bridgewater 28 June 1696; d. E. Bridgewater 25 April 1781
ae 85; dau. of Nathaniel and Elizabeth (-----) Hayward.
    On 20 Sept. 1731 Josiah and Isaac Hayward, Joseph
Latham and wife Sarah, and others, all of Bridgewater, sold
to their brother Nathaniel Hayward, their rights in land
laid out to "our father Nathaniel Hayward" of Bridgewater
deceased. The will of Nathaniel Hayward of Bridgewater
dated 17 Jan. 1733/4 names wife Elizabeth, and includes
dau. Sarah (no last name).
    Joseph Latham of Bridgewater deeded land to his sons
as follows: to son Joseph Latham of Bridgewater, 1 June
1752; to son Thomas Latham of Bridgewater, 16 May 1754; to
son Nathaniel Latham who lived with him, 15 Feb. 1757; and
to youngest son Seth Latham who lived with him, 15 Feb.
1757.
    The will of Joseph Latham of Bridgewater, "enlisted
to go to Canada," dated 2 June 1758 probated 9 Oct. 1758,
indicates his four sons had already received land by deed;
names wife Sarah, eldest daughter Betty Latham, and daughter Sarah Latham.

    Children (LATHAM) bp. E. Bridgewater "of Joseph": BETTY[6] bp.
1732; JAMES bp. 1732; JOSEPH bp. 1732; THOMAS bp. 1732; NATHANIEL bp.
1732; SARAH bp. 1733; and SETH bp. 1738.

References: VR BRIDGEWATER, E. BRIDGEWATER. BRIDGEWATER BY MITCHELL
         pp. 182, 231. Plymouth Co. PR 7:53-4(Nathaniel Hayward);
15:78-9(Joseph Latham). Plymouth Co. LR 33:184(Josiah and Isaac Hayward). BRIDGEWATER EPITAPHS p. 210.

    89 BETTY LATHAM[5] (James[4], Susanna Winslow[3], Mary[2]
Chilton, James[1]) b. prob. Bridgewater ca. 1701; bp. E.
Bridgewater 6 June 1725; d. Bridgewater 14 Oct. 1782 ("in
82 yr" W. Bridgewater).
    She m. Bridgewater 5 Jan. 1725 Judge DANIEL JOHNSON,
b. Hingham 20 April 1700; d. Bridgewater 6 March 1785 ae
86; son of Isaac and Abigail (Leavitt)(Lazell) Johnson.

Daniel Johnson of Bridgewater gave to son James Johnson of Bridgewater 20 June 1768 all his real estate in the
east and west precincts of Bridgewater containing the
dwelling where he lived after his wife's decease, reserving to his son Leverett the privilege to live in the house.

Children (JOHNSON) b. Bridgewater: DANIEL[6] b. 1726, d. 1743;
JAMES b. 1728; JOSEPH b. 1730, d. 1745; ISAIAH b. 1734; LEVET (or
Leverett) b. 1736; BETTIE b. 1738/9, d. 1743; and DANIEL b. 1747.

References: VR BRIDGEWATER, E. BRIDGEWATER, W. BRIDGEWATER. BRIDGE-
WATER BY MITCHELL p. 211. HINGHAM HIST 2:385. MD 15:89;
16:188. Plymouth Co. LR 42:219; 49:109; 66:112(Daniel Johnson).
BRIDGEWATER EPITAPHS p. 25, 27.

90 JONATHAN WASHBURN[5] (Hannah Latham[4], Susanna Winslow[3], Mary[2] Chilton, James[1]) prob. d. Bridgewater 26 Dec.
1766 "old."
     He m. (1) Sandwich 27 Dec. 1711 REBECCA PERRY, b.
Sandwich 2 Oct. 1689; dau. of Ezra and Rebecca (Freeman)
Perry, and a descendant of Pilgrim William Brewster.
     The will of Ezra Perry Sr. of Sandwich, dated 21 Oct.
1728 presented 10 Feb. 1729/30, mentions "the three children [unnamed] of my daughter Rebecca by her husband Jonathan Washburn."
     He pos. m. (2) Boston 17 Dec. 1719 "of Bridgewater,"
REBECCA JOHNSON "of Hingham." No children found.

Children (WASHBURN) b. Bridgewater to Jonathan and first wife:
SILAS[6] b. 1712/3; LEMUEL b. 1714; and another child, living Oct. 1728.

References: MD 15:48; 30:64. VR BRIDGEWATER. BOSTON VR 28:86.
          NEHGR 115:91-3[No confirmation found in Plymouth Co. that
third child was named Japhet.]. HINGHAM HIST 2:385. WASHBURN DESC.
p. 54. BRIDGEWATER BY MITCHELL pp. 339, 341. Barnstable Co. PR 4:516
(Ezra Perry). Plymouth Co. LR 28:5(Rebecca Perry).

91 JOSEPH WASHBURN[5] (Hannah Latham[4], Susanna Winslow[3],
Mary[2] Chilton, James[1]) d. Leicester in 1759.
     He m. Bridgewater in 1716 HANNAH JOHNSON, b. Hingham
17 Jan. 1694/5; d. Leicester in 1780 ae 87, "Hannah J.
wife of Joseph"; dau. of Isaac and Abigail (Leavitt)
(Lazell) Johnson.
     Joseph was a blacksmith. Joseph Washburn and wife
Hannah both of Bridgewater 11 Dec. 1738 sold their homestead in Bridgewater, acknowledged by both 19 March 1738/9,
and moved to Middletown CT. Leaving son Joseph there,
they moved to Leicester about 1745.

No probate records were found in Worcester County for
either Joseph or Hannah, and no evidence was found to substantiate a daughter Hannah proposed in *Washburn Desc*.

Children (WASHBURN) all prob. b. Bridgewater, last three bp. E.
Bridgewater:* JOSEPH[6] b. bef. 1720; SETH b. 1723; ELIJAH b. bef.
1726; MARY b. bef. 1726; ABIAH (or Abiel) b. bef. 1729; SARAH b. bef.
1729; and EBENEZER b. bef. 1734.

References: MD 2:66-70. VR BRIDGEWATER, E. BRIDGEWATER, LEICESTER.
          BRIDGEWATER BY MITCHELL p. 341. LEICESTER HIST pp. 249,
412-3. WASHBURN DESC pp. 54, 56b-57. HINGHAM HIST 2:385. HANCOCK NH
HIST p. 965. Plymouth Co. LR 35:86(Joseph Washburn).

92 MILES WASHBURN[5] (Hannah Latham[4], Susanna Winslow[3],
Mary[2] Chilton, James[1]) d. NY ca. 1772.
   He m. SUSANNA PERRY of Sandwich, b. there 27 Dec.
1701; dau. of Benjamin and Dinah (Swift) Perry.
   Miles lived in Plympton where his children were born.
He acknowledged a deed "of Plympton" 27 Sept. 1738. About
1750 he moved to Amenia NY. No evidence was found to con-
firm a son Joel indicated in *Washburn Desc*.

Children (WASHBURN) b. Plympton: MARY[6] b. 1724; DANIEL b. 1726;
HANNAH b. 1728; DINAH b. 1731; MERIBAH b. 1736/7.

References: VR PLYMPTON. NEHGR 115:98-9. MD 29:30. BRIDGEWATER BY
          MITCHELL p. 339. WASHBURN DESC. pp. 54-5. Plymouth Co.
LR 36:189(Miles and Edward Washburn). NYGBR 35:63-5.

93 EBENEZER WASHBURN[5] (Hannah Latham[4], Susanna Winslow[3], Mary[2] Chilton, James[1]) d. prob. Kent CT ca. 1767.
   He m. (1) New Milford CT 29 June 1721 PATIENCE MILES,
b. Derby CT 20 Sept. 1704; d. Kent in 1743; dau. of Stephen and Patience (Wheeler) Miles.
   Ebenezer was a blacksmith. In 1720 he was living in
Bridgewater when given land by his father, Joseph. Ebenezer was in New Milford when he bought land there in 1722;
in Dover, Dutchess County, NY in 1725; New Milford again
in 1726 when his wife Patience was admitted to the church;
and in Kent in 1741 when Patience "Washbarn" was admitted
or administered "special ordinance" to the Congregational
Church. He sold land in New Milford in 1742. No applic-
able probate records were found in CT for either Ebenezer
or Patience.
   In a tax list of Kent 1766 are Jonathan, Miles, Stephen, Eben[r] and Joseph Washburn. In a 1767 list, Ebenezer
is missing, the others are still there.

*The Mayflower Society has accepted lineages based on a purported
daughter Hannah, for whom no substantiating evidence was found.

He apparently m. (2) ca. 1744 ----- -----, the mother of his last four children.

Children (WASHBURN) b. to Ebenezer and Patience, the first eight in New Milford CT, the others bp. in Kent CT: PATIENCE[6] b. 1722; SUSANAH b. 1725; JOSEPH b. 1727; EUNICE b. 1729; MILES b. 1730/1; JONATHAN b. 1732/3; STEPHEN b. 1734/5; REBECKAH b. 1736/7; MERCY bp. 1741; PATIENCE bp. 1741; and MARY bp. 1742/3.

Children (WASHBURN) b. to Ebenezer and second wife, baptized Kent CT: HEPSIBAH bp. 1744; EBENEZER bp. 1746; ANNA (or Annice) bp. 1748; and DAVID bp. 1750.

References: CSL Barbour Index: Derby, New Milford. CT MARR 3:108. WASHBURN DESC pp. 57-60, 107-8. DERBY CT HIST p. 746. TAG 5:1184[indicates wrong mother of Patience]. KENT CT HIST pp. 24, 57. CSL Ch Rec: Kent p. 170. Plymouth Co. LR 15:41(Joseph Washburn). Kent CT LR (tax lists) and 1:70-1(Griswold to Washburn). New Milford CT LR 5:139(Ebenezer Washburn). New Milford CT Cong. Ch Recs 1712-1805 ms. CT State Library(#974.62 fN 4651C) pp. 9, 24, 39, 41, 42, 43, 45.

94[2] EPHRAIM WASHBURN[5] (Hannah Latham[4], Susanna Winslow[3], Mary[2] Chilton, James[1]) d. Plympton bef. 16 July 1755.
He m. Plympton 13 Jan. 1725/6 MARY POLEN (or Poland or Pollard) of Plympton, prob. b. Plymouth 28 Feb. 1706; dau. of John and Lydia (Tilson) Polland; d. Plympton bef. 9 Sept. 1784.
On 16 July 1755 William Washburne of "Plimton" was appointed administrator of the estate of Ephraim Washburn late of Plimton deceased. A division of 24 April 1758 was made among the widow Mary Washburn; eldest son William; other children: Lydia Norrise wife of Samuel Norrise, Elizabeth Benson wife of Consider Benson, Marcy Washburn, Stephen Washburn, Isaac Washburn, Phebe Washburn, Jemimah Washburn, Japhet Washburn, and Joshua Washburn [this Joshua is called John in the order to divide].
William Washburne of Plimton, cooper, was appointed guardian of Japhet Washburne, minor son of Ephraim Washburne late of Plimton 4 Jan 1763; Samuel Benson of Middleborough signed as surety.

Children (WASHBURN) first seven b. Plympton: WILLIAM[6] b. 1726; LYDIA b. 1728; ELEZEBETH b. 1732; MARCY b. 1734; STEPHEN b. 1736; ISAAC b. 1738; PHEBE b. 1740; JEMIMA; JAPHET; and JOSHUA (or John?).

References: MD 3:122; 13:208, 14:71. VR PLYMPTON. WASHBURN DESC pp. 54-5. Plymouth Co. PR 13:487; 14:512-6; and #21965 (Ephraim Washburn); #22009(Japhet Washburn).

95₂ EDWARD WASHBURN[5] (Hannah Latham[4], Susanna Winslow[3], Mary[2] Chilton, James[1]) d. 1757/8?
    He m. Plympton 20 April 1732 JUDITH RICKARD, b. Plymouth 1 Feb. 1701; dau. of Eleazer and Sarah (-----) Rickard.
    Eleazer Rickard of Plympton sold his cedar swamp in 1736 to his son Eleazer and son-in-law Edward Washburn "both of Plimton." On 27 April 1741 Edward Washburn of Plympton sold 1/4 share of cedar swamp formerly his father-in-law's, Eleazer Rickard. The family appears to have moved out of town. No probate record was found in Plymouth County for either Edward or Judith.

    Children (WASHBURN) bp. Plympton "of Edward": SARAH[6] bp. 1736; JOHN bp. 1736; PHEBE bp. 1738; and NOAH bp. 1740.

    References: VR PLYMPTON. MD 3:13. WASHBURN DESC pp. 54-5. Plymouth Co. LR 30:82(Eleazer Rickard); 34:125; 35:19(Edward Washburn).

96 BENJAMIN WASHBURN[5] (Hannah Latham[4], Susanna Winslow[3], Mary[2] Chilton, James[1])
    He m. as "Benjamin 3rd" Middleboro 1 Sept. 1740 ZERVIAH PACKARD "both of Bridgewater," b. Bridgewater 22 May 1713; dau. of Israel and Hannah (-----) Packard.
    The will of Israel Packard Jr. of Bridgewater dated 18 April 1752 proved 4 May 1752 names wife Ruth; "my brothers and sisters": Seth and Robert Packard, heirs of Mehitable West, Hannah Phillips, Zeruiah Washburn. Among creditors was Zerviah Washburn wife of Benjamin Washburn, who accepted a bond payable twelve months after the decease of Israel Packard, father to the above deceased. No Plymouth County probate record of Benjamin or Zerviah Washburn was found. Benjamin was a housewright.

    Children (WASHBURN) b. to Benjamin and Zerviah or bp. to Benjamin: ZERVIAH[6] bp. N. Bridgewater (now Brockton) 1741; BENJAMIN bp. N. Bridgewater 1742; HANNAH b. Bridgewater 1743/4; SUSANNA bp. N. Bridgewater 1746; SARAH b. Bridgewater 1748, bp. N. Bridgewater 1748; and EBENEZER b. Bridgewater 1750, bp. N. Bridgewater 1751.

    References: VR BRIDGEWATER, BROCKTON. MD 13:253. BRIDGEWATER BY MITCHELL pp. 265, 344. Plymouth Co. PR 13:10, 217 (Israel Packard Jr.). Plymouth Co. LR 42:81(Benj. Washburn third).

97 ROBERT LATHAM[5] (Joseph[4], Susanna Winslow[3], Mary[2] Chilton, James[1]) b. prob. Providence RI; d. Smithfield RI 14 April 1762 (inventory).
    He m. (1) prob. CATTERN [Catherine?] BOWDISH; d. bef. 1756; dau. of Nathaniel and Mary (-----) Bowdish. The

will of Mary Place of Smithfield, widow of Elder Peter
Place deceased, dated 25 May presented 31 May 1740, names
sons Joseph and Moses Bowdish and several daughters including "Cattern Latham."
   He m. (2) Smithfield 10 June 1756 LYDIA (-----) PATT,
living 3rd Mon. May 1762; widow of David Patt. The inventory of David Patt was exhibited by his widow Lydia Patt
1752; her account naming three children was allowed 31 May
1756.
   Robert Latham lived in Providence where he was a hog
constable in 1720; he later was of Smithfield where he was
admitted freeman in 1748. In Dec. 1759 William Latham of
Johnston RI applied to administer the estate of his
brother Arthur Latham who died at Surinam 9 Sept. 1759;
Joseph Latham and Robert Latham Jr. both of Smithfield
signed the bond.
   The will of Robert Latham of Smithfield husbandman
"antient," dated 3 April proved 3rd Mon. May 1762 presented by widow Lydia, executor, names wife Lydia; daughter Phebe Latham to receive "chest that was her mother's";
daughter Mary Latham the pot and platter "that was her
mother's"; four youngest children: John, Susanna, Zoriah
and Benoni; other children: Joseph, Robert, William,
"Elener" and Katherine. His death date is given in the
inventory.

   Children (LATHAM) b. Providence or Smithfield to Robert and Cattern: PHEBE[6]; MARY; JOSEPH; ROBERT b. ca. 1731; WILLIAM b. ca. 1735;
ARTHUR; ELENER; and KATHERINE.

   Children (LATHAM) b. Smithfield to Robert and either Cattern or
Lydia (except the last to Lydia): JOHN; SUSANNA; ZORIAH; and BENONI
b. 1759.

References: Smithfield RI Council and PR 1:157(Mary Place); 2:74-5,
        208-9(David Patt); 2:411(Robert Latham). Johnston RI PR
#A1766 and 1:10-11(Arthur Latham). RI VR Smithfield p. 46. RI GEN
DICT p. 154. PROVIDENCE GAZETTE 4 June 1796(d. Wm. Latham). Latham
Fam. Cemetery Rec., Knight Mem. Library, Providence(Robert and Ben-
oni Latham). PROV TOWN PAPERS 13:37. TAG 53:170-1.

   98 PHEBE LATHAM[5] (Joseph[4], Susanna Winslow[3], Mary[2]
Chilton, James[1]) b. prob. Providence RI; living 1737.
   She m. Providence 12 March 1726/7 JOHN MANTON, b.
prob. Providence bef. 1699; d. Johnston RI 15 March 1767
(inventory); son of Edward and Elizabeth (Thornton) Manton.
   John Manton of Johnston yeoman sold land to his son-
in-law Benjamin Waterman Jr. of Johnston 2 June 1759. He
also gave land in Johnston to his son-in-law Joshua Green
and his wife Mehitabel 26 Nov. 1763. An agreement was

reached on his real estate 14 May 1768 by the heirs of
John Manton late of Johnston deceased, namely Joshua
Greene and wife Mehitabel, Ephraim Pearce and wife Phebe,
all of Johnston, and Lydia and Betty the children of Benjamin Waterman by Anne his late wife.

  Children (MANTON) b. prob. Providence RI: ANNA[6]; PHEBE b. 1735;
and MEHITABEL b. 1737.

References: RI VR: Providence p. 117; Johnston p. 25. RI GEN DICT
        pp. 74, 343. Johnston RI PR(in Providence PR) 1:42-5;
3:52; 4:454(John Manton). Providence RI PR 2:153(Edward Manton).
WATERMAN GEN 3:107. Manton Fam. Johnston RI LR 1:12, 155(John Manton); 1:19(Joshua Green); 1:334(Benjamin Waterman et al.); 1:344, 374
(Josiah King, admr.); 3:158, 478(Phebe Manton).

  99[2] SUSANNA COOKE[5] (Elizabeth Latham[4], Susanna Winslow[3],
Mary[2] Chilton, James[1]) b. ca. 1689; d. Halifax in Oct.
1769 in 80 yr.
  She m. Plympton 15 Feb. 1710/1 JAMES STURTEVANT, b.
ca. 1687; bp. Plymouth 1689; d. Halifax 8 May 1756 ae 69
"Capt."; son of Samuel and Mercy (Cornish) Sturtevant.
  The will of James Stertevant of Halifax, dated 30 Nov.
1742 presented 20 May 1756, names wife Susanna; sons
Frances, Caleb and James; daus. Susanna, Lydia, Mary, Sarah
and Elizabeth; executors, wife Susanna and son Frances.

  Children (STURTEVANT) all b. Plympton except Mary and Elizabeth:*
FRANCIS[6] b. 1711/2; CALEB b. 1715/6; JAMES b. 1718; SUSANAH b. 1720/1;
LIDIA b. 1723/4; MARY b. 1728; SARAH bp. 1732; and ELIZABETH b. 1734,
d. Halifax 1747.

References: VR PLYMPTON. MD 5:207; 10:9-10; 18:147. WATERMAN GEN
        1:681. PLYMOUTH CH RECS 1:264. Plymouth Co. PR 14:144
(James Stertevant).

  100[2] ROBERT COOKE[5] (Elizabeth Latham[4], Susanna Winslow[3],
Mary[2] Chilton, James[1]) b. ca. 1691; d. Kingston 20 Jan.
1731/2.
  He m. (1) Plympton 29 Nov. 1716 ABIGAIL HARLOW, b.
Plymouth 27 Jan. 1692/3; d. Kingston 25 Oct. 1727 in 35
yr.; dau. of Nathaniel and Abigail (Church) Harlow.
  He m. (?) ca. 1728 LYDIA TILDEN, living 17 May 1731;
d. bef. 20 Dec. 1744.
  The will of Robert Cooke, dated 17 May 1731 sworn 7
Feb. 1731/2, names wife Lediah, eldest son Charles, "my
children": Charles, Nathaniel, Robert, Sarah, Francis
Cooke, son Semion Cooke; brother Caleb Cooke executor.

_____
*The Francis Cooke Family will give greater detail and one further
generation.

Division was made 20 Dec. 1744 among sons Charles Cooke, Simeon Cooke, Francis Cooke, Robert Cooke, dau. Sarah Cooke and son Nathaniel Cooke [widow Lydia not named].

 Children (COOKE) b. to Robert and Abigail, first four b. Plymouth:* CHARLES[6] b. 1717; NATHANIEL b. 1719; ROBERT b. 1721; SARAH b. 1724; and FRANCIS b. ca. 1726.

 Children (COOKE) b. Kingston to Robert and Lydia:* SAMUEL b. 1729, d. 1729; and SIMEON b. 1730.

References: MD 2:17; 7:26; 13:171; 16:150-6; 18:147. GEN ADVERTISER
        2:5. VR KINGSTON, PLYMPTON.

 101 CALEB COOKE[5] (Elizabeth Latham[4], Susanna Winslow[3], Mary[2] Chilton, James[1]) b. ca. 1694; d. Kingston 19 Aug. 1762 ae 68 "Lt."
    He m. Plympton 4 March 1724/5 HANNAH SHURTLEFF, b. Plymouth 31 July 1705; d. Kingston 14 Nov. 1789 ae 84; dau. of Abiel and Lydia (Barnes) Shurtleff.
    The will of Caleb Cook, gentleman, of Kingston, dated 13 May presented 3 Sept. 1762 left to wife Hannah the homestead farm his father Francis Cook gave him; names grandsons Bartlett and Amos Cook, sons of his deceased son Caleb; sons Benjamin and Ephraim Cook; daus. Hannah Cook, Rebeccah Cook and Lidia Cook; executor, son Benjamin.

 Children (COOKE) b. Kingston:* CALEB[6] b. 1727; BENJAMIN b. 1729; LYDIA b. 1731, d. 1733; ISAAC b. 1732/3, d. in third yr; ELKNAH d. in 13th month of his age; EPHRAIM b. 1737; HANNAH b. 1739; REBECKAH b. 1741/2; LYDIAH b. 1744; SARAH b. 1747, d. 1754; FEAR b. 15 Feb., d. same day (ca. 1748); and AMOS b. 1749, d. 1754.

References: GEN ADVERTISER 2:121-2. MD 2:79; 16:148. VR KINGSTON,
        PLYMPTON. SHURTLEFF DESC. 1:32, 43-4. Plymouth Co. PR
 16:374(Caleb Cook).

 102 FRANCIS COOKE[5] (Elizabeth Latham[4], Susanna Winslow[3], Mary[2] Chilton, James[1]) b. ca. 1696; d. "on Plymouth shore" 4 May 1724 in 28th yr.(VR PLYMPTON).
    He m. Plympton 4 Feb. 1719 RUTH SYLVESTER, b. Scituate 26 June 1702; d. bef. 17 Nov. 1779 (Phinney will); dau. of Israel and Ruth (Turner)(Prince)Sylvester, and a descendant of Pilgrim William Brewster. She m. (2) Plympton 1724/5 Samuel Ring (a Hopkins descendant); and she m. (3) Kingston 1770 John Phinney (a Rogers descendant).
    Widow Ruth of Plympton was made administratrix of the estate of her husband Francis Cooke on 20 June 1724. The inventory was sworn 4 April 1725 by Ruth Ring, administratrix of the estate of her former husband Francis Cooke Jr.

The Francis Cooke Family will give greater detail and one further generation.

In 1725 Mr. Samuel Ring was appointed guardian of Ruth
Cooke and Susannah Cooke. On 14 April 1725 a settlement
was made among the widow, Ruth Ring, now wife of Samuel
Ring, and the two children.

    Children (COOKE) b. Plympton to Francis and Ruth:* RUTH[6] b.
1721/2; and SUSANNAH b. 1723.

References: MD 7:26; 16:149-50; 22:169-70. VR PLYMPTON, KINGSTON,
         SCITUATE. NEHGR 85:363-4. Plymouth Co. PR 30:362(John
Phinney).

   103₂ SARAH COOKE[5] {Elizabeth Latham[4], Susanna Winslow[3],
Mary[2] Chilton, James[1]) b. ca. 1698; d. Plymouth 26 Oct.
1730 ae ca. 32 "wife of Ephraim."
    She m. Plympton 16 May 1717 EPHRAIM COLE, b. Plymouth
3 Feb. 1691; d. there bef. 2 March 1730/1; son of Ephraim
and Rebecca (-----) Cole.
    The will of Ephraim Cole of Plymouth, dated 2 March
1730/1 proved 21 May 1731, names wife Rebecca, and includes grandchildren Rebecca and Sarah Cole. On 15 March
1733/4 Rebecca Cole widow was appointed guardian of
Rebecca and Sarah Cole daughters of Ephraim Cole Jr. deceased, both under 14. The will of Rebecca Cole of Plymouth, widow relict of Mr. Ephraim Cole Sr. deceased, dated
4 May 1737 presented 25 Sept. 1742, names granddaughters
Rebecca Cole and Sarath (*sic*) Cole, both under 13, and
names Mr. Joseph Bartlett of Plymouth as overseer and
guardian of both. Real estate left by Ephraim Sr. was
distributed in 1743 including part to Rebecca and Sarah
Cole. In 1749 Joseph Bartlett signed receipts as guardian
of Rebecca and Sarah Cole.

    Children (COLE) b. Plymouth:* EPHRAIM[6] b. 1718, d. 1730; SARAH
b. ca. 1723, d. 1730 ae 7 yrs; REBECKAH b. 1727; and SARAH b. 1730.

References: MD 2:20; 13:32; 18:148. VR PLYMPTON. (PLYMOUTH) BURIAL
         HILL p. 16. PLYMOUTH CH RECS 1:243. Plymouth Co. PR
#4673 and 6:52; 9:119(Ephraim Cole); 6:436-7; 11:334(gdn. of Rebecca
and Sarah); 8:537(Rebecca Cole).

   104 ELIZABETH COOKE[5] (Elizabeth Latham[4], Susanna Winslow[3], Mary[2] Chilton, James[1]) b. ca. 1707; d. Bridgewater
6 June 1750 in 43 yr. "wife of David."
    She m. Kingston 22 Jan. 1734 DAVID LEACH, b. Bridge-
water 20 May 1706; d. Bridgewater bef. 6 Dec. 1756; son of
David and Hannah (Whitman) Leach. David m. (2) Bridgewater
1751 the widow Hannah Newcomb.

The Francis Cooke Family will give greater detail and one further
generation.

Francis Cooke of Kingston leased to "my son David
Leach of Bridgewater" dwelling and barn 24 Apr. 1741.
Hannah Leach, widow of Bridgewater, was appointed administratrix of the estate of David Leach late of Bridgewater deceased 6 Dec. 1756. On 26 April 1759 Hannah Edson, formerly Leach, filed an account on the estate of her
husband David Leach late of Bridgewater deceased mentioning "provisions spent in the family."

Children (LEACH) first four b. Kingston, fifth b. Bridgewater,
two "child of David" deaths Bridgewater:* JAMES[6] b. 1734; ELIZABETH
b. 1734/5; MARCY b. 1737/8; SARAH b. 1739/40; SUSANNA b. 1743; child
of David d. 1744; and pos. child of David d. 1756.

References: VR BRIDGEWATER, KINGSTON. GEN ADVERTISER 2:44. BRIDGE-
            WATER BY MITCHELL p. 239[error in mar. date; widow Hannah
Edson assigned to wrong David]. Plymouth Co. PR 14:184, 457-8; 15:119
(David Leach). LEACH GEN 1:13, 27[error in mar. date; gives only one
dau., Susanna]. BRIDGEWATER EPITAPHS p. 94. Plymouth Co. LR 36:24
(Francis Cooke); 36:123(David Leach).

105 CHARLES LATHAM[5] (Chilton[4], Susanna Winslow[3], Mary[2]
Chilton, James[1]) b. Bridgewater 18 Mar.1701; d. there 5
July 1788 ae 87y 4m.
He m. Bridgewater in March 1724 SUSANNA WOODWARD, b.
Bridgewater 30 May 1709; d. E. Bridgewater 18 Feb. 1761;
dau. of Capt. Nathaniel and Elizabeth (Willis) Woodward.
The recorded copy of the will of Nathaniel Woodward of
Bridgewater, dated 16 Feb. 1746, names wife Elizabeth and
daughters Sarah Latham and Sarah Tucker. [Unfortunately
the original papers in this case are missing, which undoubtedly would name daughter Susanna Latham.] The executors were wife Elizabeth and Charles Latham.
On 24 March acknowledged 30 May 1761, Charles Latham
of Bridgewater sold to his son Woodward Latham of Bridgewater all his farm and buildings where he dwelt.

Children (LATHAM) b. Bridgewater: BETTIE[6] b. 1725; SUSANNA b.
1727; WOODWARD b. 1729; MARY b. 1735; and twins CHILTON and JANE b.
1739.

References: VR BRIDGEWATER, E. BRIDGEWATER. BRIDGEWATER BY MITCHELL
            pp. 231, 373. BRIDGEWATER EPITAPHS p. 209. Plymouth Co.
PR 11:142-3(Nathaniel Woodward). Plymouth Co. LR 48:25(Charles
Latham).

106 ARTHUR LATHAM[5] (Chilton[4], Susanna Winslow[3], Mary[2]
Chilton, James[1]) b. Bridgewater 16 Sept. 1705; d. there
1736.

---

*The Francis Cooke Family will give greater detail and one further
generation.

He m. Bridgewater 1 Feb. 1732/3 ALICE ALLEN, b.
Bridgewater 8 Oct. 1707; d. bef. 1742; dau. of Nehemiah
and Sarah (Wormel) Allen. She m. (2) Bridgewater 1739
Jonathan Allen of Braintree (#110). Mr. Arthur Latham was
appointed administrator of the estate of Nehemiah Allen
late of Bridgewater deceased in 1733. The division of the
estate in 1734 includes Alice Latham, wife of Arthur
Latham and daughter of Nehemiah.

On Sept. 1751 Nehemiah Latham and Jane Latham, minor
children of Arthur Latham late of Bridgewater deceased,
deputed Nathan Haward as their guardian. On 1 April 1758
Jane Latham of Bridgewater sold to her brother Nehemiah
Latham of Bridgewater all rights in land on which Nehemiah
was living, which "our father Arthur Latham deceased had
of our grandfather Chilton Latham."

        Children (LATHAM) b. Bridgewater: NEHEMIAH[6] b. 1733, and JANE
b. 1736.

References: VR BRIDGEWATER. BRIDGEWATER BY MITCHELL p. 231. Plym-
        outh Co. PR 6:419-21; 7:29(Nehemiah Allen). CONANT FAM
p. 235. Plymouth Co. PR 12:339, 392(Nehemiah and Jane Latham). Plymouth Co. LR 45:91(Jane Latham). VINTON MEM pp. 304, 305.

107 JAMES LATHAM[5] (Chilton[4], Susanna Winslow[3], Mary[2]
Chilton, James[1]) b. Bridgewater 16 Aug. 1708; d. Chesterfield NH 8 July 1792 in 84 yr.

He m. W. Bridgewater 19 Dec. 1739 ABIGAIL HARVEY, b.
1694; dau. of Thomas and Elizabeth (Willis) Harvey of
Taunton.

James Latham of Bridgewater husbandman and wife Abigail sold land with dwelling house in Bridgewater 7 April
1748. Sometime after the birth of his last child, James
moved to Winchester NH, where he was living 9 Dec. 1768
when he bought land there of Thomas Byam. James Latham
of Winchester sold land there 22 Oct. 1783. Subsequently
he moved to Chesterfield NH, where son James was living.

        Children (LATHAM) first three b. Bridgewater, first three and
last two bp. E. Bridgewater: ABIGAIL[6] b. 1740; ARTHUR b. 1742; MARY
b. 1744; JAMES; SUSANNA; pos. BETTY bp. 1759; pos. SIMEON bp. 1761.

References: VR BRIDGEWATER, E. BRIDGEWATER, W. BRIDGEWATER, LOWELL.
        BRIDGEWATER BY MITCHELL p. 231. CHESTERFIELD NH HIST
p. 377. NEHGR 37:396; 38:30. NH STATE PAPERS 30:161-2. Cheshire
Co. NH LR 38:500(James Latham).

108 ROBERT LATHAM[5] (Chilton[4], Susanna Winslow[3], Mary[2]
Chilton, James[1]) b. Bridgewater 16 Aug. 1711; d. E.
Bridgewater 9 or 10 Dec. 1788 ae 77.
    He m. (1) Bridgewater 12 June 1751 MARY JOHNSON, b.
Bridgewater 29 Aug. 1729; d. E. Bridgewater 20 April 1752
in 23 yr; dau. of David and Rebecca (Washburn) Johnson.
    He m. (2) Bridgewater 17 April 175[3] (int. 31 May
1753) BETHIAH (HAYWARD) HARRIS, b. Bridgewater 2 or 23
Sept. 1715; d. E. Bridgewater 28 Aug. 1778 ae 63; dau. of
Thomas and Bethia (Brett) Hayward, and widow of Arthur
Harris. Robert and Bethiah Latham of Bridgewater on 6 May
1758 sold land received from "our grandfather William
Brett deceased."
    He m. (3) E. Bridgewater 18 Nov. 1778 JERUSHA HOOPER,
bp. E. Bridgewater 9 Oct. 1743; d. there 2 April 1829 ae
85; dau. of Thomas and Sarah (Packard) Hooper. She m. (2)
E. Bridgewater 1791 Jacob Mitchel.
    The estate of Robert Latham was declared insolvent in
1789; only the widow Jerusha was named in an account.

    Child (LATHAM) b. E. Bridgewater to Robert and Mary: ROBERT
JOHNSON[6] b. 1752, d. 1756.

References: BRIDGEWATER BY MITCHELL pp. 183, 195, 211, 232. VR
          BRIDGEWATER, E. BRIDGEWATER. Plymouth Co. PR 26:287;
30:504, 519; 31:156-7(Robert Latham); 8:367(Thos. Hayward). Plymouth
Co. LR 46:6(Robert & Bethiah Latham).

109 SUSANNA LATHAM[5] (Chilton[4], Susanna Winslow[3], Mary[2]
Chilton, James[1]) b. Bridgewater 20 May 1717; d. E. Bridgewater 4 Nov. 1800 ae 83y 6m, widow.
    She m. E. Bridgewater 26 Nov. 1746 THOMAS WADE JR.,
b. prob. E. Bridgewater ca. 1721; d. there 17 April 1777
ae 56; son of Nicholas and Anne (Latham) Wade (#86).
    Susanna Wade and Molly Wade both of Bridgewater
spinsters sold to Robert Wade 20 May 1777 their claim to
real estate of their father Thomas Wade late of Bridgewater deceased; both acknowledged 18 Oct. 1777.

    Children (WADE) all bp. E. Bridgewater "to Thomas": SUSANNA[6] b.
Bridgewater 1748, d. 1829 unm; ROBERT bp. E. Bridgewater 1750; and
MOLLEY b. 1754, d. 1845 unm.

References: VR BRIDGEWATER, E. BRIDGEWATER. BRIDGEWATER BY MITCHELL
         p. 336. BRIDGEWATER EPITAPHS p. 193, 223. Plymouth Co.
LR 59:99(Susanna and Molly Wade).

110 MARY LATHAM[5] (Chilton[4], Susanna Winslow[3], Mary[2]
Chilton, James[1]) b. Bridgewater 6 July 1720; living 26
March 1764.

She m. Bridgewater 3 June 1742 JONATHAN ALLEN, b.
Braintree 8 Feb. 1711/12; d. bet. 26 March and 9 July
1764; son of Samuel and Abigail (-----) Allen. He m. (1)
1739 Alice (Allen) Latham, widow of Arthur Latham (#106),
and sister-in-law of his second wife.
    The will of Jonathan Allen of Braintree yeoman, dated
26 March presented 9 July 1764, arranges for support of
his mother [unnamed]; names wife Mary; sons Jonathan and
Samuel, both under 21; daus. Reliance, Mary, "Unis" and
Esther; wife Mary and son Jonathan, executors.

    Children (ALLEN) b. Braintree to Jonathan and Mary: RELIANCE[6]
b. 1747; JONATHAN b. 1748; SAMUEL b. 1751; MARY b. 1753; EUNICE b.
1755; and ESTHER b. ca. 1759.

References: VR BRIDGEWATER. BRAINTREE VR pp. 690, 793, 795, 799,
             802, 806. BRIDGEWATER BY MITCHELL pp. 93, 193. VINTON
MEM p. 305. Suffolk Co. PR 63:238(Jonathan Allen).

    111[2] MARY SOUTHWORTH[5] (Desire Gray[4], Mary Winslow[3],
Mary[2] Chilton, James[1]) b. Plymouth 3 April 1676; d. there
2 Feb. 1757.
    She m. Plymouth 10 March 1706/7 JOSEPH RIDER, b.
Plymouth ca. 1671; d. there 29 Dec. 1766 in 95 yr.
    The will of Joseph Rider of "Plimouth," dated 21
April 1764 proved 2 Feb. 1767, mentions two daughters
Jemima Samson and Phillipa Loring; children of daughter
Hannah Cooper; grandson Southworth Samson; and son Joseph
Rider, executor.

    Children (RIDER) first three b. Hull, others prob. b. Plymouth:
DESIAR[6] b. 1707; HANNAH b. 1709; JEMIMMAH b. 1712; JOSEPH b. ca. 1714;
and PHILLIPA.

References: VR HULL. MD 1:142; 14:36; 31:114. SOUTHWORTH GEN p. 86.
             (PLYMOUTH) BURIAL HILL p. 39. Plymouth Co. PR 19:421-2
(Joseph Rider).

    112[2] ICHABOD SOUTHWORTH[5] (Desire Gray[4], Mary Winslow[3],
Mary[2] Chilton, James[1]) b. Plymouth ca. middle of March
1678/9; d. Middleboro 20 Sept. 1757 in 79 yr. "Capt."
    He m. Taunton ca. 1707 ESTHER HODGES, b. Taunton 17
Feb. 1677; d. Middleboro between 26 Dec. 1759 and 1 July
1760; dau. of Henry and Esther (Gallop) Hodges. The will
of Henry Hodges Sr. of Taunton, dated 17 Sept. 1717, names
wife Esther and includes dau. Esther Southworth.
    On 29 Sept. 1757 Rowland Hamond and Samuel Shaw both
of "Plimton" were appointed administrators of the estate
of Ichabod Southworth of Middleboro gentleman deceased.

Two accounts were subsequently filed, but no heirs were indicated.

The will of Esther "Southerd" of Taunton widow, dated 26 Dec. 1759 proved 1 July 1760, names dau. Abigel Sawdey wife of Benjamin Sawdey of Tiverton, grandson Ichabod Maccomber son of Deacon Nathaniel Maccomber "my son-in-law", dau. Mary Hammond wife of Rowland Hammond, and dau. "Desier" Shaw wife of Samuel Shaw; Nathaniel Maccomber was named executor.

Children (SOUTHWORTH) b. Middleboro: DESIRE[6] b. 1707; PRISCILLA b. 1709/10; NATHANAEL b. 1711/12, d. 1731; MARY b. 1713; ABIGAIL b. 1716; and WILLIAM b. 1719.

References: MD 3:84; 8:28; 15:7-8; 19:26; 21:73-6, 96. MIDDLEBORO DEATHS p. 171. SOUTHWORTH GEN pp. 86-87[correction: Abigail[6] did marry]. VR TAUNTON. HODGES GEN pp. 75, 81-2. Plymouth Co. PR 14:460; 15:255, 387, 591(Ichabod Southworth). Bristol Co. PR 17:57-8(Esther Southworth).

113 NATHANIEL SOUTHWORTH[5] (Desire Gray[4], Mary Winslow[3], Mary[2] Chilton, James[1]) b. Plymouth 18 May 1684; d. Middleboro 8 April 1757 in 72 yr.

He m. prob. Middleboro ca. 1709 JAEL HOWLAND, b. Middleboro 13 Oct. 1688; d. there 9 Nov. 1745 in 67 yr.; dau. of Isaac and Elizabeth (Vaughan) Howland, and granddau. of Pilgrim John Howland. The will of Isaac Howland of Middleboro, dated 6 Feb. 1717/8, names wife Elizabeth and includes dau. Jael Southworth.

The will of Nathaniel Southworth of Middleboro, dated 25 Dec. 1755 proved 2 May 1757, names sons Gideon Southworth and Nathaniel Southworth; "my brother Ichabod"; two grandchildren, heirs of son Samuell Southworth deceased; two daus. Fear Leonard and Hannah Sprout; son Nathaniel, executor.

Children (SOUTHWORTH) b. Middleboro:* [FE]AR[6] b. 1709/10; ICHABOD b. 1711, d. 1727; HANNAH b. 1714; GIDEON b. 1718; SAMUEL b. 1721/2; and NATHANIEL b. 1728/9.

References: MD 1:223; 2:107; 3:84, 234; 5:37; 6:147-9, 180; 7:242; 15:7-8; 29:87. MIDDLEBORO DEATHS p. 171. Plymouth Co. PR 14:318-20(Nathaniel Southworth). SOUTHWORTH GEN pp. 87-8. FAM OF PILGRIMS p. 113.

114 ELIZABETH SOUTHWORTH[5] (Desire Gray[4], Mary Winslow[3], Mary[2] Chilton, James[1]) bp. Plymouth 1687; d. prob. Middleboro bef. 1729.

---

*The John Howland Family will give greater detail and further generations.

She m. Scituate 5 June 1712 JAMES SPROUT, b. Scituate
in Feb. 1673/4; d. prob. Middleboro after 14 Sept. 1748;
son of Robert and Elizabeth (Samson) Sprout, and grandson
of Pilgrim Henry Samson. He m. (2) Scituate 8 Jan. 1728/9
Rachel (Buck) Dwelly, widow of John Dwelly.

James Sprout of Middleboro husbandman sold land to
son Robert Sprout of Middleboro millwright in 1737, and to
son Nathaniel Sprout of Middleboro in 1748.

Children (SPROUT) b. to James and Elizabeth:* ROBERT[6] b. Scituate 1713, d.y.; ROBERT b. Scituate 1715; MERCY b. Middleboro 1719;
and NATHANIEL b. Middleboro 1723.

References: VR SCITUATE. MD 3:235; 6:180; 9:87. HANOVER BY DWELLY
            p. 154. SOUTHWORTH GEN p. 86. Plymouth Co. LR 32:122;
39:198(James Sprout).

115 EDWARD SOUTHWORTH[5] (Desire Gray[4], Mary Winslow[3],
Mary[2] Chilton, James[1]) b. Plymouth 1688 or 1689, bp. 1690;
d. Bridgewater 26 April 1749 in 61 yr.

He m. Hull 25 June 1711 BRIDGET BOSWORTH, b. Hull 2
June 1691; dau. of Nathaniel and Mary (Morton) Bosworth.
She m. (2) No. Bridgewater (now Brockton) 1749 [prob. 1750
was meant] Capt. John Phillips.

Edward Southworth of Middleboro husbandman sold to
his brother Ichabod Southworth of Middleboro in 1720 land
received from his father Lt. Nathaniel Southworth of Middleboro deceased, in "the range of my brother Nathaniel
Southworth." In 1738 and 1740 he sold 90 acres of his
Middleboro homestead to his son Ebenezer Southworth. On
15 March 1744/5 Edward sold to Nathaniel Southworth a
dwelling and meadow in Middleboro "where I now dwell,"
bounded by land sold to brother Ichabod, but reserving a
life interest.

On 4 Dec. 1801 equal distribution among the heirs of
Benjamin Southworth[6] deceased, after thirds were set off to
his widow Mary, was made to: the heirs of Constant Southworth, of Edward Southworth, and of Ebenezer Southworth,
all deceased; Lemuel Southworth; heirs of Bridget Collyer,
of Sarah Edson, of Mary Jones, and of Theophilus Southworth, all deceased.

Children (SOUTHWORTH) b. Middleboro: CONSTANT[6] b. 1712; BRIDGET
b. 1714; EBENEZER b. 1716; EDWARD b. 1718; THEOPHILUS b. 1720/1;
SARAH b. 1723/4; twins BENJAMIN and LEMUEL b. 1728; and MARY b
1731/2.

References: MD 3:86, 233, 234; 6:179; 7:240; 9:48; 15:7. VR BROCK-
            TON, HULL. MIDDLEBORO DEATHS p. 171. BRIDGEWATER BY

The Henry Samson Family will give greater detail and further generations.

MITCHELL p. 320. BOSWORTH GEN 2:200; 3:311-2. SOUTHWORTH GEN pp. 88-9. Plymouth Co. PR 37:9-14(Benjamin Southworth). Plymouth Co. LR 32:122; 38:39; 43:218(Edward Southworth).

116 EDWARD ARNOLD[5] (Elizabeth Gray[4], Mary Winslow[3], Mary[2] Chilton, James[1]) b. Marshfield 20 March 1679/80; d. Duxbury bef. 21 March 1748.
    He m. Duxbury 8 Oct. 1706 MERCY BREWSTER, b. Duxbury 7 Dec. 1685; dau. of William and Lydia (Partridge) Brewster, and descendant of Pilgrim William Brewster.
    Edward Arnold lived in Duxbury where he was a justice of the peace. The will of Edward Arnold of "Duxborough," dated 30 Dec. 1741 probated 21 March 1748, names son Ezra Arnold and wife Mercy, executor.

    Children (ARNOLD) b. Duxbury: EZRA[6] b. 1707; and WILLIAM b. 1718, d. 1718.

References: VR DUXBURY. BREWSTER GEN 1:39-40, 57. Plymouth Co. PR
             11:394(Edward Arnold). MD 9:26.

117 DESIRE ARNOLD[5] (Elizabeth Gray[4], Mary Winslow[3], Mary[2] Chilton, James[1]) d. bef. 11 Dec. 1715 (father's will).
    She m. in Duxbury 14 Nov. 1709 ICHABOD BARTLETT, b. 1664; d. Duxbury bef. 1 Jan. 1716/7; son of Benjamin and Sarah (Brewster) Bartlett, and descendant of Pilgrims William Brewster and Richard Warren. He m. (1) Marshfield 1699 Elizabeth Waterman by whom he had Josiah, Nathaniel, Joseph and Elizabeth.
    Administration of the estate of Ichabod Bartlett of Duxbury was granted 1 Jan. 1716/7 to Edward Arnold and John Thomas. In April 1717 Mr. Edward Arnold of Duxbury was appointed guardian of his sister's son and dau., Seth and Sarah Bartlett, both under 14 yrs. A distribution was made 12 April 1717 to eldest son Josiah, second son Nathaniel, third son Joseph, dau. Elizabeth, youngest son Seth and youngest dau. Sarah.

    Children (BARTLETT) b. to Ichabod and Desire: SARAH[6] b. Marshfield 1710; and SETH bp. Marshfield 1713.

References: VR DUXBURY. MARSHFIELD VR pp. 25, 42, 43, 44, 352. MD
             25:16-20; 31:120. BREWSTER GEN 1:32[but was Desire Arnold
of Lebanon CT?]. WATERMAN GEN 1:60-1.

118 BENJAMIN ARNOLD[5] (Elizabeth Gray[4], Mary Winslow[3], Mary[2] Chilton, James[1]) d. bet. 19 Jan. 1715/6 and 16 July 1718.

He m. Duxbury 8 March 1713/4 HANNAH BARTLETT, b. ca.
1690; d. Duxbury 16 Jan. 1763 ae 73 yrs; dau. of Samuel and
Hannah (Pabodie) Bartlett, and a descendant of Pilgrims
John Alden, William Brewster and Richard Warren. She m.
(2) Marshfield 1719 Joseph Delano.

    Child (ARNOLD) b. Duxbury to Benjamin and Hannah: SAMUEL[6] b.
1715/6, d. bef. 1719.

References: VR DUXBURY. MARSHFIELD VR p. 38[date corrected in TAG].
            TAG 37:143-4.

    119 ELIZABETH ARNOLD[5] (Elizabeth Gray[4], Mary Winslow[3],
Mary[2] Chilton, James[1]) d. bet. 25 March 1729 and 1731.
    She m. (1) Marshfield ca. 1709 ANTHONY WATERMAN, b.
Marshfield 4 June 1684; d. there 3 April 1715 in 31 yr; son
of Joseph and Sarah (Snow) Waterman, and a descendant of
Pilgrim Richard Warren. Elizabeth Waterman, widow of
Anthony Waterman late of Marshfield, was made his adminis-
tratrix 31 June 1715.
    Division of the estate of Anthony Waterman was made 5
Jan. 1731 among eldest son Thomas, sons Joseph and Zebulon
Waterman, and daughter Orphan Waterman.
    She m. (2) Marshfield 17 Jan. 1717/8 JONATHAN ALDEN,
b. prob. Duxbury ca. 1686; d. Gorham ME 10 July 1770 ae 84y
4m; son of Jonathan and Abigail (Hallett) Alden, and a descendant of Pilgrim John Alden. He m. (2) Bridgewater 1731
Mehitable Allen by whom he possibly had son William.
    Jonathan Alden of Marshfield and wife Elizabeth, who
was a "daughter of Seth Arnold late of Duxbury," quitclaimed land in Duxbury and Tiverton RI to Edward and James
Arnold of Duxbury 3 April 1727. Jonathan was a housewright
of Duxbury in deeds dated 1733 and Jan. 1735/6. In Nov.
1766 he went to live with his son Austin in Gorham ME.

    Children (WATERMAN) b. Marshfield to Anthony and Elizabeth:
THOMAS[6] b. 1710; [JOS]EPH b. 1711/2; ZEBULON b. 1713; and ORPHAN b.
1715 (after father's death).

    Children (ALDEN) b. Marshfield to Jonathan and Elizabeth:
JONATHAN b. 1718/9; ANTHONY b. 1720; SETH b. 1721/2; JOSIAH b. 1724;
and AUSTIN b. 1729.

References: MD 14:140-2; 24:146; 31:168. MARSHFIELD VR pp. 11, 32,
            33, 36, 40, 45, 48, 87, 389. WATERMAN GEN 1:62-3. VR
BRIDGEWATER, GORHAM ME. ALDEN MEM pp. 9, 20. GORHAM ME HIST p. 387.
Plymouth Co. PR 3:353(Anthony Waterman). Plymouth Co. LR 22:61; 28:44,
46, 115-6(Jonathan Alden).

120   JAMES ARNOLD[5]   (Elizabeth Gray[4], Mary Winslow[3], Mary[2]
Chilton, James[1])   bp. Marshfield 20 Oct. 1700; d. Duxbury
24 Sept. 1755 ae 55 yrs.
       He m. Duxbury 19 Feb. 1734/5 JOANNA SPRAGUE, b. April
1715 prob. Duxbury; d. there 19 March 1766 ae 50y 11m; dau.
of John and Bethia (Snow) Sprague, and a descendant of Pilgrim Richard Warren. The will of John Sprague Sr. of Dux-
boro [Duxbury], dated 27 Nov. 1739, includes dau. Joanna
wife of James Arnold.
       On 6 Oct. 1755 Joanna Arnold of Duxboro was appointed
administratrix of the estate of James Arnold late of Dux-
boro. In a distribution 7 May 1759 all real estate was al-
loted to eldest son Bildad Arnold, after reserving his
mother's dower; he was to pay his brothers Luther, James
and Benjamin Arnold. Guardians were appointed for the two
minor sons, James and Benjamin Arnold, 9 July 1759.

       Children (ARNOLD) b. Duxbury: BILDAD[6] b. 1735; LUTHER b. 1737;
JAMES b. 1740, d. 1742; JAMES b. 1745, bp. 1744(*sic*); and BENJAMIN bp.
1752.

References: VR DUXBURY. NEHGR 124:118-20. Plymouth Co. PR 8:147-9
       (John Sprague); 13:551(James Arnold).

121   SARAH LITTLE[5]   (Sarah Gray[4], Mary Winslow[3], Mary[2]
Chilton, James[1])   b. Marshfield 23 July 1685; d. Little
Compton RI 19 March 1742 ae 57.
       She m. Little Compton 25 May 1703/4 the Rev. RICHARD
BILLINGS, b. Dorchester 21 Sept. 1675; d. Little Compton 20
Nov. 1748; son of Ebenezer and Hannah (Wales) Billings. He
graduated from Harvard in 1698, and received his master's
degree in 1701. He was ordained at Little Compton 30 Nov.
1704.
       The will of Richard Billings of Little Compton, dated
14 Nov. exhibited 6 Dec. and administration granted to
Richard Billings of Newport 9 Dec. 1748, names son Richard
Billings, executor; daughters Sarah Coggeshall, Hannah Collick and Elisabeth Tisdel; granddaughter Mary Throop (under
18); daughters Abigail Foster and Comfort Grinell.

       Children (BILLINGS) b. Little Compton RI:* SARAH[6] b. 1704;
RICHARD b. 1706; HANNAH b. 1708; ELIZABETH b. 1709; MARY b. 1712;
ABIGAIL b. 1714; and COMFORT b. 1716.

References: RI VR:Little Compton pp. 39, 81. DORCHESTER VR 21:14.
       LITTLE COMPTON FAMS p. 43. Little Compton RI PR 1:46-8
(Richard Billings). HARVARD GRADS 4:393-4.

_____
The Richard Warren Family will give greater detail and a further
generation.

122 SAMUEL LITTLE[5] (Sarah Gray[4], Mary Winslow[3], Mary[2]
Chilton, James[1]) b. Marshfield 7 Nov. 1691; d. Bristol RI
8 Jan. 1739/40 ae 49 or 50.
     He m. (1) Little Compton RI 10 May 1714 MARY BRIGGS,
d. Bristol 19 July 1729.
     He m. (2) Bristol RI 29 Oct. 1730 HANNAH (-----)
WILSON of Rehoboth; living Boston 30 March 1741. She m.
(3) Boston 1740 Josias Byles (she then of Newport).
     Samuel Little of Bristol mariner was appointed admin-
istrator 19 Feb. 1739/40 of his father Samuel Little late
of Bristol gentleman deceased. On the same day Mrs. Hannah
Little of Bristol widow was made guardian of her daughter
Haile Little, also daughter of Samuel Little late of Bristol gentleman deceased.
     In identical deeds Mary Little and Samuel Little mari-
ner, both of Bristol and children of Capt. Samuel Little
late of Bristol deceased, sold to Thomas Lawton their portions of a farm in Bristol, not including any portion
which might fall to them upon the decease of either of the
children of their father or his granddaughter Mary--after
the debts were paid this ought to amount to one-fifth part
for each; Samuel and wife Hannah signed 2 Dec. 1740, Mary
signed 6 April 1741. Josias Byle of Boston shopkeeper and
wife Hannah, late wife of Samuel Little of Bristol deceased, sold to Thomas Lawton her dower in the above-men-
tioned farm on 30 March 1741.

     Children (LITTLE) b. Bristol RI to Samuel and Mary:* THOMAS[6] b.
1714; SAMUEL b. 1715/6; and MARY b. 1718.

     Child (LITTLE) b. Bristol to Samuel and Hannah: HAILE.

References: RI VR:Bristol pp. 33, 88, 145. REHOBOTH VR p. 471.
          Bristol Co. PR 9:333(Samuel Little & gdn. Haile); 9:377
(Samuel Little). LITTLE COMPTON FAMS pp. 43, 399[error in his death].
BOSTON VR 28:234. Bristol Co. LR 28:435(Samuel Little); 30:53(Josias
Byles); 30:123(Mary Little).

123 EDWARD LITTLE[5] (Sarah Gray[4], Mary Winslow[3], Mary[2]
Chilton, James[1]) bp. Marshfield 17 July 1698; d. bet.
April 1776 and Oct. 1777.
     He m. (1) Bristol RI 7 Nov. 1717 MARY WALKER, b. Bris-
tol 28 July 1693; d. there 25 Jan. 1739/40; dau. of Thomas
and Elizabeth (Parris) Walker.
     He m. (2) Norwich CT 18 June 1741 MARY (KINSMAN) BURN-
HAM, b. Ipswich 20 Jan. 1707/8; living 2 Oct. 1777; dau. of
Robert and Rebecca (Burley) Kinsman, and widow of Benjamin
Burnham. The will of Robert Kinsman Sr., dated at Norwich
CT 6 Sept. 1750, names daughter Mary Little. Distribution

_____
*The Richard Warren Family will give greater detail and a further
generation.

of the estate of Rebecca Kinsman 2 Oct. 1777 includes widow
Mary Little, eldest daughter.
    Edward moved with his family from Bristol to Middle-
town CT about 1747, and some time after 1750 to New Haven
CT.

    Children (LITTLE) b. Bristol RI to Edward and Mary (Walker):*
SARAH[6] b. 1718 [did not d. 1718]; EDWARD b. 1720, d.y.; MARY b.
1721; THOMAS b. 1722; ELIZABETH b. 1724/5; LEMUEL b. 1726; NATHANIEL
b. 1729; EDWARD b. 1733; and REBECCA b. 1736/7.

    Children (LITTLE) first three b. Bristol to Edward and second
wife Mary (Kinsman): WILLIAM b. 1742, d. 1759; BENJAMIN b. 1744; LUCY
b. 1746; and SAMUEL b. Middletown or New Haven 1750.

    References: NGSQ 60:83-7. RI VR:Bristol pp. 33, 88, 110, 145. FALES
        FAM pp. 43, 49, 51-2(evidence for m. of first dau. Sarah).
NORWICH CT VR pp. 136-7.

    124 ANN(A) GRAY[5] (John[4], Mary Winslow[3], Mary[2] Chilton,
James[1]) b. Plymouth 5 Aug. 1691; d. Kingston 6 Sept. 1730
ae 39y 1m.
    She m. Plymouth 30 Dec. 1714 JOHN TINKHAM (or Tincom),
b. Plymouth 27 March 1689; d. Kingston 12 May 1730; son of
Helkiah and Ruth (-----) Tinkham, and a descendant of Pilgrim Peter Brown.
    On 1 Jan. 1730/1 Samuel Gray was appointed guardian of
John Tinkham's children: Edward, John, Ephraim, Joseph and
Anna. In a division 12 July 1746 of the real estate of
John Tinkham deceased, eldest son Edward Tinkham took all,
and was to pay John Tinkham, Ephraim Tinkham, Joseph Tinkham and Ann Tinkham.

    Children (TINKHAM) first two b. Plymouth, last three b. Kingston:
MARY[6] b. 1718, d. Kingston 1730; EDWARD b. 1719/20; JOHN b. ca. 1721;
EPHRAIM b. 1724; ANN** b. 1726; and JOSEPH b. 1728.

    References: VR KINGSTON. MD 4:111; 7:221-2; 13:33; 14:37. GEN
        ADVERTISER 2:39. Plymouth Co. PR 5:745, 820-2; 7:454;
8:11-12; 10:205-7(John Tinkham and gdns.). PN&Q 1:111.

    125 JOANNA GRAY[5] (John[4], Mary Winslow[3], Mary[2] Chilton,
James[1]) b. Plymouth 29 Jan. 1695/6; d. Kingston 25 Sept.
1776.

_____

The Richard Warren Family will give greater detail and a further
generation.

**For a further generation of Ann Tinkham see *The Samuel Fuller Family*
in *Mayflower Families*, volume one, page 62.

She m. Kingston 21 June 1721 EBENEZER FULLER, b. Plymouth 24 March 1695; d. Kingston 2 May 1759 in 65 yr; son
of Samuel and Mercy (Eaton) Fuller, and a descendant of
Pilgrims Francis Eaton and Samuel Fuller.

Children (FULLER) first three b. Plymouth, the rest b. Kingston:*
JOSIAH[6] b. 1721 or 1722; SAMUEL b. 1723, d. 1724; REBECCA b. 1725;
HANNAH b. 1727, d. 1736; MERCY b. 1730, d. 1733/4; LOIS b. 1733;
EUNICE b. 1736; and EBENEZER b. 1737/8.

References: VR KINGSTON. MD 3:14; 13:170. Plymouth Co. PR 21:192
              (Ebenezer Fuller).

126 SAMUEL GRAY[5] (John[4], Mary Winslow[3], Mary[2] Chilton,
James[1]) b. Plymouth 23 Dec. 1701/2; d. Kingston in Oct.
1738.
      He m. Duxbury 7 Dec. 1727 PATIENCE WADSWORTH, b. Dux-
bury 20 Aug. 1706; d. Kingston 23 April 1782 ae 76; dau. of
Elisha and Elizabeth (Wiswall) Wadsworth. The will of
Elisha Wadsworth of Duxbury dated 12 Jan. 1741 names dau.
"Patince" Gray.
      In 1771 the widow Patience Gray petitioned for her
dower rights to be included in the estate of Samuel Gray
for distribution among his heirs. A division was made 22
July 1771 with two parts to John Gray, and one part each
to Mary wife of Benjamin Cook, to Samuel Gray, and to the
heirs of Wait Gray.

Children (GRAY) b. Kingston: MARY[6] b. 1728, d. 1728; JOHN b.
1729; MARY b. 1731; ELIZABETH b. 1734, d. 1740; SAMUEL b. 1736; and
WATE b. 1739.

References: VR DUXBURY, KINGSTON. MD 7:88. Plymouth Co. PR 8:5, 63;
              21:4(Samuel Gray); 13:424(Elisha Wadsworth).

127 MERCY GRAY[5] (John[4], Mary Winslow[3], Mary[2] Chilton,
James[1]) b. Plymouth 4 Feb. 1703/4; d. Kingston 13 Aug.
1782 in 79 yr. "widow of Jabez."
      She m. int. Kingston 13 Oct. 1733 JABEZ FULLER, as his
second wife, b. Plymouth "in the beginning of June" 1701;
d. Kingston bef. 20 May 1757; son of Samuel and Mercy
(Eaton) Fuller, and a descendant of Pilgrims Francis Eaton
and Samuel Fuller.
      Mercy Fuller on 20 May 1757 was appointed administra-
trix of "your husband" Jabez Fuller late of Kingston
laborer deceased.

---

*For a more extensive account of these children see *The Samuel Fuller
Family* in *Mayflower Families,* volume one, page 60.

Children (FULLER) b. Kingston to Jabez and Mercy:* THOMAS[6] b. 1734, d. 1738; JOANNA b. 1736; JAMES b. 1737; JABISH (JABEZ) b. 1739; JOHN b. 1742; and MERCY b. 1747.

References: VR KINGSTON. MD 3:14. Plymouth Co. PR 14:238(Jabez Fuller).

128 BENJAMIN POLLARD[5] (Mary Winslow[4], Edward[3], Mary[2] Chilton, James[1]) b. Boston 6 June 1696; d. there 26 Dec. 1756 in 61 yr.
     He m. Boston 14 Aug. 1746 MARGARET WINSLOW, b. Boston 28 April 1724; d. there 25 March 1814 ae 90; dau. of Joshua and Elizabeth (Savage) Winslow (see #129ii).
     Benjamin was a High Sheriff for Suffolk County for over thirteen years. His will, dated 25 Dec. 1756 probated 21 Jan. 1757 "late of Boston, Esquire," names wife Margaret and children Jonathan, Benjamin, Margaret, Joshua and Peter, each to receive a share of his estate when they reach 21. The widow Margaret was accepted as executrix.

     Children (POLLARD) b. Boston: BENJAMIN[6] b. 1747, d. 1750; JONATHAN b. 1749; BENJAMIN b. 1752; PEGGY SAVAGE b. 1754; JOSHUA b. 1755; and PETER b. 1756.

References: BOSTON VR 24:168, 264, 271, 280, 285, 287, 289; 28:258.
           BOSTON NEWS OBITS 1:241. POLLARD FAM 1:71-3. Suffolk
Co. PR 52:30(Benjamin Pollard). NEHGR 67:211. MA OBITS 4:3603.

129 JOSHUA WINSLOW[5] (Edward [4-3], Mary[2] Chilton, James[1]) b. Boston 12 Feb. 1694/5; d. there 9 Oct. 1769 in 75th yr.
     He m. Boston 8 Feb. 1720 ELIZABETH SAVAGE, b. Boston 29 Sept. 1704; d. there 7 Aug. 1778 ae. 74; dau. of Thomas and Margaret (Lynde) Savage. Joshua Winslow of Boston, merchant, and wife Elizabeth, one of the daughters of Thomas Savage late of Boston deceased and his wife Margaret also deceased, quitclaimed rights to the estate of "our said father and mother" 1 March 1725.
     He was a merchant and Justice of the Peace. The will of Joshua Winslow Esq. of Boston, dated 29 Sept. 1769 presented 18 Oct. 1769, names sons Isaac, Joshua, John and Edward (eldest) and son-in-law John Winniet; mentions several married daus., but names only Martha and [Elizabeth] Winniet; states eleven children now living; names grandson John Winniet (under 21); executors, wife Elizabeth and brother Isaac Winslow. On 2 Oct. 1778 both executors were dead, so David Jeffries and John Winnie(t) were certified as administrators.

_____

*For a more extensive account of these children see _The Samuel Fuller Family_ in _Mayflower Families_, volume one, page 66.

Children (WINSLOW) b. Boston: EDWARD[6] b. 1722; MARGARET b. 1724;
HANNAH b. 1725/6; ELIZABETH b. 1729; SUSANNA b. 1730/1, d. 1786 unm;
MARY b. 1732; KATHARINE b. 1733; twins MARTHA and ANN b. 1734/5, Ann d.
1735; JOSHUA b. 1736/7; ANN b. 1738, d. 1751; THOMAS ALFORD b. 1740, d.
1765 unm; JOHN b. 1742; ISAAC b. 1743; WILLIAM b. 1747, d. 1751; and
HENRY b. 1748, d. 1751.

References: BOSTON VR 24:32, 158, 168, 173, 195, 200, 210, 214, 219,
             227; 28:90. NEHGR 67:211. BOSTON NEWS OBITS 1:332.
Suffolk Co. PR 68:305; 77:523(Joshua Winslow). BOSTON MEM HIST 2:543
[error: says Eliz. Savage m. *John* Winslow]. Suffolk Co. LR 47:91
(Joshua Winslow).

130 HANNAH WINSLOW[5] (Edward[4-3], Mary[2] Chilton, James[1])
b. Boston 8 March 1697; d. 17 April 1775 ae 79, widow.
     She m. Boston 26 Jan. 1715 WILLIAM DAVIS, prob. son of
Benjamin and Sarah (-----) Davis, b. Boston 16 Feb. 1686;
d. 14 March 1745/6.
     Hannah Davis, widow of Boston, was appointed adminis-
trator of her husband William Davis late of Boston deceased
"physitian" on 28 March 1746; she swore to the inventory 24
Dec. 1747. No further probate nor any land records were
found connecting their children.

     Children (DAVIS) b. Boston: SARAH[6] b. 1719; HANNAH b. 1722; and
WILLIAM b. 1726.

References: BOSTON VR 24:140, 155, 175; 28:57. BOSTON NEWS OBITS
             1:87; 2:288. Suffolk Co. PR 38:477; 40:331(William
Davis).

131 EDWARD WINSLOW[5] (Edward[4-3], Mary[2] Chilton, James[1])
b. Boston 8 Feb. 1702/3; drowned off Land's End, England,
23 Dec. 1733 "Capt."
     He m. Boston 1 Dec. 1726 HANNAH SAVAGE, b. Boston 29
Jan. 1708; d. Charlestown 30 March 1755; dau. of Habijah
and Hannah (Phillips) (Anderson) Savage. She m. (2) Boston
1754 John Austin of Charlestown.
     Widow Hannah Winslow of Boston on 25 Nov. 1754 sold to
Arthur Savage all rights in real estate set off to her near
Arthur's mansion house. John Austin of Charlestown
leather-dresser on 12 June 1755 sold a tenement and land in
Boston to Thomas Savage that was bounded by a lot set off
to Thomas from the estate of his late mother Mrs. Hannah
Savage--a building assigned to Mrs. Hannah Winslow, late
wife deceased of John Austin, from the estate of her late
mother Mrs. Hannah Savage. No probate records were found
in either Middlesex or Suffolk Counties for either Edward
or Hannah.

Child (WINSLOW): EDWARD[6] prob. d. soon after 1748.

References: BOSTON VR 24:58; 28:158; 30:13. BOSTON NEWS OBITS 3:580.
CHARLESTOWN BY WYMAN 1:35; 2:847, 1042. NEHGR 67:212-3.
Suffolk Co. LR 86:84(Hannah Winslow); 87:77(John Austin).

132 SAMUEL WINSLOW[5] (Edward[4-3], Mary[2] Chilton, James[1])
b. Boston 29 May 1705; d. Louisburg, N.S. 7 Sept. 1745.
    He m. Boston 8 June 1729 REBECCA CLARK, b. Boston 28
Jan. 1708; living 13 Aug. 1748 (will of Edward Winslow[4]);
dau. of Dr. William and Sarah (Bronson) Clarke.
    John Winslow of Boston was appointed administrator 6
Dec. 1745 on the estate of his brother Samuel Winslow, late
of Boston merchant, "but last a Midshipman on Board his
Majesty's Ship of War the *Vigilant*." The will of his
father Edward Winslow[4] in a codicil dated 13 Aug. 1748
names the children of son Samuel[5]: Sarah, Edward, Joshua
and Rebecca, and his widow Rebecca Winslow.

    Children (WINSLOW), prob. b. Boston: SARAH[6]; EDWARD; JOSHUA; and
REBECCA.

References: MD 10:106-8. BOSTON VR 24:55; 28:152. NEHGR 17:160(error
in date of Samuel's death).

133 ISAAC WINSLOW[5] (Edward[4-3], Mary[2] Chilton, James[1])
b. Boston 2 May 1709; d. New York City 23 March 1777.
    He m. (1) Boston 14 Dec. 1747 LUCY WALDO, b. Boston 23
Jan. 1724; d. Roxbury 7 Nov. 1768 ae 43; dau. of Samuel and
Lucy (Wainwright) Waldo. A letter of administration on
"your late father...Samuel Waldo late of Boston deceased,"
dated 1759, appointed Isaac Winslow of Roxbury, among
others, to administer the estate.
    He m. (2) Boston 25 Nov. 1770 JEMIMA DEBUC (or Debuke),
b. Boston 5 May 1732; d. London, England 27 March 1790; dau.
of Thomas and Jemima (Reed) Debuke.
    Isaac graduated from Harvard College 1727, and re-
ceived a second degree there 1730. He was a merchant
living in Boston until 1752, then a year in Milton, then
back to Boston, and finally to Roxbury after 1755. A
Loyalist, he returned to Boston in April 1775, left for
Halifax with his family (eleven strong) in March 1776, and
later moved to New York City.
    The will of Isaac Winslow, residing in Nova Scotia
about to embark with my family for New York, bearing no
date, left bequest to his wife; the rest of his real and
personal estate to his children and grandchild George
Erving; named Lucy Winslow as mother of George Erving; executors to be nephews Isaac Winslow Jr., Jonathan Clarke
and Isaac Winslow Clarke. This was committed in Boston 28

Oct. 1785 as the "will of Isaac Winslow late of Halifax, N.
S. merchant deceased" to his nephew Isaac Winslow Jr., one
of the executors. In two accounts of distribution both
dated 26 July 1802 the heirs named were: Isaac Winslow,
John Wall and wife Hannah, Elizabeth Winslow, Samuel Winslow, Capt. Thomas Winslow, Samuel Waldo and wife Sarah T.,
and George William Erving.

        Children (WINSLOW), Lucy and Hannah b. Boston, rest b. or bp.
Roxbury to Isaac and Lucy: LUCY[6] b. 1749; prob. child b. ca. 1752;
HANNAH b. 1755; SAMUEL b. 1757; ELIZABETH bp. 1759; GRIZEL (or
GRIZZEL) b. "dau." 1760, bp. "son" 1760; ISAAC b. 1763; and SARAH
TWING[prob. TYNG] bp. 1765.

        Child (WINSLOW) bp. Roxbury to Isaac and Jemima: THOMAS bp.
1772.

References: VR ROXBURY. BOSTON VR 24:167, 207, 272, 288, 293, 298,
            300, 307; 28:267; 30:330. BOSTON NEWS OBITS 3:580, 581.
HARVARD GRADS 8:333-9. Suffolk Co. PR #18543 and 81:379; 84:643-4;
85:177; 87:85; 92:109; 97:699; 100:318, 321(Isaac Winslow); 54:446
(Samuel Waldo). LOYALISTS BY SABINE 2:446. NGSQ 66:203.

        134 ₁ELIZABETH WINSLOW[5] (Edward[4-3], Mary[2] Chilton,
James[1]) b. Boston 16 Feb. 1712/3; d. Boston 22 Aug. or 3
Sept. 1765 ae 53.
        She m. Boston 3 May 1733 RICHARD CLARKE, b. Boston 1
May 1711; d. London, Eng. 27 Feb. 1795; son of William and
Hannah (Appleton) Clarke. He m. (1) ----- -----, by whom
he had one child.
        He was a merchant. He graduated from Harvard College
1729, and took an MA in 1732. He was one of the consignees
of tea destroyed in the Boston Tea Party; he went to London, arriving 24 Dec. 1775, and remained there until his
death.

        Children (CLARKE) b. Boston: HANNAH[6] b. 1733/4, d. Boston
1761 in 29 yr.; WILLIAM b. 1734/5; ELIZABETH b. 1735/6; EDWARD b.
1737; JOSEPH LEE b. 1740; MARY b. 1741; JONATHAN b. 1744; SUSANNA FAR-
NUM b. 1745; ISAAC WINSLOW b. 1746; SARAH b. 1750; LUCY b. 1752; and
RICHARD b. 1756.

References: BOSTON VR 24:74, 211, 224, 227, 231, 241, 244, 255, 259,
            273, 279, 288; 28:181. BOSTON NEWS OBITS 1:61. HARVARD
GRADS 8:550-62. LOYALISTS BY SABINE 1:316. CABOT GEN p. 214, 220.
NEHGR 84:156, 170.

135   KATHERINE DOWSE[5]   (Katherine Winslow[4], Edward[3], Mary[2]
Chilton, James[1])   b. Charlestown 17 May 1706; d. Concord 8
Nov. 1782.
      She m. (1) Charlestown 12 Nov. 1724 THOMAS WYER, b.
Charlestown 14 Oct. 1704; d. bef. 1747; son of William and
Eleanor (Jenner) Wyer. The only probate or land evidence
found in Middlesex County for Thomas Wyer or his children
is the will of William Wyer of Charlestown, dated 15 Jan.
1747 probated 20 Feb. 1748/9, which mentions "grandson
William Wyer, son of deceased son Thomas."
      By an indenture 7 May 1747 Katherine Wyer of Charles-
town widow sold to Isaac Johnson of Charlestown mariner one
moiety of her tenement and land adjoining in Charlestown,
bounded by land of Richard Foster deceased.
      She m. (2) Charlestown 12 May 1747 ISAAC JOHNSON, b.
Charlestown 5 Oct. 1705; d. bef. 1 Aug. 1748; son of Eleazer and Susanna (Johnson) Johnson. He m. (1) 1725 Mary
Remick, by whom he had Eleazer, two Marys, Isaac and Jacob.
Isaac was a sea-captain.
      Administration of the estate of her husband, Capt.
Isaac Johnson late of Charlestown deceased, was granted 1
Aug. 1748 to Katherine Johnson. An account of "Katherine
Johnson formerly Wyer" widow of Capt. Isaac Johnson mari-
ner deceased including the items "support of Samuel young-
est child of the deceased from 14 Jan. 1749 until seven
years of age," and "to her lying in with Samuel, being
posthumous," was allowed 27 May 1769.

      Children (WYER) b. Charlestown to Thomas and Katherine: WILLIAM[6]
b. 1728; and KATHERINE b. 1731.

      Child (JOHNSON) b. Charlestown to Isaac and Katherine: SAMUEL b.
1748 (posthumous).

References: CHARLESTOWN BY WYMAN 1:305, 557-8; 2:1054-5. DOWSE FAM
             p. 23. DOWSE DESC p. 158. Middlesex Co. PR #12673
(Isaac Johnson); #25799(Wm. Wyer). Middlesex Co. LR 46:217(Katherine
Wyer).

136   JOSEPH DOWSE[5]   (Katherine Winslow[4], Edward[3], Mary[2]
Chilton, James[1])   b. Charlestown 14 Jan. 1708/9; d. Salem
30 Jan. 1785 ae 76.
      He m. Boston 14 Dec. 1734 JANE STEEL, b. Boston 20
April 1709; bur. Boston 24 March 1788 ae 79; dau. of Thomas
and Jane (Allen) Steel.
      Joseph lived in Boston until 1760 when he moved to
Salem as Surveyor of the Port. Jane Dowse and her children
returned to Boston after Joseph died. Oliver Smith was appointed administrator on the estate of Joseph Dowse late of
Salem 1 March 1785, upon petition of widow Jane Dowse of

Salem, supported by daughters Margaret, Katherine and Isabella; she stated that her two sons [Loyalists] were out
of the country. Oliver Smith, attorney for Jonathan Dowse
of Wales, Great Britain, quitted his right in the estate
of his father Joseph Dowse late of Salem on 1 Jan. 1786 to
Margaret, Catherine and Isabella Dowse.

Children (DOWSE) all presumed to be b. Boston: MARGARET[6] b.
1735, d. Boston 1807 unm; KATHERINE b. 1737, d. Boston 1798 unm; JONA-
THAN b. 1739; SAMUEL bp. and bur. 1741; ISABELLA bp. 1743, d. Boston
1797 ae 54 unm; JOSEPH bp. 1745, d.y.; JOSEPH b. 1747; JANE b. 1749,
bur. 1751; and THOMAS bp. 1752, d. Salem 1775.

References: CHARLESTOWN BY WYMAN 1:305-6; 2:898. BOSTON VR 24:65,
             221, 228, 236; 28:328. VR SALEM. BOSTON NEWS OBITS
2:320. DOWSE FAM pp. 23-5. DOWSE DESC pp. 158-63. MA OBITS 2:1380-
1. Essex Co. PR #8285(Joseph Dowse). Suffolk Co. LR 186:235(Oliver
Smith).

137 ELIZABETH DOWSE[5] (Katherine Winslow[4], Edward[3],
Mary[2] Chilton, James[1]) b. Charlestown 13 Nov. 1710; liv-
ing 5 Oct. 1746.
      She m. int. Boston 18 Aug. 1730 MOREAU SARRAZEN of
Boston; had he d. bef. 25 Oct. 1746, when Samuel Dowse be-
queathed to "my sister Elizabeth Sarrazin"? No appropri-
ate probate or land records were found in Middlesex or
Suffolk counties, nor any records in Suffolk Superior
Court.

Child (SARRAZIN) bp. Boston: JONATHAN[6] bp. 1731, n.f.r.

References: CHARLESTOWN BY WYMAN 1:305. BOSTON VR 24:168. DOWSE
             DESC pp. 163-4.

138 NATHANIEL DOWSE[5] (Katherine Winslow[4], Edward[3],
Mary[2] Chilton, James[1]) bp. Charlestown 6 Feb. 1714/5; d.
Malden bef. 9 Dec. 1782.
      He m. int. Charlestown 11 Jan. 1746 MARGARET TEMPLE,
b. ca. 1724; bur. Boston 18 June 1771 ae 47; dau. of
Robert and Mehitabel (Nelson) Temple. The will of Robert
Temple, dated 9 April probated 22 April 1754, mentions
daughter Margaret Dowse. Nathaniel was a sea-captain.
      On 13 March 1759 the selectmen of Concord warned out
Samuel, Nathaniel, Pascal, Robert and Edward Dowse "who
came from Charlestown about three months preceding the
twenty-first of Feb. last." Nathaniel Dowse of Charlestown with consent of his wife Margaret sold his dwelling
and barn in Charlestown 7 Jan. 1762; both acknowledged 16
Jan. 1762.

Nathaniel Dowse merchant of Charlestown was granted administration of the estate of Nathaniel Dowse late of Charlestown mariner 3 Feb. 1783.

Children (DOWSE) baptized at Boston: NATHANIEL[6] bp. 1748; CATHERINE bp. 1749; MEHITABLE bp. 1751, bur. 1751; PASCAL bp. 1752; SAMUEL bp. 1754, bur. 1764; ROBERT bp. 1755, prob. d. shortly after 1759; EDWARD bp. 1756; and MARY bp. 1758.

References: CHARLESTOWN BY WYMAN 1:305-6; 2:938. DEDHAM CH pp. 133, 255. BOSTON NEWS OBITS 2:320. DOWSE FAM pp. 25-8. DOWSE DESC pp. 164-5. Middlesex Co. PR #6399(Nathaniel Dowse). Middlesex Co. LR 71:77(Nathaniel Dowse). Cambridge Court of Quarter Sessions: May 1748 to May 1761: Court convened 13 March 1759 p. 526 (Selectmen of Concord).

139   JOSEPH SCOTT[5] (Elizabeth Winslow[4], Edward[3], Mary[2] Chilton, James[1]) b. Boston 23 Nov. 1694; d. Boston bet. 14 May 1750 and 26 Aug. 1751.
     He m. (1) Boston 14 Jan. 1719[1719/20] MEHITABLE WEB-BER, living 1733; d. bef. 1739; pos. dau. of Thomas and Mehitable (-----) Webber.
     He m. (2) Boston 21 Feb. 1739 ELIZABETH BRIDGE, living 6 July 1763.
     Joseph Scott of Boston brazier sold a wharf and ware-house in Boston, wife Elizabeth relinquishing dower, which both acknowledged 14 May 1750. Elizabeth Scott widow and Joseph Scott brazier, both of Boston, were appointed ad-ministrators 26 Aug. 1751 of the estate of Joseph Scott late of Boston brazier. Dower was set off to the widow Elizabeth 6 July 1753, including land in Boston and Plymp-ton. A division, ordered 2 July 1761 to exclude the widow's thirds, was made 4 June and allowed 3 Dec. 1762 among eldest son Joseph Scott, other sons Edward Scott (one half the iron works in Plympton), John Scott and Daniel Scott, a minor; and daus. Mehitable Chamberlain (part of the farm in Plympton where she dwells) and Eliza-beth Colburn (other part of the Plympton farm). Abner Hall of Plympton and wife Mehitable sold to Joseph Scott of Boston merchant, 8 Nov. 1764 and both acknowledged 18 Nov. 1764, all their rights "to our mother-in-law's right of dower or thirds of our father Joseph Scott" late of Boston deceased, partly in Boston, partly in Plympton.

Children (SCOTT) b. Boston to Joseph and Mehitable: JOSEPH[6] b. 1720; JOSHUA b. 1722; MEHETABEL b. 1723; ELIZABETH b. 1725; JOHN b. 1727, d.y.; SARAH b. 1728; EDWARD b. 1730; KATHARINE b. 1732; and JOHN b. 1733.

Children (SCOTT) b. Boston to Joseph and Elizabeth: MARTHA b. 1740; DANIEL b. 1744; and STEPHEN b. 1749.

References: BOSTON VR 24:147, 157, 162, 173, 183, 189, 199, 209, 213,
            241, 254, 272; 28:85, 212, 269. MD 10:144. NEHGR 34:
192; 37:58. Suffolk Co. PR 45:334; 48:237; 59:79; 61:251-2(Jos.
Scott). Suffolk Co. LR 78:106(Jos. Scott); 103:101(Abner Hall).

140 SAMUEL HINCKS[5] (Elizabeth Winslow[4], Edward[3], Mary[2]
Chilton, James[1]) bp. Portsmouth NH 19 April 1717; d.
Bucksport ME 1804.
    He m. Truro 10 Nov. 1755 SUSANNA DYER, b. Truro 28
Jan. 1735/6; dau. of Jonathan and Susanna (-----) Dyer.
    Samuel lived in Boston with his parents from 1725
until he graduated from Harvard ca. 1740. He then went to
Truro as a schoolmaster until about 1795 when he moved to
Buckstown (now Bucksport) ME. In 1800 Winslow Hincks was
in Bucksport with a family of three males and five females,
the oldest male being 45 or older (presumably Samuel).

    Children (HINCKS) b. Truro: ELIZABETH[6] b. 1757; SUSANNA b. 1759;
JOHN b. 1760; PHEBE b. 1764; ANNA b. 1765; WINSLOW b. 1766; SAMUEL b.
1769; RUTH b. 1771; ELISHA b. 1774; and JESSE YOUNG b. 1776.

References: TRURO VR pp. 34, 56, 76, 139. NEHGR 29:315; 105:283.
            HARVARD GRADS 5:72-3. SMALL DESC. 3:1277.

141 JOHN TAYLOR[5] (Ann Winslow[4], Edward[3], Mary[2] Chilton,
James[1]) b. Boston 30 Aug. 1704; d. Milton 26 Jan. 1750 in
46th yr.
    He m. (1) 9 April 1730 ELIZABETH ROGERS, b. ca. 1708;
d. Milton 17 or 27 April 1735 ae 27; dau. of Rev. Nathaniel
and Sarah (Parkiss) Rogers of Portsmouth NH. This is not a
Mayflower Rogers line.
    He m. (2) DOROTHY (SHERBOURNE)(RYMES) ROGERS, d. 25
Jan. 1761; dau. of Henry Sherburne, and widow of his first
wife's brother. She m. (4) Milton 1751 Peter Gilman of
Exeter NH.
    John Taylor was a graduate of Harvard College 1721,
and took a master's degree there. He was ordained minister at Milton in 1728. The will of John Taylor of Milton,
clerk, dated 11 Oct. 1748 probated 23 Feb. 1749, names
wife Dorothy, and five children: John, Ann, Nathaniel,
William and Dorothy Taylor; executor, wife Dorothy. An
account of Dorothy Gilman, executrix of her former husband
the Rev. Mr. John Taylor late of Milton, 12 Nov. 1751, re-
mitted money in favor of her children: Nathaniel, William,
Anne and Dorothy.

    Children (TAYLOR) b. Milton to John and Elizabeth: JOHN[6] b.
1731, d. bef. 1751; ANN b. 1732, prob. d. bef. 1747; NATHANIEL b.
1734; and WILLIAM b. 1735.

Children (TAYLOR) bp. Milton to John and Dorothy: DOROTHY bp.
1747; ANN bp. 1747; and EDWARD bp. 1747, d.y.

References: MD 1:89-90; 21:121. HARVARD GRADS 6:569-71. VR MILTON.
           Suffolk Co. PR 43:364; 45:501(John Taylor). MILTON HIST
pp. 254-7, 477. GILMAN FAM p. 224.

142   ELIZABETH TAYLOR[5]   (Ann Winslow[4], Edward[3], Mary[2]
Chilton, James[1]) b. Jamaica, West Indies 8 Nov. 1712; d.
5 June 1793 ae 80y 7m.
      She m. (1) Boston 27 June 1729 NATHANIEL GREENE, b.
Boston 14 May 1709; d. Surinam, South America 4 Jan.
1737/8 ae 28y 4m; son of Nathaniel and Ann (Gold) Greene.
      In Jan. 1742 guardians were appointed for children of
Nathaniel Green late of Boston merchant deceased: Nathan-
iel Green aged about 11, and John Green aged about six.
      She m. (2) 2 July 1759(?) PETER COFFIN, b. Exeter NH
9 Dec. 1713; d. there 13 Dec. 1777 ae 64; son of Eliphalet
and Judith (Coffin)(Noyes) Coffin. Peter graduated from
Harvard College in 1733, and was ordained minister at E.
Kingston NH 14 Nov. 1739, where he remained until 1772.
He m. (1) 1739/40 Dorothy Gookin by whom he had Peter,
Eliphalet, Dorothy, Judith and Nathaniel. The Rev. Peter
and Elizabeth had no children.

      Children (GREENE) b. to Nathaniel and Elizabeth: NATHANIEL[6] b.
and d. 1730; ANN b. Boston 1731, d. 1733; NATHANIEL b. Boston 1733,
d. Boston 1773; ELIZABETH b. Boston 1734, d. 1735; and JOHN b. Para-
maribo, Surinam 1736.

References: MD 32:145-7. BOSTON VR 24:61, 202, 212, 217; 28:149.
           BOSTON NEWS OBITS 2:228, 456. GREENE FAM pp. 94, 149.
NEHGR 24:310. HARVARD GRADS 9:288-91. Suffolk Co. PR 36:256(gdns. of
Nathl. & John Green).

143   WILLIAM TAYLOR[5]   (Ann Winslow[4], Edward[3], Mary[2] Chilton, James[1]) b. Jamaica, West Indies 18 May 1714; d. Milton 16 Feb. 1789 ae 75.
      He m. (1) Boston 19 Feb. 1735 FAITH WINSLOW, b. Marsh-
field 2 Feb. 1712; d. by 1765; dau. of Kenelm and Abigail
(Waterman) Winslow, and a descendant of Pilgrim Richard
Warren.
      He m. (2) Boston 22 Oct. 1765 SARAH (CHEEVER) SAVAGE,
d. Milton 5 or 6 Dec. 1812 ae 86 "widow of Col. William";
dau. of Ezekiel and Elizabeth (Jenner) Cheever of Charlestown, and widow of Thomas Savage. Administration of the
estate of Ezekiel Cheever Esq. late of Charlestown deceased was granted in 1770. A settlement of the estate
was made on son David Cheever, who was to pay an amount to
sister Sarah; William Taylor signed an assent 10 Sept. 1771.

William was a Loyalist. He went to Halifax NS 1776
and was proscribed and banished 1778. The will of William
Taylor Esq. of Milton, dated 18 Dec. 1776, mentions late
son John, dau. Abigail, sons Joseph, William and Thomas,
and son-in-law Jonathan Amory; executors, wife Sarah, son
Joseph and Jonathan Amory. A codicil 29 June 1788 indicates that son John had received his share, and that son
Joseph may be esteemed an alien. The estate was probated
14 April 1789. On 17 Oct. 1814 Thomas Taylor, a trader of
Boston, sought appointment of an administrator to replace
William Taylor who died in 1809 without settling the estate of his father, William Taylor.

Children (TAYLOR) b. Boston to William and Faith: WILLIAM[6] b.
1736, prob. d.y.; JOHN b. 1738; ABIGAIL b. 1739; ELIZABETH b. 1741,
d. 1743; WINSLOW b. 1743; JOSEPH b. 1745; and JOSHUA b. 1748, d. 1748.

Children (TAYLOR) b. Milton to William and Sarah: WILLIAM b.
1766; and THOMAS b. 1768.

References: MILTON VR pp. 61, 178, 247. MARSHFIELD VR p. 41. BOS-
         TON VR 24:227, 235, 238, 244, 250, 258, 268, 313; 28:194;
30:328. (BOSTON) KINGS CHAPEL p. 181. Suffolk Co. PR 88:145; 112:551
(William Taylor). CHARLESTOWN BY WYMAN 1:209; 2:847. MILTON HIST pp.
254-5. Middlesex Co. PR #4319(Ezekiel Cheever). WATERMAN GEN 1:61-2.
MA OBITS 5:4411-2. WINSLOW MEM 1:209.

144 REBECCA TAYLOR[5] (Ann Winslow[4], Edward[3], Mary[2] Chilton, James[1]) b. Jamaica 25 Feb. 1715; d. prob. Durham NH
ca. 1757.
    She m. bef. 1743 Rev. MOSES EMERSON, b. Haverhill 22
Dec. 1717; d. Philadelphia PA 14 May 1779; son of Jonathan
and Hannah (Day) Emerson. He m. (2) int. Ipswich 1761
Abigail Burnham, by whom he had son Jeremiah. He m. (3)
Lydia Burnham of Durham NH.
    Moses graduated from Harvard College 1737, and took a
second degree in 1740. He taught school at Milton start-
ing in 1738. In 1746 he went to Haverhill; about 1750 to
Dover NH; in 1755 to Albany NY as a commissary, returning
to Durham NH in 1757. By 1770 Moses was in Hopkinton NH.
He was commissioner of accounts ca. 1776 at Hartford CT
when called by Congress to Philadelphia.

Children (EMERSON) b. to Moses and Rebecca: MOSES[6] bp. Marshfield 1743, d.y.; MOSES bp. Milton 1746, d. Haverhill 1748; ANNE bp.
Haverhill 1749, prob. d.y.; and EDWARD WINSLOW b. Durham NH 1755 (he
named a son John Taylor Emerson!).

References: VR HAVERHILL. MD 32:19. EMERSON GEN 1:44-5, 76; 2:17.
         DURHAM NH HIST 2:188. HARVARD GRADS 10:166-8. DOVER NH
VR pp. 158, 211.

145 TOBIAS PAYNE[5] (William[4], Sarah Winslow[3], Mary[2]
Chilton, James[1]) b. Boston 25 June 1697; d. Virgin Is-
lands either 1730 or 1733.
     He m. Marshfield 14 Oct. 1728 SARAH WINSLOW, b.
Marshfield 3 Dec. 1704; d. 8 Feb. 1770; dau. of Kenelm
and Abigail (Waterman) Winslow, and a descendant of Pilgrim Richard Warren. She m. (2) Boston 1737 Samuel Smith
of Eastham.
     Tobias, while sailing with his uncle Christopher Tay-
lor, was captured by pirates; he subsequently escaped and
lived in Barbados where he was master of a sloop. He returned to Boston where he was married, and was a ship
captain until his decease. Mary Payne, "only child of
Tobias Payne late of Boston deceased," was under guardianship of Kenelm Winslow Jr. in a deed dated 23 Sept. 1747.

     Child (PAYNE): MARY[6] b. ca. 1729.

References: MARSHFIELD VR pp. 26, 146. PAYNE & GORE FAM p. 17. BOS-
          TON VR 28:165, 228; 30:305. WATERMAN GEN 1:61. Suffolk
Co. LR 74:221(John Payne et al.).

146 MARY PAYNE[5] (William[4], Sarah Winslow[3], Mary[2] Chilton, James[1]) b. Boston 6 Jan. 1700/1; living there 19
Oct. 1747.
     She m. Boston 8 Oct. 1724 JONATHAN SEWALL, b. Salem
7 Feb. 1692/3; d. Nov. 1731; son of Stephen and Margaret
(Mitchell) Sewall. He prob. m. (1) Boston 1718 Elizabeth
Alford, by whom he had daus. Elizabeth and Mary. Jonathan
was a merchant.
     Samuel Sewall of Boston was appointed 13 Dec. 1731
administrator of the estate of his brother Jonathan Sewall
late of Boston, merchant, in response to a petition by
widow Mary Sewall. In Dec. 1742 widow Mary Sewall of Boston was appointed guardian to her children, the children
of Jonathan Sewall deceased: Margaret about 16, Jonathan
about 13, and Jane about 11.
     Mary Sewall of Boston widow, a daughter of William
Payne late of Boston gentleman and his wife Mary both deceased, quitclaimed rights to her brother Edward Payne 19
Oct. 1747.

     Children (SEWALL) b. to Jonathan and Mary, first recorded Boston:
MARGARET[6] b. 1725; JONATHAN b. 1728; and JANE b. 1731.

References: PAYNE & GORE FAM pp. 17-8[too many Margarets and Jona-
          thans appear allotted]. BOSTON VR 24:147, 162, 173; 28:
78, 122. VR SALEM. Suffolk Co. LR 74:122(Mary Sewall). Suffolk Co.
PR #6339 and 16:548(new) and 29:313(Jonathan Sewall); 36:217-8(gdn.
Mary Sewall).

147   SARAH PAYNE[5] (William[4], Sarah Winslow[3], Mary[2] Chilton, James[1]) b. Boston 15 June 1704; living 1744.

She m. Boston 26 Dec. 1734 JOHN COLMAN (or Coleman), b. Boston 2 March 1703; d. there 25 March 1771; son of John and Judith (Hobbey) Colman. John was a brewer.

The will of the Rev. Benjamin Colman, dated 25 March presented 5 Sept. 1747, bequeathed to John and Benjamin Colman, who were grandchildren of his brother John Colman and sons of his nephew John Colman. On 2 Jan. 1756 John Colman, a minor aged 18, selected Richard Tripe as guardian for such portion as accrued to him in the right of his uncle, Benjamin Colman late of Boston. On 20 Jan. 1756 Benjamin Colman, aged over 14 and son of John Colman of Boston, selected his uncle Edward Payne of Gloucester as guardian of what accrued from the will of the Rev. Dr. Benjamin Colman late of Boston.

Children (COLMAN) second and fourth recorded Boston: SARAH[6] b. 1736; JOHN b. 1737/8; WILLIAM b. 1739, d.y.; BENJAMIN b. 1740; and WILLIAM b. 1744.

References: BOSTON VR 9:217; 24:20, 228, 239; 28:182. PAYNE & GORE FAM p. 18. BOSTON NEWS OBITS 1:67. Suffolk Co. PR 40:150-1(Rev. Benjamin Colman); 50:734(John Colman); 51:51(Benjamin Colman).

148   EDWARD PAYNE[5] (William[4], Sarah Winslow[3], Mary[2] Chilton, James[1]) b. Boston 4 Feb. 1721/2; d. there 5 March 1788 ae 67.

He m. int. Boston 28 Sept. 1756 REBECCA AMORY of Boston, b. 25 June 1725; d. Boston 14 Feb. 1799 ae 74; dau. of Thomas and Rebecca (Holmes) Amory.

Edward moved to Gloucester in 1752 and remained there for nine years before returning to Boston. The will of Edward Payne of Boston, merchant, dated 15 Feb. 1787 probated 11 March 1788, names wife Rebecca, daughters Mary and Sarah Payne, son William Payne, daughter Rebecca Gore, and sister Jane Payne; wife and son William to be executors.

Children (PAYNE) all recorded Boston, first three b. Gloucester: twins MARY[6] and SARAH b. 1757; REBECCA b. 1759; WILLIAM b. 1762; and EDWARD b. 1765, d. 1765.

References: PAYNE & GORE FAM pp. 19-21. BOSTON VR 24:168, 292, 297, 304; 30:21. NEHGR 10:62-3. BOSTON NEWS OBITS 1:232, 233. MA OBITS 4:3460. VR GLOUCESTER. Suffolk Co. PR 87:134(Edward Payne).

149 SARAH GIBBS[5] (Mary Middlecott[4], Sarah Winslow[3],
Mary[2] Winslow, James[1]) b. Boston 13 Sept. 1696; prob.
bur. St. John Parish, Barbados 19 Oct. 1748.
     She m. St. Michael Parish, Barbados 24 June 1721
ALEXANDER SCOTT, prob. bur. Barbados, either St. Michael
Parish 15 Sept. 1728 or St. John Parish 21 Aug. 1753. She
went to Barbados from Boston in 1719 with her step-father
Othaniel Hagget.

     Children (SCOTT) bp. St. Michael Parish, Barbados: SUSANNA[6] b.
Jan. 1724; SARAH b. Dec. 1724; and JANE b. 1727.

References: PAYNE & GORE FAM pp. 12-4. CARIBBEANA p. 167(will of
     Nathaniel Hagget mentions nieces Sarah and Jane Scott).
Barbados Archives RL 1/2:191(mar.); RL 1/2:314; RL 1/29:34(d. Alexander); RL 1/2:247, 263, 290(bp. and b. children); RL 1/29:32(d. Sarah).

150 OTHANIEL (or Othniel) HAGGET[5] (Mary Middlecott[4],
Sarah Winslow[3], Mary[2] Chilton, James[1]) b. Barbados; bur.
St. Michael Parish, Barbados 27 Nov. 1735 "the Honorable
...Esq."
     He m. RUTH LAMBERT, d. Boston bet. 23 Dec. 1748 and
14 Feb. 1749; dau. of Simon and Susanna (-----) Lambert
(Othniel's step-mother's daughter). She m. (2) St.
Michael Parish, Barbados 1744 the Rev. Dudley Woodbridge.
     Othaniel went to England in 1717 "to be brought up in
University there"; he returned to Barbados where he mar-
ried, had a child and died. He was a judge. The will of
"the Honble" Othniel Haggatt Esq. of the Parish of St.
Michael, dated 20 Nov. 1734 probated 6 Dec. 1735, mentions
wife Ruth; an estate which lately was Simon Lambert's; dau.
Susannah, under 21; brothers Nathaniel and William (brother
Nathaniel to pay testator's wife the legacy left by her
father Simon Lambert deceased); sister Mary Haggatt; his
mother Susannah Haggatt. A codicil dated 26 Nov. 1735 indicates dau. Susannah had died.

     Child (HAGGET) b. and bp. St. Michael Parish, Barbados: SUSANNA[6]
bp. 1732, bur. 1735.

References: PAYNE & GORE FAM p. 14. CARIBBEANA p. 168. Barbados
     Archives RL 1/2:373(bp. Susanna); RL 1/2:409(bur. Sus-
anna); RL 1/2:418(bur. Othniel); RL 1/3:86(m.(2) Ruth); RB 6/24:536
(will of Othniel Haggatt).

151 NATHANIEL HAGGET[5] (Mary Middlecott[4], Sarah Winslow[3],
Mary[2] Chilton, James[1]) b. Barbados; bur. Mitcham, Richmond, Surrey Co., England 17 Oct. 1762.
     He m. Barbados 6 Feb. 1730 JANE LAMBERT, bur. Mitcham
5 May 1755; dau. of Simon and Susanna (-----) Lambert of

Barbados and Bristol, England.

Nathaniel went to Boston in 1718, later to England and Dublin, Ireland for his education. He returned to Barbados and married his step-mother's youngest daughter. On 23 Aug. 1733 Nathaniel Hagget of Barbados "now resident in Boston" appealed to the Massachusetts General Court, stating that he holds a share of lands in Boston in common with others, descendants of Richard Middlecott deceased, several of whom are minors in Barbados.

The will of Susannah Haggatt, made 18 Nov. 1751 proved 13 Jan. 1752, includes her granddau. Susannah Haggat, "daughter of my son-in-law Nathl. Haggatt"; and daughter Jane Haggat, wife of said Nathaniel Haggatt. [This is Susanna (-----) Lambert who m. (2) Othniel Haggatt, widower of Mary (Middlecott) (Gibbs) Haggatt (see #43).]

The will of Nathaniel Haggatt late of Barbados, now of Richmond, Surrey County, England, Esq., dated 17 Jan. 1761 and proved 4 Dec. 1762, names daughter Susannah and her husband Dr. Edward Barnard; nephew William Haggatt and niece Sarah Haggatt, children of his brother Rev. William Haggatt of Barbados deceased; nieces Sarah and Jane Scott; and son William Haggatt, under 21.

Children (HAGGATT) b. Barbados, last three St. Michael Parish: NATHANIEL[6] b. 1736; SUSANNAH b. 1738; SIMON OTHNIEL bp. and bur. 1739; MARY b. 1740, bur. 1742; and WILLIAM b. 1743.

References: PAYNE & GORE FAM p. 14. CARIBBEANA pp. 167-9(includes will Nathaniel). NEHGR 15:308(footnote). MA HOUSE JL 11:269. Barbados Archives RL 1/2:487(bp. Simon); RL 1/3:21(b. Mary); RL 1/3:75(b. William); RL 1/2:487(bur. Simon); RL 1/3:44(bur. Mary); RB 6/25:27(will Susannah Haggatt).

152 WILLIAM HAGGET[5] (Mary Middlecott[4], Sarah Winslow[3], Mary[2] Chilton, James[1]) b. Barbados; bur. St. Michael Parish, Barbados, 3 Oct. 1747.

He m. St. Michael Parish, Barbados, 5 Oct. 1742 SARAH DOTTIN, "spinster." She prob. m. (2) St. John Parish, Barbados, 1750 Col. Richard Rous Estwicke. William went to Boston in 1718, then to England with brother Nathaniel, and later to Dublin, Ireland for his education. He "entered Holy Orders," and after his return to Barbados was "inducted into St. Michael's Parish" 17 April 1742.

The will of William Haggatt[6] of the Parish of St. Andrew, Barbados, made 29 Dec. 1778 proved 11 Nov. 1779, names nephews William Haggatt Mellowes and Benjamin Mellowes; nieces Sarah Haggatt Mellowes and Elizabeth Mellowes; and sisters Sarah Mellowes and Elizabeth Estwick.

Children (HAGGET) b. Barbados to Rev. William and Sarah: WIL-LIAM[6] b. 1743, and SARAH b. 1744.

References: CARIBBEANA pp. 167-70(will of brother Nathaniel names children). PAYNE & GORE FAM p. 14. Barbados Archives RL 1/3:70, 89(b. William and Sarah); RL 1/3:43(mar.); RL 1/28:8(mar. Estwicke); RL 1/3:182(bur. William); RB 6/23:194(will of William Haggatt).

153 EDWARD MIDDLECOTT[5] (Edward[4], Sarah Winslow[3], Mary[2] Chilton, James[1]) b. Warminster, Wiltshire, England bef. 1708; living there 17 March 1728.
    He m. Bishopstrow, England 15 June 1727 ELIZABETH TEMPLE.
    Edward[5] was appointed administrator on the estate of his father Edward Middlecott of Warminster, Wiltshire, England 17 March 1728.

    Prob. child (MIDDLECOTT) b. England: EDWARD[6] b. 1728.

References: P.C.C. Wills and Administrations 1650/1730:1728(Edward Middlecott). "Births and Baptisms of Dissenters' Children," 1720/88. Parish Rec. of Bishopstrow(at Society of Genealogists, London).

154 ANNE BOUCHER[5] (Sarah Middlecott[4], Sarah Winslow[3], Mary[2] Chilton, James[1]) b. Boston 7 April 1703; d. there 31 March 1736.
    She m. Boston 27 Aug. 1722 NATHANIEL CUNNINGHAM of Boston, d. London, England 7 Sept. 1748 "Cap." He m. (2) Boston 1738 Susanna Gerrish, by whom he had no children.
    The will of Nathaniel Cunningham of Boston merchant, dated 1 May 1745 presented 13 Dec. 1748, mentions wife Susanna, and her marriage contract; brother-in-law Charles Paxton; mother Ruth Cunningham; daus. Sarah and Ruth (under 21) each to receive 1/4 of estate; son Nathaniel Cunningham to receive 1/2 estate.

    Children (CUNNINGHAM) b. Boston: NATHANIEL[6] b. 1725; RUTH b. 1729; SARAH b. 1731; and pos. ANN d.y.; and pos. TIMOTHY d.y.

References: PAYNE & GORE FAM p. 14. BOSTON VR 24:169, 191; 28:105. BOSTON NEWS OBITS 1:79; 2:268. Suffolk Co. PR 42:125 (Nathaniel Cunningham).

155 SARAH BOUCHER[5] (Sarah Middlecott[4], Sarah Winslow[3], Mary[2] Chilton, James[1]) b. Boston 6 Oct. 1706; d. Charlestown bef. 2 Dec. 1771 [unnamed] "widow of John."

She m. Boston 23 Oct. 1729 JOHN FOYE, b. Boston 5
Jan. 1705/6; d. Charlestown bet. 10 July 1770 and 16 Dec.
1771; son of John and Sarah (Lynde) Foye.
   The will of John Foye of Charlestown merchant, dated
10 July 1770 presented 16 Dec. 1771, left real estate to
wife Sarah, sons John and Lovis, and dau. Elizabeth Munroe; upon demise or remarriage of wife, her portion to be
divided in four parts among: sons John and Lovis, dau.
Elizabeth, and granddau. Sarah Dizer (the latter receiving
the part which should have belonged to his dau. Ann); a
bequest was left in trust for his dau. Ann, then to her
children; executors, wife and sons John and Lovis, and son
David Munroe. A division was made 6 May 1784 among John
Foye, David Munroe's wife Elizabeth, Francis Dizer's wife
Ann, and Lovis Foye's heirs.

   Children (FOYE) first two b. Boston, rest b. Charlestown:
SARAH[6] b. 1731/2; ANNE b. 1733, d.y.; JOHN b. 1734; ELIZABETH b.
1735; ANNE b. 1737; and LEWIS (or Lovis) b. 1738/9.

References: BOSTON VR 28:149. PAYNE & GORE FAMS p. 15. CHARLESTOWN
          BY WYMAN 1:373. BOSTON NEWS OBITS 2:397. Middlesex Co.
PR #8413(John Foye).

   156₂ SARAH COOKE[5] (Jane Middlecott[4], Sarah Winslow[3],
Mary[2] Chilton, James[1]) b. Boston in April 1711; d. there
11 July 1740.
   She m. Boston 7 Sept. 1732 JOHN PHILLIPS, d. Boston
bet. 17 Oct. 1741 and 12 June 1747. He m. (2) Boston 17
Oct. 1741 Margaret Payne (see #42 xii).
   The will of John Phillips of Boston merchant, dated
22 Sept. 1740 presented 12 June 1747, left several houses
in Boston to his children: eldest son Elisha, sons John,
William and Thomas, and dau. Mary (all under 21). Because his wife was ignored in his will, administrators
were appointed on his intestate estate "with will annexed"
Sept. 1747. In the 1763 account, annuities were to be
paid to Margaret Phillips.

   Children (PHILLIPS) b. Boston to John and Sarah: ELISHA COOKE[6]
b. 1733; JOHN b. 1735; WILLIAM b. 1736; THOMAS b. 1737, d. 1741; and
MARY b. 1739, d. 1741.

References: PAYNE & GORE FAM pp. 13, 15. BOSTON VR 24:213, 223, 226,
          230, 238; 28:179, 257. Suffolk Co. PR 39:630; 40:138;
62:394(John Phillips).

   157₂ MARY COOKE[5] (Jane Middlecott[4], Sarah Winslow[3],
Mary[2] Chilton, James[1]) b. Boston ca. 1723; d. Haverhill
25 Dec. 1804 ae 81.

She m. (1) Boston 3 July 1744 Judge RICHARD SALTON-
STALL, b. Haverhill 14 June 1703; d. there 20 Oct. 1756 in
54th yr; son of Col. Richard and Mehitable (Wainwright)
Saltonstall. He m. (1) Haverhill 1725/6 Abigail Waldron,
by whom he had five children of whom Abigail and Richard
survived youth. He m. (2) Boston 1738 Mary Jekyll.
    Richard graduated from Harvard College in 1722, and
stayed on for a second degree. He was justice of the
peace and a judge of superior court (1736-1755). Toward
the end of his life most of his property went to creditors.
On 10 June 1756 Richard Saltonstall Esq. of Haverhill,
with wife Mary surrendering her dower, deeded homestead
land to Enoch Bartlett trader of Haverhill.
    The will of Richard Saltonstall Esq. of Haverhill,
signed 2 Oct. 1756 sworn 22 Nov. 1756, names Enoch Bartlett both as principal heir and as executor. In 1759 a
mortgage on property of Richard Saltonstall was fore-
closed; at this time Enoch Bartlett stated he had purchased from Mary Harrod, wife of Benjamin Harrod of Boston,
her right of dower.
    She m. (2) int. Boston 3 Nov. 1757 BENJAMIN HARROD,
d. either Haverhill or Newburyport 31 Dec. 1780 ae 65 "of
Boston." He m. (1) int. Boston "in Andover" 1736 Phebe
Stevens of Andover by whom he had Phebe, John, Benjamin,
Susanna, Jonathan, Joseph, James and Phebe between 1737
and 1755. No children were found of Benjamin and Mary.
    Administration was granted to Benjamin Harrod, mer-
chant of Newburyport, 10 March 1781 on the estate of Benjamin Harrod, yeoman of Haverhill deceased.
    On 25 Oct. 1790 Mary Harrod of Haverhill widow sold
to her son Nathaniel Saltonstall of Haverhill, physician,
and to her son-in-law Moses Badger of Providence RI, clerk,
and to her daughter Mary Badger, his wife, 1/3 of a house
and barn in Boston, which was the property of her son
Leverett Saltonstall of Boston, who died after his father,
unmarried and intestate--the 2/3 descended to Mary, Nathaniel and Mary Badger as his only surviving heirs.
    Administration of the estate of Mary Harrod of Haver-
hill widow deceased was granted 5 Aug. 1805. Heirs included Richard Badger, Nathaniel Badger and George Badger.
A surety on the bond was Nathaniel Saltonstall Esq. of
Haverhill.

    Children (SALTONSTALL) b. Haverhill to Richard and Mary:
NATHANIEL[6] b. 1746; MARY b. 1749; MIDDLECOTT COOKE b. and d. 1752; and
LEVERETT b. 1754, d. unm.

References: VR ANDOVER, HAVERHILL, NEWBURYPORT. BOSTON NEWS OBITS
          3:337. MA OBITS 2:491; 3:2098. BOSTON MEM HIST 1:579,
582; 2:549. WATERTOWN BY BOND pp. 923, 927-8. BOSTON VR 24:229, 233,
243, 250, 256, 263, 277, 287; 28:230, 278, 330; 30:26, 224. HARVARD
GRADS 7:117-21. BOSTON REC COM 20:33, 133, 198. MA HIST COLL
80:69-81, 99, 551(Saltonstall Papers). Essex Co. PR #24543(Richard

Saltonstall); #12568(Benjamin Harrod); #12569(Benjamin Harrod); #12571
(Mary Harrod). Essex Co. LR 103:71, 75(Richard Saltonstall); 105:253
(Enoch Bartlett); 119:246(Enoch Bartlett and Samuel Winthrop). Suf-
folk Co. LR 89:108(Richard Saltonstall); 168:205(Mary Harrod); 91:7
(prenuptial agreement bet. Benjamin Harrod, Mary Saltonstall and
James Otis).

158 ROBERT CRANNELL[5] (Mary Winslow[4], Joseph[3], Mary[2]
Chilton, James[1]) b. prob. New York City 1696; d. 1740,
bur. Trinity Churchyard, New York City.
     He m. CATHERINE -----, bur. Trinity Churchyard.
Robert Crannell Jr. was a sheriff in New York in 1725. No
estate has been located, but a tombstone record was uncovered: "Here lies the body of Robert Crannell also
Catherine wife of Robert Crannell deceased Jany. 26th 1781
aged 65* years, and Thomas son of Thomas and Gartruyd
Fisher, grand Son of Robt. and Cath. Crannell."

     Children (CRANNELL) b. New York City: GARTRUYD[6], and BARTHOLO-
MEW b. ca. 1721.

References: [see References accompanying #47] DUTCHESS CO NY HIST
             SOC YRBK 37:58, 85. (NY) ABSTRACTS OF WILLS 3(Liber 12):
144. MIN COUNCIL NY 4:499. "Calendar of NY" Mss. by English 67:79
(NYGB Soc.). "Tombstones, Trinity Churchyard" Mss. (vault, NYGB Soc.).

159 WILLIAM CRANNELL[5] (Mary Winslow[4], Joseph[3], Mary[2]
Chilton, James[1]) b. prob. New York City ca. 1703; d.
Albany NY 7 Jan. 1757.
     He m. Albany 4 or 11 June 1726 MARGARITA BENNOIT (or
Margaret Bennewe), bp. Albany 16 Aug. 1702; d. there 22
Oct. 1758; dau. of Pierre and Henderkie (Van Schoonhoven)
Bennoit (or Benneway). In 1717 William was apprenticed
for seven years, from which it may be assumed he was then
fourteen years old.

     Children (CRANNELL) bp. Albany NY: ROBERT[6] bp. 1726; PETRUS bp.
1728, d.y.; PETRUS bp. 1732; WILLIAM WINSLOW bp. 1738/9; pos. HENRY;
pos. JOHN b. ca. 1735; and pos daughters.

References: [see all References accompanying #47] NYGBR 4:117. AM
             ANC p. 19. HOLLAND SOC YRBK 1906 pp. ?, 22. ALBANY NY
SETTLERS pp. 18, 34-5. ALBANY NY HIST 4:97, 110. DAR PATRIOT INDEX
p. 162 [says William b. 1749].

160 SAMUEL WINSLOW[5] (Joseph[4-3], Mary[2] Chilton, James[1])
prob. b. ca. 1725.
     He m. bef. May 1752 HANNAH ----- (deed). Is he the
Samuel Winslow living in Amenia, Dutchess Co.,NY in 1790,

---

*If this age is correct, Robert must have had an earlier wife, mother
of Bartholomew.

two males 16 and over, one male under 16, and three females?

Child (WINSLOW) bp. Rumbout, Dutchess Co. NY: JOHN[6] bp. 1752.

References: NYGBR 68:292. 1790 CENSUS: NY p. 72.

161 SARAH WINSLOW[5] (Joseph[4-3], Mary[2] Chilton, James[1])
b. ca. 1725-30; d. by 1764.
    She m. Rumbout, Dutchess Co. NY 28 Jan 1755 DANIEL
CUNNINGHAM, said to be b. Ireland. He m. (2) Rumbout (?)
1764 Abigail Richmond.

Children (CUNNINGHAM) b. to Daniel and Sarah: CHARLES[6] b. Beek-
man, Dutchess Co.,1757; and PATIENCE.

References: NYGBR 69:286, 380. BULL FAM 5:77 on. Rev. Pension
           #S12661 (Chas. Cunningham). PIONEER LIFE p. 659.

162 MARY FOSTER[5] (Parnell Winslow[4], Isaac[3], Mary[2] Chilton, James[1]) b. Charlestown 16 Feb. 1691/2; d. there 23
Dec. 1718 ae 26y 10m.
    She m. Charlestown 9 Dec. 1712 Capt. SAMUEL CARY (or
Carey), b. Charlestown 18 (1mo) 1683; d. there 28 Feb.
1740/1 ae ca. 58; son of Jonathan Cary. He m. (2) Boston
1722/3 Mary Martin, by whom he had eight children.
    The will of Samuel Cary of Charlestown Esq., dated 18
Feb. 1739 presented 16 March 1740/1, names wife Mary; son
Samuel (house in Boston); son Richard (given the "workt bed
which my late wife his mother workt"); son Nathaniel; son
Edward under 21; dau. Sarah Cary under 18; dau. Mary Cary
under 18; dau. Hannah Cary under 18; dau. Abigail Cary under 18; executors: wife, son Richard, brother-in-law Jacob
Hollyoke.

Children (CARY) b. Charlestown to Samuel and Mary (Foster):
SAMUEL[6] b. 1713; RICHARD b. 1716/7; and JONATHAN bp. 1718, d. 1718/9.

References: CHARLESTOWN BY WYMAN p. 179. BOSTON VR 28:105. Middle-
           sex Co. PR #4072(Samuel Cary). FOSTER GEN p. 503.

163 RICHARD FOSTER[5] (Parnell Winslow[4], Isaac[3], Mary[2]
Chilton, James[1]) b. Charlestown 23 March 1693/4; d. there
29 Aug. 1774 ae 82.
    He m. (1) SARAH EMERSON, b. Charlestown 7 Aug. 1695;
d. there 16 Nov. 1724 ae 29; dau. of John and Sarah (Carter) Emerson.
    He m. (2) Charlestown 21 Oct. 1725 MARY FOYE, b.
Charlestown 9 April 1704; d. there 26 Oct. 1774 ae 72;

dau. of Capt. John and Sarah (Lynde) Foye. Richard was
justice of the Court of Common Pleas.

Heirs of Richard Foster Esq. and those who were heirs
of Mrs. Mary Foster his late relict agreed to an audit 3
Nov. 1779: Samuel, in behalf of his mother Mrs. Sarah
Bradstreet; Eben. Breed in behalf of his mother Mrs. Mary
White; Richard Boyleston, John Austin Jr., John Sprague,
Isaac Codman for himself and for Margaret Foster, John
Sprague also for Mary Cheever.

Heirs to the widow's thirds 15 March 1781 were Richard and Parnel Boyleston, Margaret Foster, John and Ann
Austin, John and Katherine Sprague, Isaac and Abigail Codman, Ephraim Hall Jr. and wife Mary.

Children (FOSTER) b. Charlestown to Richard and Sarah: SARAH[6]
bp. 1718; RICHARD b. 1720, d. 1721/2; MARY bp. 1722; and KATHARINE b.
1724, d. ae 5 mo.

Children (FOSTER) b. Charlestown to Richard and Mary: ELIZABETH
b. 1726; RICHARD b. 1727/8; PARNELL b. 1729; HANNAH b. 1730/1; WIL-
LIAM b. 1732; MARGARET b. 1734; ANN b. 1736; KATHARINE bp. 1737/8;
ABIGAIL bp. 1738/9; JOHN bp. 1741; and MARTHA bp. 1742.

References: CHARLESTOWN BY WYMAN p. 363. Middlesex Co. PR #8252
(Richard Foster). FOSTER GEN 2:516-20. NEHGR 25:69-70.

164 PARNELL FOSTER[5] (Parnell Winslow[4], Isaac[3], Mary[2]
Chilton, James[1]) b. Charlestown 25 Aug. 1696; d. there 15
Sept. 1752 ae 56.

She m. Charlestown 1718 Capt. JOHN CODMAN, b. 29 Sept.
1696; d. Charlestown 30 June 1755; son of Stephen and
Elizabeth (Randall) Codman.

He was a sea captain. On 18 Aug. 1755 John Codman
gentleman of Charlestown was bonded as administrator of
the estate of Mr. John Codman late of Charlestown deceased.
The inventory 13 Aug. 1755 included land in Bridgewater.

Richard Codman of Falmouth, Cumberland county [now
ME] merchant; Joshua Moody of Falmouth merchant and wife
Mary, formerly Mary Codman, a dau. and heir of John Codman
of Charlestown, Middlesex county merchant deceased; John
Butler of Falmouth and wife Ann, another dau. of said John
Codman deceased; Benjamin Codman of Charlestown, now in
the island of Jamaica merchant; Isaac Codman of Charlestown mariner son of said John deceased; and Parnel Codman,
Elizabeth Codman and Katharine Codman all of Charlestown,
spinsters and daus. of said John Codman deceased, appointed their brother Mr. John Codman of Charlestown merchant
as their attorney for the sale of land in Bridgewater 6
Sept. 1764. On 22 May 1771 John Codman of Charlestown for
himself, and as attorney for Richard Codman of Falmouth
[ME], Parnel Codman of Haverhill, Catherine Codman of

of Charlestown, Joshua and Mary Moody of Falmouth, Isaac
Codman of Charlestown, Elizabeth Codman of Charlestown,
and John Butler and wife Ann of Falmouth sold land in
Bridgewater.[Benjamin's name was absent.]

Children (CODMAN) b. Charlestown: JOHN[6] b. 1719/20; STEPHEN b.
1721; PARNEL b. 1723; ELIZABETH b. 1724; MARY b. 1726; RICHARD b.
1729; BENJAMIN b. 1730/1; ANN b. 1732; BENJAMIN bp. 1735; ISAAC bp.
1737; and KATHARINE b. 1739.

References: CHARLESTOWN BY WYMAN p. 224. Middlesex Co. PR #4727
            (John Codman). BOSTON NEWS OBITS 2:225. FOSTER GEN p.
504. Plymouth Co. LR 81:127-8(Richard Codman et al.).

165 ANNE FOSTER[5] (Parnell Winslow[4], Isaac[3], Mary[2] Chilton, James[1]) b. Charlestown 8 Nov. 1699; d. W. Bridgewater 7 July 1750 in 51 yr.
    She m. Walpole 6 Nov. 1721 Rev. DANIEL PERKINS, b.
Topsfield 15 June 1697; d. W. Bridgewater 29 Sept. 1782;
son of Tobias (or Tobijah) and Sarah (Denison) Perkins.
He m. (2) by 1752 Mary (Hawke) (Thaxter) Hancock, mother
of Gov. John Hancock, by whom he had stillborn twins.
    Daniel graduated from Harvard College in 1717, and
received his master's degree in 1720. He was ordained 4
Oct. 1721 at the old church in Bridgewater (now W. Bridgewater).
    The will of Daniel Perkins of Bridgewater clerk,
dated 22 July 1768 presented 7 May 1783 by the executor
Richard Perkins, names wife Mary, dau. Anne Bridge, and
only son Richard Perkins.

Children (PERKINS) b. Bridgewater to Daniel and Anne: DANIEL[6]
b. 1722, d. 1726; ANNE b. 1724; SARAH b. 1725/6, d. 1745; DANIEL b.
1727, d. 1745; RICHARD b. 1729; and WILLIAM b. 1731/2, d. 1745/6.

References: VR BRIDGEWATER, W. BRIDGEWATER, TOPSFIELD. MD 15:88.
            HARVARD GRADS 6:208-11, 317-9. CHARLESTOWN BY WYMAN
1:362; 2:738. BRIDGEWATER BY MITCHELL p. 279. FOSTER GEN 2:504.
HINGHAM HIST 2:294-5; 3:232. Plymouth Co. PR 29:6-7(Daniel Perkins).

166 SARAH FOSTER[5] (Parnell Winslow[4], Isaac[3], Mary[2]
Chilton, James[1]) b. Charlestown 16 Nov. 1701; d. there
bet. 3 Nov. 1735 and 19 May 1736.
    She m. Charlestown 19 July 1723 PETER CALEF, b. ca.
1700; d. Charlestown 11 Oct. 1735 in 36 yr.; prob. son of
Robert and Margaret (-----) Calef.
    Sarah Calef widow of Charlestown on 3 Nov. 1735 was
appointed administrator on the estate of Peter Calef physician late of Charlestown deceased. On 19 May 1736 Richard Foster and Joseph Calef were appointed administrators

on the unadministered estate of Peter Calef, his widow
Sarah having deceased. Guardians were appointed as follows: Joseph Calef (in 15 yr.) chose Richard Foster in
1738; Sarah Calef (about 15) chose her uncle John Codman
in 1741; and also in 1741 John Codman was appointed guardian of Peter Calef (in 13 yr.), Mary (about 8) and Parnel
(about 6), all children of Peter Calef deceased.

The will of Sarah Calef of Charlestown spinster,
dated 31 May 1748 sworn 27 May 1749, mentions her father,
Dr. Peter Calef late of Charlestown, and her two sisters
Mary and Parnel Calef.

In a distribution dated 1750 Joseph, the eldest son,
was to pay heirs of his sister Sarah, and then pay his
sister Mary; Parnel was to pay Mary, and then to pay heirs
of her brother Peter. On 26 Nov. 1750 there was an agreement of division among Joseph Calef, Mary Calef and Parnel
Calef.

Children (CALEF) b. Charlestown: JOSEPH bp. 1724; SARAH bp.
1726/7, d. 1749 unm; MARY b. 1728, d.y.; PETER b. 1729, d. 1749; MARY
b. 1732; PARNEL b. 1733, d.y.; and PARNEL [dau.] b. 1734.

References: CHARLESTOWN BY WYMAN 1:166, 362. Middlesex Co. PR #3874
            (Peter Calef); #3875(gdns.); #3877(Sarah Calef). BOSTON
NEWS OBITS 2:173. FOSTER GEN p. 504.

167 ISAAC FOSTER[5] (Parnell Winslow[4], Isaac[3], Mary[2]
Chilton, James[1]) b. Charlestown 3 Jan. 1703/4; d. there
27 Dec. 1780/1.

He m. Charlestown 24 Aug. 1732 ELEANOR WYER, b.
Charlestown 14 July 1714; d. there 5 March 1798 ae 84;
dau. of William and Eleanor (Jenner) Wyer. The will of
William Wyer of Charlestown Esq., dated 15 Jan. 1747 probated 20 Feb. 1748/9, mentions daughter Eleanor Foster and
grandson William Foster. Receipts dated 29 March 1751
were signed by Isaac Foster of Charlestown "marriner" and
wife Eleanor for Eleanor, and by Isaac Foster for all William Wyer's Foster grandchildren who were alive at William's decease and are still alive: William Foster, Isaac
Foster and Eleanor Foster.

The will of Isaac Foster merchant of Charlestown,
dated 26 April 1775 proved 11 March 1783 in Boston, left
all estate to wife Eleanor; after her decease to be equally divided between his two children, Isaac and Eleanor.
"Ellener Foster" of Boston, widow of Isaac late of Boston
merchant deceased, as authorized in his will sold land in
Charlestown in 1783, and again in 1787.

Children (FOSTER) b. Charlestown: WILLIAM[6] b. 1733, d. 1759;
ISAAC bp. 1738, d.y.; ISAAC b. 1740; THOMAS bp. 1741, d.y.; EDWARD bp.
1744, d.y.; ELEANOR b. 1746; and RICHARD bp. 1748, d.y.

References: CHARLESTOWN BY WYMAN 1:363-4; 2:1054. NEHGR 25:70; 84:
            150. BOSTON NEWS OBITS 2:391. FOSTER GEN 2:520-1. Mid-
dlesex Co. LR 85:144; 96:376(Ellener Foster). Middlesex Co. PR #25799
(Wm. Wyer). Suffolk Co. PR 82:472(Isaac Foster).

168 ELIZABETH FOSTER[5] (Parnell Winslow[4], Isaac[3], Mary[2]
Chilton, James[1]) b. Charlestown 21 Aug. 1706; d. there 20
Oct. 1766 in 62 yr.
    She m. TIMOTHY McDANIEL, d. Charlestown 10 Nov. 1766
in 62 yr. [Gravestone erected by "sons Timothy, Isaac and
Jacob."] A Timothy McDaniel was captain of the ship *Mary*
during a trip from London to Boston in 1739. On 30 Oct.
1766 the selectmen of Boston found Capt. Timothy McDaniel
to be non-compos.
    The will of Timothy McDaniel of Boston, master mari-
ner, dated 6 April 1765, names wife Elizabeth and three
sons: Timothy, Isaac and Jacob; wife, son Timothy and a
friend Mr. Thomas McCarthy, executors.
    Timothy McDaniel[6] of Boston mariner and Jacob McDaniel
of Boston merchant, sons of Capt. Timothy McDaniel late of
Boston mariner deceased, sold rights to dwelling and land
in Boston to their brother Isaac McDaniel of Boston mariner
on 26 Feb. 1767.

    Children (McDANIEL) b. Charlestown: ISAAC[6] bp. 1734/5 ae 7 or 9
mos., d.y.; ISAAC b. 1735; JACOB; TIMOTHY bp. 1739; and MARY b. 1741.

References: CHARLESTOWN BY WYMAN 1:362; 2:642-3. BOSTON REC COM 15:
            218-9; 20:235. FOSTER GEN 2:504. Suffolk Co. PR 65:426
(Timothy McDaniel). Suffolk Co. LR 110:30(Timothy McDaniel et al.).

R I C H A R D   M O R E

of the

M A Y F L O W E R

Compiled by

Robert Sidney Wakefield, F.A.S.G.

and

Lydia Ropes Dow Finlay, C.A.L.S.

Robert Sidney Wakefield is a descendant of Pilgrims Stephen Hopkins and John Howland. He is a member of the California Mayflower Society. He supervises a large staff of computer programmers for the Southern Pacific Transportation Company at San Francisco. A Fellow of the American Society of Genealogists, he is known for articles on Massachusetts and Rhode Island families, and has already done extensive research on another Mayflower Family--that of Peter Brown. He is responsible for the primary source research for the More family.

Lydia Ropes Dow Finlay is a descendant of Pilgrim Richard More. Widow of Christopher A. Finlay, she and two daughters are members of the Massachusetts Mayflower Society. Mrs. Finlay is the head administrative clerk in the Salem Massachusetts District Court. A Certified American Lineage Specialist, she is author of the *History of the First District Court of Essex*, published in 1977 in connection with the dedication of the new courthouse. She is responsible principally for research into published sources for the More family.

RICHARD MORE

Richard More was baptized 13 November 1614 in Shipton
Parish, Shropshire, England. His mother, Catherine (More)
More, could claim descent from Kings Malcolm III and David
I of Scotland, and in all probability from Edward I of
England as well. Catherine, 23 year old heiress to Larden
Hall, had married in 1610 her 16 year old third cousin,
Samuel More of Linley--a marriage apparently arranged to
keep property in the family, but destined for neither hap-
piness nor permanence.

Catherine gave birth to four children who were baptized in Shipton as children of Samuel More: Elinor in
1612, Jasper in 1613, Richard in 1614, and Mary in 1616.
Subsequent divorce proceedings, however, cast doubt upon
their paternity. Mistreated and rejected by their mother,
the four children became the concern of Samuel. He first
arranged to board them with his father's tenants, but
eventually in July 1620 entrusted them to Thomas Weston,
Robert Cushman and John Carver, making provision for
transportation of the four to the New World, and including
payment for their passage, food and clothing, as well as
arrangements for each ultimately to receive 50 acres of
land. He wrote that he

"upon good and deliberate advise hath thought fitt...to provide
for the educac̄on & maintenance of these children in a place remote
from these partes where these great blotts and blemishes may fall upon
them and therefore tooke the opportunity of sendinge them when such
yonge ones as they went over wth honest and religious people."

Thus it transpired that the *Mayflower* passengers included four young Mores: Jasper assigned to John Carver,
Ellen to Edward Winslow, Richard and undoubtedly Mary (although Bradford called her a brother) to William Brewster.
In his list of passengers under "Mr. William Brewster,"
Bradford wrote "and a boy put to him called Richard More,
and another of his brothers." Only young Richard survived
that dreadful first winter; in the cattle division of 1627
he was still with the Brewsters. So, far from being a
poor waif from the streets of London, as several writers
have claimed, Richard More was the offspring of landed
gentry with assured royal ancestry.

It is possible that sometime after 1627 Richard More
returned to England. At least among the passengers listed
for departure from London, England, in June or July 1635
on the ship *Blessing* bound for Boston was "Richd. More,"
age 20. On this same ship were Richard Hollingsworth and
his family of twelve which included Christian Hunter, age

20, destined within little more than a year to be the
bride of Richard More.

Richard More married Christian Hunt(er) in Plymouth
on 20 October 1636. The couple did not stay in Plymouth
Colony, for on 1 November 1637 Richard sold his house and
land in Duxbury, and was granted half an acre of land in
Salem on 1:11mo[January]:1637/8. Here he apparently settled down--at least as nearly as can a mariner and ship-
captain, who sailed to England and the West Indies.

The week from 27 February to 6 March 1642/3 was a
busy one for Richard More: He joined the First Church in
Salem on 27 February, became a freeman next day, and had
two sons baptized on 6 March. In early Puritan New England church membership was required to become a freeman,
and generally one parent, at least, must be a member before children might be baptized. Writing in 1650 of the
Pilgrim Company's "decreasings and increasings," Bradford
noted "Richard More, his Brother dyed the first winter;
but he is married, and hath 4 or 5 children, all living."

In 1653 Captain Richard More was paid for "ye Dutch
expedition." He was at Port Royal, Nova Scotia, when the
French fort "was reduced to English Obedience" in 1654,
and from thence a bell was later brought to Salem "in
Capt. Moor's Ketch." In Virginia about 1662 he "bought
Mary, now wife of Gyels Cory out of a London ship" (as deposed by his son Caleb in 1678); and he was there again in
1668 when appointed guardian of William Henfield of Salem,
mariner, son of Capt. Robert Henfield deceased.

He was not forgotten by the Pilgrim company at Plymouth. He was included with the "Ancient Freemen" in receiving land granted by the General Court and purchased
from the Indians, and thus obtained lots in Sepecan [Roch-
ester], in 1660 near the "Falls" [Fall River], and was
"one of the first purchasers of the Freemen's lots" in
Swansea. He sold land at Mattapoiset "he of Massachusetts
Colony" on 1 March 1667/8; and "formerly of Plymouth now
of Salem" sold lots in Swansea and Sepecan on 30 August
1673, his wife Christian yielding her right of dower.

On 5 May 1675 Richard More "sen'r marrener" granted
to "my sons" Caleb and Richard, and to "my daughters" Susanna and Christian More, the "dwelling house in Salem
where I now live." The absence of similar deeds to his
other children suggests that they were by then deceased,
or far from Salem. His wife Christian died on 18 March
1676 aged 60, followed on 4 January 1678/9 by son Caleb
aged 34 and unmarried. The town shortly thereafter

granted Capt. Richard More liberty to "fence in his wife's
and son Caleb's graves."

Some time later Richard married again. His new wife,
Jane, was widow of Samuel Crumpton,* but her surname and
birthplace, as well as the date and place of their marriage, remain unknown. No children were born to this marriage. Jane died in Salem on either 5 or 8 October 1686
aged 55 years.

In a series of depositions Richard More related some
of his history, but managed to befuddle his age. On 27
September 1684 giving his age as "seaventy yeares or
thereabouts" he attested "that being in London att the
House of Mr Thomas Weston Ironmonger in the year 1620 He
was from thence transported to New Plymouth in New England." He deposed on 1 April 1690 aged about 78 that he
was a retainer and laborer in the service of "my ffather
in Law Richard Hollingsworth Senr aboute fivety six years
agoe." Later in 1690 he deposed again aged 78 naming "my
ffather in Law Richard Hollinsworth Sener of Salem de-
sesed." From the latter two depositions the conclusion
has been drawn that Richard More's second wife was an un-
recorded daughter of Richard Hollingsworth. However, the
discovery that his first wife Christian was a member of
the Hollingsworth family (though the exact relationship
has not been clarified) accounts for his Hollingsworth
connection, and indicates that Jane's surname must be con-
sidered unknown.

The "fivety six years agoe" in the second deposition
would support the speculation that Richard returned to
England, for the Hollingsworth family had not left their
mother country in 1634. Unfortunately Richard's claim in
the same deposition to an age of 78 is questionable, since
it would make him an unlikely two-year old at the time of
his baptism. Evidently conclusions cannot be safely based
on an exact application of his stated number of years.

It is equally unfortunate that Richard More's date of
death was not recorded. He was last alive of record 19
March 1693/4 when he witnessed his daughter Susanna's bond
as administratrix of her deceased husband Samuel Dutch.
By 20 April 1696 Richard More Sr. was mentioned as "lately
deceased" (in a deed of John Cromwell). Upon his grave-
stone--the only known stone of a *Mayflower* passenger erected at the time of death--originally appeared the legend

---

*Samuel Crumpton was killed in ambush at Deerfield 18 Sept. 1675 in
King Philip's War. His widow Jane administered her husband's estate
on "21:10m:1675," declaring that there were "noe relations of her husbands known of in this country." She was then aged 44 years.

"HERE LYETH BURIED Y^e BODY OF CAP^T RICHARD MORE AGED 84
YEARS." Sometime between 1901 and 1919 someone added the
mis-information "DIED 1692 A MAYFLOWER PILGRIM." This
death year is obviously incorrect, because the aforemen-
tioned deed establishes that he was alive in 1693/4. The
age at death is apparently wrong also, because we know he
was dead by April 1696. Baptized in 1614, probably on the
Sunday following his birth, Richard would not have turned
84 until the year 1698.

Tracing Richard More's family is complicated by the
various spellings in the records, used interchangeably, of
More, Moor and Moore, as well as by the large number of
early Moore immigrants. In particular, following his son
Richard Jr., assuming he left Salem, is rendered virtually
impossible by the popularity of the name Richard; for example, before 1678 six men named Richard Moore were transported to Maryland, and seven to Virginia, not to mention
one in Maine in the 1640's, and another in Lynn MA by
1661. We know that Richard More Jr. sailed to and from
Barbados. It is possible that he and others of his family
moved either to the West Indies or to one of the southern
colonies; no proof of such move has been found.

References: MD 3:193-201; 13:84; 22:49-51, 78-85. TAG 40:77-84. VR
SALEM. NEHGR 38:335; 50:203; 114:163-8; 124:85-7. NYGBR
36:213-9. SAVAGE 3:229-30. HOTTEN'S PERSONS pp. 93, 108. FAM OF
PILGRIMS pp. 119-20. MA PIONEERS pp. 317-8. SALEM BY FELT 1:418;
2:272, 504. SALEM BY PERLEY 1:376; 2:1-2, 9-10, 287, 348, 356, 371,
398, 403; 3:64-5, 80, 82, 88, 140, 421. SALEM RECS 1:63; 2:282.
ESSEX QUARTERLY COURTS 1:50; 7:111, 148, 310-12, 323. SALEM FIRST CH
pp. 11, 14, 18. Plymouth Col. LR 3:83(Plymouth Court); 3:101, 303
(Richard More). Essex Co. PR #8420(Samuel Dutch). Essex Co. LR
4:114(Richard More); 11:184(John Cromwell). WESTMORELAND CO VA DEEDS,
PATS, etc. 1665-1677, abstracted by John F. Dorman 1:47(Wm. Henfield).
MQ 43:45. Essex Co. Quarterly Cts. 49:75(Richard Moore). BRADFORD'S
HIST (1912) 2:399, 403. MARYLAND SETTLERS pp. 321-2. CAVALIERS &
PIONEERS pp. 109, 117, 167, 257, 273, 337. SAVAGE 3:230.

FIRST GENERATION

1 RICHARD[1] MORE bp. Shipton, Shropshire, England 13
Nov. 1614; d. Salem after 19 March 1693/4 but before 20
April 1696.
    He m. (1) Plymouth 20 Oct. 1636 CHRISTIAN HUNT (or
Hunter), b. England ca. 1615 (aged 20 in 1635); d. Salem
18 March 1676 ae 60. She came to Salem in 1635 as a member of the family of Richard Hollingsworth.
    He m. (2) Salem, JANE (-----) CRUMPTON, b. ca. 1631;
d. Salem 5 or 8 Oct. 1686 ae 55. She m. (1) Samuel Crumpton who d. 1675.

    Children (MORE) bp. Salem, all by first wife Christian:

       i   SAMUEL[2] bp. 6:1m:1642; living 1650; n.f.r.*
      ii   THOMAS bp. 6:1m:1642; living 1650; n.f.r.
     iii   CALEB bp. 31:1m:1644; d. Salem 4 Jan. 1678/9 ae 34, unmar.
      iv   JOSHUA bp. 3:3m:1646; living 1650; n.f.r.
    2 v   RICHARD bp. 2:11m:1647
    3 vi   SUSANNA bp. 12:3m:1650
    4 vii CHRISTIAN bp. 5:7m:1652

References: VR SALEM. SALEM BY PERLEY 1:376; 2:1-2, 9-10; 3:88.
             FAM OF PILGRIMS pp. 119-20. MD 3:193-201; 13:84; 22:49-
51, 78-84. SAVAGE 3:229-30. TAG 40:77-80. BRADFORD'S HIST (1912)
2:403.

SECOND GENERATION

2 RICHARD[2] MORE (Richard[1]) bp. Salem 2:11m:1647;
prob. living 1 May 1696 (deed).
    He m. by 1673 SARAH -----, living Salem 19 June 1691.
    Richard was commander of the *William and Mary* on a
trip which left Boston for Barbados in 1670. Richard More
Jr. of Boston was master of the *Hopewell* on a voyage to
Barbados and back in 1676-7. On 12:11:84 Richard Jr. of
Salem was abated 5 shillings in taxes. Richard More
(either father or son) received an abatement in 1691.
Richard More Jr. of Salem "marriner" and wife Sarah on 1
May 1690 sold land "given to me by my father Richard More
with dwelling" etc., acknowledged by both 19 June 1691.
In a deed of 1 May 1696 reference is made to the "North
West corner of Richard More Jun[r] his garden, that late

---

*Although Perley claims that <u>Samuel</u> and Sarah More had a son Samuel
b. 15 Nov. 1673, this is clearly a misidentification of the son
Samuel b. to <u>Richard</u> and Sarah More (see #2). Hence there is no
evidence that Samuel lived past 1650, or that he married.

was,...that part of the house which was lately Richard
Mores Jr...." The absence of death and probate records,
as well as deeds, conveys the implication that Richard
More and his family moved somewhere else.

The discovery of a will of Richard Moore of the Par-
ish of St. Phillips [Barbados], planter, made 27 Dec. 1704,
proved 2 March 1704/5, leaving all his estate to wife
Sarah Moore was rendered less than exciting with the subsequent find of a will of Sarah Moore of the Parish of St.
George [Barbados], made 13 Nov. 1733 proved 29 Oct. 1734,
naming her eight children: John Gadsby, Eliz[a] Fox, Ann
Fox, Wm. Fox, Sarah Fox, Alice Fox, Wm. Moore and Thos.
Moore; and as executors, her brother Gabriel Jemmott and
Archibald Moore. If this Sarah is the widow of the Richard who made the above will, this is not our Richard Jr's.
family.

        Children (MORE) all b. Salem:

    i   SAMUEL[3] b. 15 Nov. 1673; d. Salem 24 Nov. 1673 ae 9 days.
    ii -----(unreadable) bp. Dec. 1674; n.f.r.
    iii THOMAS bp. 1 June 1679; n.f.r.
    iv CHRISTIAN bp. Aug. 1681; n.f.r.
    v   SARAH bp. Jan. 1683/4; n.f.r.
    vi CALEB bp. 15 April 1688; n.f.r.

References: FAM OF PILGRIMS p. 120. MD 3:197, 199-200; 22:49-51,
        82-3. VR SALEM. SALEM REC 2:282; 3:123, 251. Essex Co.
LR 9:18(Richard More Jr.); 8:95(Richard More Sr.); 12:82(Wm. Browne et
al.). Barbados Archives RB 6/16 p. 213(will Richard Moore); RB 6/24
p. 377(will Sarah Moore). COL SOC MA (Suffolk Court Rec) 30:822-3.

    3 SUSANNA[2] MORE (Richard[1]) bp. Salem 12:3m:1650;
living Ipswich 30 Oct. 1728.

She m. (1) prob. Salem ca. 1675 SAMUEL DUTCH, b. ca.
1645; d. July 1693 (calculated from Susanna's account);
son of Osmon(d) and Grace (Pratte) Dutch. Samuel was a
mariner. Susannah Dutch of Salem widow posted bond 19
March 1693/4 to administer the estate of Samuel Dutch late
of Salem deceased, mariner. In a 6 Jan. 1695/6 account,
Susannah Dutch alias Hutton, administratrix of Samuel
Dutch, included expenses for bringing up one child two and
one half years.

She m. (2) bet. July 1693 and 6 Jan. 1695/6 RICHARD
HUTTON of Wenham, poss. d. Wenham 22 June 1713 "in his 96
yr." He m. (1) Elizabeth Killam, by whom he had at least
five children. Richard took the oath of fidelity in Nov.
1653 when he was sworn in as constable of Wenham. In a
receipt dated Boston 15 Dec. 1696 Richard Hutton was named
"the new husband of the relict of Samuel Dutch late of
Salem." Joseph Fowler posted bond as administrator 22

April 1714 of the estate of Richard Hutton late of Wenham
deceased. Richard and Susanna had no children.
   She m. (3) int. Wenham 11 April 1714 JOHN KNOWLTON,
father of her son-in-law; d. bef. 24 Aug. 1728; son of
William and Elizabeth (Balch) Knowlton. He m. (1) 1669
Bethia Edwards, by whom he had eleven children. John and
Susanna had no children. The will of John Knowlton,
signed 9 Jan. 1713/14 and probated 24 Aug. 1728, fails to
name his wife; but Susanna signed a receipt for money
paid to her by "my son John Knowlton...out of my husbans
estat" 30 Oct. 1728.

      Children (DUTCH) bp. Salem:

      i   BARBARA³ bp. 2 Dec. 1677; d. Salem 10 April 1678 ae 8 mos.
      ii SUSANNA bp. 28 Sept. 1679; d.y.
   5 iii SUSANNA bp. 22 Sept. 1683
      iv CHRISTIAN bp. June 1689; d.y.

References: SALEM BY PERLEY 2:1; 3:104, 303. SAVAGE 2:514. MA
         PIONEERS p. 147. FAM OF PILGRIMS p. 121. TILTON ANCY
pp. 96-9. VR SALEM, WENHAM. KNOWLTON ANCY p. 26. KNOWLTON ERRORS
pp. 7-8. MD 3:197, 199-200; 22:49-51. Essex Co. PR #8420(Samuel
Dutch); #14445(Richard Hutton); #39521(John Knowlton). ESSEX QUARTER-
LY COURTS 1:320(Richard's oath of fidelity); 7:292; 8:18, 26, 160,
163, 384, 436; 9:113, 204, 457, 584(Richard Hutton depositions).
ESSEX CO PR 2:100(Austin Killam); 2:100-101(Alice Killam).

   4 CHRISTIAN² MORE (Richard¹) bp. Salem 5:7m:1652; d.
there 30 May 1680 ae 28 yrs.
   She m. Salem 31 Aug. 1676 JOSHUA CONANT, b. Salem 15:
4m:1657; d. there between 11 July 1702 and 7 June 1705;
son of Joshua and "Seeth" (Gardner) Conant. He m. (2)
1690/1 Sarah Newcomb, by whom he had Keziah, Caleb, Sarah
and John.
   Joshua was a mariner, and for several years a gunner
at the fort on Winter Island near Salem. In 1694 he petitioned the state to be paid for his services, for which on
15 March 1700/1 the legislature granted him £10. On 11
July 1702 Joshua Conant late master of the ketch *Dragon*,
defendant at Salem court, was granted right of appeal
(which he failed to do). On 7 June 1705 Sarah Conant,
widow relict of Joshua Conant late of Salem deceased, petitioned the legislature for money based on Joshua's un-
paid service, her husband having left her very poor "with
fore small children." Payment was approved 10 Nov. 1705.
   It is claimed that Joshua and his family moved to
Eastham (the part now Truro) about 1700; but from the
foregoing such was evidently not the case.

Child (CONANT) born Salem to Joshua and Christian:

   i JOSHUA[3] b. 12 May 1678; n.f.r.

References: FAM OF PILGRIMS p. 121. CONANT FAM pp. 136-7, 162-3. VR
        SALEM. MD 3:200; 22:49-51. SALEM BY PERLEY 1:79. MA
BAY ACTS & RESOLVES 7:277, 672-3; 8:144, 537-8. TAG 30:155.

THIRD GENERATION

    5 SUSANNA DUTCH[3] (Susanna[2] More, Richard[1]) bp.
Salem 22 Sept. 1683; d. after 18 Aug. 1762.
    She m. Beverly 26 Dec. 1705 BENJAMIN KNOWLTON, b.
Ipswich ca. 1674; d. Ipswich Hamlet (now Hamilton) in Dec.
1764; son of John and Bethia (Edwards) Knowlton.
    Benjamin and Susanna "Nolton" owned the covenant at
the Wenham Congregational Church in 1709, where dau. Susanna was baptized. They were dismissed to the "Hamlet" 3
Oct. 1714. Benjamin Knowlton, weaver, and wife Susanna of
Ipswich sold land in Gloucester 20 July 1730, she being
called the "late Susanna Dutch daughter of Samuel Dutch of
Salem deceased." The will of Benjamin Knowlton Sr. of
Ipswich, signed 5 Aug. 1759 probated 17 Dec. 1764, names
wife Susanna, daughters Susanna Dodge and Elizabeth Brown,
and "only son" Benjamin Knowlton.

    Children (KNOWLTON):

6   i   SUSANNA[4] bp. Wenham 16th 3m 1714
7   ii ELIZABETH bp. Ipswich 20 Jan. 1716/7
8 iii BENJAMIN bp. Ipswich 23 Nov. 1718

References: VR BEVERLY, IPSWICH, SALEM. TILTON ANCY pp. 46-9.
          KNOWLTON ANCY p. 34. KNOWLTON ERRORS pp. 7-9. FAMS OF
PILGRIMS p. 121. NEHGR 61:335, 337; 62:45, 48. Essex Co. PR #16055
(Benjamin Knowlton Sr.). Essex Co. LR 61:24(Benjamin Knowlton).

FOURTH GENERATION

    6 SUSANNA KNOWLTON[4] (Susanna Dutch[3], Susanna[2] More,
Richard[1]) bp. Wenham 16th 3m 1714; d. Granville, Annapolis Co., Nova Scotia in June 1788.
    She m. Wenham 30 March 1739 JOSIAH DODGE, b. Wenham
10 Jan. 1718/9; d. Granville 17 July 1805; son of Josiah
and Prudence (Fairfield) Dodge. Josiah m. (2) Annapolis,
N.S., 1789 Martha Wheelock.
    About 1743 Josiah with his family and parents moved
from Ipswich to Lunenburg, where both Josiahs were active

in town affairs. The last record of the father was the
transfer in March 1772 of all his lands and buildings to
his youngest son. Josiah the son, husband of Susanna,
consistently in deeds called Josiah Dodge Jr., traded land
in Lunenburg from 1749 until 1762 when he sold the last of
his property, and moved to Nova Scotia. In 1770 Capt.
Josiah Dodge headed a household in Granville comprising
one man, two boys, one woman and one girl, all indicated
to be American.

The will of Josiah Dodge of Granville, dated 21 Dec.
1785, names wife Susannah, sons Josiah and Asahel, dau.
Susannah, youngest son Benjamin, and daus. Rhoda, Sarah
and Phebe. A codicil dated 10 April 1799 indicates wife
Susannah was deceased, and names present wife Martha,
grandson Joseph Hinds (not of age) son of deceased dau.
Rhoda, and dau. Sarah. A codicil dated 2 Aug. 1802 names
son Benjamin.

Children (DODGE) first two b. Ipswich, the others b. Lunenburg,
all to Josiah and Susanna:

9	i	JOSIAH[5] (or Josias)	b. 8 Sept. 1740
10	ii	SUSANNA	b. 3 Feb. 1742
11	iii	RHODA	b. 25 Aug. 1744
12	iv	SARAH	b. 24 May 1749
13	v	ASAHEL	b. 26 Aug. 1752(or 1751)
14	vi	BENJAMIN	b. 1 May 1754
14A	vii	PHOEBE	b. 23 Sept. 1759

References: VR IPSWICH, WENHAM. CONANT FAM pp. 235-6. DODGE GEN
1:61, 100, 157-60. LUNENBURG RECS pp. 121, 141, 186,
198, 248, 281-2. NEHGR 62:48. ANNAPOLIS CO NS HIST pp. 501-2[con-
fuses Josiah[5] with his father]. ANNAPOLIS CO NS SUP p. 68. 1770
CENSUS NS:11. Worcester Co. LR 40:300; 44:143(Josiah Dodge); 37:472,
40:299(Brewer to Dodge); 43:494; 45:273; 97:523(Josiah Dodge Jr.).
Granville NS township rec. pp. 46, 345. BRIDGETOWN NS HIST [incor-
rectly places Josiah Dodge in Granville in 1759].

7 ELIZABETH KNOWLTON[4] (Susanna Dutch[3], Susanna[2]
More, Richard[1]) bp. Ipswich 20 Jan. 1716/7; d. there 27
Nov. 1798 "widow of Nathan."
She m. int. Ipswich 19 Aug. 1737 NATHAN BROWN, bp.
Ipswich 30:1m:1712 [30 March 1712]; d. there 7 April 1794;
son of John and Mary (Fellows) Brown. A cordwainer and
yeoman, he spent his life in Ipswich.
The will of Nathan Brown of Ipswich yeoman, signed 15
Nov. 1787 and presented 2 June 1794, names his wife Eliza-
beth; children: Susanna, Hannah Boardman, Jeremiah, John,
Nathan and Abraham; granddau. "Christien Giddinge"; the
four sons to be executors. On 29 May 1794 Jeremiah Brown

declined the appointment "considering his remote situa-
tion" in Lyndeborough NH.

    Children (BROWN) baptized at Ipswich:

15   i   CHRISTIAN[5] b. ca. 1738
     ii   JAMES bp. March 1739; prob. d.y.
    iii   ELIZABETH bp. 4 May 1740 [prob. 1741 was intended]; prob.
            d.y.
     iv   NATHAN bp. 12 Feb. 1743; d. Ipswich 16 Feb. 1747.
16   v   JEREMIAH bp. 9 Nov. 1746
17   vi   HANNAH bp. 1 Jan. 1748
    vii   SUSANNA bp. 25 Nov. 1750; pos. the Susanna who d. Ipswich
            31 Jan. 1826. Abraham Brown and his wife Sarah 6 Jan.
            1815 transferred land and house in Ipswich to Nathan Brown
            Jr. of Ipswich "reserving bedroom in house occupied by
            Susanna Brown," which was left to her in her father's will
            "so long as she should remain unmarried."
18 viii   NATHAN bp. 19 Nov. 1752
19   ix   JOHN bp. 28 March 1756
20   x   ABRAHAM bp. 9 Dec. 1759

References: VR IPSWICH. POTTER FAM p. 5. CANDLEWOOD pp. 38, 95, 97-
            8. MD 22:51. ESSEX ANTIQUARIAN 12:157, 160, 170. Essex
Co. PR #3744(Nathan Brown). Essex Co. LR 206:275(Abraham Brown).

    8 BENJAMIN KNOWLTON[4] (Susanna Dutch[3], Susanna[2] More,
Richard[1]) bp. Ipswich 23 Nov. 1718; d. there 2 April 1781
ae 63.
    He m. (1) Ipswich 28 Feb. 1738 SUSANNA POTTER, bp.
Ipswich 18 Oct. 1719; d. bet. 25 April 1754 and 22 April
1756; dau. of Nathaniel Potter. The will of Nathaniel
Potter Sr. of Ipswich, dated 25 April probated 13 May 1754,
names dau. Susanna as married without indicating her surname.
    He m. (2) int. Ipswich 22 April 1756 ABIGAIL DANE,
prob. the dau. of Nathaniel and Esther (Kimball) Dane, bp.
Ipswich 5 Oct. 1734; d. there 20 May 1790 ae 55. The will
of Nathaniel Dane Sr. of Ipswich, dated 26 May and pro-
bated 23 June 1760, names wife Esther and a dau. Abigail
without indicating her surname.
    Benjamin gave patriotic service during the Revolution.
Richard Dodge was bonded as administrator of the estate of
Benjamin Knowlton late of Ipswich yeoman on 7 April 1781.
The heirs are enumerated many times; in the division 2
Aug. 1790 of the dower which had been set off to his widow
Abigail Knowlton, there are named sons Moses and Benjamin
Knowlton, eldest son Ezra, dau. Hepsibah Cummings, sons
Nehemiah, Malachi, Edmund and Ephraim Knowlton, daus. Abi-
gail Knowlton, Hannah Knowlton and Esther Knowlton, the

legal representatives of dau. Susanna Poland deceased, and
daus. Annis Knowlton and Betty Knowlton.
        In an earlier enumeration 7 Feb. 1786, Ephraim Knowl-
ton was of Wenham, Moses Knowlton was of Gloucester, and
the grandchildren, children of Nathaniel Poland and his
late wife Susanna deceased, were named: Nehemiah, Susanna, Benjamin and Esther Poland; their father Nathaniel
released his rights to his father-in-law's estate to his
children 7 Feb. 1786.
        On 5 July 1790 Malachi Knowlton posted bond as ad-
ministrator of widow Abigail Knowlton late of Ipswich. An
expense item included "for Daniel Rust and Esther Rust."
        On 7 May 1781 Abigail Knowlton of Ipswich was made
guardian of her minor children, children of the late Benjamin Knowlton: Abigail aged 17, Betty aged 7, Annis aged
10, Esther aged 12, Hannah aged 14, and Benjamin aged 15.
Later, 8 May 1790, Elizabeth Knowlton chose Col. Robert
Dodge as guardian; Annis Knowlton "more than 19" and
Elizabeth Knowlton 17 signed a discharge 8 June 1790.
Hannah Knowlton and Oliver Norton signed discharge 16 Dec.
1790.
        Ezra Knowlton of Hamilton, Edmund Knowlton of Hamil-
ton, Ephraim Knowlton of Hamilton cooper, Benjamin Knowlton of Beverly cordwainer, Jonathan Lamson of Beverly
mariner, Jonas Cummings of Topsfield, Oliver Norton of
Ipswich baker, Daniel Rust of Hamilton cooper, Annis
Knowlton and Elizabeth Knowlton of Hamilton, Benjamin Poland and Thomas Smith Jr. both of New Boston NH sold to
Malachi Knowlton of Hamilton land lately belonging to
"father Benjamin Knowlton's estate...[to] which we are
heirs" 18 July 1794.

        Children (KNOWLTON) all b. prob. Ipswich, first seven to Benja-
min and Susanna, last ten to Benjamin and Abigail:

21	i	EZRA[5] bp. Ipswich 29 July 1739
22	ii	SUSANNA bp. Ipswich 14 Dec. 1740
	iii	BENJAMIN bp. Ipswich 2 Jan. 1742/3; d.y.
23	iv	NEHEMIAH b. Ipswich 19 April 1745
24	v	EDMUND b. ca. 1747
25	vi	MOSES
	vii	JAMES d. bef. April 1781; served in Revolution.
26	viii	EPHRAIM b. 26 June 1758
27	ix	MALACHI b. Ipswich 10 Jan. 1759
28	x	HEPZIBAH b. ca. 1762
29	xi	ABIGAIL b. ca. 1764
30	xii	BENJAMIN b. ca. 1766
31	xiii	HANNAH b. Ipswich ca. 1767
32	xiv	ESTHER bp. Ipswich 1 Jan. 1769
33	xv	ANNIS bp. Ipswich 6 Dec. 1770
34	xvi	BETTY bp. Ipswich 19 Dec. 1773
	xvii	CATHARINE bp. Ipswich 14 April 1776; d. 17 Sept. 1778 ae 2.

References: VR HAMILTON, IPSWICH. MD 22:51. KNOWLTON ANCY pp. 44-5.
        KNOWLTON ERRORS p. 29. Essex Co. PR #16056(Benjamin
Knowlton); #16045, 16046(Abigail Knowlton and guardian); #22580
(Nathaniel Potter); #7121(Nathaniel Dane). Essex Co. LR 336:1(Ezra
Knowlton et al.). DAR PATRIOT INDEX (Third Supp.) p. 29.

FIFTH GENERATION

9 JOSIAH DODGE[5] (Susanna Knowlton[4], Susanna Dutch[3],
Susanna[2] More, Richard[1]) b. Ipswich 8 Sept. 1740; d. prob.
bef. 1790.
     He m. Lunenburg 8 Nov. 1761 HANNAH CONANT "of Leomin-
ster," b. Concord 12 Feb. 1740; pos. living Harpersfield
NY 6 July 1810; dau. of Ebenezer and Ruth (Pierce) Conant.
She pos. m. (2) ----- Brainerd, father of Reuben Brainerd.
     Until his marriage Josiah lived in Lunenburg. He
then went to Nova Scotia, where Josiah Dodge Jr. of Granville, N.S., husbandman, on 10 June 1762 traded land with
his father (witnesses Sarah and Susanna Dodge). In 1770
Josiah Dodge headed a household in Annapolis NS comprising two men, one woman, one boy and three girls, indicated
to be one Englishman, two Americans and four Acadians. In
May 1776 Josiah and Hannah sold their property and moved
to Machias ME, where in Nov. 1776 he enlisted as a private
for about one month; he re-enlisted as a sergeant in July
1777 for approximately five months.
     The children of Josiah and Hannah appear in the re-
cords of Ashburnham MA, though only Ebenezer's date of
birth is given. It is possible that after Josiah's death
the widow Hannah moved to Ashburnham, where her parents
had been living since 1762, and had the town clerk enter
her children in his records. There was a Hannah Dodge in
1790 with household comprising two females in Ashburnham.
No probate or land records were found in Machias ME or in
Worcester County MA for Josiah, nor a marriage record of
Hannah to Mr. Brainerd.

     Children (DODGE) first seven b. Granville or Annapolis NS, last
b. prob. Machias ME, all recorded in Ashburnham MA: EUNICE[6] b. 1762;
MARY b. 1764; JOSIAH b. 1767; ANNA b. 1769; ELIZABETH b. 1771; REUBEN
b. 1773; DANIEL b. 1775; and EBENEZER b. 1779.

References: VR ASHBURNHAM, IPSWICH, LEOMINSTER. CONCORD VR p. 167.
        LUNENBURG RECS p. 248. DODGE GEN pp. 157-8, 229. 1770
CENSUS NS:3. CONANT FAM pp. 190, 235. NEHGR 13:8. ASHBURNHAM HIST
pp. 641, 682. ANNAPOLIS CO NS SUP p. 68. DAR PATRIOT INDEX p. 197

[says Josiah d. after 1799]. 1790 CENSUS:MA:211. BRAINERD GEN 2:pt 5:48, 60. Granville NS township rec. pp. 19, 373. NS Archives RG 47 reel 21 book 1 p. 34 (1768); RG 47 reel 21 book 3 p. 60(Josiah Dodge Jr. deeds). MSSR 4:828.

10 SUSANNA DODGE[5] (Susanna Knowlton[4], Susanna Dutch[3], Susanna[2] More, Richard[1]) b. Ipswich 3 Feb. 1742; d. Granville, Annapolis Co., Nova Scotia 26 Jan. 1788 in 46 yr.
    She m. Granville NS 29 March 1762 ISRAEL FELLOWS, bp. Ipswich 4 Jan. 1740/1; d. Granville 23 April 1815 ae 76; son of Benjamin and Eunice (Dodge) Fellows. He m. (2) Joanna Smith. The will of Benjamin Fellows of Ipswich, dated 15 April 1791 and probated 2 Dec. 1794, names son Israel. On 10 [Sept.?] 1773 Josiah Dodge of Granville gave land to his dau. Fellows for love, etc., and for £7 paid by Israel Fellows of Granville; the deed was signed by both Josiah and Susanna Dodge.
    Israel served in the attack on Montreal in 1760. In 1761 he moved to Nova Scotia, and in 1770 was in Granville with a household comprising one man, one woman, one boy and three girls, all called Americans.
    The will of "Isreal" Fellows of Granville, Annapolis Co., Nova Scotia, yeoman, names wife "Joana"; two granddaughters Mariah and Phebe Chesley; daughters Eunice Troop, Susannah Dunn, Prissila Elliott; surviving children of my deceased daughter Barysintha Foster; grandson Isreal Burton Chute (under 21); my son Joseph Fellows Sr., my son-in-law Samuel Chesley Jr., my friend James Chute Sr., and my grandson Isreal Fellows Jr. to be executors. This was dated 17 March 1815, presented 18 May 1815.

    Children (FELLOWS) b. Granville NS to Israel and Susanna:
EUNICE[6] b. 1763; JOSEPH b. 1764; SUSANNA b. 1767; PRISCILLA b. 1769; ANNA b. 1772; CYNTHIA (or Berecinthia) b. 1775; PHEBE b. 1777, d. 1793; SARAH b. 1780, d. 1803 unm.; EBENEZER b. 1782; and HEPZIBAH b. 1787.

References: VR IPSWICH. DODGE GEN. P. 159. 1770 CENSUS NS:11. ANNAPOLIS CO NS HIST p. 509. IPSWICH HIST 2:197. CANDLEWOOD p. 76. Essex Co. PR #9340(Benjamin Fellows). Granville NS township rec. pp. 10, 23. NS Archives: Cemeteries, Annapolis Co. pp. 7-9; RG47 reel 21 book 2 p. 82(Josiah Dodge deed). NEW ADVENTURE pp. 108-9. YARMOUTH (NS) TELEGRAM issue of 9 March 1934 ("New Englanders in NS"). Annapolis Royal NS Probate Register F:14(Israel Fellows).

11 RHODA DODGE[5] (Susanna Knowlton[4], Susanna Dutch[3], Susanna[2] More, Richard[1]) b. Lunenburg 26 Aug. 1744; d. bef. 10 April 1799 prob. in Nova Scotia.

She m. Granville, Annapolis Co., NS 11 Sept. 1762
BENJAMIN HINDS.
In a deed dated 9 Aug. 1769 Benjamin Hinds of Wilmot,
Annapolis Co., sold land in Granville. No other records,
beyond the births of children, were found for either
Benjamin or Rhoda. The child Joseph Hinds was named in
his grandfather's will.

Children (HINDS) first nine b. Granville NS: ABRAHAM[6] b. 1763;
MOLLY b. 1767; NABBY b. 1770; EDITHA b. 1771; SIMEON b. 1773; PHEBE b.
1775; LEVI b. 1777; SUSANNA b. 1779; RHODA b. 1781; and JOSEPH b. ca.
1790, bp. 1791 ae 1 yr.

References: DODGE GEN p. 159. ANNAPOLIS CO SUP p. 68. Granville
            NS township rec. pp. 16, 365. NS Archives: MG4 #34
(bp. Joseph); Annapolis Co. LR.

12 SARAH DODGE[5] (Susanna Knowlton[4], Susanna Dutch[3],
Susanna[2] More, Richard[1])   b. Lunenburg 24 May 1749; d.
Wilmot (now Paradise), Annapolis Co., Nova Scotia 15 July
1823 (or 1824?) ae 75.
She m. Granville, Annapolis Co., NS 1 Nov. 1764 JONA-
THAN STEWART LEONARD, b. Lyme CT ca. 1740; d. Wilmot (now
Paradise) 4 May 1802 ae 61.
Jonathan was in Granville NS in 1770 with a household
comprising one man, one woman, one boy and one girl.
The will of Sarah Leonard of Wilmot, Annapolis Co.,
NS widow, dated 15 Sept. 1815 and probated 23 Sept. 1824,
mentions children of late dau. Phebe Wade, dau. Betsy wife
of Samuel McCormick Jr., children of son Abiel, children
of son Putnam, children of dau. Mary late wife of Samuel
Bent, grandson William Starret (under 21), and son Seth;
son Seth and Samuel Elliott, executors.

Children (LEONARD) b. Granville NS: PHEBE[6] b. 1765; SETH b.
1767, drowned 1786; MOLLY b. 1770; JONATHAN b. and d. 1772; DEBORAH b.
and d. 1773; ABIEL b. 1775; BETTY b. 1777; PUTNAM b. 1779; SUSANNA b.
1782, d. 1801; and SETH b. 1787.

References: DODGE GEN p. 159. 1770 CENSUS NS:11. ANNAPOLIS CO NS
            HIST p. 539. Granville NS township rec. p. 20. NS
Archives(will Sarah). Annapolis Royal PR(Sarah Leonard).

13 ASAHEL DODGE[5] (Susanna Knowlton[4], Susanna Dutch[3],
Susanna[2] More, Richard[1])   b. Lunenburg 26 Aug. 1752; d.
Wilmot, Annapolis Co., NS 12 Sept. 1798.

He m. Granville, Annapolis Co., NS 10 April 1773 ANN
WALKER, living after 26 Aug. 1798 but d. bef. 14 Oct. 1814;
dau. of Robert Walker. On 18 May 1776, acknowledged 3
Sept. 1784, Asahel Dodge of Granville yeoman and wife Ann
quitclaimed to Ann Walker spinster of Granville, administratrix of the late Robert Walker of Annapolis deceased,
their rights of inheritance from Robert's estate, but reserved right to inherit from the heirs of Robert.
    The administration of the estate of Asahel Dodge late
of Wilmot, Annapolis Co., deceased, was granted to his wife
Ann Dodge. Two deeds dated 14 Oct. 1814, which involve a
settlement of the property of Asahel Dodge late of Wilmot
yeoman deceased intestate, indicate his deceased widow,
five sons and four daughters--the children and their
spouses being named as follows: Josiah Dodge, Thomas
Dodge and wife Sarah, Lott Phinney and wife Ann, Asahel
Walker Dodge, Mary Dodge spinster, Sarah Dodge deceased,
William Dodge and his guardian John Wiswall, Benjamin
Dodge and wife Elizabeth, all of Wilmot, and Donald Logan
and wife Susannah of Pictou, Halifax Co.

    Children (DODGE) b. Granville NS: ANN[6] b. 1774; JOSIAH b. 1776;
SARAH b. 1777; SUSANNAH b. 1779; MARY b. 1781; THOMAS b. 1784; BENJA-
MIN b. 1787; ASAHEL WALKER b. 1793; and WILLIAM MILLER b. 1795, bp.
Aylesford NS 1797.

References: DODGE GEN pp. 159-60. ANNAPOLIS CO NS HIST pp. 502, 622
[errors in mar. date and names of children]. ANNAPOLIS
CO NS SUP p. 68. Granville NS township rec. pp. 18, 356. NS Archives: M6 Two Burials in Wilmot & Aylesford; MG9 Baptisms in Wilmot & Aylesford; RG4 reel 61(est. Robert Walker); RG47 reel 21 book 4
pp. 101, 367(Ann wid. Robert Walker); book 24 pp. 54-6; reel 26 book
16 pp. 193-8(children); RG47 reel 30 book 23 pp. 145-9(Josiah Dodge);
RG43 reel 22 vol. D(original papers Josiah Dodge); Annapolis Co. LR
5:205.

    14 BENJAMIN DODGE[5] (Susanna Knowlton[4], Susanna Dutch[3],
Susanna[2] More, Richard[1]) b. Lunenburg 1 May 1754; d. Granville, Annapolis Co., NS 1 March 1825 ae 71.
    He m. Granville NS 26 Dec. 1776 TABITHA PERKINS, d.
Granville in Nov. 1817.
    They lived in Granville. The will of Benjamin Dodge
of Granville, Annapolis Co., esquire, names sons Benjamin
Knowlton Dodge and Reuben Dodge; daughter Esther Longly;
Susannah Roads (under 18 unmarried), William Henery Roads
(under 21) and Reuben Pirkins Roads (under 21) (no relationship indicated); and grandson Jesse Dodge (under 21);
the two sons to be executors. The will was dated 24 July
1823 and probated 9 March 1825.

Children (DODGE) b. Granville NS: ESTHER[6] b. 1780; RUTH b. 1784, d. 1820 unm.; SUSANNA b. 1786, d. 1804 unm.; BENJAMIN KNOWLTON b. 1790; and REUBEN b. 1793.

References: DODGE GEN p. 160. ANNAPOLIS CO NS HIST p. 502. Granville NS township rec. p. 15. Annapolis Royal NS Probate Register(Benjamin Dodge). NS Archives: MG4 #34 p. 3(Granville Parish Ch. rec.); Estate papers RG43 reel 22 D:31(Benj. Dodge will). ACADIAN RECORDER of 19 March 1825(death Benjamin).

14A PHEBE DODGE[5] (Susanna Knowlton[4], Susanna Dutch[3], Susanna[2] More, Richard[1]) b. Lunenburg 23 Sept. 1759; prob. d. Annapolis Co., Nova Scotia 21 May 1808 ae 49.
    She prob. m. PARDON SANDERS (or Saunders) Jr., b. Rosette (now Round Hill), Annapolis Co., NS ca. 1656; d. Annapolis Co., NS 19 Jan. 1823 ae 67; son of Pardon and Hannah (Olivier) (Sampson) Sanders.
    In his will "reg. 1823" Pardon Sanders of Annapolis, Nova Scotia mentions daughters Louisa and Caroline, and sons Josiah, Pardon, William and Benjamin.

    Children (SANDERS) b. Nova Scotia to Pardon, and so probably to Phebe: PARDON b. 1783; JOSIAH bp. 1785; MARY bp. 1787; SUSAN bp. 1787; WILLIAM bp. 1789; BENJAMIN bp. 1792; LOUISA b. 1794; PHEBE bp. 1798; FREDERICK LeMONT bp. 1798; and CAROLINE.

References: NS Archives: Annapolis Royal Anglican Ch. parish recs.; RG48 reel 53 vol. S(estate papers, wills of Pardon Sanders Sr. & Jr.); MG1 Whiston Collec. ANNAPOLIS NS HIST, A. E. Marble, Cemeteries of Annapolis Co. #309, 310. Granville NS township book pp. 128, 242. Annapolis Royal NS township book p. 199. "Some Historical Facts and Reminiscences of Pardon Sanders and Family" by his great-great-granddaughter Enna Sanders LeCain (read at the Annual Meeting of the Hist. Assoc. of Annapolis Royal NS 2 Nov. 1930). ARCADIE GRAVESTONES pp. 43, 45, 46, 49, 50, 51.

15 CHRISTIAN BROWN[5] (Elizabeth Knowlton[4], Susanna Dutch[3], Susanna[2] More, Richard[1]) b. Ipswich 1738 or 1739; d. after 11 Feb. 1762 and bef. 4 Nov. 1766.
    She m. Ipswich 13 April 1758 FRANCIS GOODHUE, bp. Ipswich 7 Dec. 1735; d. Weathersfield VT 10 Feb. 1810 ae 74; son of Francis and Sarah (Fowler) Goodhue. He m. (2) Ipswich 1766 the widow Lucy Lord; they had son Francis.
    The will of Nathan Brown names granddau. "Christien Giddinge" (Christian[6] Goodhue m. Ipswich 1781 Isaac Giddings). Francis Goodhue Jr. joiner of Ipswich and his wife Christian[5] sold land in Ipswich 11 Feb. 1762. In 1790 Francis Goodhue was living alone in Ipswich. In 1800

a Francis was living in Swanzey NH, but this appears to be son Francis[6]. SWANZEY HIST claims father and son lived in Swanzey. Francis Goodhue Jr. of Swanzey bought land, house and store in Weathersfield VT in 1803, and apparently he and his father moved there soon afterward.

The will of Francis Goodhue of Weathersfield, Vermont, dated 19 July 1809 probated 7 March 1810, names wife Lucy; dau. Christian Giddings; grandchildren Joseph Goodhue, Wally Goodhue, and Lucy Goodhue, all under 21, sons and dau. of Francis Goodhue Jr. esquire; son Francis Goodhue Jr. esquire to be executor.

>   Child: (GOODHUE):   CHRISTIAN[6] b. ca. 1760 prob. Ipswich

References: VR IPSWICH. SWANZEY NH HIST pp. 79, 246, 523. Essex Co. LR 109:281(Francis Goodhue). Weathersfield VT LR 6:24-5 (will of Francis Goodhue); 4:464(Luke Parsons to Goodhue). Misc. Recs. & Cem. Recs microfilm #F2515, State Library, Montpelier VT(d. Francis p. 60 of Cem. Recs. Weathersfield). 1790 CENSUS MA:77. 1800 CENSUS NH:40. Brattleboro VT Records, by A. H. Clapp(d. Francis Goodhue Esq. 1839 ae 71).

16   JEREMIAH BROWN[5] (Elizabeth Knowlton[4], Susanna Dutch[3], Susanna[2] More, Richard[1]) bp. Ipswich 9 Nov. 1746; d. Lyndeborough NH bet. 12 Sept. 1828 and 18 Aug. 1829.

He m. Ipswich 16 Aug. 1770 LUCY POTTER, prob. the Lucy bp. Ipswich 5 Nov. 1752; dau. of Samuel and Lucy (Brown) Potter; living 12 Sept. 1828 (husband's will).

Jeremiah was a private in the Revolution. Jeremiah Brown of Ipswich bought land in Lyndeborough NH of Benjamin Bullock of Salem 26 Jan. 1789. In 1790 Jeremiah's household in Lyndeborough comprised three men, three boys and four women; in 1800 there were one man over 45, one man between 16 and 26, one woman over 45, one female between 16 and 26, one between 10 and 16, and one girl under 10.

The will of Jeremiah Brown of Lyndeborough NH, signed 12 Sept. 1828 presented 18 Aug. 1829, names wife Lucy; sons Jeremiah, Josiah, Israel, Allen and Nathan; daus. Betsey Brown (principal heiress), Lucy Giddings and Hannah Kidder; wife Lucy to be executrix.

Children (BROWN) all b. Ipswich: ELIZABETH[6] bp. 1771; JEREMIAH bp. 1772; JOSIAH bp. 1774; LUCY bp. 1776; ISRAEL bp. 1777; ALLEN bp. 1780; NATHAN bp. 1783; HANNAH bp. 1786; and ----- b. ?, d. 1788.

References: DAR PATRIOT INDEX p. 92. VR IPSWICH. ESSEX ANTIQUARIAN 12:163. Hillsborough Co. NH PR #0842(Jeremiah Brown).

Hillsborough Co. NH LR 22:460(Benj. Bullock). 1790 CENSUS NH:49.
1800 CENSUS NH:97. CANDLEWOOD p. 101.

     17 HANNAH BROWN[5] (Elizabeth Knowlton[4], Susanna Dutch[3],
Susanna[2] More, Richard[1]) bp. Ipswich 1 Jan. 1748; d.
Lyndeborough NH 12 Aug. 1818 ae 70.
     She m. bef. 1774 THOMAS BOARDMAN (or Bordman), bp.
Ipswich 18 Feb. 1749; d. Lyndeborough 10 Dec. 1836 ae 87;
son of Thomas and Elizabeth (How) Boardman. Thomas Boardman signed a receipt for his portion of the estate of his
father Thomas Boardman on 3 Nov. 1783.
     On 4 Sept. 1791 Thomas Boardman of Ipswich sold 77
acres of Boardman farm with dwelling and barn, wife Hannah
releasing her dower right; and on 11 Oct. 1791 he bought
land in Lyndeborough NH of widow Esther Dodge. Thomas was
in Lyndeborough in 1800. On 13 Feb. 1815 Thomas Boardman
Jr. of Lyndeborough quitclaimed to Daniel N. Boardman of
Lyndeborough all his rights in the farm "owned and occupied
by my father Thomas Boardman of Lyndeborough." On 18 Jan.
1822 Thomas Boardman of Lyndeborough transferred to Daniel
N. Boardman, gentleman, the farm in Lyndeborough "where I
and the said Daniel now live"; and Daniel N. Boardman
"demised leased and to farm let" the same farm to Thomas
"during the term of his life" and promised to provide for
Thomas.

     Children (BOARDMAN) all baptized Ipswich: LANGLEY[6] bp. 1774;
HANNAH bp. 1776; THOMAS bp. 1778; JOHN bp. 1780; and DANIEL NOYES bp.
1792.

References: VR IPSWICH. ESSEX ANTIQUARIAN 9:151; 12:160. Essex Co.
         PR #2737(Thos. Boardman). Hillsborough Co. NH LR 28:160
(Esther Dodge); 124:266; 134:402(Thos. Boardman); 134:403(Daniel N.
Boardman). LYNDEBOROUGH NH HIST p. 663[doubtful he mar. Ann Noyes].
Tombstones, North Lyndeborough NH Cemetery. 1790 CENSUS MA:76. 1800
CENSUS NH:97(Boroman). CANDLEWOOD p. 98. Essex Co. LR 154:85(Thomas
Boardman).

     18 NATHAN BROWN[5] (Elizabeth Knowlton[4], Susanna Dutch[3],
Susanna[2] More, Richard[1]) bp. Ipswich 19 Nov. 1752; d.
Ipswich 10 Jan. 1823 ae 70.
     He m. int. Ipswich 11 July 1776 ABIGAIL BOARDMAN, bp.
Ipswich 30 May 1756; d. there 27 Sept. 1831 ae 76; dau. of
Thomas and Elizabeth (How) Boardman.
     Abigail Brown received her share of the estate of her
father Thomas Boardman on 3 Nov. 1783; receipt was signed
by Nathan Brown Jr. and Abigail Brown.

The will of Nathan Brown of Ipswich, dated 7 Jan.
1823 probated 4 March 1823, names wife Abigail; children
Nathan, Langley, Francis, Susan, Sarah N. Brown and Elizabeth Hosmer; and grandson Daniel Brown. On 4 Feb. 1823
Abigail Brown of Ipswich, widow, quitclaimed to Francis
Brown of Ipswich all rights in real estate of her late
husband Nathan Brown.

    Children (BROWN) b. or bp. Ipswich: RHODA[6] bp. 1777; SUSANNA bp.
1778; ABIGAIL bp. 1781, d. 1808; ELIZABETH bp. 1784; NATHAN bp. 1786;
LANGLEY bp. 1791; SARAH N. bp. 1793, d. Cambridge unmar. 1824 ae 31;
and FRANCIS B. b. 1798.

References: VR IPSWICH, ROXBURY(d. Francis B.).   ESSEX ANTIQUARIAN
            12:163; 9:150. Essex Co. PR #2737(Thos. Boardman); #3745
(Nathan Brown). Essex Co. LR 232:283(Abigail Brown). 1790 CENSUS MA:
76. CANDLEWOOD pp. 38-9, 101-2.

    19 [2]JOHN BROWN[5] (Elizabeth Knowlton[4], Susanna Dutch[3],
Susanna[2] More, Richard[1]) bp. Ipswich 28 March 1756; d.
there 9 Jan. 1817 ae 61. He was a cordwainer.
    He m. "Chebacco" section of Ipswich 1 Dec. 1789 HANNAH
PROCTOR, bp. Ipswich 4 March 1770; d. there 21 Dec. 1843
"widow of John ae 74"; dau. of Samuel and Lucy (-----)
Proctor. The will of Samuel Proctor of Chebacco section of
Ipswich, signed 1 Feb. 1800 probated 3 Nov. 1806, names
wife Lucy and dau. Hannah Brown; this was "read to Mr. John
Brown and wife" 15 Oct. 1806.
    Administration on John Brown late of Ipswich, who died
9 Jan. 1817, was granted to John Proctor. Hannah Brown
widow 2 Dec. 1817 was named guardian of ten children of
John Brown late of Ipswich deceased: Clarissa ae 20, Fanny
and Lucy ae 19, Lepha ae 15, Elizabeth ae 13, Samuel ae 12,
Abigail ae 10, Sally ae 8, Mary Jane ae 5, and John ae
nearly 3. Signing heirs' receipts of notice 31 May 1819
were Hannah Brown, Hannah Brown, Lois Brown, Clarissa
Brown, Lucy Brown and Fanny Brown.
    Theodore Gibbs and wife Lucy, formerly Lucy Brown, of
Essex sold to John Brown 3rd land in Ipswich and Hamilton
of their late father John Brown of Ipswich, rights in re-
version in dower of her mother Hannah Brown, and rights
in her deceased sisters: Clarissa Brown, Lois Brown and
Abigail Brown 13 April 1836.
    In 1820 the household of Hannah Brown comprised one
boy under ten, one girl under ten, one girl between ten
and sixteen, five girls between sixteen and twenty-five,
one woman between twenty-six and forty-five, and one woman
over forty-five.

Children (BROWN) all but Abigail bp. Ipswich: SAMUEL PROCTOR[6]
bp. 1791, d.y.; JOHN bp. 1792, d. Ipswich 1808; HANNAH bp. 1793, d.
Ipswich 1841 ae 48 unm.; LOIS bp. 1795, d. Ipswich 1830 ae 34 unm;
CLARISSA bp. 1796, d. Ipswich 1830 unm.; twins FANNY and LUCY bp.
1798; LEFA (Relief) bp. 1802; ELIZABETH b. 1804; SAMUEL bp. 1808, pos.
d. Ipswich 1830 ae 25; ABIGAIL GILBERT b. 1807, d. Ipswich 1832 ae 24
unm.; SALLY b. 1809; MARY JANE b. 1812; and JOHN b. 1815.

References: VR IPSWICH. Essex Co. PR #22884(Saml. Proctor); #3653
          (John Brown); #3490(Clarissa Brown et al.). Essex Co. LR
290:203(Theodore Gibbs). 1790 CENSUS MA:76. 1820 CENSUS MA:Ipswich.
CANDLEWOOD pp. 38-9, 97, 98, 102.

     20 ABRAHAM BROWN[5] (Elizabeth Knowlton[4], Susanna
Dutch[3], Susanna[2] More, Richard[1]) bp. Ipswich 9 Dec. 1759;
d. Derry NH in Jan. 1832.
     He m. Ipswich 10 Jan. 1780 SARAH BOARDMAN, bp. Ipswich
3 Sept. 1758; d. Methuen 27 Jan. 1848 ae 89 "widow of Abraham"; dau. of Thomas and Elizabeth (How) Boardman. Sarah
Brown received her share of the estate of her father Thomas
Boardman 3 Nov. 1783; she and Abraham Brown signed the
receipt.
     They lived in Ipswich, moved to Gloucester ca. 1788
where they were living in 1790, later back to Ipswich, then
ca. 1815 to Londonderry NH.
     Abraham Brown of Ipswich and wife Sarah sold to Nathan
Brown Jr. house and land in Ipswich 6 Jan. 1815. Abraham
and John Brown both of Ipswich yeomen bought land in Londonderry NH of Currier Fitts 15 Feb. 1815. Abraham Brown
of Londonderry NH and wife Sarah sold to Joseph Boardman
real estate of their father Thomas Boardman which was
assigned to his widow their mother, Elizabeth Boardman,
later Elizabeth Homan, 12 July 1816. On 16 Aug. 1823 John
Brown and Abraham Brown husbandmen both of Londonderry with
wives Ruth and Sally respectively sold land in Windham NH.
On 28 Dec. 1819 and 16 June 1821 respectively Priscilla
Brown and Sally N. Brown both singlewomen of Londonderry
agreed to quitclaim rights to their father Abraham Brown's
estate within six months of his decease, and gave bond to
John Brown husbandman of Londonderry. On 1 March 1831
Abraham Brown of Derry leased his part of the farm where
he lived and which he owned in common with John Brown of
Derry to said John; in turn John "farm let" the property to
"my father Abraham Brown" during his natural life.

     Children (BROWN) all baptized Ipswich: -----[6] d. Ipswich 1781;
PRISCILLA bp. 1782; ABRAHAM bp. 1785, d.y.; JOHN bp. 1788 "son of
Abraham and Sarah of Gloucester"; and SARAH N. bp. 1798.

References: VR GLOUCESTER, IPSWICH, METHUEN. ESSEX ANTIQUARIAN
            9:150; 12:163. Essex Co. PR #2737(Thos. Boardman).
Essex Co. LR 206:275; 214;256(Abraham Brown). Rockingham Co. NH LR
207:51(Currier Fitts); 233:308-9(Priscilla & Sally Brown); 263:122
(Abraham Brown); 261:44(John Brown); 243:334(John & Abraham Brown).
1790 CENSUS MA:71. WINDHAM NH HIST p. 350. CANDLEWOOD pp. 102-3.

   21   EZRA KNOWLTON[5]   (Benjamin[4], Susanna Dutch[3], Susanna[2] More, Richard[1])   bp. Ipswich 29 July 1739; d. Hamilton 24 Aug. 1814 ae 76.
   He m. Ipswich 11 Feb. 1762 ABIGAIL DODGE, d. Hamilton
(not named) "wife of Ezra" 25 Oct. 1812 ae 72; pos. the
Abigail bp. Ipswich 4 July 1742, dau. of Samuel Dodge.
   In 1790 Ezra was living in Ipswich; his household
consisted of one man, three boys, and seven females. He
was of Hamilton in his will, dated 11 Feb. 1808 probated
2 Jan. 1815, which names son Levi as executor; makes provision for his unnamed wife and his children: Susanna,
Abigail, Ame and Nancy. Ezra served against the French at
Lake George 1758 and was a private in the Revolution.

   Children (KNOWLTON) first three b. Wenham; others bapt. Ipswich:
SUSANNA[6] b. 1763; TAMASON b. 1765; EZRA b. 1768, d. unm. 1792; ABI-
GAIL bp. 1771; AME bp. 1773; NANCY bp. 1777; JOSEPH bp. 1780, d. West
Indies 1802 or 1803 ae ca. 24; and LEVI bp. 1782.

   References: VR HAMILTON, IPSWICH, WENHAM. DAR PATRIOT INDEX p. 394.
            KNOWLTON ANCY pp. 44, 67. KNOWLTON ERRORS pp. 29, 40,
41. Essex Co. PR #16070(Ezra Knowlton). 1790 CENSUS MA:76. IPSWICH
HIST 2:189.

   22   SUSANNA KNOWLTON[5]   (Benjamin[4], Susanna Dutch[3],
Susanna[2] More, Richard[1]) bp. Ipswich 14 Dec. 1740; undoubtedly the unnamed "wife of Nathaniel Jr." who d. Ipswich 14 March 1782 ae 44.
   She m. prob. Ipswich 31 Oct. 1765 [in record she mis-
called Susanna Whipple] NATHANIEL POLAND Jr. (or Porland),
bp. Ipswich in Sept. 1740; living 7 Feb. 1786; son of
Nathaniel Poland. The will of Nathaniel Poland of Ipswich
yeoman, signed 1783 and probated 6 June 1786, left house
and barn to son Nathaniel. He m. (2) Manchester 1786 Abigail Tarring, living New Boston NH in 1820, prob. the Mrs.
Poland who d. New Boston 16 Dec. 1828 age 80.
   Papers in the estate of Benjamin[4] Knowlton in 1786
name his four grandchildren, children of Nathaniel Poland
and his deceased wife Susanna: Nehemiah, Susanna, Benjamin and Esther. In 1790 the household of Nathaniel Poland
in Ipswich comprised one man, one boy under sixteen, and
three females. In 1800 a Nathaniel Pollard and one female,
both over 45, dwelt in New Boston NH.

Children (POLAND) b. prob. Ipswich, where last three baptized:
NEHEMIAH[6]; SUSANNA bp. 1769; BENJAMIN bp. 1772; and ESTHER bp. 1774.

References: MD 22:51. KNOWLTON ANCY p. 44. KNOWLTON ERRORS p. 29
            [error in name of husband]. VR IPSWICH, MANCHESTER. NEW
BOSTON NH HIST p. 350. 1790 CENSUS MA:76. 1820 CENSUS NH 61:573.
Essex Co. PR #16056(Benjamin Knowlton). 1800 CENSUS NH:102.

    23 NEHEMIAH KNOWLTON[5] (Benjamin[4], Susanna Dutch[3],
Susanna[2] More, Richard[1]) b. Ipswich 19 April 1744; d.
Sandy Bay (now Rockport) 13 Aug. 1834 ae 90.
    He m. (1) Ipswich 14 Nov. 1769 ELIZABETH POTTER "both
of Hamlet" (now Hamilton), undoubtedly the dau. of Daniel
Potter bp. Ipswich 5 Nov. 1749; d. Ipswich either 5 April
or 9 Oct. 1770.
    He m. (2) Ipswich 11 Oct. 1771 SUSANNA FELLOWS, bp.
Ipswich 2 July 1749; d. there 23 Oct. 1773 ae 24 "wife of
Nemiah"; dau. of Joseph and Susanna (Giddings) Fellows.
No children found.
    He m. (3) Ipswich 22 Nov. 1774 MARTHA TILTON, b. ca.
1748; d. Boylston bef. 25 Aug. 1832 ae 84; dau. of Joseph
Tilton of Ipswich. Nehemiah Knowlton and wife Martha with
others conveyed land in Ipswich of their late father
Joseph Tilton of Ipswich 3 March 1779.
    In 1790 Nehemiah was living in Ipswich; his household
comprised one man, five boys and two females. He was in
Hamilton when he and wife Martha sold several lots in
Hamilton to Malachi Knowlton 24 March 1815.
    In his application for Federal pension for service in
the Revolution, Nehemiah Knowlton of Boylston attested 6
Sept. 1832 aged 88 that he was born in Ipswich (in the part
now Hamilton) 19 April 1744, and moved to Boylston in 1815.
The will of Nehemiah Knowlton of Gloucester, signed 4 Aug.
1833 probated 2 Sept. 1834, names sons Nehemiah, Charles,
Asa, Benjamin and dau. Martha Cummings; grandchildren
Mary K. Knowlton, Thomas W. Knowlton, Josiah Knowlton and
Hannah S. Knowlton; and mentions children of "my late son
Josiah Knowlton deceased." An affidavit that he was a
Revolutionary War pensioner and died 13 Aug. 1834 was
signed 3 Aug. 1835 by Sarah and James Haskell.

    Children (KNOWLTON) b. to Nehemiah and Martha prob. Ipswich:
NEHEMIAH[6] b. 1775; ASA b. 1777, d.y.; MARTHA b. 1779; BENJAMIN b.
1701; ASA bp. 1784; JOSIAH b. 1784; and CHARLES b. 1789.

References: VR GLOUCESTER, IPSWICH. KNOWLTON ANCY pp. 44, 68. KNOWL-
           TON ERRORS pp. 29, 41[some birthdates differ from Glou-
cester and Ipswich]. MA OBITS 3:2677. DAR PATRIOT INDEX p. 394. Rev.
Pension #S29951. 1790 CENSUS MA:76. Essex Co. PR #16092(Nehemiah
Knowlton). Essex Co. LR 141:256; 206:260(Nehemiah Knowlton). CANDLE-
WOOD p. 76.

24   EDMUND KNOWLTON[5]   (Benjamin[4], Susanna Dutch[3], Susanna[2] More, Richard[1])   b. Ipswich ca. 1747; d. Hamilton 24 Nov. 1827 ae 80.

He m. Ipswich 7 Sept. 1774 MARY AUSTIN, prob. b. ca. 1757; d. Hamilton 13 Oct. 1841 ae 76 (not named) "widow of Edmund."*

They resided first in Ipswich, where in 1790 the household comprised one man, two boys and three women, but by 1794 were living in Hamilton.   Edmund was a private in the Revolution.

The will of Edmund Knowlton of Hamilton, signed 14 Feb. 1827 presented 3 June 1828, names wife Mary; sons Edmund, Moses and James; granddau. Esther Hardy; grandson Timothy Burnham; son Edmund, executor.

Children (KNOWLTON) b. Ipswich: MARY[6] (or Polly) b. 1775 (from d. Mary Burnham); MOSES bp. 1781; JAMES bp. 1783; and EDMUND bp. 1791.

References: VR HAMILTON, IPSWICH. KNOWLTON ANCY pp. 44, 67. KNOWLTON ERRORS pp. 29, 41. DAR PATRIOT INDEX p. 394. Essex Co. PR #16065(Edmund Knowlton). 1790 CENSUS MA:76. 1830 CENSUS MA: Hamilton. 1840 CENSUS MA: Hamilton.

25   MOSES KNOWLTON[5]   (Benjamin[4], Susanna Dutch[3], Susanna[2] More, Richard[1])   b. ca. 1758; d. Poland ME bef. 21 Nov. 1835.

He m. Gloucester 27 Dec. 1781 POLLY (or Mary) PULSIFER (or Pulcifer), b. Gloucester 23 Aug. 1763; living Gloucester 21 May 1819; dau. of David and Hannah (Pulsifer) Pulcifer Jr.

Moses Knowlton of Gloucester and wife Mary conveyed to Malachi Knowlton of Ipswich 29 Jan. 1785 his inheritance from his father Benjamin Knowlton late of Ipswich deceased, "my part in my mother's thirds, as well as the two thirds which now falls to me."   In 1790 "Moses Knoulton" headed a household in Gloucester comprising one man, one boy and five females.   Moses Knowlton and wife Mary of Gloucester sold land in Gloucester on 21 May 1819.   By 22 June 1819 "Moses Nolton" was in Poland ME when he bought of Josiah Dunn 100 acres there, which on 15 Dec. 1820 he sold to David Knowlton.

On 25 Aug. 1828 David granted the northeast half of this land to "my father Moses Knowlton" of Poland.   David Knowlton of Poland 21 Nov. 1835 sold this same half as administrator of the estate of Moses Knowlton late of Poland.

---

*The 1830 Census lists Mary Knowlton over 70 living with one female over 40 in Hamilton. Mary is presumably the female over 80 living with Edmund Knowlton (over 50) and family in Hamilton in 1840. Either the age at death given for the "widow of Edmund" is in error, or else Edmund had a second wife Mary.

Children (KNOWLTON) bp. Gloucester "of Moses": HANNAH[6] bp. 1782; MOSES bp. 1784; a dau. (pos. MARY) bp. 1787; twins ESTHER and SUSANNA bp. 1789; BENJAMIN bp. 1801 [1791?], d. Gloucester 1803 ae ca. 12; ELIZABETH bp. 1801; DAVID bp. 1801; and BENJAMIN bp. 1805.

References: VR GLOUCESTER. KNOWLTON ANCY pp. 44, 68[errors!]. Essex Co. LR 166:141; 221:75; 357:171(Moses Knowlton). Cumberland Co. ME LR 89:78(Moses Knowlton); 89:138(Josiah Dunn); 114:221: 148:376(David Knowlton). 1790 CENSUS MA:73. POLAND [ME] PAST & PRESENT, Chap. II p. 12[cites wrong dau. of David Pulsifer as Moses' wife].

   26 EPHRAIM KNOWLTON[5] (Benjamin[4], Susanna Dutch[3], Susanna[2] More, Richard[1]) bp. Ipswich 26 June 1758; d. Thomaston ME "formerly of Hamilton" 13 May 1831 ae 74.
   He m. Ipswich 11 Sept. 1780 MOLLY (or Mary) MURPHY, b. Manchester 3 March 1754; bur. Salem 11 Sept. 1838 ae 84 yrs; dau. of Thomas and Mary (Belsher) Murphy.
   Ephraim was a cooper and lived in Ipswich, Wenham, Hamilton by 1794, Beverly, and finally Thomaston ME by 1803. He was a private in the Revolution. In 1790 Ephraim's household in Ipswich comprised one man, one boy and five females.
   Administration of the estate of Ephraim Knowlton of Thomaston, Lincoln Co., ME was recorded at Salem MA (and evidently not at Wiscasset ME). The widow and heirs requested 4 Feb. 1832 appointment of John S. Williams as administrator and signed: Molly Knowlton, Eunice Smith, Fanny Fernandes, James Richardson for self and wife, and J. B. Winchester who mar. grandchild Cynthia Richardson. On 19 April 1823 Jacob S. Ulmer sold land to Ephraim Knowlton Jr. and Benjamin Knowlton of Thomaston; assuming Benjamin was then at least 21, he was probably a son of Ephraim[5]. Also marrying in Thomaston were Lucy and Sarah Knowlton; however they might be grandchildren of Ephraim[5]. Molly's dower included a section of a house in Hamilton, and other land. Included among debts of Ephraim's estate, 3 May 1832, was money due to Ebenezer Clark for house rent for wife of sd. Knowlton for six years. It appears that Ephraim and wife Molly had been living apart for some time.

   Children (KNOWLTON): POLLY[6] bp. Ipswich 1781; KATIE (or Catherine) b. ca. 1783; EPHRAIM bp. Ipswich 1785; EUNICE bp. Ipswich 1787; ENOS bp. Ipswich 1791; TEMPLE (son) bp. Ipswich 1793, bur. Salem 1812; child b. and d. Hamilton 1795; FANNIE b. Hamilton 1798; and prob. BENJAMIN.

References: VR BEVERLY, HAMILTON, IPSWICH, MANCHESTER, SALEM. DAR PATRIOT INDEX p. 394. KNOWLTON ANCY pp. 44, 69[includes other children prob. of Ephraim[6]]. KNOWLTON ERRORS pp. 29, 41, 42. MA OBITS 3:2677(Ephraim Knowlton). THOMASTON ME HIST 2:302. 1790

CENSUS MA:76. Essex Co. LR 145:104(Ephraim Knowlton). Essex Co. PR #16066(Ephraim Knowlton). Lincoln Co. ME LR 53:122(Thompson & Totman to Ephraim Knowlton); 122:93(Jacob Ulmer to Ephraim Knowlton Jr. and Benjamin Knowlton). MSSR 9:382.

27 MALACHI KNOWLTON[5] (Benjamin[4], Susanna Dutch[3], Susanna[2] More, Richard[1]) b. Ipswich 10 Jan. 1759; d. Hamilton, run over by his wagon, 13 Sept. 1830 ae 72.
He m. Wenham 14 June 1781 ABIGAIL PATCH, b. 6 Sept. 1762; d. Hamilton 21 or 22 Aug. 1839 ae 77. No record of her parents found in birth records or Essex Co. probates.
Malachi served in the Revolution as a fifer, and participated at the surrender of Burgoyne. He lived in Ipswich until 1794, then in Hamilton. In 1790 his household comprised one man, three boys and two females.
The will of Malachi Knowlton of Hamilton, husbandman, signed 29 May 1822 presented 5 Oct. 1830, names wife Abigail, mentions the pew bought of his father Patch, sons Michael and Azor, and daus. Lavinia, Marcy and Anna; son Ivers, executor.
In a disallowed claim for pension in 1839 by Abigail Knowlton of Hamilton widow are found the birth dates of both Malachi and Abigail, their marriage in Wenham, birth dates of their six children, and Malachi's death.

Children (KNOWLTON) first four bp. Ipswich, last two b. Hamilton, all births on a paper evidently written by Malachi: MICHAEL[6] b. 1782; AZOR b. 1784; LAVINIA b. 1785; IVERS b. 1790; MERCY b. 1800; and ANNA b. 1802.

References: VR HAMILTON, IPSWICH. KNOWLTON ANCY pp. 44, 68. KNOWL-
            TON ERRORS pp. 29, 41. 1790 CENSUS MA:76. DAR PATRIOT
INDEX p. 394. ESSEX INST COL 51:216. Essex Co. PR #16087(Malachi
Knowlton). Rev. Pension #R6039(Malachi Knowlton).

28 HEPZIBAH KNOWLTON[5] (Benjamin[4], Susanna Dutch[3], Susanna[2] More, Richard[1]) b. 1762 prob. Ipswich; d. there 6 Jan. 1818 in 56 yr.
She m. Ipswich 16 Aug. 1787 JONAS CUMMINGS "of Topsfield," b. Ipswich 22 Oct. 1763; d. Topsfield 16 Jan. 1804 ae 40; son of Thomas and Lois (Boardman) Cummings. Jonas was living in Topsfield in 1790 with four females.
Widow Hephzibah was bonded as administratrix of the estate of Jonas Cummings late of Topsfield on 17 April 1804. On 7 May 1804 she was appointed guardian of three minor children of Jonas Cummings late of Topsfield: Sarah age 16, Elizabeth 14 and Hephsibah 7. In 1815 Joseph Choate and wife Sally, John Choate Jr. and wife Elizabeth, both of Ipswich, and widow Hepzabeth Cummings of Topsfield transferred land in Hamilton; Sally and Elizabeth signed

"in their own right," acknowledging their signatures 5
April 1815. No deed was found involving daughter Hepsibah[6].

   Children (CUMMINGS) first two bp. Ipswich, last bp. Hamilton:
SARAH[6] bp. 1788; ELIZABETH bp. 1790; and HEPZA bp. Hamilton 1796.

References: VR ESSEX, IPSWICH, HAMILTON, TOPSFIELD. Essex Co. PR
             #6715(Jonas Cummings); #6738(Hephzibah Cummings gdn.).
Essex Co. LR 210:69; 216:270(Joseph Choate et al.). KNOWLTON ANCY p.
45[error]. 1790 CENSUS MA:99.

     29 ABIGAIL KNOWLTON[5] (Benjamin[4], Susanna Dutch[3], Su-
sanna[2] More, Richard[1]) b. 1764 prob. Ipswich; d. Beverly
20 Oct. 1808 in 45th year "wife of Jonathan."
     She m. Ipswich 2 Feb. 1792 JONATHAN LAMSON (or Lamp-
son) 3d, b. Hamilton 1768; d. there 1 March 1848 ae 80 yrs
widower; son of Jonathan and Bethiah (Whipple) Lamson.
[Marriage record gives her name as "Elizabeth," but intention shows "Abigail."] He m. (2) Beverly 1809 Lydia
Appleton, by whom he had Thomas Appleton, Isaac Dean,
Lydia and Jarvis.
     Jonathan Lamson is revealed to be an heir of Benjamin
Knowlton in a deed (see #8). He lived in Beverly. The
will of Jonathan Lamson, yeoman of Hamilton, dated 3 April
1846 presented 4 April 1848, names son Jarvis principal
heir; dau. Abigail widow of Joseph Conant; dau. Lydia A.
wife of Jacob L. Patch of Hamilton; sons Albert, Thomas A.
and Jonathan.

   Children (LAMSON) b. Beverly to Jonathan and Abigail: JONATHAN[6]
b. 1793; BENJAMIN b. 1794; HENRY b. 1795; -----(son) b. and d. 1798;
ABIGAIL b. 1801; and ALBERT b. 1805 [is this the ALFRED bp. 1805 "son
of Jonathan"?].

References: VR BEVERLY, HAMILTON, IPSWICH. LAMSON FAM pp. 89, 137.
             KNOWLTON ANCY pp. 45, 69. KNOWLTON ERRORS pp. 29, 42
[errs in naming Abigail's husband as Jonathan *Larcom*]. Essex Co. LR
336:1(Ezra Knowlton et al.). Essex Co. PR #44848(Jonathan Lamson).

     30 BENJAMIN KNOWLTON[5] (Benjamin[4], Susanna Dutch[3],
Susanna[2] More, Richard[1]) b. Ipswich 1766; d. Beverly 28
May 1839 ae 73.
     He m. (1) Beverly 1 Dec. 1789 ABIGAIL LARCOM, b.
there 7 Aug. 1770; d. there 18 or 20 Dec. 1824 ae 54 "wife
of Benjamin"; dau. of Jonathan and Abigail (Ober) Larcom.
     He m. (2) Beverly 4 April 1826 ABIGAIL (HOOPER)
HOOPER, b. Manchester 30 Aug. 1772; d. Beverly or Manchester 16 or 18 Feb. 1845 ae "72 y 1 d"(*sic*); dau. of Edward

and Mary (Edwards) Hooper, and widow prob. of Jonathan Hooper.

Benjamin was a cordwainer, and so designated in the settlement of his father's estate; he is thus distinguished from the Capt. Benjamin Knowlton who died in Beverly in 1822 ae 56 (also born in 1766). Administration on the estate of Benjamin Knowlton of Beverly cordwainer was declined by his widow Abigail 3 June 1839, but accepted by his son Hezekiah Knowlton. Named as heirs at law 3 June 1839 were Hezekiah Knowlton, Joseph Williams, Abigail Williams, Ira Knowlton, Elizabeth Knowlton and Hannah Knowlton; all except Elizabeth [undoubtedly the wife of Ira] signed as heirs 28 Aug. 1839.

Records of the estate of Abigail Knowlton of Beverly widow indicate her death 18 Feb. 1845, her only son Andrew Hooper administrator, and only dau. Abigail Russell.

Children (KNOWLTON) b. Beverly to Benjamin and the first Abigail: DAVID[6] b. 1790, lost at sea 1813; ABIGAIL b. 1792; IRA b. 1797; HEZEKIAH b. 1801; and HANNAH b. 1803.

References: VR BEVERLY, MANCHESTER. KNOWLTON ANCY pp. 45, 69. KNOWLTON ERRORS pp. 29, 42. Essex Co. PR #16059(Benjamin Knowlton); #44713(Abigail Knowlton).

31 HANNAH KNOWLTON[5] (Benjamin[4], Susanna Dutch[3], Susanna[2] More, Richard[1]) b. Ipswich 1767; d. after 17 April 1801 but bef. 1804.

She m. Ipswich 27 Sept. 1792 OLIVER NORTON, bp. Ipswich 16 March 1766; d. So. Berwick ME 11 May 1819 ae 53 "formerly of Ipswich"; son of George and Sarah (Whipple) (Appleton) Norton. In his will signed and probated 1803 George Norton of Ipswich mentions wife Sarah and son Oliver. Oliver m. (2) bet. 1801 and 1804 Betsy -----. He m. (3) Berwick ME 1804 Bathsheba Roberts, by whom he had sons William and George.

Oliver was a baker, and lived in Ipswich until 1801, when he and wife Hannah sold "the tenement whereon I live-- dwelling house and barn" 17 April 1801. He moved to Berwick ME, where on 1 Dec. 1802 Winthrop B. Norton sold land in Berwick to Oliver Norton of Berwick baker.

In the absence of a probate record, the following deeds confirm Oliver's children. Nirum Norton of So. Berwick, trader, granted to Oliver Norton of Boston, joiner, "All my right...in the estate of our late father Oliver Norton deceased...I being an heir to one undivided fifth part of the same" 12 Oct. 1822. Oliver Norton with wife Mary H. of So. Berwick, joiner, quitclaimed to widow Bathsheba Norton of So. Berwick right to the estate of Oliver Norton deceased including the "house where I now dwell" 18 Sept. 1828. Charles E. Norton of So. Berwick, esquire,

quitclaimed to George Norton of Dover NH, cabinet maker,
rights in real estate in So. Berwick which "belonged to
our late honoured father Oliver Norton deceased" and "heir
at law of Sally Norton and William Norton both deceased"
15 June acknowledged 31 July 1832. George Norton of Dover
NH, cabinet maker, transferred to Oliver Norton of So.
Berwick, joiner, the home lot of his late father Oliver
Norton deceased "which I inherited from my mother Bathsheba Norton of So. Berwick deceased" 16 June 1832.

     Children (NORTON) first six b. Ipswich to Oliver and Hannah:
SALLY[6] b. 1793, d. So. Berwick 1823 unm.; NIRAM b. 1795; CHARLES E. b.
1795 (a twin?); twin sons b. and d. 1797; OLIVER b. 1798; and pos.
HANNAH (though she may have been born to second wife Betsy) d.y.

References: VR HAMILTON, IPSWICH. MA OBITS 4:3309. Tombstones, So.
          Berwick ME Cemetery. Essex Co. LR 172:93(Oliver Norton).
Essex Co. PR #19697(George Norton). ESSEX INST HIST COLL 74:337.
KNOWLTON ANCY p. 45. KNOWLTON ERRORS p. 29. York Co. ME LR 68:235
(Winthrop B. Norton); 110:179(Nirum Norton); 137:240; 164:234(Oliver
Norton); 143:70; 273:93(Charles E. Norton); 164:234(George Norton).
Berwick ME town rec. So. Berwick ME town rec. SOU BERWICK ME REC BK
pp. 61, 63. Bible Rec., Sanford (ME) Hist. Soc.(Roberts Family).

     32 ESTHER KNOWLTON[5] (Benjamin[4], Susanna Dutch[3], Su-
sanna[2] More, Richard[1]) bp. Ipswich 1 Jan. 1769; d. Hamilton 1 Nov. 1831 ae 63 "wife of Daniel".
     She m. Hamilton 2 Feb. 1794 DANIEL RUST, b. 1765; d.
Hamilton 9 Feb. 1845 ae 79y 7m "married." He m. (2) Salem
1832 Mrs. Hannah Kinsman, d. Hamilton 1841. He m. (3)
Hamilton 1842 Betsy Patch, by whom he had Esther (d.y.)
and Ruth. Daniel was a farmer and cooper.
     Administration of the estate of Daniel Rust of Hamil-
ton, cooper, was granted to eldest son Daniel Rust of
Hamilton on 18 Feb. 1845. Named as heirs 6 Jan. 1846 were
widow Betty Rust; Edward Pousland attorney for Betty Rust
and attorney and guardian of Ruth Rust; N. W. Hazen guardian of the three children of Seth and Mary Shearman of Andover deceased; Samuel Rust; William and Louisa Meady; and
"one child about two years of age" [Ruth].
     Daniel and Samuel Rust of Hamilton, cordwainers, and
William and Louisa Meady of Salem sold three undivided
fifth parts of a woodlot in Hamilton formerly owned by
Daniel Rust deceased, signed also by Hitty Rust wife of
Daniel the grantor, 26 July 1845.

     Children (RUST) b. Hamilton to Daniel and Esther: RUTH[6] bp.
1795, d. 1814; JOHN b. 1796; ESTHER b. 1798, d. 1825 unm.; DANIEL b.
1800; LOUISA b. 1802; HANNAH b. 1804; MEHITABEL bp. 1806, d. 1834 unm.;
child b. 1807; child b. 1808; SAMUEL bp. 1809; MARY b. 1810; and RUTH
b. 1814, d. Andover 1832.

References: VR ANDOVER, HAMILTON, IPSWICH, SALEM. KNOWLTON ANCY p.
45. KNOWLTON ERRORS p. 29. Essex Co. PR #52367(Daniel
Rust); #53137(gdn. for Shearmans). Essex Co. LR 353:12(Wm. Meady);
358:29(Nathan W. Hazen); 362:79(Daniel Rust et al.). MA VR: Beverly
deaths 256:191.

    33 ANNIS (or Anne) KNOWLTON[5] (Benjamin[4], Susanna
Dutch[3], Susanna[2] More, Richard[1]) bp. Ipswich 6 Dec. 1770;
d. Hamilton 14 June 1852 ae 82, "b. Hamilton, wife of William Foster Sr."
    She m. Hamilton 22 June 1797 WILLIAM FOSTER, bp. Ips-
wich 11 March 1770; d. Hamilton 8 Dec. 1856 ae 86y 8m
"shoemaker"; son of Reynold and Elizabeth (Conant) Foster.
    The will of William Foster of Hamilton, signed 15
Sept. 1856 presented 1 Feb. 1857, names dau. Abigail D.
Witham and grandchildren Cynthia Foster Gibbs, Elea Sophia
Foster and Charles Warren Foster; the latter to be executor. (The will of William Foster[6] Jr. of Hamilton [his
son] dated 11 April 1856 probated 6 May 1856, names wife
Sophia C.; son Charles Warren, dau. Elea Sophia.)

    Children (FOSTER) b. Hamilton: WILLIAM[6] b. 1798; IVERS b. 1801,
d. Andover 1822 ae 21; CYNTHIA b. 1804; ABIGAIL DEAN bp. 1809, d.
Hamilton 1813 ae 4; and ABIGAIL DANE b. 1814.

References: VR ANDOVER, HAMILTON, IPSWICH. MA VR (State House, Bos-
ton) Hamilton deaths 66:117; 102:122. Essex Co. PR
#39520(Wm. Foster); #39519(Wm. Foster Jr.). KNOWLTON ANCY pp. 45, 70.
KNOWLTON ERRORS p. 29. 1850 CENSUS MA:Hamilton. Hamilton Town Clerk
Rec.

    34 ELIZABETH KNOWLTON[5] (Benjamin[4], Susanna Dutch[3], Su-
sanna[2] More, Richard[1]) bp. Ipswich 19 Dec. 1773; d. Portland ME 6 June 1862 ae 88.
    She m. Hamilton 14 Feb. 1797 DANIEL CUMMINGS, b.
Topsfield 10 April 1774; d. Freeport ME 2 Aug. 1854; son
of Thomas and Lois (Boardman) Cummings. He was a farmer,
carpenter and church builder.
    Daniel went to Freeport shortly after his marriage.
He was called a housewright of Freeport when in 1803 he
bought land of Barnabas Bartol. On 4 June 1805 Daniel
Cummings of Freeport gentleman and wife Betsey sold some
Freeport land. Daniel of Freeport, housewright, sold land
in Topsfield to Malachi Knowlton in Feb. 1807, and also
transferred land to "Hipzebeth" Cummings widow of Topsfield (see #28).
    On 22 Jan. 1844 Daniel Cummings of Portland ME house-
wright, with Elizabeth Cummings releasing dower, sold land
in Portland to Daniel Cummings Jr., trader. On 19 March
1850 Freeman G. Cummings of Portland, carpenter, leased
unto Daniel Cummings of Portland, carpenter, and his wife

Elizabeth "for and during the terms of their natural
lives" land and building in Portland.

    Children (CUMMINGS) all b. Freeport, except last b. Portland:
CLARISSA[6] b. 1798; ELIZABETH b. 1799; JOHN BOARDMAN b. 1801; PERLEY
DODGE b. 1802, d. 1804; THOMAS b. 1804; FREEMAN GRIDLEY b. 1806; PER-
LEY DODGE b. 1808; LOUISA DODGE b. 1810; DANIEL b. 1812; MARY HYDE b.
1815; and JOSEPH PORTER b. 1817.

References: VR HAMILTON, TOPSFIELD. KNOWLTON ANCY p. 45. KNOWLTON
              ERRORS p. 29.   ME GEN 2:1042. Essex Co. LR 180:69; 206:
155(Daniel Cummings). CUMMINGS GEN pp. 173, 373-5. Cumberland Co. ME
LR 44:31(Barnabas Bartol); 46:370; 182:268(Daniel Cummings); 220:453
(Freeman G. Cummings). Portland ME Cemetery Rec. (city clerk).

T H O M A S   R O G E R S

of the

M A Y F L O W E R

Compiled by

Alice Wilma Andrews Westgate

Alice Wilma Andrews Westgate is a descendant of Pilgrims John Alden, Isaac Allerton, Francis Cooke, John Howland, Richard Warren and William White. Widow of Rodman Edwin Westgate, who was also a descendant of Pilgrim William White, she has served on the Board of Assistants of the Massachusetts Mayflower Society. This is her first published genealogical work.

THOMAS ROGERS

Little is known about Pilgrim Thomas Rogers, and nothing at all is known about his ancestry. His alleged descent from John Rogers the Martyr was disproved in the 19th
century by Joseph Chester and Henry F. Waters. Banks notes
that taxpayers named Thomas Rogers, Christopher Martin and
John Hooke appear in the London parish of St. Bartholomew
the Great early in 1620, but there is no proof that these
were the *Mayflower* passengers.

Our earliest known encounter with Pilgrim Thomas
Rogers was on 25 June 1618 when he became a citizen of Lei-
den, Holland, vouched for by William Jepson, formerly of
Worksop, Notts., and by Roger Wilson, formerly of Sandwich,
Kent Co., England. Banks therefore speculates that Rogers
might have been from one of those towns. On 1 April 1620
Thomas sold his Leiden house on the Barbarasteeg for 300
guilders, in preparation for the journey to New England.

Governor Bradford says in his history of the Plymouth
settlement that on board the *Mayflower* were "Thomas Rogers
and Joseph his son; his other children came afterwards....
Thomas Rogers died in the first sickness but his son Joseph
is still living [1650] and is married and hath six children. The rest of Thomas Rogers' [children] came over and
are married and have many children." Therefore we know that
Thomas and his son Joseph arrived at Cape Cod aboard the
ship *Mayflower*, and on 11 November 1620 according to their
calendar, or 21 November on ours, Thomas was one of forty-
one signers of the Mayflower Compact. Thomas did not live
through the rigorous winter which carried off half the
group, but young Joseph, like so many of the children, did
survive.

Recent discoveries show that Thomas had a family living in Leiden, Holland, when the 1622 Poll Tax was taken.
In the Over 't Hoff Quarter, in a house with other Pilgrim
families in St. Peter's Churchyard west-side, were Jan
Thomasz, orphan from England without means; Elsgen Rogiers,
widow of Thonis Rogiers, an Englishwoman; and Lysbeth and
Grietgen her children, poor people. Translated this could
read John, son of Thomas; Elizabeth Rogers, widow of
Thomas; and Elizabeth and Margaret, her children. At that
period the word orphan meant that either or both parents
were dead.

In the 1623 Plymouth Colony land division, Joseph
Rogers was allotted two acres--one for himself and one on
behalf of his late father. He may have been living in the
household of Governor Bradford with whom he was grouped on

22 May 1627, in the division of cattle. Joseph and twelve
other inhabitants of Plymouth received "an heyfer of the
last year which was of the Great white-back cow that was
brought over in the *Ann*, and two shee goats."

Governor Bradford's statement that the rest of Thomas
Rogers' children came over and married and had children,
seems clearly to indicate that more than one of his children came to New England after 1620. We know that his son
John came to Plymouth about 1630. Although many other
male Rogers immigrants have been claimed as sons of Thomas
the Pilgrim, none of the claims has been proved, and some
have been disproved.* Therefore it seems likely that at
least one of the Rogers daughters who were living in Holland in 1622 came over. John[2] and Joseph[2] Rogers each
named a daughter Elizabeth, perhaps thereby indicating
that their sister Elizabeth lived in New England. Unfortunately extensive research has failed to uncover any
further evidence.

John[2] Rogers came to Plymouth about 1630, when the
last of the Leiden contingent arrived, and was in Plymouth
Colony on 25 March 1633 when he was taxed 9 shillings.
The proof of his identity lies in a grant made 6 April
1640 to "Joseph Rogers and John Rogers his brother...fifty
acres apeece of upland...at the North River." Both then
had growing families to carry forward the Rogers heritage,
although only Joseph's descendants would carry forward the
Rogers name beyond the fourth generation.

References: BANKS ENGLISH ANCESTRY p. 78. DEXTER p. 632. TAG 52:
         110-3. PLYMOUTH COLONY RECS 1:11, 144; 12:4, 12. JAMES
ROGERS OF NEW LONDON CT AND HIS DESCENDANTS, by James S. Rogers (Boston 1902) p. 13. BRADFORD'S HIST (1952) pp. 442, 446.

---

*For proof that William Rogers of Connecticut and Long Island was not
a son of the Pilgrim see NYGBR 60:102-4.

FIRST GENERATION

1   THOMAS[1] ROGERS   prob. b. England; d. Plymouth "in the
first sickness" age and parentage unknown.
      He m. ELSGEN -----, prob. b. England; d. prob. Leiden,
Holland, after 1622, age and parentage unknown.
      Elsgen was apparently living in Leiden, Holland, in
1622 in a house with other Pilgrim families and her children John, Elizabeth and Margaret. No further record of
any of these, except John, has yet been found, except
Governor Bradford's statement that the rest of Thomas'
children came over and married and had children. There
are no probate records for Thomas or Elsgen.

         Children (ROGERS) b. England or Holland:

   2   i   JOSEPH[2] b. 1610 or earlier
   3   ii   JOHN b. ca. 1614
         iii   LYSBETH (or Elizabeth) living 1622; n.f.r., but may have
                  come to New England and married.
          iv   GRIETGEN (or Margaret) living 1622; n.f.r., but may have
                  come to New England and married.

References: MQ 43:103-4. TAG 52:110.

SECOND GENERATION

2   JOSEPH[2] ROGERS (Thomas[1])   b. England or Holland 1610
or earlier; d. bet. 2 and 15 Jan. 1677/8; bur. Eastham in
Old Cove Burial Ground.
      He m. HANNAH ----- who was named in his will 2 Jan.
1677/8. She may not have been his only wife, and may not
have been the mother of his children.
      Joseph came to Plymouth with his father in 1620 aboard
the *Mayflower*. In the 1623 land division, he received two
acres, one for himself and one on behalf of his father.
Joseph may have been living in the household of Governor
Bradford with whom he received his share of cattle in 1627.
Joseph was made a freeman in 1633 and was taxed 25 March
1633, just before the birth of his first child. On 2 March
1635/6 he was granted permission to operate a ferry over
the Jones River near his house, and on 7 June 1636 he was
first recorded as serving on a jury. He was granted 30
acres of land on 5 Nov. 1638, and was made a constable of
Duxbury 3 March 1639/40. On this latter date, Joseph was
one of the purchasers or "old comers" to whom land was
granted, and on 6 Apr. 1640 he and his brother John were
each granted 50 acres of upland. Joseph was one of a

group of Duxbury inhabitants who were to lay out land 20
Oct. 1645.

Joseph apparently moved to Eastham, then called
Nauset, about 1647 for on 1 June of that year he was appointed lieutenant to exercise the men in arms there. He
apparently spent a brief time at Sandwich in the early
1650's. He served on the council of war in June and Oct.
1658. Lt. Rogers was freed from his lieutenancy 1 Oct.
1661, but reestablished 8 June 1664. He was a selectman
at Eastham 1670. On 31 Jan. 1672 Lt. Joseph Rogers of
Eastham sold a piece of land. No wife was mentioned in
any of his deeds.

The original will of Joseph Rogers is no longer in
existence. A copy of his will, written in the Plymouth
Colony Record Book at the time of his death, does not
mention his daughter Mary, but reads as follows:

I Joseph Rogers seni^r: of Eastham of Good understanding and
prfect memory being weake in body; and not knowing the the day of my
departure out of this life, doe thinke meet to Leave this as my Last
will and Testament

Imp^r: I Comend my soule to God that Gave it; whoe is my God, and
father in Jesus Christ, and my body to the earth by decent buriall;

firstly And Concerning my temporall estate that God hath poses-
sed me off; I doe make my son Thomas Rogers whole and sole executor
which I will should be disposed of as followeth:

Imp^r I doe Give unto my Loveing son James Rogers and his heires
Lawfully begotten of his body: or the next of kinn; my house and housing and Land with ffences or the like appurtenances, that I now dwell
in and Improve adjoyning to my house be it more or lesse; as it is
Recorded & bounded on the Towne book, I say I doe Give it to him and
to his heires Lawfully begotten of his body forever or the Next kin-
dred;

Item I doe give To my sonnes John and James Rogers all my meddow
Ground that I bought of the Indians ffrancis and Josiah, Lying att
Pottammacutt and therabouts; I say I doe give and will it to them and
theire heires forever equally to be devided

Item I doe Give to my sonnes Thomas and John Rogers and theire
heires all my meddow and sedge lying on the otherside of the Cove, on
keeskagansett syde; I say I doe Give it to them and theire heires Lawfully begotten of theire bodys forever;

I doe Give to my Daughter Elizabeth higgens the wife of Jonathan
higgens six acrees of Land lying Neare the Barly neck, by a swamp
Called Ceader swamp; as it is Recorded and bounded in the Towne book,
I say I Give this six acrees To her and her heires of her body for
ever; shee nor they shall not sell hier farm it out, directly nor In-
directly to any p^{r}son whatsoever, except in Case of Removall it shalbe
lawfull for my sonnes or theire heires to buy or purchase it;

Item I Give to Benjah higgens my Grandchild on Condition hee
live with mee untill I die; I say I Give to him and his heires, one
third p^{r}te of all my upland and meddow att Paomett, purchased and unpurchased.

Item It is my will That the Remainder of my lands or marshes, both att the barly necke, Pochett Iland Paomett Billingsgate or elswher purchased or unpurchased not disposed of p^{r}ticularly in my will; I say it is my will that all those lands be equally devided betwixt my three sonnes Thomas John and James Rogers; and the heires lawfully of theire bodyes for ever; Noteing that my son Thomas his twenty acrees of upland that alreddy hee hath in the barly necke be p^{r}te of his devision of my land in the barly Necke;

Item I doe Give unto my daughter hannah Rogers, if shee be not disposed of in Marriage before my decease, and my wifes decease, then I say I doe Give to her my bed and beding with all the furniture therto belonging or that shall belonge therto att our decease;

Alsoe it is my will that shee shall have her Choise of one Cow before my Cattle be distributed, and the use of three acrees of Tillage Ground; ffenced in, with the arable Ground of her bretheren in the barly necke if shee desirs, it soe longe as shee lives unmarryed;

Item it is my will that Benjah higgens shall have one of my Cowes after mine and my wifes decease

Item it is my will Concerning my Loveing wife hannah Rogers that shee live in My house as longe as shee lives, and shalbe Comfortably maintained by my stocke and to have the use of all my houshold stuffe, That shee Needs as longe as shee lives for her Comfort and that none of my household furniture or stocke be disposed of, as longe as shee lives, save onely hannahs Cowe

Item I will that ten shillings of my estate be disposed off for the use of the Church of Christ in Eastham as shalbe Judged most Nessesarie

Item I will that the Remainder of my Stocke estate houshold furniture that my wife shall Leave att her decease Not disposed of in my will before written; be equally devided between all my Children; and Benjah higgens to have an equall share with each of them; This is my Last will and Testament as witnes my hand and seale this 2^{cond} of January 1677,

Joseph Rogers and A seale

Joseph's inventory was taken 15 Jan. 1677/8 and the will was probated 5 March 1677/8. Depositions of Jonathan Sparrow and Samuel Berry show that the grandson called "Benjah Higgens" in the will was also known as Beriah Higgens. Son Thomas Rogers died before completing the settlement of the estate and so Capt. Sparrow and remaining son John Rogers were impowered to handle the settlement.

Children (ROGERS) recorded Sandwich to Lt. Joseph Rogers:

   i   SARAH[3] b. prob. Duxbury 6 Aug. 1633; d. 15 Aug. 1633.

  ii JOSEPH b. prob. Duxbury 19 July 1635; d. Eastham 27 Dec. 1660. He m. Eastham 4 Apr. 1660 SUSANNA DEANE, b. Plymouth ca. 1634; prob. d. Eastham bef. April 1701; dau. of Stephen and Elizabeth (Ring) Deane. She m. (2) Eastham 1663 Stephen Snow, a descendant of Pilgrim Stephen Hopkins.

At the 5 March 1660/1 court held at Plymouth, John
Hawes of Yarmouth was found not guilty of "takeing away
the life of Josephth Rogers of Eastham by giveing him a
most deadly fall, on the 25 of Dec. 1660 in the towne of
Eastham, whereof he...about 48 hours after died." Also
on 5 March 1660/1 the Governor was authorized to give
oath to Susanna the wife of late deceased Joseph Rogers
for the inventory of his estate, and on 1 March 1663/4
Thomas Rogers of Eastham was appointed to administer the
estate of Joseph Rogers Jr., as his heir. On the 8th of
the third month [May] 1674 Thomas Rogers husbandman, heir
of his brother Joseph Rogers of Eastham, deeded to his
loving sister [in-law] Susanna Snow, late wife of Joseph
Rogers, and to her husband Steven Snow his rights to the
estate of Joseph, except lands and housing given him by
his father Rogers or the town.
        Apparently Joseph and Susanna had no children.

```
4   iii  THOMAS     b. prob. Duxbury 29 March 1638
5   iv   ELIZABETH  b. prob. Duxbury 29 Sept. 1639
6   v    JOHN       b. prob. Duxbury 3 April 1642
7   vi   MARY       b. prob. Duxbury 22 Sept. 1644
8   vii  JAMES      b. Eastham 18 Oct. 1648
9   viii HANNAH     b. Sandwich or Eastham 8 Aug. 1652
```

References: MD 3:67-71; 6:202; 7:109; 16:238. TAG 42:200. PLYMOUTH
             COLONY RECS 1:4, 11, 39, 42, 101, 141, 144; 2:4, 88, 117,
177; 3:138, 153, 205-6; 4:5, 55, 64; 5:35; 12:4, 12, 136. Plymouth
Col. LR 3:267(Jos. Rogers); 3:320(Rogers to Snow).

    3 JOHN[2] ROGERS (Thomas[1]) b. England or Holland ca.
1614; d. Duxbury bet. 26 Aug. 1691 and 20 Sept. 1692.
    He m. Plymouth 16 April 1639 ANNA CHURCHMAN, who was
certainly living in May 1665, and prob. alive 23 Aug. 1670;
parentage unknown.*
    John was living in Leiden, Holland, in 1622 with his
mother and sisters, in a house with other Pilgrim families.
He came to New England about 1630 with the last of the
Leiden Pilgrim community, and was first taxed in Plymouth
Colony 25 March 1633. On 20 Oct. 1634 he bought a lot of
land "on Duxbery side." The proof that John Rogers of Duxbury is the son of Pilgrim Thomas Rogers lies in a grant of
50 acres of land each at the North River [at Marshfield]
made 6 April 1640 to "Joseph Rogers and John Rogers his
brother." He first served on a jury 7 Dec. 1641, was admitted a freeman as early as 1 March 1641/2, and was first
appointed a Duxbury highway surveyor 5 June 1644. He
served as a deputy at court on 3 June 1657. On 3 June 1662
he was one of the "ancient freemen" who was given land on
the northerly side of Taunton.

---

*She is apparently not a daughter of Hugh Churchman of Lynn since his
will in 1640 does not mention daughter Anna or Rogers grandchildren.

John Rogers Sr. of Duxbury yeoman sold half his meadow northwest of "Joanes River" in May 1664, with consent
of wife Anna, the only time she is called by name other
than at their marriage. John was appointed a constable of
Duxbury 5 June 1666, and on 2 July 1667 was granted 100
acres on Coteticutt River [Titicut River between Middleboro and Taunton?]. On 23 Aug. 1670 John Rogers of Duxbury weaver "and his wife" acknowledged a deed made 30 Oct.
1654, in which he had sold the 50 acres granted to him in
1640. He was given another 100 acres on the northeast
side of Taunton 4 July 1673. In his last recorded land
transaction, John Rogers Sr. of Duxbury weaver, on 5 Jan.
1680, sold an acre of Duxbury land to Wrestling Brewster,
acknowledging his signature 12 Dec. 1685.

The original will of John Rogers is not in existence
today, but the copy made in the Plymouth County records at
the time of his death, proved 20 Sept. 1692, reads:

On the 26 August in the year of our Lord 1691:
In the Name of God Amen. I John Rogers sen[r] of Duxborough in
the County of New Plimouth Being Sick and weak of Body but of Sound
and perfect mind and memory Praise be therefore Given to Almighty God
Doe make and ordain this my present last will and Testament in maner
and forme following that is to say first and Principally I comend my
soul into the hands of Almighty God Hoping through the merits Death
and Passion of my Saviour Jesus Christ to have full and free pardon
and forgiveness of all my sins and to Inherit Everlasting Life. And
my Body I Commit to the earth to be decently Buried at the discretion
of my Executor hereafter named. And as Touching the Disposall of all
Such Temporall Estate as it hath Pleased God to bestow upon me I Give
and Dispose thereof as followeth . first I will that my debts and
funerall charges be paid.
Item I Give unto my Grandson John Rogers all my houses and Lands
Lying and being in the Township of Duxborough in the County aforesaid
to him and his heires forever. I Give also unto my Grandson John Tisdall for the use of his mother Anne Terrey one half of my Land Divided
and undivided lying and being in the Township of Middleborough Excepting my Right in the Majors Purchase And my Will is that this Land be
disposed of according to his mothers mind. Item I Give unto my Daughter Elizabeth Williams the other half of sd tract of Land in the Township of Middleborough as aforesaid to her and heires. All my Cattell
I Will that they be Equally divided Between my daughter Elizabeth
Williams and my Grandson John Rogers and my Grandson John Tisdall.
Item I Give all my houshold Stuff and moneys whatsoever unto my Grandson John Rogers out of which he shall pay forty shillings to his sister Elibeth Rogers and twenty shillings apeece to his other three
sisters Hannah Bradford Ruth Rogers and Sarah Rogers. Also I Give that
twenty shillings a year which is my due for fourscore acres of land
which I sold to my two Grandsons Joseph Richmond and Edward Richmond
which said twenty shillings a year I Give to my daughter Abigail Richmond. I Doe hereby Constitute make and appoint my Loving Son John

Rogers sole Executor and Administrator of this my last Will and Testament.

John Rogers & a (seal)

Children (ROGERS) prob. b. Duxbury:

10   i   JOHN³ b. ca. 1640
11   ii   (H)ANNA b. bet. 1640 and 1650
12   iii   ABIGAIL b. ca. 1640
13   iv   ELIZABETH b. bef. 1652

References: MD 5:205-6; 13:85. TAG 54:97. PLYMOUTH COLONY RECS
             1:31, 111, 144; 2:33, 72; 3:115; 4:12, 19-20, 123, 161;
5:127; 7:25. Plymouth Col. LR 3:37; 6:65(John Rogers). ESSEX CO PR
1:32(Hugh Churchman). TAG 52:110.

THIRD GENERATION

4 THOMAS³ ROGERS (Joseph², Thomas¹) b. prob. Duxbury 29
March 1638; d. prob. Eastham bet. 5 March 1677/8 and 7 Aug.
1678.
     He m. Eastham 13 Dec. 1665 ELIZABETH SNOW, b. Eastham
ca. 1640; d. there 16 June 1678; dau. of Nicholas and
Constance (Hopkins) Snow, and a descendant of Pilgrim
Stephen Hopkins. The will of Nicholas Snow of Eastham,
drawn 14 Nov. 1676, names only wife Constant and five sons,
but mentions "all my children."
     Thomas Rogers left no will, but his inventory was
taken 7 Aug. 1678, and includes gun, sword, bandoliers,
canoe and Rhemish testatment. On 8 July 1704, 26 years
after the decease of Thomas Rogers late of Eastham, intestate, the Barnstable court ordered an additional settlement made to his dau. Hannah, a minor at the time of his
death, but now wife of Amaziah Harding. Payment was to be
made by sons Thomas and Eleazer Rogers, and by the heirs
of Joseph Rogers, eldest son of the deceased. On 30 Oct.
that year, John Rogers, brother of the deceased, complained
that the settlement still had not been completed.

     Children (ROGERS) b. Eastham:

        i   ELIZABETH⁴ b. 8 Oct. 1666; d. bef. 1704.
14   ii   JOSEPH b. 1 Feb. 1667
15   iii   HANNAH b. 20 March 1669
       iv   THOMAS b. 6 March 1670/1; d. 15 March 1670/1.
16   v   THOMAS b. 6 May 1672
17   vi   ELEAZER b. 3 Nov. 1673
      vii   NATHANIEL b. 18 Jan. 1675; d. bef. 1704.

References: MD 3:167; 6:14; 11:179-180. NEHGR 6:235; 47:82-3; 48:71
             [contain errors]. Plymouth Col. PR 3:2:131(inv.).

5 ELIZABETH[3] ROGERS (Joseph[2], Thomas[1]) b. prob. Duxbury 29 Sept. 1639; d. Eastham bet. 2 Jan. 1677/8 and 4
July 1679.
    She m. Eastham 9 Jan. 1660 JONATHAN HIGGINS, b. Plym-
outh in July 1637; d. after 21 May 1711; son of Richard
and Lydia (Chandler) Higgins. He m. (2) Hannah[3] Rogers,
sister of his deceased wife (see #9).
    There are no probate records for Jonathan Higgins in
Barnstable County. Two deeds confirm most of his children: On 28 May 1711 Joseph Higgins Sr. of Eastham sold to
Jonathan Higgins Jr. and Elisha Higgins both of Eastham
land in Eastham given to our deceased mother Elizabeth
Higgins by our deceased grandfather Lt. Joseph Rogers. On
29 Jan. 1714/5 Nicholas Paine and wife Hannah sold to
their brother Jonathan Higgins Jr. land given by our
grandfather Lt. Joseph Rogers to our mother Elizabeth Higgins deceased.

    Children (HIGGINS) first three b. Eastham, others prob. b.
there, to Jonathan and Elizabeth:

18   i   BERIAH[4] b. 29 Sept. 1661
19   ii   JONATHAN b. "latter end of Aug. 1664"
20   iii JOSEPH b. 14 Feb. 1666[1666/7]
      iv   JEMIMA prob. a twin of Joseph as she d. Eastham 8 May 1723
           in 57th yr. She m. 1 Nov. 1699 JOHN MULFORD, b. Eastham
           in July 1670; d. there 20 April 1730 in 59th yr.; son of
           Thomas and Elizabeth (Barnes) Mulford. John m. (2) East-
           ham 25 Dec. 1723 Mercy Harris [see page 71]. John and
           Jemima had no children.
21   v   HANNAH b. ca. 1672
22   vi   ELISHA b. ca. 1677

References: MD 3:67-71; 6:15; 7:16; 8:4, 245; 17:200-1. HIGGINS DESC
             pp. 41-3, 47-9, 595-6. TAG 40:197-8. NEHGR 123:147-8.
PLYMOUTH COLONY RECS 6:19-20.

6 JOHN[3] ROGERS (Joseph[2], Thomas[1]) b. prob. Duxbury 3
April 1642; d. Eastham bet. 27 April 1713 and 10 Aug. 1714.
    He m. Eastham 19 Aug. 1669 ELIZABETH TWINING, d. East-
ham 10 March 1724/5; dau. of William and Elizabeth (Dean)
Twining. The will of William Twining of Newtown, Bucks
Co. PA, made 26 day 4th mo. 1697, bequeathed to dau. Elizabeth Rogers during her life and then to her youngest living son by John Rogers.
    John Rogers Sr. of Eastham "stricken in years" made
his will 27 April 1713 giving his son John Rogers Jr. land
in Harwich which was laid out in the right of my deceased
father Joseph Rogers. He also gave to sons Judah of Harwich, Joseph of Eastham, Eleazer of Harwich, and Nathaniel
Rogers; three daus. Elizabeth, Mehitable and Hannah

Rogers; grandson John Rogers; wife Elizabeth and son John
Rogers executors. The inventory was taken 10 Aug. 1714,
and the will proved 21 Sept. 1714.

Children (ROGERS) b. Eastham:

	i	SAMUEL[4] b. 1 Nov. 1671; d. 3 Dec. 1671.
23	ii	JOHN b. 4 Nov. 1672
24	iii	JUDAH b. 23 Nov. 1677
25	iv	JOSEPH b. 22 Feb. 1679
	v	ELIZABETH b. 23 Oct. 1682; living 7 April 1713; perhaps was the one who m. Thomas Mayo (see #43).
26	vi	ELEAZER b. 19 May 1685
27	vii	MEHITABLE b. 13 March 1686/7
28	viii	HANNAH b. 5 Aug. 1689
29	ix	NATHANIEL b. 3 Oct. 1693

References: MD 8:90-1; 11:180-1; 15:34. TWINING FAM pp. 27, 29.
           NEHGR 6:235.

7 MARY[3] ROGERS (Joseph[2], Thomas[1]) b. prob. Duxbury 22
Sept. 1644; d. Barnstable after 19 April 1718.
     She m. Barnstable 10 Aug. 1664 JOHN PHINNEY, b. Plym-
outh 24 Dec. 1638; d. Barnstable bet. 19 April 1718 and 9
March 1718/9; son of John and Christiana (-----) Phinney.
     John Phiney of Barnstable weaver made his will 19
April 1718 giving bequests after the decease of his wife
to daus. Mary Eastland, Mercy Crocker and Reliance Morton;
sons John, Joseph, Thomas, Ebenezer, Samuel, Benjamin and
Jonathan Phinney. Son John was to be executor. The inventory was taken 9 March 1718/9, and the will probated 19
June 1719.

Children (PHINNEY) b. Barnstable:

30	i	JOHN[4] b. 5 May 1665
	ii	MELATIAH b. mid Oct. 1666; d. Nov. 1667.
31	iii	JOSEPH b. 28 Jan. 1667 [prob. 1667/8]
32	iv	THOMAS b. Jan. 1671
33	v	EBENEZER b. 18 Feb. 1673
34	vi	SAMUEL b. 4 Nov. 1676
35	vii	MARY b. 3 Sept. 1678
36	viii	MERCY b. 10 July 1679
37	ix	RELIANCE b. 27 Aug. 1681
38	x	BENJAMIN b. 18 June 1682
39	xi	JONATHAN b. 30 July 1684
	xii	HANNAH b. 28 March 1687; bp. 7 Apr. 1689; d. 10 Feb. 1689 [1689/90].

References: MD 3:254; 11:130-1; 20:142-3. Barnstable Co. PR 3:595
           (John Phinney). NEHGR 10:346; 60:67. BARNSTABLE FAMS

1:225. FINNEY-PHINNEY p. 2. MORSE GEN p. 68.

8 JAMES[3] ROGERS (Joseph[2], Thomas[1]) b. Eastham 18 Oct.
1648; d. Eastham 13 April 1678.
       He m. Eastham 11 Jan. 1670 MARY PAINE, b. bef. 1655; d.
after 1705; dau. of Thomas and Mary (Snow) Paine, and a
descendant of Pilgrim Stephen Hopkins. She m. (2) Eastham
24 April 1679 Israel Cole, a descendant of Pilgrim Stephen
Hopkins, by whom she had two children. The will of Thomas
Paine of Eastham, made 12 May 1705 and proved 2 Oct. 1706,
names dau. Mary wife of Israel Cole, and her three eldest
children: James Rogers, Mary Cole and Abigail Yeats.
       On 6 May 1678 the court settled the estate of James
Rogers of Eastham deceased to provide for the widow Mary
Rogers and her small children, with the eldest, Samuel, to
have a double portion and the rest to have equal parts according to the will of their grandfather. The widow was
appointed administratrix. (The birth record of the eldest
son shows that he was originally named Samuel, but in 1680
was to be called James.)

       Children (ROGERS) b. Eastham:

40   i   JAMES[4] (originally named Samuel) b. 30 Oct. 1673
41   ii MARY   b. 9 Nov. 1675
42   iii ABIGAIL b. 2 March 1677/8

References: MD 5:195-6; 6:203; 15:189-190. NEHGR 6:44; 47:186-7.
           CAPE COD HIST 2:369. Barnstable Co. PR 3:360(Thomas
Paine). Plymouth Col. PR 3:2:121(James Rogers).

9 HANNAH[3] ROGERS (Joseph[2], Thomas[1]) b. Sandwich or
Eastham 8 Aug. 1652; d. after 17 Oct. 1690.
       She m. after 16 July 1679 JONATHAN HIGGINS, b. Plym-
outh July 1637; d. after 21 May 1711; son of Richard and
Lydia (Chandler) Higgins. He m. (1) Elizabeth[3] Rogers,
sister of Hannah (see #5).
       There are no probate records for Jonathan Higgins in
Barnstable Co. Evidence that Jonathan married second Hannah Rogers consists of (1) a court record of July 1679
when Jonathan Higgins was fined for his relationship "with
his wife's sister after his wife's death," (2) the prompt
and regular birth of children to him after that date, and
(3) the names of four of those children, identical with
the names of Hannah's siblings.

       Children (HIGGINS) b. Eastham to Jonathan and Hannah:

43   i   ELIZABETH[4] b. 11 Feb. 1680 [prob. 1680/1]
44   ii MARY b. 22 Jan. 1682 [prob. 1682/3]

45   iii   REBECCA b. 30 Nov. 1686
46   iv   JAMES b. 22 July 1688
47   v   SARAH b. 18 Oct. 1690

References: HIGGINS DESC pp. 41-2. MD 5:23; 6:15. NEHGR 123:147-8.
             PLYMOUTH COLONY RECS 6:19-20(m. Higgins-Rogers).

10   JOHN[3] ROGERS (John[2], Thomas[1])   b. ca. 1640; d. Barrington RI 28 June 1732.
     He m. (1) Duxbury in Nov. 1666 ELIZABETH PABODIE, b.
Duxbury 24 April 1647; d. bet. 4 May 1677 and Oct. 1679;
dau. of William and Elizabeth (Alden) Pabodie, and a granddau. of Pilgrim John Alden. The will of William Pabodie of
Little Compton [now RI] aged, dated 13 May 1707, mentions
"heir of dau. Elizabeth," last name not given.
     He m. (2) 21 Oct. 1679 HANNAH (HOBART) BROWNE, b.
Hingham 15 May 1638; d. Bristol RI 11 Sept. 1691; dau. of
Rev. Peter Hobart, and widow of John Browne of Salem. The
will of Rev. Peter Hobart of Hingham, dated 16 Jan. 1678,
mentions his dau. Hannah Browne of Salem, widow of John.
On 10 June 1680 John Rogers of Duxbury and wife Hannah,
and other children of Rev. Peter Hobart, sold his real
estate.
     The will of Hannah Rogers formerly Browne now of Bris-
tol [RI], made 9 June 1691, inventory taken 31 Oct. 1691,
appoints her brothers Gershom and Nehemiah Hobart overseers
of her possessions. John and Hannah had no children.
     He m. (3) after 22 March 1692/3 MARAH (COBHAM) BROWN-
ING b. Salisbury 21 May 1652; d. in 1739 "late of Rehoboth"; dau. of Josiah and Mary (Haffield) Cobham, and widow
of Joseph Browning (or Bruning) of Boston. A prenuptial
agreement between John Rogers of New Bristol and Marah
Browning of Boston widow was made 22 March 1692/3. John
and Marah had no children.
     John Rogers was a merchant and lived in Duxbury, Bos-
ton, Taunton, Swansea, Bristol and Barrington [RI]. He
left no will, but on 30 Aug. 1732 a petition was presented
by Peleg, Perez and Ichabod Richmond, Nathaniel Fisher,
Ephraim Atwood and Peleg Heath, stating that their aunts
Mrs. Bradford and Mrs. Searles desired that one of their
family assist in administering upon the estate of our
honored grandfather Mr. John Rogers of Barrington, dec.,
and asked that our brother William Richmond be appointed
to that purpose. On 5 Sept. 1732 Mr. Perez Bradford of
Milton, Suffolk Co., gent., and William Richmond and
Nathaniel Searle both of Little Compton [RI] were appointed
to administer, the widow and two daughters refusing to do
so. Probate papers refer to the period of John Rogers'
"darkness" (blindness).

Children (ROGERS) b. Duxbury to first wife:

48   i   HANNAH[4] b. 16 Nov. 1668

     ii JOHN b. 22 Sept. 1670; d. Boston 2 Nov. 1696. The inventory of his estate was taken 17 Nov. 1696. He was apparently unmarried.

49   iii ELIZABETH b. 16 April 1673

     iv RUTH b. 18 April 1675; d. 28 April 1725, bur. Little Compton in 50th yr. She m. Bristol RI 12 July 1694 JAMES BENNETT, b. Charlestown 31 May 1666; d. 17 Feb. 1729/30, bur. Little Compton in 64th yr.; son of John and Mary (Cobham) Bennett. (James' mother and Ruth's stepmother Marah were sisters.) James m. (2) Little Compton 1725 Mercy Simmons, a descendant of Pilgrims John Alden and Richard Warren, and had 4 children.

           On 18 July 1694 James Bennet of Roxbury, Suffolk Co., and wife Ruth sold to John Rogers of Bristol RI land in Little Compton which John gave to his four daus. ten years ago, of whom Ruth was one.

           The will of James Bennett of Little Compton, cordwinder, very sick names wife Marcy, executrix, sons James and John (both under 21), and dau. Marcy Bennett. The will was dated 1 Feb. 1729/30, witnesses deposed 21 April 1730. Search of Suffolk, Plymouth and Bristol Co. PR and LR, and Little Compton RI PR and LR disclosed no children by Ruth.

50   v SARAH b. 4 May 1677

References: VR TAUNTON, DUXBURY. RI VR:Bristol:7; Little Compton:8. MD 6:129-132; 19:187-192; 20:1-11, 19-23, 39-41. Plymouth Co. PR 1:249(John Rogers). Bristol Co. PR file (James Bennett). CHARLESTOWN BY WYMAN p. 78. BOSTON VR 9:229. NEHGR 115:261. HINGHAM HIST 3:335.

11 (H)ANNA[3] ROGERS (John[2], Thomas[1]) b. bet. 1640 and 1650; d. after 8 June 1704.

    She m. (1) Taunton 23 Nov. 1664 JOHN TISDALE Jr., b. England; d. Taunton "about the last of Dec." 1677; son of John and Sarah (Walker) Tisdall. The will of John Tisdale Sr. of Taunton, probated 2 Nov. 1676, gave land to "eldest son John Tisdall" and to "grandchild John Tisdall."

    John Tisdale Jr. left no will, but on 5 March 1677 [1677/8] widow Anna Tisdall of Taunton was appointed to administer his estate. Division was made into five parts giving the son (unnamed) a double part, he paying his sisters (unnamed) their portions.

    Anna m. (2) bet. March 1677/8 and 25 Jan. 1683 THOMAS TERRY b. ca. 1631; d. Freetown in Oct. 1691.

    Thomas Terry was living at Braintree in 1660, on Block Island RI from 1662 to 1677 and was a Block Island Selectman in 1664. He was in Taunton as early as 1679, and was

one of the first Freetown Selectmen in 1685. He was commissioned a lieutenant in 1686, and was a representative
to the General Court in 1689.

The will of Thomas Terrey of Freetown, aged 60 years
or thereabouts, was written in his own hand on 10 Aug.
1691, but was refused probate 30 Oct. 1691 for lack of his
signature. The document mentions land at Lyme CT, Long
Island NY, Quinebaug CT, Rye NY and Block Island. He
named his sons: eldest Thomas, John and Benjamin, and his
wife "Hana." He named guardians for each son and specified they be put to school. His Freetown lands were
divided 8 June 1704 when Anna Williams of Taunton, widow
of Thomas Terrey of Freetown, for herself and her youngest
son Benjamin Terrey who was under age, agreed with Thomas's
other sons Thomas and John to a partition "made by advice
of John Rogers, uncle of said parties." Son Thomas was to
have a double part. The agreement was signed by Benjamin
on 28 Aug. 1713.

Anna m (3) bet. Oct. 1691 and Aug. 1697 SAMUEL WIL-
LIAMS, b. Taunton ca. 1637/8; d. Aug. 1697; son of Richard
and Frances (Dighton) Williams. Samuel had m. (1) Mary
Gilbert, by whom he had six children. Samuel and Anna had
no children.

The will of Samuel Williams of Taunton tailor, drawn
6 Aug. 1697, inventory presented 31 Aug. 1697, names sons
Seth, Daniel and Samuel; daus. Sarah Doan, Mary Andros and
Hannah Bun. He gave liberty to his wife (unnamed) to live
with his son Seth.

Children (TISDALE) b. Taunton to John and Anna:

51   i   ABIGAIL[4] b. 15 July 1667
52   ii   JOHN b. 10 Aug. 1669
53   iii   ANNA b. 27 Jan. 1672
54   iv   REMEMBER b. 8 July 1675

Children (TERRY) b. to Thomas and Anna:*

55   v   THOMAS[4] b. bef. 1679
56   vi   JOHN b. bef. 1684
57   vii   BENJAMIN b. after 1683

References: MD 5:205; 19:108; 21:29, 34-5. VR TAUNTON. GRANBERRY
             FAM p. 340. EARLY REHOBOTH 1:57. BLOCK ISLAND HIST pp.
14-5. RI LE 1:161, 173, 183. PLYMOUTH COLONY RECS 6:168, 189. Plymouth Col. LR 3:181. New Shoreham Rec. Book 1:69. NEHGR 16:328; 17:
236; 19:155. Bristol Co. PR 6:275-7(Thos. Terry); 1:199(Samuel

---

*The will of Thomas Terry, carefully allocating his resources to his
wife and sons, and the division of the property, make invalid a claim
for a dau. Abigail who m. Selah Strong on Long Island as claimed by
Strong Desc. 1:597, 726-7. Abigail was prob. a child of another
Thomas Terry who had holdings at Southold, Long Island.

Williams). Bristol Co. LR 4:404-6(Thos. Terry).

12 ABIGAIL[3] ROGERS (John[2], Thomas[1]) b. ca. 1640; d.
Taunton 1 Aug. 1727 ae 86 yrs.
    She m. by 1663 JOHN RICHMOND, b. ca. 1627; d. Taunton
7 Oct. 1715 ae 88; son of John Richmond. He m. (1) prob.
Bridgewater 1653 Susanna Hayward, by whom he had Mary,
John (d.y.), Thomas and Susanna; all but John were men-
tioned in the order to divide the estate of deceased
Thomas.
    There are no probate records for either Abigail or
John, but in a 1706 account of the estate of his son
Thomas, John Richmond listed items in the hands of his
sons Ebenezer, Joseph, Samuel and Edward, and sons-in-law
Richard Godfrey and James Walker.

        Children (RICHMOND) b. to John and Abigail, all b. Taunton ex-
cept Ebenezer:

    58   i   JOSEPH[4] b. 8 Dec. 1663
    59   ii EDWARD b. 8 Feb. 1665
    60   iii SAMUEL b. 23 Sept. 1668
    61   iv SARAH b. 26 Feb. 1670
    62   v   JOHN b. 5 Dec. 1673
    63   vi EBENEZER b. Newport RI 12 May 1676
    64   vii ABIGAIL b. 26 Feb. 1678/9

References: VR TAUNTON. TAG 36:137-8; 54:96-7. MD 9:58-9. RICHMOND
             FAM pp. 3-5. Plymouth Colony LR 5:184. Bristol Co. PR
original papers(Thomas Richmond).

13 ELIZABETH[3] ROGERS (John[2], Thomas[1]) b. bef. 1652; d.
after 7 March 1703.
    She m. Taunton 17 Nov. 1668 NATHANIEL WILLIAMS, b.
Taunton 17 Nov. 1639; d. there 16 Aug. 1692; son of
Richard and Frances (Dighton) Williams.
    Inventory of the estate of Nathaniel Williams was
taken 26 Dec. 1692, and division of the estate of Nathan-
iel Williams, late of Taunton dec., was made 25 July 1698,
naming relict Elizabeth Williams, eldest son John, 2nd son
Nathaniel, their grandmother Williams, and only daughter
Elizabeth, under age 18 and unmarried.
    Elizabeth Williams left no probate records, but she
was living 7 March 1703 when her mother-in-law Frances
Williams of Taunton made a bequest to the widow of her son
Nathaniel.

        Children (WILLIAMS) b. Taunton:

    65   i   JOHN[4] b. 27 Aug. 1675

66   ii NATHANIEL b. 9 or 29 April 1679
67   iii ELIZABETH b. 18 April 1686

References: VR TAUNTON. MD 22:60. Bristol Co. PR 1:223(Nathaniel
             Williams). WILLIAMS FAM (1926) pp. 19, 26, 35, 36.
TAG 10:24-9.

FOURTH GENERATION

14 JOSEPH[4] ROGERS (Thomas[3], Joseph[2], Thomas[1]) b. Eastham 1 Feb. 1667; d. Eastham 24 April 1696. Deacon John
Payne wrote, "Joseph Rogers died of a Strang distemper of
which he had long lain Sick."
     He m. by 1691 PRUDENCE -----, living Truro 28 July
1713 (birth of child). She m. (2) at Eastham 1700 Michael
Atwood, by whom she had six children at Truro, including
Nathaniel who m. Phebe (Young) Dyer (see #180).
     The estate of Joseph Rogers of Eastham, inventory
taken 19 May 1696, was settled 22 May 1696, with one third
going to widow Prudence, and the rest to be divided among
the three children Joseph, Sarah and Elizabeth Rogers. On
that same day John Rogers of Eastham, uncle of the deceased, was appointed administrator of the estate.

     Children (ROGERS):

       i SARAH[5] b. Eastham 20 Nov. 1691; living 22 May 1696; n.f.r.
      ii ELIZABETH b. Eastham 22 Sept. 1693; did she m. 1722 Thos.
           Mayo Jr. (#43)?
     iii JOSEPH b. ca. 1694-6; living 22 May 1696. Was he the one
           admitted to the Haddam Neck Church [CT] 22 Jan. 1744 who
           d. 1751 ae 47, with a wife Dorothy who d. 1779 ae 74?

References: MD 8:16, 182; 9:7; 11:178; 28:112; 31:56. MAYO (JOHN)
             DESC p. 24. TRURO VR p. 23. NEHGR 48:71. Barnstable
Co. PR 2:21-2(Joseph Rogers).

15 HANNAH[4] ROGERS (Thomas[3], Joseph[2], Thomas[1]) b. Eastham 20 March 1669; d. prob. Eastham bef. July 1733.
     She m. bef. 1694 (A)MAZIAH HARDING, b. 1 Nov. 1671;
"executed at Barnstable, for the murder of his wife, 5 June
1734"; son of Joseph and Bethia (Cooke) Harding.
     The will of "Maziah Harding" of Eastham husbandman,
dated 20 April 1734, presented 5 July 1734, names sons John,
Nathan and Cornelus, the latter under 21; daughters Elizabeth Fish, Hannah Fish and Phebe Rogers; grandchildren
Thomas and James Harding, sons of son James; grandchildren
Mary and Elizabeth Clark, daughters of daughter Mary Clark;
son John my rights to land in Windham CT; son John executor.

Children (HARDING) b. Eastham:

68   i   HANNAH[5]   b. 15 Feb. 1694
69   ii JOHN
     iii THOMAS   b. 13 Nov. 1699; d. bef. 14 Dec. 1722 when admini-
         stration on his estate was granted to his father.
70   iv JAMES   b. 2 Nov. 1702
71   v   MARY   b. 2 April 1706
72   vi ELIZABETH   b. April 1708
     vii PHEBE   b. April 1710; m. Plymouth 13 Oct. 1732 BENJAMIN
         ROGERS (see #106).
73   viii NATHAN   b. 29 Oct. 1711
74   ix CORNELIUS   b. 31 March 1716/17

References: MD 3:180; 7:13. BOSTON NEWS OBITS 2:484. Barnstable Co.
              PR 5:180(Maziah Harding).

16   THOMAS[4] ROGERS   (Thomas[3], Joseph[2], Thomas[1])   b. East-
ham 6 May 1672; d. Middletown CT 23 Sept. 1749.
       He m. (1) 10 Dec. 1700 SARAH TREAT, b. Eastham 20 June
1678; d. Truro 26 Sept. 1728 in 47th yr. (sic); dau. of
Samuel and Elizabeth (Mayo) Treat.
       He m. (2) Eastham 11 Feb. 1730/31 REBECCA (SPARROW)
COLLINS, b. Eastham 23 Dec. 1684; d. bef. 10 June 1765;
dau. of John and Aphiah (Tracey) Sparrow. The will of John
Sparrow of Eastham, dated 10 May 1731, names dau. Rebecca
Rogers. She m. (1) Eastham 1703 Joseph Collins.
       On 3 Aug. 1741 Thomas Rogers of Truro bought land at
Middletown CT. Rebecca Rogers was dismissed from the
church in Eastham to Middle Haddam CT on 10 Feb. 1744/5.
On 5 June 1750 Rebekah Rogers of Middletown CT gave her
bond as administratrix on the estate of Thomas Rogers late
of Middletown; on 10 June 1765 Oliver Bosworth gave his
bond as administrator on Rebecca Rogers' estate.

       Children (ROGERS) first two b. Eastham; rest Truro:

     i   SARAH[5]   b. 27 Oct. 1701; bp. Truro 30 June 1717; n.f.r.
     ii   PHEBE   b. 1 Nov. 1703; bp. Truro 30 June 1717; n.f.r.
75   iii ELIZABETH   b. 27 March 1706
76   iv   LUCY   b. 6 June 1708
     v   HANNAH   b. 6 April 1710. She m. Truro 25 Dec. 1755 JOSHUA
          COOKE, prob. b. ca. 1704; son of Josiah and Mary (-----)
          Cooke. Joshua is said to have gone to Middletown CT bef.
          1726. No known children.
77   vi   THOMAS   b. 11 Dec. 1712
     vii JOSEPH   b. 24 March 1715; d. Truro 8 Aug. 1728.
     viii HULDAH   b. 13 Aug. 1717; bp. 22 Sept. 1717; n.f.r.

References: MD 6:203; 9:10, 13; 11:22, 232; 17:32. NEHGR 126:83-4.
              TRURO VR pp. 32, 56. MANWARING 3:629. TREAT FAM p. 178.
MD 8:243; 9:56; 14:94.

CAPE COD HIST 2:381. CT PR Middletown #2834(Thomas Rogers); #1767
(Rebecca Rogers); Hartford #4622(Thomas Rogers). Middletown CT LR
9:233(Thomas Rogers).

17 ELEAZER[4] ROGERS (Thomas[3], Joseph[2], Thomas[1]) b. Eastham 3 Nov. 1673; living Plymouth 10 Dec. 1739 (acknowledged
a deed).
      He m. bef. 1698 RUHAMAH WILLIS who d. after 10 Dec.
1739 (acknowledged a deed); dau. of Richard and Patience
(Bonum) Willis. On 28 Jan. 1698/9 Eleazer Rogers of Plymouth, with consent of Ruhamah Willis now wife of Eleazer,
deeded land. On 24 April 1719 Eleazer Rogers of Plymouth
innholder and wife Ruhamah, only dau. and heir of Richard
Willis of Plymouth, sold land.
      Eleazer Rogers was a seafaring man in at least one
deed. He and Ruhamah left no Plymouth County probate records.

          Children (ROGERS) b. Plymouth:

          i   ELIZABETH[5] b. 15 Oct. 1698; bp. 17 Feb. 1705/6; did she
                 m. 1722 Thomas Mayo (se #43).
   78   ii   THOMAS b. 8 Oct. 1701
   79   iii HANNAH b. 26 Feb. 1703
   80   iv   EXPERIENCE b. 28 April 1707
          v   ELEAZER b. 2 Oct. 1710. It was prob. his namesake nephew
                 (family #78) who m. int. Plymouth 1756 Bethiah Savery
                 and had Bethia, Thomas, Samuel and Priscilla 1758-69.
          vi WILLIS b. 22 April "1011"; bp. 1712; d. 27 May 1713.
   81   vii ABIJAH b. 4 Aug. 1714
          viii MORIAH b. 21 Oct. 1716; d. 27 Jan. 1723/4.
          ix RUTH b. 1718; d. 18 April 1720.

References: MD 3:123; 25:30-5, 139. NEHGR 48:72; 121:312[corrects
             identity of dau. Elizabeth]. PLYMOUTH CH RECS pp. 200,
212. (PLYMOUTH) ANC LANDMARKS 2:221. Plymouth Co. LR 3:174; 14:159;
19:104(Eleazer Rogers).

18 BERIAH[4] HIGGINS (Elizabeth[3] Rogers, Joseph[2], Thomas[1])
b. Eastham 29 Sept. 1661; d. bef. 27 April 1699 (deed calls
him deceased).
      He probably married before 1697, since his son Joseph
must have been at least 21 when he sold land in 1718, but
his wife's name has not been found.
      On 2 Jan. 1677 Joseph[2] Rogers willed to his grandson
"Benjah" Higgins land in Pamet (now Eastham). Witnesses
attested on 5 March 1677/8 that Joseph Rogers, a few days
before he died, said that "Beriah" Higgins lived with him a
great while. In various records Beriah is referred to as
Briah, Bryan, Brian and Bryant.

Beriah was a mariner, and lived in or near Dover and Portsmouth NH. He was on a Newcastle NH ketch in 1684. He signed a petition in 1689/90 with NH settlers regarding Dover, and received a grant of 50 acres there in 1693/4. In 1696/7 he bought land in Portsmouth from Samuel Cutt. On 27 April 1699 Elianor Cutt of Portsmouth, executrix of Samuel Cutt deceased, deeded land bounded by land of Beriah Higgins deceased.

Joseph Higgins in Eastham, mariner, on 30 May 1718 sold land in Portsmouth NH which his father Beriah Higgins bought of Samuel Cutt late of Portsmouth. On 13 Jan. 1726/7 Joseph Higgins of Eastham sold his right title and interest in a 50 acre grant in Dover "made to my father Beriah Higgins now deceased and descending to me."

Child (HIGGINS):

    i JOSEPH[5] b. prob. bef. 1697; living 13 Jan. 1726/7, mariner.

References: MD 3:70. CAPE COD HIST 2:377. ME-NH DICT p. 41. NH Provincial Papers 2:37, 79; 9:165(Beriah Higgins). YORK DEEDS 6:38(Gabriel Tetherly, witnessed by Beriah). NH Provincial LR 5:218(Saml. Penhallow, witnessed by Beriah); 6:93(Samuel Cutt); 6:324; 9:242, 479(Beriah named in deeds of Eleanor Cutt, Thomas Phipps and Jos. Jones); 20:359; 29:342(Joseph Higgins).

19 JONATHAN[4] HIGGINS (Elizabeth[3] Rogers, Joseph[2], Thomas[1]) b. Eastham "latter end of Aug. 1664"; d. there bet. 2 Nov. 1753 and June 1754.

He m. after 31 May 1687 LYDIA (SPARROW) FREEMAN, b. after 19 Nov. 1660; d. after 16 March 1708/9; dau. of Jonathan and Rebecca (Bangs) Sparrow. Lydia m. (1) ca. 1684 William Freeman. On 5 Oct. 1708 Jonathan Higgins Jr. and wife Lydia were among those children and grandchildren of Jonathan Sparrow deceased who deeded a piece of land.

Jonathan Higgins left no probate records; but on 2 Nov. 1753 he conveyed to his son Samuel Higgins, carpenter, land in Eastham; and on 25 June 1754 Jonathan Higgins Jr. sold land laid out to his father Jonathan Higgins now deceased.

Children (HIGGINS) b. Eastham:

        i THANKFUL[5] b. ca. 1692; d. 13 July 1712 in 20th yr.
82   ii SAMUEL b. 5 Oct. 1694
83   iii HANNAH b. bef. 1697
84   iv JONATHAN b. ca. 1697
85   v EXPERIENCE b. ca. 1699

References: MD 3:177; 8:3; 14:1-4, 195; 31:35. HIGGINS DESC pp. 67-9.

20   JOSEPH[4] HIGGINS (Elizabeth[3] Rogers, Joseph[2],
Thomas[1]) b. Eastham 14 Feb. 1666 [1666/7]; d. Chatham
bef. 21 May 1729.
    He m. ca. 1689 RUTH ----- who d. after 10 July 1739
(deed).
    On 9 June 1714 Joseph Higgins Jr. sold to Jonathan
Higgins Jr. land in Eastham and land which he had bought
from his brother Beriah, all of which our great-grand-
father Lt. Joseph Rogers gave to our grandmother Higgins
in his will.
    On 21 May 1729 widow Ruth Higgins was appointed ad-
ministratrix on the estate of Joseph Higgins late of
Chatham deceased intestate; probate records do not name
his heirs.

        Children (HIGGINS) b. Eastham:

    86   i   JOSEPH[5] b. 1 Oct. 1690
    87   ii   BERIAH b. ca. 1692
    88 iii   RUTH b. 11 Sept. 1700

References: MD 3:179. Barnstable Co. PR 4:491(Joseph Higgins).
             HIGGINS DESC pp. 69-71. NEHGR 8:219.

21   HANNAH[4] HIGGINS (Elizabeth[3] Rogers, Joseph[2],
Thomas[1]) b. prob. Eastham ca. 1672; d. there 24 Jan.
1731/2.
    She m. ca. 1699 NICHOLAS PAINE, d. prob. Eastham bef.
17 Nov. 1733; son of Thomas and Mary (Snow) Paine, and a
descendant of Pilgrim Stephen Hopkins.
    On 29 Jan. 1714/5 Nicholas Paine and wife Hannah sold
to their brother Jonathan Higgins Jr. land given to our
mother Elizabeth Higgins dec. by the will of our grandfather Lt. Joseph Rogers.
    The will of Nicholas Paine of Eastham, dated 29 July
1732 and admitted to probate 17 Nov. 1733, mentions
daughter Priscilla and her husband William Norcut, grandchildren Thankful Smith and Lois Freeman, daughters Abigail Higgins and Lydia Young, and "cousin" William Paine.

        Children (PAINE) b. Eastham:

    89   i   THANKFUL[5] b. 14 March 1699/1700
    90   ii   PRISCILLA b. 16 Oct. 1701
         iii PHILIP b. 18 Nov. 1704; d. 10 Apr. 1725 unm.
    91   iv   LOIS b. 29 Sept. 1705
    92   v   ABIGAIL b. 3 Aug. 1707
         vi   HANNAH b. 24 Sept. 1709; n.f.r.*
    93 vii   LYDIA

---

*She is not the Hannah Paine who m. Truro 1736 Joshua Snow.

References: MD 4:33-4. HIGGINS DESC pp. 48-9. Barnstable Co. PR
            5:174(Nicholas Paine). NEHGR 22:188.

22 ELISHA[4] HIGGINS (Elizabeth[3] Rogers, Joseph[2],
Thomas[1]) b. prob. Eastham ca. 1677; d. there bet. 19
Sept. 1749 and 7 Aug. 1750.
      He m. (1) Eastham 30 Sept. 1701 JANE COLLINS, b.
Eastham 3 March 1684/3(*sic*); d. bef. 1739; dau. of Joseph
and Ruth (Knowles) Collins.
      He m. (2) Eastham int. 23 Nov. 1739 ELIZABETH (-----)
BROWN, b. ca. 1681; d. Dec. 1744 in 63rd yr.; widow of
George Brown.
      He m. (3) Harwich 24 April 1746 RACHEL (LINCOLN) HOP-
KINS of Harwich, widow of Benjamin Hopkins. She prob. m.
1751 Theophilus Mayo.
      The will of Elisha Higgins of Eastham, husbandman,
gave to wife Rachel what she brought to me when I married
her; made bequests to dau. Ruth Higgins singlewoman; son
Elisha Higgins; daus. Martha Done, Else Doane, Aphiah
Doane and Elizabeth Mayo; sons Philip, Bariah, Jonathan
and Barnabas Higgins. He named his wife and son Philip
executors. The will was signed 19 Sept. 1749 and the
witnesses deposed 7 Aug. 1750.

          Children (HIGGINS) b. Eastham, all by Jane:

94   i   ELISHA[5] b. 3 Jan. 1701/2
95   ii   MARTHA b. 5 Jan. 1703/4
96   iii BERIAH b. 15 Jan. 1705/6
97   iv   ALICE b. 22 Nov. 1707
98   v   APPHIA b. 22 Nov. 1709
99   vi   JONATHAN b. 8 Oct. 1711
100   vii ELIZABETH b. 1713
       viii JOSEPH b. 1717; d. bef. 19 Sept. 1749.
       ix   RUTH b. 1719; living unm. 19 Sept. 1749.
101   x   BARNABAS b. 1722
102   xi   PHILIP b. 4 March 1724/5

References: HIGGINS DESC pp. 71-4. HIGGINS SUP p. 10. Barnstable
             Co. PR 8:387(Elisha Higgins). MD 3:230; 7:18; 8:3;
16:34; 25:101; 29:101.

23 JOHN[4] ROGERS (John[3], Joseph[2], Thomas[1]) b. Eastham 4
Nov. 1672; d. Harwich 10 Jan. 1738/9.
      He m. (1) Eastham 23 April 1696 PRISCILLA HAMBLIN, b.
Barnstable 3 April 1670; d. bet. 3 Jan. 1714 and April
1728; dau. of John and Sarah (Bearse) Hamblin. The will of
John Hamblin Sr. of Barnstable mentions "daughter Rogers"
on 3 Jan. 1714. On 10 April 1734 when Priscilla's brother
John of Barnstable made his will he named his sister Pris-
cilla deceased.

John Rogers m. (2) Harwich 18 April 1728 SARAH (WIL-LIAMS) NICKERSON who d. after 16 Oct. 1744 (deed); dau. of Thomas and Elizabeth (Tart) Williams, and widow of John Nickerson.

The inventory of the estate of John Rogers late of Harwich, yeoman deceased, was taken 5 April 1739. On 1 May 1739 Ebenezer Rogers, John Rogers, Joseph Rogers, Reuben Nickerson and Sarah Rogers, all of Harwich; Jonathan Rogers of Yarmouth; and Benjamin Rogers of Kingston in Plymouth Co. agreed that Joseph should have payment from the estate of their "father and husband John Rogers deceased," for service done since 1729. The agreement was acknowledged by all except Benjamin on 29 Aug. 1739. On 28 Aug. 1739 Priscilla Nickerson, wife of Reuben and dau. of John Rogers deceased, gave her consent (on the back of the document).

Children (ROGERS) b. Harwich, all by first wife:

103   i   EBENEZER[5] b. 17 Feb. 1697/8
           ii   THANKFUL b. 24 Oct. 1699; apparently d. bef. 1 May 1739 as she was not involved in the above agreement about her father's estate.
104   iii   JOHN b. 1 Aug. 1701
105   iv   JONATHAN b. 20 March 1703
106   v   BENJAMIN b. 19 Nov. 1704
107   vi   SARAH b. 21 July 1706
108   vii   JOSEPH b. 20 Sept. 1708
109 viii   PRISCILLA b. ca. 1710

References: MD 4:175; 6:137; 9:10; 11:174; 14:213; 18:46-7; 31:106-7.
                 Barnstable Co PR 3:484 and 5:170(John Hamblin). CAPE COD HIST 2:733.

24   JUDAH[4] ROGERS (John[3], Joseph[2], Thomas[1])   b. Eastham 23 Nov. 1677; d. bet. 28 March 1738/9 and 8 Nov. 1739.

He m. Barnstable 6 April 1704 PATIENCE LOMBARD, b. Sept. 1684; d. bet. 1717 and 28 March 1738/9; dau. of Thomas and Elizabeth (Derby) Lumbert.

The will of Judah Rogers of Eastham yeoman, drawn 28 March 1738/9, names son Judah; mentions "land my father John Rogers gave me"; names three daus. Mary Cole, Patience Mayo and Hannah Rogers; my brother Eleazer Rogers; "land which I hold with Israel Cole and my brethren which was given me in my father's will"; executor to be son-in-law Gershom Cole. The witnesses gave their deposition 8 Nov. 1739.

Children (ROGERS) b. Harwich:

110   i   JUDAH[5] b. 29 Dec. 1704

111   ii   MARY   b. 1 Oct. 1706
112   iii PATIENCE   b. 9 Nov. 1710
       iv   HANNAH bp. 28 July 1717; d. after 18 Jan. 1745/6 when she
            and her husband signed a deed. She m. Eastham 11 March
            1741/2 JOSEPH AREY, poss. b. Eastham 24 March 1715, son
            of Samuel and Mary (Mayo) Arey. On 18 Jan. 1745/6 Joseph
            Ary and wife Hannah, and her siblings and their spouses
            and others, agreed to divide a piece of land. On 18 Dec.
            1752 Joseph and Hannah sold land in Harwich. Did they
            settle at Orrington ME 1774 or was that the Joseph Arey
            and Hannah (Bickford) who m. Eastham 1761? No known
            children.

References: MD 4:145, 208; 5:17; 11:97; 14:87; 15:53, 165; 16:1; 17:
              14, 175; 20:94; 31:177. MARTHA'S VINEYARD BY BANKS 3:19.

    25 JOSEPH[4] ROGERS (John[3], Joseph[2], Thomas[1])   b. Eastham
22 Feb. 1679; d. there bef. 4 Aug. 1757.
        He m. (1) Eastham 13 Oct. 1703 MERCY CRISP, b. Eastham
15 Oct. 1681; d. bef. 23 May 1746; dau. of George and Hepsibah (Cole) Crisp.
        He m. (2) Eastham 13 April 1739 SARAH (HAMILTON) HARD-
ING, dau. of Daniel and Sarah (Smith) Hamilton, and widow
of Theodore Harding. The will of Daniel Hamilton of Chatham, dated 20 Jan. 1735/6, names dau. Sarah wife of Theodore Harding.
        The will of Joseph Rogers of Eastham yeoman advanced
in age, drawn 23 May 1746, gives wife Sarah the moveables
she brought with her; names dau. Martha Cole, and sons
Elkanah and Crisp Rogers, the latter to be executor. The
will was presented 4 Aug. 1757 by Crisp Rogers, executor.

        Children (ROGERS) b. Eastham to Joseph and Mercy:

113   i   CRISP[5] b. 17 Feb. 1704/5
114   ii   ELKANAH b. 13 Feb. 1706/7
115   iii MARTHA   b. 26 Feb. 1708/9

References: MD 3:180; 8:91; 15:166-7; 19:101. NEHGR 6:44. Barnstable
              Co. PR 5:369(Daniel Hamilton); 9:302(Joseph Rogers).

    26 ELEAZER[4] ROGERS (John[3], Joseph[2], Thomas[1])   b. Eastham
19 May 1685; d. Harwich bet. 20 April 1759 and 6 May 1760.
        He m. Eastham 22 Aug. 1712 MARTHA YOUNG, b. Eastham 28
July 1695; d. Harwich bet. 4 Jan. 1764 and 10 Oct. 1769;
dau. of Henry and Sarah (Snow) Young, and a descendant of
Pilgrim Stephen Hopkins. An order to divide the estate of
Henry Young late of Eastham deceased, dated 2 July 1712,
mentions widow Sarah and daughter Martha.

The will of Eleazer Rogers of Harwich, made 20 April 1759 and probated 6 May 1760, mentions sons Moses and Eleazer Jr.; wife Martha; heirs of deceased son Henry: Jesse, Henry and Amariah; heirs of son Insign: Thomas and Insign; three daughters Elizabeth Bassett, Marcy Fuller and Martha Chase.

The will of Martha Rogers of Harwich widow advanced in years, dated 5 Nov. 1760 and presented 10 Oct. 1769, makes son Eleazer executor of her estate.

Children (ROGERS) b. Harwich:

116   i   HENRY[5] b. 19 Aug. 1713
117   ii   ELIZABETH b. 14 Nov. 1715
118   iii   MERCY b. 1 Sept. 1718
119   iv   MOSES b. 13 March 1720/1
120   v   MARTHA b. 9 Jan. 1723/4
121   vi   ELEAZER b. 15 Nov. 1726
122   vii   ENSIGN b. 9 July 1729
      viii   DANIEL b. 16 March 1732; d. bef. 20 April 1759 when his
             father drew his will. He may have m. Chatham 27 April
             1758 DEBORAH RYDER, b. Chatham ca. 1737; dau. of Nathan-
             iel and Desire (Godfrey) Rider. She m. (2) Chatham 1763
             Joshua Nickerson and (3) Harwich 1793 Thomas Doty. No
             known children born to Daniel and Deborah.

References: MD 6:56, 85; 7:14; 9:9, 34; 13:31; 17:175; 34:103. NEHGR
             121:312. Barnstable Co. PR 3:105(Henry Young); 12:37
(Eleazer Rogers); 13:462(Martha Rogers).

27 MEHITABLE[4] ROGERS (John[3], Joseph[2], Thomas[1]) b. Eastham 13 March 1686/7; d. after 16 Sept. 1760.

She m. Eastham 15 March 1721/2 NATHANIEL MAYO, b.
Eastham 7 July 1681; d. there bet. 16 Sept. 1760 and 6 Oct.
1761; son of Nathaniel and Elizabeth (Wixon) Mayo. He m.
(1) Eastham 1710 Ruth Doane, by whom he had Elizabeth,
Nathaniel, Ruth and two Abigails.

The will of Nathaniel Mayo of Eastham under bodily indisposition, dated 16 Sept. 1760 and presented 6 Oct. 1761,
names wife Mehitable, daughter Elizabeth Rogers the wife of
Judah (#110), daughter Ruth, and sons John and Nathaniel,
the latter to be executor.

Children (MAYO) b. Eastham:

     i   JOHN[5] d. 15 March 1724/5
    ii   JOHN b. 4 Oct. 1725; living 16 Sept. 1760 when he was named
         in his father's will. Poss. he was the John Mayo Jr. of
         Eastham who m. Harwich 6 April 1749 RUTH NICKERSON of
         Harwich. They were apparently listed with the Eastham
         church in 1774. No known children.

iii   ABIGAIL   b. 18 June 1728; d. there 7 Oct. 1731.
iv   MEHITABLE   b. 9 May 1732; n.f.r.
v   RUTH   b. 31 July 1734; living 16 Sept. 1760 when she was
      mentioned in her father's will.

References: MD 4:32, 140; 15:233; 28:81; 33:61. MAYO (JOHN) pp.
              35-6.

28   HANNAH[4] ROGERS   (John[3], Joseph[2], Thomas[1]) b. Eastham
5 Aug. 1689; d. after 22 Oct. 1754.
        She m. Eastham 19 Feb. 1712/3 JAMES SMITH, b. Eastham
"last week in April 1685"; d. there bet. 22 Oct. 1754 and
13 Jan. 1755; son of Daniel and Mary (Young) Smith.
        The will of James Smith of Eastham yeoman, drawn 22
Oct. 1754 and presented 13 Jan. 1755, names wife Hannah;
sons Levi, Solomon, James and Joshua; daughter Grace Smith;
sons Benjamin and Phineas; son Levi of Eastham executor.

        Children (SMITH) b. Eastham:

123   i   LEVI[5] b. 15 March 1713/4
124   ii   SOLOMON   b. 8 March 1715/6
         iii JAMES   b. 8 April 1718; living 22 Oct. 1754 when he was
              named in his father's will; it is unlikely that he is the
              one married to Azuba and having children at Suffield
              1736-57. Was he the James Smith of Middletown CT who in
              1787 sold land in Sandisfield?
125   iv   JOSHUA   b. 19 July 1720
126   v   GRACE   b. 17 Dec. 1722
127   vi   BENJAMIN   b. 3 Oct. 1724
128   vii PHINEAS   b. 7 March 1728/9

References: MD 5:197; 7:18. VR SHEFFIELD. SMITH (RALPH) DESC pp.
              23, 33. Barnstable Co. PR 9:121(James Smith). Berkshire
Co. LR 6:194; 10:480(James Smith).

29   NATHANIEL[4] ROGERS (John[3], Joseph[2], Thomas[1]) b. Eastham 3 Oct. 1693; living Middletown CT 25 June 1743 when he
signed a deed.
        He m. (1) Harwich 1 Feb. 1715/6 ELIZABETH CROSBY, b.
Eastham 15 Sept. 1693; d. ca. 1720; dau. of Simon and Mary
(Nickerson) Crosby. Division of the estate of Simon Crosby
of Harwich deceased, made 5 Aug. 1719, included his dau.
Elizabeth Rogers, wife of Nathaniel.
        He m. (2) Harwich 1 Feb. 1721 SILENCE DIMMOCK of Har-
wich. She was living 9 Apr. 1741 when her last child was
born.
        Nathaniel was living in Middletown CT as early as 30
March 1739 when he sold land and dwelling house there. On
25 June 1743 Nathaniel Rogers of Middletown exchanged land

with Nathaniel Freeman. There are no probate records for
either Nathaniel or Silence in the Connecticut State
Library, and he apparently did not deed land to any of his
children. Did some of this family return to Harwich later?

        Children (ROGERS) first two by Elizabeth, rest by Silence, all
    b. Eastham except John:

        i   SARAH⁵ b. 4 April 1717; n.f.r.
        ii   ELIZABETH b. 10 Jan. 1718/9; poss. m. Middletown CT 1740
                WM. HURLBURT.
        iii NEHEMIAH b. 31 Oct. 1723; n.f.r.
129   iv   RUTH b. 31 July 1725
130   v   JABEZ b. 30 June 1727
        vi   TEMPERANCE b. 3 Dec. 1729; poss. m. Harwich 11 July 1762
                WILLIAM SNOW, b. Rochester 21 July 1728; son of Nathaniel
                and Elizabeth (-----) Snow. He poss. m. (1) 1752 Pris-
                cilla Richmond.
        vii MEHITABLE b. 9 Dec. 1731; poss. m. Colchester CT 1759 PAUL
                GATES who was of E. Haddam CT in 1765.
        viii SARAH b. 17 Oct. 1735; poss. m. Harwich 20 Jan 1757 JOHN
                BIRGE (or Burgess), and had ch. b. Yarmouth.
        ix   NATHANIEL b. 29 April 1738; n.f.r.
        x   JOHN b. Middletown CT 9 April 1741; poss. m. Norwich VT
                1764 SARAH -----, and d. Thetford VT 1821.

References: MD 5:195; 6:83; 8:159; 15:140-1; 34:67, 105. YARMOUTH VR
             p. 115. Barnstable Co. PR 3:550-5(Simon Crosby). Mid-
dletown CT LR 6:424; 9:384; 10:321(Nath'l Rogers). Colchester CT LR
8:521(Paul Gates). CSL Barbour Index:Middletown, Colchester. Norwich
VT Rec. Book 1:256. VR ROCHESTER.

    30 JOHN⁴ PHINNEY (Mary³ Rogers, Joseph², Thomas¹) b.
Barnstable 5 May 1665; d. there 27 Nov. 1746 ae 81.
    He m. Barnstable 30 May 1689 SARAH LUMBART, b. Barn-
stable in Dec. 1666; d. there 5 May 1753 in 81st yr. (*sic*);
dau. of Thomas and Elizabeth (Derby) Lumbart.
    The will of John Phinney of Barnstable, dated 29 Nov.
1735 and presented 15 Jan. 1746, names wife Sarah; sons
John, Thomas and Jabez; daughters Elizabeth, Hannah, Sarah,
Patience and Martha; executors, wife and son Jabez.
    (Some discrepancies appear between the recorded births
and baptisms of some of the children.)

        Children (PHINNEY) b. Barnstable:

131   i   ELIZABETH⁵ b. 11 April 1690, bp. 10 May 1691
        ii   MARY b. 20 Jan. 1692, prob. bp. 24 Jan. 1691/2; d. in Jan.
                1694.
132   iii JOHN b. 8 April 1696, bp. 6 May 1694
133   iv   THOMAS b. 25 May 1697, bp. 21 June 1696

134	v	HANNAH	b. 8 April 1700
135	vi	SARAH	b. 8 Oct. 1702, bp. 9 Nov. 1701
136	vii	PATIENCE	b. 12 Sept. 1704
137	viii	MARTHA	b. 12 July 1706
138	ix	JABEZ	b. 16 July 1708

References: MD 11:97, 131-2; 20:143-4. FINNEY-PHINNEY p. 4. Barnstable Co. PR 6:510(John Phinney). NEHGR 10:347-51.

31 JOSEPH[4] PHINNEY (Mary[3] Rogers, Joseph[2], Thomas[1]) b. Barnstable 28 Jan. 1667 [1667/8]; d. Plympton 29 June 1726. He m. (1) Plymouth 15 June 1693 MERCY BRYANT, d. bef. Sept. 1706.
He m. (2) Plymouth 19 Sept. 1706 ESTHER WEST, b. Duxbury 30 Sept. 1680; living 27 July 1726; poss. the Mrs. Phinney who d. Bridgewater in 1778 ae 98; dau. of Peter and Patience (-----) West. The will of Peter West of Plympton, made 25 July 1717, names dau. Esther.
The will of Joseph Phinney of Plympton, made 27 June 1726 and presented 15 July 1726, names wife Esther; sons John, Joseph and Pelatiah; daughters Alice Hamblin, Mary Hamblin, Mercy Phinney and Patience Phinney; son John executor.

Children (PHINNEY) first three by first wife b. Plymouth, rest by second wife b. Plympton:

	i	ALICE[5] b. 1 April 1694; living 27 June 1726. She entered intentions of marriage Barnstable 21 Nov. 1724 with EBENEZER HAMBLIN Jr. and probably married him 10 Dec. 1724, although the marriage record calls him Eleazer, which was the name of her sister's husband. Ebenezer was possibly the one b. Barnstable 18 March 1698/9 to Ebenezer and Sarah (Lewis) Hamblin; n.f.r. They may have gone to Connecticut as did other Hamblins.
139	ii	JOHN b. 17 Dec. 1696
	iii	MARY b. 5 May 1700; living 27 June 1726. She m. Barnstable 25 Feb. 1721 ELEAZER HAMBLIN, poss. the one b. 22 Aug. 1699 to Isaac and Elizabeth (Howland) Hamblin. He may have been the Eleazer Hamlin of Barnstable who appeared in a Dutchess Co. NY 1746 tax list, or the "Dea. Eleazer in 76th yr." who d. 3 Oct. 1771 and is buried with widow Sarah in Sharon CT.
	iv	MARCY b. 19 Sept. 1707; living 27 June 1726; n.f.r.
140	v	JOSEPH b. 10 April 1709
141	vi	PELATIAH b. 21 March 1710/1
	vii	PATIENCE b. 19 Aug. 1713; prob. m. Plympton 1735 ROBERT COOKE and had six ch. b. Kingston, of whom Ebenezer, Seth and Silas survived infancy.
	viii	EXPERIENCE b. 8 April 1716; d. Plympton 22 Sept. 1724.
	ix	HANNAH b. 8 April 1720; d. Plympton 5 Sept. 1724.

References: MD 2:225; 5:184; 6:137; 9:173; 13:206; 14:34; 32:157.   VR
              BRIDGEWATER, DUXBURY, KINGSTON, PLYMPTON.   FINNEY-PHINNEY
p. 4.   Plymouth Co. PR 4:278(Peter West); 5:278(Joseph Phinney).   MF1:
171.   SHARON CT BUR GD pp. 28-9.

   32   THOMAS[4] PHINNEY   (Mary[3] Rogers, Joseph[2], Thomas[1])   b.
Barnstable in Jan. 1671; d. there 30 Nov. 1755.
     He m. Barnstable 25 Aug. 1698 "widow SARAH BEETLE," d.
1748 ae. 70; poss. dau. of Richard Lockwood of Kittery ME,
and widow of Christopher Beedle of Kittery (whom she is
said to have m. in 1686!).
     Neither Thomas nor Sarah left probate records at
Barnstable County.

        Children (PHINNEY) b. Barnstable:

142   i   GERSHOM[5] b. 21 March 1699/1700
143   ii   THOMAS b. 17 Feb. 1702/3
       iii   ABIGAIL b. 8 June 1704; n.f.r.
        iv   JAMES b. 15 April 1706; n.f.r.
         v   MERCY b. 24 Aug. 1708; poss. m. Barnstable 1734 JOHN LIN-
             NELL, b. Barnstable 1702; son of John and Ruth (Davis)
             Linnell.

References: MD 11:96, 132; 12:154; 33:127.   FINNEY-PHINNEY p. 5.   ME-
              NH GEN DICT pp. 86, 442.

   33   EBENEZER[4] PHINNEY   (Mary[3] Rogers, Joseph[2], Thomas[1])
b. Barnstable 18 Feb. 1673; d. there 10 April 1754.
     He m. Barnstable 14 Nov. 1695 SUSANNA LINNELL, b. ca.
1673; d. 23 Nov. 1754; dau. of David and Hannah (Shelby)
Linnell.   David Linnell's 1688 will includes wife Hannah
and dau. Susanna Linnell.
     The will of Ebenezer Phinney of Barnstable, dated 26
Nov. 1754 and presented 10 Jan. 1755, names granddaughter
Lydia Phinney; sons Samuel, Ebenezer and David; and
daughters Mehitable Higgins, Mary Davis and Rebecca Davis.

        Children (PHINNEY) b. or bp. Barnstable:

         i   MEHITABLE[5] b. 14 Aug. 1696; m. SAMUEL HIGGINS (see #82).
144   ii   MARY b. 23 March 1698
       iii   MARTHA b. 22 April 1700; n.f.r.
145   iv   SAMUEL b. 1 April 1702
146   v   REBECCA bp. 11 June 1703
        vi   poss. LYDIA bp. 7 July 1706; n.f.r.
147   vii   EBENEZER b. 26 May 1708
148   viii   DAVID b. 10 June 1710
        ix   poss. SETH b. 12 Sept. 1714; n.f.r.

References: MD 10:100-1; 11:132. FINNEY-PHINNEY p. 5. Barnstable
            Co. PR 9:122(Ebenezer Phinney).

34 SAMUEL⁴ PHINNEY (Mary³ Rogers, Joseph², Thomas¹) b.
Barnstable 4 Nov. 1676; living 1723.
    He m. Eastham 30 April 1713 BETHYA SMITH of Eastham,
poss. the one b. Eastham 16 Jan. 1681/2 to John and Mary
(Eldredge) Smith.
    There are no Barnstable County probates for Samuel or
Bethiah Smith.

    Children (PHINNEY) first, second and fourth b. at Barnstable:

      i BETHIAH⁵ b. 9 July 1715; n.f.r.
     ii THANKFUL bp. 29 July 1716; n.f.r.
    iii RHODA b. Truro 1 Feb. 1718/19; bp. there 8 March 1718/19;
            n.f.r.
     iv MARY bp. 16 June 1723; n.f.r.

References: MD 8:92; 9:57; 11:131; 15:57. WEST BARNSTABLE CH pp.
            260, 264, 265(bp. all ch. except Rhoda). TRURO VR p. 14.
FINNEY-PHINNEY p. 5.

35 MARY⁴ PHINNEY (Mary³ Rogers, Joseph², Thomas¹) b.
Barnstable 3 Sept. 1678; d. bet. 1733 and 24 Jan. 1755.
    She m. (1) Plymouth 29 Oct. 1702 JOHN EASTLAND, who d.
Plymouth bef. 24 Sept. 1726. He m. (1) Plymouth 1700
Elizabeth Jenney.
    An inventory of the estate of John Eastland late of
Plymouth deceased was taken 24 Sept. 1726, and on 1 Nov.
1726 allowance was made to the widow.
    She m. (2) int. Kingston 12 Nov. 1726 JONATHAN BRYANT,
b. Plymouth 23 March 1677; d. Plymouth bef. 3 July 1731;
son of John and Abigail (Bryant) Bryant. He m. (1) Margery
-----.
    On 3 July 1731 claims were listed against the estate
of Jonathan Bryant late of Plymouth deceased, and on 19
May 1733 dower was set off to Mary Bryant, widow of Jonathan late of Plymouth innholder deceased. Mary had apparently died before 24 Jan. 1755 when an account on the
estate was rendered by an administrator de bonis non.

    Children (EASTLAND) b. Plymouth to John and Mary:

149   i ZERUIAH⁵ b. 8 Dec. 1703
150   ii JOSEPH b. 12 Nov. 1705
151   iii ELIZABETH b. 31 Jan. 1708
       iv MAREY b. 1 Nov. 1710; d. 13 Nov. 17--.
        v HANNAH b. 13 Feb. 1712/3; d. 2 Dec. 1717.
       vi JEAN b. 15 Sept. 1715; d. 18 Dec. 1717.

    vii   JOSHUA b. 13 April 1718; d. 25 July 1719.
   viii   MARY b. 3 March 1720; n.f.r.

References: MD 1:210; 2:166; 14:34; 16:63. Jenney Fam p. 56. Plymouth Co. PR 5:200-2(John Eastland); 6:257, 353; 13:503 (Jonathan Bryant).

    36 MERCY[4] PHINNEY (Mary[3] Rogers, Joseph[2], Thomas[1]) b. Barnstable 10 July 1679; prob. d. bet. 19 Nov. 1724 and 8 July 1731.
    She m. Barnstable 26 Jan. 1715 ELEAZER CROCKER, b. Barnstable 21 July 1650; d. there bef. 6 Sept. 1723; son of William and Alice (-----) Crocker. He m. (1) Barnstable 1682 Ruth Chipman, a descendant of Pilgrim John Howland. (Children of Eleazer and Ruth will appear in *The Howland Family*.)
    On 6 Sept. 1723 the estate of Eleazer Crocker late of Barnstable deceased was appraised. On 26 Sept. 1723 Mrs. Mery (*sic*) Crocker of Barnstable was appointed guardian to Mercy Crocker, minor daughter of Eleazer deceased. Eleazer's estate was settled 19 Nov. 1724 with two shares to eldest son Nathan, and single shares to his other children: Theophilus, Able and Eleazer Crocker, Bethiah Whiteing, Sarah Bursley, Ruth Fuller, Rebacca Robins, and youngest daughter Mercy who was under 18, reserving right of dower to the widow Mercy Crocker during her lifetime. On 8 July 1731 Isaac Hinkly of Barnstable was appointed guardian to Mercy Crocker, minor daughter of Eleazer late of Barnstable.

    Child (CROCKER) b. prob. Barnstable to Eleazer and Mercy:

152   i MERCY[5] b. ca. 1717

References: MD 3:150; 14:227; 18:158-165.

    37 RELIANCE[4] PHINNEY (Mary[3] Rogers, Joseph[2], Thomas[1]) b. Barnstable 27 Aug. 1681; d. Plymouth 4 Dec. 1735 in 55th yr.
    She m. Barnstable 27 Dec. 1705 JOHN MORTON, b. Plymouth 20 July 1680; d. there 4 Feb. 1738/9 in 59th yr.; son of Ephraim and Hannah (Finney) Morton.
    The will of John Morton of Plymouth yeoman very sick, dated 10 Nov. 1738 and proved 14 March 1738/9, gives oldest son John half the real and personal estate, and divides the rest among sons Josiah, James and David.
    In Sept. 1739 John Morton, Josiah and David Morton all of Plymouth, and James Morton of Plympton, owners of land late of our father John Morton deceased, divided their inheritance.

Children (MORTON) b. Plymouth:

    i   JOHN[5] b. 15 Nov. 1706; prob. d. Plymouth 6 April 1765 "of
         Eel River." On 21 July 1764 John Morton of Plymouth yeo-
         man gave to brother Josiah Morton of Plymouth land where
         our father last dwelt, acknowledging his signature 21
         Sept. 1764. No known marriage or children.
    ii JONATHAN b. 10 Feb. 1707/8; d. 29 Dec. 1708.
153 iii JOSIAH b. 28 Feb. 1709/10
    iv dau. b. and d. 11 Dec. 1711
154   v JAMES b. 13 May 1714
    vi DAVID b. 19 March 1716; living Plymouth 25 Nov. 1746. He
         m. Plymouth 8 May 1739 REBECCA FINNEY, bp. Plymouth 27
         Sept. 1721; living 1746; dau. of Robert and Ann (Morton)
         Finney. On 14 Jan. 1744/5 David Morton of Plymouth sea-
         faring man sold his part of the land of his father John
         Morton deceased, which was divided in 1739, with Rebecca
         also signing. On 27 Feb. 1746/7 David sold land in Plym-
         outh, one-third of what was his father John Morton's as
         given to David by his brother James deceased. No known
         children.

References: MD 1:147; 5:100; 14:88; 16:86, 254; 17:46; 20:142. PLYM-
        OUTH CH RECS pp. 220, 394. (PLYMOUTH) BURIAL HILL pp.
20, 22. Plymouth Co. PR 8:9(John Morton). Plymouth Co. LR 33:86;
37:45; 38:132, 170(David Morton); 49:143(John Morton).

  38 BENJAMIN[4] PHINNEY (Mary[3] Rogers, Joseph[2], Thomas[1])
b. Barnstable 18 June 1682; d. there bef. 19 July 1758.
    He m. (1) Barnstable 30 June 1709 MARTHA CROCKER, b.
Barnstable 22 Feb. 1689/90; d. there bef. 19 Sept. 1747;
dau. of Joseph and Temperance (Bursley) Crocker. Division
of the estate of Joseph Crocker 28 March 1728/9 names widow
Temperance Crocker and "sons-in-law and own daughters,"
among them Benjamin Phinney and wife Martha.
    He m. (2) Barnstable 5 Nov. 1747 ELIZABETH (YOUNG)
AMES, dau. of Henry and Sarah (prob. Snow) Young of Eastham, and so prob. a descendant of Pilgrim Stephen Hopkins.
Elizabeth was prob. the widow of Zephon Ames of Provincetown. On 21 Nov. 1747 Benjamin Phinney yeoman and wife
Elizabeth, and Thomas Ames cooper, all of Barnstable, sold
their interest in lands of "our deceased father and grandfather Henry Young of Eastham."
    The will of Benjamin Phinney of Barnstable yeoman,
dated 24 March 1758 and inventory dated 19 July 1758, names
wife Elizabeth, son Seth, daughters Temperance Fuller,
Malatiah (blank) and Lusannah Dimmock; five grandsons "descending of Barnabas and Zacheus as follows:" Ichabod, Benjamin, Timothy, Barnabas and Zacheus; executor, son Seth.

    Children (PHINNEY) b. Barnstable to Benjamin and Martha:

155   i   TEMPERANCE[5] b. 28 March 1710
        ii MELATIAH b. 26 July 1712; m. JOSIAH MORTON (see #153).
156   iii BARNABAS b. 28 March 1715
        iv SILAS b. 16 June 1718; d. May 1720.
157   v   ZACCHEUS b. 4 Aug. 1720
158   vi   SETH b. 27 June 1723
       vii LUSANNA m. ----- DIMMOCK bef. 21 Nov. 1748, when she wit-
            nessed her step-mother's deed above; living 24 March
            1758; n.f.r.

References: MD 3:152; 11:132; 14:255-6; 17:17-18; 33:165. Barnstable
            Co. PR 4:402(Joseph Crocker); 9:389(Benjamin Phinney).
FINNEY-PHINNEY p. 6. MD 15:201-2.

    39 JONATHAN[4] PHINNEY (Mary[3] Rogers, Joseph[2], Thomas[1])
b. Barnstable 30 July 1684; d. Middleboro bet. 9 Sept.
1738 and 6 Nov. 1738.
    He m. (1) ca. 1713 ELIZABETH -----.
    He m. (2) Bridgewater 16 Oct. 1735 DEBORAH WADE, b.
Bridgewater 1691; d. after 9 Sept. 1738; dau. of Thomas
and Elizabeth (Curtis) Wade.
    The will of Jonathan Phinney of Middleboro sick and
weak, dated 9 Sept. 1738 and presented 6 Nov. 1738, gives
house and land to son Joseph; names wife Deborah; sons
Jonathan, Joshua and Timothy; daughters Thankful Phinney,
Elizabeth Phinney under 21; wife Deborah to have what she
brought with her; wife Deborah and son Joseph executors.

    Children (PHINNEY) all by first wife:

159   i   THANKFUL[5] b. Barnstable 24 Dec. 1713
160   ii   JOSEPH b. Barnstable 24 Jan. 1716
       iii JONATHAN b. Barnstable 22 Sept. 1718; d. bef. 21 Sept.
            1739 when Joseph Phinney of Middleboro yeoman was ap-
            pointed administrator on the estate of Jonathan Phinney
            of Middleboro yeoman deceased intestate.
        iv MEHITABLE bp. 17 Feb. 1720; n.f.r.
        v   TIMOTHY bp. 17 Feb. 1720; on 21 Sept. 1739 Philip Cannon
            of Middleboro was appointed guardian of Timothy, minor
            son of Jonathan Phinney late of Middleboro deceased; n.
            f.r.
161   vi   JOSHUA b. 10 Jan. 1721
       vii ELIZABETH b. after 1717; prob. m. JOHN MACOMBER (see #305).

References: MD 11:132. VR BRIDGEWATER. FINNEY-PHINNEY p. 6. Plym-
            outh Co. PR 7:445; 8:82(Jonathan Phinney); 8:88(Timothy
Phinney).

    40 JAMES[4] ROGERS (James[3], Joseph[2], Thomas[1]) b. Eastham
30 Oct. 1673; d. there 8 Sept. 1751. When James was born,
he was given the name of Samuel, but after the death of his

father, he was renamed James in his honor and so baptized
in April 1680.

He m. Eastham 17 Feb. 1697/8 SUSANNA TRACY, dau. of
John and Mary (Prence) Tracy.

The will of James Rogers of Eastham, dated 5 March
1749 and inventory taken 1 Oct. 1751, names wife Susannah;
son Isaac; daughters Mary Davis and Abigail Young; granddaughter Susannah Rogers under 21; grandsons Thomas Rogers,
James Rogers and Isaac Davis; and sons Isaac, James and
Thomas.

Children (ROGERS) b. Eastham:

162   i   MARY[5] b. 12 Nov. 1698
       ii ISAAC b. 8 Dec. 1701; d. bef. 12 May 1767, when James
           Rogers was appointed administrator of the estate of
           Isaac Rogers late of Eastham deceased. On 10 Nov. 1767
           the real estate was set off to Isaac's brother Thomas,
           nephew James Rogers and sister Abigail Young, they making
           payment to the other heirs: sister Susannah Rogers;
           [nieces and nephews] Isaac Davis, Mary Godfrey wife of
           Nathaniel, and Susannah Killey wife of Benjamin, all
           children of a daughter (*sic*) of deceased; and Prince,
           Samuel, Jonathan, Hannah and Susannah, all Rogers, child-
           ren of brother James.
       iii SUSANNAH b. 19 Jan. 1703/4; m. JUDAH ROGERS (see #110).
163   iv JAMES b. 2 May 1706
       v   ABIGAIL b. 3 Aug. 1708; d. 1785. She m. Eastham 23 Feb.
           1748 ZEBULON YOUNG, b. Eastham 1700; d. there 29 Dec.
           1788; son of Nathaniel and Mercy (Davis) Young. He m.
           (1) Eastham 1725/6 Mercy Sparrow, by whom he had Thankful,
           Nathaniel, Thankful, Zebulon, Isaac and Mercy. On 12
           Oct. 1767 James Rogers, Thomas Rogers and Abigail Young,
           all of Eastham and heirs of Isaac Rogers late of Eastham
           deceased, divided their inheritance, with Zebulon Young,
           husband to Abigail, consenting. On 4 Feb. 1779 Zebulon
           Young of Eastham and wife Abigail sold land in Harwich.
           They left no probate records at Barnstable County. No
           known children.
164   vi THOMAS b. 21 Oct. 1710

References: MD 9:11; 16:141; 19:10; 24:138. HIGGINS SUP p. 34.
             Barnstable Co. PR 8:496(James Rogers); 13:316-8(Isaac
             Rogers). YOUNG (JOHN) GEN pp. 5, 22.

  41 MARY[4] ROGERS (James[3], Joseph[2], Thomas[1]) b. Eastham
9 Nov. 1675; d. there 17 Feb. 1731/2 "wife of Lt. John
Cole."

She m. prob. bef. 1694 JOHN COLE, b. Eastham 6 March
1669/70; d. there 13 Dec. 1746; son of John and Ruth (Snow)
Cole, and a descendant of Pilgrim Stephen Hopkins. John

was a nephew of Mary's step-father. He m. (2) Eastham
Nov. 1732 Sarah (Hamblen) Higgins.
     The will of John Cole of Eastham yeoman, dated 30
July 1743 and presented 19 Jan. 1746/7, bequeaths to wife
Sarah "what is due her from her former husband's estate";
sons Joshua, Joseph, John, James and Moses; grandson Jona-
than Cole; grandchildren Nathaniel and Jesse Cole and
their mother Hope Cole, widow of deceased son Jonathan;
granddaughters Hope, Dorcas and Mercy Cole; daughters
Mercy (*sic*) Snow, Phebe Wickham and Thankful Snow; son
Joshua of Eastham executor. In a bequest to grandson
Jonathan Cole, John mentions land that belonged to my former wife. In the will of her grandfather Thomas Paine,
Mary (Rogers) Cole was given a share of his land; perhaps
this same land now passed to Jonathan Cole.

          Children (COLE) b. Eastham all to John and Mary:

165   i   JONATHAN^5 b. 4 Oct. 1694
166   ii   JOHN   b. 14 Oct. 1696
167   iii   MARY   b. 25 Aug. 1698
168   iv   JAMES   b. 23 Oct. 1700
         v   NATHAN b. 21 Jan. 1702/3; d. bef. 1743.
169   vi   JOSHUA b. 20 March 1704/5
        vii   MOSES   b. 22 July 1707; living 1743; poss. the Moses who d.
                  E. Hampton CT 20 or 27 July 1767 ae. 60, whose wife Han-
                  nah d. there 16 March 1782 or 1798 ae. 88.
       viii   PHEBE   b. 29 Oct. 1709/10; m. bef. 1743 ----- WICKHAM (or
                  Wixam); n.f.r.
        ix   THANKFUL b. 20 Oct. 1712; d.y.
170   x   JOSEPH b. 13 Oct. 1714
171   xi   THANKFUL b. 19 Oct. 1716

References: MD 9:7; 17:36. NEHGR 6:44. Barnstable Co. PR 8:39-45
             (John Cole). Letter of Geo. N. Cole, 1926, SG-Col-18,
NEHG Soc., Boston. CSL Barbour Index: E. Hampton.

     42 ABIGAIL^4 ROGERS (James^3, Joseph^2, Thomas^1) b. East-
ham 2 March 1677/8; d. bet. 18 Jan. 1745/6 and 29 May 1747.
     She m. Eastham 11 Jan. 1698/9 JOHN YATES, who d. Har-
wich bef. 31 July 1730; son of John Yates.
     On 21 July 1730 inventory was taken of the estate of
John Yates late of Harwich deceased, and on 18 April 1732
Abigail Yates was appointed guardian to Deborah, Hannah,
Mercy and John Yates, minor children of John deceased.
     Abigail was probably the Abigail Yates widow woman
whose dwelling house was mentioned in a deed 18 Jan. 1745/6.
She probably died before 29 May 1747, when John Yates and
other heirs of Mr. John Yates deceased gave their title to
land, John signing for "sisters Mercy and Hannah," and
Crisp Rogers, Elkanah Rogers, Asa Mayo and Jeremiah

Nickerson signing for themselves, with no mention of
widow's dower.

> Children (YATES) prob. b. Harwich:

> i MARY[5] m. CRISPE ROGERS (see #113).
> ii RELIANCE m. ELKANAH ROGERS (see #114).
> 172 iii EXPERIENCE
> 173 iv DEBORAH b. 1714-20
> 174 v JOHN bp. Harwich 13 April 1718
> vi MERCY b. 1714-30; living 29 May 1747; poss. the one who d. Eastham in 1779.
> 175 vii HANNAH b. 1714-1730

References: MD 5:17; 7:186; 9:12, 242; 17:14. NEHGR 7:347. Barnstable Co. PR 5:42, 44, 48, 196(John Yates).

43 ELIZABETH[4] HIGGINS (Hannah[3] Rogers, Joseph[2], Thomas[1])
b. Eastham 11 Feb. 1680 [prob. 1680/1]; d. there 4 Nov.
1721.

She m. Eastham 3 April 1701 THOMAS MAYO, b. Eastham 3
April 1678; d. there July 1769; son of Thomas and Barbara
(Knowles) Mayo. He m. (2) int. Eastham 6 Oct. 1722 Elizabeth Rogers who d. Eastham 10 May 1772, poss. dau. of
Joseph & Prudence (#14), John & Elizabeth (#6), or Eleazer
& Ruhamah (#17), by whom he had a dau. Hannah.

On 5 June 1740 Thomas Mayo and wife Elizabeth both of
Eastham bought land from Richard Mayo which had belonged to
his father Thomas deceased.

Thomas Mayo was a cordwainer. The only Barnstable
County probate record for Thomas is a bill by [son-in-law]
Benjamin Higgins for caring for his wife's parents.

> Children (MAYO) b. Eastham to Thomas and his wife Elizabeth
> (Higgins):

> 176 i ELIZABETH[5] b. 1 May 1702
> 177 ii THANKFUL b. 10 Jan. 1703/4
> 178 iii BATHSHEBA b. 27 April 1705
> iv ELIAKIM b. 1 April 1707; d. bef. 21 Dec. 1736. He "of Boston" m. Hingham 7 May 1735 ELIZABETH KENT, b. Hingham 6 Sept. 1715; dau. of Ebenezer and Hannah (Gannett) Kent. The will of Ebenezer Kent of Hingham, dated 16 June 1748, names his dau. Elizabeth Pitcher. She m. (2) bet. 1736 and 1748 ----- Pitcher. Elizabeth Mayo of Boston widow was appointed administratrix on the estate of her husband, Eliakim Mayo late of Boston mariner deceased, 21 Dec. 1736. There were no papers to indicate that there were any children born to this brief marriage.
> v SARAH b. 12 June 1710; d. 27 July 1711.

      vi JOSHUA b. 28 May 1712; n.f.r., unless he was the Joshua of
          Eastham who on 4 Jan. 1764 divided land held in common
          with Martha Rogers widow of Eleazer, Eleazer and Judah
          Rogers, Gershom Cole and wife Mary and Joseph Arey and
          wife Hannah. Or was he the Joshua Mayo of Wellfleet
          mariner whose widow Mehitable Mayo and Chillingsworth
          Foster were appointed administrators on his estate in
          1771?
179 vii MERCY b. 27 Feb. 1718/9

References: MD 8:94; 9:9-10; 14:77, 178; 15:203; 17:175; 28:112.
             HIGGINS DESC p. 49. Suffolk Co. PR 33:22(Eliakim Mayo).
HINGHAM HIST 2:404. Barnstable Co. PR 10:237; 16:1(Joshua Mayo).

   44 MARY[4] HIGGINS (Hannah[3] Rogers, Joseph[2], Thomas[1]) b.
Eastham 22 Jan. 1682 [prob. 1682/3]; d. after June 1750.
     She m. Eastham 12 Feb. 1706/7 JAMES YOUNG, b. Eastham
4 April 1685; d. Truro 18 June 1750 in 66th yr.; son of
Joseph and Sarah (Davis) Young. James was named in the
will of his father 20 Nov. 1721.
     The will of James Young, yeoman of Truro, very sick,
made 2 June 1750, names wife Mary; son Samuel; daughter
Phebe Atwood wife to Nathaniel; daughter Sarah Crowell wife
to Joshua; daughter Mary Newcomb wife to Robert; daughter
Lydia Rich wife to John; daughter Elizabeth Smalley wife
to Francis; and daughter Hannah Buell wife to Reuben. Son
James to be executor. The witnesses deposed 26 June 1750.

          Children (YOUNG) recorded Truro:

180   i   PHEBE[5] b. Eastham 3 June 1707
181   ii   SARAH b. Truro 2 Feb. 1709/10
182   iii   SAMUEL b. Truro 11 Dec. 1712
183   iv   MARY b. Truro 25 March 1715
        v   LYDIA b. Truro 17 Aug. 1717; n.f.r.
184   vi   LYDIA b. Truro 8 Sept. 1718
185   vii   HANNAH b. Truro 12 Feb. 1719/20
186 viii   ELIZABETH b. Truro 17 Sept. 1723; bp. 11 Nov. 1722 (*sic*)
187   ix   JAMES b. Truro 30 May 1725

References: MD 6:205-6; 9:75, 76, 77; 14:100. TRURO VR pp. 1, 2.
             Barnstable Co. PR 8:420(James Young). HIGGINS DESC p. 49.

   45 REBECCA[4] HIGGINS (Hannah[3] Rogers, Joseph[2], Thomas[1])
b. Eastham 30 Nov. 1686; d. Colchester CT 25 Dec. 1776 ae
92.
     She m. Eastham 11 Aug. 1715 JACOB HURD, b. Eastham 12
Jan. 1695; d. Colchester CT bet. 1764 and 1776; son of John
and Deborah (-----) Hurd.
     There are no probate records in CT for Rebecca or
Jacob.

Children (HURD):

188   i   REBECCA[5] b. ca. 1718
189   ii JACOB b. Harwich 17 Dec. 1720
190   iii ELIZABETH b. prob. Harwich ca. 1722

References: HIGGINS DESC pp. 49-50. MD 6:85; 15:55.

46 JAMES[4] HIGGINS (Hannah[3] Rogers, Joseph[2], Thomas[1])
b. Eastham 22 July 1688; d. there 11 July 1777 in 89th yr.
    He m. (1) SARAH MAYO who d. bef. Dec. 1726; dau. of
Samuel and Ruth (Hopkins) Mayo, and a descendant of Pilgrim Stephen Hopkins. The will of Samuel Mayo of Eastham,
dated 9 April 1734, mentions "heirs of my dau. Sarah Higgins, wife to James Higgins, now deceased."
    He m. (2) Eastham 12 Dec. 1726 SARAH BIXBIE, b. Box-
ford 3 Aug. 1685(?); d. Eastham 10 Dec. 1774 in 90th yr.;
dau. of Joseph and Sarah (Gould) Bixbie.
    On 26 March 1711 James Higgins was granted land in
Eastham near the house of his father Jonathan Higgins.
The will of James Higgins of Eastham laborer "old", dated
6 Dec. 1775, names grandson Hezekiah Higgins; dau. Dorcus
Taylor; heirs of two dec. daus. Rebecca Rogers wife of
Thomas, and Hannah Higgins wife of Benjamin; and granddaughter Hannah Freeman. Grandson Hezekiah Higgins was
named executor. The will was proved 12 Aug. 1777.

    Children (HIGGINS) all prob. b. Eastham:

       i   REBECCA[5] b. ca. 1716; m. THOMAS ROGERS (see #164).
191   ii JAMES b. ca. 1718
192   iii HANNAH b. ca. 1720
193   iv DORCAS b. bef. 1731

References: VR BOXFORD (shows --rah b. 1 Dec. 1699, no b. 1685). MD
             7:185; 10:165; 16:146; 29:10. Barnstable Co. PR 5:455
             (Samuel Mayo); 20:80(James Higgins). HIGGINS DESC pp. 50, 74-5. Mayo
             Desc. pp. 38-9.

47 SARAH[4] HIGGINS (Hannah[3] Rogers, Joseph[2], Thomas[1]) b.
Eastham 18 Oct. 1690; d. after 1741.
    She m. Eastham 10 April 1717 WILLIAM MITCHELL of
Chatham, b. ca. 1691; d. after 8 Dec. 1767; son of William
and Mercy (Nickerson) Mitchell. He m. (1) Chatham 1712/3
Tabitha Eldredge.
    William and Sarah left no probate records in Barn-
stable or Bristol counties. But on 10 Jan. 1767 William
Mitchell of Dartmouth, yeoman, sold land to his grandson
David Mitchell of Dartmouth, laborer, son of my son Wil-
liam; William acknowledged the deed 8 Dec. 1767.

Children (MITCHELL) first four b. Chatham, last two Dartmouth, to William and Sarah:*

194   i   JAMES[5] b. 4 Nov. 1718
195   ii   TABITHA b. 19 July 1720
196 iii   MERCY b. 4 May 1722
197   iv   WILLIAM b. 31 June 1725
        v   SETH b. 11 Dec. 1738/9; said to be living 1800. No Barn-
            stable or Bristol county probate or land records found
            for him. Was he of Bridgewater, or of Woodbury CT?
198   vi   BETTY b. 22 March 1741

References: MD 4:184-5; 15:54. NEHGR 23:178. VR DARTMOUTH. CHATHAM
            HIST p. 249. HIGGINS DESC p. 50. HIGGINS SUP pp. 8-9.
Bristol Co. LR 51:77(William Mitchell).

   48 HANNAH[4] ROGERS (John[3-2], Thomas[1]) b. Duxbury 16 Nov.
1668; d. prob. Hingham bet. 1 June 1747 and 5 Nov. 1754.
     She m. Plymouth 31 July 1689 SAMUEL BRADFORD, b. Plym-
outh ca. 1667; d. Duxbury 11 April 1714 ae 46; son of William and Alice (Richards) Bradford, and a descendant of
Pilgrim William Bradford.
     The will of Samuel Bradford of Duxbury, made 26 Jan.
1713/4 and probated 16 June 1714, names eldest son Gershom,
son Perez, father William Bradford deceased, and youngest
son Gamaliel under 21; daughter Hannah Gilbert wife of
Nathaniel of Taunton; daughters Elizabeth, Jerusha and
Welthea Bradford all under 21; wife Hannah; negro servant
William; executors wife Hannah and son Gershom Bradford.
     The will of Hannah Bradford of Duxbury widow, dated 16
April 1734, codicil 1 June 1747, sworn to at Hingham 5 Nov.
1754, names sons Gershom, Peres and Gamaliel Bradford, and
daughters "Hannah Gilburd, Elizabeth Whiton, Jerusha Gay
and Welthean Lane"; son[in-law] Peter Lane to be executor.

     Children (BRADFORD) b. Plymouth:

199   i   HANNAH[5] b. 14 Feb. 1689[/90]
200   ii   GERSHOM b. 21 Dec. 1691
201 iii   PEREZ b. 28 Dec. 1694
202   iv   ELIZABETH b. 15 Dec. 1696
203   v   JERUSHA b. 10 March 1699
204   vi   WELTHEA b. 15 May 1702
205 vii   GAMALIEL b. 18 May 1704

References: VR DUXBURY. MD 2:18; 9:160; 13:205; 16:116; 20:21.
            PLYMOUTH CH RECS 1:197. BRADFORD DESC p. 10. Suffolk
Co. PR #12505(Hannah Bradford).

---

*No evidence was found in confirmation of a dau. Desire and a son
Hallet, claimed in CHATHAM HIST and HIGGINS SUP.

49 ELIZABETH[4] ROGERS (John[3-2], Thomas[1]) b. Duxbury 16
April 1673; d. Little Compton RI 23 Oct. 1724 in 52nd yr.
     She m. 1693 SILVESTER RICHMOND, b. Little Compton ca.
1673; d. Dartmouth 20 Nov. 1754 in 81st yr.; son of Edward
and Abigail (Davis) Richmond. Silvester m. (2) Duxbury
1727/8 Deborah (Cushing) Loring, widow of Thomas Loring.
     The will of Silvester Richmond of Dartmouth esquire,
dated 29 Dec. 1752 and probated 3 Dec. 1754, names wife
Deborah; sons William, Silvester, Peres, Peleg, Ichabod
and Rogers; daus. Elizabeth, Ruth and Mary (no last names);
grandchildren: Gamaliel Richmond, son of son Peleg; Mary
Pain, dau. of dau. Sarah deceased; grandson and granddaughter Fisher, children of dau. Elizabeth; Silvester
Richmond, son of son Silvester; Joshua Richmond, son of son
Peres; Silvester Richmond, son of son William; and Richmond Loring, son of dau. Mary. "My negro man Natt and
woman Cate to be free at my decease." Son Ichabod to have
the use of "one Room at the west End of my Dwelling house
...also one bed" (indicating that he was not married at
the time). Son Peres was named executor.

     Children (RICHMOND) b. Little Compton RI to Silvester and
Elizabeth:

206   i   WILLIAM[5] b. 10 Oct. 1694
207   ii   ELIZABETH b. 10 May 1696
208   iii   SILVESTER b. 30 June 1698
209   iv   PELEG b. 25 Oct. 1700
210   v   PEREZ b. 5 Oct. 1702
211   vi   ICHABOD b. 27 Feb. 1704
212   vii   RUTH b. 7 March 1705
      viii   HANNAH b. 9 July 1709; d. 20 Jan. 1728 in 20th yr., bur.
             Little Compton.
213   ix   SARAH b. 31 Oct. 1711
214   x   MARY b. 29 Nov. 1713
215   xi   ROGERS b. 25 May 1716

References: MD 21:12-18. NEHGR 115:265. RI VR: Little Compton:50,
             151. COMPTON FAMS pp. 514-5. RICHMOND FAM p. 34.

50 SARAH[4] ROGERS (John[3-2], Thomas[1]) b. Duxbury 4 May
1677; d. Little Compton RI 19 Jan. 1769 or 1770 in 92nd
yr.
     She m. Little Compton in 1694, NATHANIEL SEARLE, b.
Dorchester 9 June 1662; d. Little Compton 5 Feb. 1749/50
in 88th yr.; son of Robert and Deborah (Salter) Searle.
     The will of Nathaniel Searle of Little Compton weaver,
drawn 3 Oct. 1744 and presented 3 April 1750, names wife
Sarah; son Nathaniel executor to have all housing; and
daus. Deborah Pearce and Sarah Dring.

Children (SEARLE) b. Little Compton:

216   i   DEBORAH[5] b. 17 Nov. 1695
       ii   JOHN b. 12 March 1698; drowned 20 March 1714, and bur. 23
            May ae 16y 14d (*sic*).
217   iii SARAH b. 2 April 1700
218   iv NATHANIEL b. 26 April 1703

References: DORCHESTER VR p. 8. RI VR: Little Compton:53, 157.
            NEHGR 115:261. Little Compton RI PR 1:72(Nath'l Searle).
LITTLE COMPTON FAMS p. 549.

51 ABIGAIL[4] TISDALE (Anna[3] Rogers, John[2], Thomas[1]) b.
Taunton 15 July 1667; d. bet. 10 May 1718 and 1 March
1731/2.
        She m. Taunton 2 Dec. 1685 WILLIAM MAKEPEACE, b. Bos-
ton 1662/3; d. Taunton in Dec. 1736; son of William and
Ann (Johnson) Makepeace. He m. (2) Taunton 1732 Ann Cudworth.
        The will of William Makepeace of Taunton, made 16 Nov.
1736 and witnesses deposed 21 June 1737, mentions sons
Seth, William and Thomas; six ch. of my dau. Abigail dec.
(unnamed); and daus. Annah, Mary, Susannah, Lydia, Deborah,
Remember and Persilla; Lydia and Susannah to be execu-
trixes. On 23 Feb. 1736[1736/37] the petition of Ann Makepeace, widow of William late of Taunton deceased, was presented asking that she be allowed one-third of his estate
as he had not made any provision for her. On 21 June 1737
Lydia and Susannah, wives of Simeon Witheril and Joseph
Godfrey of Norton, were granted administration of the
estate.

        Children (MAKEPEACE) b. to William and Abigail, first seven b.
Freetown:

219   i   ABIGAIL[5] b. 25 Nov. 1686
       ii   ANNA b. 4 May 1689; d. bet. 16 Nov. 1736 and 11 Dec. 1750
220   iii MARY b. 22 March 1691
        iv SUSANNA b. 23 Sept. 1694; d. bef. Dec. 1748. She m. bef.
            1737 JOSEPH GODFREY, b. Taunton 1 March 1694/5; d. Norto:
            after 11 Dec. 1750; son of Richard and Mary (Richmond)
            Godfrey. He m. (2) Norton 1748 Mrs. Hannah White. The
            will of Joseph Godfrey of Norton, drawn 11 Dec. 1750,
            witnesses deposed 1 Jan. 1750, names wife Hannah, cousin
            David Gaschet, cousin William Makepeace, brothers Richar

---

*The Mayflower Society has accepted descent through a claimed mar-
riage to Joseph Staples. The Bristol County vital records, probate
records and land records were searched but no proof was found that
Anna was the wife of Joseph Staples and mother of Mary Staples who m
Jonathan Hoar about 1732, as claimed by HOAR GEN, or that Anna ever
married.

and John Godfrey, brother-in-law Thomas Makepeace, and
four sisters-in-law Mary Gould, Deborah Gurley, Remember
Porter, and Priscilla Aldridge who were to have "all my
personal estate after the death or marriage of my wife."
No children found.

221   v   LYDIA b. 4 Nov. 1696
      vi   DEBORAH b. 13 Jan. 1699; living 11 Dec. 1750 when she was
           mentioned in the will of brother-in-law Joseph Godfrey.
           She m. bef. 1748 GEORGE GURLEY of Norton. On 23 Dec.
           1748 George Gurley of Norton, ropemaker, sold land to
           Seth Makepeace, with wife Deborah releasing her dower.
           He acknowledged the deed at Norton 3 March 1748/9. n.f.r.
           There was no indication that they moved to CT where there
           were many Gurleys living.
222   vii SETH b. 23 June 1702
223 viii WILLIAM b. Taunton ca. 1704
224   ix REMEMBER b. ca. 1707
225   x PRISCILLA b. Taunton ca. 1710
226   xi THOMAS b. prob. Taunton

References: VR NORTON, TAUNTON. MD 21:140-2. FREETOWN VR p. 1.
       MAKEPEACE FAM pp. 27, 34, 37-8, 41-6. Bristol Co. PR
12:479(Joseph Godfrey); file(Jos. Staples). GEN ADVERTISER 4:33.
Bristol Co. LR 36:450(Geo. Gurley); 14:389(William Makepeace).

52 JOHN[4] TISDALE (Anna[3] Rogers, John[2], Thomas[1]) b.
Taunton 10 Aug. 1669; d. there 26 Jan. 1728 ae 57 (*sic*).
       He m. (1) ca. 1700 DEBORAH DEANE b. ca. 1675; d. ca.
1702/3; dau. of Thomas and Katharine (Stephens) Deane.
The will of Thomas Dean of Taunton, drawn 7 Aug. 1690,
names wife Katherine and dau. Deborah. The will of Katherine Dean of Taunton, widow of Thomas, dated 14 March 1725/6
names grandson John Tisdel Jr.
       He m. (2) bef. 1707 prob. ABIGAIL BURT, b. Taunton 28
Jan. 1676/7; living 1737; poss. dau. of Richard and Charity
(Hill) Burt. The will of Richard Burt, dated 7 Sept. 1685,
names dau. Abigail and wife Charity.
       John Tisdale of Taunton drew his will 26 Jan. 1727/8,
probated 5 Feb. 1727/8, naming wife Abigail; eldest son
John; second son Abraham under 21; other sons Israel under
21, Ephraim and Jedediah; daus. Deborah Tisdale, Abigail
Tisdal and Anna Tisdal. On 11 April 1728 Seth Burt was
appointed guardian to Ephraim Tisdale, over 14, son of
John Tisdale dec.

     Children (TISDALE) first by Deborah, rest by Abigail:

227   i   JOHN[5] b. ca. 1702
      ii   ABRAHAM b. bet. 1702 and 1714; d. Taunton bet. 30 June and
           20 Sept. 1737. The will of Abraham Tisdale of Taunton,
           dated 30 June 1737 and proved 20 Sept. 1737, names his

> mother Abigail Tisdale; brothers Israel and Ephraim;
> brother John Tisdale's eldest son John; my three sisters
> (unnamed); minister Thomas Clapp.

iii ISRAEL b. ca. 1708; d. Taunton 27 Oct. 1769 in 62nd yr.
"Lt."; m. Taunton 7 Aug. 1735 MARY TISDALE, dau. of
Joseph Tisdale. Mary m. (2) Israel Dean. The will of
Joseph Tisdale of Taunton dated 27 May 1739 names wife
Ruth and dau. Mary wife of Israel Tisdale.

   The will of Israel Tisdale of Taunton, made 30 Aug.
1769 and probated 22 Nov. 1769, made bequests to wife
Mary; "Abraham Hewit son of my sister Hewit", half my
real estate; Mordicai Lincoln; sister Anna Dean; Benoni
Tisdale son of brother Ephraim, under 21; and John Tisdale. A petition of Abigail Hewet widow regarding a debt
not paid her from the estate of Israel Tisdale by the administratrix Mary Tisdale "who has since married Israel
Dean of Taunton" was dated 29 Jan. 1783. Israel apparently had no children.

228 iv DEBORAH b. ca. 1709
229   v ABIGAIL b. ca. 1711
230 vi EPHRAIM b. bef. 1714
     vii JEDEDIAH prob. b. ca. 1715; d. 1735/7. He was living 20
         June 1735, when Seth Burt guardian of Jedediah Tisdale
         sold land, but was not mentioned in the will of his bro-
         ther Abraham in 1737.
231 viii ANNA b. ca. 1718

References: VR TAUNTON. Bristol Co. PR 1:183(Thos. Dean); 6:66(John
             Tisdale); 6:96(Ephraim Tisdale); 8:509(Abraham Tisdale);
21:75-7 & orig. papers(Israel Tisdale); 5:346(Katherine Dean); 9:241
(Joseph Tisdale). Bristol Co. LR 23:492(Ephraim Tisdale et al.).
Plymouth Colony LR 5:364-5(will of Rich. Burt). TAG 54:17-18.

53 ANNA[4] TISDALE (Anna[3] Rogers, John[2], Thomas[1]) b.
Taunton 27 Jan. 1672; d. Sept. 1733 ae 61 years.
     She m. (1) Taunton 4 July 1695 GEORGE LEONARD, b.
Taunton 18 April 1671; d. Norton 5 Sept. 1716 in 46th yr.;
son of Thomas and Mary (Watson) Leonard. On his gravestone
he is credited with being the first settler of Norton 1696.
     On 6 Dec. 1708 George Leonard of Taunton and wife
Anna sold 200 acres formerly of their father John Tisdale
late of Taunton dec. Anna acknowledged her signature 24
Apr. 1726.
     The will of George Leonard of Norton in 44th year,
made 30 Aug. 1716 and inventory taken 29 Oct. 1716, names
wife Anna; five daus. Phebe, Anna, Abigail, Marcy and Mary;
eldest son George, second son Nathaniel and son Ephraim; my
sisters Elizabeth Williams and Mary Tisdal.
     Anna m. (2) Norton 3 Sept. 1730 NATHANIEL THOMAS, b.
Marshfield 18 Oct. 1664; d. Plymouth 24 Feb. 1738[/9] in
75th yr.; son of Nathaniel and Deborah (Jacobs) Thomas.

Nathaniel m. (1) Marshfield 1694 Mary Appleton; he had a
wife Mary when he drew his will in 1737.

Anna Thomas wife of Nathaniel of Plymouth Esq., being
authorized by agreement between my husband and myself before our intermarriage to make a will, named son George
Leonard of Norton Esq.; son Nathaniel Leonard; granddau.
Anna, dau. of Nathaniel; son Ephraim; son Abiel Leonard to
have pewter which was his grandmother Leonards; dau. Phebe
Reynolds wife of Mr. Joseph of Bristol to have my gold
necklace; dau. Abigail Williams wife of Warham of Watertown; dau. Mary Clap wife of Rev. Thomas of Taunton;
friends Joseph Avery and Joseph Hodges both of Norton
executors. Her will was dated 15 Aug. 1733 and the
witnesses swore to their signatures on 19 Dec. 1733. On 20
Sept. 1733 Nathaniel Thomas late husband of Anna approved
and allowed the will. Anna's estate included many colorful
garments of satin, velvet and other fine materials which
she left to her daughters.

In his will, drawn 5 Oct. 1737, sworn 13 March 1738,
Nathaniel Thomas of Plymouth mentioned his third wife, his
children and grandchildren, a niece, and the Rev. Nathaniel Leonard [son of his wife Anna (Tisdale) Leonard].

Children (LEONARD) b. Norton:

232	i	PHEBE[5] b. 11 March 1696
233	ii	GEORGE b. 4 March 1698
234	iii	NATHANIEL b. 9 March 1699/1700
	iv	ANNA b. 16 Dec. 1701; d. Norton 31 Jan. 1724/5 in 24th yr.
235	v	ABIGAIL b. 20 Oct. 1703
236	vi	EPHRAIM b. 16 Jan. 1705 or 1706
	vii	MARCY b. 29 April 1708; d. bet. 30 Aug. 1716 and 17 July 1720, when Anna Leonard, widow and administratrix of Major George Leonard, signed a receipt noting that the Major had in his will ordered payment to Mercy Leonard who is now deceased.
	viii	JONATHAN b. 30 Oct. 1710; d. Norton 13 Jan. 1710/11.
	ix	JOSHUA b. 13 May 1712; d. Norton 29 June 1712.
237	x	MARY b. 17 Jan. 1713/14
	xi	ABIEL bp. June 1717; d. spring 1739. The will of Abiel Leonard of Plymouth dealer, "in 22nd year," made 15 Jan. 1738/9, sworn to by the witnesses 16 May 1739, names brothers George, Nathaniel and Ephraim; three sisters Phebe, Abigail and Mary.

References: VR NORTON, TAUNTON. MARSHFIELD VR pp. 7, 17, 19. (PLYM-
OUTH) BURIAL HILL p. 21. BOSTON NEWS OBITS 3:455. Bristol Co. PR 3:289(Geo. Leonard). Bristol Co. LR 18:87(Geo. Leonard);
27:249(Joseph Reynolds). Plymouth Co. PR 6:415(Anna Thomas); 8:6
(Nath'l Thomas); 8:41(Abiel Leonard). NEHGR 5:407-8.

54 REMEMBER[4] TISDALE   (Anna[3] Rogers, John[2], Thomas[1])   b.
Taunton 8 July 1675; d. Dighton bet. 1710 and 1712.
      She m. Taunton bef. 1696 NICHOLAS STEPHENS, b. Taunton
ca. 1669; d. there bef. 7 July 1747; son of Richard and
Mary (Lincoln) (Hacke) Stephens. He m. (2) Dighton 1712/3
Anne Spur, by whom he had Mary, Anna and Robert. There is
no record of Nicholas Stephens' birth, but a deposition of
Jonathan Lincoln of Norton, made 9 Nov. 1768, mentions
Richard Stephens of Taunton, "an old man when I was young"
...married a Mary Linkon and had four sons...[of whom]
Nicholas is deceased and left six sons: Richard and
Nicholas, both dec., Joseph, Isaac and Josiah, now living,
and [of] Robert I know nothing. Joseph eldest son of
Nicholas that is living, lived in Taunton until he was 26,
then moved to Norton.
      The will of Nicholas Stephens of Taunton yeoman,
dated 3 Jan. 1735, proved 7 July 1747, names wife Ann; son
Richard Stephens or his legal representatives; dau. Ann
Elmes wife of Robert of Scituate; sons Nicholas and Josiah
Stephens; dau. Mary Goddard; dau. Anna Holland wife of
James; sons Joseph, Isaac and Robert Stephens, the latter
under age. Since the names of his sons and daughters ap-
pear in chronological order, except for Josiah, daughter
Hannah or Ann by Remember is accepted to be the one who
married Robert Elmes.

      Children (STEPHENS) b. Dighton to Nicholas and Remember:

        i   dau. b. 29 April 1696; d.y.
238   ii   RICHARD[5] b. 21 April 1698
239   iii   NICHOLAS b. 24 Feb. 1702
240   iv   JOSEPH b. 23 April 1704
        v   ISAAC b. 11 Oct. 1706; d. after 9 Nov. 1768 (deposition).
             He m. after 1727 ANNA -----, who was living 30 May 1758
             when Isaac Stephens of Dighton sold land in Taunton ex-
             cept what my father gave a deed of to my sister Anna
             Jones. Wife Anna gave up her dower rights. Isaac may
             have been living in 1786 when Isaac Stephens of Raynham
             laborer sold land in Taunton which Nicholas Stephens
             deeded to his dau. Anna Jones dec. wife of Joseph. No
             children found to this couple.
241   vi   JOSIAH b. 23 Nov 1707
242   vii   (H)ANNAH b. 6 Oct. 1710

References: VR TAUNTON. DIGHTON VR pp. 4, 5, 17. Bristol Co. PR
             11:307 and original will on file(Nicholas Stephens).
Bristol Co. LR 37:116; 39:270; 43:124; 68:133(Isaac Stephens); 53:514
(Jonathan Lincoln deposition).

55 THOMAS[4] TERRY (Anna[3] Rogers, John[2], Thomas[1]) b. bef.
1679; d. Freetown bef. 15 June 1757.
     He m. Taunton 4 Jan. 1699/1700 ABIGAIL DEAN, b. Taun-
ton 16 Nov. 1680; d. bef. 9 April 1760 (deed of children);
dau. of Isaac and Hannah (Leonard) Dean. The will of
Isaac Dean of Taunton, made 15 Dec. 1709, names dau. Abigail Terry.
     Thomas Terry was a justice of the peace, representa-
tive to the General Court, selectman and treasurer for
Freetown at various times. The will of Thomas Terry of
Freetown, made 5 May 1748 and probated 15 June 1757, names
wife Abigail, son Thomas "not of sound mind" to have a
guardian, and daughter Lydia Jones; son Abiel was named
executor.

     Children (TERRY):

243   i   LYDIA[5] b. bef. 1701
       ii THOMAS living 1748.
244   iii ABIEL b. Freetown 3 Dec. 1714

References: VR TAUNTON. FREETOWN VR p. 42. Bristol Co. PR 15:380
             (Thomas Terry). TERRY FAM pp. 264-5.

56 JOHN[4] TERRY (Anna[3] Rogers, John[2], Thomas[1]) b. bef.
1684; d. Freetown bef. 6 Nov. 1711.
     He m. Taunton 3 April 1705 REMEMBER FARRAH (or Far-
row), b. Hingham 3 Feb. 1682/3; d. bet. 25 Feb. and 21
March 1718/9; dau. of John and Mary (Hilliard) Farrow.
Remember m. (2) Dighton 2 Sept. 1716 Thomas Gaige. The
will of John Farrow of Hingham, drawn 10 Feb. 1707/8,
names daughter Remember Terry.
     The inventory of John Terry of Freetown, blacksmith,
was taken 6 Nov. 1711. The will of Remember Gage, now wife
to Thomas of Freetown, formerly widow of John Terry of
Freetown deceased, names two sons Silas Terry and John
Terry, both under lawful age; husband to have estate bequeathed me by my father late of Hingham deceased; she
specified that Jacob Hathaway of Freetown and James Tisdale of Dighton be executors of her will. The will was
dated 25 Feb. 1718/9 and the witnesses swore to it 18 Mar.
1718/9.
     John and Remember Terry had only two children who
survived infancy as shown by the settlement of John's estate 2 Feb. 1749: John Terry blacksmith; Remember Davis,
dau. of Silas Terry dec. and widow of David Davis late
dec.; and Jonathan Davis yeoman and wife Sarah, late relict of Silas Terry late dec.; said John and Silas, the
only children of John Terry deceased, all of Freetown, received all John Terry's moveables from the executor of the
will of Remember Gaige, former relict of John Terry.

Children (TERRY) b. Freetown:

245   i   SILAS[5] b. 8 April 1707
246   ii JOHN b. 26 May 1708

References: HINGHAM HIST 2:215. VR TAUNTON. FREETOWN VR p. 21.
             DIGHTON VR p. 18. Bristol Co. PR 3:59(John Terry); 3:
517(Remember Gaige); 13:554(John Terry). Suffolk Co. PR 19:90(John
Farrow).

57 BENJAMIN[4] TERRY (Anna[3] Rogers, John[2], Thomas[1]) b.
after 1683; d. Freetown bet. 28 June 1768 and 29 March
1773.
    He m. (1) after 31 July 1710 JOANNA SPUR, dau. of
John and Mercy (-----) Spur. On 31 July 1710 John Spur of
Taunton gave to dau. Joanna Spur half his homestead in
Taunton, after decease of himself and wife Mercy, and on
27 Feb. 1753 Robert[6] Terry of Freetown sold part of the
homestead of John Spur dec. which descended to Spur's dau.
Joanna Terry.
    He m. (2) bef. 30 Nov. 1723 MARGARET HOLLOWAY, living
28 June 1768; dau. of Nathaniel and Deliverance (Bobet)
Holloway. On 16 Feb. 1729/30 Deliverance Holloway of Middleboro, widow of Nathaniel, and Benjamin Terry of Freetown and wife Margaret, one of the children of deceased
Nathaniel, sold land belonging to the deceased.
    The will of Benjamin Terry of Freetown yeoman, made
28 June 1768 and sworn 29 March 1773, names wife Margaret,
eldest son Robert, who had received land from his grandfather Spur's estate, 2nd son Benjamin, 3rd son John, 4th
son George of Swansea, 5th son William, 6th son Solomon,
eldest daughter Mary Warren, daughter Johanna Gibbs, 3rd
daughter Lydia Winslow, 4th daughter Phebe Daggett, 5th
daughter Margaret Lewing, 6th daughter Meriam Tisdale, 7th
daughter Sarah Winslow, 8th daughter Dinah Terry unmarried;
son Solomon executor.

    Children (TERRY) first four prob. by Joanna, rest b. Freetown by
Margaret:

247   i   MARY[5] b. prob. Freetown ca. 1715
248   ii   ROBERT b. prob. Freetown ca. 1717
249   iii BENJAMIN b. ca. 1719
250   iv   JOHN b. ca. 1721
251   v   GEORGE b. 30 Nov. 1723
252   vi   JOANNA b. 6 July 1725
253   vii LYDIA b. 10 Oct. 1726
254   viii PHEBE b. 15 Sept. 1729
255   ix   WILLIAM b. 17 April 1731
256   x   MARGARET b. 22 Oct. 1732
257   xi   SOLOMON b. 13 Jan. 1734

258 xii MIRIAM b. 18 May 1737
259 xiii SARAH b. 13 Aug. 1739
     xiv DINAH b. 7 Sept. 1741; d. after 3 March 1792 (see #257).
          She m. Freetown 22 Dec. 1768 NATHANIEL LEWIN (or Luen) of
          Swansea. There are no probate records for Dinah or
          Nathaniel at Bristol County. A Nathaniel Lewen headed a
          household at Swansea in 1790 consisting of one male over
          15 and 7 females. No record of children found.

References: FREETOWN VR pp. 28, 114. Bristol Co. PR 22:456(Benj.
             Terry). Bristol Co. LR 13:113(John Spur); 43:2(Robert
Terry). Plymouth Co. LR 26:52(Deliverance Holloway). 1790 CENSUS:
MA:55.

58 JOSEPH⁴ RICHMOND (Abigail³ Rogers, John², Thomas¹)
b. Taunton 8 Dec. 1663; d. bet. 13 July 1724 and 8 Dec.
1735.
     He m. Taunton 26 June 1685 MARY ANDREWS, who d. after
14 Feb. 1737; dau. of Henry and Mary (Wadsworth) Andrews
of Taunton. Joseph and Mary Richmond received her share of
the estate of her father Henry Andrews on 19 July 1701.
     Although Joseph Richmond left no will, deeds provide
evidence for four of his children: In 1720 Joseph Richmond and his wife Mary of Taunton sold land to their two
sons Joseph Richmond Jr. and Henry Richmond, both of Taunton, he acknowledging the deed 13 July 1724, she 11 March
1726; in 1724 Joseph Richmond of Taunton deeded land to
son John of Middleboro, a lot which had been John Rogers';
and in 1733/4 Christopher Richmond of Middleboro sold land
which had belonged to his father Joseph Richmond Sr.
     However, "The will of Mary Richmond of Taunton, mother
of the wife of William Reed...makes mention of children as
follows: son Joseph Richmond; daughters Margaret Richmond,
Mary Reed, Abigail Gooding; sons John Richmond, Christopher
Richmond, Henry Richmond, Josiah Richmond; and two daughters of son William Richmond. Dated 14 Feb. 1737." (This
is an abstract of a will, apparently never probated, which
was owned in 1841 by Edgar H. Reed and quoted in his Reed
Genealogy.)

     Children (RICHMOND) prob. b. Taunton:

260   i   JOSEPH⁵ b. ca. 1686
261   ii CHRISTOPHER b. ca. 1689
262 iii HENRY
263   iv JOHN
264   v ABIGAIL
265   vi MARY b. ca. 1699
266 vii WILLIAM
267 viii JOSIAH b. ca. 1700
      ix MARGARET living 1737; n.f.r.

References: VR TAUNTON. Bristol Co. LR 37:119(Jos. Richmond). Plym-
          outh Co. LR 29:63(Christopher Richmond). Reed Gen. MS. by
Edgar H. Reed(Old Colony Hist. Soc., Taunton). NEHGR 52:17. RICHMOND
FAM p. 10.

   59 EDWARD[4] RICHMOND (Abigail[3] Rogers, John[2], Thomas[1])
b. Taunton 8 Feb. 1665; d. bef. 9 Dec. 1741.
       He m. MARY -----, who was living 3 June 1738.*
    The land records of Bristol County from 1685 to 1795,
which include the bulk of deeds drawn before 1747 for
eastern Rhode Island towns such as Little Compton, show
that Edward was continually in Taunton and associated with
his father and brothers: On 5 Dec. 1705/6 (sic) John
Richmond Sr. of Taunton deeded to sons Edward Richmond of
Taunton and Ebenezer Richmond of Plymouth 70 acres in Taunton where his deceased son Thomas had lived. On 21 March
1712/3 John Richmond grandsenior of Taunton gave to son
Edward Richmond of Taunton 100 acres in Taunton bounded by
land Edward had improved [used] for about 20 years. On 1
March 1734 Edward Richmond of Taunton sold to John Richmond
of Taunton gent. [prob. his brother] a dwelling and 50
acres in Taunton where John Reed lived, bounded by land in
possession of Edward Richmond Jr., with wife Mary giving up
her dower. These deeds seem to prove that Edward, son of
John and Abigail[3] (Rogers) Richmond, was the one who made
his will in 1738 naming four sons and six daughters, none
of whose birth records survived the fire damage to the
Taunton vital records. Unfortunately only one of the
deeds for Edward[4] mentioned a wife either directly or in-
directly, and that was the 1734 deed with wife Mary.
    The will of Edward Richmond of Taunton, dated 3 June
1738 and witnesses appeared 9 Dec. 1741, names wife Mary;
son Edward to have land in Taunton bounded by land formerly
of my brother John; son Josiah "now dwelling in Middleboro"; sons Nathaniel and Seth; and my daughters Mary Burt,
Mercy Walker, Priscilla Hackett, Sarah Crane, Elizabeth
Hatheway and Phebe Eliot. He reserved a quarter acre for
himself and posterity "where the burying place is already
begun." Son Seth was named executor.

*No evidence was found in Bristol County land records that Edward had
wives Mercy ----- or Rebecca Thurston as accepted by the Mayflower
Society. On the other hand, Little Compton Families claims that the
Edward who married Rebecca Thurston at Little Compton in 1711 was son
of Edward and Sarah and grandson of Edward and Amy (Bull) Richmond,
therefore not a Mayflower line. It may be pure coincidence that
Edward and Rebecca had daughters Sarah, Mary and Priscilla born about
the same time as the daughters of Edward[4] (Abigail Rogers[3]).

Col. Robert C. Brown, (Ret.)
3 Stockridge Place
Beverly Hills
Asheville, NC 28805

Children (RICHMOND) prob. b. Taunton:

    i MERCY[5] b. ca. 1694; d. Taunton 27 Jan. 1760 in 67th yr.
        She m. EDWARD WALKER, b. ca. 1692/3; d. Taunton 9 Dec.
        1752 in 60th yr.; son of Peter and Hannah (-----) Walker.
        The will of Edward Walker of Taunton yeoman, under bodily
        infirmity, drawn 24 Oct. 1752 and sworn to 6 Feb. 1753,
        names wife Mercy; kinsman [nephew] Josiah Richmond that
        lives with me, to have my homestead after the marriage or
        death of my wife; three daughters of my sister Hannah
        Atwood: Elizabeth Place, Hannah Place and Mary Place;
        Phebe Richmond daughter of kinsman Josiah under 21; kins-
        man Elisha Walker son of my brother James Walker de-
        ceased; Eleazer Walker grandson of my brother Peter;
        Nathan Walker son of my kinsman Nathan Walker; wife Mercy
        to be executor with Josiah Richmond. No known children.
268   ii EDWARD b. ca. 1696
269 iii JOSIAH b. ca. 1697
    iv NATHANIEL b. ca. 1700; d. bet. 1739 and 1744. He m. Mid-
        dleboro 2 Nov. 1732 ALICE HACKETT, prob. the one b. 18
        Jan. 1714/5; d. after 22 Nov. 1763; dau. of John and
        Elizabeth (Elliott) Hackett (see #274). The will of
        John Hackett of Middleboro, dated 22 Nov. 1763, names
        daughter Alice Finney. She is prob. the one who m. (2)
        Taunton 1744/5 Onesimus Campbell (prob. b. Raynham 1704);
        and (3) Taunton 1762 Joseph Finney of Bridgewater (see
        #140). There are no probate records for Alice, Onesimus,
        Joseph or Nathaniel. No known children.*
270   v SETH
271   vi ELIZABETH
272 vii PHEBE b. ca. 1713
273 viii SARAH
    ix MARY d. after 1738. She m. bef. 1738 ----- BURT. No evi-
        dence was found proving that he was Edmond Burt as
        claimed in RICHMOND FAM. No known children.
274   x PRISCILLA

References: VR TAUNTON, BRIDGEWATER. RICHMOND FAM pp. 10, 25-8. MD
        6:226; 9:47. RI VR:Little Compton p. 151. Bristol Co.
PR 10:111(Edward Richmond); 13:303(Edward Walker); 20:4(John Hackett);

---

*No probate or land records were found in Bristol County which prove
that Nathaniel and Alice had the children ascribed to them in RICHMOND
FAM; nor do what published vital records there are for the Bridge-
waters, Dighton, Freetown, Norton, Raynham and Taunton list any children. Nathaniel and Gidoen Richmond, said to be two of their children,
married daughters of John and Dighton (Myrick) Richmond, through whom
their offspring have Rogers ancestry (see #285).

23:244(James Burt). Bristol Co. LR 5:49; 7:617; 27:22(Edward Richmond).

60 SAMUEL[4] RICHMOND (Abigail[3] Rogers, John[2], Thomas[1])
b. Taunton 23 Sept. 1668; d. there bet. 11 June and 20
July 1736.
     He m. (1) Taunton 20 Dec. 1694 MEHITABLE ANDREWS who
d. after 1704; dau. of Henry and Mary (Wadsworth) Andrews
of Taunton. On 22 Jan. 1694/5 Samuel Richmond and wife
Mehitable gave receipt for their portion of the estate of
her father Henry Andrews late of Taunton dec.
     He m. (2) after 1706/7 ELIZABETH (KING) HALL, b. bef.
1680; d. 16 June 1757; dau. of Philip and Judith (Whitman)
King, and widow of John Hall. The will of Philip King of
Taunton, drawn 12 [-] 1706/7, mentions his wife Judith and
dau. Elizabeth Hall.
     The will of Samuel Richmond of Taunton, dated 11 June
1736, names his wife Elizabeth to have moveables she
brought with her; sons Samuel, Oliver, Thomas and Silas;
daughters Hannah Booth, Lydya Thomas and Mehitable Horton.
Son Thomas was named executor with "my cozen Joseph Richmond" as advisor. The witnesses made oath to the will 20
July 1736.

     Children (RICHMOND) first five by first wife:

275   i   SAMUEL[5] b. Taunton 16 Oct. 1695
276   ii   OLIVER b. Taunton 25 Aug. 1697
     iii   THOMAS b. Middleboro 10 Sept. 1700; living Taunton 13 Sept.
             1737. He m. Bristol RI 21 April 1725 HANNAH FRY, perhaps
             the one b. Bristol 4 June 1702 to John and Deliverance
             (-----) Fry. There is no probate for either Thomas or
             Hannah at Bristol RI or Bristol County MA, but he was
             living 24 March 1737 when Samuel Richmond of Middleboro,
             Thomas Richmond of Taunton and Silas Richmond of Litch-
             field CT, all sons of Samuel Richmond late of Taunton
             deceased, sold land in Taunton our father died siezed of.
             The deed was acknowledged by Thomas 3 Sept. 1737, by
             Samuel 13 Sept. 1737 and by Silas at Taunton 12 Jan. 1738.
             No known children.
277   iv   HANNAH b. Middleboro 29 Aug. 1702
278   v   LYDIA b. Middleboro 14 May 1704
279   vi   SILAS prob. b. Middleboro ca. 1710
280 vii   MEHITABLE prob. b. Middleboro ca. 1712

References: VR TAUNTON. NEHGR 52:17. MD 2:104-5; 21:44. RICHMOND
          FAM p. 11, 28. RI VR 6:Bristol:46, 77. Bristol Co. PR
2:172(Henry Andrews); 3:32 1/2(Philip King). Bristol Co. LR 25:356
(Samuel Richmond).

61 SARAH[4] RICHMOND (Abigail[3] Rogers, John[2], Thomas[1])
b. Taunton 26 Feb. 1670; d. there 27 Nov. 1727 in her 57th
year.
      She m. Taunton 6 Oct. 1699 JAMES WALKER, b. Taunton
24 Dec. 1674; d. there 12 Sept. 1749 ae 74-8-19; son of
James and Bathsheba (Brooks) Walker. When John Richmond[3]
administered the estate of his son Thomas in 1706/7 he mentioned his son-in-law James Walker (see #12). James m.
(2) Sarah (-----) ----- who d. 1759 ae ca. 75.
      The will of James Walker of Taunton, gentleman ad-
vanced in years, names [second] wife Sarah to have what
she brought with her of her former husband's estate; eldest son James; sons Eliakim, Elnathan and Peter; dau.
Sarah Leonard wife of Thomas; grandson Elnathan Walker,
under 21, that lived with me. The will was dated 3 Nov.
1747 and the witnesses swore to their signatures 3 Oct.
1749.

      Children (WALKER) prob. b. Taunton*:

281   i   SARAH[5]
282   ii   JAMES b. ca. 1704
283   iii ELIAKIM b. ca. 1705
284   iv   ELNATHAN b. ca. 1707
       v   PETER b. ca. 1710; d. Taunton 6 Aug. 1767 in 58th yr.; m.
            HELEN BAYLIES, b. England; dau. of Thomas and Esther
            (Sergeant) Baylies. Helen m. (2) Rev. John Lyon. The
            will of Peter Walker, 2nd of that name in Taunton, names
            wife Helen and nephew Peter Walker, son of my brother
            Elnathan, to have gun and ivory-headed cane of my
            father's, and land which fell to me from my uncle Nehe-
            miah Walker late of Taunton dec. Executor was Elnathan.
            "to be buried in yard of St. Thomas' church with rites of
            the Church of England." The will was dated 25 July 1767
            and the witnesses gave their oath 18 Aug. 1767.

References: VR TAUNTON. RICHMOND FAM p. 12. MD 9:59. Bristol Co.
             PR 12:80(James Walker); 20:152(Peter Walker).

62 JOHN[4] RICHMOND (Abigail[3] Rogers, John[2], Thomas[1]) b.
Taunton 5 Dec. 1673; d. there bef. 24 June 1760.
      He m. Scituate 28 Nov. 1709 HANNAH OTIS, b. Scituate
16 May 1686; d. bef. 16 Oct. 1739; dau. of Stephen and Hannah (Ensign) Otis. The will of Capt. Stephen Otis of Scituate, drawn 16 May 1729, names his dau. Hannah Richmond.
      The will of John Richmond of Taunton, drawn 16 Oct.
1739, gives to son Stephen land I bought of my brother Edward Richmond; son John to have homestead; daughter Mary

_____

*David Walker who m. (1) about 1703 Mary -----, and then (2) Esther
(Paul) Dillingham, was of course a brother, not a son, of James.

Richmond unmarried; son John executor. The witnesses deposed 24 June 1760.

    Children (RICHMOND) prob. b. Taunton:

285   i   JOHN[5] b. ca. 1710
        ii   MARY b. ca. 1711-15; living 16 Oct. 1739; n.f.r.
286   iii   STEPHEN b. ca. 1719

References: RICHMOND FAM p. 12. VR SCITUATE, TAUNTON. Bristol Co.
             PR 17:45(John Richmond). Plymouth Co. PR 6:403(Stephen
Otis). OTIS FAM pp. 71, 84.

  63 EBENEZER[4] RICHMOND (Abigail[3] Rogers, John[2], Thomas[1])
b. Newport RI 12 May 1676; d. Middleboro bet. 7 April and
12 May 1729.
      He m. bef. 1701 ANNA SPROAT, b. Scituate in March
1671/2; d. after 7 Dec. 1739; dau. of Robert and Elizabeth
(Samson) Sproat, and a granddau. of Pilgrim Henry Samson.
The will of Robert Sproat of Middleboro, dated 23 Nov.
1711, names dau. Anna Richmond.
      The will of Ebenezer Richmond of Middleboro, made 7
April 1729, with the heirs agreement 12 May 1729, names
wife Annah, eldest son Ebenezer, sons Robert and Silvester,
daughters Annah Richmond, Rachel Richmond, and Elizabeth
Worshbon wife of Edward; son Ebenezer to be executor.

    Children (RICHMOND) b. Middleboro:

287   i   EBENEZER[5] b. 31 March 1701
288   ii   ROBERT b. 18 Sept. 1702
289   iii   ANNA b. 14 Oct. 1704
        iv   RACHEL b. 6 May 1707; living 29 June 1730 when she acknow-
             ledged her signature on the heirs agreement; n.f.r.
290   v   ELIZABETH b. 1 Sept. 1708
291   vi   SYLVESTER b. 25 Nov. 1711

References: RICHMOND FAM p. 12. VR SCITUATE. MD 2:43, 105, 201;
             6:8-11; 21:187-8. FAM OF PILGRIMS p. 134.

  64 ABIGAIL[4] RICHMOND (Abigail[3] Rogers, John[2], Thomas[1])
b. Taunton 26 Feb. 1678/9; d. Taunton 28 Feb. 1763 in her
84th yr.
      She m. Taunton 29 July 1708 NATHAN WALKER, b. 28 Jan.
1677/8; d. Taunton 23 Dec. 1747 in his 70th yr.; son of
James and Bathsheba (Brooks) Walker.
      The will of Nathan Walker of Dighton, advanced in
years, names wife Abigail, sons Nathan and William, daughter Abigail Austin wife of Jacob, daughters Phebe, Lydia
and Deborah (no last names given). Son Nathan to be

executor. The will was drawn 13 April 1739 and the witnesses affirmed their signatures 5 April 1748.

Children (WALKER) b. Dighton:

292	i	NATHAN[5] b. 27 Oct. 1709
293	ii	ABIGAIL b. 3 Dec. 1711
294	iii	PHEBE b. 29 Sept. 1713
295	iv	WILLIAM b. 17 Aug. 1715
296	v	LYDIA b. 31 July 1717
	vi	DEBORAH b. 13 Aug. 1719; d. prob. Taunton bet. 6 Nov. 1792 and 22 Dec. 1796. She m. int. Dighton 29 Jan. 1763 WILLIAM AUSTIN, prob. the one bur. Taunton 16 Jan. 1797; prob. son of Jonah. He had been married previously, and had at least two children to whom he deeded land. Deborah's marriage is proved through two deeds wherein heirs of Nehemiah Walker divided land: A deed 10 May 1762 calls her Deborah Walker of Dighton, child of Nathan; another 9 Aug. 1764 calls her Deborah Austin, wife of William of Taunton, and groups her with her sisters. Neither William nor Deborah left probate records, and there are no deeds to show that there were any children born to this late marriage. In 1768 William and Deborah sold the land from Nehemiah Walker; they were still in Taunton 6 Nov. 1792 when William deeded land with Deborah releasing her dower. She was apparently dead by 22 Dec. 1796 when William Austin of Taunton sold his house lot and buildings. No known children.

References: VR TAUNTON. DIGHTON VR pp. 6, 109. RICHMOND FAM p. 13. Bristol Co. PR 11:433(Nathan Walker); 14:307(Jonah Austin). Bristol Co. LR 46:391(Deborah Walker); 47:431; 54:84; 71:314; 75:282(Wm. Austin).

65 JOHN[4] WILLIAMS (Elizabeth[3] Rogers, John[2], Thomas[1]) b. Taunton 27 Aug. 1675; d. there 18 Aug. 1724 in 49th yr.
He m. HANNAH ROBINSON, b. 8 March 1670; d. 2 Dec. 1757; dau. of Increase and Sarah (Penniman) Robinson.
On 20 Oct. 1724 the widow Hannah Williams and Nathaniel Williams were appointed administrators of the estate of John Williams late of Taunton deceased. On 2 Oct. 1730 Hannah Williams widow of Taunton was appointed guardian to Simeon Williams (under 14) son of John deceased. On 11 Jan. 1753 Silas and Timothy Williams, both of Easton, and Simeon Williams of Taunton, all yeomen, sold house and land in Taunton of [their brother] Nathaniel Williams late of Taunton deceased, with the widow Hannah Williams joining "with my children" in the sale.

Children (WILLIAMS) b. Taunton:

    i NATHANIEL[5] b. 30 Dec. 1702; d. Taunton 29 Dec. 1746. He
        m. SARAH DEAN, b. 1711; d. 3 April 1799; dau. of ----- and
        Hannah (Bird) Dean. She m. (2) Capt. Joseph Hall of
        Taunton. The will of Nathaniel Williams of Taunton yeo-
        man, infirm, dated 22 May 1745 with the witnesses giving
        their oath 6 Oct. 1747, gives wife Sarah goods she brought
        with her; land set off to him from his father's estate to
        go to his three brothers--Silas, Timothy and Simeon Wil-
        liams; sister Experience Hodges wife of Nathan of Norton
        to have a legacy; three brothers to be executors.
297   ii EXPERIENCE b. 30 Nov. 1705
298 iii SILAS b. 16 Jan. 1707
    iv JOHN b. 31 Oct. 1708; d. bef. 21 Sept. 1736 when Nathan
        Hodges of Norton was appointed administrator of the es-
        tate of John Williams late of Taunton deceased, at request
        of his mother and brothers. Inventory of the estate of
        John Williams, late of Taunton singleman deceased, was
        taken 12 May 1738.
299   v TIMOTHY b. 28 Sept. 1714
300   vi SIMEON b. 21 Feb. 1717

References: VR TAUNTON. Bristol Co. PR 4:427; 7:95(John[4] Williams);
           8:406; 9:152(John[5] Williams); 11:330(Nathaniel Williams).
Bristol Co. LR 39:385(Silas Williams et al.). WILLIAMS FAM (1926) p.
39.

  66 NATHANIEL[4] WILLIAMS (Elizabeth[3] Rogers, John[2], Thomas[1]) b. Taunton 9 or 29 April 1679; d. there 24 Aug.
1726 "ae 47 in April."
    He m. 9 Jan. 1709/10 LYDIA KING, b. 3 March 1688; d.
prob. Raynham 31 March 1748; dau. of Philip and Judith
(Whitman) King. Lydia m. (2) Raynham 1733 John Macomber,
widower of her first husband's sister Elizabeth (see #67).
    The will of Nathaniel Williams of Taunton, drawn 23
Aug. 1726, proved 21 Feb. 1726/7, names wife Lydia, sons
Edmund and Nathaniel, and daughters Lydia, Bethia, Judith
and Elizabeth. Wife Lydia was executor.
    On 19 Jan. 1747 Lydia Macomber widow, late of Taunton
now of Raynham, quitclaimed land to sons Edmond and Nathaniel Williams, both of Raynham.

    Children (WILLIAMS) all prob. b. Taunton:

301   i EDMUND[5] b. 4 Dec. 1710
302   ii NATHANIEL b. 4 Jan. 1711/2
    iii LYDIA b. ca. 1713; d. Abington 19 Jan. 1796. She m. (1)
        Raynham 17 Oct. 1734 ICHABOD KEITH, b. Bridgewater 14
        March 1709; d. there 27 Sept. 1753; son of Joseph and
        Elizabeth (Fobes) Keith. In the division of real estate

of Ichabod Keith late of Bridgewater dec., made 25 Feb.
1754, widow Lydia Keith received her thirds, and the rest
was divided among his mother and siblings.

She m. (2) Weymouth 1 July 1755 Dr. NATHANIEL WHITE, b.
Weymouth 3 Sept. 1701; d. there 23 Nov. 1758; son of Thomas and Mary (White) White.

She m. (3) Abington 24 April 1759 Dr. DANIEL JONES, b.
Abington 21 Feb. 1715/6; d. there 10 Jan. 1783. He left
no probate records.

The will of Lydia Jones of Abington, dated 3 June 1793
and presented 1 Feb. 1796, names brother Edmond Williams,
cousin Hannah Alden wife of Samuel, and Daniel Alden executor. No know children were born to Lydia by any of
her husbands.

iv BETHIA b. Taunton 1 Nov. 1716; d. bet. 26 May 1742 and 21
Jan. 1746. She m. Taunton 23 March 1737 NOAH WILLIAMS,
b. 18 March 1718; d. after 1742; son of Samuel Williams.
On 21 Jan. 1746 Edmond and Nathaniel Williams, both of
Raynham, and Ichabod Keith of Bridgewater and wife Lydia
sold two pieces of land granted to their father Nathaniel
Williams late of Taunton deceased, in one of which was
included four acres that belongs to the heirs of Bethiah,
deceased wife of Noah Williams late of Taunton. Witnesses testified in March 1749 they had seen Noah "who is
since deceased or out of the government" sign a deed with
wife Bethia in 1742. The will of Samuel Williams of
Taunton 28 July 1764 mentions son Noah "if he be living
and return to Taunton," otherwise grandson Noah to have
40 shillings. [Young Noah was probably not a son of
Bethia.] No known children were born to Noah and Bethia.

v JUDITH b. ca. 1721; d. Taunton 1 Oct. 1743 in 23 yr. She
m. Taunton 10 Feb. 1742 ELIJAH MACOMBER (see #308).

vi ELIZABETH b. Taunton 21 March 1721. She m. Berkley 18 May
1742 HENRY PITTS, b. Dighton 1 Dec. 1716; living 9 April
1759; son of Henry and Ann (Carey) Pitts. He may have
m. (2) Dighton 1746 Sarah Pitts. Henry was of Dighton
when he deeded land 9 April 1759. Henry and Elizabeth
had no known children.

References: VR ABINGTON, BRIDGEWATER, TAUNTON, WEYMOUTH. DIGHTON VR
pp. 9, 18, 63, 88. MD 23:1-7. Berkley TR 1:243. NEHGR
53:436. WILLIAMS FAM (1926) p. 40. WEYMOUTH BY CHAMBERLAIN 4:733,
735. Bristol Co. PR 19:11(Samuel Williams). Bristol Co. LR 34:550
(Lydia Macomber); 43:340(Henry Pitts). Plymouth Co. PR 13:349; 35:545
(Ichabod Keith); 35:464(Lydia Jones).

67 ELIZABETH[4] WILLIAMS (Elizabeth[3] Rogers, John[2], Thomas[1]) b. Taunton 18 April 1686; d. there 2 May 1732 in
her 47th yr.

She m. Taunton 17 March 1707/8 JOHN MACOMBER, b.
Taunton 18 March 1681; d. there 14 Dec. 1747 in his 67th

yr.; son of John and Ann (Evans) Macomber. He m. (2) Raynham 1733 Lydia (King) Williams, widow of his first wife's
brother (#66).

John Macomber was impressed for service in Queen
Anne's War in 1701 and again in 1711. The will of John
Macomber of Taunton yeoman, dated 28 Dec. 1742 and sworn 5
April 1748, names wife Lydia; sons Nathaniel, Josiah and
John Jr., who were to have land in Middleboro; sons James,
Elijah and Joseph (under 21); daughters Elizabeth Roun-
sevell wife of William, Abiah Macomber and Ann Macomber
(under 18); executor son Nathaniel. No receipts of the
estate mention daughter Anna.

Children (MACOMBER) b. Taunton to John and Elizabeth:

303   i   NATHANIEL[5] b. 9 Feb. 1709
304   ii   JOSIAH b. 19 Feb. 1711
305   iii JOHN b. 10 Feb. 1713
306   iv   ELIZABETH b. 15 March 1715
307   v   JAMES b. 12 Sept. 1717
308   vi   ELIJAH b. 25 Oct. 1718
        vii MARY b. 30 July 1721; d. bef. 28 Dec. 1742 (not in
             father's will).
        viii ABIAH b. 8 June 1724; living 28 Dec. 1742. She is said to
             have married ISRAEL DEAN, and died Taunton 1 March 1750
             in her 25th year, leaving no children.
        ix   ANNA b. 2 Jan. 1726; living 28 Dec. 1742; n.f.r.*
309   x   JOSEPH b. 28 March 1732

References: VR TAUNTON. WILLIAMS FAM (1926) p. 36. MACOMBER GEN pp.
        12-3, 17 ("record preserved in a branch of descendants
...in Augusta ME"). Bristol Co. PR 11:426(John Macomber). CONTRIBU-
TIONS BY PEIRCE pp. 199-201.

FIFTH GENERATION

68 HANNAH[5] HARDING (Hannah[4] Rogers, Thomas[3], Joseph[2],
Thomas[1]) b. Eastham 15 Feb. 1694; d. after 10 Aug. 1727.
She m. Eastham 9 Oct. 1716 BARTHOLOMEW FISH, b. Fal-
mouth 16 June 1687; d. after 10 Aug. 1727; son of Nathan
and Deborah (Barnes) Fish.
There are no Barnstable County probate records for
Bartholomew or Hannah.

Children (FISH): LEMUEL[6] b. Sandwich 1727, and JEDIDIAH (dau.)
bp. Falmouth 1738.

---

*The Mayflower Society has accepted descent through a claimed marriage
of Anna to John Smith, intention 1749, who had five children baptized
at Taunton. No proof was found that John's wife was the daughter of
John and Elizabeth (Williams) Macomber.

References: MD 15:55; 30:58. VR FALMOUTH.

69 JOHN[5] HARDING (Hannah[4] Rogers, Thomas[3], Joseph[2],
Thomas[1]) b. Eastham; d. there bet. 9 Jan. and 20 March
1761.
    He m. Eastham 23 Sept. 1731 ELIZABETH YOUNG, b. East-
ham 24 May 1711; d. after 1752; dau. of Elisha and Elizabeth (Merrick) Young.
    The will of John Harding of Eastham, made 9 Jan. 1761
and proved 20 March 1761, mentions an unnamed wife, sons
John, Archelas, Joshua and Nathaniel Harding, and dau.
Mary.

    Children (HARDING) b. Eastham: MARY[6] b. 1732; JOHN b. 1734;
HANNAH b. 1736; ARCHELAS b. 1740; JOSHUA b. 1743; NATHANIEL b. 1746;
EBENEZER b. 1749; and HANNAH b. 1752.

References: Barnstable Co. PR 12:202(John Harding). MD 3:180;
           16:199; 17:34; 33:13. YOUNG (JOHN) DESC p. 22.

70 JAMES[5] HARDING (Hannah[4] Rogers, Thomas[3], Joseph[2],
Thomas[1]) b. Eastham 2 Nov. 1702; d. there 30 April 1732.
    He m. Harwich 8 Oct. 1724 MARY NICKERSON, b. Harwich
13 Aug. 1701; living Eastham 1774; dau. William and Mary
(Snow) Nickerson, and a descendant of Pilgrim Stephen Hopkins. Mary m. (2) Eastham 1732/3 Samuel Betee (or Batee)
by whom she had 5 children.
    There are no Barnstable County probate records for
James Harding or Mary Betee.

    Children (HARDING) first b. Harwich, others b. Eastham:
THOMAS[6] b. 1725; EBENEZER b. 1727/8, d. by 1734; and JAMES b. 1731.

References: MD 5:202; 8:160; 10:166; 16:198; 17:35, 37.

71 MARY[5] HARDING (Hannah[4] Rogers, Thomas[3], Joseph[2],
Thomas[1]) b. Eastham 2 April 1706; d. bef. 27 Jan. 1737/8,
and prob. bef. 20 Apr. 1734 (father's will).
    She m. Eastham 7 Nov. 1728 LAUNCELOT (or Lot) CLARK,
b. Yarmouth 30 Dec. 1703; living 1775; son of John and
Mary (Benjamin) Clark. Launcelot m. (2) int. Eastham
1737/8 Patience Brown by whom he probably had five more
children.
    There are no probate records at Barnstable County for
Mary or Launcelot.

    Children (CLARK) b. Chatham to Launcelot and Mary: MARY[6] b.
1729/30, and ELIZABETH b. 1731.

References: MD 5:142; 7:249; 16:204; 28:117, 180.   CLARK FAM p. 8.
             YARMOUTH VR 1:18.

72   ELIZABETH[5] HARDING   (Hannah[4] Rogers, Thomas[3], Joseph[2],
Thomas[1])   b. Eastham in April 1708; d. after 1751.
      She m. Eastham 16 Feb. 1730/1 ROWLAND FISH, b. Fal-
mouth 25 July 1708; d. after 1751; son of Nathan and
Deborah (Barnes) Fish.
      There is no probate record at Barnstable County for
either Rowland or Elizabeth.

      Children (FISH) b. Falmouth: NATHAN[6] b. 1733; EBENEZER b. 1734;
RUFUS b. 1740; CORNELIUS b. 1743; JAMES bp. 1745; JAMES bp. May 1747;
JAMES b. Oct. 1747; LOT b. 1748; and PRINCE b. 1751.

References: VR FALMOUTH.   MD 17:33.

73   NATHAN[5] HARDING   (Hannah[4] Rogers, Thomas[3], Joseph[2],
Thomas[1])   b. Eastham 29 Oct. 1711; d. Easthampton CT 27
March 1801 ae 89.
      He m. (1) Easthampton CT int. 8 Jan. 1736/7 ANNA BROWN
who d. Middletown CT in Nov. 1749.
      He m. (2) Middletown CT 15 Nov. 1750 ABIGAIL WEST, b.
Middletown 23 July 1716; d. there 28 Sept. 1785 ae 69; dau.
of Benjamin and Hannah (West) West.
      Nathan Harding was of Middletown on 13 Oct. 1741 when
he and Stephen Griffith divided a piece of land there.

      Children (HARDING) first b. Eastham, others b. Middletown CT or
bp. Easthampton CT to Nathan and Anna: EBENEZER[6] b. 1739; LYDIA b.
1741; twins ELEAZER and TABITHA b. 1742; ELIZABETH b. 1743, d. 1749;
ANNA b. 1745, d. 1749; NATHAN b. 1746; and GEORGE b. 1748, d. 1749.

      Children (HARDING) b. Middletown to Nathan and Abigail: EPHRAIM
b. 1752; BENJAMIN b. 1756; and ABIGAIL b. 1762.

References: CSL Barbour Index:Easthampton and Middletown.   CSL Ch Rec:
             Easthampton(formerly Chatham).   MD 28:180.   Middletown
CT LR 9:435(Nathan Harding).

74   CORNELIUS[5] HARDING   (Hannah[4] Rogers, Thomas[3], Joseph[2],
Thomas[1])   b. Eastham 31 March 1716/7.
      He m. int. Eastham 21 Nov. 1740 PRISCILLA CURTIS of
Eastham.
      A Cornelius and a Nathan Harding were living in Well-
fleet in 1779. No evidence found for a second wife of
Cornelius, or a son John.

Children (HARDING) b. Eastham to Cornelius and Priscilla:
PHEBE[6] b. 1742; JOSEPH b. 1744; PRISCILLA b. 1747; LUCIA b. 1750;
NATHAN b. 1752; CORNELIUS b. 1754; and SETH b. 1756.

References: MD 15:227-8; 29:11. NGSQ 49:139; 51:47. ANC PURITANS
              4:9, 10, 13.

75 ELIZABETH[5] ROGERS (Thomas[4-3], Joseph[2], Thomas[1]) b.
Truro 27 March 1706; d. after Sept. 1750.
      She m. Truro 13 June 1728 BENJAMIN LEWIS, b. Eastham
8 Oct. 1700; d. after Sept. 1750; son of Thomas and Joan
(-----) Lewis.

      Children (LEWIS) b. Truro: SARAH[6] b. 1729; LUCE b. 1731; BENJA-
MIN b. 1733; JOSEPH b. 1735; THOMAS b. 1738; GEORGE b. 1740; MOSES b.
1742; JOSHUA b. 1744; JOSHUA b. 1745/6; ELEAZER b. 1748; and BETTE b.
1750.

References: MD 4:141. TRURO VR pp. 21, 43-4. TREAT FAM p. 216.

76 LUCY[5] ROGERS (Thomas[4-3], Joseph[2], Thomas[1]) b. Truro
6 June 1708; d. there 1 June 1758 in 45th yr. (_sic_).
      She m. (1) Truro 15 Oct. 1734 NEHEMIAH SOMES, b.
Gloucester 22 Aug. 1704; d. after 1737; son of Timothy and
Elizabeth (Robinson) Somes. Nehemiah m. (1) 1730 Abigail
Collins, and had Abigail d.y.
      Lucy m. (2) Boston 6 Oct. 1749 ELISHA SMALL(E)Y, bp.
Truro 25 Nov. 1711; d. bef. 1774; son of Daniel Smally.
Elisha m. (1) ca. 1735 Bethia -----.

      Children (SOMES) b. Gloucester to Nehemiah and Lucy: LUCY[6] b.
1735; and NEHEMIAH b. 1737.

References: MD 9:55; 14:96. VR GLOUCESTER. BOSTON VR 28:261. TRURO
             VR p. 39. TREAT FAM p. 217. GLOUCESTER HIST pp. 160-1.
GLOUCESTER NOTES part I:73. SMALL DESC p. 192.

77 THOMAS[5] ROGERS (Thomas[4-3], Joseph[2], Thomas[1]) b.
Truro 11 Dec. 1712; d. Middletown CT 10 Oct. 1749.
      He m. Middletown CT 21 June 1744 ANN BARTLETT, b.
Guilford CT 9 Aug. 1723; d. after 1765; dau. of Daniel and
Ann (-----) Bartlett. Ann m. (2) Woodbury CT 1751 Timothy
Strong. The will of Daniel Bartlett of Guilford, dated 19
April 1765, names wife Lydia and dau. Ann Strong.
      On 15 Nov. 1749 Benjamin Harris of Middletown CT gave
bond as administrator of the estate of Thomas Rogers late
of Middletown, with Daniel Bartlett of Guilford as co-
signer. On 27 Aug. 1751 widow Ann Rogers was appointed
guardian to Anna Rogers, three-year old daughter of Thomas

Rogers deceased; and one week later, the widow was allowed
money for keeping one child about two years.

Children (ROGERS) b. Middletown CT: JOSEPH[6] b. 1746, prob. d.
y., and ANN b. 1747.

References: CSL Barbour Index: Guilford, Middletown, Woodbury. MAN-
            WARING 3:629-30. CT PR Hartford #4623(Thos. Rogers);
Guilford(Daniel Bartlett).

   78 THOMAS[5] ROGERS (Eleazer[4], Thomas[3], Joseph[2], Thomas[1])
b. Plymouth 8 Oct. 1701; d. after 1740.
       He m. Plymouth 31 Oct. 1721 PRISCILLA CHURCHILL, b.
Plymouth 27 Nov. 1701; d. after 1740; dau. of John and
Desire (Holmes) Churchill.
       There are no Plymouth County probate records for
Thomas or Priscilla.

       Children (ROGERS) b. Plymouth: RUTH[6] b. 1722; PRISCILLA or
KEZIA b. 1723, d. 1723/4; DESIRE b. 1725; WILLIS b. 1727, d. 1730;
SAMUEL b. 1728; THOMAS b. 1730; HANNAH b. 1734; ELEAZER b. 1735/6;
PRISCILLA b. 1738/9, d. 1747; and JOHN b. 1740.

References: MD 2:225; 13:174; 14:39. PLYMOUTH CH RECS pp. 232, 435.
            CHURCHILL FAM p. 10.

   79 HANNAH[5] ROGERS (Eleazer[4], Thomas[3], Joseph[2], Thomas[1])
b. Plymouth 26 Feb. 1703; d. certainly bef. 1736, and prob.
bef. Nov. 1732.
       She m. Plymouth 4 Nov. 1723 JOSEPH LEWIN. He ("of
Plymouth") may have m. (2) Eastham 1732 Rejoice Walker, a
descendant of Pilgrim Stephen Hopkins.
       Joseph Lewin of Plymouth mariner sold his homestead in
Plymouth on 29 Dec. 1730. He left no probate record at
Plymouth or Barnstable Counties. In 1736 John and Meriah,
the "grandchildren of Eleazer and Ammi [Ruhamah] Rogers,
by their daughter Lewin deceased," were baptized.

       Children (LEWIN): JOHN[6] b. 1727, and MERIAH b. 1730.

References: PLYMOUTH CH RECS p. 438. MD 12:123; 13:202; 14:40; 17:
            37. Plymouth Co. LR 26:39(Joseph Lewin).

   80 EXPERIENCE[5] ROGERS (Eleazer[4], Thomas[3], Joseph[2],
Thomas[1]) b. Plymouth 28 April 1707; d. after 2 April 1750.
       She m. Plymouth 17 April 1727 SAMUEL TOTMAN, b. Scitu-
ate 20 July 1693; d. Plymouth bef. April 1750; son of
Stephen Totman. Samuel m. (1) Plymouth 1714 Deborah Buck,
by whom he had son Simeon.

Samuel and Experience went to North Yarmouth ME [then in MA] about 1729. He was a bricklayer when he purchased land in North Yarmouth in 1729, and in 1738 he helped build the town school. In Nov. 1744 Samuel Totman from North Yarmouth was admitted to the Plymouth Church.

On 2 April 1750 Experience Totman received an allowance as widow of Samuel Totman late of Plymouth deceased.

Children (TOTMAN) first two and last two b. Plymouth, rest No. Yarmouth: JOSHUA[6] b. 1727, d. 1727; SAMUEL b. 1729; DEBORAH b. 1731/2; HANNAH b. 1734; JOSHUA b. 1737; EXPERIENCE b. 1740, d. 1740/1; and EXPERIENCE b. 1743/4.

References: MD 2:78; 12:87; 14:37, 72. VR SCITUATE. (PLYMOUTH) ANC
           LANDMARKS 2:138, 266. Plymouth Co. PR 11:329; 12:33-4
(Samuel Totman). OLD TIMES pp. 681, 740-1, 830, 1214. PLYMOUTH CH
RECS p. 525.

81 ABIJAH[5] ROGERS (Eleazer[4], Thomas[3], Joseph[2], Thomas[1])
b. Plymouth 4 Aug. 1714; d. after 1755.

She m. Plymouth 14 Sept. 1738 THOMAS WRIGHT of Plymouth, who d. after 1755.

There are no Plymouth County probate records for Abijah or Thomas.

Children (WRIGHT) b. Plymouth: ELIZABETH[6] b. 1738/9, d. 1739; ELIZABETH b. 1740; WILLIAM b. 1743; SARAH bp. 1748; HANNAH bp. 1752/3; and PRISCILLA bp. 1755.

References: MD 14:158; 15:163. (PLYMOUTH) ANC LANDMARKS 2:295[Abijah
           wrongly called Abigail]. PLYMOUTH CH RECS pp. 444, 448,
449.

82 SAMUEL[5] HIGGINS (Jonathan[4], Elizabeth[3] Rogers,
Joseph[2], Thomas[1]) b. Eastham 5 Oct. 1694; d. there 25 July
1776 in 83rd yr.

He m. Barnstable 9 Oct. 1718 MEHITABLE PHINNEY, b. Barnstable 14 Aug. 1696; d. 28 May 1778; dau. of Ebenezer and Susannah (Linnell) Phinney, and a descendant of Pilgrim Thomas Rogers (see #33i).

Samuel and Mehitable left no probate records.

Children (HIGGINS) b. Eastham: HANNAH[6] b. 1719; EBENEZER b. 1721; MARTHA b. 1723; SUSANNA b. 1725/6; JONATHAN b. 1728; SAMUEL b. 1730; ELIAKIM b. 1732/3; SILVANUS b. 1736; PRINCE b. 1741; and poss. LYDIA b. 1737.

References: MD 7:185-6; 14:227; 15:68, 142. HIGGINS DESC pp. 94-5.

83   HANNAH[5] HIGGINS   (Jonathan[4], Elizabeth[3] Rogers,
Joseph[2], Thomas[1])   b. bef. 1697; d. after 12 June 1764.
     She m. Eastham 29 Sept. 1715 EBENEZER BAKER, b. bef.
1690; d. prob. 1 May 1776 in Yarmouth; son of Daniel and
Elizabeth (Chase) Baker.
     The will of Ebenezer Baker of Yarmouth, drawn 12 June
1764, names wife Hannah, sons Reuben and Joseph, daus.
Lydia Crowel and Betty Crowell. Reuben was named executor
and gave his bond 24 May 1776.

     Children (BAKER) b. Yarmouth: JOSEPH[6] b. 1716; RUBIN b. 1718;
LYDIA b. 1721/2; and ELIZABETH b. 1724.

References: YARMOUTH VR p. 44, 280. MD 15:54-5. Barnstable Co. PR
             17:333(Ebenezer Baker). HIGGINS DESC p. 69. Baker Fam
p. 19.

84   JONATHAN[5] HIGGINS   (Jonathan[4], Elizabeth[3] Rogers,
Joseph[2], Thomas[1])   b. Eastham ca. 1697; d. there 30 Jan.
1792 in 95th yr.
     He m. Harwich 5 April 1722 REBECCA HOPKINS, b. ca.
1698; d. 19 March 1780 ae 83; dau. of Stephen and Sarah
(Howes) Hopkins, and a descendant of Pilgrim Stephen Hopkins. The will of Stephen Hopkins of Harwich yeoman,
dated 9 Jan. 1732/3, names wife Sarah and daus. including
Rebecca Higgins.
     The will of Jonathan Higgins of Eastham "advanced in
years," dated 23 May 1791 and presented 12 June 1792, names
two granddaughters Rebecca Taylor and Abigail Young; two
great-granddaughters Rebecca Sears and Kate Sears; and
grandsons Edward and Benjamin Taylor, the latter to be
executor.

     Child (HIGGINS) b. Eastham: PHEBE[6] b. 1722/3.

References: MD 8:159; 16:70. HIGGINS DESC pp. 95-6. Barnstable Co.
             PR 27:324(Jonathan Higgins); 5:112(Stephen Hopkins).
NEHGR 102:51-2.

85   EXPERIENCE[5] HIGGINS   (Jonathan[4], Elizabeth[3] Rogers,
Joseph[2], Thomas[1])   b. ca. 1699; d. Yarmouth 21 July 1777.
     She m. Eastham 3 March 1719/20 JOHN CROWELL, b. Yar-
mouth 29 Oct. 1695; d. there in Nov. 1776; son of John and
Sarah (-----) Crowell.
     John and Experience left no probate records.

     Children (CROWELL) b. Yarmouth: JOHN[6] b. 1720/1; RUTH b. 1722;
JASHAR b. 1724; ABNER b. 1726; SHUBALL b. 1728; THOMAS b. 1731;
JEDEDIAH b. 1733/4; and JENNE b. 1736.

References: MD 11:113; 15:144. HIGGINS DESC p. 69. YARMOUTH VR pp.
            30, 57-8, 280, 281.

86 JOSEPH[5] HIGGINS (Joseph[4], Elizabeth[3] Rogers, Joseph[2],
Thomas[1]) b. Eastham 1 Oct. 1690; d. Lyme CT 21 Dec. 1783
aged 94 years.
      He m. Eastham 18 Feb. 1718/9 MERCY REMICK, b. Eastham
29 July 1698; d. Lyme CT 22 Nov. 1768 ae 71; dau. of Abraham and Elizabeth (Freeman) Remick.
      Capt. Joseph Higgins moved to Saybrook CT ca. 1736,
and bought land in Lyme CT in 1740. He settled his property on his sons by deed: 28 Nov. 1757 to son Christian
and son Josiah Burnham, husband of dau. Thankful; and 6
June 1769 to sons Sylvanus and Joseph Jr. The will of Jos--
eph Jr. 1811 mentions four siblings and their children.

      Children (HIGGINS) first three b. Eastham: JOSEPH[6] b. 1721;
REBECCA b. 1724; CHRISTIAN (male) b. 1726; MERCY b. ca. 1728; THANKFUL;
SYLVANUS b. ca. 1737; JEMIMA b. ca. 1737; and JOSEPH b. ca. 1740.

References: HIGGINS DESC pp. 96-9. MD 7:238; 8:89; 15:75; 17:88-9.
             LYME CT VR p. 5. CT PR New London Dist #2606(Joseph
Higgins).

87 BERIAH[5] HIGGINS (Joseph[4], Elizabeth[3] Rogers, Joseph[2],
Thomas[1]) b. Eastham ca. 1692; d. after 1736.
      He m. ca. 1716 DESIRE COOK, b. Eastham 14 June 1694;
d. after 17 May 1736; dau. of Josiah and Mary (Godfrey)
Cooke, and a descendant of Pilgrim Stephen Hopkins.
      No Barnstable County probate records were found for
Beriah and Desire. It is barely possible they moved to
Middletown or Saybrook or Lyme CT.

      Children (HIGGINS) first three b. Truro, rest Provincetown:
THANKFUL[6] b. 1717; JEMIMA b. 1719; DESIRE b. 1724; DEBORAH b. 1725;
BERIAH b. 1727; and PHOEBE b. 1736.

References: HIGGINS DESC p. 99. HIGGINS SUP p. 13(no evidence found
             for sons Jethro, Josiah or Joseph). DAWES-GATES 2:505.
NEHGR 8:219. MD 7:238; 9:101-2; 11:47. TRURO VR p. 14.

88 RUTH[5] HIGGINS (Joseph[4], Elizabeth[3] Rogers, Joseph[2],
Thomas[1]) b. Eastham 11 Sept. 1700; d. prob. Nova Scotia
after 13 March 1762 (deed).
      She m. (1) Eastham 11 Oct. 1716 EBENEZER STEWART "of
Chatham", d. after 1728 (witnessed will); son of Hugh and
Waitstill (Denne) Stewart of Yarmouth.
      Ebenezer left no probate record, and apparently he and
Ruth had no children.

She m. (2) bef. 1733 JAMES ELDRIDGE, d. Chatham 19
July 1757. He poss. m. earlier ----- -----, mother of his
children Seth and Mary.
The will of James Eldridge of Chatham, made 16 May
1757 and presented 26 July 1757, names wife Ruth; sons
Abner and James, both under 21; son Seth living in Rhode
Island; son Zephaniah; daughters Mary Eldredge, Rebecca
Collings and Ruth Bearse; wife Ruth and brother-in-law
Solomon Collings of Chatham, executors.
Widow Ruth accompanied sons Abner and Zephaniah to
Liverpool NS in the 1760's.

Children (ELDRIDGE) b. Chatham to James and Ruth: ZEPHANIAH[6] b.
1733; REBECCA b. 1735; RUTH b. 1737; ABNER b. 1738; JAMES b. 1742; and
poss. SETH and MARY (if not b. to an earlier wife).

References: MD 15:55; 17:88-9. NGSQ 62:102. HIGGINS DESC pp. 71,
           598. YARMOUTH VR 1:125. Barnstable Co. PR 9:292(James
Eldridge).

89 THANKFUL[5] PAINE (Hannah[4] Higgins, Elizabeth[3] Rogers,
Joseph[2], Thomas[1])   b. Eastham 14 March 1699/1700; d. bef.
15 Sept. 1722.
She m. Eastham 20 Oct. 1720 JONATHAN SMITH, prob. the
one b. Eastham 5 July 1693 to Thomas and Mary (-----)
Smith. Jonathan m. (2) int. Eastham 1722 Priscilla Hig-
gins; no children recorded to them in Eastham.
There are no Barnstable County probate records for
Jonathan, though land of Jonathan Smith in Eastham is men-
tioned in deeds of 1750 and 1778. Did he possibly move to
Connecticut?

Child (SMITH) prob. b. Eastham: THANKFUL[6].

References: (Preliminary data supplied by the Hopkins family worker).
           MD 4:142; 15:229; 16:175; 17:206; 28:112.

90 PRISCILLA[5] PAINE (Hannah[4] Higgins, Elizabeth[3] Rogers,
Joseph[2], Thomas[1])   b. Eastham 16 Oct. 1701; d. Middletown
CT 16 Sept. 1752.
She m. Eastham 4 Aug. 1726 WILLIAM NORCUT, b. Marshfield 6 May 1690; d. Middletown 15 Sept. 1752; son of William and Experience (-----) Norcut. He m. (1) Eastham
1718/19 Ruth Mayo, by whom he had son William b. 1719.
On 1 Nov. 1752 an inventory was made of the estate of
William Norket late of Middletown deceased, who departed
this life 25 (sic) Sept. 1752, and of the wearing apparel
of Priscilla, widow of William, who died 26 (sic) Sept.
1752. On 4 Nov. 1754 William Norket of Middletown was appointed guardian to Sylvanus, Nicolas, Abner and Priscilla,

minor children of William Norket deceased. On 28 Jan. 1755
distribution was made to eldest son William, "the two
daughters," second son Abner, third son Nicholas and son
Silvanus.

Children (NORCUT) first six b. Eastham, last two Middletown CT:
RUTH[6] b. 1728; JOSIAH b. 1730/1; HANNAH b. 1733; EXPERIENCE b. 1735;
ABNER b. 1738; PRISCILLA b. 1739/40; NICHOLAS b. 1741; and SILVANUS b.
1743.

References: MARSHFIELD VR p. 21. MD 10:75; 15:75-6; 16:145. Middletown CT PR 1:7, 18, 28, 320(Wm. Norket). CSL Barbour
Index:Middletown. NEHGR 22:188.

91 LOIS[5] PAINE (Hannah[4] Higgins, Elizabeth[3] Rogers,
Joseph[2], Thomas[1]) b. Eastham 29 Sept. 1705; d. bef. 25
Sept. 1729.
She m. Eastham 22 April 1725 EDMUND FREEMAN, b. ca.
1702; d. 22 July 1782 ae 80; bur. Orleans; son of Edmund
and Sarah (Mayo) Freeman, and a descendant of Pilgrim William Brewster. He m. (2) Eastham 1729 Sarah Sparrow, by
whom he had Jonathan, Edmond, and prob. Abner and John.
The will of Edmund Freeman of Eastham, dated 9 Feb.
1778 and presented 13 Aug. 1782, mentions wife Sarah;
daughter-in-law Thankful Freeman widow of son Jonathan;
daughter Lois Snow; grandsons Edmund Snow and Abner Freeman; sons Abner and John Freeman; grandson Philip Young;
and minor granddaughters Rebeckah, Sarah, Hannah and Lois
Freeman.

Child (FREEMAN) b. Eastham to Edmund and Lois: LOIS[6] b. 1726.

References: (Preliminary data supplied by Hopkins family worker).
FREEMAN GEN pp. 64-5. MD 8:65-71; 16:74. Barnstable Co.
PR 14:136, 140(Edmund Freeman).

92 ABIGAIL[5] PAINE (Hannah[4] Higgins, Elizabeth[3] Rogers,
Joseph[2], Thomas[1]) b. Eastham 3 Aug. 1707; living 1742.
She m. Eastham 12 Oct. 1727 THOMAS HIGGINS Jr., b.
Eastham 24 June 1704; d. Wellfleet ca. 1789; son of Benja-
min and Sarah (Freeman) Higgins.
There are no Barnstable County probate records for
Thomas and Abigail.

Children (HIGGINS) b. Eastham: PHILIP[6] b. 1727/8; THOMAS b.
1729/30; BENJAMIN b. 1731/2; JONATHAN b. 1734; JESSE b. 1736; THANKFUL
b. 1738; SARAH b. 1740; and SOLOMON b. 1742.

References: (Preliminary data supplied by the Hopkins family worker).
MD 7:15; 16:196, 197. HIGGINS DESC pp. 87, 123-4.

93 LYDIA[5] PAINE (Hannah[4] Higgins, Elizabeth[3] Rogers,
Joseph[2], Thomas[1])   b. Eastham bet. 1707 and 1714; living
1731. Did she d. Boston bef. Sept. 1793 ae 87?
     She m. Eastham 5 March 1729/30 DANIEL YOUNG, b. East-
ham 4 April 1704; d. Portland CT in 1752; son of Benjamin
and Sarah (Snow) Young.

     Children (YOUNG) b. Eastham: MOSES[6] b. 1730; HANNAH b. 1731;
and poss. DANIEL; ELIZABETH; MARY; and LYDIA.

References: (Preliminary data supplied by the Hopkins family worker).
             MD 8:246; 16:204. YOUNG (JOHN) DESC. MA MAG p. 315.

94 ELISHA[5] HIGGINS (Elisha[4], Elizabeth[3] Rogers, Joseph[2],
Thomas[1]) b. Eastham 3 Jan. 1701/2; d. Bennington VT 22
Jan. 1777 in 77th yr.
     He m. (1) Eastham 19 Oct. 1721 SARAH LEWIS, b. East-
ham 2 June 1702; d. there after 15 Oct. 1733; dau. of
Thomas and Joan (-----) Lewis.
     He m. (2) Eastham 24 Jan. 1733/4 HANNAH (DOANE) AT-
WOOD, b. Eastham 5 March 1703/4; d. Bennington VT 22 Sept.
1776 in 74th yr.; dau. of David and Dorothy (Horton) Doane
of Eastham, and widow of Samuel Atwood of Eastham. The
will of David Doane of Eastham, yeoman, dated 25 Jan.
1738, names daus. Hannah Higgins and Rachel Higgins.
     Elisha moved with his family from Eastham to Hardwick
about 1742, perhaps lived in Palmer from 1764 to 1769,
then moved to Vermont or New York, ultimately residing in
Bennington VT. He gave patriotic service during the Revolution.

     Children (HIGGINS) first four by Sarah, rest by Hannah, all
except Uriah b. Eastham: JANE[6] b. 1722/3; SARAH b. 1725; ELISHA b.
1727; EDWARD b. 1733; JOSEPH b. 1734/5; ABIGAIL b. 1737; ABIAL b.
1740; and URIAH b. Hardwick 1742.

References: MD 4:141; 7:17; 16:27; 17:82. VR HARDWICK. NYGBR 44:
             285-6. DAR PATRIOT INDEX p. 327. HIGGINS DESC pp. 99-
101. Barnstable Co. PR 8:228(David Doane).

95 MARTHA[5] HIGGINS (Elisha[4], Elizabeth[3] Rogers, Joseph[2],
Thomas[1]) b. Eastham 5 Jan. 1703/4; d. after 5 Dec. 1775.
     She m. Eastham 8 Aug. 1723 JONATHAN DOANE, b. Eastham
7 July 1702; d. there 24 Jan. 1780 in 78th yr.; son of David
and Dorothy (Horton) Doane.
     The will of Jonathan Doane of Eastham, made 5 Dec.
1775 and proved 8 Feb. 1780, names sons Elisha, James,
Jesse (who was to receive dower land which Jonathan's
mother received from his father), Nathan, Silvanus and Seth

Doane; daus. Dorothy Doane and Elizabeth Snow wife of
Jabez; and wife Martha.

Children (DOANE) b. Eastham: ELISHA[6] b. 1724; HANNAH b. 1726;
JAMES b. 1728; DOROTHY b. 1731; ELIZABETH b. 1733; JESSE b. 1735; SETH
b. 1737; SILVANUS b. 1740; and NATHAN b. 1742/3.

References: MD 7:17; 8:110; 16:32. HIGGINS DESC p. 73. Barnstable
          Co. PR 11:78, 84(Jonathan Doane).

96 BERIAH[5] (or Briah) HIGGINS (Elisha[4], Elizabeth[3]
Rogers, Joseph[2], Thomas[1]) b. Eastham 15 Jan. 1705/6; d.
after 1774.
     He m. (1) Eastham 1 June 1730 JEMIMA WITHERELL, d.
Eastham 7 Sept. 1754; poss. dau. of John and Mercy (-----)
Witherell.
     He prob. m. (2) int. Eastham 15 Oct. 1755 ABIGAIL
HIGGINS, b. Harwich 27 Nov. 1738; d. 5 Nov. 1759; dau. of
Paul and Rebecca (-----) Higgins. They had Ephraim and
Briah.
     Beriah left no probate records.

     Children (HIGGINS) b. Eastham to Beriah and Jemima: BRIAH[6] b.
1731; MERCY b. 1733; JEMIMA b. 1735, d. 1736; JOSEPH b. 1737; JEMIMA
b. 1738; ANNA b. 1740; JOHN b. 1742; LOT b. 1745, d. 1746; LOT b.
1746/7, d. 1765; JANE b. 1748; and RACHEL b. 1750.

     Prob. Children (HIGGINS) b. Eastham to Briah and Abigail:
EPHERIM[6] b. 1757, d. 1759; and BRIAH b. 1759.

References: MD 8:106; 16:200; 28:172. HIGGINS DESC p. 101. WITHER-
          ELL FAM pp. 121-2.

97 ALICE[5] HIGGINS (Elisha[4], Elizabeth[3] Rogers, Joseph[2],
Thomas[1]) b. Eastham 22 Nov. 1707; d. after March 1786.
     She m. Eastham 3 Aug. 1727 SOLOMON DOANE, b. Eastham
8 Nov. 1705; d. there Dec. 1789; son of Samuel and Martha
(Hamblen) Doane.
     The will of Solomon Doane, made 5 March 1786 and pro-
bated 15 Dec. 1788, names sons Solomon and Noah; father
Samuel; son Joshua; daughter Dorcas Doane, apparently not
well; son Joseph; daughter Betty Cole; unnamed granddaughter who was the wife of Josiah Linkonner [Lincoln?]; and
minors, all Doanes: Samuel Dill, Elijah, Nehemiah, Mehitable, Alice and Lydia. Guardianships 30 March 1790 show
that the six minor Doanes were children of Lydia Doane, and
grandchildren of Solomon Doane, late deceased.

Children (DOANE) b. Eastham: SOLOMON[6] b. 1730; NOAH b. 1732;
SARAH b. 1733; DORCAS b. 1735; NEHEMIAH b. 1737; JOSEPH b. 1739; ISAAC
b. 1741; BETTY b. 1742; and JOSHUA b. 1744/5.

References: MD 8:17; 16:196. HIGGINS DESC p. 73. Barnstable Co. PR
             5:403; 22:172; 24:44(Solomon Doane).

98 APPHIA[5] HIGGINS (Elisha[4], Elizabeth[3] Rogers,
Joseph[2], Thomas[1]) b. Eastham 22 Nov. 1709; living 24
April 1784.
     She m. Eastham 1 Oct. 1730 SIMEON DOANE, b. Eastham 1
Dec. 1708; d. there 4 Dec. 1789 [prob. 1787 intended] in
80th yr., son of Samuel and Martha (Hamblin) Doane.
     The will of Simeon Doane of Chatham, made 24 April
1784 and probated 25 Dec. 1787, names wife Apphia; sons
Benjamin, John, Isaiah and Ephraim Doane; daus. Ruth Smith,
Abigail Eldredge and Phebe Smith.

     Children (DOANE) b. Eastham: BENJAMIN[6]; EPHRAIM; JOHN b. 1730;
ISAIAH; RUTH b. 1733/4; ABIGAIL b. 1735; PHEBE; and poss. EBENEZER.

References: MD 8:17, 110; 17:32, 145-6. ME HGR 4:288. HIGGINS DESC
             p. 73. Barnstable Co. PR 24:17; 26:386(Simeon Doane).

99 JONATHAN[5] HIGGINS (Elisha[4], Elizabeth[3] Rogers,
Joseph[2], Thomas[1]) b. Eastham 8 Oct. 1711; settled in Hardwick.
     He m. Eastham int. 28 June 1735 RACHEL DOANE, dau. of
David and Dorothy (Horton) Doane. The will of David Doane
of Eastham, dated 25 Jan. 1738, names wife Sarah and daus.
Hannah Higgins and Rachel Higgins.
     Jonathan may later have gone to Nova Scotia. Is he
or his son the Jonathan Higgins in Onslow NS in 1770?

     Children (HIGGINS) b. or bp. Hardwick: JONATHAN[6] b. 1736;
LURANIA b. 1738; HENRY b. 1740, d.y.; HENRY b. 1743; BETHIAH b. 1746;
JOSHUA bp. 1748; RACHEL bp. 1751; and PHILIP bp. 1754.

References: MD 28:178. VR HARDWICK. HIGGINS DESC pp. 73, 102. YAR-
             MOUTH NS HERALD, Tues. 22 Sept. 1931, "New Englanders in
Nova Scotia," #181. Barnstable Co. PR 8:228(David Doane). 1770
CENSUS NS p. 20.

100 ELIZABETH[5] HIGGINS (Elisha[4], Elizabeth[3] Rogers,
Joseph[2], Thomas[1]) b. Eastham 1713; d. after 1745.
     She m. Eastham 16 Jan. 1735/6 JAMES MAYO, b. Eastham
12 Aug. 1716; said to have d. Quebec; son of Joseph and
Apphia (Atwood) Mayo.

Children (MAYO) b. Eastham: JOSHUA[6] b. 1735 (*sic*), and JAMES b. 1745.

References: HIGGINS DESC p. 73. MAYO (JOHN) GEN pp. 49-50. MD 15:56; 17:142.

101 BARNABAS[5] HIGGINS (Elisha[4], Elizabeth[3] Rogers, Joseph[2], Thomas[1]) b. Eastham 1722; d. Wellfleet 18 Aug. 1799.
He m. (1) Truro 3 March 1742/3 MARY SMITH, b. Truro 14 July 1723; d. bef. 1749; dau. of Thomas and Joanna (Mayo) Smith.
He m. (2) Truro 2 March 1748/9 ABIGAIL PAINE, b. Truro 12 March 1720/1; dau. of Moses and Margery (Mayo) Paine, and a descendant of Pilgrim Stephen Hopkins. The will of Moses Paine of Truro, dated 1764, names dau. Abigail Higgins.
He m. (3) int. Wellfleet 7 May 1791 HANNAH LEWIS.

Children (HIGGINS) b. Truro, first three by Mary, rest by Abigail: JANE[6] b. and d. 1744; BARNABAS b. 1745; ELISHA b. 1747/8; DANIEL b. 1751; a son b. and d. 1755; a son b. and d. 1756; PHILIP b. 1758; and MARY b. 1760.

References: HIGGINS DESC pp. 74, 102. TRURO VR pp. 22, 45, 57, 59, 61.

102 PHILIP[5] HIGGINS (Elisha[4], Elizabeth[3] Rogers, Joseph[2], Thomas[1]) b. Eastham 4 March 1724/5.
He m. Truro 26 March 1747 PHOEBE LEWIS, b. Truro 10 July 1728; dau. of Nathaniel and Anna (Gains) Lewis.
Philip is said to have moved to Hardwick, but no evidence is found there. He is further said to have had a son David born in Nova Scotia in 1778, but this would appear more likely to be a son of Philip[6] (son of Jonathan[5] #99). No children were found for Philip and Phebe.

References: TRURO VR pp. 52, 53. HIGGINS DESC pp. 74, 103. YARMOUTH NS HERALD, Tues. 22 Sept. 1931, "New Englanders in Nova Scotia," #181 [claim Philip had son David].

103 EBENEZER[5] ROGERS (John[4-3], Joseph[2], Thomas[1]) b. Harwich 17 Feb. 1697/8; d. Lyme CT bet. 28 July 1767 and 25 June 1769.
He m. Eastham 24 March 1719/20 HANNAH COOK, b. Eastham 25 Jan. 1699/1700; d. after 28 July 1767; dau. of Richard and Hannah (Smith?) Cook.

The will of Ebenezer Rogers of Lyme CT aged about 70 years, dated 28 July 1767 and presented 25 June 1769, mentions wife Hannah; children of son Zacheus deceased; children of son Joshua deceased; children of daughter Thankful Androus deceased; children of son Richard deceased; sons Ebenezer, Samuel, Caleb and Benjamin; son Lemuel of Lyme to have land in Lyme and in Harwich MA; daughter Patience Rogers of Lyme; son Lemuel executor.

Children (ROGERS) b. Harwich: ZACHEUS[6] b. 1720; JOSHUA b. 1722; EBENEZER b. 1724; THANKFUL b. 1726; RICHARD b. 1728; SAMUEL b. 1730; CALEB b. 1732; LEMUEL b. 1734; BENJAMIN b. 1736; HANNAH b. 1739; and PATIENCE b. 1741.

References: MD 6:55; 9:13; 15:144.   CT PR Lyme(Ebenezer Rogers).

104   JOHN[5] ROGERS   (John[4-3], Joseph[2], Thomas[1])   b. Harwich 1 Aug. 1701; living Harwich 29 Aug. 1739 (acknowledged his signature).
      He m. int. Harwich 16 Nov. 1734 MARY WING, b. Harwich 13 May 1704; dau. of Ananias and Hannah (-----) Wing.
      No land or probate record was found in Barnstable Co., nor in Putnam Co. NY to indicate he moved there, though it seems likely he left Harwich.

Child (ROGERS) b. Harwich: SARAH[6] b. 1736/7.

References: MD 6:54; 19:57; 23:60. WING REG pp. 64-5, 77.

105   JONATHAN[5] ROGERS   (John[4-3], Joseph[2], Thomas[1])   b. Harwich 20 March 1703; d. Yarmouth 13 Feb. 1781.
      He m. Eastham 18 Jan. 1727/8 ELIZABETH COOKE, b. Eastham 30 Nov. 1704; d. Yarmouth 25 J---- 1778; dau. of Richard and Hannah (Smith?) Cooke.
      Jonathan was of Yarmouth 12 Feb. 1739/40 when he signed a deed. Acting on a claim that Jonathan went to Putnam County NY, land and probate records there were searched, but no evidence was turned up to indicate that he lived there.

Children (ROGERS) b. Yarmouth: CALEB[6] b. 1728, d. 1731; PRECILAH b. 1730; ABIGAIL b. 1732; and CALEB b. 1734/5.

References: MD 9:13; 14:213; 15:69. YARMOUTH VR pp. 72, 281-2.

106   BENJAMIN[5] ROGERS   (John[4-3], Joseph[2], Thomas[1])   b. Harwich 19 Nov. 1704; d. Kingston 19 Oct. 1747.
      He m. Plymouth 13 Oct. 1732 PHEBE HARDING, b. Eastham in April 1710; d. after Oct. 1747; dau. of Amaziah and

Hannah (Rogers) Harding, and a descendant of Pilgrim Thomas Rogers (see #15).

Inventory of the estate of Benjamin Rogers late of Kingston deceased was taken 23 Feb. 1747[1747/8]. An undated petition of Phebe Rogers of Kingston widow states that her husband Benjamin died leaving her six small children.

Children (ROGERS) first two b. Plymouth, rest Kingston: JOHN[6] b. 1733/4, d. 1747; HANNAH b. 1735; BENJAMIN b. 1738; CORNELIUS b. 1739; THOMAS b. 1741; JAMES b. 1744; and PHEBE b. 1746/7.

References: MD 3:180; 14:74; 15:42. VR KINGSTON. Plymouth Co. PR 11:159, 292(Benj. Rogers). NEHGR 6:46.

107 SARAH[5] ROGERS (John[4-3], Joseph[2], Thomas[1]) b. Harwich 21 July 1706; d. Barnstable 10 April 1736.

She m. int. Barnstable 29 March 1733 SAMUEL BUMPAS, bp. Barnstable 16 Oct. 1715; d. after 9 March 1739; son of Samuel and Patience (-----) Bumpas. He m. (2) Norwich CT 1738 Martha Broughton, by whom he had dau. Lydia.

Sometime between 1736 and 1738 Samuel moved to Norwich CT, but no death record is found there. On 26 Sept. 1758 Samuel Tracey of Norwich, attorney to Levi Bumpus of Norwich who was grandson to John Rogers late of Harwich, gave his receipt to Joseph Rogers (#108) of Yarmouth, guardian of said Levi, for what was due Levi as his inheritance.

Children (BUMPAS) b. Barnstable: PRISCILLA[6] bp. 1733, and LEVI b. 1734/5.

References: MD 33:123; 34:19. TAG 43:152. BARNSTABLE FAMS 1:87. Barnstable Co. PR 9:355(gdn. of Levi Bumpus). NORWICH CT VR pp. 183, 409.

108 JOSEPH[5] ROGERS (John[4-3], Joseph[2], Thomas[1]) b. Harwich 20 Sept. 1708; d. after 26 Sept. 1758, when he paid his nephew Levi Bumpus (see #107) his portion of John[4] Rogers' estate.

He m. Barnstable 19 Oct. 1738 FEAR BASSETT, b. Yarmouth 11 April 1716; d. after 15 March 1756; dau. of William and Martha (Godfrey) Bassett.

Children (ROGERS) first two recorded Harwich, rest Yarmouth: dau. b. 1739/40; DORCAS[6] b. 1741; SETH b. 1743; MELLETIAH b. 1747; JOSEPH b. 1750; SUSANAH b. 1753; and WILLIAM b. 1756.

References: MD 23:60; 33:169. YARMOUTH VR pp. 42, 225.

109 PRISCILLA[5] ROGERS (John[4-3], Joseph[2], Thomas[1]) b.
prob. Harwich ca. 1710; living there 28 Aug. 1739.
    She m. int. Harwich 28 April 1729 REUBEN NICKERSON,
poss. the one who d. Harwich 10 Dec. 1791, son of John and
Sarah (Williams) Nickerson. He may have m. (2) Eastham
1744 Ruth Arey, provided Priscilla d. bef. 1744.
    On 28 Aug. 1739 Priscilla Nickerson, wife of Reuben of
Harwich, signed an agreement relative to the estate of her
father John Rogers deceased. It is possible that her husband Reuben d. bef. 1745, in which case she may have m.
Harwich 1745 GERSHOM WHELDON of Yarmouth. Obviously both
Reuben and Priscilla did not have a second spouse; however,
further research is needed to arrive at a definite deci-
sion.

    Children (NICKERSON) b. Harwich to Reuben and Priscilla: RUTH[6]
b. 1729; ELIPHALET b. 1731; and PRISCILLA b. 1735.

    Poss. child (WHELDEN) b. Yarmouth to Gershom and Priscilla Whel-
den: LUCY b. 1749.

References: MD 7:228; 11:248; 18:47; 20:157; 23:57; 25:100. NICKER-
             SONS OF CAPE COD p. 54. YARMOUTH VR pp. 97, 183.

110 JUDAH[5] ROGERS (Judah[4], John[3], Joseph[2], Thomas[1]) b.
Harwich 29 Dec. 1704; d. Eastham 10 May 1773.
    He m. (1) Eastham 12 Dec. 1728 PATIENCE COLE, b. East-
ham 8 Dec. 1706; d. bef. June 1741; dau. of Joseph and
Elizabeth (Cobb) Cole, and a descendant of Pilgrim Stephen
Hopkins. The will of Joseph Cole of Eastham, dated 25 Feb.
1764, mentions heirs of my dau. Patience Rogers. No children found of Judah and Patience.
    Judah m. (2) Eastham 14 June 1741 SUSANNA ROGERS, b.
Eastham 19 Jan. 1703/4; living 6 Oct. 1742 when she gave
birth to dau. Susanna, but d. bef. Nov. 1743; dau. of James
and Susanna (Tracy) Rogers, and a descendant of Pilgrim
Thomas Rogers (see #40 iii).
    He m. (3) Eastham 24 Nov. 1743 LOIS YOUNG, b. Eastham
2 Nov. 1704; d. bef. Aug. 1751; dau. of David and Ann
(Doane) Young. The will of David Young of Eastham yeoman,
dated 10 April 1739, names wife Ann and dau. Louis (*sic*)
Young.
    Judah m. (4) Eastham 29 Aug. 1751 ELIZABETH (MAYO)
NICKERSON, b. Eastham 29 Sept. 1712; d. Orleans 28 May
1794; dau. of Nathaniel and Ruth (Doane) Mayo. She m. (1)
Chatham 1731 David Nickerson. The will of Nathaniel Mayo
of Eastham, dated 16 Sept. 1760, names wife Mehitable and
dau. Elizabeth, wife of Judah Rogers (see #27).
    The will of Judah Rogers of Eastham laborer, dated 4
May 1773 and presented 13 July 1773, names wife Elizabeth;
daughter Susanna Rogers to have the things that belonged to

my former wife Susanna Rogers; daughters Lois Twining and
Patience Higgins; son Judah; executors to be wife Elizabeth and son Judah.

Children (ROGERS) first by Susanna, second and third by Lois,
last by Elizabeth, all prob. b. Eastham: SUSANNA[6] b. 1742; LOIS b.
ca. 1744; PATIENCE b. ca. 1747; and JUDAH b. 1753.

References: NEHGR 6:235; 21:215. HIGGINS DESC pp. 192, 196-7.
        Barnstable Co. PR 8:93(David Young); 12:196(Nathaniel
Mayo); 13:195(Joseph Cole); 17:102(Judah Rogers). MD 4:140; 7:19,
139, 237; 9:11; 16:1, 68, 147; 17:34; 19:186; 20:156.

111 MARY[5] ROGERS (Judah[4], John[3], Joseph[2], Thomas[1]) b.
Harwich 1 Oct. 1706; living 1746.
        She m. Harwich 29 Jan. 1729/30 GERSHOM COLE, b. East-
ham 1 March 1702/3; d. poss. Eastham 1782; son of Joseph
and Elizabeth (Cobb) Cole, and a descendant of Pilgrim
Stephen Hopkins.

Children (COLE) b. Eastham: RELIANCE[6] b. 1730; PATIENCE b.
1732/3; HANNAH b. 1735; RELIANCE b. 1737; PATIENCE b. 1739; MOSES b.
1741; KEZIA b. 1743; and AZUBA b. 1746.

References: MD 7:19, 187; 11:175; 17:31.

112 PATIENCE[5] ROGERS (Judah[4], John[3], Joseph[2], Thomas[1])
b. Harwich 9 Nov. 1710; living 18 Jan. 1745/6, when she
and Isaac signed a deed.
        She m. Harwich 25 May 1732 ISAAC MAYO, b. Eastham 16
June 1708; d. there bef. 19 Jan. 1757; son of Theophilus
and Rebecca (Smith) Mayo. The will of Theophilus Mayo of
Eastham, made 15 June 1758, names grandsons Joshua and
Paul, sons of my deceased son Isaac.
        An administrator was appointed 19 Jan. 1757 on the
estate of Isaac Mayo, late of Eastham deceased cordwainer.
On 1 Feb. 1757 guardians were appointed for Isaac's minor
children: Martha Morse and Patience, Rebecca, Eunice,
Paul and Joshua Mayo. On 11 March 1757 the real estate
was divided among those same children.

Children (MAYO) b. Eastham: ISAAC[6] b. and d. 1732/3; ISAAC b.
1734; JOSHUA; PAUL; MARTHA MORSE; PATIENCE; REBECCA; and EUNICE.

References: MD 7:12-3; 13:70; 17:14, 141. Barnstable Co. PR 7:446,
        449-453; 9:328-9(Isaac Mayo); 13:10(Theophilus Mayo).

113   CRISP[5] ROGERS   (Joseph[4], John[3], Joseph[2], Thomas[1])   b.
Eastham 17 Feb. 1704/5; living 4 Oct. 1757 (father's es-
tate).
       He m. Harwich 22 Feb. 1727/8 MARY YATES (or Yeats), b.
ca. 1700; living 7 Oct. 1730 (son Joseph born); dau. of
John and Abigail (Rogers) Yates, and a descendant of Thomas
Rogers (see #42).
       This was probably the Crisp Rogers who, with wife
Mercy (*sic*) and Crisp Rogers Jr. and his wife Deborah, all
of Harwich, sold land there on 25 Dec. 1767. Was he the
Crisp Rogers of Harwich yeoman whose will, dated 13 Feb.
1770 and presented 1 May 1770, names son Crisp, daus.
Mercy Rogers and Mary Mayo, and granddaughter Apphia
Rogers?

       Children (ROGERS) b. Eastham: JOSEPH[6] b. 1730; prob. CRISP; and
poss. MERCY, and MARY.

References: MD 8:218; 15:167; 17:30; 24:64. HIGGINS DESC p. 193.
             Barnstable Co. PR 13:530(Crisp Rogers).

114   ELKANAH[5] ROGERS   (Joseph[4], John[3], Joseph[2], Thomas[1])
b. Eastham 13 Feb. 1706/7; d. there 10 Sept. 1759.
       He m. (1) Harwich 18 Feb. 1730/1 RELIANCE YATES, b.
ca. 1702; d. bef. 1748; dau. of John and Abigail (Rogers)
Yates, and a descendant of Pilgrim Thomas Rogers (see #42).
       He m. (2) int. Eastham and Harwich 25 June 1748 MERCY
(GODFREY) BURGESS, b. ca. 1714; living 7 March 1765; dau.
of Jonathan and Mercy (Mayo) Godfrey, and a descendant of
Pilgrim William Brewster. She m. (1) int. Yarmouth 1734/5
Ebenezer Burgess. The will of Jonathan Godfrey of Chatham
yeoman, dated 7 March 1765, names wife Mercy and daughter
Mercy Rogers.
       On 4 March 1760 Mercy Rogers was appointed administra-
tor on the estate of her deceased husband Elkanah Rogers of
Eastham.

       Children (ROGERS) b. Eastham, first three by Reliance, rest by
Mercy: ELKANAH[6] b. 1734, d. 1758; NATHANIEL b. 1738/9; JOSIAH b.
1741; JOSHUA b. 1755; MARTHA b. 1757; and ELKANAH b. posthumously 1
Jan. 1760.

References: NEHGR 126:239. MD 11:175; 17:147; 28:82; 33:72. Barn-
             stable Co. PR 10:51(Elkanah Rogers); 13:114(Jonathan God-
frey).

115   MARTHA[5] ROGERS   (Joseph[4], John[3], Joseph[2], Thomas[1])   b.
Eastham 26 Feb. 1708/9; d. bef. 8 Nov. 1781.

She m. Eastham 10 Dec. 1730 DANIEL COLE, b. Eastham 8 July 1709; d. there bef. 8 Nov. 1781; son of Daniel and Sarah (Hubbard) Cole.

On 8 Nov. 1781 Daniel Cole yeoman of Eastham was appointed administrator on the intestate estates of Daniel Cole yeoman of Eastham deceased, and of Martha Cole of Eastham deceased. Division of the estates of Daniel and Martha was made 5 July 1782, half going to eldest surviving son Daniel Cole, and one-quarter each to heirs of Heman Cole deceased and to Martha Cole.

Children (COLE) b. Eastham: JOSHUA[6] b. 1731/2, d. 1754; MARTHA b. 1735; DANIEL b. 1739; and HEMAN b. 1749.

References: MD 5:197; 17:33-4. Barnstable Co. PR 14:92[1], 94[1], 161[1]; 19:57(Daniel and Martha Cole).

116 HENRY[5] ROGERS (Eleazer[4], John[3], Joseph[2], Thomas[1]) b. Harwich 19 Aug. 1713; d. bef. 20 April 1759 (not in father's will).

He m. ca. 1738 ----- -----.

On 6 May 1760 Stephen Cole of Harwich was made guardian of Amariah and Henry Rogers, minor sons of Henry Rogers late of Harwich yeoman deceased; and on the same day Stephen Rogers of Harwich was named guardian of Jesse, another minor son of Henry Rogers. Henry and Jesse both married in 1761; and an Eleazer Rogers [poss. their uncle], Jesse and Amariah Rogers divided their land in 1771, mentioning land Eleazer bought of Henry (this affords a rough estimate of their birth years).

Children (ROGERS) prob. b. Harwich: JESSE[6] b. ca. 1740; HENRY b. ca. 1742; and AMARIAH b. bet. 1742 and 1750.

References: MD 15:143; 17:203-4; 34:106. HIGGINS DESC pp. 109-10. Barnstable Co. PR 11:91(Henry Rogers).

117 ELIZABETH[5] ROGERS (Eleazer[4], John[3], Joseph[2], Thomas[1]) b. Harwich 14 Nov. 1715; d. Chatham 6 Oct. 1800 ae 85.

She m. Harwich 2 Jan. 1734/5 NATHAN BASSETT, b. Chatham ca. 1713; d. there 2 Dec. 1800 ae 87; son of Nathan and Mary (Crowell) Bassett.*

Nathan was a selectman of Chatham from 1762 to 1768, and town clerk and treasurer from 1769 to 1783.

Children (BASSETT) b. Chatham: son b. and d. 1735/6; ELIZABETH[6] b. 1736/7; EBENEZER b. 1738; JOANNA b. 1740; NATHAN b. 1743; PENINNAH

---

*The Elizabeth Rogers who m. Nathan Bassett is thus not the dau. of Eleazer and Ruhamah (Willis) Rogers as claimed in _The Mayflower Index_.

b. 1745; twins DAVID and JONATHAN b. 1749; MERCY b. 1752, d. 1753; and
MERCY b. 1753, d. 1766.

References: MD 13:148; 16:214. NEHGR 121:312; 125:8.

118 MERCY[5] ROGERS (Eleazer[4], John[3], Joseph[2], Thomas[1]) b.
Harwich 1 Sept. 1718; d. after 3 May 1761, when her young-
est child was born.
     She m. Harwich 28 Oct. 1746 ELI FULLER, b. Barnstable
11 April 1720; d. after 1761; son of Isaac and Jerusha
(Lovell) Fuller, and a descendant of Pilgrim Edward Fuller.
     There are no Barnstable County probates for either
Eli or Mercy.

     Children (FULLER) b. Barnstable: MARTHA[6] b. 1747; JEDEDIAH b.
1749; DAVID b. 1751; WILLIAM b. 1753; JERUSHA b. 1756; and LYDIA b.
1761.

References: MD 23:127; 31:152; 33:60. FULLER GEN 1:76.

119 MOSES[5] ROGERS (Eleazer[4], John[3], Joseph[2], Thomas[1]) b.
Harwich 13 March 1720/1; d. there 22 March 1795 in 74th yr.
     He m. Chatham 10 Nov. 1748 ELIZABETH SMITH, b. Chatham
11 April 1732; d. there 21 Dec. 1795 in 64th yr.; dau. of
John and Elizabeth (Brown) Smith.
     The DAR Patriot Index says he served in the Revolu-
tion.
     The will of Moses Rogers of Harwich yeoman advanced
in years, dated 3 May 1791 and presented 7 April 1795,
names grandson James Kenrick, son of my daughter Mercy
Rogers; sons Abner, John, Moses, Aaron, Daniel and Mulford;
two youngest sons Enos and Reuben; unmarried daughter Mary
(or Mercy?); wife Elizabeth; five daughters (sic) Martha
Cahoon, Betty Kenrick, Elizabeth Small and Mercy Rogers.

     Children (ROGERS) b. Harwich: JERUSHA[6] b. 1749; MARTHA b. 1751;
ABNER b. 1752; JOHN b. 1755; twins MOSES and AARON b. 1757; DANIEL b.
1759; DANIEL b. 1760; MULFORD b. 1762; BETTY b. 1764; ELIZABETH b.
1766; ENOS B. 1768; MARCY b. 1769; MEHITABLE b. 1771; GEORGE b. 1772;
REUBEN b. 1775; and poss. MARY.

References: MD 4:182; 12:172; 13:178-9; 34:109. DAR PATRIOT INDEX.
               Barnstable Co. PR 24:146; 27:439(Moses Rogers).

120 MARTHA[5] ROGERS (Eleazer[4], John[3], Joseph[2], Thomas[1])
b. Harwich 9 Jan. 1723/4; living ca. 1762, when her daughter Martha was probably born.
     She m. Harwich 12 Sept. 1751 THOMAS CHASE Jr., prob.
the one b. Yarmouth in July 1728; son of Gouell and Jean
(Phillips) Chase. It is possible they moved to Maine.

No Barnstable County probates for Thomas or Martha.

Children (CHASE) b. Yarmouth: JANE[6] b. 1752; SARAH b. 1753; RELIANCE b. 1756; HENERY b. 1758; RACHEL b. 1760; and MARTHA prob. b. ca. 1762.

References: MD 34:25. YARMOUTH VR pp. 10, 108, 171. NEHGR 87:321-2.

121 ELEAZER[5] ROGERS (Eleazer[4], John[3], Joseph[2], Thomas[1]) b. Harwich 15 Nov. 1726; d. Eastham bef. 10 Aug. 1784.
    He m. Eastham 13 Nov. 1747 RUTH HIGGINS, b. Eastham 15 Aug. 1725; living 20 Aug. 1784; dau. of Joshua and Ruth (Twining) Higgins. (The marriage record says Eleazer married Rebecca Higgins, but the intentions 6 June 1747 were with Ruth, and the children were recorded born to Eleazer and Ruth. Intentions are more apt to be correct, since the principals give the information, rather than the minister.) The will of Joshua Higgins of Eastham yeoman, dated 17 July 1767, mentions wife Ruth and daughters Sarah Rogers and Ruth Rogers.
    Administration on the estate of Eleazer Rogers late of Eastham deceased was granted 10 Aug. 1784 to widow Ruth Rogers and Asa Nickerson. On 20 Aug. 1784 Ruth was granted an allowance.

    Children (ROGERS) b. Harwich to Eleazer Jr. and Ruth: JOHANAH[6] b. 1747/8; LEVI b. 1749; DAVID b. 1751; RUTH b. 1754; RUTH b. 1756; ABIGAIL b. 1759; and prob. ELEAZER b. 1769.

References: MD 24:138; 29:17; 33:71. HIGGINS DESC p. 110. HIGGINS
            SUP p. 14. Barnstable Co. PR 13:338(Joshua Higgins);
19:108; 23:361(Eleazer Rogers).

122 ENSIGN[5] ROGERS (Eleazer[4], John[3], Joseph[2], Thomas[1]) b. Harwich 9 July 1729; d. bef. 6 March 1759.
    He m. int. Chatham 5 Aug. 1755 TEMPERANCE NICKERSON, dau. of Nathaniel and Katherine (Stewart) Nickerson. She may have m. (2) Harwich 1762 William Snow.
    On 6 March 1759 Thomas Nickerson Jr. and widow Temperance Rogers, both of Chatham, were appointed administrators on the estate of Ensign Rogers late of Harwich seafaring man. On 6 May 1760 Temperance Rogers of Harwich widow was appointed guardian of Ensign and Thomas Rogers, minor sons of Ensign Rogers deceased.

    Children (ROGERS) prob. b. Harwich: THOMAS[6], and ENSIGN, both b. bef. 20 April 1759, when they were named in their grandfather's will.

References: MD 13:29; 34:105. NEHGR 121:312. Barnstable Co. PR 10:
            19^2; $11:89^2-90^2$.

123 LEVI^5 SMITH (Hannah^4 Rogers, John^3, Joseph^2, Thomas^1)
b. Eastham 15 March 1713/4; living Sandisfield 4 July 1784.
    He m. int. Eastham 8 Oct. 1737 JANE SNOW, b. Eastham
22 April 1716; d. bef. 13 April 1773; dau. of Stephen and
Margaret (Elkins) Snow, and a descendant of Pilgrim Stephen
Hopkins. In a division of the estate of Stephen Snow late
of Eastham deceased, dated 13 April 1773, the sons were to
pay the daughters including: Ruth Smith, Mercy Smith,
Sarah Smith and heirs of Jane Smith.
    On 4 July 1784 Levi, Jane, Eleazer, Martha, Elizabeth
and Priscilla Smith were admitted to the Sandisfield Congregational Church from Eastham churches.

    Children (SMITH) b. Eastham: ELEAZER^6 b. 1739; HANNAH b. 1741;
ELIZABETH b. 1743; JEAN b. 1745; RUTH b. 1748; PRISCILLA b. 1752; and
GRACE b. 1754.

References: MD 7:16; 24:141; 28:180. NEHGR 19:202. TAG 37:207.
            Barnstable Co. PR 17:95(Stephen Snow). Sandisfield Cong.
Ch. Recs. p. 228. SMITH (RALPH) DESC p. 25.

124 SOLOMON^5 SMITH (Hannah^4 Rogers, John^3, Joseph^2,
Thomas^1) b. Eastham 8 March 1715/6; d. Sandisfield 13 May
1790 ae 75.
    He m. Eastham 21 Feb. 1739/40 SUSANNAH SNOW, b. East-
ham 12 Nov. 1708; d. Sandisfield 11 June 1798 ae 90; dau.
of Benjamin and Thankful (Bowerman) Snow, and a descendant
of Pilgrim Stephen Hopkins. The will of Benjamin Snow of
Eastham yeoman, dated 1 Feb. 1747/8, names wife Thankful
and daughter Susanna Smith.
    After leaving Eastham about 1742, this family appar-
ently stopped for a while in Hebron CT, for in 1751 Solomon Smith of Hebron bought land in what was later Sandisfield. On 15 Jan. 1758 Susanna Smith, wife of Solomon,
was admitted to the Sandisfield Congregational Church from
the Eastham church. On 26 Oct. 1769 Solomon Smith of
Sandisfield sold land there to son Solomon Jr.
    Solomon did not leave a will, but on 2 June 1790 Sus-
anna Smith widow of Solomon of Sandisfield, with Solomon
Smith and Amos Smith of "the south 11,000 acres so-called,"
Ebenezer State and wife Susanna of Dorset VT, and Ezekiel
Smith of Bennington VT sold to Uriel Smith all their rights
to land and house in Sandisfield of Solomon Smith deceased.

    Children (SMITH) first b. Eastham, second and fourth Norwich CT:
SOLOMON^6 b. 1741; URIEL b. 1743; SUSANNA b. 1745; and AMOS b. 1747.

References: MD 15:55; 19:104.   NEHGR 49:202.   SMITH (RALPH) DESC. pp.
              27-32.   VR SANDISFIELD.   Sandisfield Cong. Ch. Recs. p.
226.   NORWICH CT VR 1:224.

125   JOSHUA[5] SMITH   (Hannah[4] Rogers, John[3], Joseph[2], Thomas[1])   b. Eastham 19 July 1720; d. Sandisfield 16 July
1771 ae 51.
        He m. Eastham int. 7 Jan. 1741/2 MERCY SNOW, b. East-
ham 24 Feb. 1721/2; d. prob. Sandisfield after 13 April
1773; dau. of Stephen and Margaret (Elkins) Snow, and a
descendant of Pilgrim Stephen Hopkins.   In a division of
the estate of Stephen Snow late of Eastham deceased, dated
13 April 1773, the sons were to pay the daughters including: Ruth Smith, Mercy Smith, Sarah Smith and heirs of
Jane Smith.
        Joshua was apparently living at Hebron CT 6 Dec. 1750
when he bought land in Sandisfield.   On 8 Nov. 1758 Mercy
Smith, wife of Joshua, was admitted to communion at the
Sandisfield Congregational Church, and on 6 April 1766
Joshua was admitted.
        On 13 Aug. 1771 widow Mercy Smith and Joshua Smith
were appointed administrators of the estate of Joshua
Smith late of Sandisfield deceased.   In a warrant for distribution on 10 Dec. 1771, widow Mercy Smith was to have
her thirds and the rest was to be divided into 12 shares,
two to administrator Joshua Smith (therefore the eldest
son), and single shares to sons Heman, Nathan, Joel, John,
Asa, William and David; and daughters Mercy Lee wife of
Giles, Lydia Smith and Eunice Smith.

        Children (SMITH) first b. Norwich CT, fourth through eighth b.
Hebron CT, last three b. Sandisfield: JOSHUA[6] b. 1744/5; JOHN; MERCY;
HEMAN b. 1747; NATHAN b. 1749; LYDIA b. 1750; JOEL b. 1752; EUNICE b.
1754; WILLIAM b. 1756; ASA b. 1759; and DAVID b. 1763.

References: VR SANDISFIELD.   NORWICH CT VR 1:243.   MD 7:16; 29:12.
            CSL Barbour Index:Hebron.   Sandisfield Cong. Ch. Recs.
p. 226.   Barnstable Co. PR 17:195(Stephen Snow).   Berkshire Co. PR
#843(Joshua Smith).   Berkshire Co. LR 1:626(Joshua Smith).   SMITH
(RALPH) DESC p. 37.

126   GRACE[5] SMITH   (Hannah[4] Rogers, John[3], Joseph[2], Thomas[1])   b. Eastham 17 Dec. 1722; d. after 24 Feb. 1764 when
her last child was born.
        She m. Hebron CT 7 Sept. 1749 MATTHEW WILLIAMS, b.
Hebron 8 Oct. 1720; d. after 1764; son of Matthew and Mary
(-----) Williams.
        Matthew may have been the one who, with wife Mary, was
admitted from New Marlboro to the Sandisfield Congregational Church 5 July 1767.

Children (WILLIAMS) b. Hebron CT: HANNAH[6] b. 1750; GRACE b. 1752; MATTHEW b. and d. 1754; LEVI b. 1756; TIMNA b. 1758; ISAAC b. 1762; and ACHSAH b. 1764.

References: SMITH (RALPH) DESC p. 35. Sandisfield Cong. Ch. Recs. p. 226. CSL Barbour Index:Hebron.

127 BENJAMIN[5] SMITH (Hannah[4] Rogers, John[3], Joseph[2], Thomas[1]) b. Eastham 3 Oct. 1724; d. Sandisfield 10 Feb. 1796.
    He m. Eastham 30 Nov. 1745 RUTH SNOW, b. Eastham 11 Dec. 1725; d. after 3 May 1796; dau. of Stephen and Margaret (Elkins) Snow, and a descendant of Pilgrim Stephen Hopkins. In a division of the estate of Stephen Snow late of Eastham deceased, dated 13 April 1773, the sons were to pay the daughters including: Ruth Smith, Mercy Smith, Sarah Smith and heirs of Jane Smith.
    Benjamin Smith Jr. was appointed administrator on the estate of Lt. Benjamin Smith 8 March 1796. On 3 May 1796 the estate of Benjamin Smith, Gent., was divided: one-third to widow Ruth Smith, and the rest in equal shares to the children: Benjamin, Amasa, Lot, Reuben, Dorcas Bull wife of John of Cherry Valley NY, Ruth Smith wife of Matthew, Rebecca Hurd wife of Daniel, Elizabeth Allen wife of Elihu, and Sarah Chapel wife of Richard.

    Children (SMITH) b. or bp. Sandisfield: DORCAS[6] b. 1746; RUTH b. 1748; REBECCA b. 1750; BENJAMIN b. 1752; AMASA b. 1754; LOT b. 1756; SARAH b. 1758; ELIZABETH b. 1762; REUBEN b. 1765; ELKINS bp. 1767, d. 1768; and SUSANNA bp. 1770.

References: MD 7:16; 24:87. VR SANDISFIELD. Sandisfield Cong. Ch. Recs. pp. 230-1. Barnstable Co. PR 17:195(Stephen Snow). Berkshire Co. PR #1750(Benj. Smith). SMITH (RALPH) DESC pp. 36-7.

128 PHINEAS[5] SMITH (Hannah[4] Rogers, John[3], Joseph[2], Thomas[1]) b. Eastham 7 March 1728/9; d. Sandisfield bet. 18 July 1786 and 5 Sept. 1786.
    He m. Eastham 9 Jan. 1752 RUTH DOANE, b. Eastham 3 March 1733/4; d. Sandisfield 25 Nov. 1822 ae 90; dau. of Simeon and Apphia (Higgins) Doane.
    On 12 July 1769 Phinehas Smith of Easton (*sic*), County of Barnstable, bought land in Sandisfield; and on 17 Nov. 1770 Phineas Smith and wife were admitted to the Sandisfield Congregational Church from the Eastham church.
    The will of Phineas Smith of Sandisfield, made 18 July 1786 and probated 5 Sept. 1786, names wife Ruth; four eldest children: Ebenezer, Mary, James and Levi; four younger children: Phebe, Henry, Elisha and Isaiah.

Children (SMITH) b. Eastham: EBENEZER[6] b. 1752; MARY b. 1754;
JAMES b. 1756; LEVI b. 1758; PHEBE b. 1760; HENRY b. 1763; ELISHA b.
1764; and ISAIAH b. 1766.

References: MD 17:145; 25:41-2. Sandisfield Cong. Ch. Recs. p. 227.
             Berkshire Co. PR #1339(Phinehas Smith). Berkshire Co.
LR 2:629(Phineas Smith). SMITH (RALPH) DESC pp. 38-9. VR SANDISFIELD.

129 RUTH[5] ROGERS (Nathaniel[4], John[3], Joseph[2], Thomas[1])
b. Eastham 31 July 1725; d. Norwich VT 27 Aug. 1808.
     She prob. m. Middle Haddam Parish (later Chatham) CT
20 Nov. 1746 JONATHAN LORD, b. Colchester CT 3 Oct. 1726;
d. Norwich VT 8 May 1805; son of John and Experience
(Crippen) Lord.
     They lived first at Colchester, later Bolton CT,
moved about 1773 to Hanover NH, and finally to Norwich VT.

     Children (LORD) first two b. Colchester CT, last two Bolton CT:
NATHANIEL[6] b. 1747; EXPERIENCE b. 1749/50; JONATHAN b. 1752; RUTH b.
1754; DAVID b. 1756; JOHN bp. 1760, d.y.; ICHABOD b. 1763; and JOSEPH
b. 1764.

References: CSL Barbour Index:Colchester. CT MARR 3:75. LORD DESC
             p. 91.

130 JABEZ[5] ROGERS (Nathaniel[4], John[3], Joseph[2], Thomas[1])
b. Eastham 30 June 1727; d. Tolland CT 23 May 1803 in 75th
yr.
     He m. LUCY KEEP, b. Westford 7 Nov. 1734; d. Tolland
CT 3 June 1803 in 69th yr.; dau. of Jabez and Sarah
(Leonard) Keep. The will of Jabez Keep of Harvard gentleman, dated 7 July 1773, mentions second dau. Lucy Rogers.
     Jabez Rogers was of Bolton CT by 26 April 1749 when
he bought land there.
     Neither Jabez nor Lucy left wills in the collection at
CT State Library.

     Children (ROGERS) last four b. Bolton CT: SAMUEL[6]; RUSSELL;
LEONARD b. 1754; JABEZ b. 1756; LUCY b. 1759; and NATHANIEL b. 1761.

References: CSL Barbour Index:Bolton. KEEP DESC pp. 24-5. Bolton CT
             LR 2:627(Jabez Rogers). VR WESTFORD. BOLTON CT VR p. 50.

131 ELIZABETH[5] PHINNEY (John[4], Mary[3] Rogers, Joseph[2],
Thomas[1]) b. Barnstable 11 April 1690; poss. d. Harwinton
CT 30 Dec. 1786 ae 96.
     She m. Barnstable 25 Nov. 1714 NATHAN DAVIS, b. Barn-
stable 2 March 1690; son of Jabez and Experience (Linnell)
Davis; poss. d. Harwinton CT 17 Sept. 1785 ae 96.

Was Nathan the Nathan Davis of Harwinton CT who made
a will 8 Dec. 1783, probated 11 Oct. 1785, naming wife
Elizabeth, sons Nathan and John, daughters Sarah Hopkins
and Matther [or Martha] Preston, grandsons Nathan and
Josiah (no last names)? On 24 Oct. 1785 the Hartford
Courant reported the death at Harwinton 17 Sept. of Lt.
Nathan Davis, in 97th year, leaving a widow in her 97th
year; they were married 73 years.

Children (DAVIS) b. Barnstable: JABEZ[6] b. 1715; SARAH b. and d.
1717; ELIZABETH b. 1718; ISAAC b. 1720; and poss. NATHAN b. Harwinton
CT 1735.

References: MD 4:222, 224. CSL Barbour Index:Harwinton. HARTFORD
              COURANT, 24 Oct. 1785. CT PR Litchfield Dist. #1761
(Nathan Davis). CSL Hale Cem Recs:Harwinton.

132 JOHN[5] PHINNEY (John[4], Mary[3] Rogers, Joseph[2], Thomas[1])
b. Barnstable 8 April 1696, bp. 6 May 1694 (*sic*); d. Gorham ME 29 Dec. 1780 ae 86.
    He m. Barnstable 25 Sept. 1718 MARTHA COLEMAN, b.
Barnstable 4 March 1698; d. Gorham ME 16 Dec. 1784 in 87th
yr.; dau. of James and Patience (Cobb) Coleman.
    On 29 Dec. 1762 John Phinney of Gorhamtown [ME] gent-
leman sold land in town to son James Phinney of Gorhamtown
laborer. On 26 Jan. 1763 John Phinney of Gorham sold land
in Gorham to grandsons Colman Phinney Watson, son of
Eliphalet, and John Phinney, son of John Phinney Jr., upon
payment by Eliphalet Watson "my son-in-law" and "my son
John Phinney Jr." both of Gorham.

Children (PHINNEY) first five b. Barnstable, next two Falmouth
ME, last three Gorham ME: ELIZABETH[6] b. 1721; EDMUND b. 1723; STEPHEN
b. 1725; MARTHA b. 1727; PATIENCE b. 1730; JOHN b. 1732; SARAH b.
1734; MARY GORHAM b. 1736; COLEMAN b. 1738; and JAMES b. 1741.

References: MD 4:221; 31:33[*James* Coleman m. Patience Cobb]; 32:149,
              151. FINNEY-PHINNEY pp. 4, 10. Cumberland Co. ME LR
2:483-4, 554(John Phinney). ME HGR 1:129.

133 THOMAS[5] PHINNEY (John[4], Mary[3] Rogers, Joseph[2], Thomas[1]) b. Barnstable 25 May 1697, bp. 21 June 1696 (*sic*);
d. there 10 June 1784 ae 88.
    He m. Barnstable 31 March 1726 RELIANCE GOODSPEED, b.
Barnstable 18 Sept. 1701; d. there 27 Jan. 1784 ae 83; dau.
of Ebenezer and Lydia (Crowel) Goodspeed.
    The will of Thomas Phinney of Barnstable, drawn 24
April 1780 and proved 19 July 1784, names wife Reliance;
daughters Lydia Hodge and Sarah Hinkley; children of my
late daughter Patience Bearse; son Isaac; granddaughter

Lydia Hodge; grandsons Solomon and Paul Phinney and their sister Jenny; grandson Prince Hinkley; son-in-law Sylvanus Hinkley executor. A codicil appointed son Isaac Phinney and grandson Nymphas Hinkley additional executors.

Children (PHINNEY) b. Barnstable: ELI[6] b. 1726/7; LYDY b. 1729; SARAH b. 1731/2; ISAAC b. 1734; PATIENCE b. 1736; ABIGAIL b. 1740; and ELIZABETH b. 1742.

References: MD 5:74; 32:57; 33:28. FINNEY-PHINNEY pp. 4, 10-11. Barnstable Co. PR 23:439(Thomas Phinney).

134 HANNAH[5] PHINNEY (John[4], Mary[3] Rogers, Joseph[2], Thomas[1]) b. Barnstable 8 April 1700; living there 13 Dec. 1781.
    She m. Barnstable 6 Oct. 1720 ROGER GOODSPEED, b. Barnstable 14 Oct. 1698; d. bef. 18 April 1791; son of Ebenezer and Lydia (Crowel) Goodspeed.
    The will of Roger Goodspeed of Barnstable, dated 13 Dec. 1781 and presented 18 April 1791, names wife Hannah; grandson Thomas Goodspeed; granddaughter Puella Goodspeed; sons Isaac and Joseph; daughter Elizabeth Winslow; sons Isaac and Joseph executors.

Children (GOODSPEED) b. Barnstable: THOMAS[6] b. 1721; ISAAC b. 1723; SARAH b. 1727; ELIZABETH b. 1731; and JOSEPH b. 1736.

References: MD 5:74; 32:148-9. FINNEY-PHINNEY p. 4. Barnstable Co. PR 27:51(Roger Goodspeed).

135 SARAH[5] PHINNEY (John[4], Mary[3] Rogers, Joseph[2], Thomas[1]) b. Barnstable 8 Oct. 1702, bp. 9 Nov. 1701 (_sic_); living 1738.
    She m. int. Barnstable 27 Aug. 1724 THOMAS ADAMS, b. Bristol RI 28 March 1698; living 1737; son of Edward and Elizabeth (Walley) Adams.
    No Barnstable County probate records for Thomas or Sarah.

Children (ADAMS) b. Barnstable: MARTHA[6] b. 1725; THOMAS b. 1726; ELIZABETH b. 1728; WALLEY b. 1730; SARAH b. 1732; NATHANIEL b. 1734; EDWARD b. 1736; HANNAH b. 1737/8; and poss. OBED.

References: MD 32:52; 34:116. RI VR:Bristol:5, 61. ADAMS GEN pp. 508, 520.

136 PATIENCE[5] PHINNEY (John[4], Mary[3] Rogers, Joseph[2], Thomas[1]) b. Barnstable 12 Sept. 1704; living 12 April 1773.

She m. Barnstable 12 March 1727/8 JAMES COLEMAN, b. Barnstable 11 April 1704; d. there 16 April 1781 ae 77; son of James and Patience (Cobb) Coleman.* Patience and sister Martha not only entered their intentions on the same day, but also they were married the same day (see #137).

The will of James Coleman of Barnstable yeoman advanced in years, dated 12 April 1773 and presented 10 May 1781, names wife Patience; sons James, Ebenezer and John; daughters Martha Fish, Mary Howland and Patience Coleman; sons James and Ebenezer executors.

Children (COLEMAN) b. Barnstable: MARTHA[6] b. 1728/9, d.y.; MARTHA b. 1732; JAMES b. 1735; EBENEZER; JOHN b. 1737; MARY b. 1739; and PATIENCE.

References: MD 4:221; 32:53[wrongly ascribes several of the above children to James and *Martha*]; 33:117; 34:118. Barnstable Co. PR 10:181(James Coleman).

137 MARTHA[5] PHINNEY (John[4], Mary[3] Rogers, Joseph[2], Thomas[1]) b. Barnstable 12 July 1706; living 1744.

She m. Barnstable 12 March 1727/8 JONATHAN LUMBERT, b. Barnstable 16 April 1703; living 1744; son of Joshua and Hopestill (Bullock) Lumbert. Martha and sister Patience not only entered their intentions on the same day, but also they were married the same day (see #136).

There are no Barnstable County probate records for Jonathan or Martha.

Children (LUMBERT) b. Barnstable: JONATHAN[6] b. 1729; MARTHA b. 1731; MERCY b. 1733/4; HOPESTILL b. 1737; SARAH b. 1739; SUSANNAH b. 1741; SIMEON b. 1744; and poss. JABEZ bp. 1748.

References: MD 11:98; 33:117; 34:118. LUMBERT-LOMBARD p. 7.

138 JABEZ[5] PHINNEY (John[4], Mary[3] Rogers, Joseph[2], Thomas[1]) b. Barnstable 16 July 1708; d. Barnstable 1 Dec. 1776.

He m. Barnstable 5 Oct. 1732 JANE TAYLOR, b. Barnstable 15 Oct. 1709; d. there 10 July 1787; dau. of Abraham and Mary (Butler) Taylor. The will of Abraham Taylor of Barnstable, dated 26 Aug. 1758, names dau. Jane Finney.

The will of Jabez Phinney of Barnstable, made 3 May 1771 and proved 24 Dec. 1776, names wife Jane, sons Joseph and John, and daughters Mary Phinney, Anna Shaw and Hannah Crosby.

---

*No evidence was found to substantiate the claim that this Patience Phinney was the one who married in Plymouth in 1719 Ebenezer Holmes, when she would have been under fifteen years of age. The Mayflower Society has accepted lineages based on this assumed marriage.

Children (PHINNEY) b. Barnstable: JOSEPH[6] b. 1733, d.y.; MARY
b. 1735; ANNE b. 1738; HANNAH b. 1741; JOSEPH b. 1744; and JOHN b.
1748.

References: MD 32:58; 33:23; 34:20. Barnstable Co. PR 13:109(Abraham
        Taylor); 17:472(Jabez Phinney). FINNEY-PHINNEY pp. 4, 11.

139 JOHN[5] PHINNEY (Joseph[4], Mary[3] Rogers, Joseph[2], Thomas[1]) b. Plymouth 17 Dec. 1696; d. Kingston 13 Oct. 1787
ae 89.
    He m. (1) Kingston 1 March 1721/2 REBECCA BRYANT, b.
Plymouth 6 Dec. 1702; d. Kingston 28 Aug. 1741; dau. of
Jonathan and Margaret (West) Bryant.
    He m. (2) Abington 5 April 1743 BETTY LOVELL of Abing-
ton.
    He m. (3) Plympton 25 Dec. 1770 RUTH (SYLVESTER)
(COOKE) RING, b. Scituate 26 June 1702; d. bef. 17 Nov.
1779; dau. of Israel and Ruth (Turner) Sylvester, a descendant of Pilgrim William Brewster, widow of Francis
Cooke (a descendant of Pilgrims James Chilton, Francis
Cooke and Stephen Hopkins) and of Samuel Ring (a descendant of Pilgrim Stephen Hopkins) (see p. 81).
    The will of John Phinney of Kingston, made 17 Nov.
1779 and presented 3 Dec. 1787, names friend Mary Fish
wife of Adam, brother Joseph Phinney, kinsman John Phinney
son of Pelatiah, and friend Enoch Hall to be executor.

    Children (PHINNEY) all by first wife, first two b. Plymouth,
rest b. Kingston: JONATHAN[6] b. 1722/3, d. 1734/5; JOHN b. 1724/5, d.
1734/5; JONATHAN b. 1725/6, d. 1750; REBECCA b. 1730, d. 1747; JOHN
b. 1733, d. 1751; and JOSEPH b. 1737, d. 1759.

References: MD 2:52; 18:143; 22:169. VR ABINGTON, KINGSTON, PLYMP-
        TON, SCITUATE. FINNEY-PHINNEY pp. 4, 11. Plymouth Co.
PR 30:262(John Phinney).

140 JOSEPH[5] PHINNEY (Joseph[4], Mary[3] Rogers, Joseph[2], Thomas[1]) b. Plympton 10 April 1709; d. Raynham 21 Dec. 1795.
    He m. (1) Plympton 9 Jan. 1734/5 MARY RICKARD, d.
Bridgewater 11 Sept. 1760 "wife of Joseph"; poss. the one
b. Plympton 29 Oct. 1711 to Joseph Rickard.
    He m. (2) Taunton 14 Jan. 1762 ALICE (HACKETT) (RICH-
MOND?) CAMPBELL, b. 18 Jan. 1714/5; d. after 22 Nov. 1763;
dau. of John and Elizabeth (Elliott) Hackett (see #59 iv
and #274).

    Children (PHINNEY) first three b. Plympton, rest Bridgewater, all
by first wife: EXPEARANCE[6] b. 1736; ACHSAH b. 1738; PELETIAH b. 1740;
ALICE b. 1742/3, d. 1748/9; AMY b. 1745; NOAH b. 1748; and REBECCA
b. 1750/1.

References: MD 15:171. VR BRIDGEWATER, PLYMPTON, TAUNTON. FINNEY-
            PHINNEY pp. 11-12.

141 PELATIAH[5] PHINNEY (Joseph[4], Mary[3] Rogers, Joseph[2],
Thomas[1]) b. Plympton 21 March 1710/1; living 1760.
     He m. Bridgewater 28 Dec. 1738 MERCY WASHBURN, b.
Bridgewater 29 May 1718; living 5 Oct. 1760; dau. of
Josiah and Mercy (Tilson) Washburn.
     [He was probably not the Pelatiah Phinney Jr. who m.
25 year old Mary Randall at Easton in 1764; the son of
Joseph (#140) is more likely.] No probate record found in
Bristol or Plymouth counties.

     Children (PHINNEY) b. Bridgewater: FREELOVE[6] b. 1740; LAURAINA
b. 1741; ZERVIAH b. 1742; ONESIPHORUS b. 1744; MARA b. 1745; ZERVIAH
b. 1748; ESTHER b. 1751; KEZIA b. 1753; BLISS b. 1754; HANNAH b. 1758;
and JOHN b. 1760. (One child d. 1750, another d. 1759, names not indicated.)

References: VR BRIDGEWATER. FINNEY-PHINNEY p. 12.

142 GERSHOM[5] PHINNEY (Thomas[4], Mary[3] Rogers, Joseph[2],
Thomas[1]) b. Barnstable 21 March 1699/1700; d. Harwich bef.
7 Sept. 1762.
     He m. Harwich 29 July 1725 REBEKAH GRIFFITH, b. Har-
wich 18 June 1703; d. after 4 Dec. 1761; dau. of Stephen
and Rebecca (Rider) Griffith. The will of Stephen Griffith
of Harwich yeoman, made 10 Aug. 1742, includes wife Rebecca
and dau. Rebecca Phinney.
     The will of Gershom Phinney of Harwich cooper, made
4 Dec. 1761 and presented 7 Sept. 1762, names son Isaac;
wife Rebecca; son Gershom; "three unmarried daughters";
sons Lazarus, James and Seth; daughters Thankful Taylor,
Rebecca Bangs, Temperance, Mehitable and Rhoda; son Gershom executor.

     Children (PHINNEY) bp. Brewster: GERSHOM[6] bp. 1728; LAZARUS bp.
1729; SARAH bp. 1730/1; THANKFUL; ISAAC bp. 1733; REBECCA bp. 1736;
TEMPERANCE bp. 1738; MEHITABLE bp. 1741; JAMES bp. 1743; SETH bp.
1745; and RHODA bp. 1748.

References: MD 4:177; 6:156, 217; 7:33, 94, 97, 147, 150; 8:120, 160,
            248. FINNEY-PHINNEY pp. 12-13. Barnstable Co. PR 6:498
(Stephen Griffith); 12:303(Gershom Phinney). YARMOUTH VR 1:134.

143 THOMAS[5] PHINNEY (Thomas[4], Mary[3] Rogers, Joseph[2], Thomas[1]) b. Barnstable 17 Feb. 1702/3; d. there bet. 6 June
and 30 June 1778.

He m. (1) Barnstable in Nov. 1731 MARIAH LUMBERT (or Lombard), b. Barnstable in Oct. 1700; d. bef. Nov. 1748; dau. of Bernard Lumbert.

He prob. m. (2) Barnstable 24 Nov. 1748 ABIGAIL LUMBERT (or Lombard), poss. b. Barnstable 23 April 1720 to Samuel and Mary (Comer) Lumbert.

The will of Thomas Phinney of Barnstable, made 6 June 1778 and proved 30 June 1778, names wife Abigail, sons Edmund and James, and daughters Susanna Nye, Temperance Isham and Freelove Fish.

    Children (PHINNEY) prob. b. Barnstable: EDMUND[6], JAMES, SUSANNA, TEMPERANCE, and FREELOVE.

References: MD 11:97; 14:89; 31:13; 32:57; 33:126. Barnstable Co. PR
           20:345(Thomas Phinney). FINNEY-PHINNEY p. 13. NEHGR
12:250.

144 MARY[5] PHINNEY (Ebenezer[4], Mary[3] Rogers, Joseph[2], Thomas[1]) b. Barnstable 23 March 1698; d. ca. 1796 ae 98 yr.

She m. Barnstable 22 Dec. 1724 JOB DAVIS, b. Barnstable in July 1700; d. Barnstable 4 April 1751 ae 50; son of Dolar and Hannah (Linnell) Davis.

Widow Mary Davis was named administratrix 7 May 1751 of the estate of Job Davis late of Barnstable deceased.

    Children (DAVIS) b. Barnstable: MARY[6] b. 1725, d. 1725/6; THOMAS b. 1726; SHOBAL b. 1729; MARY b. 1731; MEHITABLE b. 1733/4; SETH b. 1736; HANNAH b. 1739; and EBENEZER b. 1742.

References: MD 4:223-4; 32:148; 33:121. Barnstable Co. PR 7:206(Job
           Davis). BARNSTABLE FAMS 1:302.

145 SAMUEL[5] PHINNEY (Ebenezer[4], Mary[3] Rogers, Joseph[2], Thomas[1]) b. Barnstable 1 April 1702; living 26 Nov. 1754, when his father made his will.

He m. int. Barnstable 25 Jan. 1728/9 HANNAH RAY, b. Edgartown 16 Oct. 1712; living 29 Nov. 1745; dau. of Peter and Tabitha (Newcomb) Ray.

There are no Barnstable County probates for Samuel or Hannah.

    Children (PHINNEY) b. Barnstable: SUSANNAH[6] b. 1730/1; NATHANIEL b. 1733; PETER b. 1737; WILLIAM b. 1740; and HANNAH b. 1745.

References: MD 33:124; 34:118. VR EDGARTOWN. FINNEY-PHINNEY p. 13.

146 REBECCA[5] PHINNEY (Ebenezer[4], Mary[3] Rogers, Joseph[2], Thomas[1]) bp. Barnstable 11 June 1703; d. bet. 6 Nov. 1754 and 8 Jan. 1777.
    She m. STEPHEN DAVIS, b. Barnstable 12 Dec. 1700; d. there 4 Jan. 1782 ae 81; son of Josiah and Ann (Taylor) Davis.
    The will of Stephen Davis of Barnstable, made 8 Jan. 1777 and probated 28 Jan. 1782, names sons Prince and Jonathan; daughters Anna Cobb, Rebecca Childs, Susanna Otis, Sarah Bacon and Thankful Smith; granddaughter Sarah Davis, daughter of son Stephen deceased; and grandson Isaac Davis, son of son Isaac deceased.

    Children (DAVIS) b. Barnstable: PRINCE[6] b. 1724; ANNA b. 1726; ISAAC b. 1729; REBECCA b. 1731; SUSANNA b. 1734; SARAH b. 1737; JONA-THAN; STEPHEN; and THANKFUL.

    References: MD 4:223; 33:27. Barnstable Co. PR 14:31(Stephen Davis).
                 CAPE COD HIST 2:321.

147 EBENEZER[5] PHINNEY (Ebenezer[4], Mary[3] Rogers, Joseph[2], Thomas[1]) b. Barnstable 26 May 1708; living 26 Nov. 1754.
    He m. Plymouth 22 Sept. 1730 REBECCA BARNES, b. Plymouth 14 March 1711; living 1747; dau. of Jonathan and Sarah (Bradford) Barnes, and a descendant of Pilgrim William Bradford.
    There are no Barnstable County probate records for Ebenezer or Rebecca.

    Children (PHINNEY) b. Barnstable: SARAH[6] b. 1732; JONATHAN b. 1733; MARTHA b. 1735; LEMUEL b. 1737; SETH b. 1743, d. 1744/5; and REBECCA b. 1747.

    References: MD 7:176; 14:73; 32:155-6. FINNEY-PHINNEY p. 13. (PLYM-
                 OUTH) ANC LANDMARKS 2:12, 109.

148 DAVID[5] PHINNEY (Ebenezer[4], Mary[3] Rogers, Joseph[2], Thomas[1]) b. Barnstable 10 June 1710; d. there 23 Nov. 1793 in 84th yr.
    He m. Sandwich 27 Sept. 1733 (int. Barnstable 1 April 1733) MARY POPE, b. Sandwich in Dec. 1713; d. 11 Nov. 1797 ae. 85; dau. of John and Elizabeth (Bourne) Pope.
    The will of David Phinney of Barnstable, dated 1 July 1789 and presented 10 Dec. 1793, mentions wife Mary; daughters Sarah Gorham and Mary Taylor; grandsons David and Peter Lewis; grandchildren Seth, Elizabeth Phinney and Susannah, all Taylors; land of father Ebenezer Phinney.

    Children (PHINNEY) b. Barnstable: DEBORAH[6] b. 1735; ELIJAH b. 1738, d. 1741; ELIZABETH b. 1741, d. 1743; MARY b. 1749; and SARAH bp. 1754.

References: MD 30:65; 31:147-8; 34:19.   FINNEY-PHINNEY pp. 13-14.
              Barnstable Co. PR 27:294(David Phinney).   Barnstable East
Ch. Recs.(d. David and Mary).

149   ZERUIAH[5] (or Zerviah) EASTLAND   (Mary[4] Phinney, Mary[3]
Rogers, Joseph[2], Thomas[1])   b. Plymouth 8 Dec. 1703; living
12 Sept. 1735.
     She m. Dartmouth 12 Jan. 1723/4 BARNABAS SPOONER, b.
Dartmouth 5 Feb. 1699; d. there bet. 7 Feb. 1733 and 18
June 1734; son of John Spooner.
     The will of Barnabas Spooner of Dartmouth yeoman,
dated 7 Feb. 1733 and proved 18 June 1734, names wife
Zerviah, "my aged and honored father," daughter Jane and
son Moses, both under 21, "child my wife now goes with";
executors to be wife Zerviah and Samuel Willis Esq. of
Dartmouth.   Zerviah swore to the account 12 Sept. 1735.

     Children (SPOONER) prob. b. Dartmouth: MOSES[6] b. 1725; JANE b.
1727/8; and poss. child b. 1733.

References: VR DARTMOUTH.   SPOONER DESC 1:42.   Bristol Co. PR 8:130,
              278-9(Barnabas Spooner).

150   JOSEPH[5] EASTLAND   (Mary[4] Phinney, Mary[3] Rogers,
Joseph[2], Thomas[1])   b. Plymouth 12 Nov. 1705; d. bet. 13
March 1750/1 and 10 July 1751.
     He m. Dartmouth 6 March 1728 FREELOVE SHEPHERD, b.
Portsmouth RI 5 April 1697; d. after 3 April 1754; dau. of
Daniel and Mary (Brice) Shepherd.
     The will of Joseph Eastland of Dartmouth sadler, weak
in body, made 13 March 1750/1 and proved 7 Aug. 1751, names
wife Freelove, son John to be executor, daughters Virtue
Badcock wife of Benjamin, Mary Eastland and Reliance Eastland.   Jonathan Hathaway of Dartmouth was appointed administrator on 7 Aug. 1751, because the executor was under
age.   On 3 April 1754 widow Freelove Eastland sold land in
Bristol County, together with [son] John Eastland and his
wife Ruth.

     Children (EASTLAND) b. Dartmouth: VIRTUE[6] b. 1729/30; JOHN b.
1732; MARY b. 1733/4; and RELIANCE b. 1736.

References: VR DARTMOUTH.   Bristol Co. PR 12:615(Joseph Eastland).
              Bristol Co. LR 41:143(Freelove Eastland).   RI VR:Ports-
mouth:40, 95.

151   ELIZABETH[5] EASTLAND   (Mary[4] Phinney, Mary[3] Rogers,
Joseph[2], Thomas[1])   b. Plymouth 31 Jan. 1708.

She m. Dartmouth 7 May 1730 AMOS TABER, b. Dartmouth
29 April 1703; d. bef. 20 Dec. 1748; son of Joseph and
Elizabeth (Spooner)\ Taber, and a descendant of Pilgrim
Francis Cooke. Amos m. (1) Dartmouth 1724 Elizabeth Lapham, by whom he had Hannah and Jethro.
    The will of Joseph Taber of Dartmouth, dated 20 Dec.
1748 and probated 7 Feb. 1753, names wife Lydia and my
grandson Antipas Taber, only surviving son of my son Amos
Taber deceased, and Hannah Bennit and Rebecca Taber, sisters of Antipas.

    Children (TABER) b. Dartmouth: ANTIPAS[6] b. ca. 1731, and
REBECCA b. ca. 1733.

References: VR DARTMOUTH. Bristol Co. PR 13:289(Joseph Taber).
             TABER DESC pp. 8, 11[error in b. Amos].

152 MERCY[5] CROCKER (Mercy[4] Phinney, Mary[3] Rogers,
Joseph[2], Thomas[1]) b. prob. Barnstable ca. 1717; d. Falmouth 13 Dec. 1809 ae 92y 9m.
    She m. Falmouth 26 Oct. 1737 EBENEZER HATCH 3rd, b.
Falmouth 22 March 1709; d. Falmouth 8 Oct. 1796 ae 88; son
of Jonathan and Bethiah (Nye) Hatch. He prob. m. (1) Falmouth 1733 Hannah Davis, and had Abigail and Rebecca.
    There are no probate records for Ebenezer or Mercy in
Barnstable County.

    Child (HATCH) b. Falmouth: ELEAZER[6] b. 1740.

References: VR FALMOUTH.

153 JOSIAH[5] MORTON (Reliance[4] Phinney, Mary[3] Rogers,
Joseph[2], Thomas[1]) b. Plymouth 28 Feb. 1709/10; certainly
living 1755, prob. living 11 April 1784.
    He m. Barnstable 18 May 1732 MELATIAH PHINNEY, b.
Barnstable 26 July 1712; certainly living 24 March 1758,
and prob. living 11 April 1784; dau. of Benjamin and Martha
(Crocker) Phinney, and a descendant of Pilgrim Thomas
Rogers. The will of Benjamin Phinney of Barnstable, dated
24 March 1758, names dau. Melatiah, no last name given
(see #38 ii).
    They probably were the Josiah Morton and Melatiah Mor-
ton, wife of Josiah, who signed a Plymouth church petition
11 April 1784.

    Children (MORTON) b. Plymouth: BENJAMIN[6] b. 1733/4, d. 1735;
SETH b. 1735; BENJAMIN b. 1737, d. 1739; RELIANCE b. "1739/4"; MARTHA
b. 1742; JOHN b. 1743/4, d. 1745; MARY b. 1746; JOHN b. 1748; JOSIAH
b. 1750, d. 1751; JOSIAH b. 1752; and SARAH b. 1755.

References: MD 7:210; 11:132; 15:110; 33:124. FINNEY-PHINNEY p. 6.
            PLYMOUTH CH RECS p. 364. Barnstable Co. PR 9:399(Benja-
min Phinney).

154 JAMES[5] MORTON (Reliance[4] Phinney, Mary[3] Rogers,
Joseph[2], Thomas[1]) b. Plymouth 13 May 1714; d. Plympton
bef. Aug. 1745.
      He m. Plympton 16 Sept. 1736 MEHITABLE CHURCHILL, b.
Plympton 5 Nov. 1716; d. there 25 May 1797 ae 80y 6m 9d;
dau. of Samuel and Joanna (Bryant) Churchill. She m. (2)
Halifax 1745 Barnabas Phinney, a descendant of Pilgrim
Thomas Rogers (see #156); m. (3) Plympton 1749 James Harlow, a descendant of Pilgrim Richard Warren; and m. (4)
William Bonney.
      On 29 May 1755 James Morton, minor son of James Morton
late of Plimpton deceased, chose a guardian; and on 5 June
1760 James received his share of the estate.

      Child (MORTON) b. Plympton: JAMES[6] b. 1739.

References: VR PLYMPTON. HALIFAX VR p. 34. Plymouth Co. PR 13:467;
            15:595(James Morton). FINNEY-PHINNEY p. 14. MD 8:152.

155 TEMPERANCE[5] PHINNEY (Benjamin[4], Mary[3] Rogers,
Joseph[2], Thomas[1]) b. Barnstable 28 March 1710; living 24
March 1758, when she was named in her father's will.
      She m. Barnstable 22 Sept. 1733 JAMES FULLER, b.
Barnstable 1 May 1711; living 1753; son of Benjamin Fuller,
and a descendant of Pilgrim Edward Fuller.
      There are no probate records for James or Temperance
at Barnstable County.

      Children (FULLER) b. Barnstable or bp. W. Barnstable: MARTHA[6]
b. 1734; JOHN b. 1735[1735/6]; SILAS bp. 1739; MARY b. 1741; JAMES b.
1743[1743/4]; JOSEPH b. 1745; BENJAMIN b. 1748; and BEERSHEBA bp. 1753.

References: MD 4:227; 32:53; 34:20. FULLER GEN 1:40. FINNEY-PHINNEY
            p. 6. WEST BARNSTABLE CH pp. 248, 249, 250, 252, 253(all
8 children baptized).

156 BARNABAS[5] PHINNEY (Benjamin[4], Mary[3] Rogers, Joseph[2],
Thomas[1]) b. Barnstable 28 March 1715; d. there bef. 20
Jan. 1747.
      He m. Halifax 14 Aug. 1745 MEHITABLE (CHURCHILL) MOR-
TON, b. Plympton 5 Nov. 1716; d. 25 May 1797; dau. of Samuel and Joanna (Bryant) Churchill, and widow of James Morton (see #154). She m. (3) Plympton 1749 James Harlow, a
descendant of Pilgrim Richard Warren; and (4) William Bonney.

Inventory of the estate of Barnabas Phinney late of
Barnstable was taken 20 Jan. 1747. On 3 April 1748 Samuel
Churchill of Plymouth was appointed guardian to Ichabod
Phinney, minor son of Barnabas Phinney late of Barnstable,
and on 9 June 1750 James Harlow was appointed guardian of
Ichabod.

Child (PHINNEY) b. Barnstable: ICHABOD[6] b. 1746.

References: MD 31:83. VR PLYMPTON. HALIFAX VR p. 34. FINNEY-
            PHINNEY p. 14. Barnstable Co. PR 7:67; 8:211(Barnabas
Phinney). Plymouth Co. PR #7698(Ichabod Phinney).

157 ZACCHEUS[5] PHINNEY (Benjamin[4], Mary[3] Rogers, Joseph[2],
Thomas[1]) b. Barnstable 4 Aug. 1720; d. there bef. 1 April
1751.
        He m. Falmouth 3 March 1742/3 SUSANNA DAVIS, b. Fal-
mouth 2 Oct. 1725; living 1751; dau. of Jabez and Anna
(Dimmock) Davis. Susanna m. (2) Falmouth 1763 Theodore
Morse, a descendant of Pilgrim Edward Doty.
        Inventory of the estate of Zaccheus Phinney late of
Barnstable was taken 1 April 1751 and presented to the
court 4 July 1751 by Seth Hamblen and Susanna Phinney.

Children (PHINNEY) b. Barnstable: BENJAMIN[6] b. 1744; TIMOTHY b.
1746; BARNABAS b. 1748; and ZACCHEUS bp. 1751.

References: VR FALMOUTH. MD 31:83; 33:166. FINNEY-PHINNEY p. 14.
            Barnstable Co. PR 8:512(Zaccheus Phinney). WEST BARNS-
TABLE CH p. 247(bp. Zaccheus).

158 SETH[5] PHINNEY (Benjamin[4], Mary[3] Rogers, Joseph[2],
Thomas[1]) b. Barnstable 27 June 1723; living 24 March 1758,
when he was named in his father's will.
        He m. Barnstable 26 Oct. 1748 BETHIAH BUMP (or Bum-
pas), living 10 March 1753; poss. the one b. Barnstable 23
Aug. 1729; dau. of Samuel and Joanna (Warren?) Bump, and
so poss. a descendant of Pilgrim Richard Warren.
        There are no probate records for Seth or Bethia at
Barnstable County.

Children (PHINNEY) b. Barnstable: ZILPAH[6] b. 1749; twin sons b.
and d. 1753.

References: MD 14:256; 31:7; 32:57-58; 33:165. FINNEY-PHINNEY p. 6.

159 THANKFUL[5] PHINNEY (Jonathan[4], Mary[3] Rogers, Joseph[2],
Thomas[1]) b. Barnstable 24 Dec. 1713; living Farmington CT
3 May 1748.

She m. (1) Middleboro 23 Nov. 1738 JOHN HAYFORD (or
Haford) "of Freetown," b. Pembroke 7 Jan. 1712/3; d. Farmington 16 Oct. 1742; son of John and Lydia (Pierce) Hayford.

In 1735 John Hayford of Middleboro laborer sold one-
quarter of all land in Middleboro which my father John
Hayford late of that town died siezed of, reserving to my
mother Lydia Seelings her dower; acknowledged Freetown in
1737.

She m. (2) ----- CARRINGTON.

Administration of the estate of John Haford late of
Farmington deceased was granted to the widow Thankful Haford on 4 Oct. 1743. On 8 Oct. 1744 she was appointed
guardian of "one of the sons of John Haford aged five
years, and of [another son] John Haford aged one year five
months." On 3 May 1748 Thankful Haford alias Carrington,
administratrix, requested distribution of the estate; she
received her thirds, and the rest went to eldest son Joseph
Haford and other son John Haford.

Children (HAYFORD) b. Farmington CT: JOSEPH[6] b. ca. 1739; JOHN
d. 1742; and JOHN b. 1743 "son of John deceased."

References: MD 13:252. VR PEMBROKE. GEN ADV 1:28. Berkley Rec. Bk.
          p. 13. HAYFORD FAM pp. 39, 245. CSL Barbour Index:
Farmington. FINNEY-PHINNEY p. 6. MANWARING 3:410-11.

160 JOSEPH[5] PHINNEY (Jonathan[4], Mary[3] Rogers, Joseph[2],
Thomas[1]) b. Barnstable 24 Jan. 1716; d. Middleboro 13
Aug. 1793 in 77th yr.

He m. Middleboro 18 Sept. 1746 PHEBE COLE "of
Berkley," b. Berkley 26 July 1728; d. Middleboro 10 June
1796; dau. of John and Mary (-----) Cole.

On 23 May 1779 Joseph Phinney of Middleboro sold to
son Jonathan Finney of Middleboro a lot of land excepting
one share I gave my dau. Phebe wife of George Hacket. He
acknowledged the deed 6 March 1780.

Children (PHINNEY) b. Middleboro: JONATHAN[6] b. 1749, and PHEBE.

References: MD 18:78. FINNEY-PHINNEY p. 14. Middleboro Death Re-
          cords by Weston pp. 50-1(town hall). Plymouth Co. LR
60:67(Jos. Phinney).

161 JOSHUA[5] PHINNEY (Jonathan[4], Mary[3] Rogers, Joseph[2],
Thomas[1]) b. 10 Jan. 1721; d. Canterbury CT 4 Oct. 1787.

He m. Canterbury 16 May 1754 LUCY ENSWORTH, bp. Canterbury 17 Sept. 1732; d. there 6 June 1811; dau. of Joseph
and Mary (Cleveland) Ensworth.

Joshua Phinney bought land at Canterbury as early as 26 Feb. 1760. Neither he nor Lucy left probate records at Canterbury.

Children (PHINNEY) b. Canterbury CT: JOSHUA[6] b. 1755; SAMUEL b. 1758; and ASA (or Asael) b. 1761.

References: CSL Barbour Index:Canterbury. CANTERBURY CH REC p. 169.
            FINNEY-PHINNEY p. 14. Canterbury CT LR 7:244(Joshua
Phinney). [Marriage date in town records is in error.]

162 MARY[5] ROGERS (James[4-3], Joseph[2], Thomas[1]) b. Eastham 12 Nov. 1698; d. bef. Nov. 1767 (not among heirs of her brother Isaac).
    She m. Eastham 14 June 1733 JACOB DAVIS, b. Barnstable the last of Oct. 1699; d. after 1741; son of Jabez and Experience (Linnell) Davis. He m. (1) Harwich 1730 Keziah Crosby, by whom he had Keziah.

Children (DAVIS) b. Harwich: MARY[6] b. 1736; SUSANNA b. 1738; and ISAAC b. 1741.

References: MD 4:224; 11:175; 13:70, 71; 17:37.

163 JAMES[5] ROGERS (James[4-3], Joseph[2], Thomas[1]) b. Eastham 2 May 1706; d. East Orleans in Feb. 1759.
    He m. Chatham 21 May 1730 HANNAH GODFREY, b. ca. 1712; d. after 1765; dau. of Jonathan and Mercy (Mayo) Godfrey, and a descendant of Pilgrim William Brewster. The will of Jonathan Godfrey of Chatham yeoman, dated 7 March 1765, names wife Mercy and daughters Hannah Rogers and Mercy Rogers.
    The will of James Rogers of Eastham, made 26 Jan. 1759 and probated 12 March 1759, names wife Hannah and children James, Prince, Samuel, Silvanus, Jonathan, Lydia, Hannah and Susannah, all Rogers.

Children (ROGERS) b. Eastham: LYDIA[6] b. 1731; JAMES b. 1732; SILVANUS b. 1736, d.y.; PRINCE b. 1738; SAMUEL b. prob. 1740; SILVANUS b. 1742; HANNAH b. 1744/5; SUSANNA b. 1748; and JONATHAN b. 1750.

References: MD 17:30-1. NEHGR 126:238-9. Barnstable Co. PR 9:433
            (James Rogers).

164 THOMAS[5] ROGERS (James[4-3], Joseph[2], Thomas[1]) b. Eastham 21 Oct. 1710; d. there bet. 20 Aug. 1778 and 10 June 1779.
    He m. (1) Eastham 2 Dec. 1736 REBECCA HIGGINS, b. ca. 1716; d. bet. 1758 and 1762; dau. of James and Sarah (Mayo)

Higgins, and a descendant of Pilgrim Thomas Rogers (see #46 i).

He m. (2) Yarmouth 29 April 1763 HANNAH CROSBY, b. Yarmouth 13 March 1711/12; d. after 20 Aug. 1778; dau. of Joseph and Mehitable (Miller) Crosby.

The will of Thomas Rogers of Eastham yeoman, dated 20 Aug. 1778 and presented 10 June 1779, gives wife Hannah the things she brought with her, and names two daughters Sarah Twining and Mary Rogers who was single, and sons Thomas and Solomon who were to be executors.

Children (ROGERS) b. Eastham, all by Rebecca: SARAH[6] b. 1738; RUTH b. 1739; THOMAS b. 1742/3; ISAAC b. 1745; STEPHEN b. 1747; SOLOMON b. 1750; MERCY b. 1756; and MARY b. 1758.

References: YARMOUTH VR pp. 13, 167. MD 5:161; 17:145; 27:187. Barnstable Co. PR 20:318(Thomas Rogers). HIGGINS DESC p. 75.

165 JONATHAN[5] COLE (Mary[4] Rogers, James[3], Joseph[2], Thomas[1]) b. Eastham 4 Oct. 1694; d. bef. 30 July 1743 (father's will).

He m. Eastham 15 Feb. 1715/6 HOPE YOUNG, living 30 July 1743; prob. the dau. of Nathaniel and Mercy (Davis) Young who was b. ca. 1697.

There are no probate records for Jonathan or Hope at Barnstable County.

Children (COLE) b. Eastham: ELIZABETH[6] b. 1716; JONATHAN b. 1718; HOPE b. 1720/1; RUTH b. 1722; DORCAS b. 1724; MERCY b. 1726; NATHANIEL b. 1727; and JESSE b. 1732.

References: MD 15:54. Young Gen. by Torrey, MS., NEHG Soc., Boston, pp. 6-7.

166 JOHN[5] COLE (Mary[4] Rogers, James[3], Joseph[2], Thomas[1]) b. Eastham 14 Oct. 1696; d. Eastham bet. 12 Oct. and 6 Nov. 1753.

He m. Eastham 8 Feb. 1726/7 MERCY MAYO, living 12 Oct. 1753; dau. of Theophilus and Rebecca (Smith) Mayo.

The will of John Cole of Eastham yeoman, written 12 Oct. 1753 and proved 6 Nov. 1753, names wife Marcy; son John; land that was formerly my father Mayo's; daughter Rebecca Cole; son John to be executor.

Children (COLE) b. Eastham: JOHN[6] b. 1728/9; THEOPHILUS b. 1730; REBECCA b. 1733; and MERCY b. 1735.

References: MD 16:146. Barnstable Co. PR 9:79-80(John Cole).

167 MARY[5] COLE (Mary[4] Rogers, James[3], Joseph[2], Thomas[1])
b. Eastham 25 Aug. 1698; living 26 Oct. 1751.
     She m. Eastham 30 Jan. 1734[/5] STEPHEN SNOW Jr., b.
Eastham 19 May 1702; d. 1751; son of Micajah and Mary
(Young) Snow, and a descendant of Pilgrim Stephen Hopkins.
     The will of Stephen Snow Jr. of Eastham, drawn 26 Oct.
1751 and proved 3 March 1752, names wife Marah, sons Moses
and Heman, brother David Snow of Eastham executor.

     Children (SNOW) b. Eastham: MOSES[6] b. 1736/7; and HEMAN b. 1738.

References: MD 9:11; 17:144; 28:178. Barnstable Co. PR 8:481(Stephen
             Snow).

168 JAMES[5] COLE (Mary[4] Rogers, James[3], Joseph[2], Thomas[1])
b. Eastham 23 Oct. 1700; living 30 July 1743; poss. d.
Middletown CT 27 May 1760.
     He m. Eastham 9 Feb. 1726/7 MARY COLE.
     They moved to Connecticut sometime after 1734.

     Children (COLE) first four b. Eastham:* UNICE[6] b. 1728; SOLOMON
b. 1730, d. Middletown CT 1761 in 31 yr.; LOIS b. 1731; MARY b. 1733/4,
d. Middletown 1761 in 27 yr.; and JAMES b. ca. 1740, d. Middletown
1761 in 21 yr.

References: MD 16:146; 28:115. CSL Barbour Index:Middletown.

169 JOSHUA[5] COLE (Mary[4] Rogers, James[3], Joseph[2], Thomas[1])
b. Eastham 20 March 1704/5; d. there 1773.
     He m. Eastham 31 Jan. 1733/4 SARAH COLE, b. Eastham
8 March 1710/11; d. there 1 Feb. 1759; dau. of Joseph and
Elizabeth (Cobb) Cole, and a descendant of Pilgrim Stephen
Hopkins.
     On 12 April 1774 administration on the estate of
Joshua Cole late of Eastham deceased, yeoman, was granted to
Joshua Cole of Eastham.

     Children (COLE) b. Eastham: NATHAN[6] b. 1734/5, d. 1772; ELIZA-
BETH b. 1736, d. 1760; RUTH b. 1737, d. 1760; PATIENCE b. 1738/9, d.
1755; SARAH b. 1740; JOSHUA b. 1742, d. 1743; LIDEA b. 1743/4; JOSHUA
b. 1745/6; MARCUS b. 1750; and RACHEL b. 1752, d. 1772.

References: MD 7:184; 16:141; 17:81; 28:176. Barnstable Co. PR 15:69
             (Joshua Cole).

---

*The Mayflower Society has accepted Moses Cole, who m. Middletown CT
1766 Mary White Clark, as son of the above James and Mary (Cole) Cole.
The names of their children, b. Chatham CT (James, Eunice, Solomon and
Moses), would support this. However, Moses may have been the son of
Moses[5] (#41vii), and so a nephew of James[5].

170 JOSEPH[5] COLE   (Mary[4] Rogers, James[3], Joseph[2], Thomas[1])
b. Eastham 13 Oct. 1714; d. bet. 5 Nov. 1794 and 1 April
1796.
     He m. Eastham 2 Dec. 1736 MARY YOUNG, b. Eastham 4
May 1719; d. 1800; dau. of Nathan and Mary (Merrick) Young.
     The will of Joseph Cole of Eastham, drawn 5 Nov. 1794
and accepted 1 Apr. 1796, names wife Mary; dau. Keziah
Harding; son-in-law Joshua Crosby; son James Cole, insane;
grandsons Nathaniel, John and Seth Harding; daughters Mary
Arey and Phebe Goold; granddaughter Deborah Linnell; Meriba
(?) Crosby; grandsons James and Solomon Goold; Joseph,
Joshua and Abiel Crosby.

     Children (COLE) b. Eastham: JAMES[6] b. 1737; MARY b. 1739/40;
PHEBE b. 1741; KEZIA b. 1747; THANKFUL b. 1750; and REBECCA b. 1754.

References: MD 19:104. YOUNG (JOHN) DESC p. 21. BOSTON TRANSCRIPT
             22 June 1910: #1309. Barnstable Co. PR 24:154; 27:436
(Joseph Cole).

171 THANKFUL[5] COLE   (Mary[4] Rogers, James[3], Joseph[2], Thomas[1]) b. Eastham 19 Oct. 1716; living 30 July 1743.
     She m. Eastham 17 Sept. 1741 JOSEPH SNOW Jr., b. East-
ham 11 Oct. 1718; son of Nathaniel and Hannah (Parslow)
Snow, and a descendant of Pilgrim Stephen Hopkins.
     Neither Joseph nor Thankful left probate records in
Barnstable County.

     Child (SNOW) b. Eastham: JOSEPH[6] b. 1743.

References: MD 16:197; 19:186; 29:11.

172 EXPERIENCE[5] YATES   (Abigail[4] Rogers, James[3], Joseph[2],
Thomas[1]) prob. b. Harwich; d. prob. Eastham 3 July 1750.
     She m. int. Harwich and Eastham 4 Sept. 1731 ASA MAYO,
b. Eastham 29 July 1706; d. there in Jan. 1780; son of
Theophilus and Rebecca (Smith) Mayo.

     Children (MAYO) b. Eastham: ABIGAIL[6] b. 1732/3; LIDEA b. 1734;
SARAH b. 1736; DEBORA b. 1738; EXPERIENCE b. 1741; and ASA b. 1743.

References: MD 7:12; 13:59; 17:36; 28:174. MAYO (JOHN) REV pp. 26,
             27.

173 DEBORAH[5] YATES   (Abigail[4] Rogers, James[3], Joseph[2],
Thomas[1]) b. Harwich bet. 1714 and 1720; d. bef. Sept.
1739.
     She m. Harwich 7 Nov. 1734 JEREMIAH NICKERSON of East-
ham, who was living 29 May 1747. He prob. m. (2) Harwich

1739 Rebecca Hurd. It is not certain whether his parents
were William and Hannah (Bassett) Nickerson, or John and
Sarah (Bassett) Nickerson. He is quite possibly the Jeremiah who went to Nova Scotia and d. in Liverpool 1791.

Jeremiah was involved in a land transaction at Harwich 29 May 1747; he left no probate record at Barnstable
County.

Child (NICKERSON) b. Harwich to Jeremiah and Deborah: YEATS[6]
(or Yates) b. 1735.

References: MD 6:85; 9:239-42; 13:70, 148; 23:57. NICKERSON FAM
             1:76. NEHGR 127:50, 122.

174 JOHN[5] YATES (Abigail[4] Rogers, James[3], Joseph[2], Thomas[1]) bp. Harwich 13 April 1718; d. Eastham 1785.

He m. (1) Harwich 26 April 1750 THANKFUL KING, b. Harwich 6 March 1724/5; d. bef. 15 Sept. 1758; dau. of Roger
and Hannah (-----) King. The will of Roger King of Harwich
yeoman, dated 8 March 1768, mentions wife Hannah and heirs
of deceased dau. Thankful Yates.

He m. (2) Harwich 19 Oct. 1758 SARAH CROSBY. No children found of John and Sarah.

On 9 Aug. 1768 John Yates of Harwich yeoman was made
guardian to his minor children Reliance, Mary and John,
grandchildren of Roger King late of Harwich deceased.

Children (YATES) b. Harwich by first wife: RELIANCE[6] b. 1751;
MARY; and JOHN.

References: MD 7:187; 11:173; 33:69; 34:24, 68. Barnstable Co. PR
             13:346; 14:213[2]-215[2](Roger King). HARWICH VR n.p.

175 HANNAH[5] YATES (Abigail[4] Rogers, James[3], Joseph[2], Thomas[1]) prob. b. Harwich 1716-30; living 1767.

She m. Eastham 27 Oct. 1763 EBENEZER HIGGINS, b. East-
ham 21 July 1721; d. after 21 Apr. 1779; son of Samuel and
Mehitable (Phinney) Higgins, and a descendant of Pilgrim
Thomas Rogers (see #82). He m. (1) Eastham 1742 Martha
Burgess, by whom he had Elizabeth, Seth, Hannah, Ebenezer,
Jonathan, Abisha, Susannah, Heman and Thankful.

Ebenezer Higgins served in the Revolution, according
to the DAR PATRIOT INDEX. He left no probate records at
Barnstable County.

Children (HIGGINS) b. Eastham to Ebenezer and Hannah: ELKANAH[6]
b. 1764, and MARTHA b. 1767.

References: MD 9:242; 16:198; 20:94; 32:62. HIGGINS DESC pp. 137-8.
             DAR PATRIOT INDEX p. 327.

176 ELIZABETH[5] MAYO (Elizabeth[4] Higgins, Hannah[3] Rogers, Joseph[2], Thomas[1]) b. Eastham 1 May 1702.
     She m. Eastham 29 Nov. 1739 JOSEPH PADDOCK, b. Yarmouth 8 March 1700; d. after 1743; son of John and Priscilla (Hall) Paddock. Joseph m. (1) Harwich 1725/6 Reliance Stone, by whom he had Hannah, Keziah, Reliance, Thomas and Reliance. He m. (2) int. Yarmouth 1735 Margaret Crosby, by whom he had one dau. b. and d. the same day.
     No probate records at Barnstable or Plymouth Counties for Joseph or Elizabeth.

     Children (PADDOCK) b. Yarmouth to Joseph and Elizabeth: ELIZA-
BETH[6] b. 1740; MARGARET b. 1741; and BATHSHEBA b. 1743/4.

References: MD 5:161; 8:218; 19:103. YARMOUTH VR pp. 12, 69, 156,
     175.

177 THANKFUL[5] MAYO (Elizabeth[4] Higgins, Hannah[3] Rogers, Joseph[2], Thomas[1]) b. Eastham 10 Jan. 1703/4; d. after Nov. 1752.
     She m. (1) Eastham 7 Oct. 1725 THOMAS RICH, b. Eastham 22 Dec. 1702; d. Middletown CT 5 Sept. 1750; son of Thomas and Mercy (Knowles) Rich.
     On 13 Feb. 1746/7 Thomas Rich of Middletown bricklayer sold land bounded by that of his brother John (see #184). On 6 Nov. 1750 Thankful Rich of Middletown gave her bond as administratrix of the estate of her husband Thomas dec.
     She prob. m. (2) Middletown CT 2 Nov. 1752 LEMUEL LEE, b. Guilford CT 1 Dec. 1693; living Middletown 1752; son of Edward and Abigail (Steevens) Lee. He m. (1) Guilford 1715/6 Mary Burnet, and he m. (2) Middletown 172(?) Mary West. He had seven children by his first two wives, none by Thankful.

     Children (RICH) first five b. Eastham, other four b. Middletown
CT: AMOS[6] b. 1726; ELIZABETH b. 1728; MERCY b. 1731; BETHIAH b. 1733;
PETER b. 1735; BATHSHEBA b. 1737/8; SARAH b. 1739/40; THOMAS b. 1744;
and ELIAKIM b. 1747.

References: MD 7:236; 16:74, 75. Hartford CT PR #4467(Thomas Rich).
     CSL Barbour Index:Middletown. STEEVENS DESC pp. 34, 101.
MAYO (JOHN) REV p. 22.

178 BATHSHEBA[5] MAYO (Elizabeth[4] Higgins, Hannah[3] Rogers, Joseph[2], Thomas[1]) b. Eastham 27 April 1705; d. after 17 Nov. 1740.
     She m. Boston 8 June 1732 (int. Eastham 1 March 1731/2) JAMES ALLEN of Boston who d. after 1740; poss. either b. Boston 14 Nov. 1705 to Samuel and Lydia, or b. 26 Feb. 1706 to John and Elizabeth (Edwards) Allen.

On 27 Sept. 1737 and 21 Aug. 1738 James Allen of Boston, tailor, mortgaged his dwelling house and land in Boston, with wife Bathsheba giving up her dower.

James and Bathsheba left no probate records in Boston. (He was not the James Allen late of Boston tailor deceased, whose widow Mary gave bond as administratrix on his estate in 1763, for her account in 1767 mentions children Samuel and Joseph, apparently the ones born 1743 and 1749 to James and Mary (Adams) Allen.)

Children (ALLEN) b. Boston: SARAH[6] b. 1733; JAMES b. 1736; and JOSHUA b. 1740.

References: MD 28:175. BOSTON VR 9:235; 24:39, 45, 210, 224, 239, 248, 269; 28:175, 273, 345. Suffolk Co. PR 61:409; 65:577, 580(James Allen). Suffolk Co. LR 55:71; 57:53(James Allen).

179 MERCY[5] MAYO (Elizabeth[4] Higgins, Hannah[3] Rogers, Joseph[2], Thomas[1]) b. Eastham 27 Feb. 1718/9.

She m. Eastham 28 Oct. 1736 ELKANAH YOUNG, b. Eastham 17 June 1711; d. Eastham bef. 1 March 1763; son of Nathan and Rebecca (Shaw) Young.

On 1 March 1763 Joseph Cole Jr. of Eastham was appointed guardian to Bathsheba, Elkanah, Thomas and Deborah, the children of Elkanah Young late of Eastham dec.

Children (YOUNG) b. Eastham: BATHSHEBA[6]; ELKANAH b. 1745; THOMAS; and DEBORAH.

References: MD 8:14; 17:146. Barnstable Co. PR 11:226 1/2(Elkanah Young). YOUNG (JOHN) DESC pp. 6, 43, 59.

180 PHEBE[5] YOUNG (Mary[4] Higgins, Hannah[3] Rogers, Joseph[2], Thomas[1]) b. Eastham 3 June 1707; d. after 24 Feb. 1787.

She m. (1) Truro 18 Feb. 1724/5 JUDAH DYER, b. Barnstable in April 1701; d. Truro 19 June 1742 in 41st yr.; son of William and Mary (Taylor) Dyer.

On 20 Oct. 1742 Phebe Dier of Truro widow was appointed administratrix on the estate of her husband Judah Dier of Truro blacksmith deceased; and on 10 Nov. 1742 Ebenezer Dyer was appointed guardian of Phebe ae ca. 3 yrs., Judah ca. 13 1/2 yrs. and Elijah ca. 16 yrs., children of Judah deceased. On 27 Dec. 1743 the account of Phebe Dier now Atwood, administratrix to Judah Dier, showed the estate divided among the widow, eldest son Elijah, son Judah and dau. Phebe.

She m. (2) bef. 27 Dec. 1743 NATHANIEL ATWOOD, b. Truro 20 July 1711; d. bef. 27 Dec. 1774; son of Michael and Prudence (-----)(Rogers) Atwood. [Prudence m. (1) Joseph[4] Rogers (#14).] Nathaniel left no probate records. He m. (1) Truro 1737/8 Joanna Harding, by whom he had son Nathaniel.

She m. (3) Truro 27 Dec. 1774 JOSHUA KNOWLES, b. Eastham 6 July 1696; d. there 27 May 1786; son of John and Mary
(Sears) Knowles. He m. (1) Sarah Paine, by whom he had
several children; but he had none by Phebe.
The will of Joshua Knowles of Eastham, advanced in
age, dated 2 Nov. 1778, presented 26 June 1786, names wife
Phebe and his heirs, with his son Simeon Knowles executor.
On 24 Feb. 1787 a division of the estate set off property
to widow Phebe Knowles and the heirs of Joshua.

Children (DYER) b. Truro to Judah and Phebe: ELIJAH[6] b. 1726;
JUDAH b. 1729; ISAAC bp. 1731/2; and PHEBE b. 1739.

Children (ATWOOD) b. Truro to Nathaniel and Phebe: JOSHUA[6] b.
1744/5, and JOSEPH b. 1748.

References: MD 4:225; 8:89; 9:177, 244; 10:42; 11:20; 12:235; 25:109-
14. Barnstable Co. PR 6:189-192; 8:287-8(Judah Dyer).
TRURO VR pp. 23, 35, 39, 55, 71, 108. HIGGINS DESC p. 49. YOUNG
(JOHN) DESC p. 19.

181 SARAH[5] YOUNG (Mary[4] Higgins, Hannah[3] Rogers, Joseph[2],
Thomas[1]) b. Truro 2 Feb. 1709/10; living 2 June 1750.
She m. Truro 18 June 1730 JOSHUA COWELL "both of
Truro"; son of Edward and Rebecca (Broughton) Cowell.
Neither Joshua nor Sarah left any probate records in
Barnstable Co.

Children (COWELL) first four b. Truro: SARAH[6] b. 1731; JOHN b.
1733; RUTH bp. Truro 1735; JOSHUA b. 1738, bp. Harwich 1738; and
EDWARD bp. Harwich 1740.

References: TRURO VR pp. 16, 23. MD 7:96, 146; 9:177, 178; 10:42,
43, 150. HIGGINS DESC p. 49. YOUNG (JOHN) DESC p. 19.

182 SAMUEL[5] YOUNG (Mary[4] Higgins, Hannah[3] Rogers, Jos-
eph[2], Thomas[1]) b. Truro 11 Dec. 1712; d. Middle Haddam CT
bef. 25 Oct. 1752.
He m. ca. 1742 REBECCA BRAINERD, b. Haddam CT 15 Aug.
1722; d. after 1754; dau. of James and Anna (Risley) Brainerd. She m. (2) Middletown CT 1754 Moses Wheeler of
Chatham CT.
On 6 March 1740 Samuel Young bought land in Middle
Haddam. Inventory of the estate of Samuel Young late of
Middletown deceased was taken 25 Oct. 1752. Debts paid by
Rebecca Young, administratrix on the estate, included
charges for bringing up "One child that was three years two
months old, and one that was three months old when their
father died." On 17 April 1754 distribution was made to
Mrs. Rebekah Young and to Samuel, James, Elizabeth, Asaph
and Rebekah Young.

Children (YOUNG) bp. E. Hampton CT: SAMUEL[6] bp. 1745; JAMES bp. 1745; ELIZABETH bp. 1747; ASAPH bp. 1749; and REBECCA bp. 1752.

References: CSL Barbour Index: Middletown, E. Hampton. HIGGINS DESC
             p. 49. BRAINERD FAM p. 65. NYGBR 35:265. Middletown CT
PR #3989(Samuel Young).

183 MARY[5] YOUNG (Mary[4] Higgins, Hannah[3] Rogers, Joseph[2], Thomas[1]) b. Truro 25 March 1715; d. there 19 Sept. 1788.
     She m. (1) Truro 28 May 1734 REUBEN KELLEY (or O'Kelley or Killey), b. Yarmouth 29 Jan. 1709/10; d. bef. 8 Nov. 1744; son of Benjamin and Mary (Lambert) O'Kelley.
     On 8 Nov. 1744 Mary Killey of Truro widow was appointed administratrix of the estate of Reuben Killey of Eastham mariner deceased. Mary's account mentioned a child (unnamed) she had by the deceased.
     She m. (2) Truro 30 Nov. 1744 ROBERT NEWCOMB, b. Truro 21 June 1722; d. 13 May 1802; son of Andrew and Mercy (Oldham) Newcomb, and a descendant of Pilgrim Henry Samson.
     Neither Mary nor Robert Newcomb left probate records in Barnstable Co.

     Child (KELLEY) b. Truro to Reuben and Mary: REUBEN[6] b. 1735.

     Children (NEWCOMB)* b. Truro to Robert and Mary: DAVID b. 1747; ABIGAIL b. 1749; MARY b. 1752; and ROBERT b. 1759.

References: TRURO VR pp. 8, 49, 50, 64. YARMOUTH VR 1:14. YOUNG
             (JOHN) DESC p. 20. NEWCOMB GEN pp. 58, 102. HIGGINS
DESC p. 49. Barnstable Co. PR 6:383, 392(Reuben Killey).

184 LYDIA[5] YOUNG (Mary[4] Higgins, Hannah[3] Rogers, Joseph[2], Thomas[1]) b. Truro 8 Sept. 1718; d. Marlboro CT 11 Aug. 1809.
     She m. Truro 13 Oct. 1737 JOHN RICH "of Provincetown," b. Eastham 14 Sept. 1714; d. Middle Haddam CT 6 Aug. 1777; son of Thomas and Mercy (Knowles) Rich.
     John was a member of a committee in Truro in Oct. 1755. Although his children, all except "Bette," are recorded in Middletown CT, it appears unlikely he moved there before 1756. He was certainly there on 23 Dec. 1766 when he bought land in Middle Haddam CT.
     The will of John Rich of Chatham CT, drawn 6 May 1776 and sworn 20 Sept. 1777, names wife Liddea; sons Samuel (not well), James, John and Isaac; two daughters Mary and Elizabeth (no last names); son Isaac to be executor.

---

*No evidence was found confirming the children Thomas, John and Nancy claimed in NEWCOMB GEN.

Children (RICH) all recorded Middletown CT, except Elizabeth, but prob. b. Truro: ISAAC[6] b. 1738, d. 1752; JAMES b. 1741; MARY b. 1743; SAMUEL b. 1747; ELIZABETH bp. Truro 1751; JOHN b. 1751; and ISAAC b. 1756.

References: TRURO VR p. 9. MD 7:236; 26:122, 162. HIGGINS DESC p. 49. AUSTIN-RICH GEN pp. 24-5. Middletown CT PR #2730 (John Rich). Chatham CT LR 2:2(John Rich). CSL Barbour Index:Middletown.

185 HANNAH[5] YOUNG (Mary[4] Higgins, Hannah[3] Rogers, Joseph[2], Thomas[1]) b. Truro 12 Feb. 1719/20; living 1757.
      She m. Killingworth CT 13 June 1743 REUBEN BUELL, b. Killingworth 24 Aug. 1720; d. Clinton CT 16 Sept. 1802; son of Samuel and Abigail (Crittenden) Buell. Reuben m. (2) Haddam CT 1779 widow Anne Porter, who may have been the mother of his dau. Hannah.
      The will of Reuben Buell of Killingworth in the County of Middlesex CT in 80th year of age, dated 26 Dec. 1799 and sworn to 5 Oct. 1802, bequeathed to wife Anna the furniture she brought with her to me; sons Azariah, Reuben, Joseph, and James; daughters Elizabeth and Hannah (no last names); sons Azariah and James executors.

      Children (BUELL) b. Killingworth: AZARIAH[6] b. 1743/4; REUBEN b. 1746, d. 1751; ELIZABETH b. 1748, d. 1751; JOSEPH b. and d. 1751; REUBEN b. 1752; JAMES b. 1757; ELIZABETH; JOSEPH; and poss. HANNAH.

References: STEEVENS GEN p. 140. CT MARR 1:49. HIGGINS DESC p. 49 [it was her sister Lydia, not Hannah, who m. Reuben O'Kelley].

186 ELIZABETH[5] YOUNG (Mary[4] Higgins, Hannah[3] Rogers, Joseph[2], Thomas[1]) b. Truro 17 Sept. 1723; d. after 2 May 1760.
      She m. Truro 2 June 1743 FRANCIS SMALLEY 3d, b. Truro 30 March 1721; d. after 1759; son of Daniel and Sarah (-----) Smalley.

      Children (SMALLEY) b. Truro: JAMES[6] b. 1743/4; MARY b. 1746/7; ELIZABETH b. 1749; DANIEL b. 1751, d.y.; DANIEL b. 1755; and FRANCIS b. 1760.

References: TRURO VR p. 53, 62, 63. HIGGINS DESC p. 49. SMALL DESC p. 136.

187 JAMES[5] YOUNG (Mary[4] Higgins, Hannah[3] Rogers, Joseph[2], Thomas[1]) b. Truro 30 May 1725; d. bef. 11 May 1761.

He m. int. Falmouth (now Portland) ME 24 Aug. 1751 SARAH WEBBER, b. Provincetown 19 Jan. 1731; d. Hallowell ME after 1763; dau. of "Christoph [and] Mary (-----) Weebr." She m. (2) Truro 1761 Shubael Hinckley of Brunswick ME, son of Samuel and Mary (Freeman) Hinckley, and a descendant of Pilgrim William Brewster.

James Young left no probate records at Barnstable County.

Children (YOUNG) b. Truro: JAMES[6] b. 1751/2; SAMUEL b. 1753; JOHN b. 1756; and CHRISTOPHER b. 1758.

References: TRURO VR pp. 76, 91. MD 9:102. YOUNG (JOHN) DESC p. 43.
            HIGGINS DESC p. 49. Reminiscences and genealogy of the
Joel Hinkley and Amos Hackett Fams. by M. R. Carver and K. H. Bowers,
1971, typescript, Maine Hist. Soc., Portland.

188 REBECCA[5] HURD (Rebecca[4] Higgins, Hannah[3] Rogers, Joseph[2], Thomas[1]) b. ca. 1718; d. after 1759.

She m. (1) E. Hampton CT 10 July 1744 JAMES BRAINERD, b. Haddam CT 9 July 1725; d. 16 April 1749; son of James and Anne (Risley) Brainerd. There are no probate records for James Brainerd in CT, and no children were found.

She m. (2) Colchester CT 4 Sept. 1752 JOHN ROWLEY (or Rowlee), b. Colchester CT 7 July 1727; son of John and Deborah (Fuller) Rowley, and a descendant of Pilgrim Edward Fuller through his father.*

Children (ROWLEY) b. Colchester CT to John and Rebecca: JOSEPH[6] b. 1753; MINDWELL b. 1755; MARY b. 1757; and SETH b. 1759.

References: CSL Barbour Index:Colchester, E. Hampton, Haddam. FULLER
            GEN 1:36. NYGBR 37:6, 205. BRAINERD FAM p. 65. HIGGINS
DESC p. 49.

189 JACOB[5] HURD (Rebecca[4] Higgins, Hannah[3] Rogers, Joseph[2], Thomas[1]) b. Harwich 17 Dec. 1720; d. Middle Haddam CT in 1811 in his 91st yr.

He m. Middletown CT 28 Feb. 1745/6 THANKFUL HURLBURT, b. Middletown CT 26 April 1727; d. in 1814 ae 87; dau. of David and Mary (-----) Hurlburt.

On 23 April 1778 Jacob Hurd of Chatham CT bought land there. Neither he nor Thankful left probate records in CT.

Children (HURD) b. Middletown CT: RACHEL[6] b. 1748; JOSEPH b. 1751; ELIZABETH b. 1753; REBECCA b. 1755; MARY b. 1757; BENJAMIN b. 1759; JACOB b. 1762; JESSE b. 1765; and SARAH b. 1773.

---

*Descent from Pilgrim Edward Fuller through his mother, Deborah Fuller, has been disproved.

References: HIGGINS DESC p. 50. HURLBUT GEN pp. 28, 410. CSL Barbour Index:Middletown.

190 ELIZABETH[5] HURD (Rebecca[4] Higgins, Hannah[3] Rogers,
Joseph[2], Thomas[1]) b. prob. Harwich ca. 1722.
     She m. E. Haddam CT 21 April 1743 ROBINSON (or Robert-
son) WILLIAMS, b. E. Hampton CT 24 May 1715; son of Charles
and Mary (Robinson) Williams. He m. (1) E. Hampton 1741
Abigail Ackley. No probate or gravestone records found for
him in CT.

     Children (WILLIAMS) b. E. Haddam CT: JONATHAN[6] b. 1743/4; ABI-
GAIL b. 1745, d. 1746; SOLOMON b. 1748; LYDIA b. 1750; MARY b. 1753;
ROBINSON b. 1755; ELIZABETH b. 1758; RACHEL b. 1761; and EUNICE b.
1763.

References: CSL Barbour Index:East Haddam, East Hampton.

191 JAMES[5] HIGGINS (James[4], Hannah[3] Rogers, Joseph[2],
Thomas[1]) b. prob. Eastham ca. 1718; d. bef. 13 Aug. 1756.
     He m. Yarmouth 6 Oct. 1742 SARAH SEARS, b. Yarmouth
10 March 1720/1; living 16 May 1804; dau. of Ebenezer and
Sarah (Hawes) Sears. She m. (2) Eastham 1757 Thomas Mayo
of Harwich.
     James Higgins left no probate record at Barnstable
County, but on 16 May 1804 Isaac Freeman and wife Hannah,
and Hezekiah Higgins, all of Orleans, sold land formerly
of their father James Higgins, with widow Sarah Mayo giving up her dower rights.

     Children (HIGGINS) b. Eastham to James and Sarah: HANNAH[6] b.
1744; and HEZEKIAH b. 1750.

References: MD 19:15; 20:158; 27:105; 29:13. YARMOUTH VR pp. 49, 152.
          HIGGINS DESC p. 103. SEARS DESC p. 80. MAYO (JOHN) REV
pp. 39, 47.

192 HANNAH[5] HIGGINS (James[4], Hannah[3] Rogers, Joseph[2],
Thomas[1]) prob. b. Eastham ca. 1720; d. bef. 16 Apr. 1774.
     She m. Eastham 7 Feb. 1739/40 BENJAMIN HIGGINS, b.
Eastham 1 March 1715/6; d. there 17 Sept. 1777; son of
Benjamin and Sarah (Freeman) Higgins. He m. (2) Yarmouth
1774 Margery (Homer) Sears.
     The will of Benjamin Higgins of Eastham laborer,
dated 17 Sept. 1777, presented 15 Oct. 1777, names wife
Margret (*sic*) to have estate she brought with her; son Lot,
daughter-in-law [step-daughter] Susanna Sears; all my children: Edman, Benjamin, Lot, Elisha and Sarah; my two
grandchildren Loues and Exsperance Higgins; executor to be
son Lot.

Children (HIGGINS) b. Eastham to Benjamin and Hannah: EDMUND[6] b. 1740; BENJAMIN b. 1743; LOT b. 1745/6; ELISHA b. 1750; and SARAH.

References: YARMOUTH VR 1:317.   MD 16:148; 19:104; 29:10. HIGGINS
              DESC p. 126. Barnstable Co. PR 20:9(Benj. Higgins).

193 DORCAS[5] HIGGINS (James[4], Hannah[3] Rogers, Joseph[2], Thomas[1]) b. prob. Eastham 1731; living 6 Dec. 1775, according to her father's will.
    She m. Eastham 3 Oct. 1751 ISAAC TAYLOR of Pembroke, prob. the one b. Pembroke 1 May 1725; son of Isaac and Ruth (Green) Taylor.
    A survey of vital, land and probate records for Isaac Taylor at Pembroke seems to show that Isaac Taylor who m. Ruth Green at Scituate in 1717/18, and had children at Scituate and Pembroke, is the one who m. Jerusha Tilden at Marshfield in 1728, and had more children at Pembroke (although the VR say John was Ruth's son). The will of Isaac Taylor of Pembroke cordwainer, made 22 Feb. 1763 and presented 8 Jan. 1767, names wife Jerusha and two grand-children, Sarah and Ruth Taylor, children of son Isaac deceased. Sarah and Ruth were baptized at Pembroke 31 Aug. 1775 "daughters of Isaac Jr." He was not the Isaac Jr. who died at Yarmouth 20 July 1755 and left a will; but widow Dorcas Taylor, who was a member of the Orleans church in 1774 and died at Eastham in 1805, may have been Dorcas (Higgins) Taylor.

    Children (TAYLOR) b. bet. 1751 and 1755: SARAH[6], and RUTH.

References: MD 8:147; 10:167; 24:191; 28:79. VR PEMBROKE, SCITUATE.
             MARSHFIELD VR p. 145. Plymouth Co. PR 19:427(Isaac
Taylor). Plymouth Co. LR 33:77; 38:174; 39:259; 46:223; 50:46; 55:173
(Isaac Taylor). HIGGINS DESC p. 75.

194 JAMES[5] MITCHELL (Sarah[4] Higgins, Hannah[3] Rogers, Joseph[2], Thomas[1]) b. Chatham 4 Nov. 1718; d. after 1766.
    He m. Eastham 11 Jan. 1739/40 HANNAH HIGGINS, living 1759.
    Neither James nor Hannah left probate or land records at Barnstable, Bristol or Plymouth counties.

    Children (MITCHELL) b. Dartmouth: ELCANAH[6] b. 1740; JAMES b. 1745; HANNAH b. 1748; JONATHAN b. 1751; HALLET b. 1756; and SARAH b. 1759.

References: VR DARTMOUTH. HIGGINS SUP p. 8. MD 19:103.

195 TABITHA[5] MITCHELL (Sarah[4] Higgins, Hannah[3] Rogers,
Joseph[2], Thomas[1]) b. Chatham 19 July 1720; d. after 1766.
    She m. Dartmouth 15 March 1737/8 JOSEPH BURGESS (or
Barges) of Rochester, d. after 1766; poss. the one b.
Rochester 15 Dec. 1710, son of Benjamin and Priscilla
(Gatchel) Burges.
    Neither Joseph nor Tabitha left probate records at
Barnstable, Plymouth or Bristol counties, or land records
at Bristol County.

    Children (BURGESS) b. Dartmouth: ELIZABETH[6] b. 1738; BENJAMIN
b. 1740; LUTHER b. 1742/3; JOSEPH b. 1745; PHEBE b. 1747; TABITHA b.
1749; THOMAS b. 1752; PATIENCE b. 1760; and RUTH b. 1766.

References: VR DARTMOUTH, ROCHESTER. HIGGINS SUP p. 8.

196 MERCY[5] MITCHELL (Sarah[4] Higgins, Hannah[3] Rogers,
Joseph[2], Thomas[1]) b. Chatham 4 May 1722; d. Dartmouth 6
Feb. 1802 in 79th yr.
    She m. Dartmouth 15 Dec. 1743 NATHANIEL JENNEY, b.
Dartmouth 3 Oct. 1720; d. there 13 Jan. 1802 in 82nd yr.;
son of Lettice and Desire (Blackwell) Jenney, and a descen-
dant of Pilgrim Richard Warren. The DAR PATRIOT INDEX says
Nathaniel was a private in the Revolution.
    The will of Nathaniel Jenney of New Bedford yeoman,
dated 2 Nov. 1793 and presented 4 May 1802, names wife
Mercy, sons Israel and Weston, daughters Sarah Kemton,
Elizabeth Hathaway, Rebecca Jenne, Pernel Whitfield and
Lydia Hammond; executor son Weston.

    Children (JENNE) b. Dartmouth: SARAH[6] b. 1744; AGNES b. 1747,
d. 1763; ELIZABETH b. 1749/50; REBECCA b. 1752; PERNAL; ISRAEL; LYDIA;
and WESTON bp. 1768.

References: VR DARTMOUTH. HIGGINS SUP p. 8. Bristol Co. PR 39:88
        (Nathaniel Jenney). DAR PATRIOT INDEX p. 367. Jenney
Fam pp. 69-70.

197 WILLIAM[5] MITCHELL (Sarah[4] Higgins, Hannah[3] Rogers,
Joseph[2], Thomas[1]) b. Chatham 31 June 1725; d. Dartmouth
5 Feb. 1793 in 68th yr.
    He m. Dartmouth int. 10 Feb. 1745 PERNAL JENNEY, b.
Dartmouth 1 Sept. 1722; d. there 21 May 1784 in 60th yr.;
dau. of Lettice and Desire (Blackwell) Jenney, and a descendant of Pilgrim Richard Warren.
    The will of William Mitchell of New Bedford yeoman,
dated 23 Jan. 1793 and presented 7 May 1793, names son
David, and daughter Ruth Studson; grandson Seth Mitchell;
housekeeper Abigail Chubbuck; grandsons William Mitchell,
and William and Mitchell Studson, all under 21;

granddaughters Pernal and Elizabeth Studson; son David executor.

       Children (MITCHELL) b. Dartmouth: DAVID[6] b. 1748/9, and RUTH b. 1752.

References: VR DARTMOUTH. HIGGINS SUP p. 9. Bristol Co. PR 32:188
          (Wm. Mitchell). Jenney Fam pp. 57-9.

198 BETTY[5] MITCHELL (Sarah[4] Higgins, Hannah[3] Rogers,
Joseph[2], Thomas[1]) b. Dartmouth 22 March 1741; living 26
March 1788.
       She m. int. Plymouth and Dartmouth 22 Sept. 1759
WILLIAM RYDER Jr., b. Plymouth 25 May 1732; living 26 March
1788; son of Benjamin and Hannah (Stephens) Rider.
       On 26 March 1788 William Rider of Plymouth yeoman sold
land in Plymouth willed to him by his father Benjamin in
1773. Wife Betty released her rights.
       No Plymouth County probates were found for William or
Betty, or for their son Hallett.

       Child (RYDER) b. Plymouth: HALLETT[6] b. 1760.

References: MD 13:169; 20:70; 25:188. Plymouth VR 2:37. Plymouth Co.
          PR 60:121(Benj. Ryder). Plymouth Co. LR 24:32(William
Ryder).

199 HANNAH[5] BRADFORD (Hannah[4] Rogers, John[3-2], Thomas[1])
b. Plymouth 14 Feb. 1689/90; d. Berkley 28 Jan. 1772.
       She m. Duxbury 16 June 1709 NATHANIEL GILBERT, b.
Taunton 19 July 1683; d. Berkley 17 Aug. 1765; son of
Thomas Gilbert.
       The will of Nathaniel Gilbert of Berkley gentleman,
advanced to old age, dated 2 June 1757 and proved 11 Sept.
1765, names wife Hannah; eldest son Thomas; father Mr.
Thomas Gilbert; grandson Nathaniel Gilbert, son of son
Nathaniel late of Taunton deceased; land in Taunton where
I have buried two of my daughters; grandson George Gilbert;
son Samuel Gilbert to have my mansion house in Berkley;
children of late daughter Hannah Smith wife of Ebenezer
deceased: Lemuel, John, Ebenezer and Mary Smith; Sibel
wife of Doget (*sic*) my granddaughter; Hannah and Abigail,
daughters of my daughter Hannah; daughter Mary Godfrey of
Norton; daughter Welthia Hathaway wife of Ebenezer Jr.;
son Thomas administrator.

       Children (GILBERT) prob. b. Taunton:* NATHANIEL[6] b. ca. 1710;
HANNAH b. 1712; THOMAS b. ca. 1714; MARY b. ca. 1717; SAMUEL; WELTHIA
b. ca. 1720; and a dau. who d. bef. 1757.

The William Bradford Family will give greater detail and one further
generation.

References: VR DUXBURY, TAUNTON.   MD 2:18; 11:23; 21:117-120.   BRAD-
FORD DESC p. 26.

200 GERSHOM[5] BRADFORD (Hannah[4] Rogers, John[3-2], Thomas[1])
b. Plymouth 21 Dec. 1691; d. Bristol RI 4 April 1757 ae
66.
        He m. (2) Plymouth 23 Oct. 1716 PRISCILLA WISWALL, b.
Duxbury 25 July 1690; d. Bristol RI 12 Sept. 1780 in 90th
yr.; dau. of Ichabod and Priscilla (Pabodie) Wiswall, and
a descendant of Pilgrim John Alden.
        On 2 May 1757 Daniel Bradford was appointed adminis-
trator on the estate of his father Capt. Gershom Bradford
late of Bristol deceased. The Plymouth County land records
show that a meadow in Plympton, once owned by Samuel Bradford and then belonging to heirs of Gershom Bradford of
Bristol RI gent. deceased, was divided into eight parts,
with four of his children selling their shares: Alexander
Bradford of Stonington CT gent. sold his share 4 Nov. 1763;
Solomon Bradford of Bristol RI laborer sold his share to
Joseph Nash 2 July 1762; Daniel Bradford of Bristol Esq.
sold his to Joseph Nash 25 May 1769; and Joseph Nash
of Providence RI and wife Hopestill sold half a lot [four
shares] of land that was our father's Capt. Gershom Bradford of Bristol on 9 June 1763.

        Children (BRADORD) prob. b. Plymouth:* SOLOMON[6], ALEXANDER,
DANIEL, and HOPESTILL, and poss. PRISCILLA, NOAH, RACHEL, JOB, and
JEREMIAH.

        References: RI VR: Bristol p. 119(death yr. and age wrong). MD 2:18;
                14:38; 19:1. NEHGR 110:44-50. BRADFORD DESC p. 26.
Bristol RI PR 1:243, 247(Gershom Bradford). Plymouth Co. LR 48:166
(Alex. Bradford); 49:34(Solomon & Daniel Bradford & Jos. Nash).

201 PEREZ[5] BRADFORD (Hannah[4] Rogers, John[3-2], Thomas[1])
b. Plymouth 28 Dec. 1694; d. Attleboro 19 June 1746.
        He m. Dedham 14 April 1720 ABIGAIL BELCHER, b. Dedham
23 Aug. 1695; d. Attleboro 15 Nov. 1746; dau. of Joseph
and Abigail (Thompson) Belcher.
        The will of Perez Bradford of Attleboro Esq., drawn
12 June 1746 and proved 5 Aug. 1746, names wife Abigail;
eldest son Perez under 21; sons Joel, George, John and
Joseph; dau. Abigail Lee wife of Samuel Jr.; daus. Hannah,
Elizabeth and Mary Bradford. Abigail was to be executrix.

        Children (BRADFORD) first b. Dedham, others b. Swansea or bp.
Milton:* ABIGAIL[6] b. 1721; HANNAH; ELIZABETH; PEREZ bp. 1728/9; JOEL
bp. 1730; GEORGE bp. 1732; JOHN b. 1734; JOSEPH b. 1737; and MARY.

---

*The William Bradford Family will give greater detail and one further
generation.

References: MD 2:18. VR MILTON. SWANSEA VR. DEDHAM VR pp. 46, 48.
            Bristol Co. PR 11:168-170(Perez Bradford).

202 ELIZABETH[5] BRADFORD (Hannah[4] Rogers, John[3-2], Thomas[1]) b. Plymouth 15 Dec. 1696; d. Norwich or Stonington
CT 10 May 1777.
        She m. (1) Hartford CT 10 Jan. 1716/7 CHARLES WHITING
(or Whiton), b. Hartford 5 July 1692; d. Montville CT 7
March 1738; son of William and Mary (Allyn) Whiting.
        On 11 Dec. 1738 Elizabeth Whiting petitioned the
court to appoint Joseph Bradford Jr. administrator on the
estate of Charles Whiting late of New London deceased.
        She "of New London" m. (2) Stonington CT 13 March
1739 JOHN NOYES, b. Stonington 13 Jan. 1685; d. there 17
Sept. 1751; son of James and Dorothy (Stanton) Noyes. He
m. (1) 1714/15 Mary Gallup, by whom he had eight children.
        Proof that Elizabeth (Bradford) Whiting took a second
husband named Noyes is found in a Plymouth County deed
dated 9 Oct. 1780 in which the heirs of Elizabeth Noyes deceased sold land in Kingston which had been given to her
and [her sisters] Jerusha Gay, Hannah Gilbert, and Wealthea
Lane by their grandmother Hannah Bradford late of Hingham
deceased. These heirs were: Mary Gardner of Hingham;
Gamaliel Whiting of Great Barrington; Sibel Noyes of Gro-
ton CT; [heirs of John Whiting] James Houghton and wife
Philena, Elizabeth Leffingwell, Mary Whiting and James
Woolf Whiting of Norwich; William B. Whiting of New Canaan,
Albany Co. NY; Elizabeth Goodrich of Hebron CT; Honor Beld-
ing of Wethersfield CT, administratrix to Charles Whiting
late of Norwich deceased; Ebenezer Whiting; and Dorothy
Noyes of Norwich.
        A Suffolk probate record gives receipts dated 1787,
where most of the above heirs of Elizabeth Noyes received
payment for sale of land in that county given them under
Hannah's will. Distribution was held up until Martin Gay,
a staunch Loyalist who left Boston for Nova Scotia in 1776,
returned for a visit in 1787.

        Children (WHITING) prob. b. New London (now Montville) CT:*
MARY[6] b. 1717; JOHN b. 1719; SYBIL b. 1722; twins CHARLES and ELIZA-
BETH b. 1725; GAMALIEL b. 1727; WILLIAM BRADFORD b. 1731; BERNICE b.
1733; and EBENEZER b. 1735.

        Child (NOYES) b. Stonington CT: DOROTHY b. 1740.

References: MD 2:18. BRADFORD DESC p. 27. HARTFORD CT FAMS pp. 677-
             9. STONINGTON CT HIST p. 489. MONTVILLE CT HIST pp. 715-
6. CSL Barbour Index: Hartford, New London, Stonington. CT PR New
London #5691(Chas. Whiting). Suffolk Co. PR #12505(Hannah Bradford).
Plymouth Co. LR 60:112(Mary Gardner et al.).

---

*The William Bradford Family will give greater detail and one further
generation.

203 JERUSHA[5] BRADFORD (Hannah[4] Rogers, John[3-2], Thomas[1])
b. Plymouth 10 March 1699; d. Hingham 19 Aug. 1783.
      She m. Duxbury 13 Nov. 1719 Rev. EBENEZER GAY, b.
Dedham 15 Aug. 1696; d. Hingham 18 March 1787 ae 91;
son of Nathaniel and Lydia (Starr) Gay.
      He was graduated from Harvard College in 1714, and
began preaching at Hingham in 1717. On 30 Sept. 1760 Ebenezer Gay of Hingham and wife Jerusha sold to son Martin
Gay of Boston their rights to land in Boston which was
set off from the estate of John Rogers late of Swanzea
Esq. deceased to his daughter Hannah Bradford, and in her
will was given to her four daughters: Hannah Gilbert,
Elizabeth Noyce, Jerusha Gay and Welthea Lane.
      The will of Ebenezer Gay of Hingham, clerk [minister],
dated 23 Oct. 1783 and probated 1 May 1787, names four
children: Martin, Jotham, Abigail and Jerusha Gay, and
granddaughter Christiana Jones.

      Children (GAY) b. Hingham:* SAMUEL[6] b. 1721; ABIGAIL b. 1722,
d. 1728/9; twins CALVIN and ABIGAIL b. 1724; MARTIN b. 1726; ABIGAIL
b. 1729; CELIA b. 1731; JOTHAM b. 1733; JERUSHA b. 1735; EBENEZER b.
1737, d. 1738; PERSIS b. 1739, d. 1752; and JOANNA b. 1741, d. unm.

References: MD 2:18; 11:239. VR DUXBURY. DEDHAM HIST REG. DEDHAM
            VR p. 27. BRADFORD DESC p. 27. Plymouth Co. PR 86:246,
247, 627(Eben. Gay). Suffolk Co. LR 95:198(Eben. Gay). HINGHAM FAMS
3:264-5. HARVARD GRADS 6:59-64.

204 WELTHEA[5] BRADFORD (Hannah[4] Rogers, John[3-2], Thomas[1])
b. Plymouth 15 May 1702; d. Hingham 2 June 1755.
      She m. ca. 1723 PETER LANE, b. Hingham 25 May 1697;
d. there 17 March 1764; son of Ebenezer and Hannah (Hersey)
Lane.
      On 13 May 1760 Peter Lane yeoman, George Lane gent.,
Samuel Johnson mariner and wife Hannah, Syble Lane and
Sarah Lane both singlewomen, all of Hingham; Ebenezer
Wiswall and Irania his wife, Daniel Johnson and Lucie his
wife, all of Worcester; all children and heirs of Welthian Lane deceased, late wife of Peter Lane, sold to Martin
Gay of Boston their share of land in Boston, formerly part
of the estate of John Rogers Esq. of Swansea deceased,
which was set off to his eldest daughter Hannah Bradford
and was by her will given to her four daughters of which
said Welthian was one.

      Children (LANE) b. Hingham:* HANNAH[6] b. 1724; IRENE b. 1725/6;
LUCY b. 1728, d. 1733/4; GEORGE bp. 1731; LUCY b. 1734/5; ELIZABETH;
stillborn child b. 1739; SYBIL b. 1741; and SARAH bp. 1745.

The William Bradford Family will give greater detail and one further
generation.

References: MD 2:18. Suffolk Co. LR 95:197(Peter Lane et al.).
            BRADFORD DESC p. 28. HINGHAM HIST 3:414-5.

205 GAMALIEL[5] BRADFORD (Hannah[4] Rogers, John[3-2], Thomas[1])
b. Plymouth 18 May 1704; d. Duxbury 24 April 1778.
     He m. Duxbury 30 Aug. 1728 ABIGAIL BARTLETT, b. Dux-
bury 18 March 1704; d. there 30 Aug. 1776; dau. of Benjamin
and Ruth (Pabodie) Bartlett, and a descendant of Pilgrims
John Alden and Richard Warren.
     The will of Gamaliel Bradford of Duxbury Esq., dated
4 April 1778 and proved 6 July 1778, mentions my grandchildren, children of my eldest son Samuel Bradford deceased; sons Gamaliel, Seth, Peabody, Peter and Andrew;
land in township of Winslow, Cumberland Co. [now ME];
three daughters Abigail Wadsworth, Hannah Stanford and Ruth
Sampson; executors Seth and Peter Bradford.

     Children (BRADFORD) b. Duxbury:* ABIGAIL[6] b. 1728; SAMUEL b.
1729/30; GAMALIEL b. 1731; SETH b. 1733; PEABODY b. 1735; DEBORAH b.
1738, d. 1739; HANNAH b. 1740; RUTH b. 1743; and twins PETER and
ANDREW b. 1745.

References: MD 2:18. VR DUXBURY. BRADFORD DESC p. 27-9. Plymouth
            Co. PR 25:17(Gamaliel Bradford).

206 WILLIAM[5] RICHMOND (Elizabeth[4] Rogers, John[3-2],
Thomas[1]) b. Little Compton RI 10 Oct. 1694; d. there 22
Feb. 1770.
     He m. Little Compton 8 July 1720 ANNA GRAY, b. Little
Compton 29 Jan. 1702; d. Bristol RI 9 Oct. 1762 ae 61;
dau. of Thomas and Anna (Little) Gray, and a descendant of
Pilgrim Richard Warren. The will of Thomas Gray, dated 21
Sept. 1721, names dau. Anna Richmond.
     William Richmond was a judge, and from 1753 to 1755
was an assistant to the governor of RI. His will, dated
5 July 1766 and proved 3 April 1770, names sons Barzilla,
Ephraim, William, Perez, Thomas (not well) and Sylvester;
daughters Elizabeth Brownell wife of Jonathan, Mary Ware
wife of Dr. George, Sarah Walker wife of David, and Abigail Pitts wife of Peter; daughter-in-law Hannah Richmond
wife of my son William; grandson Gilbert Richmond, son of
my son Ichabod Richmond deceased; grandchildren, children
of son Ephraim, including his daughter Anna Richmond under
18; son William to have my negro man Solomon and care for
my negro woman Amy; son Perez to have my negro man Ebenezer; sons William and Perez to be executors.**

---

*The *William Bradford Family* will give greater detail and one further
generation.

**LITTLE COMPTON FAMS is wrong in saying that the will was dated in
176_5_, and in listing a son Ebenezer.

Children (RICHMOND) b. Little Compton RI: BARZILLA[6] b. 1721;
EPHRAIM b. 1723; ELIZABETH b. 1725; WILLIAM b. 1727; PEREZ b. 1729;
ICHABOD b. 1731; THOMAS b. 1733; MARY b. 1735; SARAH b. 1738; SILVES-
TER b. 1740; and ABIGAIL b. 1744.

References: RI VR: Bristol p. 159; Little Compton pp. 50, 119, 151,
             152. LITTLE COMPTON FAMS pp. 515-6. RICHMOND FAM p. 34.

207 ELIZABETH[5] RICHMOND (Elizabeth[4] Rogers, John[3-2],
Thomas[1]) b. Little Compton RI 10 May 1696; d. Dighton 23
Sept. 1765 in her 70th yr.
     She m. Little Compton RI 15 Dec. 1715 NATHANIEL
FISHER, b. Dedham 5 April 1687; d. Dighton 30 Aug. 1777 ae
91; son of Daniel and Mary (Fuller) Fisher.
     Nathaniel Fisher was a Harvard graduate, receiving
his bachelor's degree in 1706, and his master's degree in
1709. He was minister of Dighton in 1710.
     Nathaniel and Elizabeth left no wills, but on 6 March
1781 an account was presented by Nathaniel Fisher as administrator on the estate of Nathaniel Fisher late of
Dighton deceased.

     Children (FISHER) all presumably b. Dighton: ABIGAIL[6]; ELIZA-
BETH; NATHANIEL b. 1725, d. 1728; JEREMIAH b. 1728; NATHANIEL b. 1733;
DARRIEL; and poss others.

References: DIGHTON VR pp. 25, 26. DEDHAM VR p. 22. HARVARD GRADS
             5:312-5. RI VR:Little Compton p. 27. LITTLE COMPTON
FAMS p. 514. Bristol Co. PR files(Nathaniel Fisher). RICHMOND FAM p.
35.

208 SYLVESTER[5] RICHMOND (Elizabeth[4] Rogers, John[3-2],
Thomas[1]) b. Little Compton 30 June 1698; d. Dighton 14
Jan. 1783 in 85th yr.
     He m. Little Compton ca. 1720 ELIZABETH TALBUT, b.
Dighton 14 Jan. 1699; d. there 23 June 1772 in 73rd yr.;
dau. of Jared and Rebecca (Hathaway) Talbut. Jared called
Sylvester his son-in-law in a 1723 deed drawn about the
time Sylvester moved to Dighton, where he served as sheriff
of Bristol Co. and as a colonel in the French and Indian
Wars.
     Sylvester Richmond left no will, but on 20 Jan. 1783
Ezra Richmond of Dighton was appointed administrator of the
estate of Sylvester Richmond Esq. late of Dighton dec. The
inventory included land at Little Compton.

     Children (RICHMOND) first two b. Little Compton RI, rest Digh-
ton: EZRA[6] b. 1721; REBECCA b. 1723; ELIZABETH b. 1726; SYLVESTER b.
1729; HANNAH b. 1731; MARY b. 1733/4; RUTH b. 1736/7; and twins JOHN
and NATHANIEL b. 1738/9.

References: DIGHTON VR pp. 11-12. RI VR: Little Compton pp. 50, 152.
            RICHMOND FAM pp. 35-36. LITTLE COMPTON FAMS p. 516.
Bristol Co. PR 148:143(Sylvester Richmond).

209 PELEG[5] RICHMOND (Elizabeth[4] Rogers, John[3-2], Thomas[1])
b. Little Compton RI 25 Oct. 1700; d. Rehoboth 13 Aug.
1783.
      He m. (1) Little Compton RI 14 Dec. 1727 PATIENCE
PALMER, b. Little Compton 19 Feb. 1704; d. there 27 Dec.
1728 in 25th yr.; dau. of William and Mary (Richmond) Palmer.
      He m. (2) Little Compton in Jan. 1733 MARY (PEIRCE)
VIALL "of Barrington MA" [now RI], b. ca. 1704; d. 19 April
1781 ae 77; dau. of John and Mary (Cobham) Pierce, and
widow of James Viall. On 25 June 1733 Peleg Richmond and
wife Mary, both of Barrington, conveyed land in Boston belonging to the estate of our mother Mary Pierce, which was
held in partnership with heirs of John Rogers of Barrington dec.
      Peleg Richmond lived in Barrington RI and in Rehoboth.
The will of Peleg Richmond of Rehoboth yeoman, dated 4 May
1767 and witnesses deposed 10 Nov. 1783, names wife Mary;
son Gamaliel; son John Roger Richmond; dau. Mary Bullock
wife of Jabez; dau. Elizabeth Bucknell wife of Amos of
Ashford; dau. Sarah Richmond; and grandson Peleg Richmond,
son of John R. Richmond, executor.

      Children (RICHMOND) first by Patience b. Little Compton RI, rest
by Mary, fifth and poss. others b. Barrington RI: GAMALIEL[6] b. 1728;
PELEG b. 1733/4, d.y.; JOHN R. b. 1737; MARY b. 1740; PELEG b. 1743/4;
ELIZABETH; JAMES; and SARAH.

References: RI VR: Little Compton pp. 50, 152; Barrington p. 35. VR
            REHOBOTH. RICHMOND FAM p. 38. LITTLE COMPTON FAMS p.
516. Bristol Co. PR 27:593(Peleg Richmond).

210 PEREZ[5] RICHMOND (Elizabeth[4] Rogers, John[3-2], Thomas[1])
b. Little Compton RI 5 Oct. 1702; d. Dartmouth 15 Sept.
1770.
      He m. Little Compton 11 March 1731 DEBORAH LORING, b.
Duxbury 9 Dec. 1710; d. Little Compton 14 April 1782 in
72nd yr.; dau. of Thomas and Deborah (Cushing) Loring.
      Perez Richmond was commissioned a captain in 1742, and
was a freeman at Little Compton in 1752.
      The will of Perez Richmond of Dartmouth gentleman,
dated 29 May 1765 and proved 24 Sept. 1770, names wife
Deborah; sons Joshua, Edward, Perez and Benjamin; daus.
Hannah Jacobs wife of David, Elizabeth Jacobs wife of
Joshua, and Deborah, Mary and Lucy, all unm. Sons Edward
and Perez to be executors.

Children (RICHMOND) b. Little Compton RI: HANNAH[6] b. 1732; JOSHUA b. 1734; EDWARD b. 1736; LORING b. 1738; PEREZ b. 1741; DEBORAH b. 1742; BETSEY b. 1743; BENJAMIN b. 1747; MARY b. 1749; and LUCY b. 1751.

References: RI VR: Little Compton pp. 50, 151, 152. VR DUXBURY. RICHMOND FAM pp. 38-9. NEHGR 115:265. LITTLE COMPTON FAMS p. 517. Bristol Co. PR files(Perez Richmond).

211 ICHABOD[5] RICHMOND (Elizabeth[4] Rogers, John[3-2], Thomas[1]) b. Little Compton 27 Feb. 1704; d. Bristol RI 29 Sept. 1762 ae 59.
        Did he m. (1) 1753 MARY ----- of Bristol? No children found.
        He m. Pembroke in Sept. 1757 ABIGAIL FORD, b. Pembroke 25 April 1727; d. 27 Aug. 1789; dau. of John and Mary (Cushing) Ford. The will of John Ford of Pembroke yeoman, dated 8 April 1774, names wife Mary and daughter Abigail. Abigail m. (2) Bristol RI 1765 Benjamin Cushing of Providence.
        Ichabod Richmond was a physician, and was living in Little Compton in 1740, Dartmouth in 1758, and Bristol by 1760. The will of Ichabod Richmond physician of Bristol, made 23 April 1762 and proved 1 Nov. 1762, names wife Abigail and son Nathaniel, under 21.

        Child (RICHMOND) b. Bristol RI:* unnamed son b. 1760, and NATHANIEL[6] b. 1761, d.y.

References: RI VR:Bristol p. 159; Little Compton pp. 50, 152. VR PEMBROKE. RICHMOND FAM p. 39. LITTLE COMPTON FAMS p. 517. Bristol Co. LR 28:336(Ichabod Richmond). Bristol RI PR 2:28-9 (Ichabod Richmond). Plymouth Co. PR 24:169(John Ford). Ford Fam 1:1141.3.

212 RUTH[5] RICHMOND (Elizabeth[4] Rogers, John[3-2], Thomas[1]) b. Little Compton RI 7 March 1705; d. Dighton 15 Nov. 1776 in 71st yr.
        She m. Little Compton 27 Aug. 1724 EPHRAIM ATWOOD, b. ca. 1689; d. Dighton 14 Aug. 1776 in 87th yr.; son of Joseph and Esther (Walker) Atwood.
        In 1733 Ephraim was a shipwright at Dighton.
        The will of Ephraim Atwood of Dighton yeoman "in an advanced age", dated 21 June 1776 and witnesses deposed 24 Sept. 1776, names wife Ruth, eldest son Sylvester, son Ephraim, and only dau. Ruth Shaw late wife of Samuel lately of Dighton dec.; executor son Sylvester.

---

*Gilbert Richmond b. Little Compton 1754 is not a son of this Ichabod.

Children (ATWOOD) b. Dighton: SYLVESTER[6] b. 1725; RUTH b. 1727; EPHRAIM b. 1737; PELEG b. and d. after 1737; and poss. an unnamed son.

References: DIGHTON VR p. 26. RI VR:Little Compton p. 6. RICHMOND
          FAM p. 40. Bristol Co. PR 24:244(Ephraim Atwood). Bristol Co. LR 33:226(Ephraim Atwood).

213 SARAH[5] RICHMOND (Elizabeth[4] Rogers, John[3-2], Thomas[1])
b. Little Compton RI 31 Oct. 1711; d. Barrington RI 9 Oct. 1739 in 28th yr.
        She m. Little Compton 19 Nov. 1730 PELEG HEATH of Barrington, b. Roxbury 26 July 1700; d. Warren RI 5 Oct. 1748; son of William and Anne (-----) Heath. He m. (2) Barrington 1740 Bethiah Peck; and m. (3) Barrington 1743 Jerusha Peck, by whom he also had sons Nathaniel and Peleg.
        Peleg Heath graduated from Yale with a bachelor's degree in 1721, and received his master's degree in 1724. He was ordained a minister at Barrington in 1728, and was a freeman at Warren in 1747. In a deed of gift dated 11 Aug. 1748, Jerusha and Peleg gave to their minor sons, Nathaniel and Peleg, land of Jerusha's "father Joseph Peck of Rehoboth."
        The will of Peleg Heath of Warren RI gentleman, dated 12 Aug. 1748 and exhibited 7 Nov. 1748, names his wife Jerusha, provides for a possible posthumous child, names son Nathaniel and Peleg [both by Jerusha], and dau. Mary Heath, who was to have land in Woodstock, Worcester Co. [now in CT], and the "Bible that was her mother's, my first wife."

        Children (HEATH) b. Barrington RI to Peleg and Sarah: MARY[6] b. 1731/2; PELEG b. 1734, d. 1735/6; PELEG b. 1735/6, d. 1740; and NATHANIEL b. 1737/8, d. 1740.

References: VR ROXBURY. RI VR Barrington pp. 11, 28; Little Compton
          p. 33. HARVARD GRADS 7:629-631. RICHMOND FAM p. 40.
Warren RI PR 1:41(Peleg Heath). Warren RI LR 1:74(Peleg Heath).

214 MARY[5] RICHMOND (Elizabeth[4] Rogers, John[3-2], Thomas[1])
b. Little Compton RI 29 Nov. 1713; d. No. Yarmouth ME 15 Sept. 1803.
        She m. Little Compton 16 Feb. 1737 NICHOLAS LORING "of No. Yarmouth", b. Hull 1 Sept. 1711; d. No. Yarmouth 31 July 1763; son of John and Jane (Baker) Loring.
        Nicholas Loring graduated from Harvard in 1732, and received his master's degree there in 1735. He was ordained a minister at North Yarmouth in 1736.
        On 5 Jan. 1798 Bezaleel Loring and Lucretia Mitchell, ch. of Rev. Nicholas Loring late of No. Yarmouth, clerk [minister] dec.; and John Prince and wife Mary, Joseph

Gray, Charlotte Gray, Allen Drinkwater and wife Hannah,
Watson Gray, Loring Gray, Reuben Gray, and Ebenezer Gray,
all ch. of Mary Gray dec. dau. of Nicholas Loring, in con-
sideration of being cleared of the support of "our mother
and grandmother Mary Loring" widow of said Nicholas and of
the negro woman living with her, sold to Richmond Loring,
Levi Loring, Thomas Loring, Jeremiah Loring and Humphrey
Chase and wife Elizabeth, all of No. Yarmouth and ch. of
said Nicholas, their interest. [Although living Watson
Gray did not sign the deed and Loring Gray apparently
signed as Nicholas L. Gray.]

Children (LORING) b. No. Yarmouth ME: RICHMOND[6] b. 1738; BEZA-
LEEL b. 1739; LEVI b. 1740; LUCRETIA b. 1742; MARY b. 1744; ELIZABETH
b. 1746; RACHEL b. 1748; THOMAS b. 1751; NICHOLAS b. 1755; and JERE-
MIAH 1758.

References: OLD TIMES p. 879. PORTLAND GAZETTE 26 Sept. 1803(Mary
Loring). HARVARD GRADS 9:179-83. LORING GEN p. 53.
RICHMOND FAM p. 40. Cumberland Co. ME LR 55:531, 533-4(Bezaleel Lor-
ing). Bristol Co. MA Gen. Sess. 1714-38 p. 335(Nicholas Loring of No.
Yarmouth). RI VR:Little Compton p. 39.

215 ROGERS[5] RICHMOND (Elizabeth[4] Rogers, John[3-2], Thomas[1]) b. Little Compton RI 25 May 1716; d. Bristol RI bet.
11 Jan. 1762 and 1 March 1762.
    He m. Bristol RI 17 May 1739 SUSANNAH (VIALL) LEE, b.
Swansea 15 Nov. 1712; d. Bristol 6 July 1776 ae 64; dau.
of Samuel and Susannah (Flint) Viall, and widow of George
Lee. The will of Samuel Viall of Bristol Esq., dated 3
May 1746, names dau. Susannah Richmond.
    Rogers was a freeman at Bristol in 1747.
    The will of Rogers Richmond of Bristol yeoman, dated
11 Jan. 1762 and proved 1 March 1762, authorized John Waldron as executor not to sell any of my negroes; and mentioned wife Susannah who has "her own estate," and three daughters Elizabeth, Mary and Sarah Richmond.

Children (RICHMOND) b. Bristol RI: SUSANNAH[6] b. 1740; VIALL b.
1740/1; SAMUEL VIALL b. 1742; ELIZABETH b. 1743/4; MARY b. 1745; and
SARAH b. 1746.

References: RI VR: Bristol pp. 46, 101, 160. SWANSEA VR p. 134.
RICHMOND FAM p. 41. VIALL GEN p. 18. Bristol RI PR 1:63
(Samuel Viall); 2:24(Rogers Richmond).

216 DEBORAH[5] SEARLE (Sarah[4] Rogers, John[3-2], Thomas[1]) b.
Little Compton RI 17 Nov. 1695; d. there 16 May 1776.
    She m. Little Compton 20 Feb. 1717 GEORGE PEARCE, b.
Little Compton 2 March 1697; d. there 22 Feb. 1764; son

of George and Alice (Hart) Pearce.
    The will of George Pearce of Little Compton yeoman,
dated 23 Nov. 1763 and sworn 6 March 1764, names wife
Deborah; sons Jephthah, Nathaniel, Richard; and daus. Alles
Dwelly, Temperance Sebury, Sarah Sawyer, Ruth Horswill,
Annatruce Tabour and Deborah Pearce, unmarried. The will
of Deborah Pearce of Little Compton widow, written 8 Oct.
1770 and sworn 4 June 1776, names the same children but
calls youngest dau. Deborah Manchester.

    Children (PEARCE) b. Little Compton RI: ALICE[6] b. 1718; SARAH
b. 1720, d. 1721; JEPTHIAH b. 1722; TEMPERANCE b. 1724; JEREMIAH b.
1725; NATHANIEL b. 1727; SARAH b. 1729; RUTH b. 1731; ANTRACE b. 1733;
DEBORAH b. 1735; and RICHARD b. 1736.

References: RI VR: Little Compton pp. 45, 144-5. Little Compton PR
            2:8(George Pearce); 2:345(Deborah Pearce). LITTLE
COMPTON FAMS p. 468.

217 SARAH[5] SEARLE (Sarah[4] Rogers, John[3-2], Thomas[1]) b.
Little Compton RI 2 April 1700; d. there 16 Feb. 1783.
    She m. Little Compton 28 June 1725 THOMAS DRING, b.
Little Compton 23 April 1704; d. there in Sept. 1787; son
of Thomas and Mary (Butler) Dring.*
    The will of Thomas Dring of Little Compton, dated 23
April 1782 and sworn 4 Dec. 1787, names wife Sarah; sons
Benjamin and Phillip; daus. Tabatha Barny, Hannah Stoddard
and Abigail Carr; and grandson Nathaniel Searle, son of
son Nathaniel.

    Children (DRING) b. Little Compton RI: TABITHA[6] b. 1725; BENJA-
MIN b. 1727; PHILIP b. 1729; HANNAH b. 1731; RUTH b. 1732; NATHANIEL
b. 1734; ABIGAIL b. 1736; and MARY b. 1737.

References: RI VR: 18:394; Little Compton pp. 25, 113, 114; Tiverton
            p. 22. LITTLE COMPTON FAMS p. 245. Little Compton RI PR
3:157(Thomas Dring).

218 NATHANIEL[5] SEARLE (Sarah[4] Rogers, John[3-2], Thomas[1])
b. Little Compton RI 26 April 1703; d. there 8 Dec. 1781
in 79th yr.
    He m. Little Compton in Dec. 1725 ELIZABETH KINNECUTT,
b. 1701; d. Little Compton 11 Dec. 1781 in 80th yr.
    The will of Nathaniel Searle of Little Compton, Esq.,
dated 3 Dec. 1781 and sworn 5 Feb. 1782, names wife Elizabeth; sons John, Nathaniel and Comfort; grandson Joel
Searle; "each of my son Constant's children"; three

---

*The Thomas Dring who served as a gunner during the Revolution, and
was captured by the British and imprisoned, was a younger Thomas born
about 1758 at Newport RI and died at Providence RI 1825.

granddaughters, daughters of son James; three granddaughters, daughters of son Daniel; and daughters Betty Atwill
and Sarah Runnels (Reynolds?).

Children (SEARLE) b. Little Compton RI: JOHN[6] b. 1726; CONSTANT
(son) b. 1728; DANIEL b. 1730; BETSEY b. 1732; SARAH b. 1733; NATHAN-
IEL b. 1735; JAMES b. 1737; RUTH b. and d. 1740; and COMFORT (son) b.
1742.

References: RI VR: Little Compton pp. 53, 157. LITTLE COMPTON FAMS
            p. 550. NEHGR 115:261. Little Compton RI PR 3:19
(Nathaniel Searle).

219 ABIGAIL[5] MAKEPEACE (Abigail[4] Tisdale, Anna[3] Rogers,
John[2], Thomas[1]) b. Freetown 25 Nov. 1686; d. bet. 4 July
1720 and 17 Feb. 1724/5.
     She m. ca. 1703 EMANUEL WILLIAMS, b. prob. England ca.
1680; d. Taunton shortly bef. 2 Nov. 1719.
     On 10 June 1703 William Makepeace, formerly of Free-
town now of Taunton, gave to his son-in-law Mr. Immanuel
Williams of Taunton 50 acres of land on which Immanuel
lived.
     Inventory of the estate of Amanuell Williams, late of
Taunton dec., was taken 2 Nov. 1719 and on 4 July 1720
Abigill Williams, administratrix of the estate of her husband, made oath to the inventory. She had apparently died
by 17 Feb. 1724/5 when William Makepeace was appointed administrator de bonis non on the estate. Guardianships of
the children in 1730 give their approximate ages. A division of the real estate was made 28 Oct. 1730 among eldest
son John, second son Gersham, and third son Simion, eldest
daughter Ann wife of William Barney, second daughter Lydia,
and third daughter Phebe.

Children (WILLIAMS) b. to Emanuel and Abigail were: ANN[6]; JOHN
b. bef. 1708; GERSHOM b. ca. 1708; LYDIA b. ca. 1712; PHEBE b. bef.
1716; and SIMEON b. after 1716.

References: MD 21:136-140. Bristol Co. LR 8:25(Wm. Makepeace).

220 MARY[5] MAKEPEACE (Abigail[4] Tisdale, Anna[3] Rogers,
John[2], Thomas[1]) b. Freetown 22 March 1691; living 11 Dec.
1750, when she was named in the will of her brother-in-law
Joseph Godfrey.
     She m. bef. 4 Nov. 1717 NATHANIEL GOULD, d. after 5
May 1753; prob. the son of John Gould of Taunton whose
estate was divided in 1713, with Nathaniel receiving land
on Prospect Hill.
     On 4 Nov. 1717 William Makepeace of Taunton gave 300
acres there to daughter Mary Gould and her husband

Nathaniel of Taunton. On the same day William sold a
piece of land to Nathaniel Goold of Taunton, feltmaker.
Nathaniel Gould was living in Union CT by 15 June 1734
when he bought 60 acres there. On 15 Nov. 1750 Nathaniel
Gould of Union, Windham Co. CT, hatter, and wife Mary, one
of the daughters of William Makepeace late of Taunton, sold
their inheritance, acknowledging the deed 25 Jan. 1750/1.
     Nathaniel and Mary Gould left no probate records, and
the birth of only Phebe is recorded. However, Nathaniel
deeded land in Union to "son William" 28 Aug. 1752, "son
Seth" 25 June 1752, and "son Nathaniel" 2 March 1753,
acknowledged 5 May 1753.

     Children (GOULD) b. to Nathaniel and Mary were: WILLIAM[6];
NATHANIEL; SETH; PHEBE b. 1733; and poss. MARY and JOHN.

References: Union CT Gens, MS., Hartford State Library (1908) p. 90.
          Bristol Co. PR 3:165(John Gould). Bristol Co. LR 38:185
(Nath'l. Gould); 11:446-7(Wm. Makepeace). Union CT LR 1:31, 79, 80,
85(Nath'l. Gould). bk. 1:grantor index:G(birth Phebe Gould).

221 LYDIA[5] MAKEPEACE (Abigail[4] Tisdale, Anna[3] Rogers,
John[2], Thomas[1]) b. Freetown 4 Nov. 1696; d. Norton 9 July
1748 in 52nd yr.
     She m. int. Norton 1 Oct. 1723 SIMEON WITHEREL, b.
Norton 24 May 1693; d. there 16 Nov. 1778 ae 85-6-8; son
of John and Susanna (Newland) Witherill. Simeon m. (2)
int. Norton 1749 Sarah (Sampson) Walker, a descendant of
Pilgrim Miles Standish, by whom he had Simeon, Sarah,
Susannah and Levi.
     The will of Simeon Witherel of Norton, made 7 Nov.
1778 in his 86th year and probated 1 Dec. 1778, names wife
Sarah; sons Simeon and Levi; daughters Sarah Shaw and
Susannah Blanding; and granddaughter Lydia, dau. of my dau.
Lydia the deceased late wife of Samuel Wild.

     Child (WITHEREL) born Norton to Simeon and Lydia: LYDIA[6] b.
1732.

References: WITHERELL FAM pp. 119-120, 128-9. Bristol Co. PR 23:351-
          2(S. Witherel). VR NORTON.

222 SETH[5] MAKEPEACE (Abigail[4] Tisdale, Anna[3] Rogers,
John[2], Thomas[1]) b. Freetown 23 June 1702; d. Norton bef.
10 July 1749.
     He m. Norton 21 June 1732 MARY WARE, b. Wrentham 4
Aug. 1705; d. Norton 5 Jan. 1799; dau. of John and Mehitable (Chapin) Ware.
     On 10 July 1749 the widow Mary Makepeace was named
administratrix of the estate of Seth Makepeace of Norton.

Seth's real estate was divided 13 Dec. 1755 among the widow Mary Makepeace and her children: Mary Witherel wife of George, second dau. Mehitable Makepeace, third dau. Hannah Makepeace, fourth dau. Abigail Makepeace and fifth dau. Sarah Makepeace. Husbands of the daus. are revealed in the division of the real estate of dau. Mary, dec. wife of George Witherel of Norton, which was made 2 Aug. 1765 among widow Mary Makepeace mother of the dec. Mary Witherel; Hannah Witherel wife of William and sister of dec. Mary; Mehitable and Sarah Makepeace, also sisters of dec.; and Abigail Capron wife of Elisha and sister of deceased.

Children (MAKEPEACE) b. Norton: MARY[6] b. 1733; MEHITABLE b. 1735; HANNAH b. 1738; ABIGAIL b. 1741; and SARAH b. 1744.

References: VR NORTON, WRENTHAM. Bristol Co. PR 12:22, 370(Seth Makepeace); 19:205(Mary Witherel).

223 WILLIAM[5] MAKEPEACE (Abigail[4] Tisdale, Anna[3] Rogers, John[2], Thomas[1]) b. Taunton ca. 1704; d. Norton 15/16 April 1740 in 36th yr.
He m. Norton 14 Jan. 1724/5 EXPERIENCE ALDRICH, b. Norton 11 Nov. 1702; dau. of Peter and Experience (Cook) Aldrich. On 18 June 1731 William and Experience Makepeace received land and moveable estate from their mother Experience Aldrich of Norton, administratrix of the estate of their father Peter Aldrich.
Administration of William Makepeace's estate was granted 19 Aug. 1740 to his widow Experience Makepeace. Division of the estate was made 3 April 1753 to the children: eldest son Peter, George, William and Abigail Makepeace; each of the four received "a share of deceased child's estate" (therefore dau. Experience was dead by then).

Children (MAKEPEACE) b. Norton: EXPERIENCE[6] b. 1725, d. bef. 1753; WILLIAM b. 1727/8, d.y.; PETER b. 1730; ABIGAIL b. 1732; GEORGE b. 1735; and WILLIAM b. 1738.

References: VR MENDON (Cook-Aldrich m.), NORTON. ALDRICH GEN 1:38. Bristol Co. PR 15:445(Wm. Makepeace). Bristol Co. LR 8:264, 362(Wm. Makepeace).

224 REMEMBER[5] MAKEPEACE (Abigail[4] Tisdale, Anna[3] Rogers, John[2], Thomas[1]) b. ca. 1707; living 11 Dec. 1750, when she was named in the will of her brother-in-law Joseph Godfrey.
She m. bef. 1733 SAMUEL PORTER, poss. son of Samuel Porter of Hadley, Hampshire Co., who bought land in Lebanon CT in 1710 and was living there in 1732. In a deed

drawn 3 March 1749/50 Samuel Porter of Lebanon and wife
Remember, a dau. of William Makepeace late of Taunton,
sold land.
    There are no Connecticut probate records for Remember
or Samuel, but he may have been living as late as 7 May
1778 when a Samuel Porter of Lebanon sold land.

        Children (PORTER) b. Lebanon CT: JACOB[6] b. 1733; ISRAEL b.
1735; LYDIA b. 1738; SARAH b. 1741; twins ISRAEL and LYDIA b. 1743;
and JACOB again.

References: Bristol Co. LR 35:592(Samuel Porter). CSL Barbour Index:
             Lebanon. Lebanon CT LR 2:243; 3:159; 4:450; 13:16(Samu-
el Porter).

225 PRISCILLA[5] MAKEPEACE (Abigail[4] Tisdale, Anna[3] Rogers,
John[2], Thomas[1]) b. Taunton ca. 1710; d. after 1750.
    She m. bef. 1732 PETER ALDRICH, b. Norton 2 June 1707;
poss. d. there (or was it his son?) 2 Oct. 1805; son of
Peter and Experience (Cook) Aldrich.
    On 20 Dec. 1748 Peter Aldredge of Norton and wife
Priscilla sold land. This was their last Bristol County
deed, and there is no probate for either of them.

        Children (ALDRICH) b. Norton: PRISCILLA[6] b. 1732/3; ABIGAIL b.
1734; PETER b. 1737; and EXPERIENCE b. 1739.

References: VR MENDON (Cook-Aldrich m.), NORTON. ALDRICH GEN 1:38.
             Bristol Co. LR 37:62(Peter Aldredge).

226 THOMAS[5] MAKEPEACE (Abigail[4] Tisdale, Anna[3] Rogers,
John[2], Thomas[1]) b. prob. Taunton; living 11 Dec. 1750,
when he was mentioned in the will of his brother-in-law
Joseph Godfrey; prob. d. Taunton Oct. 1781 "old."
    He m. Taunton 20 March 1734 CHARITY STAPLES of Taun-
ton, prob. dau. of Joseph Staples, for on 24 Feb. 1736 Thomas Makepeace of Taunton and wife Charity deeded "a messuage in Taunton which Joseph Staples owned in his lifetime
or died siezed of."
    Neither Thomas nor Charity left probate records, and
they did not deed any land to children. On 1 Dec. 1767
Thomas Makepeace of Taunton laborer sold "all the rest of
what I own" in Taunton. No evidence was found to substantiate the claim of the MAKEPEACE FAM that Thomas and Charity had: Thomas, William, Seth,* Abigail, Charity and
Wealthy.

---

*The Mayflower Society has accepted members through descent from Seth,
as son of Thomas and Charity.

References: VR TAUNTON. MAKEPEACE FAM pp. 46-7. Bristol Co. LR
34:404; 51:27(Thomas Makepeace).

227 JOHN[5] TISDALE (John[4], Anna[3] Rogers, John[2], Thomas[1])
b. ca. 1702; d. bef. 7 Oct. 1755.
He m. bef. 1729 JUDITH HALL, dau. of John and Eliza-
beth (King) Hall. On 19 June 1729 John and Judith Tisdale
received from their brother John Hall of Taunton their
portions of the estate of their father John Hall, late of
Taunton dec., and of the estate of their grandmother Hanna
Hoskins.
Administration on the estate of John Tisdale, late of
Taunton deceased gentleman, was granted to John Tisdale of
Taunton 7 Oct. 1755. On 7 Sept. 1756 John Tisdale, Elijah
Tisdale and Thomas Tisdale, all of Taunton, children
of John Tisdale late of Taunton gentleman deceased intes-
tate, sold part of the land of John Hall and Israel Tisdale
deceased.

Children (TISDALE) b. 1729-35 or earlier: JOHN[6], ELIJAH, and
THOMAS.

References: Bristol Co. PR 14:548(John Tisdale). Bristol Co. LR
42:171(John Tisdale); 24:72(John Tisdale et al.).

228 DEBORAH[5] TISDALE (John[4], Anna[3] Rogers, John[2], Thomas[1]) b. prob. Taunton ca. 1709; d. after 1759, prob. the
unnamed "wife of Josiah" who d. Taunton "about 20 Oct.
1763."
She m. (prob. the 16 Jan. 1731 marriage at Taunton of
Josiah Lincoln), JOSIAH LINCOLN, b. Taunton bef. 1701; d.
Taunton 30 May 1774; prob. the son of "John the first of
that name in Taunton" who on 6 Nov. 1722 sold to son Josiah
42 acres of land in Taunton North Purchase, bounded by land
of sons Thomas and Daniel. He m. (2) Taunton 1774 Jane
Bolton.
It is difficult to assign exact dates to this family
for lack of vital records. However, the quitclaim of
Josiah Linkon of Taunton and wife Deborah, to Ephraim Tis-
dale of Taunton yeoman, of all lands of Deborah's brother
Jedidiah Tisdale's intestate estate; and of land sold by
Abiel Dean and wife Anna, another sister of Jedediah, on
4 Dec. 1759, proves that Josiah's wife was indeed Deborah[5]
Tisdale.
The will of Josiah Linkon of Taunton yeoman, dated 4
March 1774 and sworn 28 June 1774, names son Josiah; chil-
dren of son Simeon: Simeon, Silvester, Charity, Abigail and
Sibbel Lincoln; wife Jane; dau. Charity the wife of Silves-
ter Jones; Mary and Katherine Hack under 18, children of
daughter Katherin Hack; Silvester Jones Jr. and Cornelius

Jones both under 21, and Deborah Jones under 18, children
of daughter Deborah Jones; Appollos Jones under 21 and Sibble Jones under 18, ch. of dau. Charity Jones; William
Linkon and Joseph Waterman Linkon both under 21, ch. of
late son Mordecai dec. Son Josiah to be executor.

Children (LINCOLN) prob. b. Taunton: MORDECAI[6] b. ca. 1734;
JOSIAH b. bef. 1740; CHARITY b. ca. 1747; SIMEON b. bef. 1742; KATHER-
INE; and DEBORAH.

References: VR TAUNTON [either the church m. rec. is in error, or
            Deborah m. (1) ----- Vickery]. TAG 54:15. MIDDLETOWN
UPPER HOUSES p. 642. Bristol Co. PR 23:264 (Josiah Lincoln). Bristol
Co. LR 15:108; 44:38 (Josiah Lincoln).

229 ABIGAIL[5] TISDALE (John[4], Anna[3] Rogers, John[2], Thomas[1]) b. ca. 1711; d. Taunton in May 1790 in 80th yr.,
"wid. James."
     She m. bet. 1728 and 1730 JAMES HEWETT, b. Marshfield
21 Nov. 1706; d. Bridgewater bef. 4 May 1750; son of Solomon and Sarah (Waterman) Hewett, and a descendant of Pilgrim Richard Warren. In the 1715 will of his father, James
Hewett received several pieces of Middleboro land which he
sold in 1728 and 1729, when he was a resident of Dighton.
     On 4 May 1750 inventory was taken of the estate of
James Hewett, late of Bridgewater bloomer deceased intestate, and on 4 June 1750 Israel Tisdale of Taunton gentleman [Abigail's brother] was appointed administrator. Mention of Abigail in her brother Israel's will in 1769, and
her Jan. and Dec. 1783 petitions for money due from his
estate, added to the inscription on her gravestone, prove
that she lived for 40 years following James Hewett's
death.

Children (HEWETT) b. Bridgewater: ABIGAIL[6] b. 1730; SARAH b.
1732; SUSANNAH b. 1733; BATHSHEBA b. 1735; unnamed son b. 1737; ABIAH
b. 1739; and ABRAHAM b. 1742.

References: VR BRIDGEWATER, TAUNTON, W. BRIDGEWATER. MD 24:145 (Jos.
            Waterman's will). WATERMAN GEN 1:28, 29, 56-8. Plymouth
Co. PR 3:416 (Solomon Hewitt); 11:442; 12:67 (James Hewett). Plymouth
Co. LR 23:137; 26:4 (James Hewett). MARSHFIELD VR p. 25.

230 EPHRAIM[5] TISDALE (John[4], Anna[3] Rogers, John[2], Thomas[1]) b. bet. 1702 and 1714; d. Taunton 8 Dec. 1778 "old."
     He m. (1) Taunton 24 Feb. 1736 SARAH HODGES, b. Norton
26 June 1719; d. ca. 1737; dau. of Samuel and Mary Hodges.
On 12 Jan. 1739/40 Ephraim Tisdale of Taunton joiner sold
land which was set off to Sarah, dec. dau. of Samuel Hodges
late of Norton dec. Ephraim and Sarah had no children.

He prob. m. (2) Taunton 7 Nov. 1738 SUSANNAH GARSHET (or Gatchell), dau. of Henry and Sarah (Haskins) Garshet.
He m. (3) after 1754 CORALINA (or Caroline) LEONARD, b. Raynham 3 July 1738; d. Taunton early in 1788; dau. of Thomas and Sarah (Walker) Leonard, and a descendant of Pilgrim Thomas Rogers (see #281).
On 5 Jan. 1779 Ephraim Tisdale, second son of Ephraim Tisdale of Taunton dec., petitioned for guardians for his two young brothers because of land left by the will of Abraham Tisdale; of the "four male heirs" two were of age and two under 14. Widow Coralina Tisdale and eldest son Abraham Tisdale of Bridgewater were to appear at the guardianship hearing. Division of the real estate of Ephraim Tisdale late of Taunton dec. was made 28 Jan. 1779 to son Ephraim, eldest son Abraham, and sons Thomas and Seth.
The will of Coralina Tisdale, widow and relict of Ephraim late of Taunton dec., dated 30 Dec. 1785 and presented 1 April 1788, names granddau. Corlina Willbore "for her name"; daus. Prudence Tisdale, Hannah Tisdale and Silence Tisdale who was under 18; sons Seth and Thomas Tisdale both under 21; dau. Ruth Willbore; brother Gamaliel Leonard to be executor.

Children (TISDALE) poss. b. Berkley, first three to Susanna, rest to Coralina: BENONI[6] b. after 1748; ABRAHAM b. bef. 1758; EPHRAIM b. bef. 1758; RUTH b. bef. 1765; PRUDENCE; HANNAH; THOMAS b. after 1765; SETH b. after 1765; and SILENCE b. after 1767.

References: VR NORTON, TAUNTON. NEHGR 53:436; 54:17[Sarah Sulker should be Sarah Walker]. Bristol Co. PR 9:60(Henry Goshet); 25:514 & file (Ephraim Tisdale); 29:458(Coralina Tisdale). Bristol Co. LR 26:366; 34:29(Ephraim Tisdale).

231 ANNA[5] TISDALE (John[4], Anna[3] Rogers, John[2], Thomas[1]) b. ca. 1718; d. 29 April 1793 in 76th yr.
She m. Taunton 28 Nov. 1741 ABIAL DEANE, b. Taunton ca. 1720; d. Raynham 31 March 1781 ae 61; son of Israel and Ruth (Jones) Deane.
The will of Abiel Dean of Raynham, oldest of that name in this town, dated 18 Dec. 1780 and sworn 5 Feb. 1782, names sons Abiel, Abiather, Samuel and Benaiah; daus. Anna Dean, Susanna Britton wife of Ebenezer Jr. of Westmoreland, and Elizabeth Dean; son Abiather, executor. (No wife named in record book copy or in original will.)

Children (DEANE) prob. b. Raynham: ANNA[6]; SUSANNA; ELIZABETH; ABIAL; ABIATHAR; SAMUEL; BENAIAH; and poss. ALICE; and JEDEDIAH.

References: VR TAUNTON. DEAN GEN p. 79. Bristol Co. PR 27:50 and file(Abial Dean).

232 PHEBE[5] LEONARD (Anna[4] Tisdale, Anna[3] Rogers, John[2],
Thomas[1]) b. Norton 11 March 1696; d. Bristol RI 18 Dec.
1744 aged 49 unnamed "wife of Joseph."
     She m. Norton 26 Aug. 1718 JOSEPH REYNOLDS of Bristol
RI, b. Boston 29 Dec. 1676; d. Bristol RI 16 Jan. 1759 ae
82y 0m 7d; son of Nathaniel and Priscilla (Bracket) Reynolds. Joseph is buried in the old cemetery in Bristol
center under a stone carved with a coat-of-arms. On 26
Oct. 1744 Joseph Reynolds of Bristol and wife Phebe received from their brother Ephraim Leonard of Norton a
legacy of "our father George Leonard Esq." Joseph was a
lieutenant in the RI Militia.
     The will of Joseph Reynolds of Bristol tanner, drawn
16 Feb. 1757 and witnesses took oath 5 Feb. 1759, names
son Joseph to have my dwelling house in Bristol where I
dwell and land in CT; dau. Phebe Waldron wife of Daniel to
have my stone wharf and negro woman Dinah who is not to be
sold out of my family; son Samuel the drawer that came
from Norton; apprentice Peter Aldredge under 21; beloved
grandchildren John and Elizabeth Watson children of dau.
Elizabeth Watson of Plymouth dec.; son Joseph, executor.

     Children (REYNOLDS) b. Bristol: JOSEPH[6] b. 1719; GEORGE b. 1721;
ELIZABETH b. 1722; PHEBE b. 1725; SAMUEL b. and d. 1727; SAMUEL b.
1728/9; and JONATHAN b. 1732, d. 1753.

References: VR NORTON. BOSTON VR 9:139. RI VR: Bristol pp. 100, 159.
       REYNOLDS DESC pp. 1-2. REYNOLDS HIST pp. 80, 101. Bris-
tol Co. PR 23:614(Joseph Reynolds). Bristol RI PR 1:267(Joseph Reynolds).

233 GEORGE[5] LEONARD (Anna[4] Tisdale, Anna[3] Rogers, John[2],
Thomas[1]) b. Norton 4 March 1698; d. there 4 Dec. 1778 ae
81.
     He m. Scituate 9 Nov. 1721 RACHEL CLAPP, b. Scituate
29 May 1701; d. Norton 23 April 1783 in 82nd year; dau. of
Stephen and Temperance (Gorham) Clapp, and a descendant of
Pilgrim John Howland.
     George Leonard was a probate judge, and left a size-
able estate. The will of George Leonard of Norton Esq. in
73rd year, made 16 Feb. 1771, with codicil 14 Jan. 1777 and
probated 5 Jan. 1779, names wife Rachel; son George; oldest
dau. Rachel Barnes the wife of David of Scituate; and 2nd
dau. Anna Chandler wife of Gardner Esq. of Worcester.

     Children (LEONARD) b. Norton: RACHEL[6] bp. 1727; GEORGE b. 1729;
ANNA; and THOMAS b. and d. 1743.

References: VR NORTON, SCITUATE. Bristol Co. PR 25:379(Geo. Leonard).
       NEHGR 5:408.

234 NATHANIEL[5] LEONARD (Anna[4] Tisdale, Anna[3] Rogers,
John[2], Thomas[1]) b. Norton 9 March 1699/1700; d. there 11
June 1761 ae 62.

He m. int. Ipswich 22 Oct. 1724 PRISCILLA ROGERS, b.
ca. 1701; d. Haverhill 20 Nov. 1773 ae 72; dau. of Dr.
Daniel and Sarah (Appleton) Rogers of Ipswich. [She is
not a descendant of Pilgrim Thomas Rogers.]

Rev. Nathaniel Leonard graduated from Harvard College
in 1719, and was ordained 29 July 1724 at Plymouth. He
served there until 1756 when his health failed.

The will of Nathaniel Leonard of Norton, drawn 3 June
1761 and probated 15 June 1761, names wife Priscilla;
eldest daughter Sarah LeBaron now a widow; second daughter
Anna Torrey wife of Nathaniel of Plimoth; dau. Priscilla
McKinstry wife of William of Taunton; unmarried daus.
Elizabeth and Margaret; eldest son Nathaniel; and other
sons Abiel, George and Thomas.

Children (LEONARD) b. Plymouth: ANNA[6] b. 1725, d. 1725/6; SARAH
b. 1726; ANNA b. 1728; MARY b. and d. 1729; NATHANIEL b. 1730; PRIS-
CILLA b. 1732; DANIEL b. and d. 1733/4; MARY b. 1735, d. 1735/6; ELIZA-
BETH b. 1736; EPHRAIM b. and d. 1737; MARY b. 1738, d. 1739; ABIEL b.
1740; MARGARET b. 1741; GEORGE b. 1742; THOMAS b. 1744; and PHEBE b.
1746.

References: VR IPSWICH, NORTON. MD 13:199, 202. HARVARD GRADS 6:324-
7. BOSTON NEWS OBITS 3:58. (PLYMOUTH) BURIAL HILL pp.
13, 15, 20. Plymouth VR 1A:144, 151. Bristol Co. PR 17:436, 439
(Nathaniel Leonard).

235 ABIGAIL[5] LEONARD (Anna[4] Tisdale, Anna[3] Rogers, John[2],
Thomas[1]) b. Norton 20 Oct. 1703; d. Waltham 18 Sept. 1789
aged 86 "widow of Rev. Warham Williams."

Abigail m. Norton 23 May 1728 WARHAM WILLIAMS of Waltham, b. Deerfield 16 Sept. 1699; d. Waltham 22 June 1751
in 52nd year; son of Rev. John & Eunice (Mather) Williams.

When Warham was only four years old, he and his family
were taken captive by Indians in a raid on Deerfield and
held in Canada for three years, a tale told by his father
in *The Redeemed Captive*. Warham was a graduate of Harvard
in 1719, and was ordained 11 June 1723.

On 22 July 1772 Abigail Williams of Waltham, widow of
Rev. Warham Williams, gave receipt to her brother Ephraim
Leonard of Norton for a legacy from the estate of her
father George Leonard.

Children (WILLIAMS) all but last three b. Watertown, last three
born Waltham (which was set off from Watertown in 1738): JOHN[6] b. and
d. 1728/9; ABIGAIL b. 1729/30; ANNA b. 1732; EUNICE b. 1733/4, d. 1743;
SAMUEL b. 1735, d. 1742/3; SARAH b. 1737; LEONARD b. 1739; ELEAZER b.
1741/2, d. 1742/3; and SAMUEL b. 1743.

References: VR NORTON, WALTHAM. WATERTOWN REC **:88, 89, 96, 99,
            103, 109. HARVARD GRADS 6:361-4. WATERTOWN BY BOND pp.
654-5. NEHGR 5:411. THE REDEEMED CAPTIVE. Bristol Co. PR 23:614
(Abigail Williams).

236 EPHRAIM[5] LEONARD (Anna[4] Tisdale, Anna[3] Rogers, John[2],
Thomas[1]) b. Norton 16 Jan. 1705 or 1706; d. Mansfield 2
May 1786 in 81st yr.
     He m. (1) Norwich CT 28 May 1739 JUDITH PERKINS, b.
Norwich 2 March 1714/5; d. Mansfield 4 Sept. 1740 in her
26th yr., "wife of Capt. Ephraim"; dau. of Jabez and Hannah
(Lothrup) Perkins.
     He m. (2) Wrentham 15 July 1745 MELATIAH (FISHER)
(WARE) WARE, b. Wrentham 6 Oct. 1705; d. Mansfield 3 Oct.
1758 in 52nd yr., "formerly wife Jonathan Ware and also
wife Benjamin Ware M.D."; dau. of Ebenezer and Abigail
(Elles) Fisher.
     He m. (3) Easton 18 March 1760 Mrs. ABIGAIL WILLIAMS
"of Easton," d. Mansfield 27 July 1771 in 61st yr., bur.
Easton.
     He m. (4) Rochester 21 Oct. 1773 Mrs. ANNA (CLAP)
(WOODWORTH) RUGGLES, b. Scituate 1 March 1705/6; d. Mansfield 7 Oct. 1782 in 77 yr., "former wife of Elisha Woodworth and also wife of Timothy Ruggles"; dau. of Joseph
and Abigail (-----) Clap.
     Ephraim was a judge, but left no probate records in
Bristol Co. On 12 May 1762 Ephraim Leonard of Norton Esq.
gave to son Daniel Leonard of Norton gentleman 50 acres of
his farm. Apparently Daniel was his only child, for no
other deeds were found to his children.

     Child (LEONARD) b. Norton to Capt. Ephraim and Judith: DANIEL[6]
b. 1740.

References: VR MANSFIELD, NORTON, ROCHESTER, SCITUATE, WRENTHAM.
             Bristol Co. LR 46:311(Ephraim Leonard). NEHGR 5:409.
NORWICH CT VR 1:8.

237 MARY[5] LEONARD (Anna[4] Tisdale, Anna[3] Rogers, John[2],
Thomas[1]) b. Norton 17 Jan. 1713/14; d. Scituate 27 June
1741 ae 28 "wife of Thomas Esq."
     She m. Norton 9 Sept. 1731 THOMAS CLAPP of Taunton, b.
Scituate 11 Nov. 1705; d. there 31 May 1774 in 69th yr.
"Colonel"; son of John and Hannah (Gill) Clapp. He m. (2)
Scituate 1745 Mrs. Esther Chandler, by whom he had Hannah,
Calvin, Augustus, Chandler and Rufus.
     Thomas Clapp graduated from Harvard in 1725, and was
ordained at Taunton in 1728/9. After a few years he moved
to Scituate leaving the ministry. He served several terms
in the Massachusetts House of Representatives, and was a
judge of the County Court.

The will of Thomas Clapp of Scituate Esq., made 11
Nov. 1769 and proved 1 June 1774, names wife Esther; son
John; five younger children Mary, Hannah, Augustus, Chand-
ler and Rufus Clapp; son Thomas to have a porringer that
was his mother's; grandson John, son of son John. Wife
Esther and dau. Mary were named executors.

Children (CLAPP) b. Scituate to Thomas and Mary: JOHN[6]; THOMAS;
MARY b. 1739; and CALVIN b. 1740, d. 1741.

References: VR NORTON, SCITUATE. HARVARD GRADS 7:494-8. BOSTON NEWS
OBITS 2:209. Bristol Co. PR 25:379, 384(Thos. Clapp).
Bristol Co. LR 30:354(Thos. Clapp). Plymouth Co. PR 21:380(Thos.
Clapp). NEHGR 5:411; 7:325.

238 RICHARD[5] STEPHENS (Remember[4] Tisdale, Anna[3] Rogers,
John[2], Thomas[1]) b. Dighton 21 April 1698; d. bet. 19 Oct.
1731 and 9 Nov. 1768 (deposition with #54).
He m. Dighton 14 May 1725 PRISCILLA JONES of Dighton,
poss. dau. of Ebenezer Jones of Dighton to whom Richard
Stephens, late of Dighton now of Taunton millwright, mortgaged four acres of my father Nicholas Stephens's on 26
June 1731. The mortgage was paid 19 Oct. 1731.
There are no probate records at Bristol County for
Richard or Priscilla, and no land records there to indicate
they moved, but the will of Nicholas Stephens, drawn in
1735, mentions his "son Richard or his legal representa-
tives" implying that Richard was no longer living in the
Taunton vicinity. It is possible that Richard's son Ebe-
nezer moved to Rhode Island (and Richard and Priscilla
moved there and died), for in 1781 an Ebenezer Stephens of
Johnston RI and wife Sarah sold land to son Ebenezer of
Taunton.

Children (STEPHENS) b. Dighton: HANNAH[6] b. 1725/6; EBENEZER b.
1728; and MARY b. 1730.

References: DIGHTON VR pp. 19, 29. Bristol Co. LR 60:335(Ebenezer
Stephens).

239 NICHOLAS[5] STEPHENS (Remember[4] Tisdale, Anna[3] Rogers,
John[2], Thomas[1]) b. Dighton 24 Feb. 1702; d. there 30 April
1753.
He m. Jamestown RI 2 Aug. 1724 RACHEL ANDREWS ("he of
Dighton, she of Jamestown"), b. East Greenwich RI 12 July
1702; living 19 April 1753; dau. of John and Robbana
(-----) Andrews. She may have m. (2) int. Brookfield 1759
Peter Abbott.
On 25 Nov. 1751 Nicholas Stephens, shipwright of Digh-
ton, and others sold land with wife Rachel releasing her

dower. The will of Nicholas Stephens of Dighton yeoman,
dated 19 April 1753 and sworn 25 May 1753, mentions wife
Rachel; sons George and Nicholas; iron works in Dover NY;
sons Zephaniah and Elkanah to have my lands in Woodstock
and Thompson [CT]; dau. Sarah Beels; sons Isaac and Peletiah; and daughter Judia Stephens; executors, wife Rachel
and Jacob Wiley of Woodstock CT. The probate files include
a 1753 bond of Josiah Stephens of Taunton cordwainer as
guardian of Judah Stephens under 14, daughter of Nicholas
of Dighton. There was no indication in the probate file,
and no land records in Bristol County, to prove that
Rachel married Peter Abbott.

     Children (STEPHENS) b. Dighton: JOHN[6] d. 1732; GEORGE b. 1726;
NICHOLAS b. 1730; SARAH b. 1732; ZEPHANIAH b. 1734/5; ELKANAH b.
1736/7; ISAAC 1738/9; PELATIAH b. 1742; and JUDAH (dau.) b. bef. 1753.

References: RI VR:Jamestown p. 13; East Greenwich p. 94. DIGHTON VR
             pp. 5, 31. VR BROOKFIELD. Bristol Co. PR 13:397(Nicho-
las Stephens). Bristol Co. LR 38:289(Nicholas Stephens).

240 JOSEPH[5] STEPHENS (Remember[4] Tisdale, Anna[3] Rogers,
John[2], Thomas[1])   b. Dighton 23 April 1704; d. there bet.
9 Nov. 1768 and 30 Jan. 1776.
     He m. bef. 1731 LYDIA BRIGGS, who was living in Digh-
ton 31 Dec. 1777; dau. of Matthew and Abigail (Burt)
Briggs. The will of Matthew Briggs of Dighton yeoman,
dated 20 Dec. 1763, names dau. Lydia Stephens. On 31 Dec.
1777 Lydia Stephens of Dighton widow sold land of her husband Joseph dec., which they purchased of "my father Matthew Briggs late of Dighton dec."
     Lydia posted bond as administratrix of Joseph Stephens
late of Dighton on 30 Jan. 1776.

     Children (STEPHENS) b. Dighton: ABIGAIL[6] b. 1731; RUTH b. 1733;
JUSTUS b. 1737/8; REMEMBRANCE b. 1739; REBECCA b. 1742/3; MARCY b.
1745; and ASA b. 1756.

References: DIGHTON VR p. 39. Bristol Co. PR 24:359(Joseph Stephens).
             Bristol Co. LR 18:330(Matthew Briggs); 58:120(Lydia
Stephens).

241 JOSIAH[5] STEPHENS (Remember[4] Tisdale, Anna[3] Rogers,
  2
John[2], Thomas[1])   b. Dighton 23 Nov. 1707; d. there bet. 19
May 1784 and 6 Sept. 1784.
     He m. (1) Dighton 20 March 1734/5 SARAH POOL, b. Digh-
ton 21 Dec. 17--; dau. of Benjamin and Hannah (Whitmarsh)
Pool.
     He m. (2) Dighton 27 Sept. 1739 MARY TUELS, living 19
May 1784; dau. of Benjamin Tuels. The will of Benjamin

Tuels Sr. of Dighton yeoman, dated 24 June 1745, names
wife Joanna and dau. Mary Stephens.
    Josiah Stephens was a cordwainer in 1753 when he gave
his bond as guardian to Judia Stephans, his niece.
    The will of Josiah Stephens of Dighton yeoman, made
19 May 1784 and witnesses deposed 6 Sept. 1784, names wife
Mary; daughter Mary Linkon wife of Elisha; sons Elisha,
Josiah, John, Benjamin and Thomas; two grandchildren,
children of son Elijah deceased: Elisha and Sarah
Stephens; son Samuel executor.

    Children (STEPHENS): MARY[6], ELISHA, JOSIAH, JOHN, BENJAMIN,
THOMAS, ELIJAH, and SAMUEL.

References: DIGHTON VR pp. 53, 88. Bristol Co. PR 28:104(Josiah
             Stephens); 11:126(Benjamin Tuels). Bristol Co. LR 37:116
(Josiah Stephens).

242   (H)ANNAH[5] STEPHENS   (Remember[4] Tisdale, Anna[3] Rogers,
John[2], Thomas[1])   b. Dighton 6 Oct. 1710; perhaps the Ann
who d. Scituate 11 Aug. 1803 ae 86y 3m(?) "widow of Robert."
    Ann "of Taunton" m. int. Scituate 9 June 1732 ROBERT
ELMES, b. Scituate 26 Sept. 1707; d. there 4 March 1786 ae
77y 3m(?); son of Jonathan and Patience (-----) Elmes.
    On 15 Sept. 1749 Robert Stephens of Taunton [Ann's
half-brother] and Robert Elmes of Scituate quitclaimed to
Isaac and Josiah Stephens of Taunton land in Berkley which
their father Nicholas Stephens bought of John Spur in 1744.
    The will of Robert Elmes of Scituate yeoman, dated 27
June 1775 and presented 22 March 1786, names wife Nanc;
daughter Catherine White; granddaughters Ledy (or Lydia)
Stetson and Nanc Stetson, both under 21; other grandchildren all Stetsons: Susanna, James, Zibiah, Leah and Benjamin, all under 21; grandchildren Job Vinen, Ignatius Vinal
and Patience Vinal, all under 21; son Robert, executor.
[The names Nancy and Hannah were interchangeable with the
name Ann in the 1700's.]

    Children (ELMES) b. Scituate: ANN[6] b. 1733; ZIBIAH b. 1735;
PATIENCE bp. 1737; KATHARINE bp. 1738; ROBERT bp. 1741; and JOHN SPUR
bp. 1744.

References: VR SCITUATE. Plymouth Co. PR 29:464(Robert Elmes).
             Bristol Co. LR 37:115(Robert Stephens).

243 LYDIA[5] TERRY   (Thomas[4], Anna[3] Rogers, John[2], Thomas[1])
b. bef. 1701; living 3 May 1762.
    She m. Dighton 18 Feb. 1719/20 BENJAMIN JONES, b. 24
Sept. 1697; d. Taunton 24 July 1767; son of Benjamin

and Susanna (Beal) Jones.

On 9 April 1760 Abiel Terry of Freetown Esq. and Benjamin Jones of Dighton gentleman and wife Lydia sold land in Raynham, part of the estate of Isaac Dean deceased, which was divided to Thomas Terry Esq. and wife, both deceased, and to others. (This deed proves the parentage of Benjamin Jones' wife.)

The will of Benjamin Jones of Dighton gentleman, dated 16 May 1755 "under weakness of body" and sworn 31 Oct. 1768, names wife Lydia; son Ephraim who has bequest from "a near relative"; sons John, Abiel, Thomas and Zephaniah; dau. Abigail Nichols wife of John; four younger daus. Mary, Hannah, Elizabeth and Lydia (no last names); kinswoman Hannah Winslow; son Benjamin an infirm man; son Abiel was appointed executor, and was to support testator's aged mother.

Children (JONES) b. Dighton: BENJAMIN[6] b. 1721; EPHRAIM b. 1722; ABIGAIL b. 1724; JOHN b. 1726; MARY b. 1729; HANNAH b. 1730; ABIAL b. 1732; ELIZABETH b. 1734/5; THOMAS b. 1737; ZEPHANIAH b. 1738/9; and LYDIA b. 1742.

References: DIGHTON VR p. 28. Bristol Co. PR 20:396-9(Benj. Jones). Bristol Co. LR 45:462(Abiel Terry).

244 ABIEL[5] TERRY (Thomas[4], Anna[3] Rogers, John[2], Thomas[1]) b. Freetown 3 Dec. 1714; d. bet. 24 Aug. 1787 and 4 March 1793.

He m. int. Freetown 20 July 1738 HANNAH TISDALE, d. after 21 April 1792; dau. of Joseph and Ruth (Reed) Tisdale. The will of Joseph Tisdale of Taunton, 27 May 1739, names wife Ruth and daughter Hannah Terry.

Abiel served as Freetown Town Clerk, and was commissioned as Captain and eventually as Lt. Colonel. The last record of Abial Terry of Freetown Esq. was when he and John Anthony sold land in Middleboro 24 Aug. 1787.

The will of Abiel Terry of Freetown "under bodily indisposition" was dated 2 March 1776 and presented 4 March 1793. He named wife Hannah; eldest son Abiel to have rights to land on Long Island [NY] and Block Island [RI]; son Zebedee to have land "provided he return home from his present exile"; Zebedee's eldest son Zebedee; children of son Zebedee: Seth Williams, Thomas, N. Luscombe, Hannah Terry, and Mary Eels Terry, and child son Zebedee's wife may be pregnant with; son Joseph; son Abiel to be executor. A codicil was made 12 March 1778 and presented 5 March 1793, the executor being deceased. Zebedee, Mary Eels, Seth Williams and Nathaniel Luscombe, all Terrys, protested that the will had been revoked by the deceased before his death, but the judge dismissed the protest. The guardians

of the children of Abiel Terry Jr. deceased, and Hannah
Terry, widow of Col. Abiel Terry late of Freetown, agreed
to set off her dower 21 April 1792.

Children (TERRY) b. Freetown: ABIAL[6] b. 1740; ZEBEDEE b. 1741;
JOSEPH b. 1743; HANNAH b. 1746, d. 1747; and THOMAS b. and d. 1747.

References: Freetown VR pp. 42, 43, 81. Plymouth Co. LR 71:248(Abiel
              Terry). Bristol Co. PR 36:543(Abiel Terry); 9:241(Jos.
Tisdale). Bristol Co. LR 73:325(Hannah Terry). TERRY FAM p. 265.

245 SILAS[5] TERRY (John[4], Anna[3] Rogers, John[2], Thomas[1])
b. Freetown 8 April 1707; d. there bet. 2 June and 11 Aug.
1729.
     He m. SARAH -----, who d. after 2 May 1753. She m.
(2) Dighton 1730 Jonathan Davis, and had five children by
him; she is mentioned in his will dated 1753.
     The will of Silas Terry of Freetown, dated 2 June
1729, inventory taken 11 Aug. 1729, left to wife Sarah the
moveables she brought with her and the income of land which
belongs to my child, according to this will; it decreed
that enough inheritance from my mother and father be given
my brother John Terry to make his portion equal to that of
my child Remember; it mentioned my father Gage; and it
named uncle Thomas Terry executor, to divide my lands,
which were my father's, with uncle Benjamin Terry.

Child (TERRY) b. Freetown: REMEMBRANCE[6] b. 1728.

References: Freetown VR pp. 32, 78. DIGHTON VR p. 33. Bristol Co.
              PR 6:264(Silas Terry); 13:368(Jonathan Davis).

246 JOHN[5] TERRY (John[4], Anna[3] Rogers, John[2], Thomas[1]) b.
Freetown 26 May 1708; d. bet. 18 Feb. 1774 and 2 Sept.
1776.
     He m. Freetown 10 Feb. 1731/2 LYDIA WILLIAMS, b. ca.
1712; living 18 Feb. 1774; dau. of Emmanuel and Abigail
(Makepeace) Williams, and a descendant of Pilgrim Thomas
Rogers (see #219). On 15 June 1737 John Terry of Freetown,
blacksmith, and Lidia his wife, who was dau. of Immanuel
Williams late of Taunton dec., sold their part in the homestead of said Williams.
     The will of John Terry of Freetown yeoman names wife
Lydia, eldest son Zephaniah, son Ebenezer, daughter Rachel
wife of John Crance, son Silas, daughter Hannah wife of Job
Pain, son Job, daughter Welthe wife of Thomas Jones, daughter Lydia Terry; son Job, executor. The will was signed
18 Feb. 1774 and the witnesses appeared 2 Sept. 1776.

Children (TERRY) b. Freetown: RACHEL[6] b. 1732; HANNAH b. 1734;
LYDIA b. 1736; JOHN b. 1738; ZEPHANIAH b. 1740; WELTHY b. 1743; EBE-
NEZER b. 1747; SILAS b. 1750; and JOB b. 1753.

References: Freetown VR pp. 29-30, 79. FREETOWN MARR p. 56. Bristol
              Co. PR 24:233(John Terry). Bristol Co. LR 26:71(John
Terry).

247 MARY[5] TERRY (Benjamin[4], Anna[3] Rogers, John[2], Thomas[1])
b. prob. Freetown ca. 1715; d. after 28 June 1768 (father's
will).
     She m. int. Freetown 4 Sept. 1735 JAMES WARREN, b.
Middlcboro 24 Feb. 1710/11; d. Westport 1790; son of Samuel
and Elinor (Billington) Warren, and a descendant of Pilgrims John Billington and Richard Warren.
     Although not a soldier, James rendered patriotic ser-
vice in the Revolution. On 4 Dec. 1788 James Warren of
Westport sold to sons Cornelius of Westport and Gamaliel
of Tiverton 16 acres in Westport; James acknowledged the
deed at Newport RI 26 Dec. 1788.

     Children (WARREN) first and last b. Freetown, others Middleboro:
SAMUEL[6] b. 1737; MARY b. 1739; CORNELIUS b. 1741; GAMALIEL bp. 1744;
and JAMES b. 1745.

References: Freetown VR pp. 27, 80. MD 2:201; 15:122; 21:104. NEHGR
              55:170. Bristol Co. LR 67:382(James Warren). DAR
PATRIOT INDEX p. 718.

248 ROBERT[5] TERRY (Benjamin[4], Anna[3] Rogers, John[2], Thomas[1]) b. prob. Freetown ca. 1717; d. Freetown bet. 6 Jan.
and 1 June 1802.
     He m. int. Freetown 1 March 1737/8 REBECCA LAWTON of
Freetown.
     The will of Robert Terry of Freetown, drawn 6 Jan.
1802 and presented 1 June 1802, names sons Silas and Benjamin; eldest daughter Abigail Hopkins; other daughters Mary
Warren, Rebecca Spaulding and Phebe Reed; son Robert to
have use of real estate, and *his* eldest son Silas to have
use of real estate in his turn, the property then being
inherited by Silas' eldest son; Robert was named executor.

     Children (TERRY) prob. b. Freetown: SILAS[6], BENJAMIN, ABIGAIL,
MARY, REBECCA, PHEBE, and ROBERT.

References: Freetown VR p. 81. Bristol Co. PR 39:123(Robert Terry).

249 BENJAMIN[5] TERRY (Benjamin[4], Anna[3] Rogers, John[2], Thomas[1]) b. ca. 1719; d. Exeter RI bet. 3 March 1787 and 6 Oct. 1794.

He m. Dartmouth 15 Dec. 1741 JOANNA POPE, b. Dartmouth 20 Feb. 1717/8; d. prob. Exeter after 3 March 1787; dau. of Elnathan and Margaret (-----) Pope. The division of property of Elnathan Pope of Dartmouth on 8 April 1746 names widow Margaret and dau. Joanna Terry, wife of Benjamin.

Benjamin moved to Exeter RI sometime between 16 Sept. 1775, when "Benjamin Tearey of Darkmouth" yeoman bought land in Exeter, and 18 March 1781, when he and Joanna Terry, both formerly of Dartmouth, gave to son Thomas land in Dartmouth which was part of our farm where we lived. They acknowledged the deed at Exeter, Kings Co., RI on 2 May 1781.

The will of Benjamin Terry of Exeter yeoman, dated 3 March 1787 and approved 6 Oct. 1794, names son Thomas Terry of Dartmouth, son Benjamin Terry of Dartmouth, and sons Elnathan and Seth who received land in Exeter; daughters Sarah Terry, Deborah Hammond, Joanna Greene and Patience Green; wife Joanna; and granddaughter Joanna Hammond; son Thomas, executor.

Children (TERRY) first six recorded at Dartmouth, last at Exeter RI: SARAH[6] b. 1742; DEBORAH b. 1745; THOMAS b. 1749; BENJAMIN b. 1750; JOANNA b. 1753; PATIENCE b. 1755; ELNATHAN; and SETH b. 1764.

References: VR DARTMOUTH. RI VR:Exeter p. 61. Bristol Co. PR 11:254 (Elnathan Pope). Bristol Co. LR 66:374-5(Benj. Terry). Exeter RI PR 6:17(Benj. Terry). Exeter RI LR 1:409(Benj. Terry). POPE FAM p. 287. NEHGR 42:53.

250 JOHN[5] TERRY (Benjamin[4], Anna[3] Rogers, John[2], Thomas[1]) b. prob. Freetown ca. 1721; d. Hardwick bef. 26 July 1790.

He prob. m. int. Dartmouth 16 Oct. 1745 "both of Dartmouth" JOANNA POPE, b. Dartmouth 8 Nov. 1728; d. Hardwick 6 Jan. 1814 ae 88; dau. of Isaac and Lydia (-----) Pope.

The will of John Terry of Hardwick yeoman, dated 22 March 1785 and filed 26 July 1790, names wife Jehannah, sons Jacob and Isaac, daughters Rebeccah Samson wife to Samuel, Lydia who was single, and Phoebe Basset; son John Terry executor.

Children (TERRY) prob. b. Freetown or Hardwick: JACOB[6], ISAAC, REBECCA, LYDIA, PHEBE, and JOHN.

References: VR DARTMOUTH, HARDWICK. HARDWICK BY PAIGE pp. 297, 512. Worcester Co. PR #A58596(John Terry).

251 GEORGE[5] TERRY (Benjamin[4], Anna[3] Rogers, John[2], Thomas[1]) b. Freetown 30 Nov. 1723; d. after 5 Aug. 1788.
     He m. Freetown 24 Feb. 1744/5 ABIGAIL GIBBS, b. Swansea 29 June 1728; d. after 18 April 1785; dau. of Robert and Hepzibeth (Tisdale) Gibbs. The will of Robert Gibbs of Swansea yeoman, dated 2 March 1746, names wife Hepzibeth and dau. Abigail Terry. On 11 Dec. 1767 George Terry of Swansea and wife Abigail quitclaimed to their brother Henry Gibbs their share in the real estate of their mother Hepzibah Gibbs late of Swansea.
     George Terry was a "corker" when he sold land in 1760. On 29 March 1785 George Terry of Swansea yeoman gave to son James of Swansea laborer half his homestead farm. On 18 April 1785 George gave the other half to his son Philip, wife Abigail giving consent.
     There are no wills for George or Abigail at Bristol Co.; but he was doubtless the one for whom a guardian was appointed 1785, and terminated 5 Aug. 1788.

     Children (TERRY) b. Swansea: HEPZIBETH[6] b. 1750; PHILIP b. 1755; BETTY b. 1757; twins JAMES and JOHN b. 1760; and PHEBE b. 1765.

References: Bristol Co. PR 12:254(Robert Gibbs); 20:200; 28:544; 29:6; 30:21(Geo. Terry). Bristol Co. LR 63:465; 64:211(Geo. Terry). Plymouth Co. LR 48:196-7(Robt. Gibbs). SWANSEA VR pp. 40, 85, 101, 102, 133, 161.

252 JOANNA[5] TERRY (Benjamin[4], Anna[3] Rogers, John[2], Thomas[1]) b. Freetown 6 July 1725; d. Somerset 29 Sept. 1815 ae 90.
     She m. Freetown 3 Oct. 1745 ROBERT GIBBS Jr. "of Swansey," b. Swansea 24 Sept. 1724; d. Somerset 21 March 1810 ae 85 "Capt."; son of Robert and Hepzibah (Tisdale) Gibbs.
     Robert and Joanna were living in Swansea on 1 March 1775 when they sold land there. There are no probate records for them in Bristol County, but their tombstones are in the Gibbs Cemetery, Buffington St., Somerset.

     Child (GIBBS) b. Swansea: SAMUEL[6]

References: Freetown VR p. 87. FREETOWN MARR p. 29. SWANSEA VR p. 85. Somerset, Gibbs Cemetery Rec. Bristol Co. LR 56:389 (Robert Gibbs). Gibbs Bible Rec.

253 LYDIA[5] TERRY (Benjamin[4], Anna[3] Rogers, John[2], Thomas[1]) b. Freetown 10 Oct. 1726; living there 5 Aug. 1787.
     She m. Freetown 17 Jan. 1765 THOMAS WINSLOW, b. Freetown 5 July 1729; living there 6 May 1790; son of Jonathan and Sarah (Kerby) Winslow, and a descendant of Kenelm Winslow. He m. (1) int. Dighton and Freetown 1749 Mary Hoar.

On 5 Aug. 1787 Thomas Winslow of Freetown yeoman sold to Barnabas Winslow of Freetown wheelwright part of a saw mill in Freetown, with wife Lydia signing. On 4 May 1790 Thomas sold to Benjamin Winslow of Freetown cordwainer part of a saw mill, acknowledging the deed 6 May 1790. In the 1790 Census, Thomas of Freetown was living with one other male over 15 and three females.

There were no probate records for Lydia or Thomas at Bristol County, and although she received land in Middleboro in her father's will, there are no Plymouth County land records showing Lydia or Thomas selling that land.

Child (WINSLOW) b. Freetown: BENJAMIN[6] b. 1766.

References: Freetown VR pp. 12, 60, 90, 107. FREETOWN MARR p. 63. DIGHTON VR p. 88. Bristol Co. LR 66:486; 69:68(Thos. Winslow). 1790 CENSUS:MA:46. WINSLOW MEM 1:102, 235.

254 PHEBE[5] TERRY (Benjamin[4], Anna[3] Rogers, John[2], Thomas[1]) b. Freetown 15 Sept. 1729; d. prob. Freetown 1806.
She m. Freetown 6 Aug. 1752 JOSEPH DAGGETT, b. Nantucket 12 Sept. 1728; d. prob. Freetown bef. 17 July 1771; son of Jacob and Hannah (Skiff) Daggett.

Phebe Dagget of Freetown widow was bonded on 17 July 1771 as administratrix on the estate of Joseph Dagget of Freetown late deceased. No probate record was found for Phebe, or land evidence to confirm children. About 1773 Phebe received land from her father's estate.

Children (DAGGETT) b. Freetown: NATHAN[6] b. 1754; BENJAMIN b. 1756; and twins HANNAH and JOANNA b. 1763.

References: VR NANTUCKET. Freetown VR pp. 66, 92. FREETOWN MARR p. 21. MARTHA'S VINEYARD BY BANKS 3:130. DOGGETT FAM p. 104. DOGGETT SUPP p. 25. Bristol Co. PR file(Jos. Daggett).

255 WILLIAM[5] TERRY (Benjamin[4], Anna[3] Rogers, John[2], Thomas[1]) b. Freetown 17 April 1731; d. Exeter RI bet. 2 July 1798 and 1 April 1799.
He m. Swansea prob. 9 Nov. 1760* MARY BAKER, b. Swansea 28 Jan. 1733; d. after 7 Jan. 1794; dau. of Ebenezer and Lydia (-----) Baker. On 2 July 1766 William Terry of Swansea sold land there that was set off to his wife Mary from the estate of her father Ebenezer Baker late of Swansea deceased.

William and Mary moved to Exeter RI sometime between 29 May 1766 when William Terry of Swansea yeoman bought 150 acres in Exeter, and 18 Jan. 1772 when William of

---

*Freetown intentions 11 Oct. 1760, but copy of Swansea rec. gives marriage 9 Nov. 1766.

Exeter yeoman bought 29 acres in Exeter. On 10 March 1781
William Terry of Exeter yeoman sold to Ebenezer Terry of
Freetown 100 acres in Freetown given him by his father
Benjamin Terry deceased; William and Mary acknowledged
their signatures that day in Swansea. In 1790 William
Terry headed a household in Exeter consisting of one male
over fifteen, three males under sixteen, and four females.
   The last record of Mary was her release of dower in a
sale of land in Exeter by William of Exeter 7 Jan. 1794.
William died between 2 July 1798 when his son William of
Voluntown CT was appointed his guardian, and 1 April 1799
when William Terry of Voluntown, son of William Terry of
Exeter deceased intestate, petitioned to administer his
estate.

   Children (TERRY): WILLIAM[6], MEREBAH, and prob. others.

References: Freetown VR p. 102. SWANSEA VR pp. 12, 28, 39, 101. RI
          VR:Exeter pp. 5, 32. Bristol Co. LR 52:66; 66:263(Wm.
Terry). Exeter RI PR 6:121, 156(Wm. Terry). Exeter RI LR 4(new):169;
1(old):190; 10(old):169(Wm. Terry). 1790 CENSUS:RI p. 42.

256 MARGARET[5] TERRY (Benjamin[4], Anna[3] Rogers, John[2], Thomas[1]) b. Freetown 22 Oct. 1732; living 3 March 1792 (see
#257).
   She m. (1) Freetown 11 March 1756 WILLIAM TURNER,
poss. b. Newport RI ca. 1720; d. bef. 16 Dec. 1762; poss.
son of William and Patience (Hall) Turner of Newport, who
were buying and selling land in Swansea in the 1740's.
   The inventory of William Turner late of Swansea deceased was taken 16 Dec. 1762.
   Margaret m. (2) Freetown 19 Nov. 1767 JOHN LEWIN of
Swansea. Was he the John Lewin of Swansea who on 18 Oct.
1794 sold his homestead in Swansea to sons Nathaniel and
Thomas of Swansea? Was he the father also of William
Lewin of Swansea who on 23 Feb. 1789 sold to Nathaniel and
Thomas Lewin of Swansea his rights to the estate of our
father John Lewin of Swansea "which might come to him by
will or otherwise"? In 1790 two John Lewens are found in
Swansea: one living with one female, and listed next to
Thomas and Nathaniel; and John Lewen 2[d] with two males
over 15 and four females.

   Child (TURNER) b. Freetown: BETTY[6] b. 1756.

References: Freetown VR p. 61, 96, 112. FREETOWN MARR pp. 40,58.
          NEHGR 41:217; 123:40-1. Bristol Co. PR 42:159, 261(John
Lewin); 18:181(Wm. Turner). Bristol Co. LR 37:229; 38:258(John Lewen
& Wm. Lewin). TAG 22:218. 1790 CENSUS:MA p. 55.

257 SOLOMON[5] TERRY (Benjamin[4], Anna[3] Rogers, John[2], Thomas[1]) b. Freetown 13 Jan. 1734; d. there bef. 3 March 1792.

He m. Freetown 8 Dec. 1763 SUSANNA WINSLOW who d. after 4 Nov. 1794.

An inventory taken 3 Mar. 1792 of the estate of Solomon Terry late of Freetown dec. was shown by Susannah Terry and her son Shubal Terry proposed administrators. In an account 4 Nov. 1794, Shubael mentions "settling a legacy with my two aunts at Swansea" and legacies paid to Margaret Lewis (*sic*), Dinah Lain (or Lewin) and Phebe Daggett. The latter were Solomon's sisters. No probate records were found for Susan at Bristol Co.

Children (TERRY) b. Freetown: ANNA[6] b. 1765; JOANNA b. 1768; SHUBAL b. 1771; BENJAMIN b. 1773; and JOHN b. 1776.

References: Freetown VR pp. 61, 106. FREETOWN MARR p. 56. Bristol
      Co. PR 31:429; 33:150(Solomon Terry).

258 MIRIAM[5] TERRY (Benjamin[4], Anna[3] Rogers, John[2], Thomas[1]) b. Freetown 18 May 1737; d. after 28 June 1768 (father's will).

She m. Freetown 13 May 1759 ELIJAH TISDALE "of Easton, resident of No(r)ton", b. bet. 1730 and 1735; d. after 1766; son of John and Judith (Hall) Tisdale, and a descendant of Pilgrim Thomas Rogers (see #227).

On 17 Dec. 1761 Elijah Tisdale yeoman of Easton mortgaged to James Dean of Easton land in Easton received from his father's estate; wife Meriam released her dower. An Elijah was living in Taunton 1790 with two females; was this our Elijah or his son? There are no Bristol County probate records for Elijah or Miriam.

Children (TISDALE) b. Easton: BETTY[6] b. 1760; ELIJAH b. 1762; LAVINIA b. 1764, d. 1765; and LAVINIA b. 1766.

References: FREETOWN MARR p. 57. Freetown VR p. 93. Bristol Co. LR
      45:387(Elijah Tisdale). Easton Town Rec p. 90. VR NOR-
TON. HALLS OF NE p. 570.

259 SARAH[5] TERRY (Benjamin[4], Anna[3] Rogers, John[2], Thomas[1]) b. Freetown 13 Aug. 1739; d. after 23 Aug. 1784.

She m. Freetown 6 July 1761 BARNABAS WINSLOW, b. Freetown 30 Sept. 1734; d. bet. 23 Aug. 1784 and 5 Sept. 1796; son of George and Elizabeth (Tisdale) Winslow.

On 23 Aug. 1784 Barnabas Winslow of Freetown, with release of wife Sarah, sold to Job Terry of Freetown part of a saw mill etc. In 1790 a Barnabas Winslow headed a household in Freetown comprising four males 16 or over,

one boy, and 2 females.
      The inventory of the estate of Barnabas Winslow late
of Freetown deceased was taken 5 Sept. 1796, and Nathan
Winslow was appointed administrator. No evidence found
for children Andrew, Henry, Elizabeth and Simon-Peter
claimed in WINSLOW MEM.

      Children (WINSLOW) b. Freetown: ELKANAH[6] b. 1761; LYDIA b. 1763;
ABIGAIL b. 1766; BARNABAS b. 1768; and JOB b. 1770.

References: Freetown VR pp. 14, 65, 102. Bristol Co. PR 34:208, 538
             (Barnabas Winslow). Bristol Co. LR 63:5(Barnabas Wins-
low). WINSLOW MEM 1:234.

260 JOSEPH[5] RICHMOND (Joseph[4], Abigail[3] Rogers, John[2],
Thomas[1]) b. prob. Taunton ca. 1686; d. Berkley bet. 2
Dec. 1750 and 5 Feb. 1750/1.
      He m. (1) Raynham int. 17 Dec. 1[   ] HANNAH DEANE,
b. Taunton 26 Dec. 1682; living 2 Feb. 1727/8; dau. of
Benjamin and Sarah (Williams) Deane. On 2 Feb. 1727/8
Joseph Richmond Jr. of Taunton and wife Hannah, and other
children of Benjamin Dean late of Taunton deceased, quitclaimed land of their father Benjamin Dean.
      He m. (2) Berkley 20 April 1736 or 1737 ABIGAIL
(PHILLIPS) FRENCH who d. after 25 Dec. 1772; dau. of James
and Abigail (Hathaway) Phillips, and widow of Joseph French
Jr. The will of James Phillips of Taunton, made 23 March
1731/2, names dau. Abigail French. A deed of 1 Nov. 1752
by Abigail Richmond of Berkley widow, late widow of Joseph
French Jr. late of Taunton deceased, settled French's estate; on 22 June 1772 Abigail Richmond of Berkley widow
sold to son Perez Richmond of Berkley her homestead farm
in Berkley, acknowledged 25 Dec. 1772.
      The will of Joseph Richmond of Berkley "very sick,"
made 22 Dec. 1750 and proved 5 Feb. 1750[/1], mentions his
wife but does not name her; sons Seth and Joseph; daughters
Sarah Dean and Hannah Richmond, the latter unmarried; son
Perez and daughter Wealthy Richmond; Seth named executor.

      Children (RICHMOND) b. Berkley, first four by Hannah, last two
by Abigail: SETH[6]; JOSEPH b. 1723; SARAH; HANNAH; WEALTHY b. 1738;
and PEREZ b. 1744.

References: VR TAUNTON. RICHMOND FAM p. 22. Bristol Co. PR 7:485
             (James Phillips); 12:495(Joseph Richmond). Bristol Co.
LR 19:297(Israel Dean); 39:191; 55:68(Abigail Richmond). Berkley VR
1:183(b. Perez and Welthey, no parent given).

261 CHRISTOPHER[5] RICHMOND (Joseph[4], Abigail[3] Rogers,
John[2], Thomas[1]) b. prob. Taunton ca. 1689; d. there 26
Jan. 1771.

He m. (1) bef. 1717 PHEBE WILLIAMS, b. Taunton 25 Sept. 1687; d. after 3 Feb. 1730/1; dau. of Joseph and Elizabeth (Watson) Williams. On 28 Dec. 1716 Christopher Richmond and wife Phebe of Middleboro sold land in Taunton which fell to Phebe Williams alias Richmond.

He m. (2) Middleboro 15 Nov. 1750 SUSANNA (DURFEY) BARDEN of Middleboro, widow of Abraham Barden.

Christopher was one of those who went to Canada on an expedition in 1711. On 4 March 1733/4 Christopher Richmond of Middleboro sold 15 acres of the land he had received from his father Joseph Richmond Sr., and on 31 March 1735 Christopher Richmond of Middleboro cordwainer sold dwelling house and homestead, mentioning lands claimed by his brother John, and lands received of his father Joseph. On 24 Dec. 1744 Christopher deposed saying he was in his 56th year.

Neither Christopher nor Susanna left probate records in Plymouth County.

Children (RICHMOND) b. Middleboro all by Phebe: JUDITH[6] b. 1717; ELIZABETH b. 1719; MARY b. 1721; ELIAKIM b. 1724/5; PHEBE b. 1726/7; and JOSEPH b. 1730/1.

References: VR TAUNTON. MD 6:179-180, 229; 12:130; 18:82, 84. RICH-MOND FAM pp. 23-4. Bristol Co. LR 10:396; 29:63; 30:29 (Christopher Richmond). WILLIAMS FAM p. 38.

262 HENRY[5] RICHMOND (Joseph[4], Abigail[3] Rogers, John[2], Thomas[1]) b. ca. 1690; d. after 24 July 1751.

He m. bef. 26 April 1737 MEHITABLE CASWELL; prob. dau. of Samuel and Ruth (Bobbitt) Caswell.

On 26 April 1737 Henry Richmond of Taunton husbandman sold his homestead in Taunton, part of the farm where my father Lt. Joseph Richmond deceased last dwelt; wife Mehitable also signed. On 8 Dec. 1735 Henry Richmond of Taunton husbandman sold to brother Joseph Richmond of Taunton his share of the dwelling house of his father Joseph deceased; deed acknowledged 24 July 1751 at Taunton.

There were no Plymouth or Bristol County probate records for Henry or Mehitable.

Children (RICHMOND) first two b. Middleboro: MEHITABLE[6] b. 1740; DEBORAH b. 1742; and poss. HENRY, ABIAH, NATHAN, ELIAB, ABEL, WILLIAM, and JOB.

References: MD 16:247. RICHMOND FAM p. 24. Bristol Co. LR 35:107; 38:123 (Henry Richmond).

263 JOHN[5] RICHMOND (Joseph[4], Abigail[3] Rogers, John[2], Thomas[1]) b. ca. 1693; prob. d. Middleboro 21 March 1767.
    He m. ca. 1718 SARAH THRASHER, b. Taunton 20 March
1697; d. after 23 Aug. 1757; dau. of John and Mercy (Crossman) Thrasher. The will of John Thrasher of Taunton, made
20 May 1727, names dau. Sarah Richmond.
    The will of John Richmond of Middleboro names wife
Sarah, son John and daughter Abigail; son John to be executor. The will was drawn 23 Aug. 1757, presented 22 May
1767.

        Children (RICHMOND) b. Middleboro: JOHN[6] b. 1720, and ABIGAIL
    b. 1723.

References: MD 4:69; 7:241. Plymouth Co. PR 19:471(John Richmond).
          Bristol Co. PR 7:572(John Thrasher). RICHMOND FAM p. 23.
    VR TAUNTON.

264 ABIGAIL[5] RICHMOND (Joseph[4], Abigail[3] Rogers, John[2],
Thomas[1]) b. ca. 1696; d. bef. 1 Nov. 1784.
    She m. bef. 1723 MATTHEW GOODING, b. Dighton 12 June
1695; d. there 15 March 1756; son of George and Deborah
(Walker) Gooding.
    On 2 Nov. 1756 widow Abigail Gooding of Dighton be-
came one of the administrators of the estate of Matthew
Gooding deceased. The distribution was made 18 April 1757
with one-third to the widow, and the rest to eldest son
George, 2nd son Joseph, 3rd son Matthew, 4th son William,
5th son Job, eldest daughter Deborah Packer and youngest
daughter Mary Gooding. The widow's dower was divided
among the children 1 Nov. 1784.

        Children (GOODING) b. Dighton: GEORGE[6] b. 1723; DEBORAH b. 1726;
    JOSEPH b. 1729; MARY b. 1731; MATTHEW b. 1734; WILLIAM b. 1736; and
    JOB b. 1739.

References: DIGHTON VR pp. 15, 16. RICHMOND FAM pp. 23-24. Bristol
          Co. PR 13:166; 18:169(Matthew Gooding).

265 MARY[5] RICHMOND (Joseph[4], Abigail[3] Rogers, John[2],
Thomas[1]) b. ca. 1699; d. Taunton 25 Dec. 1784 ae 85.
    She m. (1) Taunton 8 June 1721 WILLIAM REED who d.
Taunton bef. 16 July 1734; son of John and Bethiah (Frye)
Reed.
    The will of William Read of Taunton husbandman very
sick, dated 31 March 1726, inventory taken 15 July 1734,
names wife Marah (or Mary) executor, sons William and John
each to receive two-fifths of the estate at age 21, and
daughter Mary one-fifth when she comes of age. Widow Mary
Read made oath to the inventory 16 July 1734.

Children (REED) b. Taunton: JOHN[6] b. 1722; WILLIAM; MARY; and ABIGAIL (not named in father's will).

References: VR TAUNTON, ROCHESTER. RICHMOND FAM pp. 22-3. Bristol
           Co. PR 8:139(Wm. Read); 21:234(Stephen Andrews). Reed
Gen. MS. by Edgar H. Reed (Old Colony Hist. Soc., Taunton).

266 WILLIAM[5] RICHMOND (Joseph[4], Abigail[3] Rogers, John[2], Thomas[1]) b. ca. 1700; d. Taunton bef. 26 Feb. 1735.
     He m. bef. 1728 ----- MACOMBER, poss. dau. of John Macomber.
     The inventory of the estate of William Richmond of Taunton was taken 26 Feb. 1735, with Joseph Richmond and William Macomber as administrators. In May 1742 guardians were appointed for Bethia Richmond and Ruth Richmond, the latter over 14, both daughters of William deceased. No Bristol County deeds were found helpful.

     Children (RICHMOND) b. Taunton: RUTH[6] b. bef. 1728, and BETHIA
b. ca. 1728.

References: VR TAUNTON. RICHMOND FAM pp. 24-5. Bristol Co. PR 8:328;
           10:143-4(William Richmond).

267 JOSIAH[5] RICHMOND (Joseph[4], Abigail[3] Rogers, John[2], Thomas[1]) b. ca. 1700; living 4 Sept. 1779, when use of land was reserved to him.
     He m. (1) Dighton 14 May 1730 ELISHABE POOL; d. Dighton 2 Dec. 1743; dau. of Isaac Pool of Dighton.
     He may have filed m. int. Dighton 1745 with ANNE HART of Taunton.
     He m. (2) int. Dighton 26 Dec. 1747 JOANNAH BRIGGS; living 3 Feb. 1753.
     On 4 Sept. 1779 Nathaniel Austin of Dighton and wife Abigail, one of the daughters of Josiah and Elishabe Richmond, sold land in Dighton which was deeded by my grandfather Isaac Pool as a gift to my mother Elishabe Richmond, then wife of Josiah Richmond Sr., and from her to my brother Elishabe Richmond; the grantors reserved to Josiah Richmond Sr. the improvement of part of the property during his lifetime. On 2 March 1782 Isaac Pool of Dighton yeoman for love and good will deeded to Abigail Austin wife of Nathaniel of Dighton, to Margaret Talbut wife of Benjamin of Killingly CT husbandman, and to Mary Randell wife of Stephen of Hanover husbandman, daughters of my sister Elishabe Richmond late of Dighton deceased, rights to land in Dighton which was the homestead of my father Isaac Pool late of Dighton deceased.

Children (RICHMOND) b. Dighton, first four to Elishabah, last
two to Joanna: ABIGAIL[6] b. 1730/1; MARY b. 1732; ELISHABE (son);
MARGRET b. 1737; JOSIAH b. 1750; and JOANNAH b. 1753.

References: DIGHTON VR pp. 33, 36, 87, 88. RICHMOND FAM p. 24.
             Bristol Co. LR 60:474-5(Nathaniel Austin, Isaac Pool).
VR TAUNTON.

268 EDWARD[5] RICHMOND (Edward[4], Abigail[3] Rogers, John[2],
Thomas[1]) b. Taunton ca. 1696; d. there 16 Feb. 1771 ae
75.
     He m. (1) ELIZABETH DEANE, b. Taunton 26 March 1695;
living 2 Feb. 1727/8; dau. of Benjamin and Sarah (Williams)
Deane. On 2 Feb. 1727/8 Edward Richmond Jr. of Taunton
with wife Elizabeth and other children of Benjamin Dean,
late of Taunton deceased, quitclaimed land of their father.
     He m. (2) Middleboro 6 Nov. 1750 ELIZABETH (HODGES)
(SHAW) SAMPSON, b. ca. 1702; d. Middleboro 10 Oct. 1782 in
81st yr.; dau. of Henry and Esther (Gallop) Hodges, and
widow of Samuel Shaw of Raynham and Isaac Sampson of Plympton.
     The will of Edward Richmond of Taunton, dated 13 Oct.
1767 and probated 12 March 1771, mentions wife Elizabeth;
son Isaac, executor; son Elijah; daughters Elizabeth Haskins, Prudence Hackett, Abigail Hall, Bathsheba Richmond
and Susannah Richmond; and son Edward.

     Children (RICHMOND) most, and prob. all, by first wife: ELIZA-
BETH[6] b. 1716; EDWARD b. 1724; PRUDENCE; ABIGAIL b. 1728; ELIJAH;
BATHSHEBA b. 1743; SUSANNA; ISAAC; and ISRAEL.

References: MD 18:84. VR TAUNTON. GEN ADVERTISER 2:32, 64. RICH-
             MOND FAM p. 25. Bristol Co. PR 23:46(Edward Richmond).
Bristol Co. LR 19:297(Edward Richmond et al.).

269 JOSIAH[5] RICHMOND (Edward[4], Abigail[3] Rogers, John[2],
Thomas[1]) b. Taunton ca. 1697; d. Middleboro 30 Jan. 1763.
     He m. (1) bef. 1727 MEHITABLE DEANE, b. Taunton 6 or
9 June 1697; dau. of Benjamin and Sarah (Williams) Deane.
On 2 Feb. 1727/8 Josiah Richmond with wife Mehitable of
Middleboro and other children of Benjamin Dean, late of
Taunton deceased, quitclaimed land of their father.
     He m. (2) Middleboro 6 Feb. 1745/6 LYDIA (EDDY)
CROCKER, b. 3 Feb. 1703/4; d. after 26 Jan. 1762; dau. of
Jabez and Mary (Richard) Eddy, and widow of Theophilus
Crocker.
     Josiah moved to Middleboro between 16 Oct. 1727, when
Edward Richmond of Taunton gave his son Josiah Richmond of

Taunton 50 acres of land in Middleboro, and 2 Feb. 1727/8 when Josiah and Mehitable quitclaimed land as above.

The will of Josiah Richmond of Middleboro blacksmith, dated 26 Jan. 1762 and presented 5 April 1763, mentions wife Lydia to have the goods she brought with her; daughter Mary Leonard; sons Josiah, Gershom, Benjamin and George; daughter Mary (*sic*) Hasket; sons Ephraim, Eleazer and Lemuel; and daughters Miriam Walker and Jirah (or Zirah) Richmond.

Children (RICHMOND) prob. all by first wife: MARY[6]; JOSIAH; GERSHOM; BENJAMIN b. 1727; GEORGE; MERCY; EPHRAIM b. 1735; ELEAZER b. 1737; LEMUEL; MIRIAM; and JIRAH (or Zirah).

References: MD 18:77. VR TAUNTON. RICHMOND FAM p. 26. Plymouth Co. PR 16:399(Josiah Richmond). Plymouth Co. LR 28:149(Edward Richmond). Bristol Co. LR 19:297(Josiah Richmond et al.).

270 SETH[5] RICHMOND (Edward[4], Abigail[3] Rogers, John[2], Thomas[1]) b. Taunton; d. there 22 Oct. 1791.

He m. prob. Taunton bef. 1738 LYDIA HASKINS who d. Taunton 29 Sept. 1782.

The will of Seth Richmond of Taunton yeoman, dated 21 April 1781 and probated 3 Jan. 1792, names wife Lydia; sons Edmund of Partridgefield, Seth of Middleboro, Jonathan of Taunton; daughter Mary Wade wife of Capt. Amos of Middleboro; son Edward of Taunton; daughters Abigail Richmond, Phebe wife of Elijah Richmond of Taunton, and Lydia Macomber wife of Simeon of Middleboro; executors, sons Jonathan and Edward.

Children (RICHMOND) b. Taunton: EDMUND[6] b. 1738; PHEBE b. 1739; SETH b. 1746; JONATHAN b. 1749; LYDIA b. 1751; MARY b. 1754; WILLIAM b. 1756; EDWARD b. 1758 (bp. 1764); and ABIGAIL b. 1762 (bp. 1764).

References: VR TAUNTON. RICHMOND FAM pp. 26-7. Bristol Co. PR 31:405(Seth Richmond).

271 ELIZABETH[5] RICHMOND (Edward[4], Abigail[3] Rogers, John[2], Thomas[1]) b. prob. Taunton; d. Dighton bet. 3 June 1738 and 31 Aug. 1742.

She m. bef. 1721 NATHANIEL HATHEWAY, b. Dighton in Feb. 1694; d. there bef. 3 May 1748; son of Ephraim and Elizabeth (Talbot?) Hathaway.

The will of Nathaniel Hatheway of Dighton yeoman, made 31 Aug. 1742 and proved 3 May 1748, left his estate to his brother Seth Hathaway.

Poss. child (HATHEWAY): LYDIA[6] b. ca. 1721, d. 1722 ae 1 year.

References: DIGHTON VR p. 6. RICHMOND FAM p. 11. HATHAWAY GEN
            (1970) p. 52. Bristol Co. PR 11:532(Nathaniel Hatheway).

272 PHEBE[5] RICHMOND (Edward[4], Abigail[3] Rogers, John[2],
Thomas[1]) b. Taunton ca. 1713; d. there 9 March 1741/2 in
30th year.
      She m. bef. 1735 NOAH ELIOT, son of Thomas and Mercy
(Walker) Eliot.
      Noah Elliot joyner of Dighton bought a farm in Kill-
ingly CT from Enoch Moffat on 1 April 1757. Noah was liv-
ing in Killingly CT when he and other heirs of Nehemiah
Walker late of Dighton quitclaimed land on 9 Aug. 1764.
No probate record of Noah found in CT.

      Child (ELIOT): MARY[6] b. ca. 1735, d. Taunton 1749/50 in 16th
yr.

References: VR TAUNTON. RICHMOND FAM p. 27. Bristol Co. LR 47:431
            (Noah Eliot). Killingly CT LR 6:178(Enoch Moffat).

273 SARAH[5] RICHMOND (Edward[4], Abigail[3] Rogers, John[2],
Thomas[1]) b. prob. Taunton.
      She m. ----- CRANE (indicated in her father's will).
      Lack of a marriage record has led to speculation that
she was the Sarah Washburn who m. (2) Bridgewater 13 Feb.
1737/8 SAMUEL CRANE of Milton; d. bef. 1787; poss. son of
Stephen and Mary (Denison) Crane, b. Braintree 23 May 1687.
This Samuel and Sarah had a son Samuel. No probate records
were found for Samuel or Sarah Crane.
      There is no record of marriage of Sarah Richmond to a
Washburn. However, a Josiah Washburn d. Bridgewater 27
Jan. 1733/4; prob. son of John and Rebecca (Lapham) Washburn, b. Bridgewater 11 Feb. 1679. He had seven children
by a first wife Mercy, but no evidence was found for any
other children. Appointed administrators of his estate
were widow Sarah Washburn and Edward Richmond of Taunton
(the only fact which connects Josiah with a wife Sarah,
possibly Richmond).*
      If Sarah was wife of Samuel Crane, she had by him son
Samuel; and she prob. d. Bridgewater 9 June 1787 (unnamed)
"widow Crane, mother of Samuel ae 86."

      Poss. child (CRANE) b. Bridgewater: SAMUEL[6] b. 1738/9.

References: MILTON HIST p. 107. BRIDGEWATER BY MITCHELL pp.
            145, 339, 340. RICHMOND FAM p. 27[no *proof* found]. VR

---

*The Mayflower Society has accepted descent through a purported dau.
Silence Washburn of Josiah and Sarah, who m. Bridgewater 1748 Jesse
Washburn. No evidence has been found that she was a dau. of Josiah
Washburn and Sarah Richmond.

BRIDGEWATER. BRAINTREE VR p. 671. NEHGR 46:217. Plymouth Co. PR
7:11(Josiah Washburn). WASHBURN DESC p. 53.

274 PRISCILLA[5] RICHMOND (Edward[4], Abigail[3] Rogers, John[2],
Thomas[1]) b. prob. Taunton; d. after 20 Nov. 1763.
     She m. after 1728 JOHN HACKET, b. ca. 1689; d. Middle-
boro 11 Nov. 1767 in 79th yr.; son of John and Eleanor
(Gardner) Hackett. He m. (1) 1711 Elizabeth Eliott, and
(2) 1728 Elizabeth Richmond, and by them had John d.y.,
Edmund, Alice, Hannah, Elijah, Elizabeth, Thankful d.y.,
John again, and Benjamin.
     The will of John Hacket of Middleboro, dated 22 Nov.
1763 and proved 4 Jan. 1768, names wife Priscilla, son
Elijah Hacket to have land and pay to daughter Hannah
Walden, son Benjamin to have land and pay to daughter
Alice Finney, and son Ephraim Hacket to have land and pay
to daughter Elizabeth Richmond. There was no division or
distribution in the probate records.

     Child (HACKET) b. to John and Priscilla prob. Middleboro:
EPHRAIM[6].

References: RICHMOND FAM pp. 27-8. Plymouth Co. PR 20:4(John
              Hackett). RI VR:Little Compton:151. MD 5:38, 39; 6:226,
228. MIDDLEBORO DEATHS pp. 77-8.

275 SAMUEL[5] RICHMOND (Samuel[4], Abigail[3] Rogers, John[2],
Thomas[1]) b. Taunton 16 Oct. 1695; d. bef. 1 Aug. 1767.
     He m. bef. 1723/4 SARAH ----- who d. bef. 1 Aug. 1767.
     There is no probate record for either Samuel or Sarah
in Bristol or Plymouth Counties; however, they were apparently dead before 1 Aug. 1767, when their living children sold land of a deceased sibling: Thomas Richmond
of Freetown cordwainer, Samuel Richmond of Taunton yeoman,
and Hannah Richmond of Taunton singlewoman sold 30 acres
in Middleboro, all land Reuben Richmond bought of Samuel
Hoar. Mary wife of Thomas, and Christian wife of Samuel
gave their consent. The deed was acknowledged 8 June 1768.

     Children (RICHMOND) b. prob. Middleboro: SAMUEL[6]; THOMAS b.
1723, d.y.; REUBEN b. ca. 1725; THOMAS b. ca. 1731; and HANNAH.

References: VR TAUNTON. MD 6:180. Plymouth Co. LR 55:34(Thos. Rich-
              mond et al.). RICHMOND FAM p. 28.

276 OLIVER[5] RICHMOND (Samuel[4], Abigail[3] Rogers, John[2],
Thomas[1]) b. Taunton 25 Aug. 1697; d. prob. Killingly CT
after 26 Oct. 1763.

He m. bef. 1735 RUTH -----.
On 4 July 1753 "Oliver Richman" of Taunton yeoman bought 40 acres in Killingly CT, and on 26 Oct. 1763 Oliver Richmond of Killingly husbandman sold to Oliver Richmond Jr. of Killingly (no relationship indicated) the same 40 acres, acknowledging his signature the same day. Neither Oliver nor Ruth left probate records.

Children (RICHMOND) first b. Taunton: PHILIP[6] b. 1735; prob. OLIVER and SYBIL; and poss. DORCAS and MICHAEL.

References: RICHMOND FAM p. 28. CLS Barbour Index:Killingly(b. Philip). Killingly CT LR 5:261; 11:17(Oliver Richmond).

277 HANNAH[5] RICHMOND (Samuel[4], Abigail[3] Rogers, John[2], Thomas[1]) b. Middleboro 29 Aug. 1702; prob. living 3 May 1759.
She m. bef. 1731 ISAIAH BOOTH, b. Scituate 10 March 1702/3; d. Taunton bet. 3 May and 28 June 1759; son of Benjamin Booth.
The will of Isaiah Booth late of Middleboro now resident in Taunton, yeoman, dated 3 May 1759 and sworn 28 June 1759, names "beloved wife", four sons Isaiah, Jacob, Silas and Shadrack; dau. Hannah; wife and son Isaiah to be executors. Administration was awarded to "his widow and son Isaiah"--the executors named in the will. William Canady of Taunton on 26 June 1759 was made guardian of Hannah Booth, over 14, dau. of Isaiah Booth late of Taunton dec.

Children (BOOTH) b. Middleboro: ISAIAH[6] b. 1729/30; JACOB b. 1731; SILAS; ABRAHAM b. 1735; SHADRACH; and HANNAH b. 1741-5.

References: VR SCITUATE. RICHMOND FAM p. 11. MD 12:233. Bristol Co. PR 16:285(Isaiah Booth); 126:78-9(Hannah and Shadrack Booth).

278 LYDIA[5] RICHMOND (Samuel[4], Abigail[3] Rogers, John[2], Thomas[1]) b. Middleboro 14 May 1704; living 1737.
She m. Middleboro 9 June 1732 SAMUEL THOMAS, b. Middleboro 24 Jan. 1697/8; son of David and Abigail (Wood) Thomas.
There are no probate records for Lydia or Samuel in Bristol or Plymouth Counties.

Children (THOMAS) b. Middleboro: ZEPHANIAH[6] b. 1733; JOSIAH b. 1735; and REBEKAH b. 1737.

References: RICHMOND FAM p. 28. Thatcher Papers 3:Thomas:17. MD 8:29, 249-50; 9:47; 12:131.

279 SILAS[5] RICHMOND   (Samuel[4], Abigail[3] Rogers, John[2],
Thomas[1]) b. prob. Middleboro ca. 1710; d. New Milford CT
21 Feb. 1784 "father of Ephraim."
        He m. Litchfield CT 19 Dec. 1733 HANNAH EMMONS, dau.
of William and Sarah (Barnes) Emmons.
        Silas moved to Litchfield before 24 March 1736/7 when
he and his brothers deeded land that was their father's
(see #60iii). Other deeds show that he moved to Goshen
CT about 1750, and back to Litchfield about 1762. He apparently spent his final years in New Milford, with son
Ephraim, where he died. (His movements were thoroughly
researched by the late Donald L. Jacobus who made a full
report in 1952.)

        Children (RICHMOND) first two b. Litchfield CT, others deduced
as almost certain by Mr. Jacobus from Goshen and Litchfield records:
EPHRAIM[6] b. 1734; PHEBE b. 1736; SILAS; SAMUEL; SARAH; BARNABAS; and
HANNAH.

References: RICHMOND FAM p. 77 [no evidence was found for children
             Elizabeth and Daniel]. CSL Barbour Index:Litchfield, New
Milford. Report of D. L. Jacobus to Roy H. Elliott of Calif. 15 Jan.
1952.

280 MEHITABLE[5] RICHMOND   (Samuel[4], Abigail[3] Rogers, John[2],
Thomas[1]) b. prob. Middleboro ca. 1712; living Rehoboth 21
May 1759.
        She m. Rehoboth 19 April 1733 ELIJAH HORTON, b. Reho-
both 17 Feb. 1708/9; living there 21 May 1759; son of
Thomas and Hannah (Garnzey) Horton.
        There are no probate records for Elijah and Mehitable
in Bristol County, but the will of Thomas Horton of Rehoboth yeoman, dated 28 Feb. 1745/6, names wife Hannah; son
Elijah to have land and house in Rehoboth where I live,
already given him by deed of gift; two grandsons: Thomas,
son of David Horton, and Levi, son of Elijah Horton, to
have the house and land in Rehoboth where I live after the
decease of Elijah. The witnesses deposed 14 April 1746.
On 11 Nov. 1758 Elijah Horton of Rehoboth laborer sold his
part of lands given him by his father Thomas late of Rehoboth dec., with wife Mehitable signing, and both acknowledged their signatures 21 May 1759.

        Child (HORTON): LEVI[6] b. bet. 1733 and 1745.

References: VR REHOBOTH. RICHMOND FAM p. 11. Bristol Co. PR 11:124
             (Thomas Horton). Bristol Co. LR 48:470 (Elijah Horton).

281 SARAH[5] WALKER (Sarah[4] Richmond, Abigail[3] Rogers,
John[2], Thomas[1])   prob. b. Taunton; d. Raynham 15 Jan. 1753.
     She m. Raynham 23 June 1726 THOMAS LEONARD who d.
Raynham 1 July 1774; son of Thomas and Johanah (Pitcher)
Leonard.
     An inventory of the estate of Thomas Leonard late of
Raynham was made 24 Aug. 1774.

     Children (LEONARD) b. Raynham: MARY[6] b. 1727; SARAH b. 1729;
HANNAH b. 1731; GAMALIEL b. 1733; PAUL b. 1735; CORALINA b. 1738; and
PHEBE b. 1740.

References: NEHGR 54:17, 18; 53:436. WALKER MEM p. 31. Bristol Co.
             PR 23:401(Thomas Leonard).

282 JAMES[5] WALKER (Sarah[4] Richmond, Abigail[3] Rogers,
John[2], Thomas[1]) prob. b. Taunton ca. 1704; d. there 6
Aug. 1761 in his 58th yr. "stifled in his well."
     He m. Taunton 21 July 1761 MARY PITTS who d. after
1775. She m. (2) bef. May 1763 James Mason, by whom she
had children. Mary was living in 1775 when James Mason of
Swansea made his will. No proof was found that she m. (3)
Abner Thayer. In fact she may have been the Mary Mason,
widow ae. 74, who d. Bristol RI 3 June 1797.
     Mary Walker, widow of James of Taunton, was named ad-
ministratrix on his estate 18 Aug. 1761, one of the
sureties on her bond being Job Pitts. She had remarried
by 3 May 1763 when James Mason of Warren RI and wife Mary,
late widow of James Walker of Taunton, petitioned to be
appointed guardian to his only child--son James aged about
one year--"Mary being mother of the child." A petition
opposing this appointment was drawn 11 May 1763 by Eliakam,
Elnathan and Peter Walker claiming that their sister-in-
law, late widow of our brother James and now wife of James
Mason, had already wasted the minor's estate.

     Child (WALKER) b. prob. Taunton: JAMES[6] b. 1762.

References: VR TAUNTON. Bristol Co. PR file and 17:519(James Walker).
             RI VR:Bristol p. 147.

283 ELIAKIM[5] WALKER (Sarah[4] Richmond, Abigail[3] Rogers,
John[2], Thomas[1])   b. prob. Taunton ca. 1705; d. there 21
Feb. 1785 in 81st yr.
     He m. MARY BRIGGS, b. ca. 1707; d. Taunton in Dec.
1785 in her 79th yr.; dau. of Thomas and Abigail (Thayer)
Briggs. On 9 March 1752 Eliakim Walker gentleman of Taun-
ton and wife Mary, said Mary being a daughter of Mr.
Thomas Briggs late of Taunton deceased, with other daugh-
ters of Thomas sold his late homestead.

The will of Eliakim Walker gentleman of Taunton, made
1 Oct. 1784 and probated 5 April 1785, names sons Eliakim
and Perez; grandsons James and Perez Wares; Benjamin and
Eliakim Whitmarsh, sons of my daughter Sarah Whitmarsh; my
late father James Walker of Taunton deceased; daughter
Sarah Whitmarsh wife of David; grandson Walker Whitmarsh;
child of grandson William Ware late of Taunton deceased;
executor, son Eliakim Walker Jr., who is to make provision
for "his father and mother Walker."

      Children (WALKER) b. prob. Taunton: SARAH[6] b. ca. 1729, d. 1739
ae 10; PEREZ b. ca. 1738; SARAH; ELIAKIM b. ca. 1736; MARY; and JAMES
b. ca. 1744, d. 1761 ae 17.

      References: VR TAUNTON. NEHGR 125:89. Bristol Co. PR 28:317(Eliakim
Walker). Bristol Co. LR 39:277(Eliakim Walker).

284 ELNATHAN[5] WALKER (Sarah[4] Richmond, Abigail[3] Rogers,
John[2], Thomas[1].) prob. b. Taunton ca. 1707; d. Dighton 6
June 1775 in his 69th yr., bur. Taunton.
     He m. (1) HANNAH CROSSMAN, b. ca. 1706; d. 4 April
1728 in 23rd yr.; dau. of Nathaniel and Sarah (Merrick)
Crossman. In a division on 11 Jan. 1759 of the real estate
of Nathaniel Crossman late of Taunton dec., the 6th share
went to Elnathan Walker, legal representative of Hannah
his mother, a child of the deceased.
     He m. (2) BETHIAH TISDALE, b. ca. 1711; d. Taunton 11
May 1759 in 49th yr.; dau. of Joseph and Ruth (Reed) Tisdale.
     He m. (3) Taunton 6 Nov. 1760 PHEBE (LEONARD) KING,
b. Taunton 9 May 1714; d. Middleboro 3 April 1803 in 89th
yr.; dau. of Samuel and Katherine (Dean) Leonard, and widow of Jonathan King.
     Eliakim was a colonel in the militia, deacon of the
First Congregational Church in Dighton, selectman and
representative to the General Court. The will of Eliakim
Walker of Dighton, drawn 25 May 1775 and proved 5 Aug.
1775, names wife Phebe to have the goods she brought with
her; sons Elnathan and Ebenezer; grandson Nathaniel Fisher,
son of Jeremiah Fisher; sons Edward and Zepheniah of Dighton; lands of my late father James; sons Peter and George;
daughter Phebe Sears wife of Alden; daughter Bathsheba
Gooding wife of William; daughter Bethia Jones wife of
Ebenezer; and Abigail King daughter of my wife Phebe.

      Children (WALKER) b. Dighton, first by Hannah, last by Phebe,
rest by Bethiah: ELNATHAN[6] b. 1727/8; EBENEZER b. 1732; HANNAH b.
1734; RUTH b. 1736; EDWARD b. 1742; BATHSHEBA b. 1743; BETHIA b. 1745;
PETER b. 1747; PHEBE b. 1748; ZEPHANIAH b. 1754; and GEORGE b. 1761.

References: VR TAUNTON. DIGHTON VR pp. 67-8. Bristol Co. PR 23:557
(Elnathan Walker). WALKER MEM pp. 31, 38-41.

285 JOHN[5] RICHMOND (John[4], Abigail[3] Rogers, John[2], Thomas[1]) b. prob. Taunton ca. 1710; living there 28 Dec.
1778.
    He m. (1) Taunton 30 Dec. 1736 DIGHTON MIRICK, d. bef.
8 Feb. 1747; dau. of Isaac and Dighton (Bird) Mirick. The
will of Isaac Mirick gentleman, dated 8 Feb. 174[?], witnesses deposed 7 March 1748, mentions among issue of his
daughters "children of Dighton Richmond, wife of John,
which Dighton is late deceased." On 26 May 1768 Mary
Richmond, wife of Nathaniel of Middleboro, daughter of
Dighton Merick deceased and granddaughter of Isaac Merrick
of Taunton deceased, sold land set off to her in the division of Isaac's estate. On 19 Oct. 1768 Dighton Richmond
of Taunton singlewoman, granddaughter of Isaac Merrick,
sold land.
    He m. (2) Taunton 1 Dec. 1748 PHEBE DUNHAM, who was
living 28 Dec. 1778.
    John Richmond, although he did not fight, gave patrio-
tic service in the Revolution.
    No probate record verifies the names of children or
indicates when John had died. But on 29 March 1776 John
Richmond of Taunton yeoman sold to son John Richmond of
Taunton cooper part of his homestead. John's last recorded
deed in Bristol County is dated 11 Nov. 1778 when he sold
to Abiel Smith of Taunton all my homestead in Taunton; John
and Phebe acknowledged their signatures 28 Dec. 1778.*

    Children (RICHMOND) b. prob. Taunton, first two at least by
Dighton: MARY[6], DIGHTON, JOHN, and poss. HANNAH, ELKANAH, JOSEPH,
ABNER, PHEBE, BETHIA, NABBY, and HULDAH.

References: VR TAUNTON. RICHMOND FAM p. 29. DAR PATRIOT INDEX p.
           569. Bristol Co. PR 11:643(Isaac Mirick). Bristol Co.
LR 51:216(Nathaniel Richmond); 56:465; 59:76(John Richmond); 51:402
(Dighton Richmond).

286 STEPHEN[5] RICHMOND (John[4], Abigail[3] Rogers, John[2],
Thomas[1]) b. prob. Taunton ca. 1719; d. there 11 March 1802
ae. 83.
    He m. ca. 1742 SILENCE ROBINSON, b. ca. 1723; d. in
July 1806 in her 84th yr.; dau. of Ebenezer and Mary (Williams) Robinson. The will of Ebenezer Robinson of Raynham,

---

*RICHMOND FAM claims John died at Ashford CT in 1801 over 90 years of
age. There are no vital or probate records at the CT State Library to
prove this, and no Ashford CT land records to prove he ever owned land
there.

made 17 Nov. 1749, names dau. Silence but does not give
her last name.
     The will of Stephen Richmond of Taunton yeoman, drawn
8 Jan. 1801, names wife Silence; sons Abial, Asa and Noah
who were to support Silence; son Stephen of Middleboro and
his three daughters: Katharine, Silence and Sarah; three
daughters Silence Caswell wife of Joseph, Weltha Caswell
wife of John, and Ann Robinson wife of Ebenezer. Executors were to be sons Abial and Asa. The will was presented
29 March 1802.

        Children (RICHMOND) b. prob. Taunton: STEPHEN[6] b. ca. 1743;
ABIEL b. ca. 1747; ASA b. ca. 1755; ANNA bp. 1764; WEALTHY bp. 1764;
SILENCE b. ca. 1765; and NOAH bp. 1777.

References: VR TAUNTON. RICHMOND FAM p. 29. NEHGR 84:344. Bristol
        Co. PR 13:490(Ebenezer Robinson); 39:35(Stephen Richmond).

287 EBENEZER[5] RICHMOND (Ebenezer[4], Abigail[3] Rogers,
John[2], Thomas[1]) b. Middleboro 31 March 1701; d. Barnard
VT 6 March 1793 ae   91y 11m.
     He m. Dighton 23 April 1730 MARY (WALKER) WALKER, b.
Dighton 15 Aug. 1704; d. Barnard VT 21 April 1782 ae   77y
9m; dau. of David and Mary (-----) Walker. The will of
David Walker of Dighton, dated 9 Aug. 1759, names wife
Esther and daughter Mary wife of Ebenezer Richmond. Mary
m. (1) Dighton 1725 James Walker, by whom she had a son
Elisha.
     On 19 May 1742 Mary Richmond, wife of Ebenezer of
Taunton and late widow of James Walker of Taunton deceased,
with David Walker, guardian to Elisha Walker son of James
deceased, petitioned for division of the real estate of
the late James Walker.
     Neither Ebenezer nor Mary left probate records in
Vermont or in Massachusetts.

        Children (RICHMOND) second Ebenezer b. Middleboro, rest prob. b.
Taunton:* MOLLY[6] b. ca. 1731; EBENEZER b. 1732, d.y.; ANNA; EBENEZER
b. 1738; SALLY; RACHEL; PATIENCE; CONTENT; and AMAZIAH b. ca. 1745.

References: DIGHTON VR pp. 1, 32, 33. MD 12:130. BARNARD VT HIST
        2:342. Bristol Co. PR file (James Walker); 19:136(David
Walker). RICHMOND FAM pp. 29-30.

288 ROBERT[5] RICHMOND (Ebenezer[4], Abigail[3] Rogers, John[2],
Thomas[1]) b. Middleboro 18 Sept. 1702; prob. living Brookfield in 1775 (pension papers of prob. son Ezra).

The Henry Samson Family will give greater detail and one further
generation.

He m. (1) Bridgewater 17 May 1733 MARTHA WASHBURN, b.
Bridgewater 10 Jan. 1708/9; dau. of James and Mary (Bowden)
Washburn. The will of James Washburn of Bridgewater, dated
14 Jan. 1747, names daughter Martha wife of Robert Rich-
mond.
  He prob. m. (2) Middleboro 3 May 1751 HANNAH RAMSDEN
("he of Taunton, she of Middleboro").
  No probate record in Worcester County for Robert,
Martha or Hannah.

     Children (RICHMOND) b. Middleboro, first four to Robert and
Martha:* ELIZABETH[6] b. 1734; LUCIA b. 1736; ROBERT b. 1738; MARTHA b.
1740; and prob. MARY b. ca. 1746, EZRA b. 1752, and ANNA.

References: VR BRIDGEWATER, BROOKFIELD. RICHMOND FAM pp. 30, 64-5[no
           wife Dorcas found]. MD 14:246; 16:52; 18:84. Rev. Pen-
sion #S29414(Ezra Richmond).

289 ANNA[5] RICHMOND (Ebenezer[4], Abigail[3] Rogers, John[2],
Thomas[1]) b. Middleboro 14 Oct. 1704; d. after 3 March
1783.
  She m. Middleboro 3 May 1734 CALEB COWING, b. Scituate
7 July 1696; d. bef. 10 June 1777; son of John and Deborah
(Litchfield) Cowing.
  On 17 April 1738 Caleb Cowing of Rochester petitioned
to receive his wife's portion of the estate of our father
Ebenezer Richmond deceased. Caleb Cowing left no probate
records, but he died before 10 June 1777, when Anna Cowing
of Rochester, widow of Caleb, being aged and indigent, complained that her dower had been withheld. James Cowing of
Rochester was appointed guardian 3 March 1783 to Anna Cowing of Rochester, aged and non-compos.

     Children (COWING) in Rochester VR:* ARIADNE[6] b. 1735; DAVID b.
1738; JAMES b. 1740; and ANA ADNA bp. 2 Aug. 1741.

References: VR ROCHESTER, SCITUATE. Plymouth Co. PR 26:481; 28:545
           (Anna Cowing); #5114(Caleb Cowing). MD 2:43; 13:250;
21:189. SAVAGE 1:466.

290 ELIZABETH[5] RICHMOND (Ebenezer[4], Abigail[3] Rogers,
John[2], Thomas[1]) b. Middleboro 1 Sept. 1708; may have d.
bef. 1742.
  She m. Middleboro 12 June 1728 EDWARD WASHBURN, b.
Bridgewater 8 Dec. 1700; d. Middleboro 25 March 1792 ae
93; son of James and Mary (Bowden) Washburn. He may have
m. (2) bef. 1742 Elizabeth Snell of Bridgewater. His son
Amos would in that case not be son of Elizabeth Richmond.

---

*The Henry Samson Family will give greater detail and one further
generation.

On 24 Nov. 1733 Edward Washburn of Bridgewater and
wife Elizabeth acknowledged their signatures on an agreement of the heirs of Ebenezer Richmond of Middleboro dec.
The will of Edward Washburn of Middleboro, dated 12 Dec.
17[-]1 and filed 1793, makes son Amos executor, and names
grandson Abial Washburn under age, granddaughter Abigail
wife of John Peckem Jr., grandson Edward Washburn under 21.

Children (WASHBURN) b. Middleboro to Edward and first wife:*
ABIGAIL[6] b. 1730; JAMES b. 1731/2; EDWARD b. 1734; and poss. ABIAL,
and AMOS b. 1742.

References: MD 5:39; 15:121; 23:45. RICHMOND FAM pp. 30-1[no evi-
             dence found for son Abial; death yr. of Edward incorrect].
VR BRIDGEWATER. MIDDLEBORO DEATHS. Plymouth Co. PR #21951(Edward
Washburn). BRIDGEWATER BY MITCHELL p. 342. INDEPENDENT CHRONICLE 12
Apr. 1792(Edw. Washburn). WASHBURN DESC p. 56a.

291 SYLVESTER[5] RICHMOND (Ebenezer[4], Abigail[3] Rogers,
John[2], Thomas[1]) b. Middleboro 25 Nov. 1711; d. New Brain-
tree 9 Dec. 1804 ae 93y 2d [called "Zepheniah"].
    He m. (1) Dighton 9 Dec. 1736 ABIAH ELLIOTT who d. New
Braintree 20 July 1789 "wife of Capt. Richmond"; dau. of
Thomas and Mercy (Walker) Elliott. On 9 Aug. 1764 Sylves-
ter Richmond of New Braintree, Worcester Co., gentleman,
and wife Abiah, and other heirs of [her uncle] Nehemiah
Walker late of Dighton deceased, quitclaimed land.
    He m. (2) New Braintree 23 Sept. 1790 HANNAH (-----)
PRATT who d. New Braintree 22 July 1808 (unnamed) "widow of
Sylvester."
    Sylvester was a captain in the "Old French Wars." He
left no probate or land records to prove who his children
were.

Children (RICHMOND)*: SILVESTER[6] b. Middleboro 1746; MERCY b.
New Braintree 1750; and poss. ZEPHANIAH, LYDIA, ABIAH, WEALTHY, JAMES,
and JANE.

References: DIGHTON VR p. 64. VR NEW BRAINTREE. RICHMOND FAM p. 31.
             Bristol Co. LR 47:431(Sylvester Richmond). MD 2:201.

292 NATHAN[5] WALKER (Abigail[4] Richmond, Abigail[3] Rogers,
John[2], Thomas[1]) b. Dighton 27 Oct. 1709; d. Taunton 30
Sept. 1771 in his 62nd yr.
    He m. int. Dighton 20 Nov. 1737 DOROTHY BURT "of Berk-
ley," b. Dighton 7 May 1711; d. Taunton 22 March 1790 in her
83rd yr. (sic); dau. of John and Abigail (-----) Burt. On

The Henry Samson Family will give greater detail and one further
generation.

30 May 1768 Nathan Walker of Dighton and wife Dorothy and
other daus. of John Burt late of Dighton dec. sold land.
     There are no Bristol County probate records for either
Nathan or Dorothy.

     Children (WALKER) b. Dighton: NATHAN[6] b. 1739, and JOHN b. 1743.

References: VR TAUNTON. DIGHTON VR pp. 9, 62, 68. Bristol Co. LR
              52:437(Nathan Walker et al.).

293 ABIGAIL[5] WALKER (Abigail[4] Richmond, Abigail[3] Rogers,
John[2], Thomas[1])   b. Dighton 3 Dec. 1711; d. 13 Aug. 1749
ae 37-7-21, bur. Taunton.
     She m. bef. 1733 JACOB AUSTIN, d. bet. 10 July 1766
and 6 May 1767; prob. son of Jonah Austin. Jacob m. (2)
Dighton 1751 Mary Perry.
     The will of Jacob Austin of Dighton yeoman, signed 10
July 1766 and presented 6 May 1767, names wife Mary, sons
Benjamin and Seth, daughter Phebe Witherell wife of Henry
Jr. and son Jacob; son Seth to be executor.

     Children (AUSTIN) b. Dighton: BENJAMIN[6] b. 1733; PHEBE b. 1735;
ABIATHAR b. 1738; JOHN b. 1741; SETH b. 1743/4; and JACOB b. 1747.

References: VR TAUNTON. DIGHTON VR pp. 53, 54, 88. Bristol Co. PR
              14:307(Jonah Austin); 20:71(Jacob Austin).

294 PHEBE[5] WALKER (Abigail[4] Richmond, Abigail[3] Rogers,
John[2], Thomas[1])   b. Dighton 29 Sept. 1713; living 9 Aug.
1764.
     She m. Dighton 17 Dec. 1741 SETH FRENCH, b. Berkley
23 March 1713; d. there 9 June 1756; son of Joseph and
Sarah (-----) French.
     On 15 Sept. 1756 Phebe French of Berkley petitioned
for administration of the estate of her husband Seth French
of Berkley deceased. On 10 May 1762 Phebe French of Berkley widow, one of the children of Nathan Walker of Dighton
deceased, and an heir of Nehemiah Walker, deeded land; and
again on 9 Aug. 1764 she and other heirs granted land.

     Children (FRENCH) b. Berkley: JOSEPH[6] b. 1743; ABIGAIL b. 1744;
THOMAS b. 1745; PHEBE b. 1746; NATHAN b. 1748; SARAH b. 1749; SETH b.
1752; JOHN b. 1754; and SILENCE b. 1756.

References: Berkley Rec. Book p. 229. Bristol Co. LR 46:391; 47:431
              (Phebe French et al.). Bristol Co. PR 15:116, 121(Seth
French).

295 WILLIAM[5] WALKER (Abigail[4] Richmond, Abigail[3] Rogers, John[2], Thomas[1]) b. Dighton 17 Aug. 1715; d. 3 Aug. 1749 ae 34 "wanting 15 days."
    He m. int. Dighton 13 May 1743 HANNAH SHAW, b. Dighton 11 Jan. 1723/4; dau. of Abraham and Anna (-----) Shaw. On 26 Jan. 1748 William Walker of Dighton and wife Hannah, she being the dau. of Deacon Abraham Shaw late of Dighton dec., sold land. Hannah m. (2) int. Dighton 1752 Ephraim Hathaway Jr.
    William Walker left no probate records in Bristol County.

        Children (WALKER) b. Dighton: WILLIAM[6] b. 1743; ABIATHAR b. 1745; and GEORGE b. 1747.

    References: DIGHTON VR pp. 64, 75, 103. Bristol Co. LR 36:514(William Walker).

296 LYDIA[5] WALKER (Abigail[4] Richmond, Abigail[3] Rogers, John[2], Thomas[1]) b. Dighton 31 July 1717; d. after 9 Aug. 1764.
    She m. int. Dighton 6 Sept. 1755 WILLIAM WARE, b. Wrentham 4 July 1697; d. Dighton 11 June 1764 ae 67; son of John and Mehitable (Chapin) Ware. He m. (1) Attleboro 1726 Mary Maxcey, by whom he had Mary; he m. (2) Wrentham 1728 Zibiah Sweeting, by whom he had Lucia, William and John; he m. (3) Norton 1733 Anna Hodges, by whom he had George, Benjamin and Anna.
    On 9 Aug. 1764 Lydia Ware of Dighton, widow of William, and other heirs of Nehemiah Walker sold land.
    The will of William Ware of Dighton surgeon, drawn 23 Aug. 1763, advanced in age, gives to wife Lydia what she brought to me, she to be guardian to my three youngest children born of her body, until full age: my son Joseph, under 21, and my daughters Lydia and Abigail, under 14. The will also names sons William and George; son Benjamin at sea; daughters Mary Eddy wife of Capt. Jonathan, and Lucy Talbut wife of Nathaniel Jr.; and grandson William Ware son of William. A codicil was dated 22 March 1764, and the witnesses deposed in July 1764, when widow Lydia was made executor.

        Children (WARE) b. Dighton to William and Lydia: JOSEPH[6] b. 1756; LYDIA b. 1758; and ABIGAIL b. 1760.

    References: VR NORTON, WRENTHAM. DIGHTON VR pp. 44, 103. WARE GEN pp. 61-3. WALKER MEM p. 32. Bristol Co. PR 18:348 (Wm. Ware).

297 EXPERIENCE[5] WILLIAMS   (John[4], Elizabeth[3] Rogers,
John[2], Thomas[1])   b. Taunton 30 Nov. 1705; d. Norton 5 Oct.
1746 in 46th yr. (*sic*).
       She m. Norton 12 Dec. 1728 NATHAN(IEL) HODGES, b.
Taunton 23 Oct. 1690; d. Norton 23 April 1770 in 80th yr.;
son of John and Elizabeth (Macy) Hodges.
       On 7 June 1770 the heirs of Captain Nathan Hodges
late of Norton deceased agreed on a division of his real
estate: Sons Nathan, James, Abiel and Josiah Hodges were
to have land their father gave them; their four sisters
Hannah Gould wife of Richard, Elizabeth Wilmarth wife of
Moses, Anna Hodges and Katherine Hodges to have land in
Easton.

       Children (HODGES) first five b. Norton: NATHAN[6] b. 1729; HANNAH
b. 1730; ELIZABETH b. 1733; ANNA b. 1734; JAMES b. 1737; ABIEL; JOSIAH
b. ca. 1741; and KATHARINE.

References: VR NORTON, TAUNTON. Bristol Co. PR 21:387(Nathan Hodges).
             WILLIAMS FAM (1926) p. 39. HODGES GEN pp. 11, 59.

298 SILAS[5] WILLIAMS (John[4], Elizabeth[3] Rogers, John[2],
Thomas[1]) b. Taunton 16 Jan. 1707; d. prob. Easton 16 Oct.
1775.
       He m. (1) Easton 19 July 1737 MARY DUNHAM of Norton,
b. ca. 1715; d. Easton 14 Nov. 1757 in 42nd yr.
       He m. (2) Bridgewater ("he of Easton") 13 Oct. 1760
SUSANNA (PRATT) RICHARDS, dau. of Joseph and Lydia (Leonard) Pratt, and widow of James Richards.
       The will of Silas Williams of Easton, made 14 Oct. 1775
and probated 10 Nov. 1775, names wife Susannah; sons John
and Elijah; daughters Mary Perry, Bethia Kingley, Sarah
Wood and Susannah Williams; grandchildren Lydia and Silas
Williams, and children of deceased son Paul.

       Children (WILLIAMS) b. Easton by first wife: PAUL[6] b. 1738;
SILAS b. 1739; MARY b. 1742; NATHANIEL b. 1744, d. 1747; SARAH b.
1746; JOHN b. 1748; BETHIAH b. 1751; ELIJAH b. 1753; and SUSANNAH b.
1755.

References: VR BRIDGEWATER, NORTON(m. Silas). Easton VR (marriages)
             p. 13. Bristol Co. PR 24:5-7(Silas Williams). WILLIAMS
FAM (1926) p. 42.

299 TIMOTHY[5] WILLIAMS (John[4], Elizabeth[3] Rogers, John[2],
Thomas[1]) b. Taunton 28 Sept. 1714; d. Woolwich ME 28 April
1770.
       He m. Raynham 18 Jan. 1736/7 ELIZABETH BRITTON who d.
Woolwich ME 1 Feb. 1794; dau. of William and Lydia (Leonard) Britton.

Timothy Williams was a town clerk at Easton, and in 1748 was a cordwainer there when he sold land to his brother Simeon. Timothy of Easton and wife Elizabeth 15 Oct. 1761 sold land originally belonging to his father John Williams, sometime after which they moved to Woolwich.

Children (WILLIAMS) b. Easton: HANNAH[6] b. 1738; TABITHA b. 1741; ELIZABETH b. 1743; TIMOTHY b. 1745; NATHANIEL b. 1747; OLIVE b. 1749, d. 1772; ELEMUEL b. 1751; SIBIL b. 1754; and ANNA b. 1756.

References: WILLIAMS FAM (1926) pp. 39, 43-4. Easton VR (births) p. 67. Bristol Co. LR 37:183; 45:292(Timothy Williams). NEHGR 54:16.

300 SIMEON[5] WILLIAMS (John[4], Abigail[3] Rogers, John[2], Thomas[1]) b. Taunton 21 Feb. 1717; d. there 18 Sept. 1794 ae 78.
He m. (1) Raynham 26 Aug. 1742 ZIPPORAH CRANE of Raynham, b. ca. 1724; d. Taunton 21 May 1748 in 25th yr.; dau. of Henry and Bathsheba (-----) Crane.
He m. (2) 1749 WAITSTILL HODGES, b. Taunton 21 Dec. 1723; d. there 21 Nov. 1820 ae 97; dau. of William and Susannah (Gilbert) Hodges. The will of William Hodges of Taunton in 1757 mentions wife Susanna and daughter Waitstill, and designates Simeon Williams as co-executor. The will of Seth Hodges of Taunton in 1802 names his sister Waitstill Williams, widow of Capt. Simeon.
Simeon Williams was a deputy to the Provincial Congress. The will of Simeon Williams of Taunton gentleman, drawn 15 May 1787 with a codicil 14 Aug. 1789, names wife Waitstill; eldest son Simeon; son Nathaniel; five daughters Zipporah King, Lurana Hodges, Hannah Dean, Jemima and Cynthia; and three grandchildren, children of deceased daughter Experience Hodges: Abial, Experience and Waitstill Hodges. Wife Waitstill and son Nathaniel were named executors. The witnesses gave oath to their signatures 29 Sept. 1794.

Children (WILLIAMS) first three by Zipporah b. Easton, rest by Waitstill prob. b. Taunton: SIMEON[6] b. 1743; JOHN b. 1745, d. 1748; EXPERIENCE b. 1746; ZIPPORAH b. 1750/1; LURANNA b. 1752; NATHANIEL b. 1755; WAITSTILL b. 1758, d. 1776; HANNAH b. 1761; LEVI b. 1763, d. 1764; JEMIMA b. 1765; and CYNTHIA b. 1767.

References: VR Taunton. Bristol Co. PR 20:228(William Hodges); 39: 124(Seth Hodges); 33:116(Simeon Williams). NEHGR 54:16. WILLIAMS FAM (1926) p. 45. HODGES GEN pp. 115, 116.

301 EDMUND[5] WILLIAMS (Nathaniel[4], Elizabeth[3] Rogers, John[2], Thomas[1]) b. Taunton 4 Dec. 1710; d. Raynham 4 Dec. 1796 ae 86.
    He m. (1) Raynham 6 Nov. 1737 LYDIA CRANE, b. 14 Aug. 1719; d. Raynham 14 May 1781 ae 61; dau. of Henry Crane.
    He m. (2) Bridgewater 20 Aug. 1781 MARY (-----) HARVEY, b. ca. 1713; d. Raynham 22 Jan. 1790 ae 77.
    He m. (3) Berkley 25 May 1790 ABIAH (CRANE)(BABBETT) (HOLLOWAY) ATWOOD, b. Berkley 12 Dec. 1716; d. Middleboro ca. 1812 ae 93; dau. of Gershom and Susanna (Whitmarsh) Crane, and widow successively of Benjamin Babbett, Nathaniel Holloway and Abiel Atwood.
    The will of Edmun Williams of Raynham, dated 9 June 1791 and presented 3 Jan. 1797, names wife Abiah and the agreement he made with her on 6 May 1790; son Nathan; daughters Huldee Williams and Phebe Leonard; son Noah; grandson Silas Burt; son Stephen; grandson Silas Williams; granddaughters Susanna and Nancy both under 21 [apparently children of son Edmun]; daughter Lydia Shaw and grandson David Shaw; daughter Sarah Padelford who labored for me and for my son Jason. Executors sons Nathan and Noah.

    Children (WILLIAMS) all b. Raynham to first wife: EDMUN[6] b. 1739; LYDIA b. 1741; JASON b. 1742; ANNE b. 1744, d. 1763; SARAH b. 1746; NATHAN b. 1748; HULDAH b. 1750; STEPHEN b. 1752; DAVID b. 1754; NOAH b. 1756; SILAS b. 1758, d. 1762; and PHEBE b. 1763.

References: VR BRIDGEWATER. MD 23:1. WILLIAMS FAM (1926) p. 46.
        Bristol Co. PR 34:308(Edmun Williams). Raynham VR 1:37, 38, 53, 54, 63, 65. NEHGR 54:16; 55:42.

302 NATHANIEL[5] WILLIAMS (Nathaniel[4], Elizabeth[3] Rogers, John[2], Thomas[1]) b. Taunton 4 Jan. 1711/12; d. Raynham 24 May 1775.
    He m. Raynham 12 May 1737 MARY ATHERTON, d. Taunton 20 Oct. 1778; dau. of Joshua and Elizabeth (Leonard) Atherton.
    The will of Nathaniel Williams of Raynham, made 24 May 1775, witnesses oath given 5 June 1775, names wife Mary; sons Seth, Nathaniel, John and Joshua; daughters Mary Hall, Phebe Wade, Hannah Alden, Elizabeth Hathaway and Judith Dean; wife Mary to be executor.

    Children (WILLIAMS) prob. b. Raynham: MARY[6] b. 1738; PHEBE bp. 1740; HANNAH b. ca. 1744; an infant who d. 1745; SETH bp. 1746; NATHANIEL bp. 1748; ELIZABETH bp. 1750; JOHN bp. 1752; JUDITH b. 1753; and JOSHUA b. 1756.

References: MD 23:1, 7. WILLIAMS FAM (1926) p. 47. NEHGR 54:16.

303 NATHANIEL[5] MACOMBER (Elizabeth[4] Williams, Elizabeth[3]
Rogers, John[2], Thomas[1]) b. Taunton 9 Feb. 1709; d. there
10 Nov. 1787 in 79th yr.
    He m. Middleboro 13 Nov. 1735 PRISCILLA SOUTHWORTH,
b. Middleboro 11 Feb. 1709/10; d. Taunton 30 Oct. 1793 in
84th yr.; dau. of Ichabod and Esther (Hodges) Southworth,
and a descendant of Pilgrim James Chilton (see page 87).
    On 14 March 1788 George Macomber and Ichabod Macomber
both of Taunton, and Nathaniel Macomber of Middleboro
deeded land as heirs of our father Nathaniel Williams late
of Taunton deceased, and Priscilla Macomber, widow of deceased Nathaniel, released her dower.

    Children (MACOMBER) b. Taunton: JOB[6] b. 1737; GEORGE b. 1740;
NATHANIEL b. 1742; ICHABOD b. 1745; EZRA b. 1747, d. 1756; and JOHN
b. 1750, d. 1756.

References: VR TAUNTON. MD 3:84; 13:251; 21:73. Bristol Co. LR 67:
            131(George Macomber et al.). WILLIAMS FAM (1926) p. 41.
MACOMBER GEN p. 16(cites "an old family record"). CONTRIBUTIONS BY
PEIRCE p. 202.

304 JOSIAH[5] MACOMBER (Elizabeth[4] Williams, Elizabeth[3]
Rogers, John[2], Thomas[1]) b. Taunton 19 Feb. 1711; d. there
8 or 18 Nov. 1801 in 91st yr.
    He m. Berkley 29 Nov. 1736 RUTH PAUL, b. 4 Feb. 1711;
d. Taunton 19 Sept. 1791 in 81st yr.; dau. of Benjamin and
Ruth (-----) Paul. The will of Benjamin Paul of Berkley,
made 6 March 1749/50, names wife Ruth and dau. Ruth Macomber wife of Josiah.
    Josiah was commissioned lieutenant of the 3rd regiment
Bristol County militia in 1762.* The will of Josiah Macomber of Taunton gentleman, made 15 Jan. 1787 and presented
28 Nov. 1801, names wife Ruth; only son Abial to be executor; eldest daughter Elizabeth Haskel wife of Samuel; and
youngest daughter Rebecca Gooding wife of Joseph.

    Children (MACOMBER) prob. b. Taunton: ELIZABETH[6] b. ca. 1737;
ABIEL b. ca. 1738; RUTH b. ca. 1743, d. 1756 in 14th yr.; and REBECCA
b. ca. 1747.

References: VR TAUNTON. WILLIAMS FAM (1926) p. 41. Rev Pension
            #S33044(Josiah Macomber). Bristol Co. PR 15:282(Benj.
Paul). Berkley TR 1:260, 269. MACOMBER GEN pp. 16-17. DAR PATRIOT
INDEX p. 432.

---

*He was not the Josiah Macomber who served as a private from Berkley
in Col. Bradford's Regiment, for the latter's pension record states
that he was aged 62 in 1819. This Josiah was probably son of his
brother James (#307).

305 JOHN[5] MACOMBER (Elizabeth[4] Williams, Elizabeth[3]
Rogers, John[2], Thomas[1]) b. Taunton 10 Feb. 1713; d. poss.
Middleboro 9 Nov. 1774 ae 54 (*sic*).
     He is supposed to be the John who m. Middleboro 27
Jan. 1746/7 ELIZABETH PHINNEY, d. poss. Middleboro 14 Jan.
1775 ae 40 or 48. She was poss. dau. of Jonathan and
Elizabeth (-----) Phinney (see #39vii), b. after 1717, but
not so late as 1735 (which the ae 40 in MIDDLEBORO DEATHS
would indicate) if she married in 1746/7.
     On 14 Feb. 1775 Benjamin Reed of Middleboro cooper was
appointed administrator of the estate of John Macomber late
of Middleboro yeoman. That same day Job Macomber of Middleboro yeoman was appointed guardian to Cyrus, Enoch and
Mary Macomber, all under 14, and selected guardian by
Samuel, John and Elizabeth Macomber, all over 14, children
of John Macomber of Middleboro deceased. The order of
division of John Macomber's estate, dated 8 April 1777,
allotted 2/8 share to eldest son John, and 1/8 each to
minor sons Samuel, Cyrus and Enoch, and to daughters
Elizabeth Macomber, Mary Macomber and Abiah Reed wife of
Benjamin of Middleboro.

     Poss. children (MACOMBER) prob. b. Middleboro: ABIAH[6]; ELIZA-
BETH b. bef. 1761; JOHN b. bef. 1761; SAMUEL b. bef. 1761; CYRUS b.
after 1761; ENOCH b. after 1761; and MARY b. after 1761.

References: VR TAUNTON. MD 18:78. MIDDLEBORO DEATHS p. 107. MACOM-
          BER GEN p. 17[omits gdn. for Mary]. WILLIAMS FAM (1926)
p. 41. Plymouth Co. PR 22:46-8, 167-8, 173-4(Job Macomber gdn.);
23:60; 24:327(John Macomber).

306 ELIZABETH[5] MACOMBER (Elizabeth[4] Williams, Elizabeth[3]
Rogers, John[2], Thomas[1]) b. Taunton 15 March 1715.
     She m. (1) ca. 1735 WILLIAM ROUNSEVELL, b. Freetown
10 Oct. 1705; d. there 31 Jan. 1744; son of Philip and
Mary (Howland) Rounsevell (a descendant of Henry, not John,
Howland).
     She m. (2) int. Tiverton RI 31 May 1746 WILLIAM(S)
ASHLEY, b. Rochester 12 Dec. 1708; d. Freetown bef. 4 Nov.
1783; son of Joseph and Elizabeth (Percival) Ashley. He
m. (1) 1733 Mercy Ashley (see MF 1:115), by whom he had
Jeptha and Abraham.
     On 2 May 1753 William Ashley and wife Elizabeth, both
of Freetown, were appointed to administer the estate of
William Rounsevell late of Freetown deceased, late husband
of Elizabeth. William Rounsevill's estate was divided 30
Oct. 1765, dower being set off to Elizabeth wife of William Ashley, among children William, Joseph and Levi Rounsevill, and Elizabeth Peirce. The four signed receipts
together with Job Peirce (husband of Elizabeth).

Bond was posted 4 Nov. 1783 on Levi Rounsevill as administrator of the estate of William Ashley late of Freetown, with Micah Ashley and Ephraim Winslow as sureties. The inventory was attested 7 Dec. 1784 by Levi.

Children (ROUNSEVELL) prob. b. Freetown: WILLIAM[6] b. ca. 1735; JOSEPH; LEVI b. ca. 1739; SYLVESTER b. 1741, d. 1743; and ELIZABETH b. 1743.

Children (ASHLEY) b. to William and Elizabeth, prob. Freetown: ABIAH b. 1751; MICAH; and NOAH b. ca. 1757.

References: VR ROCHESTER, TAUNTON. Freetown VR p. 17. RI VR:Tiverton p. 7. MF 1:115. MACOMBER GEN p. 13. WILLIAMS FAM (1926) p. 41. ASHLEYS OF AMER 1:39; 2:59. Bristol Co. PR 13:379; 19:354; 21:344(William Rounseville); 28:245 and file(William Ashley). CONTRIBUTIONS BY PEIRCE pp. 200, 206-7.

307 JAMES[5] MACOMBER (Elizabeth[4] Williams, Elizabeth[3] Rogers, John[2], Thomas[1]) b. Taunton 12 Sept. 1717; d. Berkley bet. 16 Jan. 1797 and 6 April 1804.
He m. Berkley 4 Feb. 1747 RACHEL DRAKE, b. ca. 1726; d. 1 Dec. 1809 ae 83; dau. of James and Miriam (-----) Drake.
The will of James Macomber of Berkley, made 16 Jan. 1797 and inventory taken 6 April 1804, names wife Rachel; sons Elijah, Josiah and Venus; daughters Lintha Macomber wife of Stephen, Miriam Briggs wife of Ezra, and Elinor Sanford wife of Joseph.

Children (MACOMBER) prob. b. Berkley: LINTHA[6] b. 1749; ELIJAH b. 1750/1; JAMES b. 1753; JOSIAH b. 1757; MIRIAM b. 1760; ELEANOR b. 1763; and VENUS (son) b. prob. 1775.

References: VR TAUNTON. Berkley TR 1:243. Bristol Co. PR 40:395, 399(James Macomber). MACOMBER GEN pp. 17-18. WILLIAMS FAM (1926) p. 41.

308 ELIJAH[5] MACOMBER (Elizabeth[4] Williams, Elizabeth[3] Rogers, John[2], Thomas[1]) b. Taunton 25 Oct. 1718; d. there 3 Feb. 1802 in 84th yr.
He m. (1) Taunton 10 Feb. 1742 JUDITH WILLIAMS, b. ca. 1721; d. 1 Oct. 1743 in 23 yr.; dau. of Nathaniel and Lydia (King) Williams, and a descendant of Pilgrim Thomas Rogers (see #66v). They had no children.
He is said to have m. (2) SARAH PITTS, b. ca. 1729; d. Taunton 30 May 1810 in her 82nd yr.
Elijah was a captain in the militia in 1772.

The will of Elijah Macomber of Taunton, made 18 Jan.
1802 and inventory taken 2 Aug. 1802, names wife Sarah;
daughters Betsey Padelford wife of Philip, and Sally Macomber; Elijah Macomber son of my deceased brother Joseph
Macomber late of Middleboro; and grandson Elijah Padelford.

Children (MACOMBER) by second wife prob. b. Taunton: JUDITH[6] b.
ca. 1754, d. 1770 ae 16; ELIZABETH b. 1756; JANE b. 1760; and SARAH
b. 1763.

References: VR TAUNTON. MD 23:1-5. MACOMBER GEN p. 18. Bristol Co.
             PR 39:32, 184(Elijah Macomber). CONTRIBUTIONS BY PEIRCE
pp. 203-5.

309 JOSEPH[5] MACOMBER (Elizabeth[4] Williams, Elizabeth[3]
Rogers, John[2], Thomas[1])   b. Taunton 28 March 1732; d. Middleboro 25 Jan. 1800 in 68th yr.
     He m. Taunton 16 March 1762 THANKFUL CANEDY, b. ca.
1738; d. Middleboro 13 Jan. 1794 in 56th yr., "wife of Lt.
Joseph"; dau. of William and Elizabeth (Eaton) Canedy, and
a descendant of Pilgrims John Billington, Samuel Fuller
and Francis Eaton (see MF 1:20).
     Joseph served as a lieutenant in the Revolution.

Children (MACOMBER) b. Middleboro or Taunton: JOSEPH[6] b. 1762;
THANKFUL b. 1764; BETSEY b. 1765, d. 1784; NATHAN b. 1767, d. 1788;
FREDERICK b. 1768; ELIJAH b. 1770; JUDITH b. 1772; OLIVE b. 1774;
LURANEY b. 1778; and HANNAH b. 1780.

References: VR TAUNTON. MIDDLEBORO DEATHS p. 109. MF 1:20. DAR
             PATRIOT INDEX p. 432. MACOMBER GEN pp. 18-20. CONTRIBU-
TIONS BY PEIRCE pp. 205-6.

continued from page 31

84A MARTHA HAWARD[5] (prob. Susanna Latham[4], Susanna Winslow[3], Mary[2] Chilton, James[1]) b. Bridgewater ca. 1681; living there 21 March 1747.
   She m. Bridgewater 1 Feb. 1698/9 DAVID PERKINS, b. Beverly 1677; d. Bridgewater bef. 9 Aug. 1737; son of David and Elizabeth (Brown) Perkins.
   On 9 Aug. 1737 Martha Perkins of Bridgewater widow was appointed administratrix of her husband David Perkins late of Bridgewater deceased. After setting off the widow's thirds, a division was made 11 Oct. 1738 among: children of eldest son John Perkins deceased; son Abraham Perkins; daughter Sarah Perkins; daughter Martha Byram wife of Dr. Joseph Byram; son David Perkins; daughter Mary Washburne wife of Gideon Washburne of Bridgewater; son Jonathan Perkins; daughter Elizabeth Leonard wife of Solomon Leonard of Bridgewater; and daughter Susanna Allen widow of Samuel Allen late of Bridgewater.
   Martha Perkins of Bridgewater, administratrix of her husband David Perkins deceased, in 1739 sold a purchase right in Bridgewater that was given her husband by his father David Perkins deceased. Also as his administratrix she sold swamp land in Bridgewater in 1738, by a deed she acknowledged 21 March 1747.

   Children (PERKINS) b. Bridgewater: JOHN[6] b. 1700; MARY b. 1702; MARTHA b. 1704; ELISABETH b. 1707; SUSANNA b. 1709; DAVID b. 1711; JONATHAN b. 1713/4; ABRAHAM b. 1716; and SARAH.

References: VR BRIDGEWATER. BRIDGEWATER BY MITCHELL p. 277[confounds David, husband of Martha, with his father]. HOWARD GEN p. 6. LEONARD FAM p. 63. NEHGR 50:36. Plymouth Co. PR 7:327-8, 388, 451-2(David Perkins). Plymouth Co. LR 34:138; 41:111(Martha Perkins).

84B SUSANNA HAWARD[5] (prob. Susanna Latham[4], Susanna Winslow[3], Mary[2] Chilton, James[1]) b. prob. Bridgewater ca. 1683; d. bet. 12 May 1729 and 13 Feb. 1732 (father's estate).
   She m. Bridgewater 2 Dec. 1702 NATHAN(IEL) AMES (or Eames), b. Bridgewater 9 Oct. 1677; d. there bef. 24 Dec. 1736; son of John and Sarah (Willis) Ames. He m. (2) Bridgewater 1734 Mary Lindsey.
   Nathaniel Ames and wife Susanna both of Bridgewater on 28 March 1727 sold land there bounded by land of "our grandfather John Haward decd" and land of John Hayes and wife Bethiah, and of David Perkins and wife Martha. On 24 Dec. 1736 Nathaniel Ames of Dedham physician was appointed

administrator of his father Capt. Nathaniel Ames late of
Bridgewater deceased. An account included an amount "to
the widow Mary Ames." All real estate was settled on the
oldest son, Dr. Nathaniel Ames, who was to pay 1/6 share
to each of the children (no names or receipts) 20 Aug.
1737.

Children (AMES) first four b. Bridgewater to Nathaniel and Susanna: NATHANIEL[6] b. 1708; SUSANNA b. 1711; SETH b. 1712/3; SARAH b.
1716; and poss. ANN and MARY.

References: VR BRIDGEWATER. BRIDGEWATER BY MITCHELL p. 99. HOWARD
          GEN p. 6[erroneous death dates]. Plymouth Co. PR #426
and 7:248, 344-5(Nathaniel Ames). Plymouth Co. LR 23:134(Nathan Ames)

84C EDWARD HAWARD[5] (prob. Susanna Latham[4], Susanna Winslow[3], Mary[2] Chilton, James[1]) b. Bridgewater 7 Feb. 1686/7;
d. there 14 July 1771 in 85 yr.
     He m. Bridgewater 7 Feb. 1710/1 MARY BYRAM, b. E.
Bridgewater 10 March 1689/90; d. Bridgewater 11 Jan. 1767
in 77 yr.; dau. of Nicholas and Mary (Edson) Byram. The
will of Nicholas Byram of Bridgewater, dated 18 Aug. 1727,
names wife Mary, and dau. Mary wife of Edward Haward.
     The will of Edward Haward of Bridgewater gentleman,
dated 22 Dec. 1764 and probated 5 Aug. 1771, names son Edward, executor; wife Mary; son James; daughters: Sarah
Ripley and Jane Haward; children of daughter Mary [Howard]
deceased: Henry, Elijah, Mary, Martha and Abigail; granddaughter Jane Ripley. A codicil of 12 Sept. 1768 indicates
that daughter Sarah Ripley had deceased, and names her
children: Solomon, Jane and Bethiah.

Children (HAWARD) b. Bridgewater: SARAH[6] b. 1714; MARY b. 1717;
BITHIA b. 1719; JANE b. 1721; EDWARD b. 1723/4; and JAMES b. 1726.

References: MD 15:50. VR BRIDGEWATER, E. BRIDGEWATER. BRIDGEWATER
          BY MITCHELL pp. 128, 198. HOWARD GEN p. 10. BRIDGEWATER
EPITAPHS p. 19. Plymouth Co. PR 5:340(Nicholas Byram); 21:1(Edward
Haward).

84D BETHIA HAWARD[5] (prob. Susanna Latham[4], Susanna Winslow[3], Mary[2] Chilton, James[1]) b. Bridgewater ca. 1691; d.
5 Nov. 1746 in 56 yr., "relict of John Hayes."
     She m. (1) Bridgewater 12 Aug. 1712 JONATHAN RANDALL,
b. Providence RI; d. there 7 Oct. 1724 in 36 yr.; son of
William and Rebecca (Fowler) Randall.
     Jonathan Randall "chyrurgen" of Plymouth in 1716 sold
to John Hayward of Bridgewater innkeeper "my houselot in
Plymouth wheron I dwell." William Harris, a creditor, was
to take possession of all the personal estate of Dr.

Jonathan Randall of Providence, who died 7 Oct. 1724, and
render account on 7 Dec. 1724. On 2 March 1724/5 John
Haward of Bridgewater innkeeper sold to his daughter Bethia
Randall of Bridgewater land in East Bridgewater.
     She "of Bridgewater" m. (2) Plymouth 21 April 1726
JOHN HAYES of Providence; d. Providence 29 Aug. 1744.
     John Hayes resident in Providence bought land there
22 Aug. 1726. Bethiah Hayes of Providence, wife of John
Hayes tailor, on 4 Oct. 1742 gave to "my son John Randall
of Providence sadler" land in Bridgewater which "belonged
to my father John Howard innholder deceased, which he
deeded me" in 1724. John Randal of Providence, "son-in-law"
to John Hays, was made administrator of moveable estate of
his "father-in-law" on 19 Nov. 1744. The inventory of John
Hays taylor, who died 29 Aug. 1744, was presented 19 Nov.
1744. An account of John Hays' estate was presented 1
Sept. 1745 by Johan Randal (*sic*) sadler, administrator.

     Children (RANDALL) b. Providence RI to Jonathan and Bethia:
JOHN[6], and JOSEPH, and poss. MARY d.y., and JONATHAN.

     Child (HAYES) b. Providence to John and Bethia: ZEBEDEE b. 1726.

References: RI VR:Providence pp. 227, 267, 272. VR BRIDGEWATER.
          HOWARD GEN p. 6. MD 14:71. RI GEN DICT p. 158. Provi-
dence RI PR 2:210-1(Jonathan Randall); 4:146-7(John Hays). Providence
RI LR 7:65(John Hayes). Plymouth Co. LR 13:131(Jonathan Randall);
23:134(John Haward); 35:102(Bethiah Hayes). Calef, North Burial
Grounds, Providence (Mss. RI Hist. Soc.) #1197, #1198[he has Dr.
Joseph Randall]. F. A. Randall, *"Randall and Allied Families"* p. 39.

84E ROBERT HAWARD[5] (prob. Susanna Latham[4], Susanna Winslow[3], Mary[2] Chilton, James[1]) b. Bridgewater 1699; d. N.
Bridgewater (now Brockton) 17 Aug. 1779 in 80 yr.
     He m. W. Bridgewater 28 April 1725 ABIGAIL KEITH, b.
Bridgewater 20 May 1705; d. N. Bridgewater 31 Jan. 1788 in
84 yr.; dau. of Joseph and Elizabeth (Fobes) Keith. The
will of Lt. Joseph Keith of Bridgewater, dated 22 Sept.
1730, names wife Elizabeth and dau. Abigail Haward.
     The will of Robert Howard of Bridgewater, dated 20
June 1768 and probated 6 Sept. 1779, names wife Abigail,
sons John Howard, executor, Robert, Adam and Daniel Howard,
and daughters Martha Edson and Betty Howard.

     Children (HAWARD) b. Bridgewater: JOHN[6] b. 1726; MARTHA b. 1729;
KEZIAH b. 1732, d. 1749 or 1750; ROBERT b. 1734/5; ADAM b. 1736/7;
ABIGAIL b. 1740, d. 1747 or 1748; BETTY b. 1744; and DANIEL b. 1750.

References: MD 15:170. VR BRIDGEWATER, BROCKTON, W. BRIDGEWATER.
          BRIDGEWATER BY MITCHELL pp. 198, 214. HOWARD GEN pp.
10-1. Plymouth Co. PR 6:5(Joseph Keith); 25:350-1(Robert Howard).

84F SARAH HAWARD[5] (prob. Susanna Latham[4], Susanna Winslow[3], Mary[2] Chilton, James[1]) b. Bridgewater ca. 1701; d.
bet. 3 Dec. 1760 and 3 June 1768.
      She m. Bridgewater 4 May 1721 DAVID TURNER, b. Scitu-
ate 5 May 1695; d. Rehoboth 9 Aug. 1757 in 63 yr.; son of
Thomas and Hannah (Jenkins) Turner.
      David was a graduate of Harvard College in 1718, and
received his MA in 1721. He was ordained pastor of the
Second Church in Rehoboth 29 Nov. 1721. John Haward of
Bridgewater innholder sold to his son-in-law David Turner
and wife Sarah, both of Bristol County, land in Bridgewater on 2 March 1724/5.
      Sarah Turner widow and David Turner yeoman, both of
Rehoboth, were appointed administrators of the Rev. Mr.
David Turner late of Rehoboth deceased on 12 Sept. 1757.
A distribution was made 3 July 1759 among the widow Sarah
Turner; eldest son David Turner; second son Thomas Turner;
daughter Jemimah wife of Nathaniel Willson; son Nathaniel
Turner; Sarah Burr "only legal representative" of deceased
daughter Sarah, who was wife of John Burr; son Nathan Turner; and daughter Abigail wife of Nathan Dagget. An account was filed 3 Dec. 1760 by the administrators, Sarah
Turner and David Turner.
      Upon her decease, Sarah's estate was divided 3 June
1768 among sons David, Nathaniel, Nathan and Thomas Turner; heirs of daughter Sarah wife of John Burr; heirs of
daughter Abigail deceased wife of Nathan Daggett; and
daughter Jemima wife of Nathaniel Willson.

      Children (TURNER) b. Rehoboth: DAVID[6] b. 1724; SARAH b. 1725;
THOMAS b. 1726/7; NATHAN b. 1728/9; NATHANIEL b. 1730; MARY b. 1731/2;
ABIGAIL b. 1733; and JEMIMA b. 1739/40.

References: VR BRIDGEWATER. REHOBOTH VR p. 758. BRIDGEWATER BY
            MITCHELL p. 334. HARVARD GRADS 6:287. Rehoboth Grave-
stone Records, by Robert S. Trim (typescript, RI Hist. Soc.) p. 172.
Plymouth Co. LR 22:123(John Haward). Bristol Co. PR 15:461; 16:364;
17:154; 23:148(David Turner). HOWARD GEN p. 6[gives a dau. Lucy as
only child].

96A HEPZIBAH WASHBURN[5] (prob. Hannah Latham[4], Susanna
Winslow[3], Mary[2] Chilton, James[1]) b. prob. Bridgewater;
d. there 4 April 1750
      She m. Bridgewater 8 Sept. 1702 BENJAMIN LEACH, b.
Bridgewater after 1680; d. there 13 July 1764; son of Giles
and Anne (Nokes) Leach.
      Benjamin Leach Sr. of Bridgewater and wife Hepzibah gave
land in Bridgewater to their son Benjamin Leach Jr. of
Bridgewater yeoman 6 April 1745. Benjamin Leach of Bridgewater on 15 March 1749/50 sold to son Joseph Leach of
Bridgewater part of a lot in Bridgewater. No other Plymouth County land or probate records were found to confirm

children, in particular the last three for whom no birth
records were located, although *Bridgewater Corrections*
indicates a birth year for daughter Phebe. (Fourteen children appears a lot for one woman.)

Children (LEACH) b. Bridgewater: ANNE[6] b. 1703; JOSEPH b. 1705;
MARY b. 1708; SARAH b. 1711; BENJAMIN b. 1713; ICHABOD b. 1716, d.
1722; twins BENANUEL and JERAHMEEL b. 1718; NOKES b. 1720; SUSANNA b.
1722; HANNAH b. 1725; prob. PHEBE b. 1730; and poss. NATHAN, and
EUNICE.

References: VR BRIDGEWATER. BRIDGEWATER BY MITCHELL pp. 239, 339.
            LEACH GEN 1:7, 15. Bridgewater Corrections p. 16 (b. of
Phebe). Plymouth Co. LR 37:121; 40:237(Benjamin Leach).

ABBREVIATIONS

ae	aged	n.d.	no date
b.	born	n.f.r.	no further
bef.	before		record found
bet.	between	n.p.	no place
bp.	baptised	N./No.	north
bur.	buried	NS	Nova Scotia
ca.	about	N.S.	new style (date)
Cem./cem.	cemetery	O.S.	old style (date)
ch.	children	p./pp.	page(s)
Ch.	church	pos./poss.	possibly
Co.	county	PR	probate records
Col.	colony	prob.	probably
Comm.	committee	pub.	published
d.	died	rec.	record(s)
dau(s).	daughter(s)	rem.	removed
dec.	deceased	repr.	reprinted
Dist	district	res.	resided
d.s.p.	died without issue	S./So.	south
d.y.	died young	sic	copy correct
E.	east	Soc.	society
ed.	edition	TR	town record(s)
G.S.	gravestone	unm.	unmarried
gdn.	guardian	unpub.	unpublished
granddau.	granddaughter	vol(s).	volume(s)
LR	land records	VR	vital records
m.	married	W.	west
m. int.	marriage inten-	wid.	widow
	tions	-y -m -d	years, months,
MS(S).	manuscript(s)		days

When no state is indicated after a city or town, when first mentioned in a family, the reader should assume Massachu-setts. The following two-letter abbreviations are used for states:

CT	Connecticut	NJ	New Jersey
MA	Massachusetts	NY	New York
MD	Maryland	PA	Pennsylvania
ME	Maine	RI	Rhode Island
NH	New Hampshire	VA	Virginia
	VT	Vermont	

KEY TO ABBREVIATED TITLES

The following is an alphabetical list of abbreviated titles used in the references of the three family genealogies in this volume. When the abbreviated title is in capital letters, the reference is in print -- a book or periodical. When the abbreviated title is not in capital letters, it represents unpublished material -- handwritten or typed. With respect to printed vital records, the abbreviated titles VR MANSFIELD, DUXBURY etc. indicate alphabetized vital records; the abbreviated titles MARSHFIELD VR, TRURO VR etc., followed by page numbers, indicate vital records published non-alphabetically.

Other abbreviations used in the references and in the genealogies themselves, as well as in this Key to Abbreviated Titles, appear on the opposite page.

NOTE: Readers should not assume that the books listed below have been accepted as references by the Mayflower Society. Some are cited merely to call attention to their errors, or to show that they have been consulted by the authors.

ADAMS GEN
Adams, Andrew N.
Genealogical History of Henry Adams of Braintree, Mass....also John Adams of Cambridge, Mass. 1632-1897. Rutland VT, 1898.

ALBANY NY HIST
Collections on the History of Albany from its discovery to the present time... and biographical sketches of citizens deceased. 4? vols. Albany NY, 1871.

ALBANY NY SETTLERS
Pearson, Jonathan
Contributions for the genealogies of the First Settlers of the Ancient Co. of Albany, from 1630 to 1800. Albany NY, 1872.

ALDRICH GEN
Aldrich, Alvin J.
The George Aldrich Genealogy 1605-1971...also...the descendants of John and Sarah (Aldrich) Bartlett. Iowa, 1971.

AM ANC
Hughes, Thomas P.
American Ancestry: giving the name and descent, in the male line, of Americans whose ancestors settled in the United States previous to the Declaration of Independence, A. D. 1776. 12 vols. Albany NY, 1887-1899.

ANC PURITANS
Morse, Abner
Genealogical Register of Descendants of Several Ancient Puritans. 2 Vols. 1857-1859.

ANNAPOLIS CO N.S. HIST
Calnek, W. A.
History of the County of Annapolis N.S. Toronto, 1897; reprint 1972.

ANNAPOLIS CO N.S. SUP
Savary, A. W.
History of the County of Annapolis supplement. Toronto, 1913; reprint 1973.

ARBER
Arber, Edward
The Story of the Pilgrim Fathers.... Boston and New York, 1897; reprint New York, 1969.

ASHBURNHAM HIST
Stearns, Ezra S.
History of Ashburnham Mass....1734-1886. Ashburnham, 1887.

ASHLEYS OF AMER
Ashleys of America. Vol. 1-- 1970--. Published at Bridgewater MA in 1977.

Aspinwall Papers
Aspinwall, Algernon A.
Manuscripts at New England Historic
Genealogical Society, Boston.

AUSTIN-RICH
Rich, Harold A.
Austin and Rich Genealogy. Farmington
MI, 1968.

Baker Fam
Clark, Bertha W.
Baker Family. Typescript at R. I. Histori-
cal Society, Providence, & NEHGR Soc.,
Boston, 1951.

BANKS ENGLISH ANCESTRY
Banks, Charles E.
*The English Ancestry and Homes of the Pil-
grim Fathers....* New York, 1929; reprint
Baltimore MD, 1962, 1968, 1976.

Barbados Archives
Records of baptism, marriage, burials
and wills, originals used by local
researcher.

BARNARD VT HIST
Newton, William M.
*History of Barnard with family genealogies,
1761-1927....* Montpelier VT, 1928.

BARNSTABLE FAMS
Swift, C. F.
*Genealogical Notes of Barnstable Families,
being a reprint of the Amos Otis Papers.*
Barnstable, 1888-1890.

BARRINGTON NH HIST
Wiggins, Morton H.
Barrington, New Hampshire History. 1966.

BASSETTS OF CHATHAM
Chapman, Grace O.
Bassetts of Chatham and Harwich Mass.
Dorchester, 1944. Typescript at NEHG,
Boston.

BELLINGHAM HIST
Partridge, George F.
*History of the town of Bellingham Mass.
1719-1919.* Bellingham 1919.

BERKLEY HIST
Sanford, Enoch
History of the Town of Berkley, Mass....
New York, 1872.

BLOCK ISLAND HIST
Livermore, Samuel T.
*A history of Block Island from its discovery
in 1514 to ... 1876.* Hartford CT, 1877;
reprint 1961.

BOLTON CT VR
*Vital Records of Bolton to 1854 and Ver-
non to 1852.* Conn. Hist. Soc. Hartford
CT, 1909.

(BOSTON) COPP'S HILL
Bridgeman, Thomas
*Memorials of the dead in Boston ... Copp's
Hill Burying Ground.* Boston, 1852.

(BOSTON) KINGS CHAPEL
Bridgeman, Thomas
*Memorials of the Dead in Boston ... in
King's Chapel Burying Ground....* Boston,
1853.

BOSTON MEM HIST
Winsor, Justin
*The Memorial History of Boston, including
Suffolk County, Mass. 1630-1880.* 4 vols.
Boston, 1882-3.

BOSTON NEWS OBITS
*Index of Obituaries in Boston Newspapers
1704-1800.* 3 vols. Boston, 1968.

(BOSTON) OLD SOU CH
*Historical Catalogue of the Old South
Church (Third Church) Boston.* Boston,
1883.

BOSTON REC COM
Reports of the Boston Record Commissioners of Records relating to the early history of Boston. 39 vols. Boston, 1876-1909. (Does not include those keyed under BOSTON VR.)

BOSTON TRANSCRIPT
Genealogical column of the *Boston Transcript* available on microcards from Godfrey Mem. Lib., Middletown CT. Boston, 1906-1941.

BOSTON VR
Reports of the Record Commissioners. Vols. 9 and 24: births, marriages and deaths, 1630-1699 and births 1700-1800. Boston, 1883 and 1894. Vols. 28 and 30: marriages 1700-1751 and 1751-1809. Boston, 1898 and 1902; reprinted Baltimore MD, 4 vols in 2, 1977 and 1978.

BRADFORD DESC
Hall, Ruth G.
Descendants of Governor William Bradford. n.p., 1951.

BRADFORD'S HIST (1912)
Bradford, William
History of Plymouth Plantation, 1620-1647. 2 vols. Boston, 1912.

BRADFORD'S HIST (1952)
Bradford, William
Of Plymouth Plantation, 1620-1647. Edited by Samuel E. Morison. New York, 1952.

BRAINERD-BRAINARD
Brainard, Lucy A.
The Genealogy of the Brainerd-Brainard Family in America, 1649-1908. 3 vols. Hartford CT, 1908.

BRAINERD FAM
Field, David D.
Genealogy of the Brainerd Family in the United States.... New York, 1857.

BRAINTREE RECS
Bates, Samuel A.
Records of the Town of Braintree 1640-1793. Randolph, 1886.

BRIDGETOWN N.S. HIST
Coward, Elizabeth R.
Bridgetown, Nova Scotia: Its History to 1900. n.p., 1955.

BRIDGEWATER BY MITCHELL
Mitchell, Nahum
History of the Early Settlement of Bridgewater ... including an extensive family register. Boston, 1840; reprint Bridgewater, 1897 and Baltimore, 1970.

Bridgewater Corrections
Latham, Williams
Additions and Corrections to the History of Bridgewater Mass. by Mitchell. MS. New England Historic Genealogical Society, Boston.

BRIDGEWATER EPITAPHS
Latham, Williams
Epitaphs in Old Bridgewater Mass.... Report of the Committee on the Old Graveyard. Bridgewater, 1882; reprint Middleboro 1976.

BRIGHAM FAM
Brigham, W. I. Tyler
The History of the Brigham Family: A record of ... descendants of Thomas Brigham the Emigrant, 1608-1653. New York, 1907.

BRITISH STATE PAPERS
Sainsbury, W. N.
Calendar of State Papers, Colonial Series, America and West Indies, preserved in the Public Record Office. Vols. 1-40. London, 1860-1939.

BULL FAM
Bowerman, A. C.
Genealogical list of the Bull Family of the

County of Prince Edward, Ontario. Ontario Historical Society, n. d.

CABOT GEN
Briggs, L. Vernon
History and Genealogy of the Cabot Family 1475-1927. Boston, 1927.

CAMBRIDGE FIRST CH
Sharples, Stephen P.
Records of the First Church of Christ at Cambridge in New England 1632-1830. Boston, 1906.

CAMBRIDGE HIST
Paige, Lucius R.
History of Cambridge 1630-1877. With a genealogical register. Boston and New York, 1877.

CANDLEWOOD
Water, Thomas F.
Candlewood, An Ancient Neighborhood in Ipswich, with genealogy of John Brown, William Fellows and Robert Kinsman. n.p., 1909.

CANTERBURY CH REC
Records of the Congregational church in Canterbury, 1711-1844. Hartford CT, 1932.

CANTON & STOUGHTON VR
Endicott, Frederic
The record of births, marriages and deaths and intentions of marriage in the Town of Stoughton from 1727 to 1800, and in the Town of Canton from 1797 to 1845, preceded by the records of the South Precinct of Dorchester from 1715 to 1727. Canton MA, 1896.

CAPE COD HIST
Freeman, Frederick
History of Cape Cod. 2 vols. Boston, 1858-62; reprint Yarmouth Port MA, 1965.

CARIBBEANA
Oliver, Vere L.
Caribbeana. A miscellany of papers relative to history, genealogy, antiquity of British West Indies. 6 vols. n.p., 1909-1919.

CAVALIERS & PIONEERS
Nugent, Nell M.
Cavaliers and Pioneers. Abstracts of Virginia Land Patents and Grants, 1623-1666. Richmond VA, 1934; reprint Baltimore MD, 1974.

CHARLESTOWN BY WYMAN
Wyman, Thomas B.
The Genealogies and Estates of Charlestown.... 2 vols. Boston, 1879.

CHURCHILL FAM
Churchill, Gardner and Nathaniel
The Churchill Family in America. Boston, 1904.

CONANT FAM
Conant, Frederick O.
A history and genealogy of the Conant Family.... 1520-1887. Portland ME, 1887.

CONCORD VR
Concord, Massachusetts. Births, Marriages and Deaths 1635-1850. Boston, 1895.

CONTRIBUTIONS BY PIERCE
Pierce, Ebenezer W.
Contributions Biographical, Genealogical and Historical. Boston MA, 1874.

CORY ANC
Lineal Ancestors of Rhoda (Axtell) Cory, mother of Capt. James Cory. n.p., 1937.

CSL Barbour Index
Bound volumes of alphabetized vital records to about 1850, from all CT towns, as copied by Lucius B. Barbour. Also a statewide alphabetical card index of these records, interfiled with similar

entries from private sources. At CT State Library, also filmed by LDS Genealogical Society.

CSL Ch Rec
Bound volumes of alphabetized vital records from over 600 CT churches and a single alphabetical card index for them all. At CT State Library.

CSL Hale Cem Recs
Hale collection of cemetery records copied by the WPA from CT cemeteries about 1932. Bound volumes for each town, and a single alphabetical card index. At CT State Library.

CT MARR
Bailey, Frederick W.
Early Connecticut Marriages as found on ancient church records prior to 1800. 7 vols. New Haven CT, 1896-1906; reprint with additions, 7 vols in 1, Baltimore MD, 1968.

CT QUARTERLY
The Connecticut Magazine. Devoted to Connecticut in its various phases of history, literature, scenic beauty, art, science, industry. 12 vols. Hartford CT, 1895-1908.

CT VR SHARON
Van Alstyne, Lawrence
A record of births, marriages and deaths, in the Town of Sharon, Connecticut from 1721-1879. Sharon, 1897.

CUMMINGS GEN
Cummings, Albert D.
Cummings Genealogy. Montpelier VT, 1904.

DAR PATRIOT INDEX
DAR Patriot Index. Pub. by the National Society of the Daughters of the American Revolution. Washington DC, 1966; Supplements: 1, 1969; 2, 1973; 3, 1976.

DAWES-GATES
Ferris, Mary W.
Dawes-Gates Ancestral Lines: The American Ancestry of Mary Beman (Gates) Dawes and Rufus R. Dawes. 2 vols. Milwaukee WI, 1931-1943.

DEAN GEN
Ramsay, Elizabeth D.
Notes on John Dean and the first seven generations of his descendants.

DEDHAM CH
Hill, Don G.
Record of Baptisms, Marriages and Deaths ... transcribed from the Church Records in the Town of Dedham, Massachusetts. 1638-1845. Also all the epitaphs in the ancient burial place in Dedham.... Dedham, 1888.

DEDHAM HIST REG
The Dedham Historical Register. 14 vols. Dedham MA, 1890-1903.

DEDHAM VR
Hill, Don G.
Record of Births, Marriages and Deaths and intentions of Marriage in the Town of Dedham. Volumes 1 & 2 ... 1635-1845. Dedham, 1886.

DERBY CT HIST
Orcutt, Samuel
History of the Old Town of Derby CT, 1642-1880. Springfield, 1880.

DIGHTON VR
MacCormick, Elizabeth J. and Shaw, Edith W.
Town records -- Book One -- Dighton, Mass. n.p., 1939. Typescript at R. I. Hist. Soc., Providence, and NEHG, Boston.

DODGE GEN
Dodge, Joseph T.
Genealogy of the Dodge Family of Essex County, Mass. 1629-1894. Madison WI, 1894.

DOGGETT FAM
Doggett, Samuel B.
A History of the Doggett Family. Boston, 1894.

DOGGETT SUPP
Daggett, George H. & Sydney B.
A Supplement to ... John Doggett-Daggett of Martha's Vineyard [in DOGGETT FAM]. Baltimore MD, 1974.

DORCHESTER VR
Report of the Record Commissioners. Vol. 21, to 1825: Boston, 1891; *vol. 36, 1826-49:* Boston, 1905.

DOWSE DESC
Dows, Azro M.
The Dows or Dowse Family in America: A Genealogy of the Descendants of Lawrence Dows.... Lowell, 1890.

DOWSE FAM
Dowse, William B. H.
Lawrence Dowse of Legbourne Eng., his Ancestors, Descendants and Connections in England, Mass. and Ireland. Boston, 1926.

DURHAM NH HIST
Stackpole, Everett S. and Thompson, Lucien
History of the Town of (Oyster River Plantation). Durham ?, 1913.

DUXBURY RECS
Etheridge, George
Copy of the Old Records of the Town of Duxbury, Mass. from 1642 to 1770. Plymouth, 1893.

EARLY REHOBOTH
Bowen, Richard L.
Early Rehoboth. 4 vols. Rehoboth, 1945-50.

EASTON HIST
Chaffin, William L.
History of the Town of Easton, Mass. Cambridge MA, 1886; reprint 1975.

EDDY GEN
Eddy, Ruth S. D.
The Eddy Family in America, a Genealogy. Boston, 1930; reprint Ann Arbor MI, 1965.

1800 CENSUS
Heads of Families at the Second Census, 1800. Originals at US National Archives, also on microfilm, some states in print.

1810 CENSUS
Heads of Families at the Third Census, 1810. Originals at US National Archives, also on microfilm, some states in print.

1820 CENSUS
Heads of Families at the Fourth Census, 1820. Originals at US National Archives, also on microfilm, some states in print.

EMERSON GEN
Pope, Charles H.
The Haverhill Emersons. 2 vols. Boston, 1913-16.

ESSEX ANTIQUARIAN
The Essex Antiquarian, a monthly magazine devoted to biography, genealogy, history and antiquities of Essex County, Mass. 13 vols. Salem, 1897-1909.

ESSEX CO PR
Dow, George G.
The Probate Records of Essex County, Massachusetts. 3 vols. Salem, 1916-20.

ESSEX INST HIST COLL
Historical Collections of the Essex Institute.
Vol. 1-- April 1859--. Salem.

ESSEX QUARTERLY COURTS
Dow, George F. and Thresher, Mary G.
Records and Files of the Quarterly Courts of Essex County, Mass. 1636-86. 9 vols.
Salem, 1911-74.

FAIRFIELD CT FAMS
Jacobus, Donald L.
History and Genealogy of the Families of Old Fairfield. 3 vols. in 5. 1930-34; reprint Cleveland OH, 1967.

FALES FAM
Fales, De Coursey
Fales Family of Bristol, Rhode Island. Boston, 1919.

FAM OF PILGRIMS
Shaw, Hubert K.
Families of the Pilgrims. Boston, 1956.

FINNEY-PHINNEY
Finney, Howard
Finney-Phinney Families in America: Descendants of John Finney of Plymouth and Barnstable, Mass. and Bristol, R. I.; of Samuel Finney of Philadelphia, Penn.; and of Robert Finney of New London, Penn. Richmond VA, 1957.

Ford Fam
Ford, Hannibal C.
Ford Family Genealogy, a manuscript collection of Ford families, mostly descendants of William of Marshfield, but includes Matthew and Andrew, including the Corydon La Ford manuscript material from NEHG. Microfilm at Western Reserve Hist. Soc., Cleveland OH.

FOSTER GEN
Pierce, Frederick C.
Foster Genealogy: being the record of the posterity of Reginald Foster of Ipswich in New England. Also the record of all other American Fosters. Chicago IL, 1899.

FREEMAN GEN
Freeman, Frederick
Freeman Genealogy in Three Parts ... Edmund Freeman of Sandwich ... Samuel Freeman of Watertown ... Families of the name of Freeman. Boston, 1875.

FREETOWN MARR
Herbert, Mary P.
Freetown, Mass. Marriage Records 1686-1844. Glendale CA, 1934.

Freetown VR
Freetown, Mass. Vital Records, Births, Marriage Intentions and Deaths 1686-1793. Typescript in Fall River Public Library and NEHG Soc., Boston. n.d.

FULLER GEN 1
Fuller, William H.
Genealogy of some Descendants of Edward Fuller of the Mayflower. Palmer MA, 1908.

GALPIN FAM
Galpin, William F.
Galpin Family in America. Syracuse NY, 1955.

GEN ADVERTISER
Greenlaw, Lucy H.
The Genealogical Advertiser, a Quarterly Magazine of Family History. Vols. 1-4, 1898-1901; reprint Baltimore MD, 1974.

GILMAN FAM
Gilman, A. W.
Searches into the History of the Gillman or Gilman Family. London Eng, 1895.

GLOUCESTER HIST
Babson, John J.
History of the Town of Gloucester, Cape Ann, including the town of Rockport. Gloucester, 1860.

GLOUCESTER NOTES
Babson, John J.
Notes and Additions to the History of Gloucester. Part First: Early Settlers.
Gloucester, 1876.

HALIFAX VR
Bowman, George E.
Vital records of the Town of Halifax, Mass. to the end of the year 1849. Boston,1905.

GOODHUE GEN
Goodhue, Jonathan F.
Genealogy of the Goodhue Family. Rochester NY, 1891.

HALLS OF N.E.
Hall, David
The Halls of New England, Genealogical and Biographical. Albany NY, 1883.

HAMILTON FAM
Hamilton, Charles W. Jr.
Hamilton Family of America. 1933.

GORHAM ME HIST
McLellan, Hugh D. and Lewis, K. B.
History of Gorham Maine. Portland ME, 1903.

HAMLIN GEN
Andrews, H. Franklin
The Hamlin Family; a Genealogy of James Hamlin of Barnstable Mass., eldest son of James Hamlin, the immigrant, 1629-1902. Exira IA, 1902.

GRANBERRY FAM
Jacobus, Donald L.
Granberry Family and Allied Families.... Hartford CT, 1945.

HANCOCK NH HIST
Hayward, William W.
History of Hancock, N.H., 1764-1889. Lowell, 1889.

GREENE FAM
Greene, G. S.
The Greenes of Rhode Island. New York, 1903.

HANOVER BY DWELLEY
Dwelley, Jedediah and Simmons, John F.
History of the Town of Hanover, Mass. with Family Genealogies. Hanover, 1910.

HARDWICK BY PAIGE
Paige, Lucius R.
History of Hardwick Massachusetts with a genealogical register. Boston, 1882.

HARTFORD COURANT
The Hartford [CT] Courant. 1764 to date. Available on microfilm in some libraries.

HARVARD GRADS
Sibley, John L.
Biographical sketches of graduates of Harvard University in Cambridge, Mass. Cambridge, vol. 1-- 1872--.

HAYFORD FAM
Hayford, Otis
History of the Hayford Family, 1100-1900 ... its connections by the Bonney, Fuller and Phinney families, with the Mayflower 1620, Chickering family.... Canton ME, 1901.

HIGGINS DESC
Higgins, Katherine C.
Richard Higgins ... settler at Plymouth and Eastham, Mass. and at Piscataway, N.J. and his descendants. Worcester, 1918.

HIGGINS SUP
Higgins, Katherine C.
Supplement to Richard Higgins and his descendants. Worcester, 1924.

HINGHAM HIST
History of the Town of Hingham, Mass. 2 vols. in 4. Published by the town. Hingham, 1892.

HOAR GEN
Horr, Norton T.
A record of descendants of Hezekiah Hoar of Taunton, Mass.... Cleveland OH, 1907.

HODGES GEN
Hodges, Almon D. et al.
Genealogical Record of the Hodges Family of New England.... Third edition: Boston, 1896.

HOTTEN'S PERSONS
Hotten, John C.
The Original Lists of Persons of Quality; Emigrants; Religious exiles; Political Rebels; and Others who went from Great Britain to the American Plantations, 1600-1700. New York, 1880; reprint Baltimore MD, 1962.

HOWARD GEN
Howard, Heman
The Howard Genealogy. Brockton, 1902.

HUDSON-MOHAWK GEN
Edwards, Scuyler
Hudson-Mohawk Genealogies. New York, 1911.

HUNGERFORD GEN
Leach, F. Phelps
Thomas Hungerford of Hartford and New London Conn. and some of his descendants. n.p., 1924.

HURLBUT GEN
Hurlbut, Henry H.
The Hurlbut Genealogy; or Record of the descendants of Thomas Hurlbut of Saybrook and Wethersfield Conn.... Albany NY, 1888.

INDEPENDENT CHRONICLE
The Independent Chronicle. Boston 1776-1840.

IPSWICH HIST
Waters, Thomas F.
Ipswich in the Massachusetts Bay Colony. 2 vols. Ipswich Hist. Soc. 1905-1917.

332

Jenney Fam
Clark, Bertha W.
John Jenney of Plymouth and his descendants to the 7th generation. Typescript, Boston 1958-9, available at R. I. Hist. Soc., Providence RI and NEHG, Boston.

KEEP DESC
Best, Frank E.
John Keep of Longmeadow Mass. 1660-1676 and his Descendants. Chicago, 1899.

KENT CT HIST
Atwater, Francis
History of Kent Connecticut. Meriden CT, 1897.

KING PHILIP'S WAR
Bodge, George M.
Soldiers in King Philip's War. 2rd ed., 1906; reprint Baltimore MD, 1967.

KINGMAN DESC
Kingman, Bradford
Descendants of Henry Kingman -- Some Early Generations of the Kingman Family. Boston, 1912.

KNEELAND FAM
Kneeland, Stillman F.
Seven Centuries of the Kneeland Family. New York, 1897.

KNOWLTON ANCY
Stocking, Charles H. W.
History and Genealogy of the Knowltons of England and America. New York, 1897.

KNOWLTON ERRORS
Knowlton, George H.
Errata and addenda to Dr. Stocking's History and Genealogy of the Knowltons of England and America with a complete index to both books.... Boston, 1902.

LAMSON FAM
Lamson, William J.
Descendants of William Lamson of Ipswich Massachusetts, 1624-1917. New York, 1917.

Latham Fam
Estes, William W.
Latham Family. Typescript, 1942, available at R. I. Hist. Soc., Providence.

LEACH FAM
Chessman, Samuel
Leach Family Records; Descendants of Lawrence Leach of Salem Massachusetts 1629. Albany NY, 1898.

LEICESTER HIST
Washburn, Emory
Historical Sketches of the Town of Leicester Massachusetts.... Boston, 1860.

LEONARD FAM
Leonard, Manning
Memorial: Genealogical, Historical and Biographical of Solomon Leonard, 1627, of Duxbury and Bridgewater, Mass. and some of his descendants. Auburn NH, 1896.

Leonard Papers (MA)
Leonard, Elisha C.
Genealogical records of old families of Dartmouth Mass. 2 vols., typescript at New Bedford Public Library.

LEYDEN DOCUMENTS
Plooij, D. and Harris, J. Rendel
Leyden Documents Relating to the Pilgrim Fathers. Leiden, Holland, 1920.

Leyden Poll Tax
A list of residents of Leyden Holland in 1622. MSS, Town Archives, Leiden, Holland.

LITTLE COMPTON FAMS
Wilbour, Benjamin F.
Little Compton Families published by the Little Compton Historical Society from records compiled by Benjamin F. Wilbour.
Providence RI, 1967.

LONDONDERRY NH HIST
Parker, Edward L.
The History of Londonderry, comprising the Towns of Derry and Londonderry New Hampshire. Boston, 1851.

LORD DESC
Lord, Kenneth
Genealogy of the Descendants of Thomas Lord. New York, 1946.

LORING GEN
Pope, Charles H.
Loring Genealogy compiled from the chronicles or ancestral records of James Speare Loring ... from the manuscripts of John Arthur Loring and from many other sources. Cambridge, 1917.

LOYALISTS BY SABINE
Sabine, Lorenzo
Biographical Sketches of Loyalists in the American Revolution. 2 vols. 2nd edition 1864; reprint New York, 1966.

LUMBERT-LOMBARD
Otis, Amos
The Lumbert or Lombard Family. Library of Cape Cod History and Genealogy #54. Yarmouth Port MA, 1914.

LUNENBURG RECS
Davis, Walter A.
Early Records of the Town of Lunenburg, Massachusetts (1719-1764). Madison WI, 1894.

LYME CT VR
Hall, Verne M. and Plimpton, Elizebeth B.
Vital Records of Lyme, Connecticut to the end of the year 1850. Lyme CT, 1976.

LYNDEBOROUGH NH HIST
Donovan, D. and Woodward, J. A.
History of Lyndeborough New Hampshire. Tufts Co. Press, 1906.

MA BAY ACTS & RESOLVES
Acts and Resolves of the Province of Massachusetts Bay. 21 vols. Boston, 1869-1922.

MA HIST COLL
Collections of the Massachusetts Historical Society. Vol. 1-- 1792--. Boston.

MA HIST PROC
Proceedings of the Massachusetts Historical Society. Vol. 1-- 1879--. Boston.

MA HOUSE JNL
Journals of the House of Representatives of Massachusetts. Vol. 1-- 1715--. Boston.

MA MAG
Stevens, Cj
The Massachusetts Magazine: Marriage and Death Notices 1789 - 1796. New Orleans, 1978.

MA MARR
Bailey, Frederic W.
Early Massachusetts Marriages prior to 1800. 3 vols. in 1. 1897-1900; reprint Baltimore MD, 1968.

MA OBITS
Index of obituaries in the Massachusetts Centinel and the Columbian Centinel, 1784-1840 ... 5 vols. Boston, 1961.

MA PIONEERS
Pope, Charles H.
The Pioneers of Massachusetts .... Boston, 1900; reprint Baltimore MD, 1965.

MACOMBER GEN
Stackpole, Everett S.
Macomber Genealogy. Lewiston ME, 1909.

MAKEPEACE FAM
Makepeace, William
The Genealogy of the Makepeace Families in the United States, 1637-1857. Boston, 1858.

Manton Fam
Denison, Frederic
A section of the Family Records of the Mantons in the Vicinity of Providence. Typescript 1859, at R.I. Historical Society, Providence.

MANWARING
Manwaring, Charles W.
A Digest of the Early Connecticut Probate Records. 3 vols. Hartford CT, 1902-6.

MARLBORO HIST
Hudson, Charles
History of the Town of Marlborough, Middlesex County, Massachusetts from ... 1657 to 1861; with a brief sketch of the town of Northborough, a genealogy of the families in Marlborough to 1800 ... Boston, 1862.

MARSHFIELD VR
Sherman, Robert M. and Ruth W.
Vital Records of Marshfield, Massachusetts to the year 1850. Warwick RI, 1969.

MARTHA'S VINEYARD BY BANKS
Banks, Charles E.
History of Martha's Vineyard, with Genealogy. 3 vols. Boston, 1911-25; reprint Edgartown, 1966.

MARY CHILTON
Libby, Charles T.
Mary Chilton's Title to Celebrity. Boston, 1926; reprinted with _Plymouth Colony Marriages to 1650:_ Warwick RI, 1978.

MARYLAND SETTLERS
Skordas, Gust
The Early Settlers of Maryland ... Names of Immigrants ... 1633-1680. Baltimore MD, 1968.

MAYO (JOHN) DESC
Mayo, Chester G.
John Mayo of Roxbury, Mass., 1630-1688. A Genealogical and Biographical Genealogy of his Descendants. Huntington VT, 1965.

MAYO (JOHN) REV
Mayo, E. Jean
Rev. John Mayo and his descendants. Pueblo CO, 1965.

MD
Bowman, George E.
The Mayflower Descendant: a quarterly magazine of Pilgrim history and genealogy. 34 vols. Boston, 1899-1940.

MD ARCHIVES
Pleasants, J. Hall
Archives of Maryland. Maryland Historical Society. Vol 1-- 1883--. Baltimore MD.

ME GEN
Little, George T.
Genealogical and Family History of the State of Maine. New York, 1909.

ME HGR
Watson, S.M.
Maine Historical and Genealogical Recorder. 9 vols., Portland ME, 1884-1898; reprint in 3 vols., Baltimore MD, 1973.

ME-NH GEN DICT
Noyes, Sybil; Libby, C.T.; and Davis, Walter G.
Genealogical Dictionary of Maine and New Hampshire. 1928-1935; reprint Baltimore MD, 5 parts in 1, 1972.

MF1
van Antwerp, Lee D.; Radasch, Arthur H. and Katharine W.; and Sherman, Robert M. and Ruth W.
Mayflower Families Through Five Generations: Descendants of the Pilgrims who landed at Plymouth, Mass. December 1620. Vol 1 families: Francis Eaton, Samuel Fuller and William White. Plymouth, 1975.

MIDDLEBORO DEATHS
Wood, Alfred
Record of Deaths, Middleboro, Massachusetts. Boston, 1947.

MIDDLETOWN UPPER HOUSES
Adams, Charles C.
Middletown Upper Houses: a history of the north society of Middletown CT from 1650-1800 with genealogical and biographical chapters on early families and a full genealogy of the Ranney family.... NY, 1908.

MILTON HIST
Teele, A.K.
History of Milton, Massachusetts, 1640-1887. Boston, 1887.

MIN COUNCIL NY
Minutes of the Common Council of the City of New York 1675-1776. 8 vols. New York, 1905.

MONTVILLE CT HIST
Baker, Henry A.
History of Montville, formerly the north parish of New London, from 1640-1896. Hartford CT, 1895.

MORSE GEN
Morse, J. Howard and Leavitt, Emily W.
Morse Genealogy, being a revision of the Memorial of the Morses published by Abner Morse in 1850. 2 vols. New York, 1903-1905.

MORTON DESC
Allen, John K.
George Morton of Plymouth Colony and some of his descendants. Chicago IL, 1908.

MQ
The Mayflower Quarterly. Published at Plymouth MA for the General Society of Mayflower Descendants. Vol 1-- 1935--.

MSSR
Massachusetts Soldiers and Sailors of the Revolutionary War. 17 vols. Boston, 1896-1908.

NC COL RECS
Saunders, William L.
The Colonial Records of North Carolina.... 10 vols. Raleigh NC, 1886-1890.

NEHGR
New England Historical and Genealogical Register. Vol. 1-- Jan. 1847--. Published at Boston by the New England Historic Genealogical Society.

NEW ADVENTURE
Morse, William I.
The Land of the New Adventure (The Georgian Era in Nova Scotia.) London, 1932.

NEW BOSTON NH HIST
Coggswell, Elliott C.
History of New Boston, New Hampshire. Boston, 1864.

NEW MILFORD CT HIST
Orcutt, Samuel
History of the Towns of New Milford and Bridgewater Connecticut, 1703-1882. Hartford CT, 1882.

NEWCOMB GEN
Newcomb, Bethuel M.
Andrew Newcomb 1618-1686 and his Descendants: A revised edition of "Genealogical Memoir" of the Newcomb Family published 1874 by John Bearse Newcomb .... New Haven CT, 1923.

NEWTON GEN
Leonard, Ermina N.
*Newton Genealogy ... a Record of the Descendants of Richard Newton of Sudbury and Marlborough, Massachusetts 1638 with genealogies of families descended from ....
Rev. Roger Newton of Milford CT, Thomas Newton of Fairfield VT, Matthew Newton of Stonington CT, Newton of Virginia, Newtons near Boston.* DePere WI, 1915.

NEWTOWN LI ANNALS
Riker, James Jr.
Annals of Newtown in Queen's County New York ... also a particular account of numerous Long Island Families ... New York, 1852.

NEWTOWN LI MIN
Transcriptions of Early Town Records of New York ... WPA: Town Minutes of Newtown.... 2 vols. New York, 1940.

NGSQ
National Genealogical Society Quarterly. Vol 1-- 1912--. Published at Washington DC by the Society.

NH STATE PAPERS
Documents and records relating to state and towns of New Hampshire, 1623-1800. 40 vols. Manchester NH and elsewhere, 1867-1943.

NICKERSON FAM
The Nickerson Family; the descendants of William Nickerson, 1604-1789, first settler of Chatham, Massachusetts. Yarmouth, 1973.

NICKERSONS OF CAPE COD
Driscoll, Marion L.
Nickersons of Cape Cod. 1945.

NJ ARCH
Archives of the state of New Jersey. 47 vols. Trenton, NJ. 1880-1949.

NJ Library
New Jersey State Library, Trenton, NJ.

NORWICH CT VR
Vital records of Norwich, Conn., 1659-1848. 2 vols. Hartford CT, 1913.

NOVA SCOTIA CENSUSES
See 1770 CENSUS NS

NS Archives
Public Archives of Nova Scotia, presently housed on the campus of Dalhousie University, Halifax NS.

NY BY VALENTINE
Valentine, David T.
Valentine's Manual of Old New York. New York, 1916-28.

NY HIST COLL
Collections of the New-York Historical Society.... [3rd series] Vol. 1-- 1868--.

NY WILLS
Fernow, Berthold
Calendar of Wills on File and Recorded in the Offices of the Clerk of the Court of Appeals, of the County Clerk at Albany, and of the Secretary of State, 1626-1836. New York, 1896; reprint Baltimore 1967.

NYGBR
The New York Genealogical and Biographical Record. Vol 1-- 1870--. Published by the Society.

Old Colony Recs
Records housed in the Old Colony Historical Society, Taunton. MSS.

OLD TIMES
Old Times: a magazine devoted ... to the early history of North Yarmouth, Maine including ... the towns of Harpswell, Freeport, Pownal, Cumberland and Yarmouth.... 8 vols. Yarmouth ME, 1877-1884; reprinted 8 vols. in 1, Somersworth NH, 1977.

OTIS FAM
Otis, William A.
A genealogical and historical memoir of the Otis family in America. Chicago IL, 1924.

PAYNE & GORE FAM
Whitmore, W.H.
Genealogy of the families of Payne and Gore. Boston, 1875.

PIONEER LIFE
Pioneer Life on the Bay of Quinte...The Cunningham Family. Canada?, 1904.

(PLYMOUTH) ANC LANDMARKS
Davis, William T.
Ancient Landmarks of Plymouth. 2nd edition 1899; reprint of Part Two under title *Genealogical Register of Plymouth Families.* Baltimore MD, 1975.

(PLYMOUTH) BURIAL HILL
Kingman, Bradford
Epitaphs from Burial Hill, Plymouth Massachusetts, from 1657 to 1892. With biographical and historical notes. Brookline, 1892; reprint Baltimore MD, 1977.

PLYMOUTH BY THACHER
Thacher, James
History of the Town of Plymouth from its First Settlement in 1620, to the Present Time.... 3rd edition Boston, 1835; reprint Yarmouth Port, 1972.

PLYMOUTH CH RECS
Plymouth Church Records, 1620-1859. 2 vols. New York, 1920-23; reprint Baltimore MD, 1975.

Plymouth Col. LR
Also known as Old Colony Deeds. 6 vols. MSS. at Plymouth Co. Register of Deeds. Vol 1 appeared in print as Vol 12 of *Plymouth Colony Recs* (see below); Vol. 2 and Vol. 3, as far as p. 27, have been printed in MD.

Plymouth Col. PR
Also known as Old Colony Wills. 4 vols. MSS. at Plymouth Co. Register of Deeds. Vol. 1, Vol. 2 and Vol. 3 as far as part 1 p. 153 have been printed in MD.

PLYMOUTH COLONY RECS
Shurtleff, Nathaniel B. and Pulsifer, David
Records of the colony of New Plymouth in New England. 12 vols. Boston, 1855-61; reprint 12 vols. in 6, New York, 1968.

PN&Q
Bowman, George E.
Pilgrim Notes and Queries. 5 vols. Boston, 1913-1917.

POLLARD FAM
Pollard, Maurice J.
History of the Pollard Family of America. Dover NH, 1960.

POPE FAM
Pope, Charles H.
A history of the Dorchester Pope family 1634-1888. Boston, 1888.

PORTLAND GAZETTE
Portland [ME] Gazette. Portland ME, 16 April 1798 to 28 Dec. 1824.

POTTER FAM
Potter, Charles E.
Potter Families. 1888.

PRESTON CH
First Congrational Church of Preston CT 1698-1898.... Preston CT, 1900.

Prov Town Papers
Original Providence town records of all kinds, dating from 1640 to early 1800s, including the Guild papers of Richard Brown, J.P. (1676-1774). Many volumes MSS. at R.I. Hist. Soc., Providence RI.

REDEEMED CAPTIVE
Williams, John
The Redeemed Captive Returning to Zion. 1707; edited by Edward W. Clark: Amherst, 1976.

REHOBOTH VR
Arnold, James N.
Vital Record of Rehoboth, 1642-1896. Marriages, intentions, births, deaths.... Providence RI, 1897.

Rev Pension
Selected records from Revolutionary War Pension application files at the National Archives, Washington DC, and available on microfilm at some libraries such as Western Reserve Historical Society, Cleveland OH.

REYNOLDS DESC
Reynolds, George L.
Reynolds Descendants. 1920?

REYNOLDS HIST
Tillman, S.F.
Christopher Reynolds and his descendants. Chevy Chase MD, 1959.

RI GEN DICT
Austin, John O.
The Genealogical Dictionary of Rhode Island, comprising three generations of settlers who came before 1690. Albany NY, 1887; reprint Cleveland OH, 1967 and Baltimore MD, 1969.

RI HIST MAG
Rhode Island Historical Magazine. Published by Newport Historical Society. 7 vols. Newport RI, 1880-1887.

RI LE
Rhode Island Land Evidences: volume 1, 1648-1696 Abstracts. (All published.) Providence RI, 1921; reprint Baltimore MD, 1970.

RI Rec Ctr
Original colonial documents stored at the Veterans Memorial Auditorium, Providence RI, in the custody of the State.

RI VR
Arnold, James N.
Vital record of Rhode Island, 1636-1850. 21 vols. Providence RI, 1891-1912.

RICHMOND FAM
Richmond, Joshua B.
The Richmond Family 1594-1896 and Pre-American Ancestors 1040-1594. Boston, 1897.

SALEM BY FELT
Felt, Joseph B.
Annals of Salem. 2 vols. Salem, 1845-49.

SALEM BY PERLEY
Perley, Sidney
History of Salem, Massachusetts, 1626-1716. 3 vols. Salem, 1924-28.

SALEM FIRST CH
Pierce, Richard D.
The Records of the First Church in Salem, Massachusetts, 1629-1736. Salem, 1974.

SALEM RECS
Town Records of Salem, Massachusetts. 3 vols. 1868-1934.

SAVAGE
Savage, James
A Genealogical Dictionary of the first settlers of New England, showing three generations of those who came before May 1692.... 4 vols. Boston 1860-62; reprint Baltimore MD, 1965.

SEARS DESC
May, Samuel P.
The Descendants of Richard Sares (Sears) of Yarmouth, Mass., 1638-1888. With an appendix.... Albany NY, 1890.

SEATTLE BULL
Bulletin of the Seattle [WA] Genealogical Society. Vol 1-- 1952?--.

1770 CENSUS NS
Census of Nova Scotia, 1770 (Some 1773 and 1787); from report of Board of Trustees of the Public Archives of Nova Scotia for 1934. Chicago, 1972; reprint Chicago IL, 1975.

1790 CENSUS
Heads of Families at the First Census, 1790. 12 vols. Washington DC, 1907-09; reprint Baltimore MD, 1952-1966; Spartanburg SC, 1963-66.

SHARON CT BUR GD
Van Alstyne, Lawrence
Burying Grounds of Sharon Connecticut, Amenia and North East New York. Amenia NY, 1903.

SHURTLEFF DESC
Shurtleff, Benjamin
Descendants of William Shurtleff of Plymouth and Marshfield Mass. 2 vols. Revere, 1912.

SMALL DESC
Underhill, Lora A. W.
Descendants of Edward Small of New England and the allied families, with tracings of English Ancestry. 3 vols. Cambridge, 1910.

SMITH (JESSE) DESC
Smith, L. Bertrand
Jesse Smith, his Ancestors and Descendants. New York, 1909.

SMITH (RALPH) DESC
Smith, Dwight
Ralph Smyth of Hingham and Eastham, Mass. and his Descendants. New York, 1913.

SOUTHWORTH GEN
Webber, Samuel G.
A Genealogy of the Southworths (Southards), descendants of Constant Southworth, with a sketch of the family in England. Boston MA, 1905.

SPOONER DESC
Spooner, Thomas
Records of William Spooner of Plymouth, Mass., and his descendants. Vol 1. Cincinnati OH, 1883.

STEEVENS DESC
Barlow, Claude W.
John Steevens of Guilford, Connecticut: Five Generations of 17th and 18th Century Descendants with Surnames.... Rochester NY, 1976.

STODDARD
Stoddard, Francis R.
The Truth about the Pilgrims. New York, 1952; reprint Baltimore MD, 1974.

STONINGTON CT FIRST CH
Wheeler, R.A.
History of the First Congregational Church Stonington Conn. 1674-1874 with statistics of the church. Norwich CT, 1875.

STONINGTON CT HIST
Wheeler, R.A.
History of Stonington Connecticut, with genealogies.

STRATFORD CT HIST
Orcutt, Rev. Samuel
History of the Old Town of Stratford and the city of Bridgeport Connecticut. Fairfield CT, 1886.

SUFFOLK COUNTY CT
Publications of the Colonial Society of Massachusetts. Vols. 29 & 30 contain the records of the Suffolk County Court, 1671-1680. Boston, 1933.

SUFFOLK DEEDS
Suffolk [MA] Deeds. 14 vols. Boston, 1850-1906.

SWANSEA VR
Carter, Marion P.
A copy of the index of Swansea, Mass. Vital Records Book B & a few records of Book D. 1702 to 1800, Vol. VIII. Attleboro, 1930.

TABER DESC
Randall, George L.
Taber Genealogy. Descendants of Thomas, son of Philip Taber. New Bedford, 1924.

TAG
The American Genealogist. Vol 1-- 1922--. Published at Des Moines IA in 1975.

TERRY FAM
Terry, Stephen
Notes of Terry Families in the United States of America mainly descended from Samuel, of Springfield Mass., but including also some descended from Stephen, of Windsor, Conn., Thomas, of Freetown, Mass., and others. Hartford CT, 1887.

Thatcher Papers
Thatcher, Charles M.
Genealogical records of families of Middleboro Mass. MSS. 3 vols. at Middleboro Public Library and at library of the General Society of Mayflower Descendants, Plymouth.

THOMASTON ME HIST
Eaton, Cyrus
History of Thomaston, Rockland & South Thomaston [ME]. 2 vols. Hallowell ME, 1865; reprint 1972.

TILSON GEN
Tilson, Mercer V.
The Tilson genealogy from Edmund Tilson at Plymouth, N.E. 1638-1911.... Plymouth, 1911.

TILTON ANCY
Davis, Walter G.
The Ancestry of Phoebe Tilton. Portland ME, 1947.

Tisdale Fam
Hodge, Almon D.
Tisdale Family of Massachusetts and Rhode Island. MSS. in Hodges Collection at New England Historic Genealogical Society, Boston.

TOPSFIELD HIST COLL
Historical Collections of the Topsfield [MA] Historical Society. 12 vols. 1895-1908.

TREAT FAM
Treat, John H.
The Treat family: A genealogy of Trott, Tratt and Treat for fifteen generations ... in England and America.... Salem, 1893.

TRURO VR
Bowman, George E.
Vital Records of the Town of Truro Massachusetts to the end of the year 1849. Boston, 1933.

TWINING FAM
Twining, Thomas J.
The Twining family. (Revised Ed.) Descendants of William Twining, Sr. of Eastham Massachusetts, where he died, 1659. With notes of English, Welsh and Nova Scotia families of the name. Fort Wayne IN, 1905.

VIALL GEN
Viall, Harriet N.
Viall Genealogy, 1618-1941. Berwyn IL, 1941.

VR
ABINGTON 1912, ANDOVER 1912, ASHBURNHAM 1909, BARRE 1903, BELLINGHAM 1904, BEVERLY 1906-7, BRIDGEWATER 1916, BROCKTON 1911, BROOKFIELD 1909, CAMBRIDGE 1915, CHELMSFORD 1914, DARTMOUTH 1929-30, DUDLEY 1908, DUNSTABLE 1913, DUXBURY 1911, EAST BRIDGEWATER 1917, EDGARTOWN 1906, ESSEX 1908, FALMOUTH 1976, GLOUCESTER 1917-24, HAMILTON 1908, HARDWICK 1917, HAVERHILL 1910-11, HULL 1911, IPSWICH 1910, KINGSTON 1911, LEICESTER 1903, LEOMINSTER 1911, MANCHESTER 1903, MANSFIELD 1933, MARLBOROUGH 1908, MENDON 1920, MILTON 1900, NANTUCKET 1925-28, NEW BRAINTREE 1904, NEWBURY 1911, NORTON 1906, PEMBROKE 1911, PLYMPTON 1923, ROCHESTER 1914, ROXBURY 1928, SALEM 1916-25, SANDISFIELD 1936, SCITUATE 1909, TAUNTON 1929, TOPSFIELD 1903, TYNGSBOROUGH 1912, WALTHAM 1904, WENHAM 1904, WESTBOROUGH 1903, WEST BRIDGEWATER 1911, WESTFORD 1915, WEYMOUTH 1910, WORCESTER 1894, WRENTHAM 1910.

WALKER MEM
Walker, J. B. R.
Memorial of the Walkers of the Old Plymouth Colony embracing genealogical and biographical sketches of James of Taunton, Philip of Rehoboth, William of Easham, John of Marshfield, Thomas of Bristol and of their descendants from 1620 to 1860. Northampton, 1861.

WALPOLE NH HIST
Frizzell, Martha M.
History of Walpole NH. Walpole NH, 1963.

WARE GEN
Ware, Emma F.
Ware Genealogy; Robert Ware of Dedham, Massachusetts, 1642-1699 and his lineal descendants. Boston, 1901.

WASHBURN DESC
Washburn, George T.
Ebenezer Washburn, his ancestors and descendants, with some connected families. South India, 1913.

WATERMAN GEN
Jacobus, Donald L.
Descendants of Robert Waterman of Marshfield, Mass. Vols. 1 & 2, New Haven CT, 1939-42. *Descendants of Richard Waterman of Providence, R.I.* Vol. 3. New Haven CT, 1954.

WATERTOWN BY BOND
Bond, Henry
Genealogies of the families and descendants of the early settlers of Watertown [Mass.] including Waltham and Weston. 2 vols. Boston MA, 1860.

WATERTOWN REC
Watertown Records comprising the third book of town proceedings and the second book of births, marriages and deaths to end of 1737 also ... burials in Arlington Street Burying Ground. Watertown, 1900.

WEST BARNSTABLE CH
Records of the West Parish of Barnstable Massachusetts 1668-1807. Massachusetts Historical Society. Boston, 1924.

WESTMORELAND CO VA DEEDS
Dorman, J. Frederick
Westmoreland Co. Virginia Deeds, Patents, Etc. 1665-1667. 4 vols. Washington DC, 1973-1975.

WEYMOUTH BY CHAMBERLAIN
Chamberlain, G. W.
History of Weymouth with genealogies.... Boston, 1923.

Williams Family
Williams, Charles C.
Williams Family. Typescript at NEHG, Boston. Los Angeles CA, 1926.

WINDHAM CO CT BY LARNED
Larned, Ellen D.
History of Windham County, Connecticut. 2
vols. Worcester, 1874-80.

WINDHAM NH HIST
Morrison, Leonard A.
History of Windham NH, 1719-1883. Boston, 1883.

WING REG
Wing, Conway P.
A Historical and Genealogical Register of John Wing of Sandwich, Mass. and his Descendants 1662-1881. Carlisle PA, 1881.

WINSLOW MEM
Holton, David P. and Frances K.
Winslow Memorial. Family records of the Winslows and their descendants in America with the English ancestry.... 2 vols. NY, 1877-88.

WITHERELL FAM
Witherell, Peter C. and Edwin R.
History and Genealogy of the Witherell/Wetherell/Witherill Family of New England. A record of ... descendants ... of Rev. William Witherell (ca. 1600-1684) of Scituate, Plymouth Colony, and of William Witherell (ca. 1627-1691) of Taunton, Plymouth Colony. Baltimore MD, 1976.

WORCESTER BY NUTT
Nutt, Charles
History of Worcester and its people. New York NY, 1919.

YARMOUTH N.S. HERALD GEN
Genealogical columns in the *Yarmouth, Nova Scotia Herald,* Nov. 1896 to May 1902. Copies at NEHG Soc., Boston, and library of the General Society of Mayflower Descendants, Plymouth.

YARMOUTH VR
Sherman, Robert M. and Ruth W.
Vital records of Yarmouth, Massachusetts to the year 1850. Warwick RI, 1975.

YORK DEEDS
York [county] Deeds, 1642-1737. 18 vols. in 19. Portland ME, 1887-1910.

YOUNG (JOHN) GEN
Young, Elisabeth R. and Kendall A.
John Young of Eastham, Massachusetts, descent to Elkanah Young of Eastham and Mt. Desert, Maine, and his known descendants. Baltimore MD, 1950.

YOUNG (JOHN) DESC
Torrey, Clarence A.
John Young of Eastham, Mass. and some of his Descendants (Five Generations). Boston, 1923. Typescript at library of the New England Historic Genealogical Society, Boston.

INDEX OF PLACES

This index lists significant residences mentioned in this book but omits places mentioned in connection with military activity.

MASSACHUSETTS (cont.)
  Barre 54, 268
  Bellingham 67, 68
  Berkley 61, 207, 245, 260, 292, 307, 308, 312, 315
  Beverly 61, 128, 146, 147
  Boston 6, 8, 11, 12, 15-20, 25, 26, 29, 38-49, 62, 63, 75, 92, 95-110, 116, 117, 164, 187, 211, 218, 251, 252, 262, 263, 266
  Boylston 142
  Braintree 28, 41, 70, 86, 165, 298
  Brewster 238
  Bridgewater 10-11, 13-4, 21-5, 30-35, 51, 53, 55-62, 67-70, 72-5, 82-5, 115, 167, 179, 184, 201, 206-7, 237-8, 298, 306-7, 312
  Brookfield 54, 281
  Cambridge 13, 47, 48
  Charlestown 20, 50, 51, 165
  Chatham 172, 176, 189, 190, 215, 216, 220, 224, 226-9, 246, 258, 259
  Chelmsford 41
  Cohasset 18
  Concord 100, 132
  Dartmouth 189-191, 241-2, 259, 260, 266, 287
  Dedham 261, 263, 265
  Deerfield 279
  Dighton 61, 196, 204-5, 207, 265, 267, 281-5, 294-7, 303, 305, 307-9
  Dorchester 191
  Dudley 54
  Dunstable 41
  Duxbury 11, 21-5, 30, 36, 55, 89-91, 94, 156-162, 165, 179, 190, 191, 260, 261, 264, 266
  Eastham 71-2, 105, 155-6, 160-3, 168-178, 181, 183-9, 208-211, 213-222, 224-7, 229-233, 246-254, 257=8
  Easton 62, 205, 238, 280, 291, 310, 311
  Edgartown 239
  Falmouth 208, 242
  Freetown 61, 166, 192, 197-8, 245, 271-2, 284-292, 314-5
  Gloucester 106, 142, 143, 211
  Great Barrington 262

MASSACHUSETTS (cont.)
  Hadley 273
  Halifax 73, 80, 243
  Hamilton 141, 143-6
  Hanover 295
  Hardwick 54, 220, 221, 287
  Harvard 233
  Harwich 71, 161, 173-8, 185-7, 209, 214, 219, 221-9, 238, 246-7, 249, 250, 256-7
  Haverhill 52, 279
  Hingham 23, 30, 74, 164, 187, 190, 197, 262, 263
  Hull 268
  Ipswich 104, 126, 128-131, 136-149, 279
  Kingston 34, 37, 80-3, 93-4, 179, 181, 222-3, 237
  Leicester 54, 75
  Lunenburg 128, 129, 132
  Malden 67, 100
  Manchester 144, 146
  Mansfield 67, 216, 280
  Marlboro 54, 59
  Marshfield 12, 26, 36-7, 43, 89-92, 105, 194, 258
  Mendon 67
  Methuen 140
  Middleboro 35, 77-8, 86-8, 159, 184, 198-9, 201-2, 204, 208, 245, 276, 286, 293-301, 303-7, 310, 313-4, 316
  Milton 43, 97, 102, 103, 261, 298
  Newbury 16
  Newburyport 111
  New Braintree 307
  Norton 192-6, 206, 272-4, 278-280, 291
  Oakham 54
  Orleans 217, 224, 257
  Pembroke 68-9, 73, 245, 258, 267
  Plymouth 5, 6, 10, 15, 21, 25, 34-38, 49, 122, 125, 155-6, 158, 162-3, 170, 179, 181-3, 190, 194-5, 200, 212-3, 223, 237, 240-3, 260-4, 279
  Plympton 68, 69, 77, 78, 81, 101, 179, 237, 238, 243, 261
  Provincetown 5, 256
  Raynham 201, 206-7, 237, 277, 284, 292, 302, 304, 310-2
  Reading 53
  Rehoboth 26, 31, 92, 266, 268, 301
  Rochester 178, 259, 280, 306

INDEX OF NAMES

With a few exceptions, each name in the text and footnotes is indexed. The exceptions are: references to other Mayflower families, authors or titles of reference books, and heads of military units under whom a descendant or spouse served.

Each married woman is indexed under her maiden name, and also under each married name, giving her maiden name in parentheses. For example, Abiah CRANE, who married four times, appears also as Abiah (Crane) BABBETT, Abiah (Crane) HOLLOWAY, Abiah (Crane) ATWOOD, and Abiah (Crane) WILLIAMS. A married woman of unknown maiden name is shown, for example, as Mary (-----) Smith.

When variant spellings of a surname occur, they are alphabetized under the more popular spelling, followed by one or more of the alternate spellings.

This index, originally prepared by computer, has been appreciably revised and retyped by R. M. and R. W. Sherman.

CODMAN cont.
  Parnell 114, 115
  Parnell (Foster) 50, 114, 115
  Richard 114, 115
  Stephen 114, 115
COFFIN
  Dorothy 103
  Dorothy (Gookin) 103
  Eliphalet 103
  Elizabeth (Taylor) 103
  Judith 103
  Judith (Coffin) 103
  Nathaniel 103
  Peter 103
COGGESHALL
  Sarah (Billings) 91
COLBURN
  Elizabeth (Scott) 101
COLE
  Azuba 225
  Betty (Doane) 219
  Daniel 227
  Dorcas 186, 247
  Elizabeth 247, 248
  Elizabeth (Cobb) 224, 225, 248
  Ephraim 82
  Eunice 248
  Gershom 174, 188, 225
  Hannah 225
  Hannah (-----) 186
  Heman 227
  Hepzibah 175
  Hope 186, 247
  Hope (-----) 186
  Hope (Young) 247
  Israel 163, 174
  James 186, 248, 249
  Jesse 186, 247
  John 185, 186, 245, 247
  Jonathan 186, 247
  Joseph 186, 224, 225, 248, 249,
    252
  Joshua 186, 227, 248
  Kezia 225, 249
  Lidea 248
  Lois 248
  Marcus 248
  Martha 227
  Martha (Rogers) 175, 227
  Mary 186, 248, 249
  Mary (-----) 188, 245
  Mary (Cole) 248
  Mary (Paine) 163
  Mary (Rogers) 163, 174, 185,
    186, 225

COLE cont.
  Mary (Young) 249
  Mary White (Clark) 248
  Mercy 186, 247
  Mercy (Mayo) 247
  Moses 186, 225, 248
  Nathan 186, 248
  Nathaniel 186, 247
  Patience 224, 225, 248
  Phebe 186, 245, 249
  Rachel 248
  Rebecca 82, 247, 249
  Rebecca (-----) 82
  Reliance 225
  Ruth 247, 248
  Ruth (Snow) 185
  Sarah 82, 248
  Sarah (Cole) 248
  Sarah (Cooke) 34, 82
  Sarah (Hamblin) 186
  Sarah (Hubbard) 227
  Solomon 248
  Stephen 227
  Thankful 186, 249
  Theophilus 247
  Unice 248
COLEMAN see COLMAN
COLLICK
  Hannah (Billings) 91
COLLIER/COLLYER
  Bridget (Southworth) 88
  Elizabeth 35
COLLINS/COLLINGS
  Abigail 211
  Jane 173
  Joseph 169, 173
  Martha 40
  Rebecca (Eldridge) 216
  Rebecca (Sparrow) 169
  Ruth (Knowles) 173
  Solomon 216
COLMAN/COLEMAN
  Benjamin 44, 106
  Ebenezer 236
  James 234, 236
  John 44, 106, 236
  Judith (Hobbey) 106
  Martha 234, 236
  Mary 236
  Patience 236
  Patience (Cobb) 234, 236
  Patience (Phinney) 236
  Sarah 106
  Sarah (Payne) 44, 106
  William 106

CUMMINGS cont.
    Louisa Dodge 150
    Martha (Knowlton) 142
    Mary Hyde 150
    Perley Dodge 150
    Sarah 145, 146
    Thomas 145, 149, 150
CUNNINGHAM
    Abigail (Richmond) 113
    Ann 109
    Anne (Boucher) 109
    Charles 113
    Daniel 113
    Nathaniel 109
    Patience 113
    Ruth 109
    Ruth (-----) 109
    Sarah 109
    Sarah (Winslow) 113
    Susanna (Gerrish) 109
    Timothy 109
CURTIS
    Elizabeth 184
    Priscilla 210
CUSHING
    Abigail (Ford) 267
    Benjamin 267
    Deborah 191, 266
    Mary 267
CUSHMAN
    Robert 121
    Seth 68
    Susanna (Newland) 68
CUTT
    Elianor 171
    Samuel 171
DAGGETT/DOGGETT
    Abigail (Turner) 320
    Benjamin 289
    Hannah 289
    Hannah (Skiff) 289
    Jacob 289
    Joanna 289
    Joseph 289
    Nathan 289, 320
    Phebe (Terry) 198, 289, 291
    Sibel (-----) 260
DANE
    Abigail 130
    Esther (Kimball) 130
    Nathaniel 130
DAVID I (king of Scotland) 121
DAVIS
    Abigail 191

DAVIS cont.
    Ann (Taylor) 240
    Anna 240
    Anna (Dimmock) 244
    Benjamin 96
    David 197
    Dolar 239
    Ebenezer 239
    Elizabeth 234
    Elizabeth (-----) 234
    Elizabeth (Phinney) 233
    Experience (Linnell) 233, 246
    Hannah 96, 239, 242
    Hannah (-----) 40
    Hannah (Linnell) 239
    Hannah (Winslow) 96
    Isaac 185, 234, 240, 246
    Jabez 233, 234, 244, 246
    Jacob 246
    Job 239
    John 234
    Jonathan 197, 240, 285
    Josiah 240
    Keziah 246
    Keziah (Crosby) 246
    Martha 234
    Mary 239, 246
    Mary (Phinney) 180, 239
    Mary (Rogers) 185, 246
    Matther 234
    Mehitable 239
    Mercy 185, 247
    Nathan 233, 234
    Prince 240
    Rebecca 240
    Rebecca (Phinney) 180, 240
    Remember (Terry) 197
    Ruth 180
    Sarah 96, 188, 234, 240
    Sarah (-----) 96, 285
    Sarah (Terry) 197
    Seth 239
    Shobal 239
    Stephen 240
    Susanna 240, 244, 246
    Thankful 240
    Thomas 239
    William 96
DAWES/DORZ
    Jepthae 73
DAY
    Hannah 104
DEAN/DEANE
    Abiah (Macomber) 208

DURFEY
    Susanna 293
DUSTIN
    Hannah 52
DUTCH
    Barbara 127
    Christian 127
    Grace (Pratte) 126
    Osmon/Osmond 126
    Samuel 123, 126, 128
    Susanna 127, 128
    Susanna (More) 123, 126
DWELLY/DWELLE
    Alice (Pearce) 270
    John 88
    Rachel (Buck) 88
DYER
    Ebenezer 252
    Elijah 252, 253
    Isaac 253
    Jonathan 102
    Judah 252, 253
    Mary (Taylor) 252
    Phebe 252, 253
    Phebe (Young) 168, 252
    Susanna 102
    Susanna (-----) 102
    William 252
EAMES see AMES
EASTLAND
    Elizabeth 181, 241
    Elizabeth (Jenney) 181
    Freelove (Shepherd) 241
    Hannah 181
    Jean 181
    John 181, 241
    Joseph 181, 241
    Joshua 182
    Mary/Marey 181, 182, 241
    Mary (Phinney) 162, 181
    Reliance 241
    Ruth (-----) 241
    Virtue 241
    Zeruiah/Zerviah 181, 241
EATON
    Elizabeth 316
    Mercy 94
EDDY
    Jabez 296
    Jonathan 309
    Lydia 296
    Mary (Rickard) xii, 296
    Mary (Ware) 309

EDSON
    Elizabeth 35, 67
    Hannah (-----) 83
    Martha (Haward) 319
    Mary 318
    Sarah (Southworth) 88
EDWARD I (king of England) 121
EDWARDS
    Bethia 127, 128
    Elizabeth 251
    Mary 147
ELDRIDGE
    Abigail (Doane) 220
    Abner 216
    James 216
    Mary 181, 216
    Rebecca 216
    Ruth 216
    Ruth (Higgins) 216
    Seth 216
    Tabitha 189
    Zephaniah 216
ELIOT/ELLIOTT
    Abiah 307
    Elizabeth 201, 237, 299
    Mary 298
    Mercy (Walker) 298, 307
    Noah 298
    Phebe (Richmond) 200, 298
    Priscilla (Fellows) 133
    Samuel 134
    Thomas 298, 307
ELKINS
    Margaret 230, 231, 232
ELLES
    Abigail 280
ELLIOTT see ELIOT
ELMES
    Ann 283
    Ann/Annah (Stephens) 196, 283
    Hannah (Stephens) 283
    John Spur 283
    Jonathan 283
    Katherine 283
    Nanc (Stephens) 283
    Patience 283
    Patience (-----) 283
    Robert 196, 283
    Zibiah 283
EMERSON
    Abigail (Burnham) 104
    Anne 104
    Edward Winslow 104

EMERSON cont.
  Hannah (Day) 104
  Jeremiah 104
  John 113
  John Taylor 104
  Jonathan 104
  Lydia (Burnham) 104
  Moses 104
  Rebecca (Taylor) 104
  Sarah 113
  Sarah (Carter) 113
EMMONS
  Hannah 301
  Sarah (Barnes) 301
  William 301
ENSIGN
  Hannah 203
ENSWORTH
  Joseph 245
  Lucy 245
  Mary (Cleveland) 245
ERVING
  George 97
  George William 98
ESTWICKE
  Elizabeth 108
  Richard Rous 108
  Sarah (Dottin) 108
EVANS
  Ann 208
FAIRFIELD
  Prudence 128
FARNUM
  Susanna 40
FARRAH/FARROW
  John 197
  Mary (Hilliard) 197
  Remember 197
FELLOWS
  Anna 133
  Benjamin 133
  Berecinthia 133
  Cynthia 133
  Ebenezer 133
  Eunice 133
  Eunice (Dodge) 133
  Hepzibah 133
  Israel 133
  Joanna (Smith) 133
  Joseph 133, 142
  Mary 129
  Phebe 133
  Priscilla 133
  Sarah 133
  Susanna 133, 142

FELLOWS cont.
  Susanna (Dodge) 133
  Susanna (Giddings) 142
FENNER
  Arthur 33
  Mehitable (Waterman) 33
  Phebe 33
  Thomas 34
FERNANDES
  Fannie (Knowlton) 144
FINNEY see PHINNEY
FISH
  Adam 237
  Bartholomew 208
  Cornelius 210
  Deborah (Barnes) 208, 210
  Ebenezer 210
  Elizabeth (Harding) 168, 210
  Freelove (Phinney) 239
  Hannah (Harding) 168, 208
  James 210
  Jedidiah 208
  Lemuel 208
  Lot 210
  Martha (Coleman) 236
  Mary (-----) 237
  Nathan 208, 210
  Prince 210
  Rowland 210
  Rufus 210
FISHER
  Abigail 265
  Abigail (Elles) 280
  Daniel 265
  Darriel 265
  Ebenezer 280
  Elizabeth 265
  Elizabeth (Richmond) 191, 265
  Gartruyd (Crannell) 112
  Jeremiah 265, 303
  Mary (Fuller) 265
  Melatiah 280
  Nathaniel 164, 265, 303
  Thomas 112
FITTS
  Currier 140
FLETCHER
  Moses 3
FLINT
  James 53
  Susanna 269
FOBES
  Elizabeth 206, 319
FORD
  Abigail 267

FORD cont.
  John 267
  Mary (Cushing) 267
FOSTER
  Abigail 114
  Abigail (Billings) 91
  Abigail Dane 149
  Abigail Dean 149
  Ann/Anne 50, 51, 114, 115
  Anne (Brackenbury) 50, 51
  Anne/Annis (Knowlton) 149
  Barysintha (Fellows) 133
  Charles Warren 149
  Chillingsworth 188
  Cynthia (Fellows) 133, 149
  Edward 116
  Elea Sophia 149
  Eleanor 116
  Eleanor (Wyer) 116
  Elizabeth 50, 51, 114, 117
  Elizabeth (Conant) 149
  Hannah 114
  Isaac 50, 51, 116
  Ivers 149
  John 114
  Katherine 51, 114
  Margaret 114
  Martha 114
  Mary 51, 113, 114
  Mary (Foye) 113, 114
  Parnell 50, 51, 114
  Parnell (Winslow) 50
  Reynold 149
  Richard 50, 51, 99, 113-116
  Sarah 50, 51, 114, 115
  Sarah (Emerson) 113
  Sophia C. (-----) 149
  Thomas 116
  William 50, 114, 116, 149
FOWLER
  Joseph 126
  Rebecca 318
  Sarah 136
FOX
  Alice 126
  Ann 126
  Elizabeth 126
  Sarah 126
  William 126
FOYE
  Anne 110
  Elizabeth 110
  John 48, 110, 114
  Lewis/Lovis 110
  Mary 113

FOYE cont.
  Sarah 110
  Sarah (Boucher) 48, 110
  Sarah (Lynde) 110, 114
FREEMAN
  Abner 217
  Edmond 217
  Elizabeth 215
  Hannah 189, 217
  Hannah (Higgins) 257
  Isaac 257
  John 217
  Jonathan 217
  Lois 172, 217
  Lois (Paine) 217
  Lydia (Sparrow) 171
  Mary 256
  Nathaniel 178
  Rebecca 75, 217
  Sarah 217, 257
  Sarah (Mayo) 217
  Sarah (Sparrow) 217
  Thankful (-----) 217
  William 171
FRENCH
  Abigail 308
  Abigail (Phillips) 292
  John 308
  Joseph 292, 308
  Nathan 308
  Phebe 308
  Phebe (Walker) 308
  Sarah 308
  Sarah (-----) 308
  Seth 308
  Silence 308
  Thomas 308
FRY/FRYE
  Bethiah 294
  Deliverance (-----) 202
  Hannah 202
  John 202
FRYER
  Elizabeth 42
FULLER
  Beersheba 243
  Benjamin 243
  David 228
  Deborah 256
  Ebenezer 37, 94
  Eli 228
  Eunice 94
  Hannah 94
  Isaac 228
  Jabez/Jabish 38, 94, 95

GILBERT
  Elizabeth (Ballard) 42
  George 260
  Giles 27
  Hannah 60, 260
  Hannah (Bradford) 190, 260,
    262, 263
  Mary 166, 260
  Nathaniel 190, 260
  Samuel 260
  Susanna 311
  Thomas 60, 260
  Welthea 260
GILL
  Hannah 280
GILMAN
  Dorothy (Sherbourne) 102
  Peter 102
GODDARD
  Mary (Stephens) 196
GODFREY
  Desire 176
  Hannah 246
  Hannah (White) 192
  John 193
  Jonathan 226, 246
  Joseph 192, 193, 271, 273, 274
  Martha 223
  Mary 215
  Mary (Gilbert) 260
  Mary (Richmond) 192
  Mary (Rogers) 185
  Mercy 226, 246
  Mercy (Mayo) 226, 246
  Nathaniel 185
  Richard 167, 192
  Susanna (Makepeace) 192
GOFFE
  Dixe 40
GOLD
  Ann 103
GOODHUE
  Christian 136, 137
  Christian (Brown) 136
  Francis 136, 137
  Joseph 137
  Lucy 137
  Lucy (-----) 136, 137
  Sarah (Fowler) 136
  Wally 137
GOODING
  Abigail (Richmond) 199, 294
  Bathsheba (Walker) 303
  Deborah 294

GOODING cont.
  Deborah (Walker) 294
  George 294
  Job 294
  Joseph 294, 313
  Mary 294
  Matthew 294
  Rebecca (Macomber) 313
  William 294, 303
GOODRICH
  Elizabeth 262
GOODSPEED
  Ebenezer 234, 235
  Elizabeth 235
  Hannah (Phinney) 235
  Isaac 235
  Joseph 235
  Lydia (Crowell) 234, 235
  Puella 235
  Reliance 234
  Roger 235
  Sarah 235
  Thomas 235
GOOKIN
  Dorothy 103
GORE
  Rebecca (Payne) 106
GORHAM
  Sarah (Phinney) 240
  Temperance 278
GOULD see also GOLD
  Hannah (Hodges) 310
  James 249
  John 271, 272
  Mary 272
  Mary (Makepeace) 193, 271, 272
  Nathaniel 271, 272
  Phebe 272
  Phebe (Cole) 249
  Richard 310
  Sarah 189
  Seth 272
  Solomon 249
  William 272
GRAY
  Ann/Anna/Anne 9, 15, 16, 37,
    38, 93, 264
  Anna (Little) 264
  Charlotte 269
  Desire 15, 35, 38
  Dorothy (Lettice) 15
  Ebenezer 269
  Edward 7, 15, 36, 38
  Elizabeth 15, 16, 36, 94

GRAY cont.
  Hannah 269
  Joanna 37, 38, 93
  Joanna (Morton) 37
  John 15, 16, 37, 94
  Joseph 268, 269
  Loring 269
  Lydia 15
  Mary 7, 15, 38, 94, 268
  Mary (Loring) 269
  Mary (Winslow) 15
  Mercy/Marcy 37, 38, 94
  Nathaniel 15
  Nicholas L. 269
  Parnell 20
  Patience (Wadsworth) 94
  Rebecca 15
  Reuben 269
  Samuel 15, 37, 38, 93, 94
  Sarah 15, 16, 37
  Susanna 15
  Thomas 15, 264
  Wait 94
  Watson 269
GREEN/GREENE
  Ann 103
  Ann (Gold) 103
  Elizabeth 103
  Elizabeth (Taylor) 103
  Joanna (Terry) 287
  John 103
  Joshua 79, 80
  Mehitable (Manton) 79, 80
  Nathaniel 103
  Patience (Terry) 287
  Ruth 258
  Sarah (-----) 48
GREENLEAF
  Sarah 16
GREENOUGH
  Elizabeth 40
GRIFFITH
  Rebecca 238
  Rebecca (Rider) 238
  Stephen 210, 238
GRINNELL
  Comfort (Billings) 91
GURLEY
  Deborah (Makepeace) 193
  George 193
GURNEY
  Mary 58
  Ruth (-----) 12
GUSHEE see GARSHET

HACK/HACKE
  Katherine 275
  Katherine (Lincoln) 275
  Mary 275
  Mary (Lincoln) 196
HACKET/HACKETT
  Alice 201, 237, 299
  Benjamin 299
  Edmund 299
  Eleanor (Gardner) 299
  Elijah 299
  Elizabeth 299
  Elizabeth (Eliot) 201, 237, 299
  Elizabeth (Richmond) 299
  Ephraim 299
  George 245
  Hannah 299
  John 201, 237, 299
  Phebe (Phinney) 245
  Priscilla (Richmond) 200, 299
  Prudence (Richmond) 296
  Thankful 299
HAFORD see HAYFORD
HAFFIELD
  Mary 164
HAGGAT/HAGGET
  Jane 108
  Jane (Lambert) 107, 108
  Mary 46, 107, 108
  Mary (Middlecott) 17, 46, 108
  Nathaniel 46, 107, 108
  Othaniel 46, 107, 108
  Ruth (Lambert) 107
  Sarah 46, 108, 109
  Sarah (Dottin) 108
  Simon Othniel 108
  Susanna 107, 108
  Susanna (-----) 46, 107, 108
  William 46, 107-109
HALL
  Abigail 68
  Abigail (Richmond) 296
  Abner 101
  Elizabeth 66, 68
  Elizabeth (King) 202, 275
  Elizabeth (Tripp) 68
  Enoch 237
  Ephraim 114
  Jane (Harris) 68
  John 202, 275
  Joseph 206
  Judith 275, 291
  Mary 68
  Mary (Foster) 114

HALL cont.
Mary (Williams) 312
Mehitable (Scott) 101
Patience 68, 290
Priscilla 251
Ruth 68
Sarah (-----) 54
Sarah (Dean) 206
Seth 68
Susanna 68
Susanna (-----) 68
Thomas 54
Urania 68
Zurial 68
HALLETT
Abigail 90
HAMBLEN/HAMBLIN
Alice (Phinney) 179
Ebenezer 179
Eleazer 179
Elizabeth (Howland) 179
Isaac 179
John 173
Martha 219, 220
Mary (Phinney) 179
Priscilla 173
Sarah 186
Sarah (Bearse) 173
Sarah (Lewis) 179
Seth 244
HAMILTON
Daniel 175
Sarah 175
Sarah (Smith) 175
HAMMOND
Deborah (Terry) 287
Joanna 287
Lydia (Jenney) 259
Mary (Southworth) 87
Rowland 86, 87
HANCOCK
John 115
Mary (Hawke) 115
HANLEY
Catherine 16
HARDEN/HARDING
Abigail 70, 210
Abigail (West) 210
Abraham 73, 74
Amaziah/Maziah 160, 168, 169, 222
Anna 210
Anna (-----) 72
Anna (Brown) 210

HARDEN/HARDING cont.
Archelas 209
Benjamin 210
Bethia (Cooke) 168
Cornelius 168, 169, 210, 211
Deborah 72
Ebenezer 209, 210
Eleazer 210
Elizabeth 168, 169, 210
Elizabeth (Young) 209
Ephraim 210
George 210
Hannah 168, 169, 208, 209
Hannah (-----) 70, 73
Hannah (Rogers) 160, 168, 223
James 168, 169, 209
Jepthae 73
Joanna 252
John 70, 72, 73, 168, 169, 209, 210, 249
Joseph 168, 211
Joshua 209
Keziah (Cole) 249
Lucia 211
Lydia 210
Mary 73, 74, 169, 209
Mary (Nickerson) 209
Maziah see Amaziah
Nathan 168, 169, 210, 211
Nathaniel 32, 73, 74, 209, 249
Phebe 168, 169, 211, 222
Priscilla 211
Priscilla (Curtis) 210
Reuben 73
Samuel 73
Samuel (Hamilton) 175
Seth 73, 74, 211, 249
Susanna 32
Susanna (Latham) 73
Tabitha 210
Theodore 175
Thomas 168, 169, 209
HARDY
Esther 143
HARLOW
Abigail 80
Abigail (Church) 80
James 243, 244
Mehitable (Churchill) 243
Nathaniel 80
HARRICK
Dorcas (Bundy) 65

HIGGINS cont.
 Else 173
 Epherim/Ephraim 219
 Experience/Exsperance 171,
   214, 257
 Hannah 161, 171, 172, 189, 213
   214, 250, 257, 258
 Hannah (Doane) 218, 220
 Hannah (Higgins) 189, 257
 Hannah (Lewis) 221
 Hannah (Rogers) 161, 163
 Hannah (Yates) 250
 Heman 250
 Henry 220
 Hezekiah 189, 257
 James 164, 189, 246, 257
 Jane 218, 219, 221
 Jane (Collins) 173
 Jemima 71, 161, 215, 219
 Jemima (Witherill) 219
 Jesse 217
 John 219
 Jonathan 156, 161, 163, 171-
   173, 189, 213, 214, 217,
   220
 Joseph 161, 170-173, 215, 218,
   219
 Joshua 220, 229
 Lot 219, 257, 258
 Loues 257
 Lurania 220
 Lydia 213
 Lydia (Chandler) 161, 163
 Lydia (Freeman) 171
 Lydia (Sparrow) 171
 Margery/Margret (Homer) 257
 Martha 173, 213, 218, 250
 Martha (Burgess) 250
 Mary 163, 188, 221
 Mary (Smith) 221
 Mehitable (Phinney) 180, 213,
   250
 Mercy 215, 219
 Mercy (Remick) 215
 Patience (Rogers) 225
 Paul 219
 Phebe 214, 215
 Phebe (Lewis) 221
 Philip 173, 217, 220, 221
 Prince 213
 Priscilla 216
 Rachel 173, 219, 220
 Rachel (Doane) 218, 220
 Rachel (Lincoln) 173

HIGGINS cont.
 Rebecca 164, 188, 189, 215, 229,
   246
 Rebecca (-----) 219
 Rebecca (Hopkins) 214
 Richard 161, 163
 Ruth 172, 173, 215, 229
 Ruth (-----) 172
 Ruth (Twining) 229
 Samuel 171, 180, 213, 250
 Sarah 164, 189, 217, 218, 229,
   257, 258
 Sarah (Bixbie) 189
 Sarah (Freeman) 217, 257
 Sarah (Hamblin) 186
 Sarah (Lewis) 218
 Sarah (Mayo) 189, 246
 Sarah (Sears) 257
 Seth 250
 Silvanus/Sylvanus 213, 215
 Solomon 217
 Susanna 213, 250
 Thankful 171, 215, 217, 250
 Thomas 217
 Uriah 218
HILL
 Charity 193
 Ebenezer 56
 Eleazer 56
 Hezekiah 56
 Israel 56
 Jacob 56
 Moses 56
 Ruth (-----) 56
 Susanna (Leonard) 23, 56
HILLIARD
 Mary 197
HILTON
 Sarah 16
 Sarah (Greenleaf) 16
 William 16
HINCKLEY
 Isaac 182
 Mary (Freeman) 256
 Nymphas 235
 Prince 235
 Samuel 256
 Sarah (Phinney) 234
 Sarah (Webber) 256
 Shubael 256
 Sylvanus 235
HINCKS
 Anna 102
 Elisha 102

HOOPER cont.
  Thomas 85
  William 53
HOPKINS
  Abigail (Terry) 286
  Benjamin 173
  Constance 160
  Damaris 34
  Rachel (Lincoln) 173
  Rebecca 214
  Ruth 189
  Sarah (Davis) 234
  Sarah (Howes) 214
  Stephen 214
HORSWILL
  Ruth (Pearce) 270
HORTON
  David 301
  Dorothy 218, 220
  Elijah 301
  Hannah (Garnzey) 301
  Levi 301
  Mehitable (Richmond) 202, 301
  Thomas 301
HOSKINS/HASKINS
  Elizabeth (Richmond) 296
  Hanna (-----) 275
  Lydia 297
  Sarah 277
HOSMER
  Elizabeth (Brown) 139
HOUGHTON
  James 262
  Philena (Whiting) 262
HOWARD see HAYWARD
HOWE/HOWES/HOW
  Elizabeth 138, 140
  Sarah 214
HOWLAND
  Elizabeth 179
  Elizabeth (Vaughn) 87
  Isaac 87
  Jael 87
  Mary 314
  Mary (Coleman) 236
HUBBARD
  Sarah 227
HUNTER/HUNT
  Christian 121, 122, 125
HURD see HERD
HURLBURT
  David 256
  Elizabeth (Rogers) 178
  Mary (-----) 256
  Thankful 256

HURLBURT cont.
  William 178
HUTCHINSON
  Catherine (Hanley) 16
  Edward 16
  Elisha 20
  Elizabeth 16
HUTTON
  Elizabeth (Killam) 126
  Richard 126, 127
  Susanna (More) 126, 127
Indians
  Francis 156
  Josiah 156
IRISH
  Elizabeth 55
ISHAM
  Temperance (Phinney) 239
JACOBS
  David 266
  Deborah 194
  Elizabeth (Richmond) 266
  Hannah (Richmond) 266
  Joshua 266
JEFFRIES
  David 95
JEKYLL
  Mary 111
JEMMOTT
  Gabriel 126
JENKINS
  Hannah 320
JENNER
  Eleanor 99, 116
  Elizabeth 103
JENNEY/JENNE
  Agnes 259
  Desire (Blackwell) 259
  Elizabeth 181, 259
  Israel 259
  Lettice 259
  Lydia 259
  Mercy (Mitchell) 259
  Nathaniel 259
  Pernal 259
  Rebecca 259
  Sarah 259
  Weston 259
JENNINGS
  Hannah 60
  Richard 60
JEPSON
  William 153
JOHNSON
  Abigail 65

JOHNSON cont.
  Abigail (Leavett) 74, 75
  Ann 192
  Betty 32, 75
  Betty (Latham) 74
  Daniel 32, 74, 75, 263
  David 85
  Eleazer 99
  Hannah 75
  Hannah (Lane) 263
  Isaac 74, 75, 99
  Isaiah 75
  Jacob 99
  James 75
  Jane (Harris) 70
  Joseph 75
  Katherine (Dowse) 99
  Leverett/Levet 75
  Lucy (Lane) 263
  Mary 64, 85, 99
  Mary (Remick) 99
  Rebecca 75
  Rebecca (Washburn) 85
  Samuel 99, 263
  Susanna 99
  Susanna (Johnson) 99
JOLLS
  Hannah (Briggs) 18, 19
  John 19
  Thomas 18
JONES
  Abial 284
  Abigail 284
  Anna (Stephens) 196
  Appollos 276
  Benjamin 283, 284
  Bethia (Walker) 303
  Charity (Lincoln) 275,
    276
  Christiania 263
  Cornelius 275
  Daniel 207
  Deborah 276
  Deborah (Lincoln) 276
  Ebenezer 281, 303
  Elizabeth 284
  Ephraim 284
  Hannah 284
  John 284
  Joseph 196
  Lydia 284
  Lydia (Terry) 197, 283,
    284
  Lydia (Williams) 207
  Mary 284

JONES cont.
  Mary (Southworth) 88
  Priscilla 281
  Ruth 277
  Sibble 276
  Silvester 275
  Susanna (Beal) 284
  Thomas 284, 285
  Wealthe (Terry) 285
  Zephaniah 284
KEEP
  Jabez 233
  Lucy 233
  Sarah (Leonard) 233
KEITH
  Abigail 319
  Elizabeth (Fobes) 206, 319
  Ichabod 206, 207
  Joseph 206, 319
  Lydia (Williams) 206, 207
KELLEY/KILLEY
  Benjamin 185, 254
  Mary (Lambert) 254
  Mary (Young) 254
  Reuben 254
  Susanna (Rogers) 185
KEMPTON
  Joanna 37
  Sarah (Jenney) 259
KENRICK
  Betty (Rogers) 228
  James 228
KENT
  Ebenezer 187
  Elizabeth 187
  Hannah (Gannett) 187
KIDDER
  Hannah (Brown) 137
KILLAM
  Elizabeth 126
KILLEY/KELLEY
KIMBALL/KEMBLE
  Esther 130
  Mary 26
KING
  Abigail 303
  Elizabeth 202, 275
  Experience (Phillips) 23
  Hannah (-----) 250
  Jonathan 303
  Judith (Whitman) 202, 206
  Lydia 206, 208, 315
  Phebe (Leonard) 303
  Philip 202, 206
  Roger 250

KING cont.
  Samuel 23
  Susanna 23
  Thankful 250
  William 29
  Zipporah (Williams) 311
KINGLEY
  Bethia (Williams) 310
KINGMAN
  Abigail 67
  Bethia 67
  Bethia (-----) 67
  David 67
  Deliverance 67
  Desire 67
  Desire (Harris) 30, 67
  Ebenezer 67
  Elizabeth (Edson) 35, 67
  Isaac 67
  John 30, 35, 67
  Joseph 67
  Josiah 67
  Mary 67
  Seth 67
  Susanna 35
KINNECUTT
  Elizabeth 270
KINSMAN
  Hannah 148
  Mary 92
  Rebecca (Burley) 92, 93
  Robert 92
KIRBY/KERBY
  Sarah 288
KNEELAND
  Mary (-----) 25
  Solomon 25
KNOWLES
  Barbara 187
  John 253
  Joshua 253
  Mary (Sears) 253
  Mercy 251, 254
  Phebe (Young) 253
  Ruth 173
  Sarah (Paine) 253
  Simeon 253
KNOWLTON
  Abigail 130, 131, 141, 146,
    147
  Abigail (Dane) 130, 131
  Abigail (Dodge) 141
  Abigail (Hooper) 146, 147
  Abigail (Larcom) 146
  Abigail (Patch) 145

KNOWLTON cont.
  Ame 141
  Anna/Anne 145, 149
  Annis 131, 149
  Asa 142
  Azor 145
  Benjamin 128, 130, 131,
    141-144, 146, 147
  Bethia (Edwards) 127, 128
  Betty 131
  Catherine 131, 144
  Charles 142
  David 143, 144, 147
  Edmund 130, 131, 143
  Elizabeth 128, 129, 131, 144,
    149
  Elizabeth (-----) 147
  Elizabeth (Balch) 127
  Elizabeth (Potter) 142
  Enos 144
  Ephraim 130, 131, 144
  Esther 130, 131, 144, 148
  Eunice 144
  Ezra 130, 131, 141
  Fannie 144
  Hannah 130, 131, 144, 147
  Hannah S. 142
  Hepzibah 130, 131, 145
  Hezekiah 147
  Ira 147
  Ivers 145
  James 131, 143
  John 127, 128
  Joseph 141
  Josiah 142
  Katie 144
  Lavinia 145
  Levi 141
  Lucy 144
  Malachi 130, 131, 142, 143, 145,
    149
  Martha 142
  Martha (Tilton) 142
  Mary 143, 144
  Mary K. 142
  Mary (Austin) 143
  Mary (Murphy) 144
  Mary (Pulsifer) 143
  Mercy/Marcy 145
  Michael 145
  Molly (Murphy) 144
  Moses 130, 131, 143, 144
  Nancy 141
  Nehemiah 130, 131, 142
  Polly 144

LAWRENCE
  Sarah 19
  Thomas 19, 20
LAWTON
  Rebecca 286
  Thomas 92
LAZELL
  Abigail (Leavitt) 74, 75
LEACH
  Anne 321
  Anne (Nokes) 320
  Benanuel 321
  Benjamin 33, 320, 321
  David 82, 83
  Elizabeth 83
  Elizabeth (Cooke) 82
  Eunice 321
  Giles 320
  Hannah 321
  Hannah (-----) 82
  Hannah (Cooke) 83
  Hannah (Whitman) 82
  Hepzibah (Latham) 33
  Hepzibah (Washburn) 320
  Ichabod 321
  James 83
  Jerahmeel 321
  Joseph 33, 320, 321
  Marcy 83
  Mary 321
  Nathan 321
  Nokes 321
  Phebe 321
  Sarah 83, 321
  Susanna 83, 321
LEAVITT
  Abigail 74, 75
LeBARON
  Sarah (Leonard) 279
LeBLOND/LeBLONDE
  Alexander 38, 39
  Ann 39
  Ann (Gray) 38
  Gabriel 38, 39
  James 38, 39
  Mary/Mary Ann 38, 39
  Peter 38, 39
  Phillipa 38, 39
LeBROS
  Charles 19
  Sarah (Winslow) 19
LeCONSTEUR
  Phillip 18

LEE
  Abigail (Bradford) 261
  Abigail (Stevens) 251
  Edward 251
  George 269
  Giles 231
  Lemuel 251
  Mary (Burnet) 251
  Mary (West) 251
  Mercy (Smith) 231
  Samuel 261
  Susanna (Viall) 269
  Thankful (Mayo) 251
LEFFINGWELL
  Elizabeth (Whiting) 262
LEONARD/LENARD/LENERSON/LENNERSON/
  LEONARDSON etc.
  Abiel 134, 195, 279
  Abigail 21, 23, 24, 55, 56,
    194, 195, 279
  Abigail (-----) 53, 280
  Abigail (Washburn) 55
  Abigail (Williams) 280
  Abigail (Wood) 21
  Andrew 54
  Anna 194, 195, 278, 279
  Anna (Clap) 280
  Anna (Tisdale) 194, 195
  Benjamin 24, 60, 61
  Bette/Betty/Betsy 60, 134
  Beulah (-----) 54
  Caleb 61
  Coralina/Caroline 277, 302
  Daniel 279, 280
  David 58, 59
  Deborah 134
  Deborah (-----) 21
  Deliverance 24, 56
  Deliverance (-----) 24
  Deliverance (Ames?) 24
  Dorothea 61
  Ebenezer 52, 60
  Elizabeth 21, 51, 54, 55, 57,
    194, 279, 312
  Elizabeth (Hooper) 53
  Elizabeth (Perkins) 57, 317
  Enoch 22, 53, 54
  Ephraim 56, 61, 194, 195, 278-
    280
  Experience 23, 57
  Ezekiel 55
  Ezra 54
  Fear (Southworth) 87

LEONARD/LENARD/LENERSON etc. cont.
  Gamaliel 277, 302
  George 194, 195, 278, 279
  Hannah 24, 59-61, 197, 302
  Hannah (Jennings) 60
  Hannah (Phillips) 60
  Hannah (Woods) 54
  Henry 61
  Isaac 11, 24, 58-60
  Jacob 11, 23, 54, 55
  Jane 52
  Jemima 61
  Johanah (Pitcher) 302
  John 11, 22, 55
  Jonas 54
  Jonathan 134, 195
  Jonathan Stewart 134
  Joseph 22-24, 53-56, 58, 60
  Joshua 195
  Josiah 22, 53, 55
  Judith (Perkins) 280
  Katherine (Dean) 303
  Lydia 25, 52, 61, 310
  Lydia (-----) 21
  Lydia (Cooke) 52
  Marcy see Mercy
  Margaret 279
  Margene 55
  Marjoram (Washburn) 55
  Martha 25, 56, 61
  Martha (Orcutt) 55
  Mary 11, 21, 23, 25, 39, 55,
    57, 134, 194, 195, 279,
    280, 302
  Mary (-----) 24, 58
  Mary (Cudworth) 61
  Mary (Gurney?) 58
  Mary (Richmond) 297
  Mary (Watson) 194
  Mehitable 60
  Melatiah (Fisher) 280
  Mercy/Marcy 21, 51, 54, 194,
    195
  Mercy (Newton) 54
  Molly 134
  Moses 22, 23, 54, 60
  Nathan 52, 55
  Nathaniel 194, 195, 279
  Paul 302
  Phebe 22, 53, 134, 194, 195,
    279, 302, 303
  Phebe (Williams) 312
  Priscilla 279
  Priscilla (Rogers) 279

LEONARD/LENARD/LENERSON etc. cont.
  Putnam 134
  Rachel 278
  Rachel (Clap) 278
  Rebecca 60
  Samuel 11, 21, 52, 55, 303
  Sarah 11, 22, 23, 25, 58, 61,
    203, 233, 279, 302
  Sarah (-----) 22, 54
  Sarah (Chandler) 10
  Sarah (Dodge) 134
  Sarah (Walker) 203, 277, 302
  Seth 60, 134
  Solomon 10, 11, 23-25, 57, 62,
    317
  Susanna 23, 56, 57, 61, 134
  Susanna (King) 23
  Thankful 60
  Thomas 58, 59, 194, 203,
    277-279, 302
  Timothy 60
  William 61
LETTICE
  Dorothy 15
LEVERETT
  Elizabeth 48
LEWIN/LEWING/LUEN
  Dinah (Terry) 199, 291
  Hannah (Rogers) 212
  John 212, 290
  Joseph 212
  Margaret (Terry) 198, 290, 291
  Meriah 212
  Nathaniel 199, 290
  Rejoice (Walker) 212
  Thomas 290
  William 290
LEWIS
  Anna (Gains) 221
  Benjamin 211
  Bette 211
  David 240
  Eleazer 211
  Elizabeth (Rogers) 211
  George 211
  Hannah 221
  Joan (-----) 211, 218
  Joseph 211
  Joshua 211
  Luce 211
  Moses 211
  Nathaniel 221
  Peter 240
  Phebe 221

McDANIEL cont.
    Isaac 43, 117
    Jacob 117
    Mary 117
    Timothy 117
McKINSTRY
    Priscilla (Leonard) 279
    William 279
MEADY
    Louisa (Rust) 148
    William 148
MELLOWES
    Benjamin 108
    Elizabeth 108
    Sarah Haggatt 108
    Sarah (Haggatt) 108
    William Haggatt 108
MERRICK/MYRICK
    Dighton 201, 304
    Dighton (Bird) 304
    Elizabeth 209
    Isaac 304
    Mary 249
    Sarah 303
MERRIT
    John 63
MIDDLECOTT
    Edward 17, 18, 47, 109
    Elizabeth (Temple) 109
    Jane 17, 18, 48
    John 47
    Mary 17, 18, 45, 108
    Mary (-----) 17, 47
    Richard 10, 17, 18, 45-47,
       108
    Sarah 7, 9, 10, 17, 18, 47
    Sarah (Winslow) 17
    William 47
MILES
    Patience 76
    Patience (Wheeler) 76
    Stephen 76
MILLER
    Faith 43
    Mehitable 247
MILLINS
    Mary (Threeneedles) 63
    Thomas 63
MINOT
    Elizabeth 41
MITCHELL/MITCHEL
    Betty 190, 260
    David 189, 259, 260
    Deborah (Andrews) xii

MITCHELL/MITCHEL cont.
    Desire 190
    Elcanah 258
    Elizabeth 32
    Hallet 190, 258
    Hannah 258
    Hannah (Higgins) 258
    Jacob 85
    James 190, 258
    Jerusha (Hooper) 85
    Jonathan 258
    Lucretia (Loring) 268
    Margaret 105
    Mary (Wade) 73
    Mercy 190, 259
    Mercy (Nickerson) 189
    Pernal (Jenney) 259
    Ruth 259, 260
    Sarah 258
    Sarah (Higgins) 189
    Seth 190, 259
    Tabitha 190, 259
    Tabitha (Eldridge) 189
    William 189, 190, 259
MITCHELSON
    Elizabeth 29
MOFFAT
    Enoch 298
MOODY
    Hannah 40
    Joshua 40, 114, 115
    Martha (Collins) 40
    Mary (Codman) 114, 115
MOORE/MORE
    Archibald 126
    Caleb 122, 123, 125, 126
    Catherine 121
    Catherine (More) 121
    Christian 122, 125-127
    Christian (Hunt) 122, 125
    Christian (Hunter) 123, 125
    Elinor/Ellen 121
    Jane (-----) 123, 125
    Jasper 121
    Joshua 125
    Mary 121
    Richard 121-126
    Samuel 121, 125, 126
    Sarah 126
    Sarah (-----) 125, 126
    Susanna 122, 125, 126
    Thomas 125, 126
    William 126

POTTER cont.
  Lucy 137
  Lucy (Brown) 137
  Nathaniel 130
  Samuel 137
  Susanna 130
POUSLAND
  Edward 148
PRATT/PRATTE
  Grace 126
  Hannah (-----) 307
  Joseph 25, 310
  Lydia (Leonard) 25, 310
  Margene (Leonard) 55
  Susanna 310
PRENCE see PRINCE
PRESBURY
  Hannah 64
  Joseph 63, 64
  Martha (Smith) 63, 64
  William 63, 64
PRESTON
  Martha (Davis) 234
PRINCE/PRENCE
  John 268
  Mary (Gray) 268
  Ruth (Turner) 81
PROCTOR
  Hannah 139
  John 139
  Lucy (-----) 139
  Samuel 139
PULSIFER/PULCIFER
  David 143
  Hannah 143
  Hannah (Pulsifer) 143
  Mary 143
  Polly 143
PUMERY
  John 26
RAMSDEN
  Hannah 306
RAND
  Margery 42
RANDALL/RANDELL
  Bethia (Haward) 318, 319
  Elizabeth 114
  John 319
  Jonathan 318, 319
  Joseph 319
  Mary 238, 319
  Mary (Gurney?) 58
  Mary (Richmond) 295
  Rebecca (Fowler) 318

RANDALL/RANDELL cont.
  Samuel 58
  Stephen 295
  William 318
RAY
  Hannah 239
  Peter 239
  Tabitha (Newcomb) 239
REED
  Abiah (Macomber) 314
  Abigail 295
  Benjamin 314
  Bethiah (Frye) 294
  Edgar H. 199
  John 200, 294, 295
  Mary 294, 295
  Mary (Richmond) 199, 294
  Phebe (Terry) 286
  Ruth 284, 303
  William 199, 294, 295
REMICK
  Abraham 215
  Elizabeth (Freeman) 215
  Mary 99
  Mercy 215
REYNOLDS
  Elizabeth 278
  George 278
  Jonathan 278
  Joseph 195, 278
  Mary 65
  Nathaniel 278
  Priscilla (Bracket) 278
  Phebe 278
  Phebe (Leonard) 195, 278
  Samuel 278
  Sarah (Searle) 271
RHODES see ROADS
RICH
  Amos 251
  Bathsheba 251
  Bethiah 251
  Bette 254
  Eliakim 251
  Elizabeth 251, 254, 255
  Isaac 254, 255
  James 254, 255
  John 188, 251, 254, 255
  Lydia (Young) 188, 254
  Mary 254, 255
  Mercy 251
  Mercy (Knowles) 254
  Peter 251
  Samuel 254, 255

SNOW
  Benjamin 230
  Bethia 91
  Constance (Hopkins) 160
  David 248
  Edmund 217
  Elizabeth 160
  Elizabeth (-----) 178
  Elizabeth (Doane) 219
  Hannah (Paine) 172
  Hannah (Parslow) 249
  Heman 248
  Jabez 219
  Jane 230-232
  Joseph 249
  Joshua 172
  Lois (Freeman) 217
  Margaret (Elkins) 230-232
  Mary 163, 172, 209
  Mary (Cole) 248
  Mary (Young) 248
  Mercy 230-232
  Mercy (Cole) 186
  Micajah 248
  Moses 248
  Nathaniel 178, 249
  Nicholas 160
  Priscilla (Richmond) 178
  Ruth 185, 230-232
  Sarah 90, 175, 183, 218,
      230-232
  Stephen 157, 158, 230-232, 248
  Susanna 230
  Susanna (Deane) 157, 158
  Temperance (Nickerson) 229
  Temperance (Rogers) 178
  Thankful (Bowerman) 230
  Thankful (Cole) 186, 249
  William 178, 229
SOMES
  Abigail 211
  Abigail (Collins) 211
  Elizabeth (Robinson) 211
  Lucy 211
  Lucy (Rogers) 211
  Nehemiah 211
  Timothy 211
SOUTHWORTH
  Abigail 87
  Benjamin 88
  Bridget 88
  Bridget (Bosworth) 88
  Constant 35, 36, 88
  Desire 15, 87

SOUTHWORTH cont.
  Desire (Gray) 15, 35
  Ebenezer 88
  Edward 35, 36, 88
  Elizabeth 35, 36, 87
  Elizabeth (Collier) 35
  Esther (Hodges) 86, 87, 313
  Fear 87
  Gideon 87
  Hannah 87
  Ichabod 35, 36, 86-88, 313
  Jael (Howland) 87
  Lemuel 88
  Mary 36, 86-88
  Mary (-----) 88
  Nathaniel 15, 35, 36, 87, 88
  Priscilla 87, 313
  Samuel 87
  Sarah 88
  Theophilus 88
  William 87
SPARROW
  Aphiah (Tracy) 169
  John 169
  Jonathan 157, 171
  Lydia 171
  Mercy 185
  Rebecca 169
  Rebecca (Bangs) 171
  Sarah 217
SPAULDING
  Rebecca (Terry) 286
SPOONER
  Barnabas 241
  Elizabeth 242
  Jane 241
  John 241
  Moses 241
  Zeruiah (Eastland) 241
SPRAGUE
  Bethia (Snow) 91
  Joanna 91
  John 91, 114
  Katherine (Foster) 114
SPROAT/SPROUT
  Anna 204
  Elizabeth (Samson) 88, 204
  Hannah (Southworth) 87
  James 88
  Mercy 88
  Nathaniel 88
  Rachel (Buck) 88
  Robert 88, 204

WALKER cont.
    Mary 92, 303, 305
    Mary (-----) 203, 305
    Mary (Briggs) 302
    Mary (Pitts) 302
    Mary (Walker) 305
    Mercy 298, 307
    Mercy (Richmond) 200, 201
    Miriam (Richmond) 297
    Nathan 201, 204, 205, 307,
        308
    Nehemiah 203, 205, 298, 307-
        309
    Perez 303
    Peter 201, 203, 302, 303
    Phebe 204, 205, 303, 308
    Phebe (Leonard) 303
    Rejoice 212
    Robert 135
    Ruth 303
    Sarah 165, 203, 277, 302, 303
    Sarah (-----) 203
    Sarah (Richmond) 203, 264
    Sarah (Sampson) 272
    Thomas 92
    William 204, 205, 309
    Zephaniah 303
WALL
    Hannah (Winslow) 98
    John 98
WALLEY see WHALLEY
WARD
    Frances 58
WARE
    Abigail 309
    Anna 309
    Anna (Hodges) 309
    Benjamin 280, 309
    George 264, 309
    James 303
    John 272, 309
    Jonathan 280
    Joseph 309
    Lucia 309
    Lydia 309
    Lydia (Walker) 309
    Mary 272, 309
    Mary (Maxcey) 309
    Mary (Richmond) 264
    Mehitable (Chapin) 272, 309
    Melatiah (Fisher) 280
    Perez 303
    William 303, 309
    Zibiah (Sweeting) 309

WARREN
    Anna 37
    Cornelius 286
    Elinor (Billington) 286
    Gamaliel 286
    James 286
    Joanna 244
    Mary 286
    Mary (Terry) 198, 286
    Samuel 286
WASHBURN/WORSHBON
    Abial/Abiel 76, 307
    Abigail 55, 56, 307
    Abigail (Leonard) 23, 24, 56
    Amos 306, 307
    Annice 77
    Benjamin 32, 33, 78
    Daniel 76
    David 56, 77
    Deborah (Packard) 24, 56
    Deliverance 56
    Deliverance (Leonard) 24, 56
    Dinah 76
    Ebenezer 32, 33, 76-78, 307
    Edward 32, 33, 78, 204, 306,
        307
    Elijah 76
    Elizabeth 77
    Elizabeth (Irish) 55
    Elizabeth (Leonard) 55
    Elizabeth (Mitchell) 32
    Elizabeth (Richmond) 204,
        306, 307
    Elizabeth (Shaw) 70
    Elizabeth (Snell) 306
    Ephraim 32, 33, 77
    Eunice 77
    Gideon 317
    Hannah 33, 76, 78
    Hannah (Latham) 32
    Hannah (Johnson) 75, 76
    Hepzibah 33, 77, 320
    Isaac 77
    James 306, 307
    Japhet 77
    Jemima 77
    Jesse 298
    Joel 76
    John 32, 55, 57, 77, 78, 298
    Jonathan 32, 33, 75-77
    Joseph 14, 32, 33, 75-77
    Joshua 77
    Josiah 55, 238, 298
    Judith (Rickard) 78

John Rogers "her M marke

Mary her M Winslow marke Rich. Mov.

Mary Winslow Rich. Mov. John
o her M marke

M Winslow marke Rich. Mov. John Rog

low Rich. Mov. Mary
ke John Rogers her

Ch. Mov. John Rogers her M thi
ma

Mov. John Rogers Mary her M Winslow marke

John Rogers Mary her M Winslow marke Rich.

ohn Rogers Mary her M Winslow marke

M Winslow marke Rich. Mov.

Winslow marke Rich. Mov. John